History in Communist China

History in Communist China

Edited by
Albert Feuerwerker

The M.I.T. Press
Massachusetts Institute of Technology
Cambridge, Massachusetts, and London, England

Preface

By 1958, as described in the essay "China's History in Marxian Dress" (Chapter 2 of this volume), historiography in the People's Republic of China, like so many other aspects of that society, had come to an important juncture. In spite of obvious accomplishments, ten years of rewriting history had still left the political rulers of China unsatisfied with the historians' treatment of the past inherited by the Communist regime. The Great Leap Forward in the realm of historiography included a renewed emphasis on "directing historical research with theory", i.e., the thought of Mao Tse-tung; a call to "emphasize the present and de-emphasize the past", i.e., to use the study of the past to serve present-day political needs; a demand that the history of emperors, generals, and ministers be replaced by attention to the historical struggles of the labouring masses; and a call for the "broad masses of history workers" to join with workers and peasants and write histories of families, villages, communes, and factories.[1]

While the leading historians could not but offer support to the Great Leap, it is apparent that some at least were as dismayed by what the political mobilization of 1958–1959 did to the teaching and study of history[2] as many economists were by its disastrous economic aftermath. The quality and content of academic discussion following the Great Leap period—first centering on the problem of evaluating historical personages, then broadening to encompass the question of the "critical inheritance" of China's entire "cultural legacy", and finally taking the shape of a debate between the proponents of "historicism" *(li-shih chu-i)* and those who called only for a "class viewpoint" *(chieh-chi kuan-tien)* —seemed to me, when I wrote in 1960 and even in 1964 (but much less positively in the latter year), to offer the possibility that the writing of history in China, while it would never again be "bourgeois" history, might yet succeed in the successful construction of a new domestic tradition combining Marxism-Maoism and Chinese nationalism. Articles critical of the shabby quality of much current historical work were

[1] See Ch'i Pen-yü, Lin Chieh, and Yen Ch'ang-kuei, "Fan-kung chih-shih fen-tzu Chien Po-tsan ti chen mien-mu" (The True Face of Chien Po-tsan—An Anti-Communist Intellectual), *Hung-ch'i (Red Flag)*, No. 15, 1966, pp. 25–35.

[2] See Albert Feuerwerker and S. Cheng, *Chinese Communist Studies of Modern Chinese History* (Cambridge: Harvard University Press, 1961), pp. xiii–xv.

published in professional journals,[3] but also in *Hung-ch'i*,[4] the official voice of the Communist Party. A strong case was made in historical circles for what in effect was a nationalistic evaluation of the two millenia of "feudal" China that preceded the beginning of the modern revolutionary movement.[5] The discussion of "historicism" and the "class viewpoint", which became very intense from early 1963, appeared to leave some room for treatment of the past in its own terms once the proper obeisance had been made to Marxism-Maoism.[6]

Some writers to be sure, such as Professor Liu Chieh of the Department of History at Chungshan University, went beyond acceptable limits in emphasizing what was assertedly Chinese at the expense of what was assuredly Communist, and in consequence were attacked by their more politicalized colleagues. Riding on the wave of historicist criticism of the crude application of the class viewpoint, Liu in several articles written in 1962 and 1963 questioned whether the class struggle was really applicable to ancient Chinese history. "In brief, the theory of class struggle is practical and effective when applied in current politics," he wrote, "but when applied in the interpretation of ancient historical events, is it necessary to use the theory in such a dogmatic manner and so mechanically?"[7] Liu's doubts had been expressed in his contributions to discussions in philosophical circles devoted to the re-evaluation of Confucius and Confucian thought. Like a few others, notably Fung Yu-lan, who was also to be attacked, Liu had argued that Confucian *jen*, for example, was devoid of class content. He described it as an "abstract ethical concept" which "has been induced from all kinds of concrete happenings in human society from ancient times till the present." The nature of man, regardless of his times and his class, always required him to pursue *jen*.

On the one hand, Liu's position might be likened to that of some earlier predecessors who had sought to identify values in the Chinese tradition that might too, like those of the politically dominant West, be

---

[3] For example, Teng T'o, "Mao Tse-tung ssu-hsiang k'ai-p'i-le Chung-kuo li-shih k'o-hsüeh fa-chan ti tao-lu" (The Thought of Mao Tse-tung Opens the Way for the Development of Historical Science in China) *Li-shih yen-chiu (Historical Studies)*, No. 1, 1961, pp. 1–12; Fan Wen-lan, "Fan-tui fang k'ung-p'ao" (Oppose Empty Theory), *ibid.*, No. 3, 1961, pp. 1–4.

[4] Pai Shou-yi, "Li-shih k'o-hsüeh chi-pen hsün-lien yu-kuan-ti chi-ko wen-t'i" (Some Problems Concerning Fundamental Training in the Historical Sciences), *Red Flag*, No. 18, 1961, pp. 21–31.

[5] See Chapter 2 of this volume.

[6] For brief reviews of these discussions, see *Jen-min jih-pao (People's Daily)*, February 25, 1964, and *Kuang-ming jih-pao (Kuang-ming Daily)*, January 18, 1964.

[7] Quoted in *People's Daily*, June 18, 1963. I have not seen the original articles by Liu, some of which appeared in the Canton bi-monthly *Hsüeh-shu yen-chiu (Academic Studies)*, No. 1, 1962; Nos. 2, 3, 1963.

nominated as candidates for universal acceptance. That is, in re-evaluating China's philosophical heritage, Liu was to some degree expressing a nationalist attitude. This was not, however, the way in which his eccentricity was interpreted by Liu's more politically sophisticated colleagues. In numerous articles and at meetings such as that of the Kwangtung Historical Association held on October 5, 1963, he was attacked for "opposing the materialist historical viewpoint of Marxism", for espousing a theory of human nature "basically opposed to the class theory of Marxism", and for taking a "supra-class viewpoint" which was in fact the viewpoint of the capitalist class.[8] It was Liu's misfortune that in his interpretation and espousal of Confucian *jen* (which one might read as the equivalent of "humanism" or "humanitarianism") he was, intentionally or not, coming close to the very ideological sin of which the Chinese Communist Party was accusing the Soviet "modern revisionists". As Chou Yang, then Deputy Director of the Propaganda Department of the Central Committee of the CCP, put it in a speech to a conference of the Department of Philosophy and Social Science of the Academy of Sciences on October 26, 1963:

> Completely discarding historical materialism, the modern revisionists substitute the bourgeois theory of human nature for the Marxist-Leninist teachings on class struggle and proletarian dictatorship. . . . They have equated the concept of humanism, so-called, with that of scientific communism. . . . They say "communist ideology is the most humane ideology," they talk of humanism as "the highest embodiment of communism," and they assert that "humanism in the broad sense of the word merges with communism," and that "the communist system means the triumph of humaneness". . . . We are firmly opposed to substituting the theory of human nature in the abstract and the preaching of fraternity for the standpoint of class analysis and class struggle; we are against describing communism as humanism and against placing humanism above communism.[9]

But few went so far as Liu Chieh publicly, and while the channel between the Scylla of "historicism" and the Charybdis of "class viewpoint" was a narrow one, most historians seemed to be capable of negotiating it successfully.

There is irony perhaps in the fact that just when Chou Yang and others—including Liu Shao-ch'i, Chairman of the People's Republic of China, who was present at the philosophy and social science conference and reportedly delivered an "important speech"[10]—were castigat-

[8] *Kuang-ming Daily*, November 10, 1963.
[9] Chou Yang, "The Fighting Task Confronting Workers in Philosophy and the Social Sciences," *Peking Review*, January 3, 1964.
[10] New China News Agency, Peking, November 24, 1963.

ing those guilty of "modernizing the ideologies of the ancients" and asserting that "they are something which transcends classes and time",[11] the "modern revisionist" adversary himself was accusing Chinese historians of "bourgeois nationalism" for their favourable reappraisal of the thirteenth-century Mongol conquests (seen as calamitous of course by the Russians and other Europeans), for their claim that Chinese "feudalism", not European, is the classical model of this historical phenomenon, and because of their allegedly exaggerated estimate of the role of Confucian ideas and their influence on Western philosophy.[12] And even greater irony is manifest in the circumstance that Liu Shao-ch'i and Chou Yang, who in late 1963 were criticizing excessive "historicism", were in the next act of the drama to be accused as the evil powers behind the historians Wu Han, Teng T'o, Chien Po-tsan, Hou Wai-lu, Li Shu, Liu Ta-nien, Sun Tso-min, Shen Yüan, Ts'ai Mei-piao, and others who were denounced for opposing the Great Proletarian Cultural Revolution of Mao Tse-tung.

The attack, which began in November 1965, on Wu Han, specialist in Ming history, chairman of the Peking Historical Society, and deputy mayor of Peking, was perhaps the first public signal of the imminent upheaval in Chinese intellectual and political circles.[13] When all the academic verbiage is stripped aside, Wu stood accused for writing a play, *The Dismissal of Hai Jui*, produced in 1961 at the height of China's post-Great Leap economic crisis. In this play he covertly attacked the economic policies of Chairman Mao and implicitly identified the dramatic protagonist, a mid-sixteenth century official of almost legendary popularity, with the dismissed Marshall P'eng Te-huai, ousted by Mao in 1959 for opposing the Great Leap and for advocating a mending of fences with the Soviet Union. This is not the place to recount the dramatic sequence by which the campaign, launched first against Wu Han, next engulfed Ten T'o, fellow historian and writer, official of the Peking Municipal Committee of the Communist Party and editor of *Ch'ien-hsien*, theoretical organ of that Committee, and former editor of *Jen-min jih-pao*.[14] Nor how, as the Cultural Revolution gathered steam, P'eng Chen, Politburo member and mayor of Peking, Chou Yang, and many others fell from power amid assertions that their

11 *Kuang-ming Daily*, January 23, 1963; *Hsin chien-she (Reconstruction)*, No. 1, 1962, pp. 1–4.
12 See Chapter 16 of this volume.
13 See Stephen Uhalley, Jr., "The Wu Han Discussion: Act One in a New Rectification Campaign," *The China Mainland Review*, Vol. 4, No. 1, March, 1966, pp. 24–38.
14 See "The Press Campaign against Wu Han," *Current Background* (Hong Kong, U.S. Consulate), No. 783, March 21, 1966, and "Teng T'o, his 'Evening Talks at Yenshan' and the 'Three-Family Village' Group," *ibid.*, No. 792, June 29, 1966.

"anti-Party, anti-socialist" activities were directed, supported, and shielded by a person of even higher authority within the Party "who has taken the capitalist road", which of course we know referred to Liu Shao-ch'i.

The past year of confused struggle between supporters of Mao and their opponents (if one dare put it that simply), with its Red Guards, *ta-tzu-pao*, armed clashes, shadowy advances and obscure retreats, it need hardly be said, has not been conducive to academic scholarship. China's institutions of higher education were closed in June 1966 and at the time of this writing are just beginning to reopen. Efforts to reopen lower schools this past spring met with many obstacles, as teachers were barely able to manage their Red Guard charges, who were in turn reluctant to exchange the license of demonstrations, marches, and mass meetings for classroom discipline. When and how the teaching and writing of history will return to something like its pre-1966 format remains a hazardous guess.

In addition to the general distrust of "bourgeois" intellectuals characteristic of China today, the fact that Wu Han, Teng T'o, and others in their "criminal" group were historians has probably added an extra measure of resentment on the part of China's political leaders against established professional historians as a group. *Li-shih yen-chiu* (*Historical Studies*), the leading historical journal in China, ceased publication after its April 1966 number. In a front-page editorial on June 3, 1966, *Jen-men jih-pao* vituperatively attacked "bourgeois 'authorities' in the field of historical studies" for opposing the "scientific theses" of Mao Tse-tung, for denying the class struggle, and for suppressing truly revolutionary historians through their control of the leading academic positions. Individual prominent historians, among them Li Shu, editor-in-chief of *Historical Studies*, as well as the magazine itself, were similarly attacked in the same newspaper on October 23, 1966. It was charged that in 1961 Chou Yang had covertly gained control of *Historical Studies* by arranging the appointment of Li Shu as editor, and had thereafter utilized that journal to support his "counter-revolutionary" activities. Numerous "reactionary" articles by Wu Han, Teng T'o, Chien Po-tsan, and others of their ilk were allegedly solicited and printed by Li Shu in pursuance of this plot: the Taiping "renegade", Li Hsiu-ch'eng, was defended, peasant class struggles were deliberately misinterpreted, Mao's thought was basely distorted, the feudal landlord class and its emperors were extolled. Now, the article concluded, the proletarian revolutionaries have torn away the "black curtain enveloping *Historical Studies*. . . . However, we must continue to expose and criticize thoroughly the large amount of poison it has spread. We must sweep away all rubbish and wash away all dirt, and plant on the positions of historical science the proletarian, dazzling red banner of the thought of Mao Tse-tung."[15]

The future of historiography in China is, of course, unknown. Its present configuration, like so much else under the reign of Chairman Mao, is difficult to apprehend with confidence. The essays in this volume are collectively a preliminary reconnaissance of the work done by Chinese historians in the first fifteen years of the People's Republic of China. In their original drafts most of them were prepared for delivery at a conference on "Chinese Communist Historiography" sponsored by *The China Quarterly* and held at Ditchley Manor, Oxfordshire, September 6–12, 1964. Others were made available as background papers for that conference. Chapter 13, although it was not written in connection with the historiography conference, is included because of its value as a case study of how modern history is treated in Communist China. Chapter 17, also not available at the conference, touches on one important aspect of contemporary Chinese historiography not otherwise separately discussed in this volume: Chinese Communist treatment of the history of Asian countries as a whole. It displays, for those who are not already acquainted with it, the customary polemical style of many historical writings published in China today.

Chapter 1 is a summary of the discussions at Ditchley, while Chapter 2 surveys the main developments in the field of history in Communist China through the year 1959. These two contributions may serve as an introduction to the topical essays that follow.

ALBERT FEUERWERKER

Ann Arbor, Michigan
August 1967

15 Translated in *Survey of the China Mainland Press* (Hong Kong, U.S. Consulate), No. 3813, November 2, 1966.

Acknowledgments

As chairman of the historiography conference and editor of this volume, I gratefully acknowledge the major responsibility for organizing the conference and for preparing its papers for publication undertaken by Mr. Roderick MacFarquhar and *The China Quarterly* staff, in particular Mr. Gordon S. Barrass, Miss Antoinette Diniz, and Mrs. Karen H. Judd.

Chapter 2 is reprinted from the *American Historical Review*, Vol. LXVI, No. 2, January 1961, pp. 323–353. Chapter 16 appeared originally in *Voprosy Istorii*, No. 10, October 1963, pp. 3–20, and is reprinted here (with minor editorial corrections) as translated in *The Current Digest of the Soviet Press*, Vol. 16, No. 4, February 19, 1964, pp. 3–10. Chapter 17 is reprinted from *Peking Review*, No. 45, November 5, 1965, pp. 23–28. The remaining essays are reprinted from the following issues of *The China Quarterly*: Chapter 4 from No. 12, October–December 1962; Chapters 1, 9, 12 from No. 22, April–June 1965; Chapters 3, 6, 7, 8, 13 from No. 23, July–September 1965; Chapters 5, 11, 14 from No. 24, October–December 1965; Chapter 15 from No. 28, October–December 1966; Chapter 10 from No. 30, April–June 1967. The consent of authors, editors, and publishers is noted with thanks.   A.F.

Contributors

Howard L. Boorman, *Professor of History, Vanderbilt University*

Kenneth Ch'en, *Professor of Religion and Oriental Studies, Princeton University*

Cheng Te-k'un, *Lecturer in Far Eastern Art and Archaeology, University of Cambridge*

David M. Farquhar, *Assistant Professor of History, University of California, Los Angeles*

Albert Feuerwerker, *Professor of History, The University of Michigan*

C. P. Fitzgerald, *Professor of Far Eastern History, Australian National University*

James P. Harrison, *Assistant Professor of History, Hunter College*

A. F. P. Hulsewé, *Professor of Chinese and Director of the Sinological Institute, University of Leiden*

John Israel, *Assistant Professor of History, Claremont Men's College*

Harold Kahn, *Lecturer in Far Eastern History, School of Oriental and African Studies, University of London*

Joseph R. Levenson, *Sather Professor of History, University of California, Berkeley*

Liu Ta-nien, *until 1966 Deputy Director of the Third History Institute (Modern History), Chinese Academy of Sciences, and assistant editor of* Li-shih Yen-chiu *(Historical Studies)*

Maurice Meisner, *Associate Professor of History, University of Virginia*

Donald J. Munro, *Assistant Professor of Philosophy, The University of Michigan*

R. V. Vyatkin, *U.S.S.R. Academy of Sciences, Institute of the People of Asia*

S. L. Tikhvinsky, *U.S.S.R. Academy of Sciences, Institute of the Peoples of Asia*

Hellmut Wilhelm, *Professor of Chinese History and Literature, University of Washington*

Contents

Preface

Acknowledgments

Contributors

1

The Ideology of Scholarship: China's New Historiography

By HAROLD KAHN and
ALBERT FEUERWERKER

This article is a report on the conference on historiography in Communist China convened by The China Quarterly at Ditchley Park near Oxford, September 6–12, 1964. Many of the papers will appear in forthcoming issues of this Journal and will be published in book form next year. Professor Feuerwerker served as chairman of the conference, Mr. Kahn as its rapporteur.*

IDEOLOGY is, rightly considered, a datum of history. When it becomes *the* datum of history—the end of the scholar's search as well as his means—the rules of the game change and historical inquiry becomes essentially a political exercise. The historian moves from the classroom to the platform, the natural habitat of the ideologue; historiography moves from an effort to discover what actually was (Ranke's hope) to an effort to confirm what in fact should be. The past, that is, serves the present not by illuminating it but by defining it, by justifying it. This is not an unfamiliar phenomenon. Prussian scholarship served Bismarck as Soviet scholarship, after Pokrovsky, served Stalin and as Chinese scholarship today serves Mao. It is in large the scholarship of nationalism. And nationalism, being a jealous mistress, demands the creation of a particularistic history, a private affair, as it were, between the state and the people. This is all very well in the privacy of the sovereign realm, but it is awkward in the vestibule of the new ecumeni. For Marxism too is jealous and demands of her historians universality. To court both cultural uniqueness and universal applicability is a task few historians savour, yet it is one that Chinese writers today are forced to perform.

Their frequent incompatibility and the problems raised by attempting to reconcile nationalist sentiment and Marxist-Leninist theory in the writing of history are demonstrated in the controversy over " historicism " (*li-shih chu-i*) and the " class viewpoint " (*chieh-chi kuan-tien*) which

---

* This report represents in general form and without specific acknowledgment of individual contributions to the discussions a consensus of views expressed at the conference. The authors alone of course are responsible for the form those views take here.

since mid-1963 has regularly occupied the pages of historical and philosophical journals in the People's Republic of China. In the first decade of Communist China, historical writing was heavily weighted towards the "class viewpoint." That is to say, the problems to which historians addressed themselves tended to be clothed in a vulgar and schematic Marxism which failed, on the evidence of the practitioners themselves, to do justice to the scope and weight of a cultural tradition as magnificent as any that human genius has created. By the late 1950s a reaction was evident against anonymous history—dynasties without "feudal" emperors or bureaucrats, literature minus the landlord-scholar-official literatus, nameless peasant rebellions as the central matter of China's history—which emasculated as a feudal excrescence the two-thousand-year core of traditional Chinese civilisation. The "re-evaluations" which were undertaken of such hitherto malefic persons as Ts'ao Ts'ao, the emperor Han Wu-ti, the Manchu rulers K'ang-hsi and Ch'ien-lung, and most recently of Genghis Khan introduced a leaven of "historicism," or historical relativism, into the treatment of the feudal past. In brief, historians were enjoined that these men and others like them were henceforth to be judged by their "contribution to the people and to the development of the whole nation and to cultural development" rather than by the standards of the "Socialist" society in which the historian wrote.

There is evidence to suggest that this altered emphasis in Chinese historiography after 1958 or 1959 correlates with a patent quickening of Chinese nationalism in the face of increasingly severe differences with the Soviet Union. But however much diluted in practice, the observance of the old religion and the worship of its gods cannot be abandoned without calling into question the foundation of the state and undermining one's defences in the great polemic with Soviet Russia. Hence movement from a "class viewpoint" to "historicism" inevitably gives rise to counter forces. Witness the experience of Professor Liu Chieh of the Department of History at Chungshan University in Canton.

Riding on the wave of historicist criticism of the crude application of the class viewpoint, Liu in several articles written in 1962 and 1963 questioned whether the class struggle was really applicable to ancient Chinese history. "In brief, the theory of class struggle is practical and effective when applied in current politics," he wrote, "but when applied in the interpretation of ancient historical events, is it necessary to use the theory in such a dogmatic manner and so mechanically?" [1] Liu's doubts had been expressed in his contributions to discussions in

---

[1] Quoted in *Jen-min Jih-pao* (*People's Daily*), June 18, 1963. We have not been able to see the original articles by Liu, some of which appeared in the Canton bi-monthly *Hsueh-shu Yen-chiu* (*Academic Studies*), No. 1, 1962; Nos. 2, 3, 1963.

philosophical circles devoted to the re-evaluation of Confucius and Confucian thought. Like a few others, notably Fung Yu-lan, who was also to be attacked, Liu had argued that Confucian *jen*, for example, was devoid of class content. He described it as an " abstract ethical concept " which " has been induced from all kinds of concrete happenings in human society from ancient times till the present." The nature of man, regardless of his times and his class, always required him to pursue *jen*.

On the one hand, Liu's position might be likened to that of some earlier predecessors who had sought to identify values in the Chinese tradition which might too, like those of the politically dominant West, be nominated as candidates for universal acceptance. That is, in re-evaluating China's philosophical heritage, Liu was to some degree expressing a nationalist attitude. This was not, however, the way in which his eccentricity was interpreted by Liu's more politically sophisticated colleagues. In numerous articles and at such meetings as that of the Kwangtung Historical Association held on October 5, 1963, he was attacked for " opposing the materialist historical viewpoint of Marxism " for espousing a theory of human nature " basically opposed to the class theory of Marxism," and for taking a " supra-class viewpoint " which was in fact the viewpoint of the capitalist class.[2] It was Liu's misfortune that in his interpretation and espousal of Confucian *jen* (which one might read as the equivalent of " humanism " or " humanitarianism ") he was, intentionally or not, coming close to the very ideological sin of which the Chinese Communist Party was accusing the Soviet " modern revisionists." As Chou Yang, Deputy Director of the Propaganda Department of the Central Committee of the CCP, put it in a speech to a conference of the Department of Philosophy and Social Science of the Academy of Sciences on October 26, 1963 [3]:

> Completely discarding historical materialism, the modern revisionists substitute the bourgeois theory of human nature for the Marxist-Leninist teachings on class struggle and proletarian dictatorship. . . . They have equated the concept of humanism so-called with that of scientific Communism. . . . They say " Communist ideology is the most humane ideology," they talk of humanism as " the highest embodiment of Communism," and they assert that " humanism in the broad sense of the word merges with Communism," and that " the Communist system means the triumph of humaneness." . . . We are firmly opposed to substituting the theory of human nature in the abstract and the preaching of fraternity for the standpoint of class analysis and class struggle; we are against describing Communism as humanism and against placing humanism above Communism.

[2] *Kuang-ming Jih-pao (Kuang-ming Daily)*, November 10, 1963.
[3] Chou Yang, " The Fighting Task Confronting Workers in Philosophy and the Social Sciences," *Peking Review*, January 3, 1964.

3

Liu Chieh was singled out for chastisement, but the convention and theme of the philosophy and social science conference referred to immediately above—at which Liu Shao-ch'i, Chairman of the People's Republic of China, delivered an " important speech " [4] and which was attended by many Party officials as well as by scholars and research workers—indicated that there were others too guilty of " modernising the ideologies of ancients " and asserting that " they are something which transcends classes and time." [5]   The rub is that while it is easy to agree that the principles of historicism and the class viewpoint have an " internal and organic " connection, this is of little help in guiding actual historical research.   " If the unity of the class viewpoint with historicism is taken as complete agreement of content and the relations between them are regarded as necessary ones, so that possession of the class viewpoint inevitably implies possession of historicism, the resulting interpretation will be mechanical and oversimplified."   On the other hand, historical relativism which abandons " revolutionary responsibility and fervour for changing present realities " and does not ask what significance the narration and portrayal of the past has for " today's life and struggles," emasculates historicism which degenerates into merely a restoration of ancient things. [6]   To inherit " correctly " the legacy of the past, the historian must steer between Scylla and Charybdis guided only by the Maoist star that signals, " Another task in our study is to examine our historical legacy and *sum it up critically from the Marxist* approach," [7] while the shifting clouds of domestic and international policy cast doubts as to direction from which the beacon really beckons.

What happens in such circumstances to the historical record as we know it?   What contributions can be or have already been made towards illuminating a tradition once condemned out of hand as a feudalistic embarrassment?   How shall we evaluate them?   How new in fact is the current historical process?   How revisionist?   How flexible?   What are its theoretical and organisational constructs?   How accurate a barometer is it of current social and political concerns?   These are some of the questions that were discussed at the Conference on Chinese Communist Historiography.   In attempting to generalise on the conclusions reached it will be useful to consider two broad areas of inquiry: the varieties of history—the theory, methods, and organisation of historiography—and the contents of history.

[4] New China News Agency, Peking, November 24, 1963.
[5] See *Kuang-ming Daily*, January 23, 1963; *Hsin Chien-she* (*New Construction*), No. 1, 1962.
[6] Ning K'o, " Lun Li-shih-chu-i Ho Chieh-chi Kuan-tien " (" On Historicism and the Class Viewpoint "), *Li-shih Yen-chiu* (*Historical Research*), No. 4, 1963.
[7] *Selected Works of Mao Tse-tung* (Eng. ed., London: Lawrence and Wishart, 1954–56), Vol. II, p. 259; emphasis added.

THE VARIETIES OF HISTORY

It is tempting to conclude that China's new historiography is simply a variation of the old—the substitution of one orthodoxy (Maoism) for another (Confucianism) and the continuation of a tradition which emphasised the here-and-now, public, essentially political, purpose of history. This may be true, but it is also too simple. Continuities and similarities there are to be sure: The need to legitimise the present by appeals to the past, the bureaucratic historian paid to praise the "throne," the avowed didactic purpose of history, the organisation of the record from the centre, the hardening of methodology into a moralistic scholasticism, the inclusion and suppression of preferred data, the pride in preserving the record and rearranging it in vast compendia— all are common to both traditions. The differences, however, outweigh the similarities. So great are they in fact that a traditional historian would be hard put to recognise much of the new past as at all relevant to his own experience. The substantive priorities—the contents of history (see below)—are markedly different today; so are the norms and principles which guide their choice and the organisation of the effort itself.

The Chinese classically regarded history as a mirror which, properly angled, would reflect the cherished precedents of a golden age upon which present action had to be based or at least rationalised.[8] As the mirror became tarnished in the long years of methodological complacency after the Sung dynasty (960–1278) the reflection paled into a scholastic acceptance of the praise-and-blame moralism of Chu Hsi (1130–1200). History came to resemble not so much the arrangement of facts as the recitation of dogma. And even the eighteenth century reaction to this, represented by the empirical methods of the school of Han learning, ended in a rigid pedantry.

Today the mirror has been replaced by the calibrating instrument, the scientific tool, which, according to Marxist dogma, if properly read will measure the inexorable march of progress through time to the present. But the danger of rigidity remains, for the proper reading of the new instrument also depends on a set of revealed truths. History in these circumstances begins to look more like propaganda than science. Yet ironically the historiographical situation in China today seems in some ways more fluid than in the past. This is not because dogma is less strict but rather because it has not yet gained the absolute approbation which comes of old age. For the moment the new scholasticism is still in flux. The Chinese historiographers may have their Aquinases or Chu Hsis in Marx and Mao, but not all of them know the scriptures. And

---

[8] The most recent study of traditional historiography is W. G. Beasley and E. G. Pulleyblank, eds., *Historians of China and Japan* (London: Oxford University Press, 1961).

even if they did they could not be overly complacent, for the scriptural ground keeps shifting under them as exigencies of policy call for new approaches. The new history, it was agreed, is really a variety of histories, a shifting, unsure, uneven, confused ground which has a high emotional content as well as a doctrinal rationality. For the first time the question, " what, really, is this China of ours?" is being asked—a question irrelevant in the traditional historiographical context and too mortifying in the imperialist context of nineteenth and twentieth century China.

The break with tradition, then, while not complete is irrevocable. There can be no going back to the old and pre-eminent concern for the supremacy of Confucianist politics; the new order instead proclaims the transcendence of economic and social forces in history. It does not, of course, deny the primacy of political concerns, for the Marxist-Leninist canon admits as much, but rather casts them in a vocabulary of class struggle alien to the tradition. By doing so it is changing the very language of Chinese history. For emperors and courts we now read peasants and people; the cycle of history recedes before the straight line of progress; former villains—Genghis Khan, for example, or the Man-chus, even Ts'ao Ts'ao, the arch villain of popular history—become heroes and heroes—above all Confucius [9]—villains. The danger, of course, is that this will produce just one more oversimplification of the record, another static view of Chinese history just when its complexities are beginning to be appreciated. Yet it was recognised that there is promise in the new methodology as well, for behind the more egregious claptrap of Marxist ideology and language is evidence of an acceptance of new ideas, new techniques in the writing of history. It has been through Marxism-Leninism, in fact, that, sometimes in a blurred form to be sure, much of the new historical technique and methodology that developed in the modern West came to China. Notwithstanding its cramped ideological boundaries, Marxism does in some directions border upon the modern social sciences the fruits of which illicitly but undeni-ably penetrate into her confines. Marxism, moreover, in its claim to universality is more truly *historically* universal than Confucianism, which never recognised the possibility of national sub-universes, ever could be In a word, in history as in other areas of Chinese society, the new dispensation is evidence of a back-door entrée into the world of modernisation.

Historical research in Communist China is conducted by the Institute of Historical Research of the Chinese Academy of academic bodies. In addition, the Communist Party itself carries on a certain

---

[9] See Joseph R. Levenson, " The Place of Confucius in Communist China," *The China Quarterly*, No. 12, October–December, 1962.

amount of historical activity, and government archival offices, national and local, from time to time publish collections of historical source materials. The Institute of Historical Research is part of the Department of Philosophy and Social Science of the Academy of Sciences. Kuo Mo-jo, who is President of the Academy, is simultaneously Director of this Department. The Institute consists of three Offices: the First Office (Ancient History) is also headed by Kuo Mo-jo; the Director of the Second Office (Medieval History) is Ch'en Yuan, a specialist on T'ang history and the history of Buddhism; the Third Office (Modern History) is directed by Fan Wen-lan, a scholar who began his career as a student of the Chinese classics, but later turned to modern history. Research in economic history is also carried on at the Peking Institute of Economics of the Academy of Sciences, whose Deputy Director, Yen Chung-p'ing, is one of the most capable scholars in Communist China. The work of these research organs is carried on both by a permanent research staff and by leading faculty members of universities throughout China who are associated with the several institutes.

Nearly every university and college has a Department of History; in some cases there are two departments, one for Chinese history and one for foreign history. These departments, the members of which are, of course, engaged in both teaching and research, are under the general supervision of the Ministry of Higher Education. While the curricula of the several schools are not uniform, they tend to be quite similar as a consequence of the fact that many courses are taught from " pedagogical outlines " prepared by conferences of historians which are sponsored regularly by the Ministry. In general, the undergraduate history curriculum—there is very little graduate study—extends through four academic years. The ideological content of instruction and research in the field of history, as in other academic areas, is under the constant scrutiny of the Communist Party units in the universities and colleges. It has not been possible to determine how many active historians there are at present in the People's Republic of China. It was estimated by the editor of *Li-shih Yen-chiu* (*Historical Research*) that in 1957 there were 1,400 " teachers of contemporary history and history of the Revolution in institutions of higher learning in all parts of the country." This figure refers only to those who are primarily concerned with the period after 1919; it is unlikely, however, that the specialists in any other single period outnumber these modern historians.

The personnel of the new historiography are not yet unified in a single, ideologically respectable camp. Remnants of the capitalist and feudal scholarly élite active in the Kuomintang years exist side by side with representatives of the new curriculum. And the latter come and go as interpretative shifts render their works heretical or obsolete. This is

7

a period of transition. Existing scholarly resources must be mobilised and exploited even if they do not always conform to the new standards of excellence. Thus the conference was able to distinguish three groups of historians now at work: the older generation of non-Marxist trained scholars, the middle-aging party liners, and the new hotheads.

Among the first group are those, such as the eminent T'ang scholar Ch'en Yin-k'o and the old Academia Sinica archaeologists, whose reputations and expertise have until recently spared them from excessive criticism. Most notably in archaeology, a subfield of history where political pressures are minimal, are these scholars allowed to continue their work in relative methodological peace. On the whole, however, the trend seems to be to shunt them off into the obscurity of local historical commissions and boards where they are tolerated, neutralised, and counted as curios from a bygone age. The middle group is the most unstable. Its members, including Fan Wen-lan, Kuo Mo-jo, Chien Po-tsan, Hou Wai-lu, Liu Ta-nien, Shang Yüeh, and Lo Erh-kang, learned their Marxist lessons early and often too well, and in some cases have not always been able to keep up with changes in the text. Thus, for example, Fan Wen-lan has had to confess his doctrinal tardiness with every revision of his general studies of Chinese history, Shang Yüeh was left with a handful of withered sprouts when the argument for a pre-nineteenth century development of capitalism dried out, and Lo Erh-kang, the dean of China's Taiping scholars, is currently fighting a rear-guard action to save his patriot peasant hero, Li Hsiu-ch'eng, from being downgraded by the revisionists. The third group is a native product of the revolution. Its members are in a sense Mao's men, trained largely since 1949 in the new school of doctrinaire historiography and more at ease with the party line than the historical document. Academically inferior to their colleagues they are politically more enlightened and hence publicly safe and louder in their scholarly pronouncements. They represent, disconcertingly some feel, the wave of the future. The quality of Chinese historical scholarship in the next generation will in any case depend largely on their ability, or that of their students, eventually to escape the more cumbersome canonical strictures of Maoism and work out, even with the blunt tool of class analysis, a more sophisticated and hopefully more realistic past.

The performance to date has been mixed, but on the whole discouraging.[10] The exception is in the field of archaeology where the work, both in quantity and quality, has by and large maintained the

10 For a review of the accomplishments in modern history see Albert Feuerwerker and S. Cheng, *Chinese Communist Studies of Modern Chinese History* (Cambridge, Mass.: Harvard University Press, 1961).

high standards set in the 1930s.[11]   Generally, however, specialists agreed that in their respective fields little new information has appeared, the main effort rather having been confined to reinterpretations of existing data.   Monographic work has given way to the compendium, the polemic, the " proof."   The academic journals serve as forums for the latest debates but rarely for original ideas.   Curiously it is the large national newspapers, such as the *Kuang-ming Daily*, that often carry the first notices of tentative departures from the accepted norms—as if acting as a sounding board for controlled public opinion.

Doctrinally the single most important measure of success remains the ability to produce popular history—history about the people and essentially for them.   This has inevitably meant a decline in professional standards but has also led to the encouragement of a growing body of amateur historiography which may in time act as a leaven on the more portentious products of official history.   Results of the popularisation move are already in.   A janitor has been transformed into an honoured archaeological worker for his careful work in preserving an unexpected find; six million poems have been produced in the province of Szechwan alone; vast collections of folklore and songs and ethnic tales are being compiled as repositories of the most primary data of popular history. Whether or not this will eventually change our picture of the past remains to be seen.

By far the greatest contribution to international scholarship so far has been the publication of conscientiously and expertly edited collections of historical documents.[12]   Their appearance, unencumbered by moralistic trappings, has significantly expanded our knowledge of modern Chinese history.   In the field of classical scholarship and literature, too, much work has been done to simplify the record.   An ongoing programme of republication of seminal works and modern punctuation and annotation of classical texts promises to facilitate research not only by Western students but by the growing number of Chinese students who no longer can handle the earlier texts with ease.

THE CONTENTS OF HISTORY

Ever since the 1930s when Chinese Marxist scholars began the attempt to reshape history after the Socialist model, Chinese history has been caught in the artificial vice of periodisation.   This need to torture an exceptional, in many ways unique, historical experience into the classical stages of development as defined by Marx, primarily on his knowledge

---

11 See Cheng Te-k'un, *Archaeology in China*, 3 vols. to date (Cambridge: Cambridge University Press, 1959 *et seq.*).

12 For a discussion of some of these see John K. Fairbank and Mary Wright, *et al.*, " Documentary Collections on Modern Chinese History," *Journal of Asian Studies*, November 1957.

of European history, has led to endless and on the whole sterile debate over the course of Chinese history.[13] There is no indication that the controversy is near settlement and until it is, the conference agreed, much scholarly energy is doomed to be wasted on essentially peripheral matters. When the slave period ended, how long, if at all, the embarrassing (because unclassical and somehow second-class) stage of the Asiatic mode of production lasted, when the modern period begins— are questions more amenable to exegetical than historical solutions.

The problem has been compounded by a countervailing need—the need to find in China's past not just a correspondence to classical models but the models themselves. This trend, exacerbated by the Sino-Soviet split and the growth of an increasingly self-conscious nationalism, has had the effect of creating a new sinocentrism in the historical writing, a kind of classicism in reverse where China, not the West, represents the archetypal experience of progress towards Socialism.[14]

As a result of these political and ideological agonies Chinese history has emerged as a lopsided story with a beginning and an end but hardly any middle. The vast stretch of some 2,000 years from the formation of the Han states to the mid-nineteenth century constitutes a feudal embarrassment that seems safer left alone for the time being. Emphasis rather has been on the nodal points, the transitional periods of history, as defined by the Marxist-Maoist canon. These are the real problem areas of the new historiography, for upon them depends China's ultimate acceptance or rejection as a respectable historical member of the school of materialist progress. Yet even for these periods the Chinese historians have tended to restrict themselves to a limited number of topics more or less directly related to the problem of constructing a new past to replace the discarded Confucianist interpretation. Besides periodisation as a legitimate concern in its own right, they seem particularly concerned with such problems as the interpretation of peasant rebellions, the formation of the Han nation, the nature of landholding in " feudal " China, the controversy over the origins of capitalism in China, and the role of imperialism in modern Chinese history.[15]

These historians of course have not been able fully to ignore the middle period. But they approach it with notable caution. The trouble is that while doctrine defines a feudal epoch as static, history indicates that this period was decidedly dynamic. It witnessed, among other things, a radical change in class relationships, from the dominance

---

[13] For the early debates see Benjamin I. Schwartz, " A Marxist Controversy in China," *Far Eastern Quarterly*, February 1954.

[14] The Marxist-nationalist dichotomy and its effects on the substance of current historiography is examined more closely in Albert Feuerwerker, " China's History in Marxian Dress," *American Historical Review*, January 1961.

[15] See *ibid.*

of a small, monied aristocracy to the ascendence of a much broader-based land-owning commoner élite; the partial implementation for several centuries of a suspiciously egalitarian land tenure and allotment programme known as the " equal field " system; the gradual acceptance of the alienability of land and the right of private ownership; the increase in living standards, even for the peasantry, with marked improvements in agricultural techniques and handicraft trades; the growth of large cities and an urban work force; the expansion of the realm by the periodic incursion of proto-imperialists such as the Mongols and Manchus; the development from the Sung dynasty on of a thriving commercial capitalism. Many of these developments, however, were initiated or led by the throne, and it is still difficult for the Chinese historians to admit that a reactionary political force could or would energise progressive socio-economic forces. Understandably, then, the role of the " Crown," except as a negative force, has been underplayed and the role of the personalities who wore it all but ignored.

In downgrading the monarch and the court the new historiography has performed one useful service. It has rescued from traditional neglect the common man and made of him an historically relevant creature. The treatment of peasant rebellions, while often excessively enthusiastic itself, has provided a needed corrective to the old obsession with battles and kings and the sanctity of orthodox power. While it was noted that there is no brief for the claims of a progressive growth of peasant class consciousness as peasant unrest grew in intensity through the centuries, it was agreed that concentration on this shadowy area of history has brought to light much new and useful information. Popular history perhaps is being misused, but it is, nevertheless, being well documented. Unfortunately the most important rebellion still awaits definitive treatment. While much individual work has been done on the Taiping rebellion (1851–64), the very complex sociological and ideological problems it poses seem as intractable to the new Chinese methodology as they still are to various non-Chinese approaches.

In the realm of ideas much has been written but little accomplished. Studies in Buddhism, for example, both in its doctrinal and socio-economic aspects, have progressed little beyond the pre-1949 level of general surveys and hostile attacks. Part of the reason for this is the lack of trained scholars in this highly difficult field. Part, however, is the political rather than historical preoccupation of the régime with the religion. Rather than suppress the Buddhist church it has sought to reform it. It is rewriting the scriptures to emphasise the positive, progressive nature of this worldly service and the reactionary nature of superstitious belief. The pantheon, so to speak, is being brought down to earth and the sutras, together with the Maoist writ, being made the litany of the five year plans.

Classical philosophy is being restudied from a materialist base which paradoxically still seems hyper-interested in traditional metaphysical questions. Materialism itself appears ill-defined by the new historians of philosophy and they have yet to make the distinction, assumed in Western philosophy, between metaphysical or mechanical materialism, the heritage derived from Greek atomistic thought, and dialectical materialism, the heritage from German idealism. But more important than philosophical distinctions, even for the philosophers, are historical distinctions. Until the periodisation of the classical age (6th-3rd centuries B.C.) is fixed, the class affiliations of the early thinkers, upon which rests a correct evaluation of their worth, must remain strictly provisional. Not so with the neo-Confucians. As early as the May Fourth movement Chu Hsi orthodoxy was declared modern China's greatest intellectual enemy and nothing has changed to alter that view. It is recognised, nevertheless, that the early neo-Confucians of the mid and late T'ang period performed a progressive role in their attacks on Buddhism, for the Buddhism of this period is seen as the captive of an aristocratic class and Confucianism the ideology of a materialist landlord class. However, just as peasant leadership in the feudal age was corrupted by success, so neo-Confucianism was spoilt by its victory, and by the Sung had lost its materialist content to a new and odious idealism. Ever after it would be a force of reaction. In this interpretation finer distinctions than those between idealist and materialist do not occur and the class analysis is still so rough that thinkers are often assigned to classes that did not exist. Clearly the historians of philosophy have a formidable task before them. Not only will they have to refine their techniques but they will eventually have to decide what weight to give ideas in history. Are they to be considered to have played a reflective or independent history-making role, *i.e.*, did they simply reflect their times or actually affect them? The question seems still to be open.

No area of Chinese history is more beset by interpretative problems than the modern period. As events move closer to the revolution they become more sensitive, as if proximity, unless correctly handled, somehow might detract from the lustre of that event. This is well illustrated in the problem of the growth of capitalism. Essentially it is the problem of cultural pride. Did China have a legitimate history of her own which could account by domestic factors for normal development away from feudalism and into the modern age? Or did external events—the invasion of China by Western capital in the nineteenth century—determine the course of history? At first it appeared that the former was the case and the origins of capitalism were discovered in a few large-scale handicraft industries in the Ming period. But this denied to Western imperialism the full value of its dual function as exploitative villain and necessary accomplice to the growth of a modern economy and modern class-conscious revolutionary proletariat. And so for the time the second interpretation holds the field, armed with a quotation from Mao that modern history began with the invasion of the West. The sprouts of capitalism, never very hardy anyway and seeded by a fallacious assumption about the inevitable evolution of commercial capitalism into industrial capitalism, are allowed to die on the vine. The content of modern history, like that of all periods, is still decided more by fiat than fact, and meaning in history remains an elusive goal.

It was apparent from the papers presented to the conference and the lively discussions which they occasioned that the writing of history in China continues to occupy under the present régime, as under its predecessors, a critical place among the preoccupations of the ruling strata. From its beginnings, history in China has been intimately associated with the politics of the Chinese state—as a justification for bold departures which, it was claimed, were merely restoring the " golden age " of the great sages of the past, as a means of legitimising the succession of one ruling group to the throne of its predecessor, as a powerful weapon in the struggles of factions and cliques over the centuries. The Government of the People's Republic of China has been acutely aware of the political uses of history, and since coming to power in 1949 it has vigorously promoted the rewriting of the Chinese past.

The Chinese Communist reinterpretation of China's history has, in considerable part, been offered as propaganda designed to perpetuate support of the present régime among the Chinese people. But there is something more to it than this. Historical writing in China today, as viewed by the nation's leaders, also represents a genuine attempt to find legitimisation in China's past for the domestic and external developments of her most recent present. For the Confucian ideology of imperial China, the Communist government in Peking has, of course, substituted a still developing Maoist version of Marxism-Leninism as the touchstone for the assessment of the past. The deep-running current of nationalism, which surfaced in the late 1950s, would make it misleading to suppose, however, that what was peculiarly Chinese, either in motivation or in substance, has been totally expunged from the historiography of China by the Communist revolution.

2

China's History in Marxian Dress

ALBERT FEUERWERKER

ONE of the promised, though as yet unrealized, fruits of the great bustle of historiographical activity in the People's Republic of China will be a new general history of China—a *Chung-kuo t'ung-shih*. *T'ung-shih*, today the common term for "general history," is a particularly appropriate designation for the kind of product we may eventually expect from the Chinese Communist historians. In the past it was used by historiographers specifically to distinguish those writings which encompassed the events of more than one dynasty, as distinct from *tuan-tai-shih* which restricted themselves to a single dynastic period.[1] Now it implies the comprehensive rewriting of all Chinese history. Although the Chinese Communists are devoting their main energies to fitting China's modern history into Marxist-Leninist-Maoist dress, it is essential to keep in mind this larger context of historical revisionism within which modern history, while increasingly emphasized, is only a part.

The key to understanding China's history in Marxian dress lies in what I shall call the problem of meaninglessness. Joseph Levenson has pointed out that although modern Chinese intellectuals—this includes the Communist historians—*as intellectuals* have rejected their Confucian heritage, *as Chinese* this has not been a painless amputation.[2] They have not easily accepted the fact that the intellectual influences, including Marxism, which have replaced the values of the past, are preponderantly Western. Even for the men of the "New China" the cultural tug of the past demands the apotheosis of some Chinese equivalent to fill the void left by the rejected Confucian-literati tradition. Hence the effort, which I shall describe, to substitute a new past for the old, centering on the peasant revolts, urban commercial developments, and popular literature which had always before been only a substratum in the sweep of Chinese history. But the deliberate creation of a new, popular,

---

[1] See Chin Yü-fu, *Chung-kuo shih-hsüeh shih* [History of Chinese Historiography] (Shanghai, 1957, originally pub. 1941), 160–62.

[2] Joseph R. Levenson, "The Past Made to Measure: History under Chairman Mao," *Soviet Survey* (Apr.–June 1958), 32–37; see also his *Confucian China and Its Modern Fate* (Berkeley, Calif., 1958).

Marxist tradition has apparently aggravated rather than ameliorated the problem of finding meaning in the past. As a consequence, the mainland historians are paradoxically being forced to resurrect and incorporate, with some changes of course, portions of the heritage that the May Fourth generation had discarded.[3]

We can examine this process from two directions, by looking in turn at the substance of Chinese Communist historiography, and at the policy (or "line") that has guided historical research in the People's Republic of China. In what follows I shall consider first five substantive problems to which the mainland historians have turned most assiduously in their efforts to rewrite their history: the interpretation of peasant rebellions, the controversy over the origins of capitalism, "the formation of the Han nation," the place of "imperialism" in modern Chinese history, and the periodization of China's past.

The Chinese Communists in power were motivated by more than the iconoclasm of the May Fourth movement in their antipathy to the Confucian-literati tradition. Their aim was to break specifically with what they called the "feudal" past which they identified with their Kuomintang enemy. Ancient China during the Warring States period (480–222 B.C.), the age of the philosophers, perhaps had its "immortal character." But "then came the protracted stagnation of the feudal system which lasted for more than two thousand years, and during which thought, literature, and art could not break free from the patterns and rules set by the various schools of thought, particularly the Confucian school, of the Warring States era."[4] To the Com-

[3] In what follows I shall be referring continually to some of the more prominent historians in the People's Republic of China, who should be introduced briefly here: Chien Po-tsan, professor of history at Peking University and member of the Standing Committee of the Department of Philosophy and Social Science of the Chinese Academy of Sciences, studied for a year and a half at the University of California in the 1920's, and before 1949 published several works including *Chung-kuo shih kang* [An Outline of Chinese History] (2 vols., Chungking, 1943, 1944), which covers the period from prehistory through the Han. Kuo Mo-jo, president of the Academy of Sciences, is best known as a scholar for his work on ancient history, especially for his studies of bronze inscriptions. His principal works include *Chung-kuo ku-tai she-hui yen-chiu* [A Study of Ancient Chinese Society] (Shanghai, 1930) and *Shih p'i-p'an shu* [Ten Critiques] (Chungking, 1945). Fan Wen-lan is now the director of the Third Office (modern history) of the Institute of Historical Research. He began his career as a scholar of the Chinese classics, but later turned to modern history and in Yenan in 1945 completed the first volume of his *Chung-kuo chin-tai shih* [Modern History of China], which after revision was published in 1951. Pai Shou-yi has written a history of communications in China, *Chung-kuo chiao-t'ung shih* (Shanghai, 1937), and has also studied the history of the Moslem minority peoples. Hou Wai-lu is a specialist on the history of thought and with others has written *Chung-kuo ssu-hsiang t'ung-shih* [A History of Chinese Thought] (Shanghai, 1949, rev. ed., Peking, 1957). Since the 1930's Lü Chen-yü has been a leading Marxist writer on social history. Among his works are *Shih-ch'ien-ch'i Chung-kuo she-hui yen-chiu* [A Study of China's Prehistoric Society] (Peking, 1934), *Yin Chou shih-tai ti Chung-kuo she-hui* [Chinese Society in the Yin and Chou Periods] (Shanghai, 1936), and *Chung-kuo she-hui-shih chu wen-t'i* [Problems of Chinese Social History] (Shanghai, 1940).

[4] See Kuo Mo-jo, "Kuan-yü hou-chin po-ku wen-t'i" [On Emphasizing the Present and De-

munists the real history of China, in which every Chinese could take heart, was not the succession of imperial dynasties with their "feudal" landlord ruling classes, the last representatives of which had not only cruelly plundered the people but had also shamelessly surrendered to the Western imperialists. Chinese history was the history of the struggles of the peasants against their feudal masters and of the people against the imperialist aggressors.

Mao Tse-tung had said it: "These class struggles of the peasants—the peasant uprisings and peasant wars—alone formed the real motive force of historical development in China's feudal society. For each of the major peasant risings and wars dealt a blow to the existing feudal regime and more or less furthered the development of the social productive forces."[5] The past ten years have therefore seen an enormous outflow of documentary material and special studies of *nung-min ch'i-i,* "righteous uprisings of the peasantry," the use of the term *ch'i-i,* literally "uprising-righteous," rather than any one of several terms meaning "rebellion," being indicative of the general tenor of these works.[6] In one example, the history of China from the Chou dynasty to the present is depicted as pivoting on nine major peasant uprisings. The historian is enjoined to begin his narration of each period with a detailed treatment of the struggles of the peasant masses against the landlords and nobles. He is then to describe the early period of the new dynasty that arose out of this conflict, noting the "concessions" the dynastic founder and his immediate successors were forced to make to the peasantry, but also remarking on the basic "feudal contradictions" that remained unresolved. Finally, in lesser detail, he should treat of the dynasty's later development, when these contradictions led inexorably into the next round of peasant risings.[7]

The "theoretical" basis adduced in these writings for assessing the significance of the *nung-min ch'i-i* turns out to be a combination of the familiar "dynastic cycle" (but now turned on its head and viewed from the putative point of view of the masses), the lessons drawn by Mao Tse-tung from the experiences of 1927, and Lenin on the role of the peasantry. As the remarks by Mao just cited imply, China's "feudal society" is seen not as wholly stag-

---

emphasizing the Past], *Pei-ching ta-hsüeh hsüeh-pao, Jen-wen k'o-hsüeh* [Peking University Journal, Humanistic Sciences] (No. 3, 1958), 111–14.

[5] "The Chinese Revolution and the Chinese Communist Party," *Selected Works of Mao Tse-tung* (Eng. ed., 4 vols., London, 1954–56), III, 76.

[6] See, e.g., the collection of twenty-six studies covering Chinese history from the Ch'in to the Republic, *Chung-kuo nung-min ch'i-i lun-chi* [Collected Essays on the Righteous Risings of the Chinese Peasantry], ed. Li Kuang-pi, Ch'ien Chün-yeh, and Lai Hsin-hsia (Peking, 1958).

[7] T'ang Lan, "Wang-ch'ao-shih t'i-hsi ying-kai ta-p'o" [We Must Overthrow the Genre of Court History], *Hsin-chien-she* [Reconstruction], Apr. 7, 1959, 11–13.

nant, but only slow in developing as compared with feudalism in the West. Historical movement comes as a result of the overthrow of successive dynasties by peasant revolt, which also forces the new unifier (often of peasant origin himself, as in the cases of Liu Pang [reigned 206–195 B.C.], founder of the Han, and Chu Yuan-chang [reigned 1368–1398], founder of the Ming, who are the favorite examples) to relax momentarily the restrictions on society's "social productive forces," that is, to offer concessions to the peasantry in the form of land registration in order to discover landlord tax evaders, lighter taxes, assistance in the opening of new lands, relief in times of natural disaster, and the like. These measures are presumed to increase peasant security and agricultural output, with a resultant larger social surplus which is the basis on which commerce, handicraft, and urban clusters develop that will ultimately undermine the "feudal" form of society.

The Chinese Communist commentators acknowledge that herein lies a "dialectical" problem, although the implications of this admission are perhaps deeper than they would admit. Peasant revolts, it is seen, in order to have their beneficial effects, are inextricably tied to the successful establishment of a new dynasty to replace that which the revolts had overthrown. In other words, in order to realize the positive results of peasant uprisings, such disturbances must be suppressed and political order restored. This is so because the peasantry, in the orthodox Marxist-Leninist view, are incapable of organizing a new sociopolitical structure of their own. Where purely peasant movements have been successful, as in the case of Li Tzu-ch'eng (1606–1645) at the end of the Ming, they both tend to reduplicate the institutions of the imperial regime that preceded them and are incapable of carrying out the thorough reorganization of local power that would effectively check the feudal-gentry-literati forces that have been momentarily defeated, but lurk off the scene ready to rise again at the first opportunity. *Nung-min ch'i-i,* then, cannot be viewed uncritically by the mainland historians; they are not the historical equivalent of the workers' and peasants' movement led by the Chinese Communist party which successfully overthrew the "compradore-feudal" Kuomintang and established socialist political power in China.[8]

Nor, I may add, given this "dialectical" evaluation, do they seem to be a foundation solid enough on which to erect a past that will evoke unqualified commitment. While useful perhaps in satisfying an immediate emotional hunger, peasant rebellion may be a rather unsatisfactory staple historical diet. It rarely, if ever, has an independent existence in the records of the past, but

---

[8] Sun Tso-min, *Chung-kuo nung-min chan-cheng wen-t'i t'an-so* [Studies on the Question of China's Peasant Wars] (Shanghai, 1956), 8–19, 20–28, 40–54.

can only be seen—in a distorted image to be sure—through the eyes of the "feudal" officials and landlords, the literati, who are the authors of the millions of volumes of essays, memorials, history, poetry, and philosophy that comprise the awe-inspiring corpus of Chinese writing.

The subject of peasant revolts, however, is one on which there is probably considerable agreement among mainland historians. There is less unanimity in the case of a second major area of concern, the question of "incipient capitalism" (*tzu-pen chu-i meng-ya*).[9] The problem of capitalist origins follows naturally from the assertion that, however slowly, China's "feudal" economy was nevertheless developing and changing. What would have been the end product of that development if it had not been diverted from its "natural" course by foreign aggression? What was the nature of China's pre-nineteenth-century society, and what were its potentialities?

Again Mao has supplied the text to which all other answers are mere exegesis: "As China's feudal society developed its commodity economy and so carried within itself the embryo of capitalism, China would of herself have developed slowly into a capitalist society even if there had been no influence of foreign imperialism."[10] The exegesis in this instance began with the composition by Hou Wai-lu of an intellectual history of early modern China in which he ascribed the appearance of "bourgeois" thought in China to the late Ming and early Ch'ing periods, roughly the sixteenth and seventeenth centuries.[11] This theme was carried forward in 1954 in a textbook largely written by Shang Yüeh which asserted that incipient capitalist elements (*meng-ya*) were already existent in the Ming.[12] In the next year extensive discussion in literary circles of the social background of the novel *Hung-lou meng* (Dream of the Red Chamber) stimulated a spate of articles agreeing that capitalist burgeons were already to be found prior to the Opium War, but differing quite sharply as to the date of their origin and the degree of their development and significance.[13]

[9] See Albert Feuerwerker, "From 'Feudalism' to 'Capitalism' in Recent Historical Writing from Mainland China," *Journal of Asian Studies*, XVIII (Nov. 1958), 107–16.

[10] *Selected Works of Mao Tse-tung*, III, 77.

[11] Hou Wai-lu, *Chung-kuo tsao-ch'i ch'i-meng ssu-hsiang shih* [History of Early Modern Thought in China] (Peking, 1956, but written and circulated privately more than a decade earlier).

[12] *Chung-kuo li-shih kang-yao* [Outline History of China], ed. Shang Yüeh (Peking, 1954).

[13] The chief contributions to this discussion are reprinted in *Chung-kuo tzu-pen chu-i meng-ya wen-t'i t'ao-lun chi* [Collected Papers on the Problem of the Incipiency of Capitalism in China] (2 vols., Peking, 1957) and *Ming-Ch'ing she-hui ching-chi hsing-t'ai ti yen-chiu* [Studies in the Society and Economy of the Ming and Ch'ing Periods] (Shanghai, 1957). Both collections are edited by the Chinese History Seminar of the Chinese People's University of Peking.

For a time, during 1956 and 1957, it appeared that the view represented by the historian Shang Yüeh had won the day.[14] In brief, Shang and his supporters argued that the late Ming and Ch'ing economy was already protocapitalist. The central arch of this contention was the assertion of the widespread existence of factory handicrafts (*kung-ch'ang shou-kung-yeh*) which are presumed to have fulfilled the Marxist criteria for capitalist production. Their development, so the schema goes, was preceded by a proliferation of internal and external trade. These market forces acted to bring about an increasing differentiation of handicraft, traditionally a peasant ancillary occupation, from agriculture, as well as an unprecedented concentration of landholding which forced many peasants into newly growing towns where they found employment in factory handicraft. The new "bourgeoisie" of the late Ming (whose ideological leaders, it is explained, were such men as Ku Yen-wu, Huang Tsung-hsi, and Wang Fu-chih) would eventually have seized political power in combination with their peasant allies (this is the interpretation given to Li Tzu-ch'eng's rebellion which overthrew the Ming) and then proceeded to prepare the rest of the prerequisites for the development of industrial capitalism, just as their English and French counterparts are alleged to have done. But the Manchu invasion and devastation of the land in the first instance and the imperialists' aggression and exploitation which followed in the nineteenth century prevented this happy fruition.

Like the debates on the nature of Chinese society of the 1920's and 1930's, in which most of the theoretical arguments now advanced were already stated,[15] the present concern to establish that China's premodern economy was in fact evolving in accordance with the Marxist normative stages of societal development can be best understood as part of an effort to erect a new meaningful past, as the sewing of another stitch for the garment that would replace the rejected Confucian-literati habit. By claiming an identical pedigree with the West, parallel and not derivative, and of equal hoariness, the mainland historians are simultaneously discarding the Confucian past and substituting a Chinese equivalent value. To assert that Chinese society was not fundamentally different and to ascribe the humiliations endured to the conspiracy of the Manchu dynasty and its "compradore-feudal" successors with the imperialist powers is doubtless a means whereby self-respect may be preserved and the positive value of tradition maintained.

[14] See Shang Yüeh, *Chung-kuo tzu-pen chu-i kuan-hsi fa-sheng chi yen-pien ti ch'u-pu yen-chiu* [Preliminary Studies on the Origin and Development of Capitalist Relations in China] (Peking, 1956), and his preface to the collection *Ming-Ch'ing she-hui ching-chi hsing-t'ai ti yen-chiu*.

[15] See Benjamin I. Schwartz, "A Marxist Controversy on China," *Far Eastern Quarterly*, XIII (Feb. 1954), 143–53.

It may well be that, given the underdeveloped state of East Asian studies, we have until now underestimated the degree of commercialization of the premodern Chinese economy. But the step from the posited existence of extensive commerce and advanced forms of organization in handicraft manufacture to the assertion that the Chinese economy was developing toward an "industrial revolution" is an act of faith rather than a historical-scientific conclusion. Even more significant for our present purpose than the external criticism we might apply is the fact that more recently the weight of authoritative opinion seems to have swung away from Shang Yüeh.[16]

The reaction against Shang Yüeh raises some doubt about the probability that the mainland historians will be able to reach agreement on this part of the new reading of the past that they are seeking to establish. Assuming that somewhere in the writings of Mao (or Marx, Engels, Lenin, and Stalin) there is the word, which of the incomplete and frequently offhand directives provided by the "classics of Marxism" shall be followed? In this instance, the remark by Mao just cited, beginning "As China's feudal society developed its commodity economy . . ." follows immediately after a passage that reads, "Chinese feudal society lasted for about 3,000 years. It was not until the middle of the nineteenth century that great internal changes took place in China as a result of the penetration of foreign capitalism." Shang Yüeh's critics explicitly indict him for contradicting this last passage. Behind their charge is the fear that too great an emphasis on internal protocapitalist developments prior to the full impact of Western imperialism in the nineteenth century might divert attention from the villain's role assigned to foreign capitalism in transforming China into a "semicolonial, semifeudal" status. This clearly would not fit in with the need, at this stage of the Chinese revolution, to project a large share of the blame for a century and more of humiliation and weakness onto the "imperialist aggressors," a matter that I shall discuss further. Thus Shang is accused of misinterpreting the nature of the Opium War, of failing to see that it marked the beginning of "the struggle between the Chinese people's anti-imperialist, anti-feudal line which sought to transform China into an independent and prosperous nation, and

---

[16] See, e.g., Liu Ta-nien (associate editor of *Li-shih yen-chiu*, the leading mainland historical journal), "Kuan-yü Shang Yüeh t'ung-chih wei *Ming-Ch'ing she-hui ching-chi hsing-t'ai ti yen-chiu* i-shu so hsieh ti hsü-yen" [A Critique of Shang Yüeh's Preface to *Studies in the Society and Economy of the Ming and Ch'ing Periods*], *Li-shih yen-chiu* [Historical Studies] (No. 1, 1958), 1–16; a sweeping attack by the modern historians at the People's University in Peking, "P'ing Shang Yüeh t'ung-chih kuan-yü Ming-Ch'ing she-hui ching-chi chieh-kou ti jo-kan kuan-tien" [A Critique of Shang Yüeh's Views Concerning the Social and Economic Structure of the Ming and Ch'ing Dynasties], *ibid.* (No. 12, 1958), 21–35; and Li Shu, "Chung-kuo ti chin-tai shih yü ho shih?" [When Was the Beginning of Modern History in China?], *ibid.* (No. 3, 1959), 1–11.

the imperialist feudal line which sought to transform China into a colony." And this because of his false attribution of a connection between the leadership of the people's struggles in 1839–1842 and the "bourgeois urban movement" of the late Ming and early Ch'ing, with the result that "the nature of this Chinese national anti-aggressive struggle is changed into 'bourgeois' anti-feudalism."[17] Playing up the degree of China's economic development along the Marxist normative road to capitalism, moreover, may raise doubts about the historical necessity of the revolution led by the Communist party. "If 300 years ago capitalism already held such a secure position," state the critics of Shang Yüeh, "then the anti-feudal land reform led by the Communist Party could not have occurred. . . . And how could there have been any necessity for the proletariat to seize the leadership of the democratic revolution?"[18]

In sum, then, the argument that the Chinese economy was following a path of development parallel to but independent of Western Europe, because it can never be firmly based on scripture and because it appears to conflict with certain political needs of the regime that have a higher priority, has turned out to be a less than satisfactory link in the newly forged chain of the past.

An article by Professor G. V. Efimov of Leningrad University in *Voprosy istorii* in October 1953 prompted the mainland historians to consider the question of the "formation of the Han nation." Employing Stalin's four characteristics of a "nation," Efimov concluded that China from the Chou dynasty (ca. 1027–222 B.C.) onward had possessed a *narodnost'* type of collective existence. But the Chinese (or Han) nation was formed only in the nineteenth and twentieth centuries, and as a consequence of imperialist aggression it was a semicolonial bourgeois nation.[19] The first Chinese response to this formulation was an article by Fan Wen-lan which followed Efimov in applying Stalin's criteria, but argued that as early as the Ch'in-Han period (221 B.C.– A.D. 220) China already had a common language, a common territory, a

---

[17] Liu Ta-nien, "Kuan-yü Shang Yüeh t'ung-chih," 11–12.

[18] People's University historians, "Ping Shang Yüeh t'ung-chih," 22–23. Shang Yüeh, however, has not given up the fight; see his recent rebuttal to Li Shu: "Yu-kuan Chung-kuo tzu-pen chu-i meng-ya wen-t'i ti erh-san shih" [Some Matters Concerning the Question of Incipient Capitalism in China], *Li-shih yen-chiu* (No. 7, 1959), 25–50.

[19] G. V. Efimov, "K voprosu ob obrazovanii Kitaiskoi natsii" [On the Formation of the Chinese Nation], *Voprosy istorii* (No. 10, 1953), 65–78. Efimov's argument hangs on the term *narodnost'*, which the Chinese translate as *pu-tsu*, and which has no simple English equivalent other than perhaps "nationality." It is used on the one hand in contrast to "tribe" (*pu-lo*) and on the other in contrast to "nation" (*min-tsu*), and is defined as a stage in which the four Stalinist criteria of a nation are present to some degree, but not in a developed form. The common economy in particular is only incipient or potential and is not realized until the rise of capitalism produces a national market. See J. V. Stalin, "Marxism and the National Question" (1913), *Works* (Eng. ed., 13 vols., Moscow, 1952–55), II, 300–81.

common economic life, and a common psychology based on a common culture. Fan devoted considerable space to demonstrating that a common economic life was well developed, his chief argument being that Chinese "feudalism" differed from European feudalism in permitting the free alienation of land and in the degree of social mobility that was possible, and because it was characterized by the fusion of landlords and merchants. "Feudal" industry and commerce in China therefore were conducive to national unity and were the basis for the formation of a unified state (*t'ung-i kuo-chia*). "The Han race from Ch'in-Han onwards was not a *narodnost'* in a period of national disunity, nor was it a bourgeois nation of the capitalist period. It was a unique nation formed under unique social conditions."[20]

Following a conference called by the Institute of Historical Research of the Academy of Sciences in November 1954 for the purpose of discussing Fan's thesis, many articles on this subject began to appear in the historical journals. The issue of whether or not premodern China had a common economy drew the most fire. It was assumed that in asserting the existence of a unified state, Fan Wen-lan intended to confirm the existence of a Chinese nation in the Ch'in-Han period. A minority of the commentators supported this position. But the majority chose to draw a distinction between a unified state and a nation and to argue that the latter did not exist prior to the development of capitalism, without which there could be no national market and hence no common economy. And capitalism was a late development. Depending on where one stood in the *tzu-pen chu-i meng-ya* controversy, it first appeared either in the late Ming, or after 1840. They agreed, in short, with Efimov's characterization of the premodern Han race as a *narodnost'*, or nationality, rather than a nation.

The other half of Fan's assertion of China's uniqueness, that China was never a bourgeois nation, did not fare much better. Here the arguments of the majority criticized Fan for not giving enough attention to the effects of the incursion of foreign capitalism. It was due to this omission, they contended, that he failed to distinguish clearly between "feudal society" and "semifeudal, semicolonial society" and as a consequence denied that China was ever a bourgeois nation. In their view the essence of the "semifeudal, semicolonial" tag applied to post-1840 China is that Chinese "capitalism" had already begun to develop and undermine "feudal" society, hence "semifeudal." On this basis a bourgeois nation was gradually formed. But that development was stunted by imperialist encroachment, hence "semicolonial"

[20] Fan Wen-lan, "Shih lun Chung-kuo tzu Ch'in-Han shih ch'eng-wei t'ung-i kuo-chia ti yuan-yin" [Preliminary Discussion of the Reasons Why China Has Been a Unified State since the Ch'in-Han Period], *Li-shih yen-chiu* (No. 3, 1954), 15–25.

as a special characteristic of the Han nation. If there had been no Chinese bourgeois nation, it was asked of Fan, then how could one distinguish the ancient movements of the Han race against their feudal rulers and foreign aggressors from the "national liberation movement" of the past century? Fan was in error, moreover, in holding that because the proletariat led the bourgeoisie in the revolution that culminated in 1949, China could not have been a bourgeois nation. In that case, how could one understand the struggle between the proletariat and the bourgeoisie in the last fifty years for the leadership of the nation?

The significance of these arguments for the task of reinterpreting the past is not difficult to see. On the one hand Fan Wen-lan's statement that the Han race constituted "a unique nation formed under unique social conditions" represents an attempt, while still remaining within the perimeters of Marxism-Leninism, to claim for Chinese history a unique path of development. It is undoubtedly founded on the recognition that the assertion of a parallel, though separate, lineage with the capitalist West raises many difficult problems.

On the other hand, although I have referred to a "majority" as standing against Fan Wen-lan, there is no apparent unanimity on any other ground within this group. Like Fan, each writer made his bow to the "classics of Marxism," in this instance to Stalin's writings on the "national question." But when it came to specifying precisely when each of the four Stalinist criteria of a nation became operative in China, there was no agreement. Nor should one expect there to be when the writing of history sometimes consists of no more than the collection of quotations to illustrate the often inaccurate chance remarks of the doctrinal authorities. There is nothing in Stalin, or Mao for that matter, that really illuminates the development of nationalism in China. While, as I shall show below, it is to nationalism indeed that the mainland historians have in the end to turn, their effort to renew the past has benefitted little from their contemplation of the metaphysically stated "problem of the formation of the Han nation."[21]

[21] The principal contributions to this discussion are reprinted in *Han min-tsu hsing-ch'eng wen-t'i t'ao-lun chi* [Collected Papers on the Question of the Formation of the Han Nation], comp. by the editors of *Li-shih yen-chiu* (Peking, 1957). Failure to reach a definite conclusion about the formation of the Han nation has perhaps had an adverse effect on the study of a related problem, the history of the non-Chinese national minorities. If it is not clear what the Han "nation" is, consideration of its relations with non-Han minorities is doubly difficult. See Huang Yuan-ch'i, *Chung-kuo li-shih shang min-tsu-chan ti p'ing-p'an wen-t'i* [Critical Problems Concerning National Wars in China's History] (Shanghai, 1957), 7–9. The mainland historians hold that Chinese historiography prior to 1949 either totally ignored or gravely slandered the history of these "brother" nations. (For example, Chien Po-tsan, "Tsem-yang yen-chiu Chung-kuo li-shih" [How to Investigate Chinese History], in *Tsem-yang hsüeh-hsi tsu-kuo ti li-shih* [How to Study the History of Our Fatherland] (Shanghai, 1953), 23–41, esp.

One further way of rescuing the value of the past, in this case of the most recent century, is to turn the blame for the political weakness, economic chaos, and cultural discord of that century onto an external scapegoat. The singular evil, and increasingly the focus of the study of modern history in Communist China, is "imperialism."

Any reader who has turned his attention to the deluge of historical writing now pouring from the People's Republic of China will certainly be aware of a consistent, if unintended, imprecision in the treatment of this "evil" in modern Chinese history. While the Manchu dynasty, its warlord successors, and finally the Kuomintang are of course subjected to all the abuse that can be expressed through the profuse use of characters written with the "dog" radical, the ultimate degree of obloquy is reserved for the "foreign imperialist aggressors." It may be safely ventured that at the present time the principal emphasis of the mainland historians who write on the history of the past century is quite in line with Mao Tse-tung's dictum of 1940: "The history of imperialist aggression upon China, of imperialist opposition to China's independence and to her development of capitalism, constitutes precisely the history of modern China. Revolutions in China failed one after another because imperialism strangled them. . . ."[22] But for self-professed "scientific" historians the outlines of this foreign imperialist evil are remarkably shadowy and fluid.

Their imprecision is not due to any want of effort to define the enemy's

---

25–29. But post-1949 treatment of this question, despite a more positive evaluation of minority opposition to the Ch'ing, for example, continues to be colored by Chinese nationalism. Thus the conquest of the Hsiung-nu tribes by Han Wu-ti (reigned 140–87 B.C.) is interpreted as a "progressive" act because it contributed to the inevitable advancement of history through the Marxist stages, because it was motivated by the desire to protect the superior and relatively peaceful class relations—at that time—of the Han nation, because it was the Hsiung-nu ruling class that was hardest hit, and because through the conquest the more advanced Chinese culture was propagated among the Hsiung-nu. In the same vein, the revolt (ca. 1866–1877) of Yakub Beg against the Ch'ing was not "progressive" because it resulted in increased exploitation of the Moslem people, and was in fact a tool of British imperialist expansion into Turkistan. The Ch'ing suppression of Yakub Beg therefore is to be judged positively. See Huang Yuan-ch'i, *Chung-kuo li-shih shang min-tsu-chan ti p'ing-p'an wen-t'i,* 5–6, 26, 44–45. It seems manifest that in part the increased attention given to the history of non-Chinese minorities is motivated by a desire to tie them closely to Han China and to reassert and underline Chinese sovereignty over her border areas. Note, for example, the following: "Ever since ancient times Sinkiang has been an integral part of our fatherland. The history of Sinkiang is a segment of our great national history. The history of the Sinkiang peoples has its glorious past, in which we may take pride, but we must place it appropriately within the history of the fatherland, regarding it as a constituent part of that history." Chang Tung-yüeh, "Kuan-yü Hsin-chiang li-shih ti chi-ko wen-t'i" [Some Problems Concerning the History of Sinkiang], *Min-tsu yen-chiu* [Ethnological Studies] (No. 6, 1959), 14.

22 "On New Democracy," *Selected Works of Mao Tse-tung,* IV, 123. See, e.g., Hu Sheng, *Imperialism and Chinese Politics* (Peking, 1955), 53–54 and *passim;* Ting Ming-nan *et al., Ti-kuo-chu-i ch'in Hua shih* [A History of Imperialist Aggression against China] (Peking, 1958), I; and Ch'ing Ju-chi, *Mei-kuo ch'in Hua shih* [A History of United States Aggression against China] (2 vols., Peking, 1952, 1956).

nature and motives. It is the expected thing for every writer to make such explicit assertions as "the nefarious activities of the imperialists aimed at halting China's progress" were in the beginning the result of "trade disputes," that the mid-nineteenth-century conflicts between China and the West, especially England, resulted from the aggressive designs of the "rising industrial capitalists" who "were anxious to convert [China] . . . into their own market in which they could sell their surplus commodities," and that finally, in the last decade of the nineteenth century, "the dominion of monopoly finance capital gradually established itself" and the "imperialist powers . . . no longer satisfied with the privileges secured earlier in China which enabled them to dump their goods and plunder the country" now "scrambled madly to acquire leased territories in China, to establish 'spheres of influence' and to place their investments in the country."[23] Although this diachronic differentiation of motive forces is piously put forward, it is remarkable to what degree historical narration in practice tends to lump all foreign contact with China in the modern period under the heading "imperialist aggression" and to ignore any finer distinctions. The first and greatest sinner on this count is Mao himself, in whose doctrinal writings "foreign capitalism" and "foreign imperialism" are often loosely interchangeable. Thus in the long list of sins which Mao attributes to the "imperialist powers" no clear distinction such as one might have expected from a disciple of Lenin is made between preimperialist capitalism and imperialist capitalism.[24] What is the significance of this "looseness" on the part of Mao and the Communist historians who are now elaborating on his pronouncements?

Whatever we may think of the validity of his particular formulations, it is evident that for Lenin "imperialism" had a relatively specific and restricted meaning.[25] The contrast between Lenin's specificity and the looseness of Chinese Communist historians is so marked that we can hardly believe that the Chinese are not aware of it. It would be misleading to interpret the protean and omnipresent application of the touchstone "imperialism" in current mainland writing as a very serious attempt to employ even the tools

[23] Hu Sheng, *Imperialism and Chinese Politics*, 4, 7–8, 110–11. See also Ting Ming-nan *et al.*, *Ti-kuo-chu-i ch'in Hua shih*, 6–7; Hu Pin, *Shih-chiu shih-chi mo-yeh ti-kuo-chu-i cheng-to Chung-kuo ch'üan-i shih* [History of Imperialist Encroachment on China's Rights and Interests in the Late Nineteenth Century] (Peking, 1957), 7–16; a simple-minded catechism for students: Lu T'ien, *Chung-kuo chin-tai-shih hsüeh-hsi wen-ta* [Questions and Answers for the Study of Chinese Modern History] (Shanghai, 1953), 19–20, 64–65; and Tai I, *Chung-kuo chin-tai shih-kao* [A Draft History of Modern China] (Peking, 1958), I, 1–11.

[24] "The Chinese Revolution and the Chinese Communist Party," *Selected Works of Mao Tse-tung*, III, 77–81.

[25] See Alfred G. Meyer, *Leninism* (Cambridge, Mass., 1957), 235–73.

of Marxism to probe the history of the past century in order to comprehend it better, to explain its structure and dynamics. The study and writing of modern Chinese history in the People's Republic of China at the present time is primarily an ideological exercise and emotional release, repeated over and over again, the function of which is to harness and channel the real political and economic frustrations encountered in China's nineteenth- and twentieth-century experience in the interests of a new historical integration under the auspices of the Chinese Communist party. The invariable point of all synthetic work, and the implicit assumption underlying monographic research on modern history, is the unmitigated baneful result of foreign intrusions, in particular their deflection of the "normal" course of development of China's history. As Mao put it, "Revolutions in China failed one after another because imperialism strangled them."

Even while this state of affairs continues, one cannot but be aware of misgivings on the part of some of the actors. The Chinese Communist historians, as I shall show, are very much preoccupied with the question of the "periodization" of their history, a reflection of the large problems involved in making three millennia of Chinese history fit the normative Marxist stages of development. "Modern history" (*chin-tai-shih*), it now seems generally agreed, denotes the period from the first Opium War until the May Fourth movement.[26] But to accept this definition of modern history apparently can raise some embarrassing questions for the Marxist *cum* emotional nationalist Chinese historian, such as that which glimmers for a moment and then is quickly if not easily drowned in sophistry in the following remarks by Li Shu, a participant in the periodization discussions:

There remains one important question. If we employ a foreign war of aggression against China to mark a division point in the periodization of our history, do we not then become proponents of external causation? My answer is to deny this. Comrade Mao Tse-tung has pointed out that the correct use of [historical] materialism does not at all deny a role to external causative factors; but external causes only manifest themselves through internal causes. Foreign capitalist aggression against China has influenced China to undergo internal changes. This means that Chinese society internally already possessed the prerequisite for the appearance of change; and this prerequisite was the high degree of development that China had attained during the long period of feudal society. At the time of the encroachment of foreign capitalism, if China had been no more than a primitive tribal society, the appearance of a bourgeoisie and a proletariat would have been impossible, no individuals with a developed consciousness could have emerged at all, and there could not have been a conscious revolutionary movement. . . . Comrade Mao Tse-tung has pointed out that China's revolution "is not merely

[26] See *Chung-kuo chin-tai-shih fen-ch'i wen-t'i t'ao-lun chi* [Collected Essays on the Problem of the Periodization of Modern Chinese History], comp. by the editors of *Li-shih yen-chiu* (Peking, 1957).

a formless uprising produced by the incursion of Western thought. It is a war of resistance provoked by imperialist aggression." This resistance is a conscious resistance which developed steadily in the period after the Opium War. Therefore it is reasonable for us to take the Opium War as a division point to mark the great revolutionary period that followed it.[27]

Li Shu is sensitive about the problem of internal versus external causation in China's historical development. There is an obvious anxiety that to assign so large a role to foreign incursions in the structuring of China's modern history verges on abandoning the belief that this history was capable of autonomous development. This is almost to cast doubt on the value of one's own past, no small emotional wrench for the hypernationalist Chinese. An uneasy resolution is reached by asserting that "external causes only manifest themselves through internal causes" and that "Chinese society internally already possessed the prerequisite for the appearance of change."

Perhaps it is comforting to dispose of the problem in this manner, but the inherent instability of the answer is revealed in the oscillations of Chinese Communist historiography in the past few years, such as I have described in connection with the incipient capitalism controversy. There we saw that the position of Shang Yüeh has lately come under attack largely because it might seem to take some of the "heat" off the foreign aggressors as the perpetrators of China's sorrows. There is an obvious paradox, moreover, as I have already implied, in Mao's statement that "the history of imperialist aggression upon China, of imperialist opposition to China's independence and to her development of capitalism, constitutes precisely the history of modern China." Is not this assertion a form of "imperialism" itself, a self-inflicted historical imperialism as poisonous to the construction of a new and valued past for the "New China" as "foreign imperialist aggression" allegedly was to China's independence and to her economic development? Could a Western historian "get away" with putting the main dynamic force in modern China outside of the stream of Chinese history itself? That such a formulation could be long lived in China, where history has for millennia been explicitly recognized as first of all a defender of the key values of Chinese civilization, seems improbable.

Each of the foregoing problems might also be viewed as a part of a general concern to establish the periodization of Chinese history. Since 1949 there have been extensive discussions of the proper dating of the slave and feudal stages of Chinese history, of the beginnings of capitalism, and of the

[27] Li Shu, "Chung-kuo ti chin-tai shih yü ho shih?" 10–11.

periodization of modern history. The goal of the periodization discussions, even more explicitly than the other topics on which the mainland historians have concentrated, is to fit Chinese history into a Marxist suit of clothes. The end product of the procrustean tailors is to be a Chinese history that they confidently assume can be valued because it was inevitable, and because notwithstanding a long period of stagnation, in a last minute spurt it has completed the prescribed course well ahead of its competitors.

The central question in the periodization of ancient history is when did the era of slavery end in China and consequently when did the feudal era begin.[28] For it is assumed, of course, that Chinese society passed from primitive communism through slavery, feudalism, and capitalism to socialism, and that it will soon achieve the Communist paradise. The pressure to settle this question finally (and the other periodization problems as well) therefore probably stems as much from the Communist party leadership, who are anxious lest any looseness at the beginning of the developmental paradigm raise doubts about its completion, as it does from the historians themselves.

As "historical materialists," it is not surprising that the mainland historians have turned with great energy to the study of the material artifacts of their history. Since 1949 archaeological research has been greatly accelerated and significant new finds reported.[29] It is then quite appropriate that it should have been an article—only a retrospective one, however, since the records of the excavations in question are now on Taiwan—contributed by the archaeologist Kuo Pao-chun to a Peking newspaper in March 1950 that touched off the current round of discussions about the periodization of ancient history. This article described the discovery of many corpses of commoners, who had apparently been buried alive, in the Shang royal tombs at Anyang, and noted briefly that comparatively fewer such discoveries had been made for the Chou period.[30] Kuo Mo-jo, president of the Academy of Sciences and a leading student of ancient society, immediately suggested that those persons who had been buried alive were slaves, that this con-

[28] The principal contributions to the discussion of ancient history are reprinted in *Chung-kuo ti nu-li-chih yü feng-chien-chih fen-ch'i wen-t'i lun-wen hsüan-chi* [Collected Essays on the Periodization of the Slave and Feudal Eras in China], comp. by the editors of *Li-shih yen-chiu* (Peking, 1956), and *Chung-kuo ku-shih fen-ch'i wen-t'i lun-ts'ung* [Essays on the Periodization of Ancient Chinese History], comp. by the editors of *Wen-shih-che* [Literature, History, and Philosophy] (Shanghai, 1957).

[29] See *K'ao-ku hsüeh-pao* [Journal of Archaeology], which includes English extracts of its articles, and Cheng Te-k'un, *Archaeology in China*, I, *Prehistoric China* (Cambridge, Eng., 1959).

[30] *Kuang-ming jih-pao*, Mar. 19, 1950, reprinted in *Chung-kuo ti nu-li-chih yü feng-chien-chih fen-ch'i wen-t'i lun-wen hsüan-chi*, 58–60.

firmed his view that the Shang (16th century–1027 B.C.) was a slave society, and that moreover the Chou too was a slave period.[31]

In the disputation that subsequently developed, there were two principal opposing positions (with numerous subvarieties, of course) represented respectively by Kuo Mo-jo and by the historian Fan Wen-lan. Kuo's views over the years have gone through a considerable evolution. In his well-known *Study of Ancient Chinese Society* (1930) [see note 3 above], he had labeled the Shang as a matriarchal clan society in the stage of primitive communism, the Western Chou (ca. 1027–771 B.C.) as a slave society, and the Eastern Chou from the Ch'un-ch'iu period (770–481 B.C.) onward as the beginning of feudalism in China. Later, in the *Ten Critiques* (1945) and elsewhere, this schema was revised radically with primitive communism relegated to the pre-Shang period, slavery extended through the Shang, Chou, and Ch'in with some survivals even in the Han, and the beginning of the feudal period identified with the Han dynasty. By the early 1950's Kuo had arrived at a still further modification which he still holds today.[32] The Shang and Western Chou remain periods of slave society. Kuo interprets the decline in the number of burials of commoners in the Chou tombs as a sign of the development, not the decline, of slavery. As the slave system of production developed, slaves became more valuable and hence fewer were sacrificed. But sometime during the middle of the Eastern Chou, roughly at the transition from the Ch'un-ch'iu ("Spring and Autumn") period to the Chan-kuo ("Warring States"), slave society gave way to feudal society. It is of significance that for the most part these successive reinterpretations are not based on startling new evidence.

In contrast to Kuo, Fan Wen-lan and his supporters, although their arguments are based on precisely the same sources as Kuo employed, hold that the Western Chou was not a slave period at all. The Shang was a type of slave society, but the Chou conquest in the eleventh century B.C. represented a social revolution that replaced the slave system with feudalism. This is shown by the fact that the Chou abolished the practice of burying persons alive. Where, asks Fan, was the equivalent social revolution between the Western and Eastern Chou? This school of thought also contends that Chinese feudal society in its first stage, until the establishment of a unified empire by the Ch'in in 221 B.C., was characterized by the nominal ownership of the land by the Chou sovereign and the relative weakness of private property. In

[31] *Kuang-ming jih-pao*, Mar. 21, 1950, reprinted in *ibid.*, 54–58.
[32] Cf. Kuo Mo-jo's "Nu-li-chih shih-tai" [The Period of Slavery], in *ibid.*, 1–53 (written in 1952) with his "Kuan-yü Chung-kuo ku-shih yen-chiu ti liang-ko wen-t'i" [Two Problems in the Study of Ancient Chinese History], *Li-shih yen-chiu* (No. 6, 1959), 1–8.

the later stage of "absolutist feudal society," private ownership by landowners who exploited their estates with serf labor was characteristic.[33] To both Kuo and Fan, "feudalism" means essentially a landlord economy in which the exploitation of serf labor is the dominant form of agriculture. Their arguments about the beginnings of feudalism do not depend, as is the case with many non-Marxist Chinese scholars, on the identification of the Chou practice of enfeoffment (*feng-chien*) with its alleged counterpart in Western Europe. Thus despite their differences with regard to its origin, they both agree that the feudal stage in China lasted until at least the nineteenth century.

To this date the definitive periodization of ancient history has still to be achieved; the argument continues roughly along the lines outlined above. While the historians are confident that it can be settled, perhaps through the discovery of new historical sources, the variety of detailed studies of the Shang and Chou which rake over the oracle bones, bronze inscriptions, and ancient texts and quote profusely from Marx, Engels, Lenin, Stalin, and Mao remain bewildering. If a definitive periodization is ever established, it is less likely to be the result of new archaeological finds than of a prescribed reading of the Marxist classics. These texts in themselves manifestly provide no sure guide, but the trends in their interpretation seem to point in the direction of a victory for the school of thought led by Kuo Mo-jo.

Fan and those who follow him depend in part on a version of Marx's speculations about an "Asiatic mode of production." True, they do not in general go so far as to apply this tag in a wholesale fashion to Chinese society in the imperial period, thereby suggesting that this was the chief cause of China's long stagnation, as some participants in the earlier discussions on the nature of Chinese society had done. They do, however, tend to follow Lü Chen-yü, who proposed in 1940 that the Asiatic mode of production was in fact a variant of the stage of slavery in which certain elements of clan society and primitive communism have survived.[34] On this basis they claim that slave society in China was never fully developed before it was replaced by feudalism, and that it would therefore be in error to view Chou society as a further development of Shang slavery. But, in whatever

[33] Fan Wen-lan *et al.*, *Chung-kuo t'ung-shih chien-pien* [A Short General History of China] (Shanghai, 1952, 8th printing of 1948 rev. ed.), and Fan, "Ch'u-ch'i feng-chien she-hui k'ai-shih yü Hsi-Chou" [The First Period of Feudal Society Began in the Western Chou], reprinted in *Chung-kuo ti nu-li-chih yü feng-chien-chih fen-ch'i wen-t'i lun-wen hsüan-chi*, 59–73.

[34] See Lü Chen-yü, *Chung-kuo she-hui-shih chu wen-t'i*, 2, 31, and *passim*. This whole matter is further complicated by the intense debates on the "Asiatic mode of production" and "Oriental society" in the Soviet Union and among Japanese Marxists which I am unable to treat here.

qualified fashion one broaches the matter of an Asiatic mode of production as an explanation of Chinese history, there is always the danger that the fascination of this theory will lead some to "misuse" it, even to suggest that it, rather than feudal oppression and imperialist exploitation, was the cause of China's centuries of backwardness.[35] This as we have seen is politically *non grata*. Kuo, on the other hand, rejects this formulation entirely, and it is therefore probable that his version of the periodization of ancient history has stronger backing from the Communist party than that of his rival. For our purposes, the principal significance of all this quotation dropping is that the problem of periodization, like all the others we have discussed, is unsolvable except on completely arbitrary grounds, and thus makes little positive contribution to the revaluation of the past.

Relatively little attention has been given to the periodization of the two millennia of feudal society that the mainland historians assert followed the epoch of slavery. This is perhaps indicative of a reluctance to venture forth in uncharted waters.[36] The Marxist classics have had very little to say about the feudal period; their emphasis has always been on tracing the origins and development of a capitalism that successfully grew out of medieval society and much less on analyzing the antecedent feudal order. What criteria shall be applied then in dividing feudal society into neat little packets? Very much the same problem exists with respect to the periodization of China's modern history, but here the external political demand for agreement insures that the question has received close attention. The nearer we approach to the modern period, the greater is the apparent agreement among historians and the more is conformity required. With respect to modern history proper, the consensus on the main outlines and characteristics seems nearly complete.

In discussing the place assigned to "imperialism" in mainland historiography, I noted the possible drawbacks to taking the Opium War—the beginning of foreign aggression against China—as the starting place for modern history. This nevertheless is what is being done. All are agreed that during the Opium War and its aftermath Chinese feudal society was transformed into semifeudal, semicolonial society which lasted until the establishment of the People's Republic in October 1949. "Modern history" extends from 1840 to 1919 and is characterized by the gradual development of the forces

---

[35] In fact, one of Fan's supporters does just this; see Yang Hsiang-k'uei, "Chung-kuo li-shih fen-ch'i wen-t'i" [The Problem of Periodizing Chinese History] in *Chung-kuo ti nu-li-chih yü feng-chien-chih fen-ch'i wen-t'i lun-wen hsüan-chi*, 331–58, esp. 355.

[36] See, however, Shu Shih-cheng, *Chung-kuo ti feng-chien she-hui chi ch'i fen-ch'i* [China's Feudal Society and Its Periodization] (Shanghai, 1957).

of the "Old Democratic Revolution" (or bourgeois revolution) which reached its culmination in the movement led by Sun Yat-sen. From 1919 to 1949 is the period of the "New Democratic Revolution" under the leadership of the Chinese Communist party, and is referred to as "contemporary history." "Current history" or the "epoch of the People's Republic of China" began with 1949.[37] With the outline and content of modern history so fully prescribed by the political leaders of the regime, the historians have been able to do no more than turn with a vengeance to the task of elaborating the stages and substages of that century.

The discussion was initiated by an article by Hu Sheng, best known as the author of *Imperialism and Chinese Politics*,[38] in the first number of the journal *Li-shih yen-chiu* (Historical Studies), which set forth an elaborate scheme of seven stages (1840–1850, 1851–1864, 1864–1895, 1895–1900, 1901–1905, 1905–1912, 1912–1919) and attempted to justify them by postulating three great "revolutionary waves" of the class struggle with which they were related. The numerous articles on this subject that followed were all of the same kind—proposing a bewildering confusion of dates and rationalizing them by one or another Marxist criterion. Let me illustrate with three examples out of many: Sun Shou-jen, four stages (1840–1864, 1864–1894, 1894–1905, 1905–1919), determined by reference to the "principal contradictions" in Chinese society; Chin Ch'ung-chi, five stages (1840–1864, 1864–1894, 1894–1900, 1900–1914, 1914–1919), correlated with alleged social and economic changes—changes in the "mode of production"; Tai I, three stages (1840–1873, 1873–1901, 1901–1919), using the same class struggle criterion applied by Hu Sheng.[39]

For the most part, the reader's probable impression that this cutting and trimming is pointless is a correct one. What possible difference can it make whether one ends a chapter or a lecture on modern history with 1901 or ends it with 1905 when he has already squeezed the whole century into a semifeudal, semicolonial garment? What, after all, is the difference between a

---

[37] The scriptural sources for the treatment of modern history are, above all else, Mao Tsetung's *The Chinese Revolution and the Chinese Communist Party* (written in December 1939) and his *On New Democracy* (written in January 1940); see *Selected Works of Mao Tse-tung*, III, 72–101, 106–56. The principal contributions to the recent discussions of the periodization of modern history are reprinted in *Chung-kuo chin-tai-shih fen-ch'i wen-t'i t'ao-lun chi.*

[38] Hu Sheng, *Imperialism and Chinese Politics* (Eng. ed., Peking, 1955).

[39] Hu Sheng, "Chung-kuo chin-tai li-shih ti fen-ch'i wen-t'i" [The Problem of Periodizing Modern Chinese History], *Li-shih yen-chiu* (No. 1, 1954), 5–15; Sun Shou-jen, "Chung-kuo chin-tai li-shih ti fen-ch'i wen-t'i ti shang-chüeh" [A Discussion of the Problem of Periodizing Modern Chinese History], *ibid.* (No. 6, 1954), 1–15; Chin Ch'ung-chi, "Kuan-yü Chung-kuo chin-tai li-shih fen-ch'i wen-t'i ti i-chien" [Opinions on the Periodization of China's Modern History], *ibid.* (No. 2, 1955), 37–51; Tai I, "Chung-kuo chin-tai-shih ti fen-ch'i wen-t'i" [The Problem of Periodizing Modern Chinese History], *ibid.* (No. 6, 1959), 1–22.

"manifestation of the class struggle" and a "principal contradiction" as a criterion for the organization of that history when one already knows that it is the struggle of the masses against the feudal landlords and foreign imperialists that forms the content of modern history? And if either of these, or the third—the "stage of development of the mode of production"—has the "scientific" validity that the Chinese historians claim, then why is there so much disagreement about which manifestations are significant, which contradictions are the principal ones?

It would be unfair, however, to deny that some small part of the argument over the periodization of modern history does have a substantive content, although it is admittedly difficult to discover in the prolix verbiage. The views of Hu Sheng and Sung Shou-jen, for example, reveal quite opposite interpretations of the 1898 Reform Movement and the Boxer Rebellion, although both remain safely within the parameters of modern history à la Mao Tse-tung. Hu takes as the criterion for his periodization, as we have seen, the three great "revolutionary waves" of the class struggle which he identifies as the years 1850–1864 (the Taiping Rebellion), 1898–1900 (the Reform Movement and Boxer Rebellion), and 1905–1911 (the revolutionary activities of the T'ung-meng-hui culminating in the overthrow of the Ch'ing in 1911). Sung chooses to place his reliance on Mao's typology of the "fundamental contradictions" in modern Chinese society, that is, imperialism versus the Chinese nation, the people versus feudal reaction, the bourgeoisie versus the proletariat, and the "contradictions within the reactionary ruling classes themselves." From his own fortress, Sung is able to criticize Hu, because of the latter's concern with the class struggle, for ignoring what Mao has stated to be the "principal contradiction"—between imperialism and the Chinese nation. As a consequence, states Sung, Hu does not take seriously enough the program of "national and racial salvation" of the 1898 reformers and sees their reformism only as a device to head off peasant rebellion. Similarly, because he concentrates on the class struggle, Hu is accused of misinterpreting the Boxer movement and calling it a "perversion." He incorrectly characterizes Tz'u Hsi's declaration of war against the Western powers as a cunning policy aimed at getting rid of the Boxers by embroiling them with superior foreign troops. But in truth, continues Sung, this was only a secondary motive. If Hu had kept in mind the "principal contradiction," he would have seen that the Empress Dowager's decision for war was a positive response of the court to an actual threat to the existence of the dynasty and that it was made under the impact of a popular anti-imperialist movement.

These are points of considerable interest to historians of modern China, but they are unrepresentative of the general level and tenor of the periodization discussions. The articles and essays devoted to dividing up modern history are, I believe, unrivaled in their sterility anywhere else in mainland Chinese historiography. Everything of significance has been prepackaged in an airtight wrapping. Not a whiff of contingency can be allowed to adulterate the inevitable, the predetermined. If this is the way the Chinese Communist historians seek to make their recent past meaningful and valued, they have on their own admission fallen far short of their goal.

What, if I may attempt to draw up a balance sheet, has ten years of concentration on the foregoing problem areas contributed to reestablishing the meaning of the Chinese past? Peasant rebellion as the main content of Chinese history is a chimera. Too much emphasis on China's independent parallel development with the West toward capitalism has unwanted political implications. The "formation of the Han nation" leads either to the postulation of China's uniqueness, which Marxist orthodoxy cannot accept, or to metaphysical nonsense. If "imperialism" is the key to modern Chinese history, that history stands in danger of losing entirely its autonomy and hence its meaning. No definitive periodization of ancient history is possible except on arbitrary and thus meaningless grounds. This arbitrary decision has already been taken in the case of the more politically sensitive modern period, and its flummery revealed.

And from a broader perspective, consider what has been left out as well as what has been the center of historical interest. Almost no attention has been given to the two thousand years of what is referred to as the feudal period. The enormously broad and exciting question of the development and inner life of Confucianism, the analysis of China's unique and remarkably long-lived political institutions, the animation of the religious and ideological controversies in the great periods of Han (206 B.C.–A.D. 220), T'ang (618–906), and Sung (960–1279), the complex role of barbarian invaders in China's history—all this is dismissed as "protracted stagnation" and little more. It is small wonder that during the "anti-rightist campaign" of 1957 one of the principal accusations directed against the "rightist" historian Hsiang Ta was his alleged characterization of post-1949 historiography as being "at the brink of death" because of its exclusive attention to the questions of periodization, capitalist burgeons, peasant wars, the feudal land system, and the formation of the Han nation.[40]

[40] Jen-min jih-pao [People's Daily], Oct. 4, 1957; American Consulate General, Hong Kong, Survey of the China Mainland Press [SCMP], Dec. 3, 1957, 25. On Hsiang Ta, see SCMP, July 29–30, 1951, 27–28.

Above all else, the past has been seen only in terms of the inevitable present that followed it. However much talmudic exegesis is applied to the Marxist-Leninist-Maoist scriptures, the assertion that the past is meaningful cannot be combined with the simultaneous declaration that the study of the past is primarily for the purpose of discovering laws and uniformities applicable in the immediate present. Nor can it be logically professed that the movement of history is inevitable, but that this inevitable future is only realized through the meaningful decisions of historical individuals.[41] Meaning in history centers on the contingent choice of alternatives at the time that the choice is made. It is the contingent, of course, that Chinese Communist historiography completely obliterates. The past is only raw material for the present, standing in the same relationship to it as wood pulp to a printed volume of the works of Mao Tse-tung.

My over-all characterization of Chinese Communist historiography, then, is that it is in danger of being meaningless. This is a fact of which even one who does not read Chinese may satisfy himself by a look at a recent English-language volume emanating from the Foreign Languages Press in Peking and entitled *An Outline History of China*.[42] (Nothing much better in the way of an introductory general history written after 1949 is yet to be found in Chinese.) It reveals only a mechanically acted melodrama, culminating inevitably in "the great victory of the new democratic revolution" in 1949.

However indirect the references to this matter may be, the Chinese Communist historians themselves have not been able to repress the anxieties that are a concomitant of a meaningless past. The continuing, perhaps even accelerated, publication of articles devoted to the topics I have surveyed is in part motivated by the hope that these issues, if pursued relentlessly, really can yield a precipitate of meaning. Other signs of this anxiety are apparent both in the policy statements of the leading Communist historians and in the tack that the writing of history has taken most recently.

In his address to the founding meeting of the Chinese Historical Society in Peking on July 28, 1951, Kuo Mo-jo surveyed the path onto which he stated the Chinese historians "under the leadership of the Party had entered

---

[41] For typical discussions of this matter, see Chien Po-tsan, "Mu-ch'ien li-shih chiao-hsüeh chung ti chi-ko wen-t'i" [Some Present Problems in the Teaching of History], *Hung-ch'i* [Red Flag], May 16, 1959, 21–31, and Pai Shou-yi, "Li-shih chiao-hsüeh shang ti ku yü chin" [Ancient and Modern in the Teaching of History], *ibid.*, June 1, 1959, 36–44.

[42] The book was published in 1958 as part of the "China Knowledge Series," intended to introduce Western readers to Chinese civilization; the name of the author (or authors) is not given. It is of interest, too, to peruse the section on history in the *Outlines of Examinations for Matriculation to Institutions of Higher Education in 1959*, comp. by the Ministry of Education of the People's Republic of China (trans. in American Consulate General, Hong Kong, *Current Background*, Aug. 17, 1959); the same dreary story appears.

. . . with regard to their method, style of work, purpose and subject of study":

1. The old idealistic view of history was gradually being replaced by the materialistic view of history.
2. Collective research was gradually replacing individual studies.
3. Historical research, hitherto an "ivory tower" enterprise, was gradually turning to serve the people.
4. The attitude of adoration of the past and contempt for the present was gradually giving way to appreciation of the modern period.
5. Han chauvinism was gradually giving way to consideration for the national minorities.
6. Emphasis on European and American history was gradually ceding place to attention to Asian history.

Seven years later, in 1958, he admitted that in this address "I was trying to give everyone encouragement, so what I said was more or less what I hoped for. To judge from present conditions, the speed with which our historians have changed has not been so great as I expected. . . . Our scholars' understanding of Marxism-Leninism is not yet profound enough and not yet unanimous. We must still make greater efforts in our ideological revolution."[43] Taking note of the fact that Kuo's 1951 pronouncement summarizes quite succinctly the policy lines that have guided the mainland historians in the past decade, I am struck by his confession that all has gone less well than he had expected, and in particular by the statement that "Our scholars' understanding of Marxism-Leninism is not yet profound enough and not yet unanimous." This is not an isolated criticism. Among the other panjandrums of the historical profession, Pai Shou-yi, for example, has recently characterized the great majority of mainland historians as "still elementary students of Marxist theory," and Chien Po-tsan, at greater length, has declared:

At present all our historians are studying Marxism-Leninism and the thought of Mao Tse-tung, but our studies are still very much inadequate. This is revealed principally in that we have not yet comprehended how to use theory in order to analyze concrete historical questions. Thus in the teaching of history, we are unable to combine properly theory and source materials, we are not able to employ theory to penetrate the sources.[44]

[43] "Kuan-yü hou-chin po-ku wen-t'i," in which Kuo quotes his 1951 speech; *SCMP*, July 27–28, 1951, 18.
[44] Pai Shou-yi, "Li-shih chiao-hsüeh shang ti ku yü chin," 39; Chien Po-tsan, "Mu-ch'ien li-shih chiao-hsüeh chung ti chi-ko wen-t'i," 30–31. Note also the following remarks by the archaeologist Yin Ta: "[Despite progress since 1941] when closely examined the study of the science of history is still found to be seriously infected with subjectivist and dogmatic ways of working. Some historians are still unable to gain possession of detailed data and to analyze large numbers of objective historical facts in earnest for the purpose of drawing up the correct conclusions under the guidance of the theories of dialectical materialism and historical materialism. On the contrary, they frequently proceed from certain texts in the Marxist-Leninist classics to concoct various kinds of theories with their own subjective imagination. After that, they go

Why—after ten years of ideological remolding, continuous indoctrination in Marxism-Maoism, criticism and self-criticism, and all the other concomitants of political control of intellectual activity—are the historians in the People's Republic of China still told by their leaders that their major shortcoming is their lack of a profound grasp of Marxism-Leninism-Maoism? The answer, of course, is obvious. It cannot be that Marxism-Leninism-Maoism is an inadequate set of tools for the job they have undertaken—the reconstruction and revaluation of China's past. Then it must be that the historians have been clumsy with their scissors and paste.

Aside from theoretical incompetence, there has been other telling self-criticism. Why, it is asked, are there still no satisfactory textbooks or general histories (*t'ung-shih*)?[45] (The non-Marxist reader may query in turn, how can there be when the problems of periodization and the like remain unsolved?) The new crop of historians is poorly trained, having mastered neither the Chinese nor the Western classics of history and showing little competence in foreign languages or even in classical Chinese (*ku-wen*).[46] (Again, can it be that the better students prefer to enroll in the scientific and technological faculties where the political pressure, while still great, is less direct?) There has been much done with the collection and publication of source materials, which is indeed valuable, but why so little first-class monographic and synthetic work?[47] (Perhaps the publication of documents and annotated editions of sources, like concentration on premodern history or procrastination in producing a definitive periodization, which are also criticized, is a device, however feeble and temporary, to avoid control.)

What way out of this state of affairs? One way was to "emphasize the present and deemphasize the past" (*hou-chin po-ku*). The May 1958 issue of *Li-shih yen-chiu,* the most important historical journal in the People's Republic of China, led off with a string of heavyweight editorials by Kuo

---

on to quote one-sidedly certain historical data drawn from here and there in order to prove their predetermined conclusions. Such phenomena can definitely be detected in the controversies about the periodization of ancient history in China, the formation of the Han nation, and incipient capitalism. If allowed to continue, this state of affairs will lead to greater confusion; it can offer no real solutions to problems." (*Jen-min jih-pao,* May 30, 1956; trans. in *SCMP,* July 13, 1956, 31–36, slightly modified.)

[45] Yin Ta, *Jen-min jih-pao,* May 30, 1956; T'ang Lan, "Wang-ch'ao-shih t'i-hsi ying-kai ta-p'o."

[46] Pai Shou-yi, "Li-shih chiao hsüeh shang ti ku yü chin."

[47] Kuo Mo-jo, "Kuan-yü hou-chin po-ku wen-t'i" and "Kuan-yü mu-ch'ien li-shih yen-chiu chung ti chi-ko wen-t'i" [Some Present Problems Facing Historical Research], *Hsin chien-she,* Apr. 7, 1959, 1–5. For a detailed review of some of the major publications of documents on modern history, see *Journal of Asian Studies,* XVII (Nov. 1957), 55–111. *Ching-chi yen-chiu* [Economic Studies] (No. 5, 1958), 89–90, lists thirty-eight major projects under way for the compilation of source materials on modern Chinese economic history alone.

Mo-jo, Fan Wen-lan, Ch'en Yüan, Hou Wai-lu, Lü Chen-yü, and Liu Ta-nien which proclaimed that slogan, a clear sign that the party was unhappy about the condition of historical studies. *Hou-chin po-ku* had a double edge. On the one hand it was meant to be taken literally as a guide to cutting up the pie of available historical manpower and other facilities. But it also indicated a tightening of the political screws so far as the historians were concerned. Fan Wen-lan, in an address to a symposium of historians and archaeologists in April 1958, put it very neatly:

The difference between placing more emphasis on the present than on the past, and placing more emphasis on the past in preference to the present, represents a struggle between the two paths of promoting the proletariat and demoting the bourgeoisie, and of promoting the bourgeoisie and demoting the proletariat. We, of the new historians, should adhere to the Marxist standpoint and regard it as our responsibility to emphasize the present in preference to the past and to promote the proletariat and demote the bourgeoisie.[48]

If the historians had not done their assigned jobs well, if they had not been able to provide the regime with a neatly packaged past that would call forth intellectual and emotional commitment from their readers, a conclusion that follows from the criticism summarized above, it was because they were still ideologically backward. And a large measure of blame for that backwardness was attributable to their isolation from the great struggles of the masses of workers and peasants to build a socialist society. They had failed to solve the problems of ancient history because they did not adequately comprehend the present. Liu Ta-nien, an editor of *Li-shih yen-chiu* and author of a study of American "imperialist aggression" against China, stated it this way: "Marxism tells us that if we are to understand ancient China scientifically, we must emphasize the study of modern and contemporary China." The historical classics of the past and present, Chinese and foreign, he continued, have always reflected certain political and economic systems and have directly or indirectly served such systems. "The *Spring and Autumn Annals* [*Ch'un-ch'iu*] of Confucius has been revered as a 'classic,' and therefore it is a typical learned work. But it has been said that Confucius wrote the *Spring and Autumn Annals* and 'struck fear in the heart of rebellious ministers and insolent sons.' It is clear that its contents are not 'independent' and not aloof from politics." The burden of Liu's rather skillful reference to Confucius, and also, interestingly enough, to H. B. Morse's *International Relations of the Chinese Empire* as an example of a classic written from the "bourgeois" viewpoint, was to urge onto the Chinese historians an increased "politicalization" of their work in order "thoroughly to expose

48 *SCMP*, May 8, 1958, 37-39, Apr. 23, 1958, 46-48.

the hypocritical viewpoint of the bourgeoisie and establish the Marxist viewpoint instead." "We are willing to do without bourgeois learning; we need only Marxist learning," he concluded.[49]

I need hardly emphasize that pulling historians out of their ivory towers into the current "struggles of the masses" is not likely to avert the crisis of meaninglessness that Chinese historiography faces. The reluctance of the problems which the historians have set for themselves—periodization, peasant revolts, the formation of the Han nation—to yield to solution cannot be ascribed to inferior Marxist tailoring. Quite the contrary. And in the specific case of modern history, how can the historians do anything other than sterile periodization exercises? Liu Ta-nien admits that there are "some comrades" who fear to participate actively in the study of recent history. But he immediately brushes the problem aside:

Contemporary history should not evoke any fear because of its close link with present-day life which makes its practitioners more liable to criticism. That should spur us on to more and more intensive research. The phrase "let one hundred schools of thought contend" [*pai-chia cheng-ming*] has two meanings: it means free research and also free criticism. If people are free only to make public their new views but not to criticize erroneous thinking and erroneous style of work, then there would be only "crying" [*ming*] but no "contention" [*cheng*]. But we must have both crying and contention at the same time. There are those who fear that in the research and discussion of contemporary history, academic questions might easily be confused with political questions. Of course the two are related, but they are also distinguishable from each other. In order to distinguish them, and create an environment for free research, academic circles must be able to conduct academic criticism correctly.[50]

Who would decide when academic criticism was being conducted "correctly" requires no comment.

Running parallel with the *hou-chin po-ku* "line," so to speak, there has most recently appeared another candidate for the first string of Chinese Communist historiography, none other than the celebrated general and poet Ts'ao Ts'ao (155–220). The most prominent character in the exciting epoch of the downfall of the Later Han dynasty, Ts'ao Ts'ao is known to every Chinese as the villain of the famous novel *Romance of the Three Kingdoms* (*San-kuo-chih yen-i*), the tyrannic usurper who seized the last Han emperor, Hsien-ti, and in lifelong warfare contested with the heroic Liu Pei and his great min-

---

[49] Liu Ta-nien, "Hsü-yao cho-chung yen-chiu 'Wu-ssu' yun-tung i-hou ti li-shih" [We Must Stress the Study of History after the "May Fourth" Movement], *Li-shih yen-chiu* (No. 4, 1958), 9–14.
[50] *Ibid.*

ister Chu-ko Liang for universal dominion of the empire. The evaluation of Ts'ao Ts'ao among historians has more or less corresponded to that of the novel: able and crafty, but wicked and unscrupulous. In the traditional histories this judgment depended in part on the fact that the Wei dynasty (220–265) of the Three Kingdoms epoch, which was established by Ts'ao and his son, was not a "legitimate" successor to the Han, while Liu Pei who founded the Shu dynasty (221–264) was a distant relation of the Han ruling house and his rule could thus be considered legitimate. For the modern "progressive" historians the principal blot on Ts'ao's record was his brutal suppression of the peasant uprising known as the "Yellow Turbans" during the last years of the Han. But beginning with pronouncements by Chien Po-tsan and Kuo Mo-jo early in 1959, and followed by intensive discussion in the newspapers and historical periodicals, the case of Ts'ao Ts'ao has recently been reopened and, it seems, the judgment of the past completely overturned.

The discussion has centered on three issues: Ts'ao's suppression of the Yellow Turban rebellion, the policy of land reclamation that he carried out with his troops (t'un-t'ien), and his ruthless military expedition against the Wu-yuan people. Ts'ao Ts'ao, wrote Kuo Mo-jo, in putting down the Yellow Turban rebellion, did not violate the goals of that quite just peasant uprising. The Yellow Turbans were poorly organized and incapable of bringing about the improvement that they sought in the people's livelihood. When Ts'ao defeated them, many of the Yellow Turban troops voluntarily joined his forces. Would they have followed him if he were the vicious person that the historians have alleged? The t'un-t'ien policy moreover, far from being in the interest of the great landlord families or contributing to Ts'ao's own enrichment, provided his troops and the civil population of northern China with the food and other agricultural products that had been in such short supply. Ts'ao himself led a Spartan life, and with the popular support and military resources that the land reclamation policy ensured, he was able to defeat his enemies in battle and eventually to unify much of China. The suppression of the semicivilized Wu-yuan tribes was not an aggressive act against a weaker people, but a defensive war against a backward barbarian invader for which he had wide popular support. (It is of interest that on this last point Kuo quotes a poem by Mao Tse-tung in which he finds a favorable reference to Ts'ao Ts'ao's expedition against the Wu-yuan—poet and military leader Mao bowing to poet and military leader Ts'ao!) Ts'ao, Kuo admitted, had often recklessly slaughtered his enemies, and his errors and shortcomings were not to be overlooked. Yet, his strong points outweigh his shortcomings. "In my opinion . . . Ts'ao Ts'ao made a greater contribution to the development of the nation and its culture than any of his contemporaries."[51] Although there was some dissent from Kuo's call for a new estimate of Ts'ao Ts'ao,[52] the consensus strongly supported the view that Ts'ao Ts'ao's contributions to enriching and strengthening the Chinese "nation"—the key word in Kuo's brief for the defense—warranted a reappraisal of his place in China's history.[53]

Along with the refurbishing of the erstwhile villain Ts'ao Ts'ao has gone an appeal for the reevaluation of many others, not popular heroes or leaders of peasant revolts, but emperors, generals, statesmen, and scholars of the feudal past, such as King Chou, the "licentious" last ruler of the Shang dynasty, the first Ch'in emperor (reigned 221–210 B.C.), Han Wu-ti (reigned 140–87 B.C.), T'ang T'ai-tsung (reigned 627–649), and the great Manchu emperors K'ang-hsi (reigned 1661–1722) and Ch'ien-lung (reigned 1736–1796).[54]

These recent developments are potentially of great significance for the problems that the Chinese Communist historians face. Although there has been no Chinese equivalent of M. N. Pokrovsky, the approach to China's past through such topics as peasant rebellion, capitalist origins, and periodization is in a number of ways quite similar to the tendency in Soviet historiography associated with the name of that Russian historian. Pokrovsky, who dominated his profession until the 1930's, and his adherents presented their materials "in a theoretical and schematic form," writing an almost anonymous history of the movement and clash of social forces. They "portrayed all pre-Soviet institutions and personalities in a sarcastic vein. This did not meet the needs of a regime that wished to stimulate patriotism by rehabilitating selected personalities, and to present Russian history in an interesting narrative form suited to secondary school education."[55] After his death Pokrovsky was severely attacked, and Soviet historiography moved steadily onto a more nationalistic tack which culminated in the near chauvinist output of the World War II period. I suggest that the rehabilitation of Ts'ao Ts'ao and the others is analogous to the post-Pokrovsky reevaluation

---

[51] Kuo Mo-jo, "T'i Ts'ao Ts'ao fan-an" [Let Us Reopen the Case of Ts'ao Ts'ao], *Hsin-hua pan-yüeh k'an* [New China Semimonthly] (No. 8, 1959), 104–108 (reprinted from *Jen-min jih-pao*, Mar. 23, 1959).

[52] E.g., Yang Ping, "Ts'ao Ts'ao ying-tang pei k'en-ting ma?" [Should Ts'ao Ts'ao Be Viewed Favorably?] *ibid.* (No. 12, 1958), 141–45 (reprinted from *Jen-min jih-pao*, Apr. 21, 1959).

[53] See *ibid.*, 137–41, 145–49, for additional contributions to the discussion.

[54] Kuo Mo-jo, "Tui Yin Chou-wang ti i-chung k'an-fa" [One Way of Looking at King Chou of the Yin Dynasty], *Hsin chien-she*, Apr. 7, 1959, 6–7; and "Kuan-yü mu-ch'ien li-shih yen-chiu chung ti chi-ko wen-t'i."

[55] *Rewriting Russian History: Soviet Interpretations of Russia's Past*, ed. C. E. Black (New York, 1956), 15.

of Ivan the Terrible, for example, by Soviet historians. It represents a shift from an emphasis on the popular past to an emphasis on the national past. But, I hasten to add, neither need exclude the other, nor can one say with any assurance how far the change will go in China. Yet the context within which the Ts'ao Ts'ao discussion has occurred leads me to believe that it is part of the most recent attempt by the mainland historians to cope with the threat of a meaningless past.

About the same time that the matter of reevaluating Ts'ao Ts'ao was occupying a prominent place in mainland publications, Chien Po-tsan and others who had reopened the case of Ts'ao Ts'ao were also expressing their reservations about the manner in which the *hou-chin po-ku* "line" had been carried out. Writing in *Hung-ch'i,* the semimonthly theoretical organ of the Central Committee of the Chinese Communist party and manifestly the most authoritative publication in the People's Republic of China, Chien was highly critical of the fact that "some colleges have excessively reduced the proportion of ancient history in the general study of history."[56] He thought it an error, too, that a number of schools in response to "emphasizing the present and deemphasizing the past" had turned their curricula upside down and were now teaching modern history before ancient history.[57] This could only make it more difficult for the students to comprehend the laws of social development. Chien then proceeded to criticize those historians who taught an anonymous history—saying "the early Han" rather than "Ch'in Shih-huang" or "Han Kao-tsu"—and those who in their Marxist purity omitted all mention of the ruling class. "To sum it up, when teaching history, we must emphasize the explanation of the laws of social and economic development of each period, and the creative role of the masses; but we must also discuss the roles of individual historical personages." In a similar vein Kuo Mo-jo was critical of historical research.[58] It is correct, he asserted, to abandon court-centered history, but imperial dynasties nevertheless existed and cannot simply be ignored. He objected to those who omitted the *nien-hao* (reign title) and the customary honorific or temple names of the emperors and cited merely the Western calendar years and the rulers' personal names (*ming*) in the belief that to do otherwise would indicate deference or respect to these "feudal" rulers. And like Chien, Kuo took exception to the

[56] Chien Po-tsan, "Mu-ch'ien li-shih chiao-hsüeh chung ti chi-ko wen-t'i."

[57] For extremely interesting—and saddening—reports on how the several universities executed the instructions to "emphasize the present," see *Li-shih yen-chiu* (No. 8, 1958), 73–75, (No. 9, 1958), 71–76, (No. 10, 1958), 70–79, (No. 11, 1958), 71–73, (No. 12, 1958), 83–88, (No. 7, 1959), 90–93.

[58] Kuo Mo-jo, "Kuan-yü mu-ch'ien li-shih yen-chiu chung ti chi-ko wen-t'i."

tendency to write only about the masses and to give short shrift to the affairs of the ruling classes of the past.

This implied dissatisfaction with the cruder aspects of Marxist historiography, though of course not with Marxism-Maoism itself, seems to be related to the Ts'ao Ts'ao discussions in that both are part of an effort to patch up what I earlier described as the largest hole in the garment of Chinese Communist historiography, the two millennia of "feudal" void. It will doubtless remain "feudal," but it is possible that larger and larger portions of it will be reevaluated from a viewpoint that is at least as much Chinese as it is Marxist. "One of the important meanings implicit in the discussions of Ts'ao Ts'ao," stated a report of a meeting of historians in Shanghai in the spring of 1959,

is that we now know how to make a correct appraisal of the characters of history. In the course of the discussion, all participants agreed on the principles advanced by Kuo Mo-jo that we should judge a character in history from an overall point of view and assess his place in history according to his major deeds. Particularly we should see whether he made any contribution to the people and to the development of the whole nation and to cultural development. We should make an overall analysis of him and of the background of the times he was in, taking the role he played in historical development as the standard.[59]

It is too early to say what the effects of these pronouncements will be. If, however, a reevaluation of Ts'ao Ts'ao and the other "feudal" figures is in fact carried out on the basis of their "contribution to the people and to the development of the whole nation and to cultural development," the mainland historians will indeed have taken a long step toward replacing a Chinese meaning in their past. In the words of the report of the Shanghai historians' conference that I referred to earlier: if the problem of Ts'ao Ts'ao "is correctly settled, then we can gradually discover a correct attitude toward our cultural heritage, and find the solution to the question of how to tackle present problems in the light of ancient, similar cases."

Chinese history will never be "bourgeois" history again. And it is equally unlikely that the Pokrovsky-like treatment of anonymous social forces will disappear from the scene in the People's Republic of China. It is, however, possible to conceive of (perhaps, better, to hope for) a time when the importunate demands of the real world, as interpreted by the Chinese Communist leadership, will have abated enough to permit the relinquishment of belief in a single source of evil in modern history. "Imperialism" will not be banished from the mainland historical workshops, but its dimensions may

[59] U. S. Joint Publication Research Service, "Report on Academic Discussions in Shanghai," *Communist China Digest*, Aug. 31, 1959, 24–27.

be reduced as the successful construction of a new domestic tradition proceeds apace. The result will still not be the kind of history that will satisfy the Western student of China, any more than the dominant Marxism of Japanese historiography can be taken as an adequate picture of Japan's past. But some of the emotion, and aggression, will have been wrung out of the Chinese fabric. And it may be that on some matters at least the historiographical meeting of minds, East and West, will be feasible.

3

Archaeology in Communist China

By CHENG TE-K'UN

TRADITIONAL ARCHAEOLOGY

Archaeology has a long history in traditional China where it served as the handmaiden of history, lexicography and geography, as well as preserver of art and literature. References to ancient material remains are common in the early Chinese literature. In the early fifth century B.C. Feng-hu-tzu, presumably after a study of early implements, proposed a four-stage sequence for the ancient period, each characterised by a weapon made of stone, jade, copper and iron, respectively. The grand historian of the second century B.C., Ssu-ma Ch'ien, made special efforts to visit as many ancient sites and monuments as possible to substantiate his records. In the second century A.D. Hsü Shen compiled a dictionary of 10,516 characters, many of which were drawn from ancient bronze and stone inscriptions. In the sixth century Li Tao-yuan wrote his commentaries on the *Book of Rivers*, which was fully documented with archaeological data. Throughout the ages many important discoveries were recorded and large numbers of ancient art objects and literature preserved. By the twelfth century Chinese archaeology had become a specialised subject, known as *Chin-shih-hsueh*, literally, a study of bronze and stone objects. A vast literature began to accumulate, reaching its height in the last two centuries.

MODERN ARCHAEOLOGY UP TO 1949

Archaeology based on planned investigation with modern science and technology is a new adventure in China. J. G. Andersson excavated the first site in 1923, followed by a number of European and Japanese scholars who worked mainly in the outlying regions of China, including Korea and Indo-China. But the responsibility for excavating sites in China proper was in the hands of Chinese archaeologists in the Academia Sinica and the Geological Survey of China. Even at this stage there was already a division of spheres in the field. The academicians, led by Li Chi and Liang Ssu-yung, concentrated their activities on the historical sites in and around An-yang, while the geologists, notably Yang Chung-chien and Pei Wen-chung, conducted their investigations in a far wider area. With the data they had found they tried to establish

45

the prehistory of this ancient land. After a decade of careful investigation considerable advance had been made by both parties. They were sure that prehistoric China covered only the Stone Age while historic China probably began with the Shang dynasty, when a written language was introduced and a metallic industry established.

Archaeological work was interrupted by the Japanese invasion in 1937. Some archaeologists had to join the guerrillas and perished in action. Others were forced to migrate westward into the hinterland where they could still carry on some field work and research projects. With the exception of West China archaeology, the new science was practically at a standstill for more than a decade. It was not until the establishment of the People's Republic that activities in this field began to be revived.

ORGANISATION

Archaeological work in China is organised on a nationwide scale. Soon after 1949 a set of laws and regulations for the protection of relics and field excavations was promulgated, existing museums were reorganised and thousands of new ones established, and a Bureau of Cultural Relics (*Wen-wu kuan-li chu*) was set up under the Ministry of Culture. The Bureau is responsible for planning and conducting antiquarian and archaeological activities. It has encouraged exhibitions and introduced a wide variety of research methods and techniques. Its monthly journal, *Wen wu chan-k'ao tzu-liao*, with a present circulation around 10,000, reviews the work of the Bureau and promotes archaeological work.

In the summer of 1950, an exploration party was organised under the leadership of Pei Wen-chung, then Head of the Museum Section of the Bureau of Cultural Relics. Sixteen scholars and archaeologists from Peking and Tsinghua Universities, the Historical and Palace Museums and other institutions were invited to take part. All veterans in their respective fields, they were organised into two teams to survey the archaeological and architectural remains in northern Shansi. In forty days the party made a general reconnaissance of the region and excavated two Han burials. The official report, published under the title *Yen-pei Wen-wu K'an-cha-t'uan Pao-kao* (*Reports of the Yen-pei Exploration Party*), includes diaries of the teams, eight articles on archaeology and four on architecture. This first attempt, modest though it was, marks a new era in Chinese archaeology, characterised by full government support, inter-institutional co-operation, organised field work, group discussion and prompt publication of the report.

After 1949, China began to build new roads, railways, reservoirs, canals and factories in large numbers. These construction projects brought to light thousands of ancient tombs and cultural relics. The

Bureau of Cultural Relics thus found itself confronted with an enormous task of salvaging the new finds. The Bureau started a campaign to educate the people, especially the workers in the construction projects, to give them some knowledge of the underground relics and basic principles of excavation. Archaeologists were obliged to keep in close contact with them in the field. In this way it was claimed that not a single relic suffered from destruction. By 1954 a total of over 140,000 objects (not counting potsherds) had been recorded and preserved. The Bureau put 3,760 of the finer examples in a special exhibition at the Peking Historical Museum and catalogued them in two folio volumes.[1] " The protection of underground relics," concludes Cheng Chen-to, Director of the Bureau, in his introduction, " is not only . . . to preserve the cultural heritage of the past. The function and significance of this work is deeper; it is to develop the culture and art of today and tomorrow." Archaeology in China has assumed a new role, to carry out a social as well as a historical mission.

COMMITTEES OF CULTURAL RELICS AND PROVINCIAL MUSEUMS

Steps taken by the Bureau of Cultural Relics in the capital are soon followed up by the provincial authorities in every region. Regional Committees on Cultural Relics or similar organisations, usually under the leadership of a few veteran archaeologists and scholars, co-operate closely with the local museums to take stock of all relics and register them. Field teams are organised to work side by side with construction workers. Some of these ordinary labourers, while serving as apprentices in the field, have acquired the trade quite readily and distinguished themselves as worker-archaeologists.

The provincial archaeologists are just as busy preparing exhibitions and reports as they are in the field. The reports are usually produced by group discussion and published under the name of the committee or the museum or both. Provincial workers also publish a large number of monographs by their own efforts. Many of these are of very high quality in scholarship and production.[2]

The central authority in Peking also participates actively in and co-ordinates the field work in the provinces. Apart from sending archaeological teams to help the provincial workers, the Bureau and other organisations frequently sponsor joint conferences and exhibitions of provincial discoveries. In 1956 an exhibition of the important finds

---

[1] *Ch'uan-kuo Chi-pen Chien-she Kung-ch'eng-chung Ch'u-t'u Wen-wu Chan-lan T'u-lu* (*Archaeological Finds at Construction Sites*), Shanghai, 1955.

[2] See Nanking Museum, *Nanking Fu-chin K'ao-ku Pao-kao* (*Archaeological Reports on Sites around Nanking*), Shanghai, 1952; Yunnan Museum, *The Ancient Cemetery of Shi-chai-shan, Tsin-ning, Yunnan*, Peking, 1959; Li I-yu, *Nei-meng-ku Ch'u-t'u Wen-wu Hsuan-chi* (*Selected Cultural Relics from Inner Mongolia*), Peking, 1963.

from five provinces was held in the Palace Museum in Peking. More than 300 exhibits were drawn from twelve excavated sites. The catalogue was prepared by T'ang Lan, a well-known expert on Chinese bronze. His introduction is followed by a comprehensive list of site reports.[3] The exhibition was intended not only to cultivate respect for underground relics but also to pave the way for scholarly research in art and history.

INSTITUTE OF ARCHAEOLOGY

To give archaeology more status in the academic world, an Institute of Archaeology (*K'ao-ku yen-chiu so*) has been set up under the new Chinese Academy of Sciences with Liang Ssu-yung as the Deputy Director. In the spring of 1950, the Institute resumed the excavation of An-yang, an ancient site containing a wide variety of dwelling ruins and burials which provide a useful training ground for young students of the Institute. The first season's work was directed by Kuo Pao-chun, veteran excavator of the site. Soon after the excavation the finds were exhibited to the public and a report published.[4]

Later in the year, the Institute started a major excavation at Hui-hsien, employing some 500 daily workers. A Shang dwelling site and more than forty burials of the Chou and Han periods were investigated and interesting discoveries included sixty iron implements, nineteen chariots and a large quantity of jade, silver and gold articles. A final report of these finds was published as the first monograph of the Institute.[5]

To meet the demand for more archaeologists in the field, the Institute co-operated with the Bureau and Peking University in conducting a series of training courses in archaeology.[6] The first session was held in 1952 with seventy-one students. It was a three-month course covering four subjects: Government Policies, Chinese Archaeology, Regional Chinese Archaeology and Archaeological Methods and Techniques. The class work was followed by a three-month practical training at one of the excavating sites. The course, given annually for four years, had 100 students in 1953, 101 in 1954 and 69 in 1955. Many of the students are employed by the Institute whose membership increased from 37 in 1950 to 292 in 1957. The students were organised

3 T'ang Lan, *Wu-sheng Ch'u-t'u Chung-yao Wen-wu Chan-lan T'u-lu* (*Illustrated catalogue of the Exhibition of the Important Cultural Relics from Five Provinces*), Peking, 1958.
4 *Wen-wu, Chan-k'ao Tzu-liao* (*Cultural Relics*), Peking, January-June 1950, pp. 79–80; July 1950, pp. 10–11.
5 K'ao-ku yen-chiu so, *Hui-hsien Fa-chueh Pao-kao* (*Reports of the Hui-hsien Excavation*), Peking, 1956.
6 *Wen-wu*, August 1955, pp. 150–151 *et seq.*

into eleven teams which answered requests for assistance from many areas.[7]

In order to reach a wider public, the manual used in the training course was published in 1958 under the title *K'ao-ku-hsueh Chi-ch'u* (*Foundations of Archaeology*). It contains the lecture notes in three parts: I. General Chinese Archaeology, arranged in chronological order; II. Special Topics and Areas of Study, covering a number of ancient sites, Buddhist temples, art objects, palaeontology and methods of preservation and exhibition; and III. Archaeological Methods and Techniques, including photography, drawing, surveying and restoration of artifacts. The National Laws and Regulations governing the protection of cultural relics and field excavations are appended for reference. This manual became the standard textbook of Chinese archaeology.

Field teams of the Institute of Archaeology have worked in practically all the important excavation centres: besides An-yang and Hui-hsien, in Cheng-chou, Hou-ma, Lo-yang, Sian, Ch'ang-sha and many others. The final reports of these field works show invariably fine workmanship and careful research. At Pan-p'o-ts'un, near Sian, the neolithic village was so well excavated that a building was erected to protect the 10,000 square metres of ruins and Pan-p'o-ts'un has become one of the many site museums in China.[8]

The Institute also carries on an active publication programme. In 1951, the publication of the *Chung-kuo K'ao-ku Hsueh-pao* (*Chinese Journal of Archaeology*) was revived by the appearance of Volume 5. The following issue was published in 1952 under the present name, *K'ao-ku Hsueh-pao*, as a semi-annual journal. It was enlarged in 1956 into a quarterly, but its publication was interrupted by the shortage of paper in 1960, and only six issues have been produced in the last five years. The journal is devoted to scholarly articles and reports of important sites. Most of the preliminary accounts of excavation and general discussions on special topics are published in another journal, *K'ao-ku* (*Archaeology*).

K'ao-ku appeared first in 1955 as a bi-monthly under the name *K'ao-ku T'ung-hsun* (*Archaeological News*) which aimed to provide a vehicle for the publication of brief reports, to promote discussion and co-operation among archaeologists and to introduce outstanding foreign archaeological achievements. The project was itself a joint effort of the Institute, the Bureau and the University of Peking. Three years later the journal was enlarged and became a monthly. It began to use its present name, *K'ao-ku*, in 1959. To celebrate the tenth anniversary

---

[7] *K'ao-ku*, August 1958, p. 12.
[8] Institute of Archaeology and Pan-p'o Museum, *Sian Pan-p'o* (*The Neolithic Village at Pan-p'o, Sian*), Peking, 1963.

of the founding of the Republic this year, the journal began publishing a full bibliography of Chinese archaeology since 1949. This useful service has been followed in the subsequent issues.

The most important works on Chinese archaeology are being published by the Institute in four Monograph Series, *Chia*, *Yi*, *Ping* and *Ting*. They include some revised editions of pre-1949 books, collections of articles, research monographs and site reports, now numbering forty-two volumes. Apart from a few reports of excavated sites which are produced by the teams in charge, all the monographs are individual works, mostly by veteran archaeologists and scholars. The most unique monograph is Volume Six of Series Chia, entitled *Hsin Chung-kuo ti K'ao-ku Shou-hou* (*Archaeology in New China*), a summary of the field works carried out in China up to 1960. It was produced by a team of thirty-two archaeologists, young and old, representing fourteen institutes, museums and field parties, under the editorship of the Institute of Archaeology.[9] The Institute is indeed a nerve-centre of Chinese archaeology.

PEKING UNIVERSITY

At the same time that the Institute set up short-term training courses in archaeology, archaeological education was introduced at the university level in the form of a four-year course for forty students in the History Department of Peking University. After a two-year experiment, it was expanded into a five-year course. In the summer of 1959 eighty-nine students and two post-graduates graduated. In the following year 140 students were registered.[10]

The Peking University course includes three papers in Political Theory and one each in World History, Asian History and Chinese History in the first year. Archaeological subjects are introduced in the second year with General Archaeology and Field Methods followed by special topics such as Prehistoric Archaeology, Art and Archaeology, Historical Archaeology, History of Archaeology, Epigraphy and Museology. The class instruction is supplemented by three field trips which are taken at the end of the first and third and in the fifth years. A thesis on the field excavation is required for graduation.[11]

Courses in archaeology may also be found in the provincial universities of Shensi, Honan, Shantung, Kiangsi, Szechwan, Fukien and Kwangtung. Field activities of these students have often been reported in the *Wen-wu* and *K'ao-ku*. China should have by now enough trained archaeologists at her disposal.

---

9 Published in Peking, 1962. See Cheng Te-k'un, "New Light on Ancient China," *Antiquity*, No. 38, 1964, pp. 179–183.
10 *K'ao-ku*, October 1959, p. 153.
11 *Ibid*. p. 514.

50

INSTITUTE OF PALAEONTOLOGY

Before the formal establishment of the People's Republic, the new government had authorised the resumption of excavation at Chou-k'ou-tien, the home of the Peking Man. This was followed immediately by a formal demarcation of the boundaries for excavation and the construction of a museum and a rest house at the site. In 1954 Chou-k'ou-tien was linked with Peking by a new highway and became a centre for palaeontological training.[12] A research laboratory was established at Peking with Yang Chung-chien, formerly of the Chinese Geological Survey, as its director. This was expanded into a full institute, first of Vertebrate Palaeontology and later of Vertebrate Palaeontology and Palaeoanthropology.

The Institute has developed very rapidly. In 1955 Yang prepared a manual of Palaeontology for the training of field workers.[13] University courses on palaeontology were introduced into Peking University, Nanking University, the Geological Institute of Peking and other institutes of higher education. The number of palaeontologists increased from less than forty in 1949 to almost 400 in 1964.[14] The Institute sends out field teams of young recruits who work under veterans to carry out investigations from Sinkiang to Kwangsi and from Manchuria to Tibet. As a result of their work and other researches, a number of old problems in Palaeolithic China have been solved and several new fossil men and their cultures established.

The Institute maintains three learned journals [15] and a series of *Memoirs* in which four monographs on Palaeolithic men and cultures in China have been published.[16] It is clear that the Institute is taking charge of the Cenozoic researches while the Neolithic and Historic periods are in the hands of the Institute of Archaeology.

ARCHAEOLOGY AND POLITICS

It is generally accepted that the writing of history is more or less a political act. As a handmaiden of history, archaeology cannot help but be involved in politics. Chinese archaeology occupies a rather privileged position politically, and yet it is still expected to act as a branch of the political movement, now geared to Marxism-Leninism.

In the early years when the Chinese Government adopted the policy of " leaning to one side " and maintained a close alliance with the

---

12 *Wen-wu*, September 1957, p. 20.
13 *Chih-chui-tung-wu ti Yen-hua (Evolution of Vertebrates)*, Peking, 1955.
14 *Peking Review*, 1965, Vol. 13, p. 25.
15 *Acta Palaeontologia Sinica*; *Vertebrate Palasiatica*; and *Palaeovertebrata et Palaeo-anthropologia*.
16 *Tzeyang Palaeolithic Man*, Peking, 1957; *Report of the Excavation of Palaeolithic Sites at Tingtsun, Shansi, China*, 1958; *Kehe*, 1962; *Palaeoliths of Shanshi*, 1961.

U.S.S.R., Chinese archaeologists began to introduce Russian excavating techniques and research methods. Many Russian scholars were invited to China, among them S. V. Kissélev, who gave twenty-three lectures to a total audience of 22,500 people.[17]

Some of Kissélev's lectures touched on the issues of China's relations with Western Asia and Siberia and with the much-discussed problems of the Yang-shao painted pottery, the Shang bronze industry and the animal style of Ordos bronzes. He also discussed Russian theories on the controversial question of slavery in China. Some Russian historians were of the opinion that slave society in China ended with the fall of the Shang dynasty and that feudal society was introduced by the Chou people. Others believed that the two types of society continued in existence for a long time after the Chou dynasty and that slave society ended probably with the Han dynasty as a result of the active development of the non-Han peoples. Kissélev realised that all the Russian views he presented were not in complete agreement with the prevalent Chinese opinions, but he expressed his readiness to accept any challenge because "controversial arguments will lead to better and closer friendship." [18]

In return for the influx of Russian scientists the Chinese Government sent a number of exhibitions to Russia. The most successful was the 1950 Moscow exhibition of 600 cultural relics which attracted some 190,000 visitors in six weeks.[19]

A flood of articles on Russian libraries and museums and translations of Russian articles and books on archaeology and art soon appeared in the *Wen wu, K'ao-ku* and *K'ao-ku Hsueh-pao*. The movement reached its height in 1956 when A. V. Artsikhovsky's *Osnovi Arkheologii* [20] and A. L. Mongait's Introduction to *Archaeology in the U.S.S.R.*[21] were published in Chinese and widely circulated in China. A system of exchange in publications between the two countries was also introduced.

In these early cultural exchanges between China and Russia, China undoubtedly played the active role. She also took the lead in promoting cultural relations with other Communist and neutral countries in every continent.

The Sino-Russian cultural and archaeological co-operation was seriously impaired, however, when grave ideological and political conflicts began to develop between them around 1959. The curtailment of Russian technical assistance and the recall of Russian engineers in

17 *K'ao-ku*, December 1959, p. 695.
18 *Wen-wu*, January-June 1950, p. 78.
19 *Ibid*. July 1950, pp. 1–102.
20 *K'ao-ku T'ung-hsun*, Peking, 1956.
21 *K'ao-ku*, June 1956, pp. 108–117 *et seq*.

1960 forced the Chinese Government to adopt the policy of "relying on yourself and working with a will." Almost simultaneously the Chinese archaeologists stopped translating Russian works and no more articles on Russian archaeology appeared in Chinese journals.

It is interesting to note that the influx of Russian archaeology does not seem to have left much impression on Chinese archaeology. Now that the Russians are using archaeology to support their claims in the border territories [22] one wonders how long Chinese archaeologists can remain aloof from the border dispute.

Archaeologists have played their part in the even more acrimonious conflict with the United States by denouncing American cultural aggression and criminal activities of American scholars, museum directors and collectors. Lists of important cultural relics illegally acquired by Americans have been compiled.[23] The United States is held responsible for robbing such famous collections as the relics of the Peking Man and the treasure of the Palace and the Central Museums and the National Library of Peking.[24]

Internal Movements

Archaeologists in China are also involved in internal political movements. In the first few years after 1949 archaeologists were busy reorganising their works and salvaging relics which were being unearthed in the construction programmes. In 1955 a campaign was launched against spiritualism and capitalist mentality in archaeology and the handling of cultural relics. It specifically accused Hu Shih, Li Chi and Hu Feng as part of the general anti-United States, anti-Formosa campaign.[25]

The ideological struggle in Chinese archaeology was soon channelled into a more positive movement of learning from Marxism-Leninism. It was claimed that only through such study could Chinese archaeology be redeemed from the traditional capitalistic attitude and practice. In a National Symposium of Archaeological Workers attended by 180 experts from every province it was resolved that archaeological activities should seek the support of the masses and the work should proceed side by side with the people and for the people.[26]

22 A. P. Okladnikov, "The Soviet Far East in the Light of the Latest Achievements in Archaeology," *Problems of History*, January 1964.
23 *Wen-wu*, November 1950, pp. 1–106; December 1950, pp. 12–15; January 1951, pp. 64–84 *et seq.*
24 *Ibid.* June 1955, pp. 3–10; July 1955, pp. 27–59; March 1960, pp. 7–17.
25 *Wen-wu*, May 1955, pp. 12–14; June 1955, pp. 19–26; July 1955, pp. 65–66. Also *K'ao-ku*, February 1955, pp. 75–76; April 1955, pp. 01–04, 66–71; May 1955, pp. 1–8 *et seq.*
26 *Wen-wu*, March 1956, pp. 1–16.

Archaeologists responded rather slowly to the first proclamation of the Hundred Flowers and their indifference aroused much criticism. But when they were invited to participate in the campaign, more than 100 people spoke at sixteen meetings which were organised for them. Their complaints were more political than professional. It came to light that some archaeologists were bitter about party leadership in their field. They openly declared that the present system of government was no better than that of the past and the *wei-hang* (raw hands) should not be authorised to lead the *chuan-chia* (experts): "The express trains of archaeology do not need any locomotives." [27] The attack on the ruling party, however, was not joined by all the archaeologists and the complaints touched off an anti-rightist demonstration. [28] A number of the more individualistic experts were severely criticised and were obliged to leave their posts for re-education in Marxism-Leninism and self-reform through manual work.

When the Hundred Flowers gave way to the Great Leap Forward, archaeologists and museum workers voted to follow the principle of *hou-chin pao-ku* (paying more attention to the present than to the past), to serve the common people and to heed the anti-waste and anti-conservatism slogans. A large number of standard monographs and publications, including the much-used *Foundations of Archaeology*, were criticised [29] and some *pai-chuan* (white experts) denounced or criticised themselves. [30] Students began to criticise university courses in archaeology. [31] Group activities were in vogue and institutional competitions in specimen preservation and exhibit arrangement, in publicity and attracting visitors, in diligence and industry and in the production of *hung chuan* (red experts) were the order of the day. [32]

The slowing down of field excavations after 1960 gave Chinese archaeologists a breathing spell to consolidate their new discoveries. A number of excellent field reports and research articles were published. [33] Serious discussions were held on social evolution in ancient China and a three-stage sequence of development was formally adopted in the standard summary of *Archaeology in China*, namely, *yuan-shih* (primitive society in prehistoric times), *nu-li* (slave society in Shang and early Chou periods) and *feng-chien* (feudal society in late Chou and subsequent dynasties). The first stage might have developed from a

---

27 *Ibid.* June 1957, pp. 3–7; July 1957, pp. 1–10.
28 *Ibid.* September 1957, pp. 1–64; October 1957, pp. 3–13.
29 *K'ao-ku*, December 1958, pp. 1–21.
30 *Ibid.* October 1958, pp. 23–29.
31 *Ibid.* October 1958, p. 16; January 1959, p. 7; March 1959, p. 126.
32 *Wen-wu*, 1958.
33 *K'ao-ku*, October 1964, p. 485; see *Sian Pan-p'o*, Peking, 1963; *Excavations at Feng Hsi* (Peking, 1962).

matriarchal into a patriarchal society, but the division of primitive society into two sub-stages is still open to discussion.[34]

In spite of all ideological struggles and political pressures, archaeology in China manages to develop, maintaining smooth continuity with the past in personnel and organisation and in training and research. Since 1963 some of the victims of the anti-rightist campaign have begun to come back to their work and research.[35] The general tendency in the field is one of industry, purposefulness and progress. There is so much excavation and research going on and so many papers and monographs published that an individual can hardly keep up with such an explosion of information. Fortunately, summaries of new discoveries and research results have been published at every stage.[36]

[34] *K'ao-ku*, January 1961, pp. 3–11.
[35] *Wen-wu*, May 1963, pp. 32–34.
[36] *K'ao-ku*, October 1964, pp. 485–497, 503. See also Cheng Te-k'un, *Archaeology in China*, Vols. I, II, III, Supplement to Vol. I (5 vols. forthcoming).

4

The Place of Confucius in Communist China

By JOSEPH R. LEVENSON

> The entire area has, in fact, shared in this attention to the relics of
> the Sage since the creation of a special commission for the
> preservation of monuments and relics in Kufow. . . .
>
> *The Times* (July 31, 1961)

IN Chinese Communist fashions, Confucius seems to be " in " this year.
Earlier, certainly in the nineteen-twenties, revolutionaries were quite
ready to see him out, and even now, in the first decade or so of the
People's Republic, there are plenty of people with little patience for the
sage of the old intelligence. Indeed, " despise the old " and " preserve
the national heritage " have been chasing each other down the nineteen-
fifties and incipient sixties, and contemporary historians, in this area,
should perhaps not dwell too seriously on trends *pro* and *anti*, so fore-
shortened, if discernible at all, in the foreground of our age. What seems
historically significant is the range, not the petty successions, of recent
Communist options in evaluating Confucius. For all the possibilities are
equally modern, all plausible and consistent within a new Chinese view
—an essentially anti-Confucian view informing even the pro-Confucius
minds.

In the early years of the 1911 Republic, embattled radical iconoclasts,
out to destroy Confucius, and romantic conservatives, bent on preserving
him, had been equally untraditional.[1] Now, in the People's Republic of
1949, successor-radicals, with that battle behind them and those foes
crushed, may bring the romantic note into their own strain and celebrate
Confucian anniversaries in the name of the national heritage. But the
Communists who wish Confucius happy birthday only swell the chorus
that sounds him down to burial in history.

IMPERISHABILITY OF THE CONFUCIAN SPIRIT?

A grand old question : is Confucianism a religion? Certainly the problem
of Confucianism is rather different from the problem of Buddhism in the

---

[1] For this bond of " anti-traditional " and " traditionalistic " as both non-traditional,
see Joseph R. Levenson, " The Suggestiveness of Vestiges: Confucianism and
Monarchy at the Last," in David S. Nivison and Arthur F. Wright, ed., *Confucianism
in Action* (Stanford Un. Press, 1959), pp. 244–267.

Communist era; there is no organised Confucian body whose state can be statistically assessed.[2] Actually, when there had been some sort of effort, before the First World War, to conceive of it as a church, Confucianism was at its nadir, and no Communist policy about that Confucianism need or can be scrutinised. Other questions claim attention. First, is there Confucianism *in* Communism? Second (and more important here), what of Confucius himself, his current reputation and its meaning?

There are those, with a taste for paradox, who feel that the new régime is " in spirit," in real content, whatever the surface forms of revolution, Confucian forever. This implies an interpretation of continuity in terms not of process but reality; past is related to present not by sequence but by the persistence of essentials. From this point of view it is enough to remark that (give or take a few degrees) both Communist and Confucian China have been institutionally bureaucratic and despotic, intellectually dogmatic and canonical, psychologically restrictive and demanding. And for those who balk at forcing Confucianism and Communism to match, there is still the " Legalist " label for Mao's China. The principle of " sinological determinism " might thereby still be defended, a Chinese ideal type still preserved against corrosive historical thinking; and, with Mao a Ch'in Shih Huang-ti, Confucianism would still be implicitly there, an alternative or a partner, as in the days of that Legalist " First Emperor " or of later dynastic autocrats.

If, in such a timeless, noumenal version of continuity, China were " always China," the place of Confucius in Communist China would be pre-ordained, and empirical inquiry gratuitous or fussily misleading. Yet, if only out of piety to history (or, less grandly, in defence of his occupation), a historian has to assume the authenticity of phenomenal change, and, in this instance, contemplate not the ideal of a ghostly Confucius in the mere flesh of a modern Communist, but the idea of Confucius in the minds of men who publish under Communist aegis. One of them, Lo Ken-tse (editor of Volumes IV, 1933, and VI, 1938, of *Ku Shih Pien*, (*Symposium on Ancient History*), the famous collection of modern critiques of Classical historical orthodoxy), makes a point in discussing Confucius that could seem to assimilate Confucianism to Marxism. What lies behind the appearance?

In some observations about Confucius on poetry, Lo remarks that Confucius had basically philosophical, not literary, interests. Knowing that poetry had a lyrical, expressive character, he wanted to impose on it standards of moral orthodoxy, because he valued poetry from a utilitarian not an aesthetic point of view. Lo speaks of Confucius' practice

² *Cf.* Holmes Welch, " Buddhism under the Communists," *The China Quarterly*, No. 6 (April–June 1961), pp. 1–14.

57

of *tuan chang ch'ü i* (" cutting off the stanza and selecting the principle "), a proceeding traditionally related to the way the *Chung-yung* (*Doctrine of the Mean*), for example, cites the *Shih-ching* (*Book of Poetry*): to extract moral dicta. Literature was a tool for him, and rhetorical considerations *per se* played no part. That is why, though his doctrine of " seizing the word " had a great influence on the development of literary criticism, its purport was not " revise words " but " rectify names." [3]

Now, surely not only Lo's ancient subject but his contemporary patrons have a utilitarian not an " aesthetic " conception of literature. Mao as well as Confucius has viewed literature as the carrier of an ethos. Long ago, in the nineteen-twenties, it could seem like a throwback to the Confucian doctrine of " literature to convey the *tao*," when the " Creation Society," a body of writers imbued at first with a Western-tinged aestheticism, turned toward Marxist commitment.[4] Yet, in the " Creation " affair, the later commitment was quite as remote from Confucian premises as the earlier; indeed, it was the exhaustion of Confucianism, premises and all, which had rendered " art for art's sake "— though a radical slogan against a vital Confucianism—seemingly superfluous, and exposed it, in Communist eyes, as counter-revolutionary for a post-Confucian age.[5] Lo Ken-tse, some thirty years later, is just as far from simply engrossing a Confucian motif in a Marxist one. Rather, when he speaks of Confucius " imposing standards " on the *Shih-ching,* Lo (rather late in the critical day) means to release the poems from their Confucian blanket and to reveal them, by restoring their natural, poetic quality, as truly " popular." He wants to save a Classic by redeeming it from Confucian associations, thus permitting it to qualify for a Communist accolade.

THE DWINDLING SHARE OF CONFUCIAN MATTER IN INTELLECTUAL LIFE

But why should Communists care about such a salvage job? Would not revolutionaries (once we take them seriously as such) be expected to cancel the old intellectual currency, instead of converting it? At least from a quantitative standpoint, certainly, the old concerns of Confucian scholarship get relatively meagre attention. In 1958 Kuo Mo-jo, in a

---

[3] Lo Ken-tse, *Chung-kuo Wen-hsüeh P'i-p'ing Shih* (*History of Chinese Literary Criticism*) (Shanghai: Ku-tien Wen-hsüeh Ch'u-pan-she, 1957), pp. 39, 48–49.

[4] Chow Tse-tsung, *The May Fourth Movement: Intellectual Revolution in Modern China* (Harvard Un. Press., 1960), pp. 284–287, 309–310.

[5] *Cf.* Joseph R. Levenson, " The Day Confucius Died " (review article), *The Journal of Asian Studies*, XX, No. 2 (February 1961), p. 225.

briskly modern, no-nonsense mood, said that ancient studies had only a slight claim on available Chinese energies.[6]

Even so, a considerable programme of annotation, translation into modern Chinese, and publication of Classics and other early literature was reported for the next two years.[7] But with the development of a paper shortage (undoubtedly real since spring, 1961, and already blamed in 1960 for the serious cut in publications export), the ancient texts were the first to go.[8] And this is not surprising, since Shanghai publishers—typically, we may suppose—were proclaiming in 1960 the necessity of " learning about science and technology," " catching up with science and technology," and " overtaking science and technology." [9] These are the twins, not classical arts and letters, that the Communists especially foster in the educational system.

Intellectual training, then, once a Confucian preserve, is now pervaded by a spirit quite alien to the Confucian. Science and technology are there, on the one hand; and on the other, especially since 1958, some sort of material production and physical labour has been injected into the curriculum, with the avowed aim of domesticating the intellectuals, destroying any lingering Confucian assumptions about the " higher life " and its natural claim to prestige.[10]

CONFUCIAN MATTER DE-CONFUCIANISED:

(A) MILESTONES TO THE PRESENT

In a society where an anti-classical education sets the tone, what can the Classics be used for? In contemporary China, where Confucian scholars are invisible, scholars in Confucianism still do find employment. Their principal aim is not to extol antiquity, but to illustrate a theory of process.[11]

Accordingly, the Classics retain no scriptural authority; far from providing criteria for historical assessments, they themselves are

---

[6] Kuo Mo-jo, " Kuan-yü ' hou-chin po ku ' wen-t'i " (On the " broaden the new, narrow the old " question), *People's Daily (Jen-min Jih-pao)*, June 11, 1958, p. 7.

[7] *Daily Report: Foreign Radio Broadcasts*, No. 248 (December 22, 1960), BBB 10–11.

[8] CCS report (July 1961).

[9] *Weekly Report on Communist China*, No. 28 (June 3, 1960), p. 26.

[10] Leo A. Orleans, *Professional Manpower and Education in Communist China* (Washington: National Science Foundation, 1961), p. 18.

[11] For description and analysis of the use of Classics as sources in Communist periodisation of history, see Levenson, " History under Chairman Mao," *Soviet Survey*, No. 24 (April–June, 1958), pp. 32–34; Levenson, " Ill Wind in the Well-field: the Erosion of the Confucian Ground of Controversy," in Arthur F. Wright, ed., *The Confucian Persuasion* (Stanford Un. Press, 1960), pp. 268–270, 285–287; Albert Feuerwerker, " China's History in Marxian Dress," *American Historical Review*, LXVI, No. 2 (January 1961), pp. 336–340; Albert Feuerwerker and S. Cheng, *Chinese Communist Studies of Modern Chinese History* (Harvard Un. Press, 1961), pp. 2–9, 21–26, 209–213.

examined for significance in history. The authority they had is an object of historical study, instead of its premise.

Historical revisionism, whereby a Confucianist's villain becomes a Communist's hero, is widespread nowadays, but where the Classics are concerned it is the pattern rather than the praise-and-blame which is markedly revised. True, Kuo Mo-jo can stand an old judgment on its head and rehabilitate Chou Hsin of Yin, whom the *Shu-ching* (*Book of History*) made the classic example of the " bad last emperor." But when Kuo says that the latter was really competent, that he struck blows for the Chinese people's expansion and unification,[12] Kuo is fitting him into the annals of Chinese progress; and it is this orientation to progress, more than the bleaching of a blackened name, which puts Kuo in the un-Confucian stream. In Communist use of the Classics for making historical points, Marxist process is the governing idea, not, however revalued, a moralistic absolute.

Thus, history teachers should use the Classics in illustrating stages, *e.g.*, " For the waning of primitive communism and the coming of slave society, cite the *Li-yün* section of the *Li-chi* (*Book of Rites*), from ' Ta tao chih hsing yeh' to ' Shih wei hsiao-k'ang' " (*Li-chi* VII A, 2-3; Legge, " When the Grand Course was pursued, a public and common spirit ruled all under the sky. . . .").[13] This passage was dear to nineteenth-century innovators and egalitarians, T'ai-p'ing rebels and K'ang Yu-wei's Reformers.[14] But these groups (though generally far apart in their attitudes toward the Classics) used the *Li-chi* for the validity that a Classic might lend; while Communists cite the same text as illustrative, not exemplary—to corroborate a theory, not authenticate a value.

As a matter of fact, some Communists see not only their modern predecessors' *Li-yün* citations, but the *Li-yün* itself, as a falling back on authority. For the *Li-yün* attributes the " Grand Course " passage to Confucius, though it really dates from some two centuries after his time.[15] There are harsh words for one Comrade Jen Chüan, who seems to accept

12 Kuo Mo-jo, " Kuan-yü mu-ch'ien li-shih yen-chiu chung ti chi-ke wen-t'i," (" Several problems concerning present-day historical research "), *Hsin Chien-she*, April 1959, p. 5.

13 Wang Chih-chiu and Sung Kuo-chu, *Chung-hsüeh Li-shih Chiao-shih Shou-ts'e* (*Handbook for History Teachers in Middle Schools*) (Shanghai: Shanghai Chiao-yü Ch'u-pan-she, 1958), p. 56.

14 As noted, with context of " primitive communism," in Feng Yu-lan, " K'ang Yu-wei ti ssu-hsiang " (" The thought of K'ang Yu-wei "), in *Chung-kuo Chin-tai Ssu-hsiang Shih Lun-wen Chi* (*Collection of Essays on Modern Chinese Intellectual History*) (Shanghai: Shanghai Jen-min Ch'u-pan-she, 1958), p. 120.

15 Chinese Academy of Sciences, philosophical research department, history of Chinese philosophy section, ed., *Chung-kuo Ta-t'ung Ssu-hsiang Tzu-liao* (*Materials in Chinese Utopian Thought*) (Peking: Chung-hua Shu-chü, 1959), p. 1. For an indorsement of this position, see Ku Ti, " K'ung-tzu ho ' ta-t'ung ' ssu-hsiang " (" Confucius and utopian thought "), *Kuang-ming Jih-pao* (hereafter KMJP), May 24, 1961, p. 2.

the attribution uncritically.[16] And yet, while inviting this attack from a critic who denies that Confucius had any intention of " abolishing distinctions," Jen Chüan is really not in the business of praising Confucius by raising him out of his time, taking him as a validator of socialism, or socalism as validator of him. Jen Chüan suggests that Confucius (like K'ang Yu-wei, who revered this *ta-t'ung* side of him) had a vague *kung-hsiang* (fantasy) socialism, impracticable in his day. Therefore, lacking a clear road ahead to his goal, he looked back to primitive communism. Whence, " Ta tao chih hsing yeh. . . ." [17]—or, back to the *Li-yün* as reflector of primitive communism, a superseded stage.

And so for the next progressive transition, from slave society to feudalism : this is said to be reflected textually in the sequence of *I-ching* (*Book of Changes*) to *I-chuan* (*Commentary on Changes*—possibly included among the " Ten Wings," appendices to the *I-ching*). For these texts are equated, respectively, with an early Chou religious idealism (*T'ien-tao*, " Way of Heaven ") and a " Warring States " materialistic naturalism.[18]

And as materialism is a higher stage of thought than idealism, and naturalism higher than religion, so the " Warring States " advance of the doctrines of Confucius towards victory was advance indeed, in the historical sense of the word. For as a pair of authors interprets the *Lun-yü* (*Analects*), Confucius' concept of *jen* (human kindness) was both anti-aristocratic and anti-religious. *Jen*, the special mark of the *chün-tzu*, undercut the nobles by substituting individual quality for blood line in distinguishing *chün-tzu* from *hsiao-jen*, the " princely man " from the " small." And inasmuch as *jen* implied " esteeming wisdom," this was progressive, too, in its humanist agnosticism, that strain in Confucius that Feuerbach praised, when he marked the advance of capitalism on European feudalism, reflected in the attrition of religion.[19]

[16] Ku Ti, 2, referring to Jen Chüan, " K'ung-tzu Li-yün ' ta-t'ung ' ssu-hsiang " (" Confucius' *Li-yün* utopian thought "), KMJP, May 12, 1961, p. 4. Ku Ti maintains that Confucius was unconnected with *ta-t'ung* (" Great Harmony ") utopianism. His article insists that in the *Lun-yü* (*Analects*), in large part a reliable source for Confucius' thought, there is no shred of *ta-t'ung* doctrine ; and Ku Ti declines to accept the two *Lun-yü* extracts in the Academy of Science volume [note 15] as specimens of *ta-t'ung*, on the ground that the *Lun-yü* has non-utopian class-distinction (*viz.*, between *jen* and *min*) built into it.

[17] Jen Chüan, p. 4.

[18] Wang Ming, " *I-ching* ho *I-chuan* ti ssu-hsiang t'i-hsi wen-t'i " (" The problem of *I-ching* and *I-chuan* systems of thought "), KMJP, June 23, 1961, p. 4.

[19] Kuan Feng and Lin Yü-shih, " Lun K'ung-tzu ti ' jen ' ho ' li ' " (" A discourse on Confucius' *jen* and *li* "), *People's Daily* (July 23, 1961), p. 5 ; for *jen* as humanistic base of *li*, liberating thought from an original superstitious theology, see also Chi Wen-fu, *Ch'un-ch'iu Chan-kuo Ssu-hsiang Shih-hua* (*Historical Discourses on the Thought of the " Spring and Autumn " and " Warring States " Periods*) (Peking : Chung-kuo Ch'ing-nien Ch'u-pan-she, 1958), pp. 20–22, and " Chung-nan ti-ch'ü shih-hsüeh-chieh tsai Kuang-chou chü-hsing hsüeh-shu t'ao-lun-hui " (" The historical society of the Chung-nan region holds a scholarly discussion meeting in Canton "), KMJP, May 19, 1961, p. 2.

Other authors, too, appreciate the *Lun-yü* for the humanism and materialism they sometimes strain to find. One, for example, sees the message of *Lun-yü*, III, xii (" One should sacrifice to a spirit as though that spirit were present ") as, " Gods and ancestral spirits exist only in the mind." Passages indicating Confucius' preference for non-speculative direct perception, and for enriching the people before teaching them, are cited as materialist, in different senses of the word. And so is Confucius' scepticism about knowing the " Way of Heaven " (see *Lun-yü* V, xii)—a Way referred to often, superstitiously, by men recorded in the *Ch'un ch'iu* (*The Spring and Autumn Annals*), but materialistically doubted in the *Tso-chuan* (the main classical " commentary " appended to the *Annals*), Ch'ao-kung 18: " The Way of Heaven is far, the way of man is near. . . ." [20]

As the *Lun-yü* and *Tso-chuan* contribute humanism to the march of progress, so the *Shih-ching* (which we have seen already as " popular ") is said to begin a great tradition of realism, reflecting the creativity which burgeoning feudal society so abundantly released.[21] We know well enough, from modern invective, that feudalism *per se* wins no Communist admiration. It is the progressive stage, not the entity, that is praiseworthy; and a Classic is used for documenting, and praised for projecting, this progress.

Accordingly, possible Communist respect for Confucian Classics, as creative expressions of social evolution, does not usually carry over to Confucian classical scholarship. It may be said occasionally that there is much to be learned from one of its practitioners, as in recent praise of Chia I (200–168 B.C.), a Han official who made a famous critique of Ch'in rule by power alone. Such praise, far from implying Communist self-identification with the past through a Confucian fellow-feeling, reflects more likely a stung reaction to allegations of " Legalism "—the hostile way of identifying the Party with the past. And what is Chia I's virtue? It is nothing absolute, but relative to process. In what he was, he had to be imperfect: he could not escape limitations of time and place. His merit lies in where he was going.

---

20 Chang Tai-nien, *Chung-kuo wei-wu-chü-i ssu-hsiang chien-shih* (*A Brief History of Chinese Materialist Thought*) (Peking: Chung-kuo Ch'iang-nien Ch'u-pan-she, 1957), pp. 20, 22. For a more cautious discussion, locating Confucius between materialism and idealism, since he professed neither belief nor disbelief in " Heaven's decree " or " spirits," cf. Kuo Shao-yü, *Chung-kuo Ku-tien Wen-hsüeh Li-lun P'i-p'ing Shih* (*A Critical History of Classical Chinese Literary Doctrines*) (Peking: Jen-min Wen-hsüeh Ch'u-pan-she, 1959), p. 28.

21 Jen-min Wen-hsüeh Ch'u-pan-she Pien-chi-pu, ed., *Shih-ching Yen-chiu Lun-wen Chi* (*Collection of Research Papers on the Shih-ching*) (Peking: Jen-min Ch'u-pan-she, 1959), p. 1; Yu Kuan-ying, " China's Earliest Anthology of Poetry," *Chinese Literature*, No. 3, 1962, pp. 109, 111; cf. Kuo Shao-yü, p. 16, for Confucius recognising the *Shih-ching's* realism.

His lifetime (so the argument runs) coincided with a great change in feudal society, and Chia I, seeking to construct a program for a new feudal government, represented the interest of a newly rising commoner landlord class. He had a realistic viewpoint (good), and he paid special attention (very good) to Ch'in and contemporary (early Han) history—*i.e.*, for his own day, modern history.[22] Thus, the Communist favour goes to modern times, and, among men and events of the past, to the modernising forces.

For the most part, then, Confucian scholarship after classical times themselves is seen as the main line of Chinese feudal culture, the support of feudal monarchy, and feudal society (as distinct from the feudalisation of slave society) has no intrinsic virtue. Han Wu-ti (regn. 134–86 B.C.) winnowed the *Ju* (Confucianists) from out of the 'Hundred Schools' for special honour, and established their texts as authoritative. Thus the Classics became the preserve of the feudal land-holding, bureaucratic literati. And one of the aims of classical study now (runs the argument) is to show how classical study then could serve the feudal interests.[23] The Sung *li-hsüeh* neo-Confucianism—to cite an impressive school of classical scholarship—constrained thought, imposed rote, blocked science; and the " Han-chien (Chinese traitor) Tseng Kuo-fan " (1811–72) was a great patron of *li-hsüeh*, not by chance.[24]

In short, the contemporary approach to the Classics is neither *necessarily* to damn them as feudal (some do), nor to praise them (in the Confucian vein) as timeless. They are subject to scrutiny from a mental world beyond them; they do not govern the mental world (as once they did) themselves. As a Communist *Mencius* study-group expressed it : *They* (traditional intellectuals) used *Mencius* as a vehicle—Chu Hsi (1130–1200) did it to carry his neo-Confucianism, Tai Chen (1724–77) did it to correct Chu Hsi, K'ang Yu-wei (1858–1927) did it as a " modern-text " Confucian Reformer, all of them summoning up antiquity to sanction innovation. But *we* use the tool of Marxism-Leninism for an analytic critique.[25]

[22] " T'an-t'ao Chia I ssu-hsiang ho *Hsin-shu* chen-wei wen-t'i " (" An inquiry into Chia I's thought and the question of the authenticity of the *Hsin-shu* "), *People's Daily*, October 5, 1961, p. 7.

[23] Chou Yü-t'ung and T'ang Chih-chün, " Wang Mang kai-chih yü ching hsüeh chung ti chin-ku-wen hsüeh wen-t'i " (" Wang Mang's reform and the problem of modern and ancient texts in classical scholarship "), KMJP, May 16, 1961, p. 2 ; Chou Yü-t'ung and T'ang Chih-chün, " T'an-t'ao Chung-kuo ching-hsüeh wen-t'i " (" An inquiry into the problem of Chinese classical scholarship "), *People's Daily*, May 31, 1961, p. 7.

[24] Hsü Lun, *Shen-mo Shih Feng-chien She-hui (What is Feudal Society?)* (Shanghai : Shanghai Jen-min Ch'u-pan-she, 1954), p. 69.

[25] Lanchow University Department of Chinese Literature, Mencius-annotation sub-section, *Meng-tzu I-chu (Mencius: Translation and Commentary)* (Peking : Chung-hua Shu-chü, 1960), p. 13 ; and similarly, " Chung-kuo Jen-min Ta-hsüeh che-hsüeh-

This means, of course, that a Marxist commentary on Mencius conveys Marxism. In this it may seem to be doing, *mutatis mutandis*, just what Chu Hsi, Tai Chen and K'ang Yu-wei did. Yet, while such Sung and Ch'ing commentators may not, indeed, have been doing what they claimed, expounding Mencius or Confucius " authentically," still they assumed that only if they did so would their own views be valid. However individual their interpretations, however eccentric they seemed to outsiders, these earlier scholars had to establish—for their own satisfaction as much as for anyone else's—that classical Confucian authority was being duly upheld. But Marxists scout Confucian authority, considering it a specimen to be analysed (not idolised) and put in its place in history —a place in the flux of the past, not an eternal place of ever-present judgment.

That is why a Communist reversal of older radical textual critiques is comprehensible. It may seem extraordinary that a contemporary scholar in Communist China should take up the traditional Confucian line on the *Tso-chuan*: that it really was compiled by Tso Chiu-ming as a commentary on the *Ch'un-ch'iu* (which was Confucius' own).[26] Yet, despite appearances, decades of " doubting antiquity " have not gone quite for nothing. For the main point of Confucius, said to be " rectification of names," is seen as completely feudal and only feudal. And Confucius, while commendably materialistic in some ways, and incomparably important in planting history in Chinese education, was a step behind Ssu-ma Ch'ien, the " Grand Historian " of the Former Han; while Confucius did not (as so often advertised) see history as an irredeemable fall from sage-antiquity, he did see an eternity of oscillation (in the Mencius phrase, " now order, now chaos ") while Ssu-ma Ch'ien had a sense of historical progress.

We have, then, in this account of Confucius, another avowal of progress (indeed, to see progress *is* progress), not a triumphant return of an old unfaded perennial. If progress goes through Confucius (as evinced in his *Spring and Autumn*, not the first of its name, but first to deal with " the Empire " and not just a single state), it also goes beyond him. And therefore, without identity, a Communist may now agree with orthodox Confucianists on the link of *Tso-chuan* to *Ch'un-ch'iu*, because they agree on the error of the *Kung-yang* school, which had to deny the link in order to make its specious case for Confucius as the ultimate progressive. This is same stand, different standpoints; different effects

hsi t'ao-lun Meng-tzu p'ing-chiai wen-t'i " (" The Philosophy Department of the Chinese People's University discusses the problem of evaluating Mencius "), KMJP, July 28, 1961, p. 1.

26 For this reference, and others in this paragraph and the next, see Shu Shih-cheng, " K'ung-tzu *Ch'un-ch'iu* " (" Confucius' *Spring and Autumn* "), *Li-shih Yen-chiu*, No. 1 (1962), pp. 47–50, 55, 57.

from the same description. For progress matters in Communist theory, while it mattered precious little in the orthodox Confucian. In the present day, when the thrill of iconoclasm in the field of Classics has worn off—because icons no longer sacred tempt fewer men to break them—old conventional combinations (like the *Ch'un-ch'iu* and the *Tso-chuan* respectably together) are no witness at all to renascence of Confucius.

Thus, praise of Confucius (*e.g.*, for seeing the true relation between "ideology" and "reality"[27]) tends to be patronising, no reverent expression of discipleship. Confucius cannot guarantee this truth; he simply decorates the discussion. One points up a thesis, perhaps, by referring to the Classics, but legitimacy flows back from Marx (Lenin, Mao), not forward from Confucius. "Ideology" and "reality," in our example, are *wen* and *tao*, luminous classical terms—but here, metaphorical, used clearly in the expectation that no one will misunderstand. And nothing so marks the relegation of values to the past, to historical significance, as the metaphorical drift, whereby originally literal statements of content become rhetorical allusions.

CONFUCIAN MATTER DE-CONFUCIANISED:

(B) GRAVESTONES FROM THE PAST

On this showing, when writers in Communist China display some admiration of Confucius, they are not reproducing the traditional admiration. Therefore, when other contemporary writers sound unregenerately, untraditionally anti-Confucian, this is no sign of Party schizophrenia. For this is the kind of controversy that a Marxist world can contain. If one wants to put a reactionary construction on Confucius' work (holding that he feared the future and was generally "anti-people"),[28] this taste

[27] T'ai Shih-chien, "Wen yü tao" ("*Wen* and *tao*"), *People's Daily*, January 21, 1962, p. 5.
[28] Examples: For Confucius (a) loving the old, specifically to inculcate conservatism, *cf.* Chu Tung-jun, ed., *Tso-chuan Hsüan* (*Selections from the Tso-chuan*) (Shanghai: Shanghai Ku-tien Wen-hsüeh Ch'u-pan-she, 1956), p. 8. (b) On the side of a declining class of masters of slaves, or a tool (with Classics) of reactionary feudal class against the people, *cf.* "Chung-nan ti-ch'ü shih-hsüeh-chieh . . ." (note 19, above), p. 2; "Of Confucius, Fung Yu-lan and Others," *China News Analysis*, No. 398 (November 24, 1961), pp. 3, 5, 7; *Communist China Digest*, No. 17 (June 6, 1960), p. 83; Jen Chi-yü, "Ho Ch'i Hu Li-yüan ti kai-liang-chu-i ssu-hsiang" ("The reformist thought of Ho Ch'i and Hu Li-yüan"), *Chung-kuo Chin-tai Ssu-hsiang Shih Lun-wen chi* (Collected Essays on the History of Modern Chinese Thought) (Shanghai: Shanghai Jen-min Ch'u-pan-she, 1958), p. 86. (c) As an idealist and a religionist, fostering anti-materialist, anti-scientific thought, upholding traditional superstition through the doctrine of the "Will of Heaven," with its implication that the fate of society is determined from outside society, *cf.* Ch'en Po-ta, "P'i-p'an ti chi-ch'eng ho hsin ti t'an so" ("A critical inquiry into heritage and novelty"), *Red Flag* (*Hung Ch'i*), No. 13, 1959, p. 44; Kuo Shao-yü, p. 19; Kuan Feng and Lin Yü-shih, "Lun K'ung-tzu" ("On Confucius"), *Che-hsüeh Yen-chiu* (*Philosophical Research*), No. 4, July 25, 1961, pp. 54–56 (some points in this article and others in similar vein summarised in

in interpretation clashes, to be sure, with the "progressive" taste, but the tasters, all the same, have a common assumption: that history moves regularly through progressive stages, no matter which stage one sees as dear to Confucius, or to which he seems appropriate. The controversy is tame, like the more general one about when slave society ends and feudal begins. Within a framework of agreement on the historical reality of these societies in China, in that order, there can be several ideas about their boundaries.

But even if one acknowledges that the relatively pro-Confucius wing of Communist opinion is safely Communist enough, not Confucian, why did it come into being? Why does it differ not only from traditional conservatism but from traditional (earlier twentieth-century) radicalism? The fact that it can co-exist with Communist hostility to Confucius does not explain how it came to exist at all. It is challenging, surely, that after all the vitriolic treatment of Confucius so usual in the "Renaissance," the "New Tide," all the early radical intellectual groupings, we can find a scholar in mainland China, vintage 1958, with this fine antique allusion: "The Great Pheasant gives a cry, dawn comes to the world." Confucius, here no wretched feudal crow, is the "Great Pheasant," and it is his galvanising of scholarship and his diffusion of it in new milieus, non-aristocratic, that give rise to the "Hundred Schools." "This has great significance in the history of Chinese thought and Chinese education. Thereafter, literate men took Confucius as their great ancestral teacher. . . ." [29]

"Of Confucius, Fung Yu-lan and Others," p. 5): Feng Yuan-chun, *A Short History of Classical Chinese Literature* (Peking: Foreign Languages Press, 1958), p. 39; A. A. Petrov (Li Shih, tr.), *Wang Ch'ung—Chung-kuo Ku-tai ti Wei-wu-chu-i-che ho Ch'i-meng Ssu-hsiang-chia (Wang Ch'ung—An Ancient Chinese Materialist and Enlightened Thinker)* (Peking: K'o-hsüeh Ch'u-pan-she, 1956), pp. iii, 73–75. (d) As a reformist, basically conservative, seeking to harmonise class-contradictions and prevent the rising of the poor against the governing class, *cf.* Ho-nan Ta-hsüeh Li-shih-hsi, ed., *Chung-kuo T'ung-shih Tzu-liao Hsüan-chi (Compilation of Materials for a General History of China)* (Kaifeng; Honan Un., 1953), p. 40; Kuan Feng and Lin Yü-shih, "Lun K'ung-tzu," pp. 46–47; Kuan Feng and Lin Yü-shih, "Lun K'ung-tzu ti ' jen ' ho ' li,'" p. 5.

It is significant that in many of these references (*e.g.*, the last, with which compare purport of note 19), criticism of Confucius is combined with respect: both idealist *and* materialist elements, conservative *and* progressive, etc., are often noted. *Cf.* "Review of Reviews," *China News Analysis*, No. 410 (March 2, 1962), p. 3, for summary of yet another article on Confucius and *jen* and *li*, with Confucius being granted at least a relative merit while at the same time his limitations (as a member of the dominant class) are noted.

29 Chi Wen-fu, 16–17. *Cf.* also Tu Shou-su, *Hsien-Ch'in Chu Tzu Ssu-hsiang (The Thought of the Pre-Ch'in Philosophers)* (Sheng-huo Shu-tien), p. 6, and Chang Tai-nien, p. 20, for Confucius as more than the progenitor of the *Ju* school—as the first spokesman for open, public instruction in the history of Chinese education. For an account of others' emphasis on Confucius as a pioneer non-discriminatory educator, characterised by the spirit of study and eagerness for knowledge, *cf.* "Of Confucius, Fung Yu-lan and Others," pp. 2–3; and for a more grudging respect for Confucius as mildly progressive in his own day, an opinion clinched by reference to his disciples "propagating knowledge," *cf.* Feng Yuan-chun, pp. 26–27.

The big difference between early days and now for the Communists and Confucius is the difference between social and national associations. In Communist eyes originally, Confucius was simply the idol of the rulers of the old society; if those feudal rulers (or their abortively revolutionary bourgeois successors), for their part, claimed that Confucius embodied the "national essence," this was only a reactionary fiction, designed to avert the class struggle which would sweep the old away. Thus, Confucius, in trouble enough just for his traditional distinction, was further compromised by traditionalistic efforts to revive him.

For at first, in the new Republic after 1911, the old elementary education in Confucian *hsiu-shen tu-ching* (moral culture and classical reading) had fallen into abeyance, and the texts of Confucian learning were left to the universities, where a spirit of detachment—knowledge *of*, not knowledge *in*, judgment, not immersion—was expected to prevail. However, in 1915 Yüan Shih-k'ai, appealing to conservatives with his monarchical movement, put the old formula back in the lower schools. In 1923, *hsiu-shen* slipped once more, supplanted by a blandly modern "citizenship and hygiene," and *tu-ching* vanished, too, as the literary language, with its Confucian aura, yielded to the colloquial in the primary and high schools.[30] But when Chiang Kai-shek turned to the old pieties, with his "*San-min chu-i* (Three People's Principles) education" for an anti-Communist China's destiny, Confucius again turned up in school. Ch'en Li-fu's directives in January 1942 had agriculture as the basis of national life, *Ch'un-ch'iu* and *Li-chi* as the heart of instruction in ethics.[31] (And twenty years later, on Formosa, Confucius was still being enlisted against the "alien revolution.")[32]

What the Communists made of this should be easy to imagine. Confucius needed only the curse of Japanese sponsorship to make his exposure complete. Reactionary "sellers of the nation," the indictment ran, "revived the old, revered Confucius." And the predatory buyers, the Japanese fascists, pumped their own gas of "Confucius and the Kingly Way" into occupied China.[33]

[30] Chiao-yü pu, ed., *Ti-erh-tz'u Chung-kuo Chiao-yü Nien-chien (The Second Chinese Educational Yearbook)* (Shanghai: Commercial Press, 1948), pp. 205–206, 209.

[31] *Ibid.*, pp. 5, 8, 12, 355.

[32] *Cf. Shih-chieh Jih-pao (The Chinese World)*, San Francisco, April 14, 1962, p. 1, for Chiang Kai-shek blessing a commemorative effort of the "Confucius-Mencius Society" and urging everyone to study the Sages, restore the Chinese ethic, and thereby sweep the Communists aside.

[33] Wu Yü-chang, *Chung-kuo Li-shih Chiao-ch'eng Hsü-lun (Introduction to the Teaching Pattern for Chinese history)* (Shanghai: Hsin-hua Shu-tien, 1950), p. 1 (preface), p. 8. For another suggestion, from the outside, of an appropriate link between the pro-Confucian and anti-national causes (or the anti-Confucian and anti-fascist), *cf.* Ezra Pound, *Impact: Essays on Ignorance and the Decline of American Civilization* (Chicago: Regnery, 1960), p. 139: "Lady Hosie's introduction in a recent reprint tells us that the Four Classics have been relegated to University study and are no longer the main preoccupation of Chinese schools. She dates the essay 1937, which

This made two things clear. First, Confucius must be anathema to Communists as long as he seems identified with a contemporary Chinese class cause or a Japanese foreign cause: to the Communists, by no means always distinguishable. But second, Communists, preempting the *national* cause, can nationalise Confucius, freeing him of current social associations, taking him out of history from now on—by putting him back into it (in another sense), packing him away in the past as *historically* significant!

For the very fact that their enemies, foreign and domestic, *used* Confucius meant that the defence of Confucius was not their genuine end; and if these enemies, exactly like the Communists, were really concerned with present interests, their used Confucius was just as dead as a Communist might wish him. A dead man, superseded as a target, could be measured for a monument.

Publicity for a " people's tradition " against a " gentry " (Confucian) tradition [34] is not inconsistent with a restoration of Confucius. Once, during the days of the Paris Commune, Jacob Burckhardt rushed to believe a rumour of something he rather expected, the burning of the Louvre and all its contents [35]; to Burckhardt, the treasures of art and culture seemed destined for ruin in the dawning age of destruction of authority. What should they do, revolutionaries from the lower depths, but destroy the products of the old high culture, symbols of their own subservience?

But Burckhardt might have remembered the first French Revolutionaries' preservation of the Bayeux Tapestry as a national treasure, even though, as a relic of the grandeur of nobles, it had been threatened, like its associates, with destruction. [36] And Burckhardt (in a heroic feat of clairvoyance and broadening of sympathies) might have applied the lesson in envisioning the fate of Confucius: " the people," without abandoning hostility to bearers of the " other culture," can conceive of themselves as capturing it. Confucius need not be shattered; he can be preserved, embalmed, deprived of life in a glass case instead of in a cultural holocaust. He can be restored, in short, not as an authentically resurgent Confucianism (or an immanently Confucian Communism)

year brought the natural consequences of unusual idiocy in the form of Japanese invasion. If China had got to this point, naturally there would be an invasion, and quite naturally some Chinese would, as they do, hold the view that such an invasion is to be welcomed."

[34] For reference to Mao and Lenin on these " two cultures," *cf.* Miu Yüeh, " Chiang-shou Chung-kuo li-shih tui-yü wen-hua pu-fen ju-ho ch'u-li " (" How to handle the cultural portions in lecturing on Chinese history "), KMJP, May 30, 1961, pp. 2–3.

[35] Alexander Dru, ed., *The Letters of Jacob Burckhardt* (New York: Pantheon, 1955), p. 24.

[36] Frank Rede Fowke, *The Bayeux Tapestry: a History and Description* (London: Bell, 1913), pp. 6–7.

might restore him, but as a museum-keeper restores, his loving attention to " period " proclaiming the banishment of his object from any living culture. What could be more aggressive than that (new masses *vs.* old elite), and yet more soporific? Revolutionaries, in a *metaphorical* way, kissing off into the past instead of blowing up in the present, commit the destruction which Burckhardt half-literally expected. As the Communists claim to stand for the whole nation, the ancient mentor of a high, once mighty part is quietly taken over, and given his quietus. Nobody raises his voice in a National Gallery—on either side of the exhibition frames.

Under the new dispensation, then, Confucius can have all the class-associations anyone envisages, as long as they are ascribed to him *for his own day only*. Make him " slave " or " feudal," but only for late Chou. He can then belong to the modern nation by being in its history, or (to say the same thing) by being *now* de-classed: *i.e.*, out of historical action. Thus, " the feudalist system which set up his name as a symbol has gone for good; but the name of Confucius himself is, and always will be, respected and cherished by the Chinese people." [37]   And another writer, in the same business of extricating Confucius from the past for present admiration, consigns him to the past, too, as a matter of practical influence: " I myself am not a Confucianist, and I think, to speak frankly, that what he taught belongs now irrevocably to history." [38]   A biographer censures Yen Fu (1849–1921) for using Confucius after World War I as a stick for beating Western civilisation. To a Communist, this is using the ante-historical concept of " Chinese essence " to damn modernisation, and he says that Confucius' teaching had the form of the feudal consciousness, which was not for modern China, not for the modern world. But the critic is attacking Yen Fu, a late antagonist, not Confucius, a late, late one. He agrees that the thought of Confucius, *in history*, had a great position and applicability. [39]

To accept literal Confucian influence is wrong; he must be dead to the present. Therefore, even the generally favoured Hung Hsiu-ch'üan, the T'ai-p'ing ruler, may be scored off for " traditional feudal superstition " implanted by his youthful Confucian training. [40]   But to acknowledge some national Confucian ancestry, over a gulf of time unbridgeable to influence, is all right. For this means continuity, or life to the culture. Thus, an alphabetic script-reformer would preserve against obliteration Confucius and the culture which he dominated, though this culture was

[37] " Of Confucius, Fung Yu-lan and Others," p. 2.
[38] *Ibid.*, p. 5.
[39] Wang Shih, *Yen Fu Chuan (Biography of Yen Fu)* (Shanghai: Shanghai Jen-min Ch'u-pan-she, 1957), p. 96.
[40] " Ho-nan shih-hsüeh-chieh t'ao-lun Hung Hsiu-ch'üan ti ssu-hsiang yü Ju-chia ti kuan-hsi wen-t'i " (" The Historical Society of Honan discusses the thought of Hung Hsiu-ch'üan and the problem of its relationship to Confucianism "), KMJP, June 1, 1961, p. 1.

enshrined in the script that is marked for discard.[41] And the historian,
Ch'en Po-ta, avowing that " today's China is an extension of historical
China," refers to a Mao statement of 1938: " As we are believers in
the Marxist approach to history, we must not cut off our whole historical
past. We must make a summing up from Confucius down to Sun Yat-sen
and inherit this precious legacy." [42]

" Broaden the modern, narrow the old," Ch'en continues, as he makes
it clear that a line is thrown back to the past not for the sake of the past,
but for the present. (Recall the praise of the past's Chia I for attention to
his own present.) The tie is for continuity, not constraint. What, to
Ch'en, distinguishes the Communist zeal for the modern from that of
earlier iconoclasts, with their capitalist world-view and their slogans on
the order of, " Break through the web! " or " Break down the Confucianists' shop! "? What these men lack, with their capitalist-reformist
mentalities, is scientific detachment regarding ancient thought and culture. Some of their fellows try superficially to harmonise the old and
the new; they themselves go to extremes, and cut off the old from the
new absolutely. A new scholarship is needed, and the Communists will
supply it: neither Classical, nor Sung neo-Confucian, nor Ch'ing
empirical, nor late-Ch'ing reformist. It must be a scholarship fulfilling
each earlier type, transcending the accomplishments of all the preceding
Chinese.[43]

Fulfilment—neither dismissal nor resuscitation. For the former would
leave an impression of China de-nationalised, the victim of " cultural
imperialism," and the latter would leave her unmodernised, a relic of
feudalism. The great aim is to be modern *and* Chinese, that combination
so desperately sought through a century of reformist and revolutionary
exasperation at a seemingly immobile China and an all-too-kinetic West.
Thus, for all the Communists' hostility to the reactionary use of Confucius, there is an equal animus against what they see as the liberal,
bourgeois, pro-Western abuse of Confucius. Ku Chieh-kang, in a new
preface (1954) to a 1935 book on Han dynasty scholarship, censures
himself for his old unmitigated rejection of the Confucian thought of

[41] Ni Xaishu [Ni Hai-shu], " *Lunjy* " *Syanji* [" *Lun-yü* " *Hsüan-i*] (*Selected Translations
from the Lun-yü*) (Shanghai: Dungfang Shudian [Tung-fang Shu-tien], 1954), pp. 1–2.
[42] Ch'en Po-ta, p. 37. For Mao's remarks, *cf.* " The Role of the Chinese Communist
Party in the National War," *Selected Works of Mao Tse-tung* (London: Lawrence &
Wishart, 1954), II, pp. 259–260. For another reference to Mao in this vein (" learn
from the people—and learn from the ancients "), *cf.* Tang Shu-shih, " A Brief Discussion on Comrade Mao Tse-tung's Contribution to Marxist Literary Style," translated in *Communist China Digest*, No. 17, June 6, 1960, pp. 84–85.
[43] Ch'en Po-ta, pp. 37–38.

those days—an error stemming from his failings in historical material-ism.[44] And another writer, not bearing the culpability as his own but spreading it around, indicts the Chinese bourgeoisie for an overweening reverence for Western culture and disparagement of China's, though Mao had ordained that "today's China is the extension of historical China." [45]

Confucius, then, redeemed from both the class aberration (feudal) of idolisation and the class aberration (bourgeois) of destruction, may be kept as a national monument, unworshipped, yet also unshattered. In effect, the disdain of a modern pro-Western bourgeoisie for Confucius cancels out, for the dialecticians, a feudal class's pre-modern devotion. The Communists, driving history to a classless synthetic fulfilment, retire Confucius honourably into the silence of the museum. In a concrete way, this is evident in the very making of museums in Communist China.

For the Confucian temple at Sian is restored, to house a historical museum. The temple and tomb (and environs) of Confucius at Ch'ü-fu are repainted, regilded and preserved.[46] In April 1962, during the traditional " Ch'ing-ming " spring festival for worshipping at graves, streams of visitors were drawn there, in a market-fair atmosphere, officially contrived, along the route of procession from the " Confucian grove " to the temple.[47] (The K'ung-lin, " Confucian grove," had once been proposed as the Mecca and Jerusalem of Confucianism as a religion.) [48] And such acts of piety (consistent with, not confounded by, a " feudal " identification) [49] convey the Communists' sense of synthesis in arresting physical ruin. Products of the old society, which might be (and, earlier, were) deemed proper objects of iconoclasm, provocative symbols of a social type which Communists ought to attack, nevertheless had suffered neglect and depredation, not loving care, from the society which the Communists succeeded.[50] This

---

[44] Ku Chieh-kang, *Ch'in Han ti Fang-shih yü Ju-sheng* (*Taoists and Confucianists of the Ch'in and Han Periods*) (Shanghai: Ch'ün-lien Ch'u-pan-she, 1955), p. 15.

[45] Li Shu, " Mao Tse-tung t'ung-chih ti ' Kai-tsao wo-men ti hsüeh-hsi ' ho Chung-kuo li-shih k'o-hsüeh (" Comrade Mao Tse-tung's ' Reform our learning' and Chinese historical science "), *People's Daily*, June 8, 1961, p. 7.

[46] Joseph Needham, " An Archaeological Study-tour in China, 1958," *Antiquity*, XXXIII, No. 130, June 1959, pp. 116–117.

[47] *People's Daily*, April 8, 1962, p. 2; *Hua-chiao Jih-pao* (*China Daily News*), New York, April 16, 1962, p. 1; *Shih-chieh Jih-pao*, April 24, 1962, p. 1. The latter account cites Hong Kong speculation to the effect that, with a shortage of seeds for spring plowing, Mao prefers to divert attention to the Confucian associations of spring. (This does not seem to be a very powerful analysis.)

[48] Ch'en Huan-chang, *K'ung-chiao Lun* (*On the Confucian Religion*) (Shanghai, 1912), p. 27.

[49] *Cf. Glimpses of China* (Peking: Foreign Language Press, 1958): " Confucius (551–469 B.C.) was a famous thinker of ancient China. His teachings held sway in feudal society. Temples dedicated to him were built in various places. The one in Chufu, his native town, is the largest and houses a large number of precious cultural objects and relics."

[50] For impressions of this neglect of monuments, see K. M. Panikkar, *In Two Chinas: Memoirs of a Diplomat* (London: Allen and Unwin, 1955), pp. 34, 99–100.

neglect, combined with foreign plundering, comes to the fore as a cultural crime of the old society, overshadowing the inequities of the even older society which made the relics in the first place. If anything, it was the pre-Communist neglect which consigned these things to history, which stamped them *non-contemporary*. When the Marxist historicism of the current society relativises its " restored " Confucius to a remote stage of society—and preserves him for the present through the Museum's trick of dissociating art from any life at all—it only confirms the action (or inaction: the working of neglect) of the society just before this one. In a satirical fantasy from that Kuomintang era, the 1930s, the novelist Lao She, now thoroughly acceptable to the Communists, mordantly pictured two things, perceived as a combination: conservative spirit in clinging to a moribund culture, and material failure to conserve. For the museum in " Cat City " is empty, its possessions all sold to foreigners.[51]

Any contemporary assault against Confucius, then, while still a sort of ritual exercise (at the moment, in abeyance) for some writers in Communist China, is ideologically superflous. The Communists know they have living men to assail, non-Communists as modern and post-Confucian as themselves, not the stuffed men from a costume past (whose clothes they are stealing anyway, to display as their " national heritage "). The stake today is title to the prestige of science. Science, as we have suggested, sets up values alien to the Confucian, and a Confucian challenge on this issue could only be remote. But a non-Communist anti-traditionalism cannot be stripped of a claim on that title so easily. An attack on a biologist for basing himself on Darwin instead of Michurin [52] is a more typical accusation of " rightism " than an attack on grounds of Sinocentric narrowness. The Confucian literatus, who might have been narrow in that way, is so faint a memory that no one gets credit now in the Communist heaven, as a new man, just by being a Western-trained scientist. The latter is now the old man (the Confucianist is the dead man), and the " post-bourgeois " scientist is the new.

Scientists have tended lately to be less harassed by ideologues in a technologically hungry China, but the demand for " red and expert," the redder the better, has long been heard in the land,[53] and will doubtless be heard again. The question has been raised of possible affinity between this point of view and the Confucian preference for the highly indoctrinated

---

51 Cyril Birch, " Lao She: the Humourist in His Humour," *The China Quarterly*, No. 8, October–December, 1961, pp. 48–49.

52 Roderick MacFarquhar, *The Hundred Flowers Campaign and the Chinese Intellectuals* (New York: Praeger, 1960), p. 90.

53 *Cf.* Franklin W. Houn, *To Change a Nation: Propaganda and Indoctrination in Communist China* (Glencoe, Ill.: Free Press, 1961), p. 7.

universal man over the specialist.[54] If the affinity existed, then the Confucian spirit might well be thought, in a sense, imperishable. Yet, the " red and expert " formula may better be taken, perhaps, to prove the opposite: scientific expertise, specialised knowledge, far from being inferior to the general, is indispensable. It is this very indispensability that makes it such an important thing to capture; it must not be seen as independent, or anything but derived from the Marxist point of view. The Communists have to own science—or *they* will appear not indispensable.

A Chinese world in which science has to be owned, to be captured, is the very world in which Confucius can only be captured, cannot be free and dominant. Where science is all-pervasive (even seeping into the rhetoric applied to the social system), Confucius is under lock and key and glass. It is the curators, not the creators, who look to Confucius now. No longer a present incitement to traditionalists (these having been crushed), Confucius is ready for history.

But not for " the dustbin of history "—the museum, in every sense (and to one in particular) is not that by any other name. The museum where Confucius is posed may be a storehouse of value and inspiration. And " museumified " is not " mummified." Still, the " museumified " Confucius does not speak; no longer involved in the handing down of judgments, he is therefore not much involved in clamorous class struggle. One is neither quartering Botticelli nor taking his as the last word for a contemporary jury, when one hangs him on the wall, far from the social context of his patronage. The critics, by and large, call him masterly. They also call him *quattrocento*. Confucius, too, is wise today for many revolutionaries, and may grow wiser as his patrons grow deader. But Confucius is also *Chou*.

The first wave of revolution in the twentieth century had virtually destroyed him, and seemed to destroy with him a precious continuity, a historical identity. Many schools have tried to put these together again. The Communists have their own part in the search for time lost, and their own intellectual expedient: to bring it back, bring him back, by pushing him back in history. It has been a long peregrination, from the Confucian *tao*, K'ung's Way, to the past recaptured.

[54] Mary C. Wright, " The Pre-Revolutionary Intellectuals of China and Russia," *The China Quarterly*, No. 6, April–June, 1961, p. 179.

5

Chinese Communist Treatment of the Thinkers of the Hundred Schools Period

By DONALD J. MUNRO

ALTHOUGH there is no detailed definitive Chinese Communist interpretation of the thinkers of the 100 Schools Period,[1] this does not mean that one cannot isolate certain constants from which deviation is not permitted. The sayings of Marx-Engels and Mao Tse-tung which are directly relevant to the early thinkers, if not strictly about them, have obviously been the primary guidelines for the scholar in Communist China. Especially in the material produced since 1957, when relatively intensive study of the period began, one becomes aware of more specific trends in interpretation. With the basic tenets of Marx and Engels as tools for interpretation, it is axiomatic that understanding the class struggle of a given time is the key to understanding the thought of that time. The " contention " among the 100 Schools is taken to be a reflection of the intensity of class struggle in the Warring States Period. It is also axiomatic that the history of the struggle between progressive and reactionary forces is reflected in the enduring philosophical struggle between materialism and idealism. But the philosophical concepts associated with materialism and idealism are not native to China; nor are their Marxist definitions universally accepted in the history of Western philosophy. Therefore, in interpreting the thought of the 100 Schools Period, scholars most frequently cite Marx-Engels definitions as support for their own interpretations or to criticise those of others. Engels states that all those who take spirit as prior to the existence of the natural world and thus in the last analysis admit a creator (Old Testament variety or the more sophisticated Absolute Spirit of Hegel) belong in the idealist camp. Those who take the natural world as

---

[1] In the selection of works to be read for a study of this kind, one is necessarily guided in part by subjective factors. One gets the feeling from repeated exposure to articles and books on the 100 Schools Period that certain authors are the most widely discussed among their peers. Their names continually crop up in the works of other scholars, and their articles are regularly included in compilations of selected pieces on a specific topic. I have tried to concentrate on men of this calibre. But in addition to my " impressions " I had the advantage of very helpful advice from Professor Wing-tsit Chan, of Dartmouth College. Strictly speaking, the term " 100 Scholars " refers to the numerous philosophical doctrines which flourished during the Warring States Period (475–221 B.C.), *i.e.*, after the time of Confucius and Mo Tzu.

primary belong to the different schools of materialism.[2] A variation on the theme is that those who hold that physical existence determines thought, and hence regard matter as primary, are materialists. Those who hold the reverse, *i.e.*, that reality depends on consciousness to exist, are idealists. A further division is made between "objective idealism" (the view that the true nature of all things is mental, *e.g.*, Reality is one Absolute Mind) and "subjective idealism" (the doctrine that things exist only in minds). The Chinese are accustomed to making this kind of distinction which resembles the Neo-Confucian debate over the priority of *li* "principle" (or *Tao*) and *ch'i* "ether."

The statements of Mao which are quoted are more relevant to the Confucian thought of the period than to that of other schools. The first concerning human nature (*hsing*) reads, "Is there any such thing as a theory of human nature? Of course there is. But there is only concrete human nature, namely, human nature with a class background in the class society, and there is no abstract Human Nature transcendent of classes."[3] Secondly, there is no love of others (denoted by *jen* in the early works) transcending classes. Mao says, "As for the so-called 'love of humanity,' there has never been such a unified love since humanity was divided into classes."[4] A corollary of both of these statements is an affirmation of the relativity of moral values. "The concepts of morality, immorality, good and evil, are not instinctive, and cannot be deduced rationally from the so-called 'eternal truth' or from the traits of the supposedly non-changing Human Nature," says one Communist theoretical work.[5]

Chinese scholars must ask several questions in considering a thinker of the 100 Schools: Was his thought idealistic or materialistic (or predominantly one or the other)? This question frequently is broken down into sub-questions, *e.g.*, concerning the idealistic or materialistic nature of his "world view," epistemology, etc. What class did he

---

[2] As stated in Engels, *Fei-erh-pa-ha yu Te-kuo Ku-tien Che-hsueh ti Chung-chieh (Feuerbach and the Outcome of German Classical Philosophy)* (Shanghai: Jen-min Ch'u-pan She, 1955), pp. 19–20. Since the time of Engels there has been a confusion in Marxist thought between the definition of "materialism" as a belief in "the primacy of Nature over Spirit" (*i.e.*, the denial of a creator God and treatment of mind as a function of matter) and as a belief in objective reality independent of consciousness and sensation ("realism" in Western terminology). In each case "idealism" is defined as the reverse and includes the most diverse of creeds from Hegel's absolute idealism to agnosticism and scepticism. See Gustav A. Wetter, *Dialectical Materialism* (New York: Frederick A. Praeger, 1958), pp. 28–296.

[3] *Mao Tse-tung Hsuan-chi (Selected Works of Mao Tse-tung)* (Harbin: Tung-pei Shu-chu, 1948), p. 989, quoted in Dai Shen-yu, *Mao Tse-tung and Confucianism* (unpublished Ph.D. dissertation, Department of Political Science, University of Pennsylvania, 1952), pp. 150–151.

[4] *Mao Tse-tung Hsuan-chi*, pp. 973, 989, quoted in Dai, p. 163. Both remarks of Mao are frequently cited by recent commentators.

[5] Chin Shih-po and Wu Fu-heng (trans.), *On Communist Morality* (Hankow: Hsin-hua Book Co., 1950), p. 7, quoted in Dai, p. 160.

represent or the interest of which class was expressed in his thought (feudal lord, sunken slave-owner (*mo-lo nu-li-chu*), rising landlord, craftsman, peasant)? What contribution did he make to history—or was his thought progressive or conservative? Scholars are encouraged to investigate the annotation and dating of texts in order to invalidate the interpretations of later (*e.g.*, Sung) commentators who read into the early works ideas appropriate to a later age and thus to discover the original meaning.[6]

The importance of these constants as charts for interpretation and evaluation is clear to anyone who reads publications on the early thought. More dramatic evidence is available from an examination of targets of criticism. The unfortunate Liu Chieh, of the Department of History, Chungshan University, is a case in point. As a Roman commentator once said of Epicurus, he has "the whole pack of philosophers barking around him."[7] Drawing his inspiration largely from the Ch'eng-Chu school of Neo-Confucianism[8] and supplementing it with a dose of Hegel (he is classified as an objective idealist), he has violated many of the above guide-lines. He rejects the theory of class struggle as a tool for the study of ancient history, and his key for the study of Chinese thought is not the materialism/idealism struggle but simply the question of the nature of the union between Heaven and man. He and many others accept the Mencius (371–289 B.C.?) definition of human nature as an endowment to all men from Heaven and ignore its class character.[9] Unmindful of the relativity of virtues, he treats "human-heartedness" (*jen*) as an abstract concept transcending time and class, appropriate to any time and any class.[10] In fact, he treats all four cardinal virtues isolated by Mencius ("human-heartedness," "justice," "ritual" and "knowledge") in this manner.[11] It is pointed out that he clearly is unaware of the fraud in Mencius' belief that such virtues have universal validity for all people in any age. Thus he is guilty of uncritically glorifying the thought of the early Confucian thinkers and failing to see the deception in their claims of universal validity.

Liu is not alone in this error by any means. Fung Yu-lan sees some class content in *jen* (human-heartedness).[12] But, after finding what he

---

6 For example, see *Kuang-ming Jih-pao (Kuang-ming Daily)*, August 17–18, 1963.
7 Norman W. Dewitt, *Epicurus and His Philosophy* (Minneapolis: University of Minnesota Press, 1954), p. 179.
8 The so-called "Rationalistic School," one of the two major schools of Confucian thought which flourished in the Sung (A.D. 960–1279) and subsequent dynasties.
9 See the criticism of him in *Kuang-ming Jih-pao*, November 10, 1963.
10 *Jen-min Jih-pao (People's Daily)*, June 18, 1963.
11 "Marxist Theory of Class Struggle Must Be Employed in the Study of History," *Survey of China Mainland Press (SCMP)* (Hong Kong: U.S. Consulate General), No. 3128.
12 Fung Yu-lan, whose name is most associated with Chinese philosophical studies in the West, no longer seems to me to be the dominant figure in Chinese philosophy. His place seems to have been taken by Kuan Feng, whose name is frequently

believes to be Marxist sanction for his view, he goes on to accept as not entirely fraudulent the claims by members of the new (landlord) class in the Eastern Chou (770–221 B.C.) that *jen* has universal validity. His Marxist references state that, in the beginning while a new class is rising to power and while its own position is unstable, it has not yet formulated its own interests and has some interests in common with other classes.[13] Fung would include all classes as objects of " human-heartedness " in definitions of the concept of *jen*, such as " It is to love all men " [14] and " not doing to others as you would not have done to yourself." [15] But it is held that Fung's view is clearly erroneous, and that he distorted the words of Engels in seeking support for it.[16] Attempts by Liu and Fung to find universal validity in a concept such as *jen*, so that it is applicable today too, are considered not only erroneous but dangerous. They run against Chairman Mao's instruction never to carry out benevolent government to the enemy.[17]

Those scholars whose studies are not directed by the questions mentioned above but by certain others have been quickly attacked. A common error has been to inquire in what way an early thinker was modern, *i.e.*, of what truths of dialectical materialism was he aware. For example, some scholars have tried to show that the classic work, the *Chou I*, contains the principle that " practice is the source of knowledge." [18] This is considered dangerous because it leads to worship of the ancient. The value of seeing the eternal truths of Marxism in *embryonic* form in the early thinkers is not denied. But it seems that one is approaching dangerous ground when he attributes to the ancients ideas that are too sophisticated (from the Marxist point of view). For example, it would be proper to see embryonic dialectical thought in the *Chou I* but not to find therein the law of conversion from quantity to quality. Another error is to carry out one's own study and then simply

associated with the activities of the Research Institute of Philosophy of the Chinese Academy of Sciences and who was elected a deputy from Shantung to the Third National People's Congress. Kuan Feng often writes jointly with Lin Yu-shih of the same Institute, who has been connected with the Editor's Office of *People's Daily*.

13 Fung Yu-lan, " Lun K'ung-tzu kuan-yu ' jen ' ti ssu-hsiang " (" On Confucius's Thought Concerning ' Jen ' "), *Che-hsueh Yen-chiu (Philosophical Research)*, No. 5, September 1961, p. 67.

14 Confucius, *Analects*, xii.22.1.

15 *Ibid*. xii.2.

16 *Kuang-ming Jih-pao*, November 25, 1963.

17 Mao Tse-tung, *On People's Democratic Dictatorship* (Peking: Foreign Languages Press, 1961), p. 11; referred to in the critique of Liu Chieh appearing in *SCMP*, No. 3128.

18 *Kuang-ming Jih-pao*, November 25, 1963, and Tung Fang-ming, " Che-hsueh shih kung-tso-chung ti i chung chi yu-hai ti fang-fa " (" An Extremely Harmful Method in the Task of Studying the History of Philosophy "), *Che-hsueh Yen-chiu*, No. 1, January 25, 1963, pp. 33–34.

add a coating of class terms in order to achieve orthodoxy.[19] It is also erroneous to ask which ancient truths can guide our conduct today.

These, then, are the broad constants guiding the interpretation of the thought of the 100 Schools Period. Coupled with the fact that contemporary Chinese scholars of the period tend to haggle over a very limited number of the same passages in putting forth their theses, the result is an expected impression of some uniformity.

CONTROVERSY WITHIN CONSTANTS

Within the bounds of the constants, however, a great deal of lively controversy still continues to emerge. Several factors produce a climate which permits controversy. First, the periodisation of early Chinese history has not been officially established, and this may explain the failure to classify early thinkers definitively according to class. Some contemporary scholars hold that the Western Chou was feudal, that the time from the Spring and Autumn period (722–481 B.C.) to the Warring States signalled a shift from a system of feudal lords (the people as private chattels of the lords) to a new feudal landlord economic system (the people as freemen). The other and definitely more popular periodisation stems in part from Kuo Mo-jo. It takes the Western Chou as a slave society and the period from Spring and Autumn to Warring States as marking a shift from slave to feudal society, with the class struggle taking place between slave-owners and the members of the new landlord class, and also involving the struggles of the slaves and internal strife among slave-owners.[20] The landlords achieved formal power only gradually and in certain stages (e.g., Ch'i) earlier than others.[21] The gradual shift meant that Mencius lived at a time when the slave society and its system of blood-ties still had some strength, whereas at the time of Hsun Tzu (fl. 298–238 B.C.) it had been virtually dissolved,[22] and the peasantry was a rising power.[23]

Also conducive to controversy within the limits of the constants described above is the fact that the effect of class identity on a thinker's doctrines is by no means predetermined. For example, Kuan Feng

[19] Kuan Feng and Lin Yu-shih, " Tsai lun K'ung-tzu " (" Second Discussion on Confucius "), *K'ung-tzu Che-hsueh T'ao-lun Chi* (*Collected Discussions on the Philosophy of Confucius*) (Peking: Chung-hua Shu-chu, 1963), p. 306. The article first appeared in *Hsin Chien-she* (*New Construction*), No. 11, 1961.

[20] *Ibid.* p. 307.

[21] Kuan Feng, " Chuang-tzu che-hsueh p'i-p'an " (" Critique of Chuang-tzu's Philosophy "), *Chuang-tzu Che-hsueh T'ao-lun Chi* (*Collected Discussions on the Philosophy of Chuang-tzu*) (Peking: Chung-hua Shu-chu, 1962), p. 12. The article first appeared in *Che-hsueh Yen-chiu*, Nos. 7–8, 1960.

[22] Li Teh-yung, " Hsun-tzu ti ssu-hsiang " (" Hsun-tzu's Thought "), *Chung-kuo Ku-tai Che-hsueh Lun-ts'ung* (*Discussions on Ancient Chinese Philosophy*) (Peking: Chung-hua Shu-chu, 1957), pp. 89–91.

[23] *Ibid.* p. 94.

notes that the Sung/Yin school,[24] Mencius, Hsun Tzu and Han Fei Tzu (d. 233 B.C.) all represented the landlord class, but that Sung K'eng and Yin Wen, Hsun Tzu and Han Fei Tzu are materialists and Mencius an idealist.[25] Jen Chi-yu notes that simply because a man belonged to the "sunken class of slave-owners" by no means meant that he could not put forth a materialistic philosophy; Marx-Leninism had shown that such phenomena had occurred in England.[26] A final encouragement to controversy is the spirit of letting a hundred flowers bloom. This is frequently cited in disclaimers of any search for unanimity, though it seems more a slogan than a consistent policy.

THE USES OF HISTORY

Why should such studies of the early thought be carried out? There are several immediate uses for these studies. They give practice in using Marxism to analyse the philosophical systems which have emerged in history.[27] They provide the opportunity for struggle with erroneous doctrines, such as nihilism, the doctrine that denies any basis for knowledge or truth, sometimes attributed to the early Taoist thinkers. And they lead to the discovery of the laws of thought, or the laws of philosophical development, such as the law derived from the study of Chuang Tzu that any search for the beginning of things in the world, things which are without beginning and end, is bound to lead to idealism.[28] They also increase an understanding of the era in which a given thinker lived.[29] Commentators continually point to the fact that since subsequent rulers adopted many of the views of the 100 Schools thinkers, their hold remained strong.

[24] Sung K'eng and Yin Wen are early Taoists mentioned in the *Chuang-tzu, T'ien Hsia P'ien.*

[25] Kuan, "Chuang-tzu che-hsueh p'i-p'an," *op. cit.*, p. 16; Jen Chi-yu, "Chuang-tzu ti wei-wu-chu-i chih-chieh kuan" ("Chuang-tzu's Materialistic World View"), *Chuang-tzu Che-hsueh*, pp. 160–161. The article first appeared in *Hsin Chien-she*, No. 1, 1957. Kuan Feng seems to see the evil in early Taoist thought as stemming from such class ties. Jen Chi-yu on the other hand sees no ill effect on Chuang Tzu of his belonging to the slave-master class; he finds him realistic regarding the impossibility of reverting to the old order, not seeking escape into religion, and as taking a materialistic view of things.

[26] Jen Chi-yu, "Lun Lao-tzu che-hsueh ti wei-wu-chu-i pen-chih" ("On the Materialistic Essence of Lao-tzu's Philosophy"), *Lao-tzu Che-hsueh T'ao-lun Chi (Collected Discussions on Lao-tzu's Philosophy)* (Peking: Chung-hua Shu-chu, 1959), p. 45. The article first appeared in *Che-hsueh Yen-chiu*, No. 7, 1959. The article constitutes a reply to Kuan Feng and Lin Yu-shih.

[27] Kuan Feng and Lin Yu-shih, "Lun Lao-tzu che-hsueh t'i-hsi ti wei-hsin-chu-i pen-shih" ("On the Idealistic Essence of Lao-tzu's Philosophy"), *Lao-tzu Che-hsueh*, p. 227. The article first appeared in *Che-hsueh Yen-chiu*, No. 6, 1959.

[28] Kuan, "Chuang-tzu che-hsueh p'i-p'an," *op. cit.*, pp. 34–35.

[29] *Kuang-ming Jih-pao*, November 12, 1962.

But the more fundamental answer is found in Mao's statement that as Marxists, the Chinese must not cut themselves off from their historical past, but must " critically sum it up using the Marxist approach " and then proceed to " inherit this invaluable legacy." The essence is to be kept, the dross discarded. The fruits of the studies will then, among other things, become grist for the education of the youth.[30]

Thus interpretation of the early thought must be guided by the obligation to " critically inherit " that philosophical legacy. But " inheritance " is a vague word, one which must be explained in Marxist terms. Briefly stated: due to the dialectical course of history, present Chinese society contains elements of essence and dross from the past. These elements dictate the limiting conditions under which Marxism is to be applied to China. Since each country has its own tradition, Marxism must be adjusted to those traditions. A knowledge of China's legacy is of great importance in determining which elements of Marxism must be played up and which played down in China, *i.e.*, what in present-day Chinese thought, attitudes and conduct must be overcome, and what should be preserved and built upon. Within the sphere of philosophy one must look for essence in even the most erroneous world views so as to be mindful of what is vital in the heritage. Just as Marx stood the idealist Hegel on his head, so it is possible for the Chinese to inherit the positive aspects of their own idealistic philosophies.

COMMUNISTS ON CONFUCIUS

It is not possible to discuss the thought of the 100 Schools Period without making some remarks about Chinese Communist interpretation of the thought of Confucius. According to Communist writers the major struggle was between materialism and idealism, and the leaders of these two opposing camps, Hsun Tzu and Mencius, had carried on divergent threads found in Confucius.[31]

Controversies have centred on the political and religious doctrines of Confucius, especially on the progressive or conservative nature of his conceptions of *jen* and *li* (" ritual "). Whether or not *jen* is viewed as largely progressive (as Fung Yu-lan views it)[32] depends for the most part on whether or not the character *jen* (" man ") in the various phrases associated with *jen* (" human-heartedness ") is interpreted as denoting

---

30 See the reference to the article by Wang Shih-ching, " The Present Must Not be Confused with the Past," in *Selections from China Mainland Magazines (SCMM)* (Hong Kong: U.S. Consulate General), No. 405. The author's reference is primarily to the " classical literary legacy."

31 Yang Jung-kuo, " Lun K'ung-tzu ssu-hsiang " (" On the Thought of Confucius "), *K'ung-tzu Che-hsueh*, p. 396. Article originally appeared in *Hsueh-shu Yen-chiu (Academic Research)*, No. 1, 1962.

32 Fung Yu-lan, " Lun K'ung-tzu " (" On Confucius "), *K'ung-tzu Che-hsueh*, pp. 85–90. Article first appeared in *Kuang-ming Jih-pao*, July 22 and 29, 1960.

all men or simply the upper class and freemen.[33] Whether or not *li* is largely progressive depends on whether or not it is held that Confucius introduced a new content to the Chou rites (de-emphasis on outward show, elimination of oppressive activities, bringing members of even the lowest class under the obligations of *li*, new relationships between ruler and ministers based on civility and loyalty respectively).[34] Clearly the conclusion which more and more writers seem to be drawing is that there are both progressive and conservative elements in the thought of Confucius, with the emphasis mainly on the latter. The conservatism is seen particularly in his advocacy of social gradations, in his opposition to formal law, in his desire to restore the Chou system, and in his calling for a stronger affection for those close by than for others. In addition, Confucius was an idealist in his epistemology, believing in inborn sagacity (which he rated over acquired knowledge) and in truths handed down in poetry, history and ritual which need no testing in social practice.[35] However, even those who see him as most reactionary often agree that there are progressive aspects in his theory of *jen* (the reciprocity of relations, or the fact that the observances of *li* bound both sides). In addition, he first discovered man as an individual (" the commander of the armed forces of a state might be captured, but the will of even a common man could not be changed "), gave a moral connotation to the term *chun-tzu* or " superior man " and advocated government by men of worth.[36] Finally, his condemnations of tyranny and cruelty and his call for employing the people at the proper times were progressive.[37]

As to Confucian religious views, for some he had a new, perhaps materialistic, conception of Heaven (" Does Heaven Speak? The four seasons pursue their courses, and all things are continually being produced, but does Heaven say anything? "),[38] opposed naïve beliefs in spirits and advocated human effort rather than reliance on the divine.

---

[33] Kuan and Lin, " Tsai lun K'ung-tzu," pp. 319–321.

[34] An Tso-chang, " Kuan-yu K'ung-tzu di ' li ' ho ' jen ' ti hsüeh-shuo " (" On Confucius's Theories of ' li ' and ' jen ' "), *K'ung-tzu Che-hsüeh*, pp. 97–98. Kuan Feng and Lin Yu-shih oppose this tendency to attribute a new content to *li*. See Kuan and Lin, " Tsai lun K'ung-tzu," pp. 321–323. By and large such men as Kuan Feng, Lin Yu-shih and Jen Chi-yu emphasise the reactionary nature of the concepts of *jen* and *li* in the thought of Confucius; Kao Heng, Chung Chao-p'eng, An Tso-chang and in some respects Fung Yu-lan stress the progressive nature. But it must be emphasised that progressive elements are often found in a largely reactionary doctrine and vice versa.

[35] Fung Yu-lan, " Mao Tse-tung's *On Practice* and Chinese Philosophy," *SCMP*, No. 224.

[36] Kuan Feng and Lin Yu-shih, " Lun K'ung-tzu " (" On Confucius "), *K'ung-tzu Che-hsüeh*, p. 226. The article originally appeared in *Che-hsüeh Yen-chiu*, No. 4, 1961.

[37] Yang, " Lun K'ung-tzu ssu-hsiang," p. 396. See also *Kuang-ming Jih-pao*, August 5, 1960.

[38] *Analects*, xvii.19.3.

Others ask, was Heaven thus non-theistic? Doesn't the phrase really mean that Heaven can speak but does not choose to speak? [39] Does Confucius not cause men to kneel in awe of Heaven's commands?

The same historical fact will be cited with varying interpretations to prove either the progressive or reactionary class stand of Confucius. For example, in the State of Lu where Confucius lived was the powerful Chi family. Kung-shan Fu-jao revolted against them. If one believes that the Chi family represented the new landlord class (the Duke of Lu representing the slave-owners) and that Confucius sided with the rebels, one interprets Confucius as having the interests of the slave-owner class at heart. If one changes the variables around, the interpretation changes.

In the course of the controversies over political and religious doctrines, however, a general unanimity seems to have arisen about the progressive nature of Confucius's contributions to education (he was the first to educate students on a large scale privately, and he made no class distinction among prospective pupils), his methods of learning which reflected his practical experience (unceasingly study, and be mindful of when you know and not know something) and his work as historian and editor.[40]

EVALUATING MO TZU

Mo Tzu, who lived sometime during the period 479–381 B.C., was a critic of Confucianists and a man of the people who might be expected to be viewed favourably by Chinese Communist philosophers. In fact, while most Communist critics do praise him, his case is a good example of the controversy that surrounds even the most obvious candidates for canonisation.

Hou Wai-lu issued a positive evaluation of Mo Tzu, which was elaborated on by quite a few others, among them Yang Jung-kuo. According to them, Mo Tzu probably came from slave or urban craftsman stock and stood for the interests of freemen.[41] His general outlook was scientific, no nonsense. A materialist in epistemology, he emphasised sense experience as the basis of knowledge and human experience as an important test of truth. His three standards for recognising truth (testimony of the senses, testimony of the ancients

---

39 Jen Chi-yu, " Kung-tzu Cheng-chih-shang ti pao-shou li-ch'ang ho che-hsueh-shang ti wei-hsin-chu-i " (" Confucius's Conservative Political Standpoint and Philosophical Idealism "), *K'ung-tzu Che-hsueh*, p. 156. The article originally appeared in *Pei-ching Jih-pao* (*Peking Daily*), July 27, 1961. See also Hou Wai-lu, *Chung-kuo Ssu-hsiang T'ung-shih* (*General History of Chinese Thought*), I, p. 154.

40 For example, see Kuan and Lin, " Lun K'ung-tzu," pp. 253–255, and Yang Jung-kuo, " Lun K'ung-tzu ssu-hsiang," pp. 393–395.

41 Yang Jung-kuo, *Chung-kuo Ku-tai Ssu-hsiang Shih* (*History of Early Chinese Thought*) (Hong Kong: San Lien Shu-tien, 1962, p. 112.

and effect on people) were aimed at illuminating the *objective* facts. He would test the rightness or wrongness of an action by examining its actual rather than supposed effect on the people. Mo Tzu opposed this to the criterion associated with the Confucian theory of the "rectification of names," a doctrine maintaining that truth is forever fixed and can be discovered by introspection, not by experience.[42] That is, when one encounters a situation one looks within to the name and eternally fixed concept associated with the name and if there is an exact correspondence between situation and concept, a statement using the name to describe the situation is true. The policy of "rectifying names," *i.e.*, reverting to meanings of terms long since in disuse, was a Confucian attempt to revert to the tribal slave state, according to Yang Jung-kuo. Mo Tzu, however, held that the right way to correct social evils was to understand the trends in social change and development.[43] Obviously one would see, for example, that new times require new words and meanings. Whereas Confucian principles supported the tribal aristocracy, many Mohist doctrines aimed at its destruction. For example, against the Confucian "human-heartedness" with its stress on preferential treatment for kin, Mo Tzu set the levelling "universal love." In opposition to official preferment for aristocratic worthies, Mo Tzu advocated opening a new road for official advancement, devoid of favouritism, to those newly arisen from the slave class.[44] He spoke out against the extravagance in the aristocracy which was encouraged by the Confucian concern with music and rites. Finally, he rejected the notion of Heavenly decree (*t'ien ming*) as a tool of those in power for deceiving the people.

Mo Tzu does not fare as well with some other philosophers in China today. Again, the contest is between him and Confucius. In the 1940s, for example, Kuo Mo-jo saw Confucius as the enemy of belief in the power of an anthropomorphic Heaven and in the existence of traditional spirits. He dismissed Mo Tzu as superstitious and reactionary and made no attempts to explain away Mo Tzu's religious ideas (a typical attempt to do so would be to assert that Mo Tzu was the first to maintain that commoners as well as aristocrats became ghosts at death, hardly demonstrating Mo Tzu's non-superstitious character). According to Kuo Mo-jo, Confucius's notion of Heavenly decree was simply "necessitivism" (whatever occurs is an instance of the operation of inexorable natural laws), not fatalism. Mo Tzu was the "fatalist" because of his belief that all good fortune depends on obedience to spirits and to the rulers

[42] *Ibid.* p. 144.
[43] *Ibid.* p. 116.
[44] *Ibid.* p. 136.

of the slave society.[45] Kuo was not alone, and his views seem to have had other adherents in more recent times.[46]

MENCIUS AS SUBJECTIVE IDEALIST

Mencius developed the negative ideas in Confucian thought. He is commonly held to be a subjective idealist, the direct source of whose inspiration may have come from Confucius's disciple Tseng Tzu, according to Hou Wai-lu. This idealism is seen in his belief in man's innate ability to distinguish right from wrong and in his denigration of the senses,[47] leading to the conclusion that man need not exert himself to know objective reality. Through mind alone he can know human nature and Heaven. The "subjectivity" of his idealism is pinpointed in the phrase "all things are complete within me." His conservative religious ideas centred on that of the union between Heaven and man, *i.e.*, that man cannot be understood in isolation from Heaven with whom man has some kind of metaphysical contact, since Heaven is the source of man's innate moral tendencies (in the words of Mencius, "If one knows his own nature, he knows Heaven"). Thus the supernatural intervenes in the natural. In spite of his subjective idealism, he did maintain a positive concern with the world, in contrast with others such as Chuang Tzu, who held a similar position.[48] Politically conservative, he advocated *jen* and *i* as primary instruments of rule at a time when progressive thinkers were stressing rule by law. But according to Lin Keng there surely were some positive elements in his political views, such as the statement that the "people are the most valuable thing." [49]

HSUN TZU AS MAJOR MATERIALIST

Hsun Tzu is said to have inherited the progressive factors in Confucian thought, such as the naturalistic conception of Heaven (if one believes that Confucius had such a notion). Heaven was "naturalistic" in the sense that the term "Heaven" denoted simply natural *regularities*, such as regular movements of celestial bodies, regular changes of seasons, regular functioning of animal organs, etc. Hsun Tzu's study of Nature (Heaven) and of man's ability to influence it is certainly materialistic, according to Li Teh-yung.[50] Tao is treated as objective law existing independently of man. Hsun Tzu drew on all 100 Schools

[45] Kuo Mo-jo, *Shih P'i-p'an Shu (Ten Critiques)* (Chungking: Chung-i Ch'u-pan She, 1945), pp. 92–108.
[46] For example, see the discussion of the meeting of historians of Central South Region in *Kuang-ming Jih-pao*, May 19, 1961, translated in *SCMP*, No. 2514.
[47] Hou, *Chung-kuo Ssu-hsiang T'ung-shih*, I, p. 397.
[48] Kuan, "Ch'uang-tzu che-hsueh p'i-p'an," pp. 4–5.
[49] *SCMM*, No. 405.
[50] Li, "Hsun-tzu ti ssu-hsiang," pp. 76–77.

for his inspiration, and so he also drew on the positive aspects of Taoist materialism [51] in his understanding of Heaven, *i.e.*, the Taoist interest in understanding the regularity of change undergone by physical bodies and the elimination in Taoist doctrine of interference in the natural processes by an anthropomorphic deity. Another positive heritage from Confucius is Hsun Tzu's emphasis on study as the means of betterment and on the dissemination of textual learning.[52] According to Li Teh-yung, there certainly are materialistic factors in his epistemology which assigns an important role to the senses in the acquisition of knowledge and the affirmation of the knowability of the objective world.[53] Reliance on law in ruling was a progressive doctrine of the new landlord class, for it served to protect the rights of commoners and helped eliminate inherited privileges.[54] Hsun Tzu entered the progressive system by redefining *li* (" ritual ") so as to include law.[55] However, one should not overlook the idealistic residue in Hsun Tzu, such as his excessive glorification of *li* and *i* and only tacit recognition of the need for law.[56] But despite some disagreement, most mainland scholars conclude that Hsun Tzu was the major materialistic and atheistic thinker of the 100 Schools Period. The materialist stream which he inherited from Kuan Chung (d. 645 B.C.) was subsequently developed by the Han materialist Wang Ch'ung (A.D. 27–*c.* 100).

TAOISTS AND LEGALISTS: UNCERTAIN QUANTITIES

Was the Taoist Lao Tzu an objective idealist or a materialist? To some Chinese Communist philosophers such as Lü Chen-yü and Yang Jung-kuo he was an idealist because *Tao* is an absolute spirit transcending space and time, which produced all things. *Tao* is not a physical substance because it existed prior to things, and it is not natural law because it exists independently of the process of physical movement.[57] Idealism is reflected in Lao Tzu's epistemology which denies any efficacy in sensation and experience and relies on mystic intuition.[58] But others, such as Yang Hsing-shun and Jen Chi-yu, question whether Lao Tzu is *really* an idealist. His *Tao* is defined by them as a primal mass of

[51] *Ibid.* p. 78.   [52] Yang, " Lun K'ung-tzu ssu-hsiang," p. 399.
[53] Li, " Hsun-tzu ti ssu-hsiang," pp. 83–85.
[54] Jen Chi-yu, " Han Fei-tzu ti she-hui cheng-chih ssu-hsiang ti chi-ko wen-t'i " (" Some Questions Concerning Han Fei-tzu's Social and Political Thought "), *Chung-kuo Ku-tai Che-hsueh Lun-ts'ung*, p. 141. The article originally appeared in *Wen Shih Che*, April 1955. See also *Kuang-ming Jih-pao*, August 25, 1961.
[55] Yang, " Lun K'ung-tzu ssu-hsiang," p. 398.
[56] Li, " Hsun-tzu ti ssu-hsiang," p. 72.
[57] Jen Chi-yu and Feng Ching-yuan, " Lao-tzu ti che-hsueh " (" Lao-tzu's Philosophy "), *Lao-tzu Che-hsueh*, pp. 15–16; Yang Jung-kuo, " Kuan yu ' Wu-ch'ien yen ' Lao-tzu ti Ssu-hsiang " (" On the Thought of the *Tao Teh Ching* Lao-tzu "), *Lao-tzu Che-hsueh*, pp. 295–296. The article originally appeared in *Shang Yu*, No. 13, 1959.
[58] Kuan and Lin, " Lun Lao-tzu che-hsueh," p. 212.

chaotic matter from which all things derive their substance (something like the Unlimited of early Ionian philosophy) and their laws of change.[59] He denies the existence of anthropomorphic spirits; he asserts that in the Heavenly Way there is no sign of a wilful Heaven but rather of *wu wei*, and he refers to Tao as having existed *before* the Lord-on-High (an anti-religious view). All these doctrines are considered to denote a materialistic outlook.[60]

Chuang Tzu (fourth century B.C.) carried the doctrines of Lao Tzu to an extreme, and most Chinese Communist philosophers consider him a subjective idealist. He views Tao as emptiness and his total focus is introspective with no concern for the external world at all—a negativism reflecting the hopeless condition of the " sunken slave-owner " class to which he belonged.[61] But others, such as Jen Chi-yu, challenge his view. To them *Tao* is not a spiritual void but *ch'i*, whose congealing and dispersal produces all things.[62] This *ch'i* is said to constitute an objective world which exists independently of man's thought. In any case Chuang Tzu's most violent critics, such as Kuan Feng and Lin Yü-shih, see some positive factors in his views, such as his criticisms of exploitation and oppression,[63] and his opposition to religious superstition.

Most important, all contending critics agree that there was rudimentary dialectical thought in these two Taoist thinkers: in the discovery of pairs of opposites (Being-Not Being, wealth-poverty, heavy-light, etc.) and in the doctrine that things transform into their opposites and that such is the nature of change.[64]

According to Li Teh-yung the Legalists, representing the rising landlord class, developed to new heights the materialist themes so well stated by Hsun Tzu.[65] The materialist nature of Han Fei Tzu's epistemology is seen in his method of testing statements against objective facts as the only standard of verification.[66] He viewed ethical precepts as tools for use by the rulers in governing the realm and showed the

59 Jen and Feng, " Lao-tzu ti che-hsueh," pp. 19–21. See also Chan Chien-feng, " Lao-tzu ti ' Tao ' chi shih chueh-tui ching-shen ma?" (" Is Lao-tzu's ' Tao ' Really Absolute Spirit?"), *Lao-tzu Che-hsueh*, p. 159. The article originally appeared in *Li-lun Chan-hsien* (*Theoretical Front*), No. 8, 1959. It is a rebuttal of the interpretations of Kuan Feng and Lin Yu-shih.

60 Jen, " Lun Lao-tzu che-hsueh," p. 31. Even those who regard Lao-tzu as an idealist see incipient " materialistic factors " in his denial of anthropomorphic spirits and view of the Heavenly Way; see Kuan and Lin, " Lao-tzu che-hsueh," p. 176.

61 Kuan and Lin, " Chuang-tzu che-hsueh p'i-p'an," pp. 4–5.

62 Jen Chi-yu, " Chuang-tzu wei-wu-chu-i shih-chieh-kuan " (" Chuang-tzu's Materialistic World View "), *Chuang-tzu Che-hsueh*, p. 162.

63 Kuan and Lin, " Chuang-tzu che-hsueh p'i-p'an," p. 21.

64 Kuan and Lin, " Lun Lao-tzu che-hsueh," p. 205. Also Yang, " Kuan yu ' Wu-ch'ien Yen '," p. 297. Also Kuan, " Chuang-tzu che-hsueh p'i-p'an," p. 60.

65 Li, " Hsun-tzu ti ssu-hsiang," p. 96.

66 Jen, " Han Fei ti she-hui," p. 139. Also *SCMP*, No. 224.

relevance of economic factors (such as the relation between the availability of goods and the number of people in the realm) to ethical norms.[67] The Legalist call for the reign of law is considered to have been progressive because it restricted the power of the nobles and officials who would impede centralisation of government. And yet, it is held, one cannot ignore the erroneous views of Han Fei Tzu. The King replaced *Tao* as the transcendent entity, and his law was held to have some objective, universal truth.[68] Han Fei Tzu was also condemned for his failure to recognise the new power of the peasantry or to deal with their problems.

FINDING THE ESSENCE AND DROSS

No official evaluation of the philosophical legacy has yet been issued. But certain conclusions shared by almost all scholars seem to be emerging. Among these, the most important observation is that Chinese thought *even in the early period* was rich in materialistic and idealistic philosophies. This gives the thought its place in the sun and in part may explain the severity of attack on those (*e.g.*, Liu Chieh) who do not see the thought in such terms. One critic of Liu Chieh condemns his focus on the differing interpretations which scholars over the ages have lent to the notion of the " unity of man and Heaven," as the ultimate method for understanding the history of Chinese thought.

> By depriving his theory of the " unity of Heaven and man " of the substance of class struggles in Chinese history and that of the struggles of materialism against idealism, Mr. Liu has downgraded the history of Chinese thought, which is enriched with substance, into a history of the mysterious relations between Heaven and man.[69]

Clearly, then, although there is no single authoritative list of philosophers in the 100 Schools Period who had rudimentary materialist world views, there is unanimity that such views did exist. Kuan Chung is accepted as the founder of the materialist school. His progressive ideas stood in opposition to those of a man like Chang Chu, from whose ideas the idealistic doctrines developed.[70] Materialist thinking was stimulated by the Five Element thought of the late West Chou.[71] The discovery of new means of production in the Warring States Period led to the development of astronomy and other sciences which also encouraged materialist views. Among thinkers of the 100 Schools, Sung

---

[67] Jen, " Han Fei ti she-hui," p. 141. Also *Kuang-ming Jih-pao*, August 25, 1961.
[68] Jen, " Han Fei ti she-hui," pp. 147–149.
[69] Yang Jung-kuo, in *Kuang-ming Jih-pao*, November 10, 1963, translated in *Joint Publications Research Service (JPRS)* (U.S. Department of Commerce, Office of Technical Services), No. 22, 391.
[70] *Kuang-ming Jih-pao*, November 7, 1961. Also Kuan and Lin, " Lun K'ung-tzu," p. 141.
[71] Kuan and Lin, " Tsai lun K'ung-tzu," p. 324.

K'eng and Yin Wen, whose positive contributions included attacks on the Chou rites, are considered by some to have played an important role in the development of a materialistic world view, especially through their investigations of the refined matter *ching*.[72] Whether or not he is willing to treat the *Tao* of Lao Tzu and Chuang Tzu as physical substance/laws of change, no philosopher in China will deny that Hsun Tzu had a materialistic world view. So had the Later Mohists, who eliminated the religious ideas which had caused disagreement on Mo Tzu's status. The epistemology of Hsun Tzu and the Later Mohists also was materialist, for they stressed the use of sense organs as sources of knowledge of the objective world. The Mohists viewed practice as the source of knowledge. In addition there were " materialist factors " even in basically non-materialistic thinkers, as in Confucius's development of a teaching method based on his own practical experience as a student and teacher.

An important aspect of the materialistic world view is atheism, which according to Hou Wai-lu emerged concurrently with materialism towards the end of the late Chou. Tzu Ch'an (sixth century B.C. statesman) was one of the progenitors. Whether or not Confucius saw Heaven as a wilful anthropomorphic deity is debated, but his scepticism about spirits and his new focus on man is rarely contested. Lao Tzu may have conceived of Tao as absolute spirit, but he denied the existence of anthropomorphic gods.[73] No one could question the atheism in Hsun Tzu's denial of any unity between Heaven and man and in his naturalistic conception of Heaven.[74] Clearly, too, Han Fei Tzu denied the Heavenly Mandate. Instead he held that the people choose the king, and historical events are determined by non-theistic (*e.g.*, economic) factors.[75]

Another positive legacy from the early period is a rudimentary dialectical theory which developed in the late West Chou.[76] Some see it in the thought of Confucius, *e.g.*, in the dialectical relation between native " substance " (*chih*) and " refinement " (*wen*) in the cultural sphere (a union of both being necessary in the superior man), and in the internal dialectical relations of quality and quantity (as in the proposition that " doing too much is equivalent to doing nothing at all ").[77] It was

---

[72] See Kuan Feng and Lin Yu-shih, " Lun Sung Yin hsueh-p'ai " (" On the Sung-Yin School "), *Che-hsueh Yen-chiu*, No. 5, 1959, pp. 28–45. The material for the study of these early Taoists comes mainly from the text *Kuan Tzu*, possibly first century B.C., based on earlier materials. Fung Yu-lan and Hou Wai-lu dispute this attribution of materialism to the Sung/Yin School.

[73] Jen, " Lun Lao-tzu che-hsueh," pp. 33–35.

[74] *JPRS*, No. 22, 391. Also see Li, " Hsun-tzu ti Ssu-hsiang," p. 78.

[75] Jen, " Han Fei ti she-hui," p. 146.

[76] Kuan and Lin, " Tsai lun K'ung-tzu," p. 324.

[77] Jen, " K'ung-tzu cheng-chih-shang," p. 159.

developed to a high level in Taoist thought, though still with grave shortcomings. It is a key epistemological and logical law of the Later Mohists. In examining the contradictions between objective things, between two things of the same kind or between two contradictory aspects of the same thing, they occupied themselves with the mutually related states of " sameness " (*t'ung*) and " difference " (*i*), the relation being summarised as " the mutual dependency of ' sameness ' and ' difference '." [78]

This is the " essence " in the thought of the 100 Schools Period, a rudimentary materialism, an atheism, and a rudimentary dialectics. Probably other matters could be added to the list such as Confucius's views on education and teaching method, developed to a more sophisticated level by Confucianists of the Warring States Period. But this essence is always mixed with dross in the early thought. One may be pleased to find rudimentary dialectical thought in Lao Tzu but then will discover that he was an idealist and that the two are contradictory. Hence the problem of removing the dross is always present.

One of the most important pieces of dross discovered in the thought of the 100 Schools Period by present-day scholars in Communist China is the lack of any appreciation of the value of struggle between opposites. There was of course a struggle going on between materialism and idealism, but the thinkers themselves usually were totally unaware of the scientific value of struggle as they were of the incompatibility of opposites, which they often tried to " unite " or " harmonise."

Some contemporary scholars see Confucian virtues as tools to harmonise contradictions between classes or to bring about " compromises " between other contradictory phenomena. Kuan Feng and Lin Yu-shih regard the Confucian *jen* in this light. Loyalty and altruism have the function of harmonising relations between rich and poor, ruler and minister, etc. The call to " love all men " has the same end.[79] The doctrine of the " mean " was an attempt to justify compromises between mutually contradictory matters, such as belief in Heavenly *ming* and reliance on human effort.[80] In addition, Confucian discussions of an abstract " human nature " were meant to cover up class contradictions. Since later representatives of the feudal rulers adopted these doctrines, the evil was long perpetuated in China.

The failure to understand the nature of struggle between opposites is most clearly manifest in the rudimentary dialectical views of the early

---

[78] Kao Heng, " Mo Ching-chung i-ko lo-chi kuei-lu—' T'ung I Chiao-te ' " (" A Logical Rule in the Mohist Canon—' The Mutual Dependency of Sameness and Difference' "), *Chung-kuo Ku-tai Che-hsueh Lun-ts'ung*, pp. 69–70.

[79] Kuan and Lin, " Lun K'ung-tzu," p. 225.

[80] *Ibid* pp. 244–245. Also see Hou Wai-lu, *A Short History of Chinese Philosophy* (Peking: Foreign Languages Press, 1959), p. 6.

thinkers. This points to a unique deficiency in the Chinese legacy. In Western thought from the earliest time there was such an understanding. Heraclitus spoke of *strife* between opposites as essential to the coming into being of things and to ordered change. Such an idea found its way into the idealism of Hegel and thence to Marx.

Kuan Feng and Lin Yu-shih hold that dialectics and idealistic philosophies are basically contradictory, for dialectics means constant development through the clash of opposites, while in an idealism such as that of Lao Tzu all opposition disappears in the Absolute. There is no development and change in *Tao* through the clash of opposites.[81] A host of modern commentators offer variations on the interpretation that Lao Tzu's dialectic seeks to eliminate all struggle between opposites.[82] Chuang Tzu is said to carry the denial of struggle even farther to the point of seeming to deny the existence of opposites. His dialectics become an attempt to avoid contradictions.[83] He preferred to take a middle position between opposites (*e.g.*, between good and bad, strength and weakness) as an expedient means for preserving life.[84] Or he would make a " head in the sand " escape from conflict by " transcending " it with a flight into " absolute freedom " or " pure experience." [85]

Not only Taoistic dialectical theories lack an understanding of struggle. The dialectics of the Mohist school are restricted to explaining the contradictions between phenomena and to elaborating on a logical rule for analysing them. There is no conception of struggle between opposites resulting in development.[86]

The Chinese tendency to avoid struggle or to seek some compromise is not a new discovery of the Chinese Communists. It was recognised by certain figures connected with the cultural readjustment associated with the May 4th Movement of 1917–21. For example, in a joint statement, Hu Shih, pupil of John Dewey and proselytiser of pragmatism in China, and Ch'en Tu-hsiu, one of the founders of the Chinese Communist Party, said:

> The old literature, old politics and old ethics have always belonged to one family; we cannot abandon one and preserve the others. It is Oriental to compromise and only go halfway when reforming, for fear

81 Kuan and Lin, " Lun Lao-tzu che-hsueh," pp. 206–208. Lu Chen-yu takes a similar position.
82 *e.g.*, see Fung, " Lao-tzu ti che-hsueh," p. 11, and Lu Chen-yu, *Chung-kuo Cheng-chih Ssu-hsiang Shih* (*History of Chinese Political Thought*) (Peking: Jen-min Ch'u-pan She, 1961), pp. 57–59; Yang, " Kuan-yu ' Wu-ch'ien Yen '," p. 297.
83 Jen, " Chuang-tzu ti wei-wu-chu-i," p. 171.
84 Fung Yu-lan, " Lun Chuang-tzu (" On Chuang-tzu "), *Chuang-tzu Che-hsueh*, p. 126. The article originally appeared in *People's Daily*, February 26, 1961.
85 Jen, " Chuang-tzu ti wei-wu-chu-i," p. 171; Kuan, " Chuang-tzu che-hsueh p'i-p'an," p. 21.
86 Kao, " Mo Ching-chung," p. 57.

of opposition. This was the most important factor behind the failures of reform movements during the last several decades.[87]

But the negative aspects of China's philosophical legacy have left special problems for the Chinese leadership which is eager both to promote a politically conscious populace and to rid the country of the ideological dross of the past. These special problems are recognised by philosophers observing their own countrymen. In their eyes, early attempts to transcend conflict by entering the realm of " absolute freedom " where all problems disappear have their counterpart today in the " Ah Q " spirit [88] of so many Chinese who try to rationalise problems away.[89] The Taoist preference for taking a mean position between opposites is seen today in " middle-of-the-roadism," by which people hope to avoid the possibility of making a mistake.[90] The attempt to deny opposites was handed down from the early period to the present by feudal rulers who found it a useful tool for drugging the people; those who believe there is no difference between life and death, between getting and losing, will not struggle to achieve the former.[91] Liu Chieh, whose ideas are derived from Mencius and the Ch'en-Chu school, states that man must not take part in " wild and wrong acts " which may injure Heaven and damage reason, but must strive to recover his heavenly nature.[92] In other words, man's task is to devote himself to internal examination and avoid struggle.

The concern over the negative legacy takes concrete form in the attacks on scholars suspected of perpetuating the dross of the past with an overlay of Marxist terminology. Liu Chieh was one victim and the the contemporary popular philosopher Feng Ting was another. Like his predecessors in the old China, Feng Ting has been interested in studies of " human nature," in discovering what is common to all men. He takes biology as his point of departure and focuses on those environmental factors biologically favourable to the human species and the " instincts " common to all men. His " error " lies in attempting to obliterate class boundaries and reconcile class contradictions by seeking to derive an abstract human nature through biology.[93] The most recent manifestation of concern about the negative legacy is the polemic

---

[87] *Hsin Ch'ing-nien* (*New Youth*), Vol. V, 4 (October 15, 1918), quoted in Chow Tse-tsung, *The May Fourth Movement* (Cambridge: Harvard University Press, 1960), p. 289.

[88] Ah Q is the central character in " The True Story of Ah Q," by Lu Hsun (Chou Shu-jen, 1881–1936). He claims " spiritual victories " when beaten and beats those weaker than himself when he can. He was a symbol of a national defect, manifested most clearly in China's behaviour towards the other nations which threatened her.

[89] Kuan, " Chuang-tzu che-hsueh p'i-p'an," pp. 4–5.

[90] Fung, " Lun Chuang-tzu," p. 126.

[91] *Ibid.*

[92] *JPRS*, No. 22, 391.

[93] *Kuang-ming Jih-pao*, November 10, 1964.

surrounding Yang Hsien-chen, elderly philosopher at the Higher Party School of the Party Central Committee who has been under attack since the spring of 1964. In discussing dialectics Yang had talked of "the combination of two into one," a process with roots in early Chinese discussions of the unity of opposites. Yang was accused of opposing dialectical materialism because "emphasising combining two into one" instead of "dividing one into two" was said to be equivalent to stressing compromise rather than struggle.[94]

Two reasons, one international and one domestic, stand out among the main causes for the focus on struggle today. One is the tendency which the Chinese see in the doctrines and policies of the Soviet and Yugoslav "modern revisionists" to soften the relationship between capitalist and socialist countries (ideas such as "the nature of capitalism has changed," "peaceful road to socialism in imperialist countries," etc.). What is the "peaceful co-existence" of the revisionists but a policy of compromise (with capitalism)? The Chinese see their historic role as opposing a new version of the revisionism that appeared in the doctrines of men like Edward Bernstein during a similar crisis in the Marxist camp at the turn of the century.[95] The other reason is the fear of resurgent capitalism in China (demand for more private markets, for private enterprise, etc.) and other bourgeois tendencies indicating the continued presence of anti-régime voices and the consequent need to keep the pressure up.[96]

CONCLUSIONS

The best way to evaluate from a Western standpoint the work done by scholars in China is briefly to compare the kinds of questions with which

94 Numerous articles appeared on the matter in the Press. See, for example, *People's Daily*, July 17 and 19 and August 14 and 31, 1964. Also *China News Analysis* (Hong Kong), No. 535.

95 The doctrines of Edward Bernstein (1850–1932), advocating peaceful parliamentary means for attaining the workers' goals and socialism, were attacked by Lenin. Lenin stressed class struggle and proletarian dictatorship.

96 A *Hung Ch'i (Red Flag)* editorial has this to say about compromise: "Moreover, the modern revisionists give voice to pure inventions such as that the revolutionary Marxist-Leninists, whom they call 'dogmatists,' 'reject' certain necessary compromises. We would like to tell these modern revisionists that no serious-minded Marxist-Leninist rejects compromises indiscriminately. In the course of our protracted revolutionary struggle, we Chinese Communists had reached compromises on many occasions with our enemies, internal and external. For example, we came to a compromise with the reactionary Chiang Kai-shek clique. We came to a compromise, too, with the U.S. imperialists, in the struggle to aid Korea and resist U.S. aggression. For Marxist-Leninists, the question is what kind of a compromise to arrive at, the nature of the compromise, and home to bring about a compromise. . . . It is precisely in accordance with Lenin's teaching that we Chinese Communists distinguish between different kinds of compromise, favouring compromises which are in the interests of the people's cause and of world peace, and opposing compromises that are in the nature of treachery. It is perfectly clear that only those guilty now of adventurism, now of capitulation, are the ones whose ideology is Trotskyism, or Trotskyism in a new guise": *Red Flag*, No. 1, 1963, reprinted as *Leninism and Modern Revisionism* (Peking: Foreign Languages Press, 1963), pp. 9–10.

they are concerned and those deemed important by scholars outside of China.

Among the topics selected for study by Chinese scholars probably only one would rank among the subjects generally selected for study by Westerners—*i.e.*, the annotation and dating of texts and related philological studies. Chinese philological studies are of special interest to all concerned with the period. Among the especially impressive works are Kuan Feng's *Chuang Tzu Nei-p'ien I-chieh ho P'i-p'an* (*Interpretation and Critique of the Chuang Tzu Nei-p'ien*),[97] Ku Chieh-kang's explication of a chapter of the classic *The Book of History*, in *Li-shih Yen-chiu* (*Historical Research*),[98] and articles in *Wen-shih* (*Literature and History*).

Actually, the individual scholar in China working with materials of the 100 Schools Period might very well have two counterparts in the West, one person whose interest is primarily textual and the other whose interests are in philosophy (or the history of philosophy). While many questions asked by the Westerner interested in textual matters would overlap with those asked by the Chinese, a significant portion of this work reflects a Marxist orientation. There seems to be an excessive concern with etymological studies of words in the early texts relevant to social class. For example, terms such as "man" (*jen*) and "people" (*min*) seem to be favourite choices for close study. The thesis of Chao Chi-pin [99] that *jen* denoted members of the slave-master class and *min* members of the slave class seems to be widely accepted. Not only philologists but philosophers and historians in Communist China have been studying such terms for some time. Ch'en Meng-chia has made extensive studies of the terms *jen*, *chung-jen*, *chung*, *shu jen*, etc., in his attempt to isolate the terms denoting members of the ruling and ruled class in early China.[100] Kuo Mo-jo has laboured over the term *chung*. The form of the Shang bone graph (representing three men toiling under the sun according to Kuo) plus the existence of phrases such as "the king goes to repress the disorders of the *chung*" and "so-and-so many *chung* ran away" supplement the existence of headless corpses in royal

---

[97] (Peking: Chung-hua Shu-chu, 1961.)

[98] *e.g.*, Ku Chieh-kang, " Shang-shu ' Ta Kao ' Chin shih " (" Modern Explanation of the Ta Kao Chapter of *The Book of History* "), *Li-shih Yen-chiu*, No. 4, 1962, pp. 26–51.

[99] In the chapter " Shih ' jen ' ' min '." (" Explaining ' jen ' and ' min ' "), in Chao Chi-pin, *Lun-yu Hsin T'an* (*A New Study of the Analects*) (Peking: Jen-min Ch'u-pan She, 1962).

[100] Ch'en Meng-chia, *Yin-hsu Pu-tz'u Tsung-shu* (*An Account of the Oracle Bone Graphs from the Yin Wastes*) (Peking: K'o-hsueh Ch'u-pan She, 1956), pp. 610–616 and 640. Although his historical interpretations sometimes reflect a Marxist viewpoint, Ch'en himself has never been identified closely with the Party and in 1957 was declared " right-wing."

Shang graves to "prove" the existence of the early slave society demanded by a quasi-Marxist historical standpoint.[101]

When it comes to matters other than those relevant to the *explication de texte*, the Western philosopher will find most of his questions unanswered in recent Chinese studies. Much of the praise of the early thinkers for their "progressive" educational ideas or "embryonic dialectics" seems downright silly to the Westerner who measures the importance of a philosopher not necessarily in terms of the social consequences or "modern sound" of his ideas but in terms of how well he argued for them.

Due to the limitations of Marxist categories of classification, the Chinese philosopher suffers from the standard Marxist ailment of forced and often artificial attempts to fit all philosophers into the two categories of materialism and idealism (Kuan Feng is an occasional exception to this). Western philosophers are not always attracted to labels and certainly balk at being reduced to two of them if they are going to be used.

The Western philosopher working with the early Chinese materials would ask questions in categories roughly corresponding to the branches of Western philosophy. For example, because much of the thought of the 100 Schools Period is concerned with political philosophy he would be interested in the answers to such questions standard in the field as: Why should men submit to governmental authority? (self-interest? public-interest? both? will of God?). In whose hands should the political power be? (those whom the individual or majority "consents" to obey? the "wise"?). How can the limits of political power be determined, or are there individual rights, duties or freedoms outside of the jurisdiction of governmental control? What are the ends of government?

Answers to these questions can certainly be found in the early Chinese works even though the questions as phrased may not be traditional ones. Considerations pertinent to the answers in many cases are common to both Western and Chinese thought (*e.g.*, the problem of the "equality" of men which arises in discussions of the locus of political power).

Traditional factors do linger on in the Chinese Communist approach to the early thought. Such might be the preoccupation with a limited number of passages, many of which were also of primary concern to the Neo-Confucianists. The condemnations of Chuang Tzu for his "selfishness" are traditional—dating from the Sung attacks on Buddhism and

---

[101] There is a nice summary of the arguments in Ch'i Ta, "Chia-ku-wen-chung ti 'chung' shih-pu-shih nu-li" ("Does the Oracle Bone Graph 'chung' Denote a Slave?"), *Hsueh-shu Yueh-k'an* (*Academic Monthly*), No. 1 (1957), p. 18.

Taoism.[102]   But certainly no one should underestimate the extent to which the Chinese Marxists are trying to re-focus the reader's attention onto matters which have hitherto rarely (and perhaps with good reason) been studied.   An example is the emphasis on the epistemology of the thinkers of the 100 Schools Period (Fung Yu-lan and Kuan Feng are occasionally free from this criticism).   Epistemology even in the West became a major concern only with Descartes, though to look at the space allotted to it one would think the early Chinese writers were deeply interested in the matter.   Obviously one explanation in this case is the Chinese Communist concern with the relationship between " thought " and " existence " (the " number one philosophical problem " in Marxist eyes)—of special importance to a country desiring to show how " thought " (the heightened consciousness of the masses) can work miracles on " existence " (the objective world).

It is true that questions which scholars outside of China consider fundamental have gone unanswered on the mainland.   But the answers to some questions being considered are of interest to scholars in the field everywhere.   For example, the range of possible relationships between *Tao*, the laws of change, and *ch'i* seems to be narrowing considerably. Matters of ontological or epistemological interest may be brought to light even when the questions guiding the inquiry are not important from the outsider's point of view.   In short, it would be naïve not to look for some very positive advances in our understanding of the thought of the 100 Schools Period to emerge from studies whose approach is dictated by dialectical materialism.

---

[102] Yang Jung-kuo, " Chuang-tzu Ssu-hsiang t'an-wei " (" A Close Examination of Chuang-tzu's Thought "), *Chuang-tzu Che-hsueh*, pp. 289 and 291. The article first appeared in *Che-hsueh Yen-chiu*, No. 5, 1961. See also Jen, " Chuang-tzu ti wei-wu-chu-i," p. 174, and Kuan, " Chuang-tzu che-hsueh p'i-p'an," p. 6.

6

Chinese Communist Treatment of the Origins and the Foundation of the Chinese Empire

By A. F. P. HULSEWÉ

BRIEF SURVEY OF ANCIENT CHINESE HISTORY

IN antiquity, China was far from being the China we know today, neither in extent, nor in political and social organisation. To the south it did not extend beyond the Yangtze River, to the north it stopped short of the Mongolian steppe, to the north-east, only a small part of the south Manchurian plain was included, whereas in the west it merely went up to the easternmost part of what is now Kansu Province; the Szechwan plain was only included at the end of the fourth century B.C. Politically, the King of Chou was theoretically the overlord of most of this area, but in actual practice, independent rulers reigned over a congeries of larger and smaller states. As a result of wars of conquest, seven large states had come to be formed by the middle of the fifth century B.C. and these were engaged in a ceaseless struggle for supremacy. The time between the middle of the fifth century and 221 B.C., when the western state of Ch'in finally conquered all its rivals, is known as the period of the Warring States.

Organisationally the states were feudal, in so far as the states themselves were conceived as fiefs granted by the King of Chou, and the rulers of the states in turn granted fiefs to their nobles. Socially, there existed a sharp cleavage between the nobles, holders of smaller or larger fiefs, and the common people, mainly farmers who tilled the land, presumably as serfs of their noble lords. However, the creation of the large states was accompanied by a gradual change in society, including the rise of free landowners, and by the establishment, on a modest scale at first, of territorial units that were no longer granted as fiefs, but which were administered by persons directly dependent on the ruler. The Ch'in conquest of 221 B.C. saw the end of feudal land tenure and the establishment of a bureaucratic organisation over the whole realm.[1]

---

[1] The best account of Chinese ancient history in a Western language remains Henri Maspero, *La Chine antique* (Paris: Imprimerie Nationale, 1955), originally published in 1927; 2nd ed. More modern, but less detailed, are John K. Fairbank and Edwin O. Reischauer, *East Asia, the Great Tradition* (Boston: Houghton Mifflin, 1960), and A. F. P. Hulsewé, "China im Altertum," *Propyläen Weltgeschichte*, Vol. II (Berlin: Propyläen-Ullstein, 1962), pp. 479–571 (up to the end of the Han period in the early third century A.D.).

Soon after the death, in 210 B.C., of the first Emperor of Ch'in, the creator of China's unity, revolts against the Ch'in régime broke out all over the new Empire. The supreme leadership of the rebellious movements soon fell to Hsiang Yü, a noble from one of the former states of the Yangtze area. But his division of the spoils of victory did not please one of the other prominent leaders, Liu Pang, who had been created king of the Han river basin after the final victory over the Ch'in. The resulting wars ended in 202 B.C. with the victory of Liu Pang, who thereupon mounted the throne as Emperor of the new Han Empire. This was to endure for four centuries and under its aegis the Chinese realm was to expand enormously and permanently into South China, into Manchuria and northern Korea, into present-day Kansu, and, precariously, into Central Asia.

Thanks to the ancient sources, large works like the *Shih chi*,[2] China's first general history from its beginnings to the time of writing, about 100 B.C., the *Tso chuan*,[3] and the *Han shu*,[4] the history of the Han Dynasty covering the years 206 B.C.–A.D. 23, we are quite well informed about the general course of events, but these sources are far from providing us with interpretations of these events. Nor is this attempted by the voluminous historical and encyclopaedic literature of later ages such as the *T'ung tien* by Tu Yu in the ninth century[5] or *Tzu-chih t'ung-chien*,[6] " the General Mirror in Aid of Good Government," by the great and careful historian Ssu-ma Kuang (1010–86).

NEW DATA

The aim of this article is to consider whether since 1949 the historians of mainland China have furthered our insight into the developments briefly outlined above by presenting new data and, more important, new interpretations beyond those offered by modern Chinese historians since the beginning of our century.

2 The first 47 chapters of the total of 130 were translated by Ed. Chavannes in the five volumes of *Les mémoires historiques de Se-ma Ts'ien* (Paris: Leroux, 1895–1905); since then a considerable number of the other chapters have been translated, esp. by Burton Watson, *Records of the Grand Historian of China, Ssu-ma Ch'ien*, 2 vols. (New York: Columbia Univ. Press, 1961).

3 Complete translation by James Legge in Vol. V of *The Chinese Classics* (originally published in 1865, reissued by the University of Hong Kong in 1960).

4 The first 12 chapters as well as the 99th have been translated by H. H. Dubs, *The History of the Former Han Dynasty*, 3 vols. (Baltimore: Waverly Press, 1938, 1944, 1955). Several other chapters have likewise been rendered in Western languages.

5 See E. Balazs, " L'histoire comme guide de la pratique bureaucratique," in W. G. Beasly (ed.), *Historians of China and Japan* (London: Oxford University Press, 1961), pp. 78–94, esp. p. 90 *et seq.*

6 See E. G. Pulleyblank, " Chinese Historical Criticism, Liu Chih-chi and Ssu-ma Kuang," in W. G. Beasly (ed.), *Historians of China and Japan*, pp. 134–166, esp. p. 151 *et seq.*

The question about new data may be answered positively to a certain extent. Quite a number of inscribed early bronze vessels [7] have been discovered at different sites, but these can hardly be said to present new insights into the problems of social and economic history which are our major concern. Other finds, *i.e.*, of literary texts of the Han period,[8] are of eminent importance for the study of religion and literature, but again, they do not contribute to a better understanding of the historical phenomena under discussion. Of much greater interest in this respect are the archaeological finds of objects belonging to the sphere of material culture which are regularly and extensively reported in the archaeological journals. These objects, as well as their sculpted or painted representations, show the transition from bronze to iron and the development of all kinds of technical and agricultural tools and different types of weapons, whereas the sites throw light on the spread of Chinese culture, and, eventually, of political power, over originally non-Chinese regions. To a certain extent, these new discoveries have been used in the studies discussed in the following pages, but, as far as I can see, archaeological finds have on the whole remained the concern of archaeologists,[9] whose researches have, in general, been remarkably free of politically inspired interpretations, as is also stressed by Professor Cheng Te-k'un.[10]

EARLY MARXIST INTERPRETATIONS

The use of Marxist ideas for the interpretation of Chinese history did not, of course, start with the establishment of the Chinese People's Republic in 1949. Discussions were already in full swing in the late twenties, when in the wake of the May Fourth Movement [11] attempts at " the reorganisation of the nation's ancient history " were started by Ku Chieh-kang.[12] This was the time when the great scholarly journals began to appear, but it was also the time when Marxist ideas were being

---

[7] Extensively discussed in the archaeological journals by eminent epigraphers such as Kuo Mo-jo and Ch'en Meng-chia.

[8] For a brief survey, see my forthcoming contribution to the Swiss journal *Asiatische Studien*, entitled " Texts in Tombs."

[9] An excellent survey of the discoveries of recent years and their assumed implications for Chinese history is provided by Hsia Nai in his *Hsin Chung-kuo ti K'ao-ku Shou-huo (Archaeology in New China)* (Peking: Wen-wu Press, 1961), and in its sequel in *K'ao-ku*, October 1964, pp. 485–497.

[10] Cheng Te-k'un, " Archaeology in Communist China," *The China Quarterly*, No. 22, July–September 1965, p. 67.

[11] For a description of the social, political and cultural revolution which started in the summer of 1919, see the masterly work by Chow Tse-tsung, *The May Fourth Movement* (Cambridge: Harvard University Press, 1960), and Wolfgang Franke, *Chinas kulturelle Revolution* (Munich: Oldenbourg, 1957).

[12] For an outline of this movement, which envisaged particularly a " debunking " of the legendary part of China's earliest history, see Arthur W. Hummel, *The Autobiography of a Chinese Historian* (Leiden: Brill, 1931). Ku Chieh-kang initiated the series *Ku-shih Pien (Discussions on Ancient History)*, of which nine volumes appeared between 1926 and 1941.

widely used in fierce battles in the periodical Press on the social history of China.[13] The level of knowledge of Marxist writings cannot have been very high, for thirty to forty years ago, the Marxist classics had not yet been translated fully into Chinese. Moreover, acquaintance with modern Western approaches to humanistic studies in general was still neither very wide nor very deep, nor, given the lack both of translations and enough trained teachers, could it be. Added to this was the understandable but nevertheless unjustifiable parochialism of many Chinese scholars towards the whole range of Chinese studies. Still, the dialectical-materialist conception of history was known in its broad outlines and it was eagerly used.[14]

The first work which applied Marxist concepts specifically to the establishment of the Empire was, as far as I know, T'ao Hsi-sheng's study of the political organisation of the Ch'in and the Han, published in 1936, though it is quite likely that other studies had preceded this.[15] Here we find pronouncements such as: "The central unified state was the political organisation created by slavery production and merchant capital," and "The centralised power was the political power of the landlords and merchants over the small peasants and slaves."[16] Some of the catchwords are already there and they will not leave us again, although the dosage may vary according to the individual authors.

EARLY ABSENCE OF INTERPRETATION

145339

The establishment of the Ch'in-Han Empire at the end of the third century B.C. is politically an event of the greatest importance. All histories, ancient and modern, deal with the meteoric rise of the Kingdom of Ch'in, often described as backward or barbarian, and its rapid conquest of the other Warring States. All histories also dwell in great detail on the outbreak of the rebellions against the despotic Ch'in rulers, the fall of Ch'in, the wars between the brave but ruthless aristocrat Hsiang Yü and the astute but humane former village constable and bandit chief Liu Pang, ending in the establishment of the Han Empire.

However, the traditional historians only relate; they do not explain. Neither Ssu-ma Ch'ien or Pan Ku two thousand years ago, nor Ssu-ma Kuang a millennium later, attempt to indicate why the individual Warring States were doomed to disappear, or why a unified state arose on their territories. And the non-Marxist historians of modern times

---

[13] See Chung-jo Liu, *Controversies in Modern Chinese Intellectual History* (Cambridge: Harvard University Press, 1964), pp. 146–159.

[14] See Teng Ssu-yü, "Chinese Historiography in the Last Fifty Years," in *Far Eastern Quarterly* (FEQ), VIII, 1949, pp. 131–156.

[15] T'ao Hsi-sheng today serves as Chiang Kai-shek's leading ideologist on Taiwan.

[16] T'ao Hsi-sheng and Shen Chü-ch'en, *Ch'in Han Cheng-chih Chih-tu (The Political System of the Ch'in and Han Empires)* (Shanghai: Commercial Press, 1936), p. 6.

often continue in the old vein; somehow they seem to believe that it is *luce clarius* that certain events had to happen, without feeling the need to try and find the causes. Consequently few attempts at explanation are to be found.

Among these non-Marxist historians, there are excellent scholars, providing excellent surveys, but they are not very helpful when one starts to put the questions " why?" and " wherefore?" Typical in this respect is the Ch'in-Han history by the well-known Lü Ssu-mien, who apart from half a page of vague generalities in his preface—trade grew, and the influence of capital made itself felt, and simultaneously the feudal order declined—does not suggest any reasons or motives for the events he describes in no less than 835 pages![17] During the war, Ku Chieh-kang produced a useful booklet on Ch'in Shih Huang-ti, but he did not indulge either in any speculations about the reasons for the unification of China, although he gives a good general survey.[18] And even the veteran historian of the Han period, Professor Lao Kan, does not discuss the problems connected with the establishment of the Empire in his Ch'in-Han history, although he remarks significantly that the commoner origins of the first rebel or revolutionary, Ch'en She, and of the founder of the Han Dynasty, Liu Pang, are not indicative of their political ideas. They were anything but egalitarian and it is a great mistake to believe that they started a commoners' revolution,[19] an idea that is no longer entertained on the mainland.[20] Finally, even the argumentative Ch'ien Mu has passed up the occasion to say something provocative in his stimulating Ch'in-Han history.[21] In his outline of national history he merely repeats the usual arguments about the decline of the feudal nobility, the growth of centralism and the expansion of trade. However, he has interesting things to say about the critical attitude towards the feudal nobility he discerns in the teachings of the

[17] Lü Ssu-mien, *Ch'in Han Shih* (*Ch'in-Han History*) (Shanghai: Commercial Press, 1947).
[18] Ku Chieh-kang, *Ch'in Shih Huang-ti* (originally published in Chungking in approximately 1944, republished in Taipei by the Sheng-li publishers in 1954; 112 pp.). Professor Ku has remained in Peking and his latest publication which has come to my notice is an excellent article on the date of compilation of the *Yü-kung* chapter in the Book of Documents, included in *Chung-kuo Ti-li Ming-chu Hsuan-tu, ti I-Chi* (*Selected Readings in Famous Writings on Chinese Geography*) (Peking: K'o-hsueh Ch'u-pan She, 1959).
[19] Lao Kan, *Ch'in Han Shih* (Taipei: Chung-hua Wen-hua Ch'u-pan Shih-yeh Wei-yüan-hui, 1952), p. 40.
[20] See the highly enlightening article by Ch'i Li-huang, " Chung-kuo feng-chien she-hui nung-min cheng-ch'uan ti liang-chung-hsing chi-ch'i hsiang feng-chien-hsing cheng-ch'uan chuan-hua ti pi-jan-hsing " (" The Twofold Nature of Peasant Political Power in China's Feudal Society, and its Inevitable Development into a Feudalistic Political Power "), in *Li-shih Yen-chiu* (*Historical Research*), March 1962, pp. 134–142.
[21] Ch'ien Mu, *Ch'in Han Shih* (Hong Kong: Hsin Hua publishers, 1957); not so much a consecutive survey as a collection of thoughtful essays on problems connected with this period.

followers both of Confucius and of Mo Ti, and about egalitarian principles inherent in all pre-Ch'in philosophers and the idea of a society of commoners which he believes to have contributed greatly to the establishment of the Empire.[22]

That innocuousness was perhaps what the government in the thirties wanted might explain why in 1933 the textbook on Chinese history for universities, included in the series *Ta-hsueh Ts'ung-shu*, was a work by Chang Ch'in first published in 1914, very detailed and very systematic, but as traditional in its views as if there never had been any movement for the reorganisation of antiquity.[23]

Needless to say, matters are wholly different when we turn to the Chinese Marxist scholars.

THE PROBLEM OF PERIODISATION

The establishment of the Ch'in-Han Empire represents, one would expect, the beginning of a new period in Chinese history; on the other hand it is well known that the problem of periodisation has always been an important issue in Marxist historiography. No wonder, therefore, that this problem has been hotly debated in China. The intensity of the discussions on ancient history alone can be gauged by the number of articles devoted to the problem of periodisation of this early period. More than 150 articles were published in less than seven years and selections of these were republished in two voluminous collections.[24] At present the furore has more or less died down and the question seems to have been settled: slaveholding society was replaced by feudalistic society some time in the second half of the first millennium B.C. In this respect the changing views of Kuo Mo-jo have perhaps an exemplary value: in his *Nu-li-chih Shih-tai* (*The Period of the Slavery System*)[25] he tells how in 1929, in his *Chung-kuo Ku-tai She-hui Yen-chiu* (*Studies of China's Ancient Society*), he cited 770 B.C. as the critical date, the year of the transfer of the Chou royal house from the Wei valley to Lo-yang. Later (publication not specified) he placed it at the

---

22 *Kuo-shih Ta-kang* (*Outline National History*), Vol. I (Shanghai: Commercial Press, 1940; Formosa: Kuo-li Pien-i-kuan, 1958), pp. 71, 83–84.

23 Chang Ch'in, *Chung-hua T'ung-shih* (*General History of China*) (Shanghai: Commercial Press, 1933, 1936).

24 *Chung-kuo nu-li-chih yü feng-chien-chih fen-ch'i wen-t'i lun-wen hsuan-chi* (*Selected Articles on the Problem of Periodisation of the Slavery System and the Feudal System in China*) (Peking: San-lien Bookstore, 1956), 508 pp., 25 papers; and *Chung-kuo ku-tai-shih fen-ch'i t'ao-lun chi* (*Collected Discussions on the Periodisation of Chinese Ancient History*) (Peking: San-lien Bookstore, 1957), 584 pp., 19 papers and a bibliography of 153 numbers for publications between October 1949 and August 1956. Both collections were edited by the journal *Li-shih Yen-chiu*, in which a considerable number of these articles had appeared first.

25 pp. 20–25; also quoted in *Selected Articles, op cit.*, note 24, p. 19 *et seq.*

beginning of the Han (206 B.C.), and finally, in 1952, he found reasons to let the feudalistic period start in 475 B.C.

The interesting point in this arrangement of the great periods is that the establishment of the Empire, *i.e.*, of a centralised, bureaucratic state which occupied the whole of the Chinese *oikoumenè*, does not even remotely coincide with the change-over from the period of slave society to the feudalistic period. From all accounts it is evident that the Empire is not the final outcome of an important change in the methods of production. Improvements in agricultural methods and tools took place during the first two centuries of the Han Dynasty, but not earlier; even so, their results seem to have been meagre [26] and this is perhaps the reason why they did not produce any weighty consequences in the social and political organisation. The methods of production were feudalistic before the establishment of the Empire, and they remained feudalistic. The social position of the primary producer, the peasant, remained practically unchanged. In ancient times he had owed his land rent and his labour service to a noble fief-holder. With the progress of centralisation in the individual countries of the Warring States period, his obligations had been transferred eventually to the state, and in the new centralised Empire it was again the state which received the farmer's dues. " Qualitatively " these dues remained basically unaltered, regardless of effective quantitative changes introduced in Han times.[27] Nor were they affected by the reintroduction in 202 B.C. of a modified form of political feudalism (as we understand the term) which, moreover, soon was completely emasculated,

---

[26] Li Chien-nung, not a Marxist by origin, writes in his highly informative *Hsien Ch'in Liang-Han Ching-chi Shih-kao* (*A Draft Economic History of the pre-Ch'in Period and of the Two Han Dynasties*), originally written in 1936, first published in 1956, quoted according to the Peking Chung-hua Shu-chü edition of 1962, p. 149, Chap. 12, " The Development of Agriculture ": " In general, the Han people were able to continue and to extend the work of the late Chou period as regards irrigation. There was also improvement in the manufacture of agricultural tools and in the methods of cultivation. *However, the effect of these improvements and their application seems to have been very slow, and not at all as far-reaching as imagined by authors in general* " (my italics). Professor Li then shows in detail the general ineffectiveness and impermanence of waterworks (pp. 149–154), the extremely slow and uneven spread of new agricultural techniques (pp. 154–162), and the effect of natural disasters (pp. 162–164), including cattle diseases which seriously influenced the area ploughed by means of draught animals. Finally, he points out that during the Han period mechanical irrigation devices had either not yet been invented or were not used as such (p. 169).

[27] Owing to the relative scantiness of the data available for the labour service and military service under the Han, different explanations have been proffered, but on the whole the description given by Professor Yang Lien-sheng, *Harvard Journal of Asian Studies*, 13, 1950, p. 547 *et seq.* (now included in his *Studies in Chinese Institutional History* (Cambridge: Harvard University Press, 1961), p. 108 *et seq.*), has remained unaffected. Problems concerning taxation have been very carefully worked out in a series of articles by Hiranaka Reiji, now collected in one volume: Hiranaka Reiji, *Chūkoku kodai no densei to zeihō* (*Land Rent and Taxation in Chinese Antiquity*) (Kyoto: Ibundō, 1961).

and, whatever its initial political importance, never was important economically.[28]

Because the Marxist scheme of periodisation is motivated by socio-economic criteria, the Chinese Marxist is faced with a very serious difficulty, for, as indicated by Professors Etienne Balazs [29] and Benjamin Schwartz,[30] he is saddled with the enormously long stretch of the Chinese feudal period which does not allow any further subdivisions. In order to circumvent this difficulty, Chinese Marxist scholars have, quite legitimately, explored another avenue indicated by the Communist classics, *viz.*, the study of the forms of landownership, for here it seems possible to construct certain lines of development which allow the demarcation of different stages.[31] This can be done by those who maintain that state ownership of land was the dominant form, as well as by those who stress the prevalence of the private ownership of land. But as practically everybody is agreed on the point that some form of private rights on land (either absolute, or conditional—c.q. restricted—*i.e.*, rights of mere occupation or usufruct, permanently subject to some form of intervention by the state) existed several centuries before the establishment of the Empire, these studies do not contribute directly to the solution of the problem under survey.

The net result is that some of the most gifted authors have, as far as I have been able to see, avoided giving an opinion on the causes of the establishment of the Empire. In Hou Wai-lu's works, for instance, in spite of his extensive and thorough Marxist analysis of both society and ideology,[32] I could find no explanations of the origins of empire. The same applies to the stimulating studies by Yang Hsiang-k'uei, but it is interesting to observe how he does his best, Marx, Engels, Lenin and Mao in hand, to demonstrate that China's society developed along a course which differed from the standard lines. In doing so he takes

---

[28] In modern times, as far as I am aware, problems concerning the Han kingdoms and marquisates have been mostly discussed by Japanese scholars; see, *e.g.*, Kamada Shigeo, *Shin-Kan seiji seido no kenkyū*, Kyoto, 1962, pp. 123–272. In China less attention seems to have been paid to these institutions since the enlightening remarks on the subject by the great 17th- and 18th-century critics.

[29] Balazs, review of W. Eberhard, *Conquerors and Rulers*, *Etudes Asiatiques*, VII, 1953, p. 163.

[30] Paper read at the Paris conference of the " Junior sinologues " in 1956, under the title " Some Stereotypes in the Periodisation of Chinese History."

[31] Also in this case, a number of studies on the problem have been collected in a large publication, *Chung-kuo feng-chien she-huei t'u-ti so-yu-chih hsing-shih wen-t'i t'ao-lun-chi (Collected Discussions on the Problem of the Form of Landownership in China's Feudal Society)* (Peking: San-lien Bookstore, 1962), 733 pp., 39 articles and a bibliography of 132 contributions on the subject, published between October 1949 and December 1960; the final article in the collection (pp. 713–724) gives a detailed and clear survey of the different standpoints as regards the key problem: whether land was basically state property or private property.

[32] Hou Wai-lu, *Chung-kuo Ku-tai She-huei Shih-lun (Studies in Chinese Ancient Social History)* (Peking: Jen-min Ch'u-pan She, 1955) and *Chung-kuo Ssu-hsiang Shih (History of Chinese Thought)* (Peking: San-lien Bookstore, 1957), Vols. 1, 2.

the ideologically safe slave society as his subject, and ventures to refer, *inter alia*, to conditions prevailing among the present-day autochthonous tribes in South-west China.[33]

Chang Shun-hui even goes so far as to show rather explicitly that there are no clear-cut differences between periods, referring to similar remarks by Kuo Mo-jo.[34] Like Hou Wai-lu [35] both Yang Hsiang-k'uei and Lü Chen-yü (who does, however, enter into the problem of the founding of the Empire) have discovered the general Marxist tenet that during a given historical period there exist both remains of an earlier stage and germs of the next.[36] All want to show that China, with its large area, had an uneven development in different regions, with remnants of primitive village communities in some places and of the slavery system elsewhere, so that feudalism arose earlier in one area than in another.[37] Still, these speculations do not contribute directly to the problem of the genesis of the Empire.

Sometimes a Communist author plays safe, like Shang Yueh, who states blandly in his preface that at the time of writing (the early fifties) the problem of periodisation still awaited further study and that due to the limitations of his knowledge he could not find sufficient material to explain the organisation of the base and the superstructure. He also complains of the lack of reliable data on class contradictions and class struggles which forced him to restrict himself to providing material recognised as " objectively true." The surprising result was that the pages devoted to the period under review show not much more than a superficial compliance with Marxist tenets, whereas the main account is largely traditional. The cautious attitude of this textbook for the people's universities must have commended itself, for it was printed in large editions.[38]

The first edition of Fan Wen-lan's concise general history of China

---

[33] Yang Hsiang-k'uei, *Chung-kuo Ku-tai She-hui yü Ku-tai Ssu-hsiang Yen-chiu* (*Studies in China's Ancient Society and Ancient Ideology*) (Shanghai: Jen-min Ch'u-pan She, 1962), Vol. 1, pp. 1–18.

[34] Chang Shun-hui, *Chung-kuo-shih Lun-wen-chi* (*Collected Essays on Chinese History*) (Hankow: Hu-pei Jen-min Ch'u-pan She, 1956), pp. 182–185. The remarks by Kuo Mo-jo occur in the journal *Hsin Chien-she* 14/5.

[35] Hou Wai-lu, *Chung-kuo Ku-tai She-huei Shih-lun*.

[36] *Cf.* G. A. Wetter, *Sowietideologie heute*, Vol. 1, *Dialektischer und historischer Materialismus* (Frankfurt: Fischer Bücherei, 1962), p. 174.

[37] Yang Hsiang-k'uei, p. 33 *et seq.*; Lü Chen-yü in an article on " the transitional and uneven nature of the development of social conditions under the Chou—an investigation into the problem of the completion of the transition of Chinese society from slaveholding to feudalism," in his *Shih Lun-chi* (*Collection of Essays on History*) (Peking: San-lien Bookstore, 1960), pp. 147–173.

[38] Shang Yüeh, *Chung-kuo Li-shih Kang-yao* (*Outline of Chinese History*) (Peking: Jen-min Ch'u-pan She, 1954), first printing August 1954; second printing December 1954; total: 106,000 copies.

appeared in 1941, according to Teng Ssu-yü,[39] and so did Lü Chen-yü's simplified general history of China.[40] These works set the general tone, probably supported strongly by another of China's veteran Marxist historians, Chien Po-tsan.

Since there is no quantitative-qualitative change in production relationships to explain the sudden change from a number of independent kingdoms into one single Empire, the explanation is found in a gradual transformation of these relationships, from the system whereby the serf was taxed by having to perform unremunerated labour for his lord, to a system of taxation-in-kind, *viz.*, the land rent. This theory is to be found rather well formulated in an article by Teng T'o,[41] but it recurs in different forms in the writings of other authors. However, other elements are also adduced, of which, beside purely Marxist arguments, the more remarkable are the " demands of the masses " and secularised providence in the form of history.[42]

THE RISE OF THE LANDOWNER CLASS

The essential turning-point in the history preceding the establishment of the Empire is seen to be the emergence of a new class, that of the landowners; there is no text which does not deal with the " newly-risen landowner (class)." [43] So Chien Po-tsan writes [44] that from approximately the sixth century onward, the part of the land which formerly was owned by members of the noble class was gradually transferred to the newly risen landowners and the newly risen peasant class, and thereafter could be freely bought and sold. In the period of the Warring States (fifth to third century B.C.) free deals in land became even more common; at that time " the newly risen landowners' class . . . had come to form an historical force . . . it leased the land

39 " Chinese Historiography in the Last Fifty Years," *FEQ*, VIII, 1949, p. 147; Teng calls Fan " a leading Communist scholar " who had " received too much traditional training to be very radical " and who " merely puts the old wine in a new jar."

40 Fan Wen-lan, *Chung-kuo T'ung-shih Chien-pien* (*General History of China Simplified*), revised edition (Peking: Jen-min Ch'u-pan She, 1956). The most serious revision evidently took place after a critical review published in 1955, but from the preface it is clear that also earlier there had been several revisions, *i.e.*, in 1951. Lü Chen-yü, *Chien-ming Chung-kuo T'ung-shih* (Peking: Jen-min Ch'u-pan She, 1956), considerably revised in 1954.

41 Teng T'o, " Chung-kuo ch'ang-ch'i feng-chien she-hui nung-yeh sheng-ch'an kuan-hsi ti pien-hua " (" The Changes in Agricultural Productive Relations in China's Long-Enduring Feudal Society "), *Lun Chung-kuo li-shih ti chi-ko wen-t'i* (*Some Problems in Chinese History* "), (Peking: San-lien Bookstore, 1963), p. 92 *et seq.*, esp. pp. 106–113.

42 On the latter phenomenon, see the remarks in Edmund Wilson, *To the Finland Station* (London: Collins' Fontana Library, 1962), pp. 181–200; " The Myth of the Dialectic," esp. p. 191 *et seq.*; see also G. A. Wetter, *Sowietideologie*, Vol. I, pp. 150–151, 194–195.

43 Hsin-hsing ti-chu chieh-chi.

44 Chien Po-tsan, *Chung-kuo Li-shih Kai-yao*, pp. 6–7.

to the farmer directly and collected from him a fixed amount of the harvest as land rent." This landowner class "gradually grasped the pulse of social economy; going further, they demanded . . . the establishment of a centralised government of the dictatorship of the landowner class." [45] The same argument is used by Yang I-hsiang in his outline of Ch'in-Han history, but he adds: "At the same time, the large labouring population, having suffered bitterly from the long wars of the divided states, also wished for a united government, so as to enable them to work in peace. For this reason, Ch'in's labours for the sake of unification gradually obtained the support of the large mass of the population." [46] But he comes back to the landowners; like T'ao Hsi-sheng, he believes that "Ch'in's destruction of the six states was an enormous victory for the newly risen class of landowners," [47] and so says Chien Po-tsan, who calls it "the historical victory" of this class. [48] Nearly forty years ago, Maspero described the process through which there gradually emerged "une classe de petits propriétaires fonciers." [49] But how do the Marxist historians view the appearance of this new element in productive relationships, or rather, of a new form of landownership?

Lü Chen-yü brings in the concept of the manor, *chuang-yüan*, which he equates with the enfeoffed township, *i* [50]; the latter is of course the ancient term, whereas *chuang-yüan* used to be considered as a form of land tenure typical of T'ang times (seventh century and later), although at present there seems to be a tendency to place the rise of the *chuang-yüan* system at a much earlier date. [51] Lü believes that the "newly risen class of landowners" consisted of several elements. Some feudal lords, observing the increase in agricultural production on the fields tilled by free owner-farmers (according to the Marxist canon, the serf is more interested in his work than the slave, and the free farmer is keener again than the serf), [52] handed their own lands over to the occupants, demanding a land-rent in kind. Rich merchants acquired landed property by occupying the "manors" they had received as surety for loans, in case these loans were not repaid. Thus Lü assumes

[45] *Ibid.* p. 9.
[46] Yang I-hsiang, *Ch'in Han Shih Kang-yao (Outline of Ch'in Han History)* (Shanghai: Hsin-chih-shih Ch'u-pan She, 1956), p. 1.
[47] *Ibid.* p. 2.
[48] Chien Po-tsan, p. 9.
[49] Henri Maspero, p. 112, p. 135 *et seq.*
[50] *Chien-ming Chung-kuo T'ung-shih*, p. 91 *et seq.*
[51] See Liu Yü-huang, "Lun Han Chin Nan-ch'ao ti feng-chien chuang-yuan chih-tu" ("The feudal *chuang-yuan* system under the Han, the Chin and the Southern Dynasties, *i.e.*, from the 2nd century B.C. to the 6th century A.D."), *Li-shih Yen-chiu*, March 1962.
[52] See Ho Ch'ang-ch'ün, "Ch'in Han chien ko-t'i hsiao-nung ti hsing-ch'eng ho fa-chan ping lun Chen She ch'i-i ti chieh-chi kuan-hsi" ("Formation and Growth of Individual Small Peasants in Ch'in-Han Times and the Class Relationships of the Revolt of Ch'en She"), *Li-shih Yen-chiu*, December 1959.

the existence in the early fifth century of feudal "manors" side by side with remains of primitive communes, independent free farmers (threatened already by "annexation"), and land that could be bought and sold (pp. 93–94). In the fourth century B.C. the latter type of land greatly increased in extent, especially in Ch'in, where Shang Yang abolished the traditional manor, which Lü here equates with the *ching-t'ien* or "well-field" (pp. 107–108).[53]

According to Lü, the increase in agricultural production is due to the increased use of iron farm tools as a result of the invention of a smelting furnace heated by bellows (p. 94). Now all authors assume an increase in agricultural yields; Yang K'uan starts his extensive study on the period of the Warring States with a chapter on the expansion of production,[54] and Ch'i Hsia mentions the increased use of draught oxen for the plough, the use of manure and seed selection.[55]

Fan Wen-lan, who, of course, also adopts the theory of the increased production of the land, has a different hypothesis concerning the origin of the private ownership of land. He assumes that during the Eastern Chou, in the eighth or seventh century B.C., the individual household emerged as an economic unit and that, as a result, family ownership of land came to replace ownership by a noble clan. Moreover, the feudal lords rewarded their knights, *shih*, with land, and this became private property. As the number of knights increased with the incessant wars between the states, so did the extent of privately owned land.[56] Contrary to Lü Chen-yü, Fan Wen-lan holds that the merchants were only one element among many. He believes that due to the wars, the methods of exploitation changed and that therefore large numbers of serfs originally belonging to the noble clans were able to obtain their freedom, " in general " becoming small peasants.[57]

All authors agree that the freedom to deal in land led to the emergence of different types of landowners, ranging from landed magnates to rich and middle-class farmers to poor peasants. It also created an agricultural proletariat of hired labourers who had been compelled to sell their property to the exploiters; occasionally Engels is quoted

[53] The *ching-t'ien* system has formed an inexhaustible source for discussion since antiquity; for a survey of theories, see W. Eberhard, *Conquerors and Rulers* (Leiden: Brill, 1952), p. 7 *et seq.*; see also the articles in E. T. Zen Sun and John de Francis, *Chinese Social History, Translation of Selected Studies* (Washington, D.C.: American Council of Learned Societies, 1956), p. 3 *et seq.*; Yang K'uan, *op. cit.*, note 31, above, pp. 348–367.

[54] Yang K'uan, *Chan-kuo Shih* (*History of the Warring States*) (Shanghai: Jen-min Ch'u-pan She, 1955), pp. 11–39.

[55] Ch'i Hsia, *Ch'in Han Nung-min Chan-cheng Shih* (*History of the Peasant Wars During the Ch'in and the Han Dynasties, i.e., from the end of the 3rd century B.C. to the end of the 2nd century A.D.*) (Peking: San-lien Bookstore, 1962), p. 1.

[56] Fan Wen-lan, Vol. I, p. 155 *et seq.*

[57] Fan Wen-lan, p. 236.

in support of this development.[58] The obvious sign that changes had occurred in the form of land tenure is the occurrence of statements in the records that the rulers of different states imposed a tax on land. These are to be found in the *Tso chuan* and they are utilised by practically all authors, among them Kuo Mo-jo. Li Chien-nung devotes a separate appendix to the meaning of the technical terms used.[59]

INCREASED AGRICULTURAL PRODUCTION

All authors assume, or rather, postulate, that during the centuries preceding the unification, agricultural production increased significantly, for they need "a rapid growth of the social productive forces"[60] to make the other phenomena possible. Perhaps there was some increase, but it is instructive to observe the hesitant manner with which some well-informed authors approach the problem. Li Chien-nung is careful not to put too much stress on this factor,[61] and although the doctrinaire Yang K'uan devotes several pages to a description of this growth, he protests too much, using terms like "of course" and "undoubtedly"[62]; it is curious to see that the innovations Yang K'uan assumes for the Warring States' period are the very ones which Li Chien-nung demonstrates to have been still ineffective in Han times![63]

Beside an increase in the yield of agricultural production and the growth of the "newly risen class of landowners," the authors stress in varying degrees the emergence of commerce and industry. We have already seen how Lü Chen-yü has the merchants acquire land from the feudal lords. Fan Wen-lan, however, believes that trade never had a decisive effect on the whole of feudal economy, so that it is wrong to bring in the concept of "merchant capitalism" in order to explain the history of the period.[64] Contrary to this, Ho Tzu-ch'üan sees the growth of an economy using trade goods and currency as one of the chief factors, if not the very factor, which promoted the eventual establishment of the unified Empire; the strengthening of economic ties between

---

[58] Ch'i Hsia, *Ch'in Han*, p. 5; Fan Wen-lan (p. 250) notes in passing that the class struggle within this divided peasantry had not yet assumed violent forms.
[59] *Nu-li-chih Shih-tai* (*The Age of Slavery*) (Peking: Jen-min Ch'u-pan She, 1952), p. 19; *Tso chuan*, duke Hsüan, 15th year (594 B.C.) is the earliest date, referring to the State of Lu; Li Chien-nung, *Hsien Ch'in*, pp. 127–140.
[60] Ch'i Hsia, *Ch'in Han*, p. 3.
[61] *Hsien Ch'in*, p. 38, p. 44 *et seq.*
[62] *Chan-kuo Shih*, p. 26 *et seq.* For a condensed and more positive version of Yang K'uan's views, see his *Ch'in Shih Huang* (Shanghai: Jen-min Ch'u-pan She, 1956), p. 2.
[63] Li Chien-nung, *Hsien Ch'in*.
[64] Fan Wen-lan, pp. 242–243.

the states gave rise to the "demand" for political unity.[65] What Ho says briefly in a few paragraphs is worked out in great detail by Yang K'uan.[66] A special refinement, perhaps induced by English "parallels" of the eighteenth and early nineteenth century, is applied by Lü Chen-yü, who introduces the concept of the rising towns as centres of attraction for the rural population who are condemned to the utmost misery.[67]

CONDITIONS FOR THE UNIFICATION OF CHINA

Because of the reforms of Shang Yang in the middle of the fourth century B.C., the State of Ch'in became the stronghold of the power of the newly risen landlord class, which in the other Warring States was unable to gain the upper hand. Fan Wen-lan says succinctly that the whole period of the Warring States is the time of the aggressive attacks of this new power against the six states in the east, where the political authority was unevenly shared between the territorial lords and this class.[68] Fan states that Ch'in could never have unified China, had it not been for the existence of certain prerequisite conditions, viz., good communications, the need for trade and the resulting desire to eliminate all barriers erected by individual states, and finally the need for unified water control, not so much for irrigation as to prevent arbitrary actions by the individual states. This need was especially felt by both the landowners and the peasants. Besides, there were two other reasons, "abstract . . . but of tremendous importance," namely, that the working people demanded unification, for they knew from experience that the burdens, especially military service, imposed by a large state were relatively lighter. The last reason was that "the common culture demanded unification"![69]

An argument common to all authors is that the frequency and increasing size of military operations in the wars between the states, resulting in increasingly large losses of life, made everybody long for peace. All shared the view that the wars hampered production, although these same authors tell us earlier that agricultural production was increasing. Quite unexpected is the observation by several writers

---

[65] Ho Tzu-ch'üan, *Ch'in Han Shih-lueh* (*Brief History of the Ch'in-Han Period*) (Shanghai: Jen-min Ch'u-pan She, 1954), p. 4.

[66] Yang K'uan, *Chan-kuo Shih*, pp. 40–59.

[67] Lü Chen-yü, pp. 116–117. Yang K'uan is sensible enough to say only that the increase in the size of the town populations was *also* due to an influx of peasants (p. 46).

[68] Fan Wen-lan, p. 228.

[69] Fan Wen-lan, p. 258. The existence of a common culture in a politically divided area may render the political unification of that area seem logical and inevitable but the history of Western Europe (the Scandinavian countries, the German states, Italy), of India, of South America, etc., shows that historical reality is quite different. The idea that a common culture should "demand" unification is preposterous; one can only say that it might facilitate unification theoretically, or that it would be desirable as an ideal.

that the Chinese community had to be protected against alien invaders, *i.e.*, against the nomadic tribes in the north,[70] for, as far as I am aware, these tribes only came to constitute a real danger *after* the unification of China under the Ch'in because of Ch'in attacks on the nomads.

Hence, everybody wished for unification, and this wish found expression in the works of the thinkers of those days. The only way to end the wars was to end the division of the Chinese world into several contending powers. However, this could not be accomplished by " a revolution, for at that time the labouring people all lived dispersed under the domination of the individual feudal states, where in each state the concrete situation was different. The class struggle undertaken by the peasants was restricted to each single state [71] and could not yet be merged into one huge revolutionary force. Under these circumstances it was only to be hoped that a better ruler would come forward to accomplish the task of unification. Everybody realised that ' there is no greater disaster than the absence of a Son of Heaven,[72] and hoped that an ' enlightened Son of Heaven ' would appear to complete the unification." [73]

THE FIRST EMPEROR, CH'IN SHIH HUANG-TI

Of course, in view of the sources, King Cheng of Ch'in was cast for this role.[74] It remains to be seen how he accomplished the unification, given the " objective conditions " mentioned above. Here all authors first provide a more or less detailed survey of the Ch'in conquests up to the significant year 221 B.C. Then they proceed to indicate the measures he used to consolidate the unification, and finally the reasons for his ultimate failure.

A number of biographies of Ch'in Shih Huang-ti must exist, but the single one at hand is a thorough study by Yang K'uan, to which reference has already been made. According to Yang it was the success of Shang Yang's reforms that a century later enabled the first Emperor to establish " a unified landlord government power." [75] He adopted and

---

[70] Liu K'ai-yang, *Ch'in-mo Nung-min Chan-cheng Shih-lueh (Brief History of the Peasant Wars at the End of the Ch'in)* (Peking: Commercial Press, 1959), p. 3; Ho Tzu-ch'üan, *Ch'in Han*, p. 13; Yang K'uan, *Ch'in Shih Huang*, p. 9; *Chan-kuo Shih*, p. 245.

[71] Yang K'uan, *Chan-kuo Shih*, p. 82 *et seq.*, raises the interesting point that internal disturbances—peasant revolts—weakened the power of resistance of the other states against the attacks of Ch'in.

[72] *Lü-shih Ch'un-ch'iu*, Vol. XIII, No. 5, Vol. XVI, No. 2, *Chu-tzu Chi-ch'eng (Collected Texts of the Various Philosophers)*, Vol. VI, pp. 132 and 182.

[73] Yang K'uan, *Ch'in Shih Huang*, pp. 10–11.

[74] Ch'ü T'ung-tsu is the only author to say that, if Ch'in had not brought the feudal system to an end by political force, sooner or later one of the other warring states would have replaced it by a state with centralised power: *Chung-kuo Feng-chien She-huei (China's Feudal Society)* (Shanghai: Commercial Press, 1937), p. 357.

[75] Yang K'uan, *Ch'in Shih Huang*, p. 109.

expanded the ideas of the Legalists,[76] because these fitted the demands
of the contemporary socio-economic development, and " provided the
methods to solve the new historical tasks, that had been put on the
agenda . . . His measures, though violent, had the effect of strongly
promoting the creation of a unified state . . . His great achievements
are that for the first time he defined the basic parts of our present territory, that he liberated China from the disorders of the period of the
Warring States, that he put an end to the remnant influence of the nobles
in politics and in the economy, and that he consolidated the defence,
ensuring the independence of the state, promoting the growth of economy and culture." Another author, Ho Ch'ang-ch'ün, writes surpris-
ingly that the first Emperor's inscriptions (quoted in his annals in the
Shih chi [77]) show that he freed numerous slaves and serfs in the conquered states, in order to develop " the stratum of small individual
peasants." [78]

Still according to Ho Tzu-ch'üan, " although in the process of his
historical task the results he obtained were enormous, there was not a
single one of these enormous results that had not been created under
heavy difficulties by the large masses of the people. For . . . Ch'in
Shih Huang-ti was an autocratic emperor of a feudal dynasty, and all
reforms . . . were executed by means of the oppression and exploitation
of the people . . . After the completion of his historical task of the
unification . . . to satisfy his boundless lust for luxury, he used all kinds
of autocratic measures . . . and cruel means to oppress and exploit the
people . . . causing them to suffer unprecedented misery." [79]

Ho Tzu-ch'üan also concludes that, although the establishment of the
Ch'in Empire had been in harmony with the development of history and
in accordance with the interests of the people, its oriental despotism
[*sic*] and its system of statute labour could not bring peace to the people,
but on the contrary only brought them suffering, to which was added the
exploitation of the masses by the landlord class.[80] The general tenor of
all contributions on this point is that the Ch'in rulers did not give the
people rest and a chance to recuperate by lightening their taxes and
labour duties, but rather " increased their exploitation and oppression,"

[76] The Legalists are hard-headed, matter-of-fact " Realpolitiker," who owe their name
(*fa-chia*) to their reliance on a severe penal law, impartially applied to both nobles and
commoners, to aid the ruler in his efforts for centralisation; Shang Yang is the first
of these Legalists whose work has been transmitted to us. See for an outline of
Legalist policies the introduction to J. J. L. Duyvendak, *The Book of Lord Shang*
(London: Probstein, 1929). A good general survey of the measures taken by Ch'in
Shih Huang-ti is provided by D. Bodde, *China's First Unifier* (Leiden: Brill, 1938).
[77] See for this text *ibid.*, p. 2; a translation of the inscriptions is to be found in
Chavannes, *Les mémoires historiques de Se-ma Ts'ien*, Vol. II, p. 140 *et seq.*
[78] Ho Ch'ang-ch'ün, pp. 15–41, esp. p. 20.
[79] Ho Tzu-ch'üan, p. 117
[80] Ho Tzu-ch'üan, pp. 13–22.

with the result that the unprecedentedly heavy pressure of these duties seriously influenced production.[81] The Ch'in Government also took no measures against the process of *ch'ien-ping*, lit. "annexation," *i.e.*, the concentration of landed property and the accompanying pauperisation of the peasants.[82]

For Yang I-hsiang, the establishment of the Ch'in Empire is a glorious feat, and Ch'in Shih Huang-ti " in a positive way enacted policies for its consolidation, and made many important rules . . . Although he was enabled to do what he did because it accorded with the needs of the development of production and relied on the support of the labouring population," still, " he was the leader who executed the work . . . [and] . . . whose positive exertions hastened the progress of history." He is " an outstanding personality in Chinese history." On the other hand, he indulged in reactionary and cruel actions, going against the demands and the interests of the people.[83]

Very similar, if not identical, passages are to be found in the work of Fan Wen-lan, Lü Chen-yü and others. All these authors describe, of course, the measures taken in order to promote unification, paraphrasing the first Emperor's annals in the *Shih chi* about the centralisation of the government, the unification of writing, of weights and measures, and of coinage, the building of roads and canals, the abolition of custom barriers and of defence works inside the new state, etc. The forced migration of large numbers of people is also evaluated positively, not only because it destroyed the power of the magnates in the former feudal states, but also because it decreased the ancient differences in language and dialect.[84] Fan Wen-lan, traditionalist, suggests that the reason these people were mostly moved into newly conquered areas was to protect the inhabitants of Ch'in from contamination by the corrupt way of life of the eastern states.[85] Lü Chen-yü includes these migrations, however, among the reactionary acts of the first Emperor.[86]

THE BUREAUCRATIC ADMINISTRATION

The creation of the enduring framework of the long-lived Empire, *i.e.*, the establishment of the bureaucratic administration in the *chün-hsien* system,[87] is more or less taken for granted by most historians; it is

---

81 Liu K'ai-yang, pp. 3–4.
82 *Ibid.* pp. 9–10; similarly Chien Po-tsan, p. 10.
83 Yang I-hsiang, pp. 8–10.
84 See Fan Wen-lan, Vol. II, p. 14.
85 *Ibid.* Vol. I, p. 256.
86 Lü Chen-yü, p. 132 *et seq.*
87 The whole Empire eventually came to be divided into *chün*, " commanderies," which were in their turn subdivided into *hsien*, " prefectures," all governed by imperially appointed officials. Two excellent modern studies on the growth of the *chün-hsien* system are Yang Yü-liu, *Han I-ch'ien Chih Ti-fang Hsing-cheng Ch'ü-hua (Areas of*

mentioned, but, with one significant exception, hardly discussed. A typical remark is made by Yang I-hsiang, who writes only about the effect of the new system, saying that it " prevented local rivalries and struggles, and consolidated the unification of the Empire. Hence, it was beneficial for the development of economy and culture and for that reason it was a progressive system, in agreement with the social development of those times." [88] Fan Wen-lan is more old-fashioned. He considers the creation of these administrative units—in my opinion, justly—as conscious attempts by the rulers of the states, intent on centralisation, to undermine the position of their hereditary nobles.[89]

The exception is Lü Chen-yü, who, far from seeing the new administration as a creation of the territorial lords for their own purposes believes that it was the outcome of demands about their " manors " by the newly risen landlord class who had no powers in political and military matters. Because their holdings were scattered over a large area, they could not organise an administration for each separate unit, so the only feasible method was to form a " combined organ." " The *chün-hsien* system which grew from the manorial system was the form of organisation of the ' combined organ ' they (*viz.*, ' the new feudalistic landlords ') demanded." [90]

Ch'i Hsia remarks that in the " complete bureaucracy " established in Ch'in, posts at all levels were filled by " elements of the noble class and of the new landlord class," and that " in this highly stratified administrative structure even for the function of prefectural clerks, Thrice Venerables (*san-lao*), and constabulary chiefs (*t'ing-chang*), poor people could not be selected." [91] This is the only case of wilful misquotation I have discovered; the author here cites the biography of Han Hsin, Marquis of Huai-yin, which states literally: " His family was poor, [and as] he was a ne'er-do-well, he did not succeed in being selected to become an official," the commentators stressing that it was the man's lack of good behaviour which led to this. But Ch'i leaves out the crucial words " he was a ne'er-do-well," [92] and this enables him to conclude that all posts were occupied by landlord elements, with the result that " fundamentally, the tools of the autocracy were in the hands of the landlord class which exercised to the full its function of restraining and oppressing the masses of the peasants." [93] Also Hou Wai-lu shares this

Local Government before the Han Dynasty), Hsueh-shu chi-k'an, Vol. 4, Taipei, 1957, pp. 39–66, and Yen Keng-wang, *Ch'in Han Ti-fang Hsing-cheng Chih-tu (Local Government Organisation under the Ch'in and the Han Dynasties)*, Academia Sinica special publication 45, Vol. I, Taipei, 1961, pp. 1–8.
[88] Yang I-hsiang, p. 3.   [89] Fan Wen-lan, Vol. I, p. 185.
[90] Lü Chen-yü, p. 118.
[91] Ch'i Hsia, p. 14.
[92] *Han-shu Pu-chu*, 34, 1 a: " Chia p'in; wu hsing; pu te t'ui tse wei li."
[93] Ch'i Hsia, p. 14.

viewpoint, but he only speaks of the period of the Warring States; to him, the *chün-hsien* system was a compromise, in which the ancient nobility, " now transformed into local magnates," continued to play the leading role.[94]

The burning of the books and the extermination of the scholars [95] are usually condemned, but Yang I-hsiang wants it both ways: he includes these events among the measures that were necessary to protect the centralised government system and to suppress the old political ideology, aimed at the re-enfeoffment of the nobles. " From the standpoint of the consolidation of the unified government power of the newly risen landlord class, it had a certain effect . . . But . . . in actual fact this act grievously damaged culture." But this concession is taken back in the next sentence which states blandly that the Ch'in policies of consolidation were " in accord with the demands of the development of contemporary history . . . they were necessary for the promotion of the further development of economy and culture; fundamentally they all had a progressive meaning." [96]

REVOLTS AGAINST THE CH'IN

For all authors, the main, if not the only, reason for the rebellions against the Ch'in régime was the excessive burden laid on the population in the form of services: military service in the campaigns against the Hsiung-nu and to the south, and labour service, used for building the imperial palaces, the first Emperor's tomb, and the new roads.[97] Fan Wen-lan put the number of men engaged in various types of services at three million, or 15 per cent. of the total population which he estimates to have been twenty million.[98]

---

[94] Hou Wai-lu, *Chung-kuo Ku-tai She-huei Shih-lun*, p. 355 and p. 367. It is, however, undoubtedly true that the offices under the Commandery Administrator and the Prefect were staffed by members of the economically better situated stratum (who therefore had the means and the leisure to study), and these locally engaged clerks could be recommended to the central government so as eventually to become imperially appointed administrators themselves. See Masubuchi Tatsuo, *Chūkoku kodai no shakai to kokka (Society and State in Ancient China)* (Tokyo: Kobundo, 1960), p. 77 *et seq.*, and Hsu Cho-yun, " The Interaction of Social Power and Political Authority during the Former Han Dynasty," *Bulletin of the Institute of History and Philology*, Vol. 35 (Taipei: Academia Sinica, 1964), p. 261 *et seq.*

[95] Two measures taken by the first Emperor of Ch'in in order to silence criticism of his government; the books to be handed in for destruction included the Confucian classics as well as the works of the philosophers of the preceding centuries. These measures have more than anything made the first Emperor earn the undying hatred of all Confucians of later ages.

[96] Yang I-hsiang, *Ch'in Han*, p. 8.

[97] Chien Po-tsan, *Chung-kuo*, p. 10; Lü Chen-yü, *Chien-ming*, pp. 132–133.

[98] *Chung-kuo T'ung-shih Chien-pien*, Vol. II, pp. 16–18. Twenty millions seems too low in view of the figure of about 60,000,000 two centuries later, as established by H. Bielenstein, " The Census in China," in *Bulletin of the Museum of Far Eastern Antiquities*, 19 (Stockholm, 1947), p. 125 *et seq.*

Ho Ch'ang-ch'ün points to the interesting circumstance that the peasants did not demand land, not only on this occasion, but throughout the centuries up to the Sung period. For Ho, the reason is to be found in the state ownership of the land, with the accompanying statute labour which tied the peasant to the soil. Hence, the peasant rose to resist this form of "extra-economic compulsion," but not in order to demand land.[99]

FAILURE OF THE PEASANT REVOLT

Mao Tse-tung has written that the peasant wars were the moving power which created the changes in China's long feudal history.[100] Chien Po-tsan has called the study of these peasant wars one of the flowers of Marxist historiography.[101] No wonder the number of studies devoted to this subject is legion, and collections of such studies have been published.[102] There are at least sixteen articles on the rebellion under survey and it is discussed in detail in two books.[103]

In discussing the peasant revolts, Mao said that peasant movements of this type were bound to fail " because at that time there existed as yet

---

[99] Ho Ch'ang-ch'ün, pp. 39–40.

[100] Mao Tse-tung, *Selected Works*, Vol. 2, p. 629. The word "rebellion" (or "revolt") is not the right way to translate the expression *ch'i i*, as in China's long historiographical tradition this term denotes risings that from the traditionalist and legitimist point of view might be called justified or legitimate; also, they were mostly hallowed by their eventual success. In this way the T'ang histories speak of the *ch'i i* by the aristocratic founder of the T'ang Dynasty. It is, of course, generally known that the term *ko-ming*, used nowadays for an actual revolution aiming at a change of the social structure like the French revolution of 1789 or the Russian one of 1917, denoted originally merely a change of dynasty, when the heavenly mandate was changed. At present, the term *ko-ming* is likewise often used to designate risings in the "feudal" past which in actual fact merely expected a restoration of "good order" according to the traditional concept, *viz.*, the ideal functioning of the old-established social pyramid. Again another use of the term is to be found in Kuo Mo-jo's *Nu-li-chih shih-tai*, p. 29, where he describes the struggles between the ruling houses in the States of Ch'i and Chin and the leading noble families, and the changes resulting from these struggles. These changes "have to be considered as revolutionary, *ko-ming-ti*, as they were not purely political revolutions *ko-ming*, involving merely a change in the ruling house, but qualitative changes in society, social revolutions, *ko-ming*."

[101] Chien Po-tsan, "Tzu-ch'an chieh-chi yu-p'ai tsai li-shih-hsueh fang-mien ti fan-tang fan-she-huei-chu-i huo-tung" ("Anti-Party and Anti-Socialist Activities in the Field of Historical Science by Rightists of the Bourgeois Class"), *Li-shih Wen-t'i Lun-ts'ung* (*Collected Essays on Problems of History*) (Peking: Jen-min Ch'u-pan She, 1962), pp. 8–15, originally published in the Peking University Paper *Pei-ching ta-hsueh-pao* of September 23, 1957, p. 9.

[102] Li Kung-pi (ed.), *Chung-kuo Nung-min Ch'i-i Lun-chi* (*Collected Papers on Chinese Peasant Rebellions*) (Peking: San-lien Bookstore, 1958), 462 pp., 26 articles; Shih Shao-pin (ed.), *Feng-chien She-huei Nung-min Chan-cheng Wen-t'i T'ao-lun-chi* (*Collected Discussions on Problems concerning the Peasant Wars in Feudal Society*) (Peking: San-lien Bookstore, 1962), 545 pp., 34 articles and a bibliography of 398 items (partly contributions in the great daily papers) of which the first 148 discuss general principles, whereas the remainder is devoted to the separate wars.

[103] See the bibliography in Shih Shao-pin, pp. 528–529; Ch'i Hsia, pp. 41, 210. Besides the Ch'en She rebellion of 209 B.C. (which set off the other risings that caused the fall of the Ch'in) Ch'i also analyses the Red Eyebrows' revolt of A.D. 22 and the rising of the Yellow Turbans in A.D. 184. See also Liu K'ai-yang, p. 98.

no new productive forces or new production relationships, no new class strength, no progressive political party . . . [no] present-day correct guidance of the proletariat and the Communist Party. . . During and after the revolution they were used by the landowners and the nobles as tools to bring about a change of dynasty." [104]   Liu K'ai-yang quotes these words and writes that in Chinese feudal society, all political power established by peasant risings had to be taken over by the landlord class, whereas the leaders of the peasants, if they were not " butchered," necessarily became representatives of the landlords.[105]

Liu K'ai-yang gives as reasons for the failure of the rising by Ch'en She that the peasant leaders were quickly satisfied with what they had gained and then turned to luxurious living, becoming as rapacious as their former opponents. This led, of course, to the leaders' becoming divorced from the masses, and to quarrels and struggles among the leaders who then were easily tempted to surrender.[106]

Ho Tzu-ch'üan explains this miserable behaviour of the peasant leaders as determined by historical conditions: the peasants lived in scattered settlements, they were narrow-minded and backward, they lacked the guidance of a progressive class, and finally, they suffered from the evil influences exerted by the nobles. They also lacked military knowledge and true leadership, as is shown by Ch'en She, who divided his armies, allowing them to be defeated one by one.[107] This contrasts curiously with the statement of Ho Ch'ang-ch'ün, who, supported by passages from Marx and Engels, maintains that the military training the peasants had received in the recent far-flung campaigns stood them in good stead when they rose to fight the Ch'in.[108]

THE WAR BETWEEN HSIANG YÜ AND LIU PANG

Chinese historians readily concede that the first Emperor of the Han was compelled by the military situation to reinstate feudal kingdoms within the newly established empire. But the same move by Hsiang Yü a few years earlier is roundly condemned as reactionary, although Hsiang Yü's justifications were essentially the same as those of Liu Pang, the eminent founder. Less than twenty years before, the first

104 Mao Tse-tung, *Selected Works*, Vol. II, pp. 619–620, paraphrased by Chien Po-tsan, *Li-shih wen-t'i lun-ts'ung*, pp. 115–116; see also Ch'i Li-huang, on the persistence of the " feudal ideology " among the peasants.

105 Liu K'ai-yang, pp. 90–91.

106 *Ibid*. pp. 96–97.

107 Ho Tzu-ch'üan, p. 29 *et seq.*

108 Ho Ch'ang-chün, p. 35, quoting Marx's study on the *coup d'état* of Louis Napoléon; according to Ho's Chinese version of this study, Marx said that the individual small peasants, although forming a large mass, had no intensive mutual connections, their nearly self-sufficient units being like potatoes held together in a bag; having only local ties, they could not form a class and needed others to be their leaders.

Emperor of Ch'in had refused the request of his councillors to enfeoff his sons as kings, saying that this would plunge the Empire into confusion, since all the sufferings of the past were due to this system.

Ho Tzu-ch'üan considers the war between Hsiang Yü and Liu Pang as the struggle between the forces of the old and the new order, with Hsiang Yü representing the nobility, " remnants " of which had continued to exist, whereas Liu Pang stood for " the newly risen classes." As proof for his point, he notes the absence of members of the nobility among the collaborators of Liu Pang in the wars against Ch'in.[109] This is, of course, no argument, for in those days Liu Pang was still a subordinate commander recently risen from a local bandit leader.

Of considerably more interest is Ho's explanation of " the material bases " for the re-establishment of the feudal kingdoms which compelled Liu Pang to arrive at a temporary compromise with " the divided local forces." Ho thinks that the old fiefs still possessed a great traditional force, as well as material foundations, for, in spite of the development of economic ties between the different areas, production was still organised on a small scale, and the economy of these areas was still self-sufficient and quite independent, with the result that politically there was a strong demand for independence or semi-independence.[110]

Yang I-hsiang introduces more of the accepted terminology, but he possesses less insight. Hsiang Yü was reactionary and went against " the tendencies of the economic development of the landowners," as well as against " the wishes of the masses who demanded unification," whereas " the basic reason " why Liu Pang was victorious is that he " represented the interests of the newly risen class of the landowners." [111] Similarly Ch'i Hsia: " The remnant powers of the six states who had since long been scheming for their restoration, together with the elements of the nobility and the landlords who had grasped the direction of the revolutionary armies, ruthlessly robbed the fruits of victory of the peasant war." This is a surprising analysis, because usually the landlords are shown to be in favour of a thorough unification. " Hsiang Yü turned back the wheel of time . . . and so he was spit out by the revolutionary people and finally buried in the dust-heap of history." [112]

THE ESTABLISHMENT OF THE HAN EMPIRE

In principle, all authors agree that the establishment of the Han was the victory of the " newly risen landlord class," the peasants gaining only temporary respite because of general exhaustion. As Chien Po-tsan

[109] Ho Tzu-ch'üan, p. 33.
[110] *Ibid.* pp. 33–34.
[111] Yang I-hsiang, pp. 22–25.
[112] Ch'i Hsia, pp. 42–44; similarly Fan Wen-lan, *Chung-kuo*, Vol. II, p. 28.

succinctly puts it: "The establishment of the Han is the fruit of the great peasant revolution, which could, however, only overthrow the old rulers, but not the feudal system. This means that the victors in the peasant revolution would certainly end up as landowners who would then turn about and dominate the peasants. No wonder, therefore, that the Ch'in system was adopted for all Han institutions, oppressing the peasants in order to protect the property and the political interests of the landlord class. On the other hand, the strength of the peasant revolution caused the rulers to make some political and economic concessions that were advantageous for the development of the social economy." [113] Yang I-hsiang says practically the same thing. [114]

Fan Wen-lan goes into greater detail. He praises Liu Pang for the tremendous work he did in the seven brief years of his reign, "preparing the conditions to give rest to the people." He first mentions his "establishment of the regulations," *i.e.*, the compilation of the laws by Hsiao Ho: "in this way the people were able to live under definite laws . . . so that they felt at peace," a sentiment that seems rather more Roman or Western than typically Chinese. The bureaucracy "dared not to behave as rapaciously as the Ch'in officials." Then Fan mentions the repression of the merchants, which "contained an element of vengeance," as Liu Pang had seen with his own eyes how, under the Ch'in and during the wars, the merchants had profited from the people's misfortunes. Liu Pang also showed his wisdom by concluding peace with the Hsiung-nu, although it meant suffering insults, because it was beneficial to the people. Finally, he engaged in post-war reconstruction to the satisfaction of all social strata, *i.e.*, he enfeoffed his supporters, he richly rewarded his former officers and soldiers who in this way came to swell the landlord class, he decreased the land rent from one-third to one-fifteenth of the harvest, and he ordered the liberation of all persons who had become slaves because of hunger or poverty. "The peasant revolution had sacrificed large amounts of goods and many lives to obtain these concessions (*i.e.*, specifically the decrease of taxation and statute labour) from the ruling classes . . . but without paying this price, the peasants were unable to continue to live. It was only through these concessions against a high price that social production could slowly recover and expand." [115]

The policy of "giving rest to the people" is also mentioned by Fan, but this was, "of course," the only possible way for the exploiters. Or, as Ch'i Hsia puts it, although taxation was decreased and the people

[113] Chien Po-tsan, *Chung-kuo Li-shih Kang-yao*, pp. 10–11.
[114] Yang I-hsiang, p. 26.
[115] Fan Wen-lan, pp. 32–35.

suffered less oppression, "the main aim of these policies was to consolidate the rule of the landlord class, which likewise profited from this breathing space to strengthen their political and economic forces. Hence, under the conditions of the increasing acerbity of the class struggle . . . the policies and practices of the ruling group . . . were merely changing the form of class struggle, without altering its substance," [116] whatever that may mean.

To Ho Ch'ang-ch'ün, finally, inspired by passages in Marx and Engels (which were again echoed by Mao Tse-tung), the establishment of the Han empire means the recognition of the importance of "the individual small peasant" to the state, which therefore tried to protect this essential stratum against the landowners and against the big merchants. That is at least the gist of a long and needlessly complicated article, where Ho says in his conclusion: "Those whom the feudal power wanted to develop and protect were the free individual small peasants, as being both profitable for itself and for production . . . so, for more than two hundred years the Ch'in and the Han consistently applied the basic policy of 'promoting agriculture and repressing trade.'" But he cannot help pointing to "the gradual enserfment of the free farmers during the Ch'in-Han period," with the result that "the peasant disturbances and rebellions led by the free men who had fallen on evil days constitute the main form and content of the class struggle and the historical development of this historical period." [117]

EVALUATION

This is the picture which the new school of historians paints of the establishment of the Chinese Empire. Does it provide us with new insights, does it solve problems, has it answered any of the questions posed by the extraordinary development of the united, bureaucratic state? From the Marxist point of view the answer is undoubtedly yes. But the non-Marxist merely observes that a number of standard clichés have been constantly used, and that standard labels have been stuck over the glaring gaps in the argument. The more tenuous the textual proof, the more specious the reasoning. For, after all, there is so little we know definitely; there is so much that has to be supplied by a very careful handling of the fragmentary evidence, and by induction.

No, I cannot say that the new school has given us an adequate explanation of the genesis of the unified state. And, if matters remain as they are at present, that is to say, that Chinese scholars continue to operate

[116] Ch'i Hsia, pp. 55–56.
[117] Ho Ch'ang-ch'ün. The basic quotations are from Marx's *Kapital*, Engels' *Anti-Dühring*, *Origin of the Family*, *Situation of the English Working Class*, and Mao's *Selected Works*, Vol. III, p. 954.

on the one hand within a purely Chinese framework, and on the other continue to apply superannuated Marxist labels, this explanation will not be forthcoming. When thirty-five years ago the dean of China's Marxist scholars, Kuo Mo-jo, published his *Studies in Ancient China's Society*,[118] this first thorough-going application of Marxist methods for the interpretation of Chinese history was not only revolutionary, but also highly refreshing. For, whatever it was worth, this attempt showed what could be achieved by using a socio-economic approach to Chinese data. But since then it seems as if little further advance has been made.

In their day, Marx and Engels were intellectual giants who keenly absorbed the results obtained in other fields of study and tried to incorporate these into their universal scheme. Since then, nearly a century has passed. Studies in all fields have progressed immensely, especially in social and economic history, cultural anthropology, history of religion, etc. But the Chinese sinologue is prevented from looking at work done in his own field by scholars of other nations both by his parochial lack of interest in foreign developments and by obedience to the sacrosanctness of his Marxist canon. Men like Lei Hai-tsung, who during the days of the Hundred Flowers in 1956 openly complained of this attitude and its resulting backwardness, seem to be an exception.[119]

SCHOLARLY ACTIVITIES

However, the application of uniform standards has not resulted in a perfectly uniform picture. The reader will have noticed in the preceding pages that many different explanations—Marxist, of course—were offered for the same phenomena. It is also apparent that the better acquainted the Chinese scholars become with the writings of the *scholars* Marx and Engels (in contrast to those of the *political strategist* Lenin), especially with their minor studies and letters, the more vivid their picture seems to become. Although the true scholar has recognised certain historical phenomena to be *sui generis*, he still finds himself compelled to find the right passage in the canon which should be applied in this particular case. The sources are not allowed to speak for themselves.

Still, notwithstanding these restrictions, scholarship is far from dead. Even within the purely Marxist framework, a scholar is severely criticised when he oversteps the bounds and shows that he has not observed Mao Tse-tung's admonition that it is not enough to know the Communist classics, but that one must also know Chinese history.[120] And

---

118 *Chung-kuo Ku-tai She-huei Yen-chiu*, republished and subsequently revised several times.　　　　　　　　　　　　　　119 Chien Po-tsan, *op. cit.*, note 101, above.
120 Mao Tse-tung, *Selected Works*, Vol. IV, p. 18. A case in point is that Chien Po-tsan had tried to show that the Han period was no longer part of slavery society: *Li-shih Yen-chiu*, April 1954, pp. 1–24. This standpoint was attacked by three young men

although the correctness or incorrectness of an author's Marxist treatment of his subject plays a considerable role in critical reviews, the subject-matter itself is far from being neglected.

The traditional Chinese preoccupation with texts, with their philological interpretation, with textual emendation, in other words, with solid old-fashioned philology, goes on. Ancient texts continue to be studied for their own sake, and the results of such studies continue to be published in books and articles. As far as the period from high antiquity down to the Han is concerned, the subjects range from studies on the oracle bone inscriptions,[121] Shang Dynasty culture [122] and the canonical Book of Documents,[123] to critical editions of *The Discourses on Salt and Iron* [124] and of the *Han shu*.[125] Some of these are the work of old-established scholars like Kuo Mo-jo, Ch'en Meng-chia and the late Yang Shu-ta,[126] but many other contributions are certainly by much younger men.

The following are a few other outstanding scholarly productions of the last years. The photographs of the Edsin-gol archives of the Han garrison on that barren desert frontier [127] are being republished with modern transcriptions,[128] and emendations to these interpretations continue to appear, as well as studies on related problems. On economic and social problems of the Han period there appeared a collection of

who set out to prove that it still was: *Li-shih Yen-chiu*, January 1955, pp. 19–46. However, their handling and even their understanding of the primary texts proved to be so poor that they were subjected to severe counter-criticism: Tu Chin-ming, *Li-shih Yen-chiu*, November 1956, pp. 51–63. In all these discussions the splendid definitive study on the subject of slavery in the Han period was, of course, never mentioned, viz., Martin C. Wilbur, *Slavery in China under the Han Dynasty* (Chicago: Field Museum of Natural History, Anthropological Series, 1943), Vol. 34.

121 The flattened surface of a bone or a tortoise shell was heated at a prepared point by means of a glowing metal rod and the resulting cracks in the bone were interpreted by soothsayers in the same way as the folds in sheep's livers by the Acadian and Roman *haruspices*. In many cases the question to the oracle as well as the reply were inscribed beside the cracked spot.

122 The Shang rulers were overlords of the western part of the Great North China Plain between the 16th and the 11th century B.C.

123 A collection of short pieces of varying date on historical and legendary subjects. The best translation is that by B. Karlgren in the *Bulletin of the Museum of Far Eastern Antiquities*, Vol. 22, Stockholm, 1950.

124 This text, composed about 45 B.C., is a synopsis of the debates held at an economic court conference in 81 B.C. The first 29 chapters have been translated by E. M. Gale, *The Discourses on Salt and Iron* (Leiden: Brill, 1931); and *Journal of the North China Branch of the Royal Asiatic Society*, Vol. 65, 1934.

125 For this text, see note 4, above. For the critical edition referred to, see M. A. M. Loewe in *Asia Major*, Vol. 9 (London, 1962), p. 162 *et seq.*

126 He died in 1958.

127 Discovered by the Sino-Swedish expedition in 1930; see Folke Bergmann, *Travels and Archaeological Fieldwork in Mongolia and Sinkiang* (Stockholm, 1945), p. 114. These texts were published by their decipherer, Lao Kan, already in 1944; his definitive edition was published on Formosa; see my "Han time documents" in *T'oung-Pao*, 45, 1957, p. 4.

128 *Chü-yen Han-chien Chia Pien* (*Han Documents from Edsin-gol*) Vol. I (Peking: K'o hsueh Ch'u-pan She, 1959).

excellent studies by Ch'en Chih, a true Marxist, but with a great respect for the texts.[129]   Also other works might be mentioned, but it would not serve a useful purpose to enumerate all such studies in detail.   It is questionable whether these measure up in quantity (quality being equal) with the solid work done during the same period by Japanese scholars working in the same field [130]; perhaps preoccupation with modern history has to do with it, due to the slogan *hou-chin po-ku*, " less stress on the past, more stress on the present."

GROWING NATIONALISM

Another facet of modern Communist Chinese studies in ancient history that deserves attention is its tendency, particularly noticeable in the last few years, to grow more and more nationalistic.   The increasing nationalistic tone is evidently connected with the development of the Sino-Soviet dispute; no wonder, therefore, that this trend has been severely criticised by two prominent Soviet sinologues.[131]   But the roots of this nationalistic attitude lie deeper; they are emotional, they spring from the age-old feeling of cultural superiority of the Chinese over their less developed neighbours and from the still unhealed wounds which this feeling suffered during a century of contact with the West.

In ancient history this comes out in several ways.   For instance, the old concept of " 4,000 years of history," long since given up, has returned by the back-door.   Although lip-service is paid to the idea that China's recorded history began with the rise of the Shang Dynasty in the sixteenth century B.C. at the earliest, the mythical emperors of hoary antiquity who were discarded by the movement for the reorganisation of the nation's ancient history [132] have been reinstalled, now as leaders of the early Chinese community in the neolithic stage.   And " the Great Yü," the primeval hero who tamed the flood, has become the first of China's hydraulic engineers, with a statue in the historical museum in Peking.   A similar attempt to salvage legendary information may be seen in the identification of tribes and peoples mentioned in the ancient sources with members of the different neolithic cultures found within the Chinese culture area.[133]

Another symptom is the violent refusal to have any of China's attainments ultimately traced back to more westerly regions, whence they

129 Ch'en Chih, *Liang Han Ching-chi Shih-liao Lun-ts'ung* (*Collected Papers on Materials for an Economic History of the Two Han Dynasties*) (Sian: Shensi Jen-min Ch'u-pan She, 1958).
130 I am thinking in particular of scholars like Kaizuka Shigeki, Utsunomiya Kiyoyoshi, Sūdo Sōkichi, Kamada Shigeo, Masubuchi Tatsuo, Nishijima Sadao, Moriya Mitsuo, Oba Osamu, Hiranaka Reiji, Uchida Tomoo and others.
131 R. V. Viatkin and S. L. Tikhvinsky, " Some Questions of Historical Science in the Chinese People's Republic," *Voprosy Istorii*, October 1963.
132 *Op. cit.*, note 12, above.   133 Fan Wen-lan, Vol. I, p. 104.

could have come through cultural diffusion. An extreme example is to be found in the angry diatribes of Li Ya-nung,[134] who sees in such theories wilful attempts to belittle China, a kind of spiritual neo-colonialism. But to more sedate scholars also, the idea that an innovation such as the art of casting bronze might have come from some centre in western Asia is clearly repugnant.[135] Even the hypothesis that a minor thing such as the form of the " willow leaf " sword of the Chou could be of foreign origin is abhorrent.[136]

Hou Wai-lu feverishly searches for support in the writings of Marx and Engels for his contention that the ancient Chinese mode of production is of the same calibre—one is tempted to write " of the same standing "—as the " classical " mode of production worked out by Marx.[137] However, to stress the uniqueness of China's attainment and the Chinese way of development against the wide background of developments elsewhere is one thing; to stress China's uniqueness in ignorance of all other historical phenomena except for third-hand Marxist accounts is quite another. Are Chinese historical studies, save for Marxism, going back to where they were in the eighteenth century?

CONCLUSION

Ancient China's culture continues to be studied as many publications testify. Mao Tse-tung's advice that people should know Chinese history not only of today and yesterday, but also of the day before yesterday,[138] has not fallen on deaf ears among the strongly historically minded Chinese. The differences of opinion to be found in their publications— mostly, but not wholly, in the domain of Marxist interpretation—show that the study of history has not become petrified. Original work continues to be done.

The study of history in China is the handmaiden of politics, and even ancient history is made to serve propaganda purposes, to show the nation that China was always great and strong, that its labouring multitudes were industrious and brave, and that all misfortunes were due to the oppressors. As a theme, this is somewhat monotonous, nor does it bode well for the future, for it leads to an arid repetition of platitudes. The ultimate impression of Chinese historiography is therefore mixed: joy because of much excellent work, especially in the fields of material culture and philology, and misgivings as regards the validity of the narrow interpretation of the rich sources of a great tradition.

[134] Li Ya-nung, *Hsi Chou yü Tung Chou* (*Western and Eastern Chou*) (Shanghai: Jen-min Ch'u-pan She, 1956), p. 1 *et seq.*
[135] Chang Kwang-chih, *The Archaeology of Ancient China* (New Haven: Yale University Press, 1963). [136] Liu Shou-min, *Wen wu*, November 1963, pp. 50–55.
[137] Hou Wai-lu, *Chung-kuo Ku-tai She-huei Shih-lun*; pp. 1–100.
[138] Mao Tse-tung, *Selected Works*, Vol. III, p. 821; *cf.* p. 817.

7

The Chinese Middle Ages in Communist Historiography

By C. P. FITZGERALD

HISTORICAL writing in China today, whether by scholars who are members of the Communist Party, or academic writers who are not themselves Communists, has paid scant attention to the long period of time which may be called the Chinese Middle Ages, roughly from A.D. 316, the date of the partition of north and south following the nomad invasions, down to the end of the Sung Dynasty in A.D. 1278. This period of nearly a thousand years is considered by the Communist philosophy of history to be " feudal " and no real change in the social structure is supposed to have taken place under the long succession of " feudal " dynasties. Compared with the important transformation of ancient " slave society " to serf-owning feudalism, which is considered to have been completed somewhat before the Han Dynasty came to power, this long interim of feudalism drags on until, with the Ming, the first signs of nascent capitalism are to be detected, ushering in the still more dramatic events of imperialist aggression, revolution and the final triumph of the Communist Party. The scheme is not Chinese; it was borrowed, or adopted, from the Russians, who in turn seem to have based it upon a reference of Marx, contained in one of his letters, to the view that the general progression from primitive society to slave-owning monarchies, and then to feudalism, appeared to be a law of history. It may well be that this scheme is roughly applicable to several Western societies, but it is very hard to thrust Chinese history onto this procrustean bed—and still make sense of it.

One of the most awkward misfits is precisely this long gap of a thousand, or indeed, more nearly 1,500, years of " feudalism." It is not permitted to the Communist historian to make much of the fact that the first period of this millennium-and-a-half, the Han Dynasty, was a centralised empire, which was followed by fully four hundred years of division and constant internecine warfare, giving way to a second and more enduring centralised empire, first founded by the Sui and T'ang, continued by the Sung, Yuan and Ming right down to the end of the Ch'ing (Manchu) in 1912. These periods of unity and division, which old Chinese historians considered a most important aspect of their past, and which modern and Western non-Communist historians also see as highly significant, are not to be considered as anything but very minor varia-tions on the enduring pattern of " feudal " domination. It is, of course, also well known that " feudal " in Communist parlance bears a differ-ent meaning to that which Western and other non-Communist historians give to it. In our terminology, " squirearchy " or " bureaucratic squire-archy " would be the apter term.

The difficulty with those thousand years and more is that they are not allowed to exhibit any change or any advance in the social development of the Chinese people. This is disturbing: how comes it that the Chinese people move so much more slowly than the Western peoples? Why was " feudalism " so well entrenched that, in spite of its repeated dynastic convulsions, foreign invasions and periods of anarchy, it was always able to re-establish its peculiar institutions and endure for a period more than three times as long as its European counterpart? The difficulty has not really been faced; scholars tend to avoid this problem, and conse-quently the record of Communist historiography for the long Middle Ages is slight. One may wonder whether this dogma will withstand the erosion of Chinese reinterpretation for many years more, for such re-interpretations are already making a faint showing, possibly as a conse-quence of the continuing breach with Russia. So far, in the main, the formal view still prevails: the Empire under all and every dynasty was feudal; no real distinction can be drawn between Han and Six Dynasties, T'ang or Sung. Other differences and other developments, in the eco-nomy, the arts and the literature may be explored and recognised, but the political system remains inviolate.

Consequently it is wrong to see more value in one dynasty than another. The Empire, whether misgoverned by a Han Ling Ti or reor-ganised by a T'ang T'ai Tsung, was still the same engine of exploitation of the masses, ruthless, selfish, without care for the poor or real concern for the nation. Class origin determines everything: as T'ang T'ai Tsung came from the " territorial military leadership " (which he undoubtedly did), he cannot possibly have had any ideas which went against the interest of this group, nor followed policies which were of benefit to the people, least of all consciously designed for that purpose. Little atten-tion is paid to the political history of imperial China. In ten years the leading journal of historical research, *Li-shih Yen-chiu* (*Historical Research*), has published some thirty articles on the period under review, of which only two or three at most deal with political history, ten with land tenure, three or four with economics, and the remainder cover such varying fields as philosophy, contacts with foreign peoples, archaeo-logical discovery and bibliographical matters.

The Six Dynasties

The present survey starts with the period of division following the fall of Han. It is not a period which has attracted much attention from Communist historians. The " Three Kingdoms " and the Chin Dynasty do not come under their notice in the pages of *Li-shih Yen-chiu*. The southern Chinese dynasties are also neglected, but the Northern Empire under the Wei and its short-lived successors in the period immediately preceding the reunification of China by the Sui (A.D. 589) saw the beginning of certain land reforms and military organisation which attained great importance in the reunited Empire of the T'ang. These are discussed in two important articles [1]: " The Special Contradictions of Society in the Western Wei and Northern Chou Dynasties at the Time when the Fu Ping System was Established, and the Solution (of these Contradictions) " and " The Real Meaning of the *Chun T'ien* (*Equal Fields*) System in the Northern Wei Dynasty."

The author of the first article is concerned with the new measures instituted by the founder of the Northern Chou Dynasty, Yu-wen T'ai, who came to power when the Wei Dynasty was dissolved by factional struggles. Yu-wen, himself a member of the military aristocracy of Tartar descent, had received support from other such leaders, but was faced with the characteristic problem of this period, the instability of dynasties, and the difficulty of maintaining the allegiance of great aristocratic families. The author attributes the establishment of the " Fu Ping " or local troops, to this need. Yu-wen organised these forces on village lines, strengthening the dependent relation of soldiers to their commanders. He gave a fixed amount of land to each army unit, in the expectation that this would localise military power and prevent the commanders from attaining the considerable independence which they would have had if they had paid a roving army with plunder rather than with fixed land revenue.

The author considers that the land system called *chun t'ien* (equal fields) must be regarded as a complement to the *fu ping* military system. He points out that this redivision of land could only take place in areas where the original social system and land ownership had been destroyed by foreign invasion or peasant uprising; it was not a redistribution of owned land nor an attempt to equalise land ownership. He further points out that the system was designed to meet the needs of the

---

[1] Chu Wei-ch'en, " The Special Contradictions of Society in the Western Wei and Northern Chou Dynasties at the Time when the Fu Ping System was Established, and the Solution (of these Contradictions)," *Li-shih Yen-chiu* (*Historical Research*), No. 6, 1963, pp. 151–172; T'an Hui-chung, " The Real Meaning of the *Chun T'ien* (*Equal Fields*) System in the Northern Wei Dynasty," *Li-shih Yen-chiu*, No. 5, 1963, pp. 135–146.

former nomadic population (the Tartar invaders) who were now settled in agricultural districts and had abandoned their former way of life. They remained the main source of military strength, but, no longer supported by plunder, they had now to be supplied by land revenue. He notes that the social position of the soldier was at this time higher than that of the civilian. Finally he concludes that these measures were of temporary effect enabling the former nomadic people to become settled agriculturalists and " accomplishing, or nearly accomplishing, the transition from feudal lord to land lord." " Historical changes in feudal troops," he observes, " cannot be separated from the development of land relations in a feudal society."

It is interesting to note that the possibility of some changes within a " feudal society " are now accepted. The " transition from feudal lord to land lord " in this context—that of the transformation of the military aristocracy of both races which had merged in the long period of division into the " squirearchy " of later T'ang—is indeed one aspect of the major changes in Chinese society which occurred when the Empire was reunited. But hitherto it has not been very orthodox for Communists to admit that it ever took place.

A somewhat different view of this question is given by the second writer. He does not agree with those who believe that the *chun t'ien* system distributed uncultivated land to peasants so as to restrain the power of influential families. He points out that " according to Marxist teaching the spirit of legislation is always in accord with the will of the ruler." The Northern Wei, a dynasty of the Toba Tartars, had established a class system distinguishing nobility from commoner (although he does not say so, this was part of the distinction between conqueror and conquered, between Tartar and Chinese). The régime, therefore, represented the noble families, and the *chun t'ien* like other laws were conceived in their interest. He argues that it " is hard to imagine that a régime monopolised by influential families would propose a law which restricted their own interests." The system was introduced in T'ai Ho 9 (A.D. 486), rather late in the Wei Dynasty, and the author then points out that from the memorial of the promoter, Li An-shih, it is clear that it was designed to provide land for the nobility " who had many slaves and cattle but lacked suitable land." These were the nobility of Tartar origin, whose ancestors had been nomadic, but who were finding it increasingly difficult to maintain their position in an agricultural society without extending their land holding. The author believes that the *chun t'ien* system was designed to buy up land from the influential Chinese part of the nobility for the benefit of the relatively landless Tartar nobility.

The appearance of these two articles in one year on the critical subject of the role of the nobility of dual descent, Tartar and Chinese, in the late Six Dynasties seems to indicate a growing attention to the problems of Chinese medieval history from a less dogmatic point of view. Another short article in the same year, " Research into the ' Slave ' Army Uprisings at the End of the Sui Dynasty," also deals with the problem of the partly settled people of nomadic origin.[2] The name " slave " (*nu*) indicates that they were of non-Han origin, and seems, says the author, to have originally meant a member of a tribe. He considers that the effect of the rising was to destroy the old " slave " relationship, raise the social position of the former tribesmen and promote " the Sinification of the Fu tribes in these districts."

THE T'ANG DYNASTY

Non-Communist historians may award the T'ang dynasty a special place in the long panoramic roll of Chinese history: for the Communist historian it is, if special at all, only a rather more difficult example of the " feudal " régimes which have to be fitted into his framework. The T'ang is more difficult, for it can hardly be denied outright that this great period was truly formative in the development of Chinese civilisation. It has been shown by contemporary evidence, preserved either in the dynastic histories or in independent sources, that in the T'ang period China had an administrative machine far superior to that of any other contemporary state, indeed superior to any in the world, ancient or modern, until the late eighteenth century at the earliest. Even if all the artistic and cultural achievements of the period are to be attributed to the " people " and not to their rulers, it is still true that these rulers accomplished some remarkable tasks and initiated some great changes which remained the basis of the imperial system from the seventh century on. The examination system for the civil service, the reformed tax laws, the development of a professional army, were among many T'ang institutions which preceded by centuries their appearance in other parts of the world or provided a model for unacknowledged borrowings from China. Many of these developments were undeniably the work of the rulers and not the ruled.

Communist historians do seem to be genuinely interested in the important changes in China's land tenure system and economy which took place in the T'ang period. They are less willing to relate these developments to social changes, since here the ice is thin. It is permissible to argue that changes in the land tenure system or the emergence of

---

[2] Chiang Po-ch'in, " Research into the ' Slave ' Army Uprisings at the End of the Sui Dynasty," *Li-shih Yen-chiu*, No. 3, 1963, pp. 151–164.

a nascent money economy are significant but it must still be assumed that the feudal ruling class was merely adapting to new ways. It may not be suggested that the class itself was undergoing a profound transformation, for then it would no longer be possible to describe it without abandoning the all-inclusive term " feudalism."

Even in the economic field this interpretation must cross some awkward hurdles. Sun Ta-jen, writing in *Li-shih Yen-chiu* on the " Economic Content of Leases during the T'ang and Five Dynasties," [3] has discovered that the " owner of the land " was not in all cases a feudal landlord, and the lessee not always a feudal tenant. Treating eight out of eleven surviving lease contracts of the T'ang, he finds that in five cases the owner of the land was a peasant, and the lessee a landlord. Sun concludes that this unexpected relationship arose because of poverty. An eminent Japanese historian, Niida Noboru, is criticised for failing to realise this and contending that the reason for such leases was that the peasants had more land than they could manage themselves, or that it was often too scattered and therefore convenient to lease it to a man with more resources. Why peasants with more land than they could use were yet so poor is not explained.

It would appear from this and other articles on the land question that it is not orthodox to take into account the very different degree of pressure upon the land which existed in the T'ang period, when the population of the Empire did not exceed sixty millions, and the later periods of Ming and Ch'ing, when the numbers were three and four times as great. A system in which peasants leased surplus land to richer men could hardly exist in recent centuries, when surplus land in this sense was non-existent. That it did prevail in the T'ang period would suggest that the social realities of the countryside in that dynasty also differed very widely from those which the modern Chinese remembers from the pre-Communist period, and which are now assumed to have been the normal condition of all previous dynasties. Historians everywhere will be grateful for the patient research which has brought these ambivalent testimonies to the real nature of T'ang rural society to light; the facts are of great value, although the interpretations put upon them may not seem to flow naturally from the evidence.

The orthodox Communist view of the T'ang period can best be judged by the criticism meted out to one historian who seems to have strayed from the path of correct doctrine. In 1958, *Li-shih Yen-chiu* published a critical review of a history of the Sui, T'ang and Five

---

[3] Sun Ta-jen, " Analysis of the Economic Content of Leases during the T'ang and Five Dynasties Periods," *Li-shih Yen-chiu*, No. 6, 1962, pp. 97–107.

Dynasties, by Wu Feng.⁴ The book is flatly described as " bad " and its author accused of " selling bourgeois ideology under a Marxist cloak." This accusation is reinforced later on by the suggestion that the author's work is inspired by the ideology of the " counter-revolutionary Kuomintang faction."

It is interesting therefore to consider the views that have called down such severe criticism. Wu Feng, in his chapter on the reunion of China by Yang Ch'ien, who conquered the southern Ch'en Dynasty and founded the Sui, says that the military discipline of Yang Ch'ien's army was very strict, that they were forbidden to " touch a hair " of the people's property, and that when the south was conquered the people of that region welcomed the Sui army as deliverers. T'ang Hsing, in reviewing the book, declared that " apparently the feudal Sui Government was already a People's Government, and its army a People's Army." He then derided such an idea as a total misunderstanding of the nature of any feudal monarchy.

Wu Feng, discussing the founding of the T'ang Dynasty, which in agreement with most historians he regards as a major turning point in Chinese history, remarks that Li Shih-min, later the Emperor T'ai Tsung, clearly received the support of the people in Kuan Chung (modern Shensi) when he raised the revolt against the Sui. This brings the scornful rejoinder from T'ang Hsing that, " in Wu Feng's view Li Yüan (T'ang T'ai Tsu) and his son were not military territorial leaders, but are transformed into leaders of the people." When Wu Feng praises Li Shih-min as a man with an exceptional talent for government and supreme ability as a military commander—" the greatest hero in the history of our country . . . who performed a great task in the development of society," his critic admits Li Shih-min's part in the foundation of the T'ang Dynasty but denies any credit for social achievement. The improved state of the country after the foundation of the T'ang was due to " the popular upheaval at the end of the Sui, without which no T'ang Dynasty would have been possible." All that the Li family did was to use their territorial military power to profit from the victory of the popular rising and change the dynasty.

The correct view is then elaborated. " We recognise the T'ang period as one of important change and development in the period of the Middle Ages in China, but we do not attribute these developments to the leadership of heroic individuals." Just how the upheaval of the popular masses at the end of Sui brought about the important political reforms which have hitherto been associated with the reign of T'ang T'ai Tsung

⁴ T'ang Hsing, " A Critical Review of Wu Feng's History of the Sui, T'ang and Five Dynasties," *Li-shih Yen-chiu*, September 1958, pp. 47–55.

is not explained. The offence of Wu Feng is plainly shown to be that he does not attribute the proper importance to the peasant risings which have, from time to time, disturbed the rule of all dynasties. These risings represent the truly creative forces in history. It is to them that we should look to find the causes of such progress as occurred, of such advances as the economy attained.

Wu Feng said that the Yellow Turban Rebellion in the late Eastern Han period inaugurated a long period of strife and foreign invasions, which was brought to an end only by the reunion of China under the Sui Dynasty. T'ang Hsing is horrified at such obtuseness. " This means," he remarks, " that the only significance of the Yellow Turban Rebellion was that it led to a long period of darkness and chaos." As a matter of fact, this is not what Wu Feng said; he referred to incessant civil wars and foreign invasions, not to " darkness " nor to " chaos." T'ang Hsing goes on to point out that popular rebellions of the peasants were not periods of confusion, but examples of the growing power and influence of the people, and as such, creative forces in the process of history.

Wu Feng comes in for more castigation for his account of the rebellion of Huang Tsao, which really destroyed the failing power of the dynasty in the late T'ang. This rising, T'ang Hsing says, " was a heaven-frightening, earth-shaking peasant revolt "—an example of the dynamic power of the people. But poor benighted Wu Feng said that Huang Tsao's followers were " rabble, salt smugglers and mutinous soldiery," a gross libel of the people and a total failure to understand the real nature of such popular movements. Wu takes a rather traditional view of the relations between the T'ang Government and the Turki peoples who then dominated the Mongolian steppe. His observations about the Tibetans, that their often warlike contact with China had the effect of introducing a higher civilisation to Tibet, are also condemned. His point of view is reactionary, T'ang Hsing claims: the contact of Chinese and border peoples was fruitful to both sides; the traditional view of the barbarism of the nomadic tribes is quite unscientific and unhistorical; the Tibetans already had an advanced economy, and taught the Chinese many useful arts. The invasions and raids of the nomads were more often reprisals against imperialist encroachment by the feudal monarchists, a legitimate reaction to " Chinese aggression."

Wu Feng is no better when he deals with the artistic heritage of the T'ang period and its literature. He unwisely states that Po Chu-yi's poem on the death of Yang Kuei-fei, " The Everlasting Wrong," has " true human love " as its theme. T'ang Hsing indignantly asks, " Love between whom? Does Wu Feng know that at the time of her death

Yang Kuei-fei was thirty-eight and her supposed infatuated lover, the Emperor T'ang Hsuan Tsung (Ming Huang), was seventy-three?" So Wu Feng and his reactionary ideas are thoroughly discredited. It is curious that not a word of this criticism is directed at anything Wu has to say about another T'ang sovereign of great historic interest, the Empress Wu Tse T'ien. Perhaps traditional Wu Feng was not too much at fault in accepting in 1958 the old view of her reign and character, described in the dynastic histories as " the calamity of Wu." Here, at least, was a feudal monarchist whom ancient and modern could agree to condemn. But it would seem that times, and opinions, are changing.

In 1962, Professor Wu Han delivered a lecture on the Empress Wu Tse T'ien at a conference of historians held in Peking on August 5. His remarks were reported *in extenso* three days later in the literary section of the *People's Daily*.[5] It must therefore be assumed that they were not thought to be out of line with official thinking. Wu Han has been a professor of history at Tsing Hua University since 1949, and has served as deputy mayor of Peking. He is also well known as an expert on the Ming Dynasty. Wu Han first stated that the subject of his lecture, the Empress Wu Tse T'ien, was one of the greatest of women " statesmen " as well as being the only " woman Emperor " in Chinese history. The professor seems to have had some trouble with the awkward fact that the word for " empress " in Chinese means only the consort of an emperor: the language lacks such neutral terms as " monarch " or " sovereign " which can be used for rulers of either sex. Wu Han goes on to point out that in this respect the Empress Wu Tse T'ien differs from her infamous predecessor, the Empress Lu of the Han, and her recent successor, the Empress Tz'u Hsi of the Ch'ing. These were the widows of emperors and ruled as regents in the name of infant successors. The Empress Wu Tse T'ien, on the other hand, actually ascended the throne and changed the name of the dynasty. Wu Han then outlined the career of the Empress Wu and stressed the fact that she had wielded supreme power (first as regent, later as sovereign) for forty-five years (A.D. 660–705)—a much longer period than the vast majority of male emperors had attained.

He then praised her as a statesman for the following achievements:

> 1. She dealt a crushing blow to the established nobility who were politically conservative and who opposed any innovation and the employment of progressive elements. This was an expression of the nobility's attempt to monopolise state power and suppress the newly rising landlord class. By striking at the nobility Wu Tse T'ien gave a positive impetus to the political development of her period.
> 2. The Empress Wu employed men of talent irrespective of their

5 *Jen-min Jih-pao* (*People's Daily*), July 8, 1962.

family origin and upbringing. People such as Ti Jen-chieh,[6] Yao Yuan-ch'ung and Sung Ching were all promoted by her. One could say, therefore, that in this respect she had not only continued the traditions of the Chen Kuan period (the reign of T'ang T'ai Tsung), and made a contribution during her own lifetime, but also set an example for the K'ai Yuan reign (T'ang Hsuan Tsung or " Ming Huang ").

3. During the forty-five years of her reign, peace was preserved. There was not a single major peasant uprising. Even after her death, her son T'ang Chung Tsung, whom she had deposed, had to say that during her reign " she forgot her own interest in order to serve the good of the state; her subjects were able as a result to enjoy peace and prosperity." Ou-Yang Hsiu of the Sung Dynasty, who compiled the *Hsin T'ang Shu* (*New History of the T'ang Dynasty*), and who did not approve of her, had to admit that during her reign she " was able to hold those at the top to their place, and rule those below."

4. She had political talent and could also tolerate criticism; thus in evaluating her the great T'ang statesman, Lu Chih, said, " She had no hesitation in choosing people, and had complete trust in those she had chosen, nor did she ever tire in her search for the talented. She was strict in her demands and prompt in deciding promotion and demotion. She dismissed incompetent officials without the slightest hesitation, and with the same promptness and speed she elevated the talented and able. Therefore her contemporaries were of the opinion that she had the skill to know and choose the right people, with the result that in the following reigns reliance was placed in the men she had selected." " This is high praise indeed," adds Professor Wu Han.

Wu Han does not consider Wu Tse T'ien to be without defects and shortcomings. In her struggle against her opponents she mistakenly killed many good and innocent people; and while she led a simple life in her early years, she indulged in luxury and extravagance in later life. She also shared many other defects of the feudal monarchists. So if it is wrong to follow the traditional Confucian scholars in their condemnation of Wu Tse T'ien, it is equally mistaken to think that she was perfect.

This revaluation of the Empress Wu contains a number of interesting differences from the views expressed by T'ang Hsing in criticising the Sui, T'ang and Five Dynasties history of Wu Feng. Professor Wu Han not only gives Wu Tse T'ien credit for developing the political trends of her time away from the rule of the military aristocracy towards a wider distribution of power throughout the landlord scholar class, but he specifically says that in doing so she was continuing the traditions of T'ang T'ai Tsung and setting an example for T'ang Hsuan Tsung. But these traditions, and this example, when cited by Wu Feng, met only with the scornful condemnation of T'ang Hsing. It is clear that there are either two views of the great T'ang

---

[6] The original of Dr. Van Gulik's " Judge Dee."

rulers current in Chinese historical circles today, or that a new view has been expressed in recent years. In general, the opinions of Professor Wu Han are shared by Western and other "bourgeois" historians of the period, to whom they are not at all new. It is also significant that Wu Han can quote a T'ang writer in praise of Wu Tse T'ien, and also Ou-Yang Hsiu of the Sung. The opinions of such old-fashioned reactionaries would certainly not have been accepted by the critic of the historian Wu Feng.

Wu Han's lecture is not the only evidence that in the higher circles of Chinese Communist historiography a less rigidly doctrinaire standard of criticism is becoming acceptable. The literary section of the *People's Daily* of September 2, 1962, carried a long article by Feng Tzu, " Wu Tse T'ien on the Stage," reviewing a play by Kuo Mo-jo entitled *Wu Tse T'ien*. After praising the distinguished author for portraying Lo Pin-wang, one of the Empress Wu's most able opponents, not as a mere *hsiao jen* (petty fellow) but as a talented writer who lacked the gift for action, he continues:

> It has been asked, is *Wu Tse Tien* a play of historical re-evaluation? My answer is yes, and no. Yes, because the intention is to give a correct evaluation of this one-time all-powerful " woman emperor," but on the other hand, the aim of the playwright was not simply historical re-evaluation. This play aims at presenting the political and spiritual aspects of the historical figure, Wu Chao (the Empress Wu) through her struggle with the powerful nobility of her time. The play reflects the philosophy of Wu Tse T'ien that " to yield one step is to fall back a thousand miles." By means of the conspiracy between P'ei Yen and the Crown Prince the play describes the mind and feelings of an ambitious great " statesman " in the last years of her life, and depicts the loneliness and inner emptiness of a " woman emperor " during the period when she had only her own intelligence, talent and power to depend upon in order to rule. The Empress Wu repeatedly refrained from putting Shang-kuan Wan-erh to death; on the contrary she gave her important positions. This was no doubt due partly to her esteem for the talented, but it is not to be ruled out that it was also due to her desire to get spiritual support from Shang-kuan Wan-erh by making her her right hand " man." P'ei Yen, the opponent of Wu Tse T'ien, is an ambitious man; if he dared to conspire with the Crown Prince, it was because he had strong political backing. He is the representative figure of Wu Tse T'ien's enemies, and he was not isolated.

Feng Tzu, the author of this article, was a subordinate of Kuo Mo-jo when, during the war with Japan, the latter was the head of the Third Bureau of the Military Affairs Commission which was responsible for cultural matters. It becomes clear that the views of Professor Wu Han are not his alone; the same points are made, that the Empress Wu opposed and destroyed the military aristocracy, that she sought out talented people, and that she trusted those she chose. This is particularly emphasised in the points made about the lady Shang-kuan Wan-erh, granddaughter of Shang-kuan Yi, who had been one of Wu Tse T'ien's most formidable enemies during her rise to power, and had only just failed to bring about her degradation. The Shang-kuan family paid the price of failure, the head of the family was executed and lesser members and children exiled or reduced to the rank of commoners. But Wu Tse T'ien took the orphaned Wan-erh into her own household as a child, brought her up, and in time made her her confidential private secretary.

There are reasons perhaps for the Chinese Communist historians to look with a more kindly eye on Wu Tse T'ien than on other "feudal" rulers. First, she was a woman, and one who obtained the highest position; in this way she was clearly a forerunner of the modern emancipation of women. Second, she struck down the nobility and promoted men of humble origin; in this way she had some historical value as an instrument of social progress. But when Wu Han goes on to refer in favourable terms to the "traditions of the Chen Kuan period," *i.e.*, the reign of T'ang T'ai Tsung, he is clearly implying that even that "military territorial feudal landlord," as T'ang Hsing calls him, had some merits as a ruler. Moreover, there is much less about the historical role of popular rebellions in the two writers who discuss Wu Tse T'ien than in the criticism of T'ang Hsing. Wu Han indeed points out that there were no peasant rebellions in Wu Tse T'ien's reign, and attributes this fact to the merit of her rule, whereas it is clear from T'ang Hsing's comments on the foundation of the T'ang that the more doctrinaire writer would see this as merely a consequence of the popular victory in the rising against the Sui, which the Empress Wu, like T'ang T'ai Tsung, used for her own selfish ends.

Further evidence of a new willingness to reconsider the dogmas of formal Marxist interpretation as applied to "feudal" society is provided by the publication of an article [7] on the political struggle in the reign of T'ang Shun Tsung (A.D. 805–806). The statesmen of this reform movement, led by Wang Shu-wen, are known as "the Group," and came to power in A.D. 805 after the death of the Emperor T'ang Te Tsung. They retained imperial favour for only five months, but during that short space of time endeavoured to bring about an important political reform. The author decries the unfavourable treatment accorded to this group of men by the traditional histories, the *Hsin T'ang Shu* (*New History of the T'ang Dynasty*) and *Tzu Chih T'ung Chien* (*The Mirror of Government*). He points out that these works reflect "the feudal ruler's class point of view, judging people by their

[7] Wang Yi-sheng, "Historical Significance of the Political Reforms of the Two Wangs and the Eight Ssu-ma," *Li-shih Yen-chiu*, No. 3, 1963, pp. 105–130.

success or failure and following the point of view of their political enemies."

He sees the rise and activity of this group of officials as a consequence of the increasing contradictions of the society of their age: the decay of the *chun t'ien* land tenure system, the oppressive character of the new *liang sui* (double tax) taxation system, and the growing conflict between the aristocratic great landowners, who were buying up property to form very large estates, and the smaller " commoner " landlord class (" squires " would be the English equivalent) whose emergence he sees as part of the process of " differentiation of social classes." The political movement headed by Wang Shu-wen was therefore " the practical revelation of this struggle of social contradiction." The policy of the Group was to deprive the eunuchs of military power and to restrain the power of the semi-independent provincial military governors, a power which had grown as a direct consequence of the great rebellion of An Lu-shan. He believes that had the Group succeeded in these aims, the history of late T'ang would have been different, since " the decline of the T'ang Empire, besides the two fundamental contradictions between peasants and large-scale landlords, was due to the two causes stated above." He concludes, after reviewing the course of events which culminated in the overthrow of the Group by the eunuch power, that " the Group reflected the ' commoner ' landlords' class consciousness and political demands. The Group tried to change the situation of the monopoly of influential (noble) families and great landlords, and to institute political reform . . . the incident was a severe struggle between the new rising commoner landlord class and the influential families over the demand of the former for reorganisation of the feudal social system . . . the Group to some extent expressed the demands and wishes of the people at that time, so the struggle with the inner circle of the feudal ruling class also generated changes in society. The Group pushed society forward, while the aristocracy tried to hold history back. We should sympathise with the Group."

The author then points out that the failure of the Group, in spite of these merits, was that " though representing the interests and demands of the commoner class they did not act in co-operation with it or utilise this class's strength . . . without the backing of the peasantry against the privileges and interests of the influential families and (large) landlords they could not succeed."

This interpretation of the social development of the late T'ang period is not greatly at variance with that of non-Communist historians. The main points of difference are the use of the term " feudal " and the peculiar meaning attached to it by Communist writers. It is also clear that it is now possible to accept the fact of social change within the "feudal system." The rise of the "commoner landlord class," that is to say, the "scholar gentry" of Western terminology, is now acknowledged as one of the significant developments of the T'ang period. However, it is not yet apparent that this is linked, as non-Communist writers would see it, with the policy of the Court, especially of the first three great T'ang rulers, T'ai Tsung, the Empress Wu and Hsuan Tsung, who promoted this development to secure the throne against possible rivals among the high aristocracy—the bane of the dynasties of the period of partition. The Communists' unwillingness to give the emperors any credit for change, even when imperial motives are obviously self-interested, still reflects the traditional Marxist outlook. Change and progress must be generated by the People.

Perhaps the other significant difference between the treatment of these events by such historians as Wang Yi-sheng and his colleagues in other countries is the persistent refusal of the Communist writers to accept the fact that the institution of the civil service with its recruitment from T'ang onward by public examination, is the real and essential difference between the bureaucratic empire and any system which can truly be called "feudal." It is not, at bottom, an unwillingness of the non-Communist historians to recognise that this civil service state was in fact often very oppressive to the poor; it is a question of differentiating two distinct types of class rule in pre-modern ages. The civil service was in fact recruited from those families which could afford to educate their sons in a long and costly programme of classical learning. They were, therefore, inevitably recruited from landlord and official families. But if this proves the existence of a privileged ruling class (which no one would deny), it does not make this class of bureaucratic landlords "feudal" any more than the eighteenth-century English gentry were feudal.

THE SUNG DYNASTY

Interest in the Sung dynasty on the part of historians now working in China is centred on evidence that this period saw the first dawning of a new economic order—capitalism—and heralds, in fact, the overdue end of the long "feudal" period. Studies of such developments as the growth of wage labour and the progress of the handicraft industries were made several years ago, and two such articles appeared in *Li-shih Yen-chiu* in 1957 and 1959.[8] The author of the article on handicraft

---

[8] Wang Fang-chung, " Private Handicraft Industry of the Sung Dynasty," *Li-Shih Yen-chiu*, February 1959, pp. 39–57; K'o Ch'ang-chi, " Preliminary Study of Wage Labour in the Sung Dynasty," *Li-Shih Yen-chiu*, February 1957, pp. 23–48.

industry inquires whether "any relationship exists between the beginnings of capitalism and the private handicrafts of the Sung dynasty." Fortified by a quotation from Lenin's "Development of Capitalism in Russia," the author shows that handicraft industry in the Sung divides into minor and large-scale industries. The latter, including porcelain, salt and mining, used hired labour, and were not, in fact, based upon the minor industries which include silk, paper, printing, tea and sugar. The small handicraft industries "resemble feudalism much more than capitalism," and their influence on the development of capitalism was judged to be indirect.

The author of the article on wage labour considers that "the appearance of wage labour proves that both the late Middle Ages and the stage of preparation for capitalism in China began in the Sung dynasty. It also proves that if there had been no aggression by imperialist forces, Chinese society would have developed normally and in an orderly way into a capitalistic society." When the interests of the new factory masters conflicted with those of the feudal system, "they were not frightened, since they had considerable economic and social strength."

The "aggression by imperialist forces" might be supposed to mean the conquest of China by the Mongols, which certainly for a time wrecked the existing economy, particularly in North China. But it is probable that this is not what the author means. He would regard Genghis Khan as a feudal militarist, albeit a non-Chinese one. The failure of capitalism to develop from these tender shoots in the Sung period is to be charged to the heavy account payable by the later aggressors, the imperialist British, Portuguese, French and others, who distorted the "normal" pattern of China's development in ways which the Chinese Communist historians of the Ming, Ch'ing and modern periods are very interested in demonstrating. But this aspect of the treatment of Chinese history lies beyond the scope of this article.

A new trend in the Chinese treatment of the earlier periods has appeared since the development of the Sino-Soviet quarrel. There is a readiness to look at the middle period of Chinese history with more sympathy and less prejudice. As the Communist régime becomes assured, and exercises the increasing power of the Chinese state, it is to be expected that former rulers who arrived at a similar degree of authority, by succession or by dynastic revolution, will be looked upon with more toleration and fellow-feeling. Their problems are better understood in relation to those which face the rulers of today. The need to explain the "lag" in Chinese history, the long drawn out feudal period, becomes more urgent, as it seems to reflect some defect in the

Chinese people themselves, a view hardly to be tolerated by the Communist régime. The ultimate necessity of revaluing the whole Marxist scheme of rigid periods based on the history of Europe is not yet accepted. But the steady trend to exalt China and Chinese experience must bring about a reconsideration of those ages and of those rulers who, for better or for worse, did determine that, often shaken but always restored, China would remain a unified empire.

8

The Reappraisal of Neo-Confucianism

By HELLMUT WILHELM

I

As in all living scholarly traditions one can see in traditional Chinese historiography a wide range of divergent opinion as to what history is and how it should be written. On one point, however, all schools of Chinese historiography agree, and this is the clear awareness of the evaluative character of their trade. The historian of every school was an arbiter who, by passing judgment assessed the value of, and gave meaning to, events.[1] This consciously evaluative character of Chinese historiography demanded self-reliance and courage on the part of the historian, who was not only the keeper of documents and the recorder of events; his assessments assumed normative status like the sentences of a judge.

Theoretically autonomous, the historian was, however, dependent for the substantiation of his judgment upon the traditional system and the traditional hierarchy of values as accepted or ordained at a given period of time. The data of intellectual history were also considered binding on the historian. These data formed the code by which the judgment of the historian was determined. Thus the philosopher's position was further reinforced; he defined the dominant values which in turn were eternalised by the historian.

When Chinese Marxist historians followed the mandate of Mao to reassess Chinese history in Marxian terms, intellectual history presented them with an especially formidable task. Specifically the phenomenon of Neo-Confucianism[2] posed a problem, for its system of values had been accepted, and made to be accepted by imperial decree for centuries, and were reflected not only in all recent history but also in commonly assumed social and personal attitudes. What was involved in this reassessment was not just bringing about a new Marxian understanding of the data of history, but breaking down the acceptance of values and

---

[1] See H. Wilhelm, " Der Sinn des Geschehens nach dem Buch der Wandlungen," *Eranos Jahrbuch* 26, Zürich 1958, pp. 351–386, particularly p. 381 *et seq.*, and " Chinesische Historiographie," *Gesellschaft und Staat in China*, Hamburg 1960, pp. 137–142.

[2] The term " Neo-Confucianism " has been used in a variety of interpretations in recent literature. For Carsun Chang, for instance, everything that happened in the intellectual field beginning with Han Yü, down to and including Ch'en Tu-hsiu, is Neo-Confucianism. In this paper I shall place particular emphasis on the Ch'eng-Chu school which, if not philosophically the most interesting, is politically the most important trend of thought during the later centuries of Imperial China.

the dominance of attitudes which were still very much alive in 1942 and in 1949. Re-evaluation of history had to go hand in hand with re-education.

According to Marxist theory, breaking the power of these values should not have been a difficult task. Once specific contradictions in material life were removed and a specific form of social existence was modified, social consciousness should have changed automatically and values connected with this special stage of social consciousness should have gradually faded away. The Chinese Communists were to learn to their chagrin that this was not always the case.

A typology of the values which Marxian reassessors had to face in this field might contribute toward an understanding of their strategy in coping with this task. There are, I believe, certain values reflected in what Marxists call "social consciousness" which are without doubt rather closely linked to the prevailing social hierarchy. These could be called canonical values. A general, if enforced, acceptance of this type of values is expressed in the distribution of status and authority in a given society. Attitudes and symbols connected with the position of the emperor, with the ladder of success in officialdom, with the distinctions of age and sex, rest on such canonical values and may be used as a rather close indication of the prevalent social structure. Embodied in " virtues " and " rites," their prescriptions are operable in a specific social context only and they change their applicability with a change of this context. The term " loyalty," to take an example, had a different content in pre-imperial (" feudal ") and in imperial times during the periods of long lasting and of fast changing dynasties. The rituals of mourning were adapted to changing social attitudes and, just like other rituals, were even used to induce desired change. And certain virtues connected with the exercise of filial piety reflect directly the actual position of the father and other relatives in society.

Not all values do, however, exhibit this degree of social contingency. A second type, which I would like to call archetypal values, seems to be independent of the prevailing social context but derived from basic, generally human, relationships and from fundamental, generally human, urges and needs. They grow out of those strata of the human psyche which as a rule remain unconscious, and they are expressed in primordial symbols reflected in mythology and legendary, as well as legend-arised history, in religious usages and in poetic imagery. Values of this type have, of course, a cogency much beyond that of strictly canonical values; they will be found operative alongside with, and at times in opposition to, the social realities of the day. At times, in well constructed societies,[3] they will work in consonance with, and add conviction and staying power to, canonical values. This seems to have been the case in several periods of Chinese history. They retain their force, however, even under changing societal circumstances. When, for instance, the father in society is stripped of his dominant position, a filial son will dispense with the expressions of the virtue of filial piety, he will no longer consider it his duty " to scratch reverently his father's back." However, the father-son relationship still remains as an archetypal value and, directly or obversely, moulds the son's attitude toward his father. In extreme cases of contrariety between these two value systems, a schism will result, affecting not only the personality structure of the individual but also throwing culture into a crisis.[4]

A third type of values seems to be of more recent vintage. It seems to have gained general currency only when, during periods of enlightenment, the human mind achieved another step in its self-realisation. This type, which I would like to call utopian values, is expressed in seemingly abstract notions, not or not yet realised in society. Here belong the values of liberty, equality, democracy and the like, but also Science with a capital S and Industrialisation. Their future-directedness gives these values a specific emotional force which appears as cogent as those of the other two types.[5] They are embodied in " causes " for which men have fought and died. Their apparent rationality supplies them with a degree of unassailability which the other two types of values do not share. Not even the architects of a Communist society, can dare to come out openly against freedom or against democracy even though both these notions have no place in a Communist organisation. They may assail religion as an opiate for the people; but they have to profess the principle of freedom of religious belief.

II

In this configuration of problems, the task of dealing with traditional values does not rest solely on the shoulders of the intellectual historian. We are not concerned here with the emergence and the cultivation of new values. The special machinery established for their propagation is well known, the degree of its efficiency would have to be discussed in a different context. But re-evaluation of the tradition also needs social engineers as well as scientists, and, in particular, it needs special techniques of value elimination and a special apparatus to enforce these techniques. Much has been written about these techniques and their

3 See Erich Neumann, *The Origins and History of Consciousness* (New York: Pantheon Books, 1954), pp. 360–381. " Balanced " societies is Neumann's term.
4 *Ibid.* pp. 381–394.
5 See Ira Progoff, " The Dynamics of Hope and the Image of Utopia," *Eranos Jahrbuch* 1963, Zürich 1964, pp. 89–145.

enforcement, and they do not have to concern us here. We might, however, want to keep in mind that the decision that a certain value should
go necessarily leads to an application of these techniques, sometimes on
a nationwide scale. The decision as such is arrived at under the pressure
of a frightening responsibility not only intellectual but to an even greater
degree, social. The decision is not only, and as a rule not even primarily,
for the intellectual historian to take, but to the extent that he participates
in this process, the responsibility is also his. He always works in the
knowledge that the intellectual processes of analysis and reassessment
will reach far beyond the strictly intellectual scene; he forges the sword
that is then applied in battle, possibly against himself.

This pressure might, I believe, help to explain a certain diffidence
and caution among Communist China's intellectual historians. There
is a tendency to work with only a very limited armoury of intellectual
tools and to apply concepts which one can be reasonably certain are,
and will in the foreseeable future, be acknowledged and accepted elements of the political premises under which he labours. This gives
the writings of the present-day intellectual historians in China, even of
those who are known to be in complete mastery of their fields, the
appearance of a rather low level of sophistication, to say the least.
Problems of the Chinese intellectual tradition are again and again
garbed in the antitheses, materialism *versus* idealism and dialectics
versus metaphysics, so that on just about every page the reader gets the
eerie feeling of *déjà vu*.

Intellectual adventurousness has not, however, entirely disappeared
among present-day Chinese historians. In addition to caution, we find
an almost uncanny sense of the politically possible. Whenever the
political moment seems to permit, a voice or even a concert of voices
clamours for the extension of intellectual boundaries and for the
inclusion of cherished, or secretly cherished, traditional values. The
experience of the transiency of these moments which all intellectual
historians in China must share by now had not, by 1963 at least,
dampened this spirit of daring for which eventually, of course, the price
must be paid.

III

Apart from the political ambience in which they are working, the task
of the Chinese intellectual historians has been circumscribed by what
have come to be considered as the Marxist classics. Even without strictly
defining the role of the historian, dialectical materialism, as a determi-
nant concept of Marxist historiography, has implicitly set the stage for
their performance. Intellectual historians have to keep pace with what
are considered to be the laws of development of society. The historian

and particularly the intellectual historian cannot remain within the comparatively safe precincts of what has been ridiculed as " factology "; his task is to appraise and to pass judgment. In other words history under the Communists is at least as evaluative as classical Chinese historiography always has been. This puts the historian straight into the battle of values where he has to conduct himself with the same degree of responsibility, if not with the same degree of power, as the politician.

Soviet Marxist tradition has not supplied any specific criteria for this evaluative task. There is, to be sure, the general schema of historical development, whose stark simplicity, particularly after the elimination of the concept of " Oriental society " [6] gave little incentive to sophisticated thinking. Nor could Soviet sinology be tapped for specific guidelines for " bourgeois " sinologists with their " bourgeois " working methods continued to be respected. Even today such scholars as Alekseyev are still in high repute, and whatever practical services Alekseyev rendered to his Chinese colleagues, they do not measure up to his achievements in traditional sinology. The short-lived Soviet Institute of Sinology, established in 1958, and its four issues of the journal *Sovetskoe Kitaevedenie* could not have been very inspirational to Chinese scholars since they appear to have been rather closely controlled by Peking.[7]

This situation is not surprising, for the position of the Soviet intellectual historian was entirely different from that of his Chinese colleague. He did not have to cope with the intellectual tradition and values of his own country. Whatever he " appraised " was a foreign import and he could do so coolly and remain outside of the field of gravity of traditional values. For the Chinese, however, the intellectual tradition was almost identical with his cultural heritage. Once the initial urge to throw away the past was overcome, he faced names, situations, systems and concepts which for him weighed heavily one way or the other. He had to face squarely the battle of values which his Soviet colleague could easily escape. The emotion-laden decision of the Chinese not to participate in any international conference even in Moscow dealing with the Chinese tradition was certainly not only, and probably not even mainly, a reflection of the current stage of Soviet-Chinese relationships but rather of the awareness of the specific position of the Chinese historian, particularly the intellectual historian, when confronting the values of his own cultural tradition.

[6] K. A. Wittfogel, *Oriental Despotism* (New Haven: Yale University Press, 1963), p. 402 *et seq.*

[7] Mark Mancall, " Soviet Historians and the Sino-Soviet Alliance," John Keep and Liliana Brisby, ed., *Contemporary History in the Soviet Mirror* (New York: Praeger, 1964), pp. 181–184.

IV

For a closer understanding of the Chinese intellectual historians' reappraisal of Neo-Confucianism, there might be some merit in tracing, at least in outline, the zigs and zags which various political trends and attitudes imposed on their activities. A tug of war has taken place between two groups: those who worked entirely along doctrinaire lines attempting as best they could to apply to the Chinese intellectual tradition the meagre assortment of concepts provided by Marxist and Soviet theory, and those who wanted to retain room for traditional values. The latter are found, when they are found at all, mainly in the Institute of Philosophy of the Academy of Sciences where stalwarts such as Feng Yu-lan and Ho Lin had succeeded in establishing a home base. There they sometimes got a hearing, even in the face of scathing attacks from outside, particularly from the Institute of History where Hou Wai-lu and his praetorian guards were entrenched. For short periods, the more adventurous spirit of the Institute of Philosophy spilled over and was taken up by other centres in the country. At other times, such as the present, strictest orthodoxy dominated the Institute of Philosophy as well.

It might be significant that the time when serious discussions on the appraisal of the intellectual heritage gradually gathered momentum coincided with the time of the anti-Hu Shih campaign. Thus the problems were taken up not for their intrinsic interest only, but in order to combat Hu Shih's position. This combative necessity forced the discussants into points of view that they might not otherwise have assumed, and these forced assumptions limited their future freedom of action. The attempt to show that Hu Shih's evaluations of Chinese intellectual history were part of the conspiracy between Chiang Kai-shek and capitalist imperialism forced upon them a dilemma which they could not then satisfactorily solve and which has ever since determined their course of action. Hu Shih's strongly anti-Neo-Confucianist position, for instance, had to be shown to be nefarious even though Marxist ideology would have demanded the same position, if for slightly different reasons. A kind of tortured reasoning ensued in which arguments *ad hominem* had to replace sound thinking. Feng Yu-lan has the following to say in this context [8]: "As an intellectual of the comprador class, Hu Shih consistently served imperialism . . . his thought supports imperialism and also supports feudalism . . . Hu Shih's so-called objective history . . . is a deceitful device of the capitalist historian to dress up his class-mindedness. History is of the past, but historians are people belonging to a

[8] " Che-hsueh shih yü cheng-chih," *Che-hsueh Yen-chiu* (hereafter *CHYC*) (*Philosophical Research*), January 1955, pp. 70–83.

distinct, present-day class . . . Historians of philosophy of the capitalist class serve the purposes of the capitalist class. When we, who are
working in the field of philosophy, want to reveal historical truth we
have to serve the purposes of the working class. What is good for the
working class coincides with the progressive trend in history, that is why
the working class is not afraid of having historical truth revealed. Only
by revealing historical truth can we serve the purposes of the working
class." [9]

But then in 1956 a new theme was inserted into the discussion, started
by an article by Yang Yung-chih in the year's first issue of the *Che-hsueh
Yen-chiu*.[10] This article is an emotional plea for the loving preservation
of the cultural heritage of the fatherland (*tsu-kuo*). Covered by quotes
from Lenin and from Mao's *New Democracy*, Yang maintains that it
is the duty of Marxism to preserve the cultural heritage. Everything that
is valuable in thought and culture should be absorbed and transformed.
Only petty bourgeois revolutionaries, he claims, do not recognise the
importance of this task. Recent Soviet attitudes toward their own past
are also adduced as examples. To be sure, the cultural heritage should
be cleansed of all trends which Marxism opposes. Of these he finds only
two in the Chinese tradition: an attitude of nihilism and cosmopoli-
tanism, and an attitude of reactionism and chauvinism (*kuo-ts'ui*). It
becomes abundantly clear that what Yang wants to have lovingly preserved is not just the record of the past but its guiding values.

The discussions of this proposition soon gained impetus. Labels
were attached freely to personalities and concepts of the past which
would make them Marxist and therefore acceptable. One incident might
deserve special mention. In December 1956 Yang Hsing-shun delivered
a lecture in Russian, to a group of Soviet specialists, on the materialist
tradition in Chinese philosophy.[11] With pride and self-assurance, representatives of the Big Brother country were informed that the Chinese
past was much more acceptable than their own. Even the Yin people
of 1400–1100 B.C. were claimed to be materialist, witness their calen-
derological knowledge based on the yin-yang concept. Chou times
produced great astronomers and mathematicians. Technological knowledge, particularly in metallurgy and agronomy, is attested to in the
Book of Songs and then again in the *Kuo-yü* and the *Tso-chuan*. The
ch'i concept and the concept of the five elements are materialistic. From
early writings the *Tao-te-ching* is materialistic and so is Yang Chu, and
Hsun-tzu is the greatest materialist philosopher of ancient times.

---

9 For similar arguments see Chang Heng-shou, *CHYC*, February 1956, pp. 18–40; many
other contributions in *CHYC* and other journals of the time.
10 *Ibid.* January 1956, pp. 52–70.
11 Chinese translation in *CHYC*, April 1956, pp. 84–101.

Materialists of Han times include Ssu-ma Ch'ien, Yang Hsiung, Huan T'an, and above all, Wang Ch'ung. In the Six Dynasties period we have Fan Chen, in T'ang, Lü Ts'ai, and Han Yü and his disciples also argue from a materialist foundation. Neo-Confucianism is said to be a struggle between idealist and materialist trends, Chang Ts'ai holding up the materialist end. In Ming there is Li Chih and all the great thinkers of early Ch'ing such as Huang Tsung-hsi, Wang Fu-chih and Ku Yen-wu are anti-feudal and stress empirical knowledge. Then comes Tai Chen and the most progressive Kung Ting-an. The crowning achievement in late Ch'ing is then represented by T'an Ssu-t'ung out of whose leftist trend and under the banner of materialism, Sun Yat Sen's party emerged.

These discussions were summarised and scrutinised in a symposium on the object and scope of the history of Chinese philosophy and on the preservation of the cultural heritage held by the Department of Philosophy of Peking University in January 1957.[12] A rather free-wheeling exchange seems to have ensued at this time between the preservationists and the doctrinaires. Among the first group, Ho Lin seems to have been particularly persuasive. Feng Yu-lan spoke up strongly and Wang I even went so far as to propose not to treat Chinese philosophy with methods derived from reinterpretation of Western philosophy but to concentrate on special points and concepts of the Chinese intellectual heritage. The dogmatic use of terms like materialism and idealism was attacked and their value as determinants of good and bad was questioned by Ho Lin, Ch'en Hsin-chai and Chang Heng-shou. The counter-attack was not slow in coming from the doctrinaires, among them Kuan Feng, Cheng Shih-ying, T'ang Yueh, and Chang Tai-nien. But they do not seem to have won the day, at least not yet at that time, for the yearning for the preservation of the heritage seems to have been too general. Again it is abundantly clear that what was to be preserved was not just the reinterpreted record but the values contained in the record.

It did not take long, however, for this discussion to be cut short. Soon after this symposium, the charge of revisionism was hurled against the preservationists [13] and nothing was heard of the preservation of traditional values for several years. At this time the Academy journal opened its pages to "mass philosophy" or "the philosophy of workers and peasants."

It was not until the widespread hunger after the collapse of the "Great Leap Forward" had induced the régime to relax ideological

---

12 See *Pei-ching Ta-hsueh Hsueh-pao, Jen-wen K'o-hsueh* (Science section of Peking University Journal), February 1957, pp. 145–148; *CHYC*, January 1957, p. 135.
13 Sun Ting-kuo, *CHYC*, April 1957, pp. 1–8; Wu Chuan-ch'i, *ibid.* June 1957, pp. 18–37.

reins somewhat, that preservationism got another hearing. Then a profusion of propositions and discussions poured forth from some of the major centres first focusing on specific clusters of problems but soon involving the whole country in an attempt to redefine the intellectual historian's task. The attempted re-establishment of Confucius was the principal problem originating the controversy.[14] It was widely discussed in Canton, Wuhan, and far up north in Heilungchiang,[15] and in November 1962 a nation-wide symposium was organised by the Historical Society of Shantung and the Historical Institute of Shantung province with over 160 philosophers and historians from sixteen provinces attending.[16] Another lively discussion was aroused by the attempted re-establishment of the *Book of Changes*, proceeding mainly from Li Ching-fang's writings.[17] A host of other problems was pursued also, among them the question of the nature of early Taoism (Lao-tzu and Chuang-tzu) in the course of which discussions even the Yin-fu-ching was proclaimed materialist.[18] The strategy of the preservationists varied. Some resorted to the simple device of attaching acceptable Marxist labels to those parts of the heritage which they wanted to see preserved. Ho Lin, quoting heavily from Hegel, Lenin and Mao, came forward with another bold attempt to relativise the concept of materialism.[19] Feng Yu-lan was among those who attempted to ascribe class-transcending value to certain parts of the cultural heritage, but the most heated controversy on this point was aroused by Liu Chieh and his endeavour to salvage Confucianist virtues, particularly jen.[20] The counter-attack of doctrinaires was vivid and sharp but the impression is that at times they were driven to the defensive and even into certain concessions.

When, recently, the régime had abated the problem of feeding its people, and when, in consequence, the ideological reins were tightened again,[21] discussions came to a sudden end. Chang Tung-feng was chosen as the executioner. In the first 1964 issue of the *Che-hsueh Yen-chiu* [22] he summarised the entire discussion in an article entitled, " On the Methodology of the History of Philosophy and the Question of Preservation of Ethics." He calls a halt to the " beatification " of Confucius and

[14] See Joseph P. Levenson, " The Place of Confucius in Communist China," *The China Quarterly*, No. 12, Oct.–Dec. 1962.

[15] Report on the Heilungchiang discussions in *CHYC*, April 1963, p. 83.

[16] See report in *CHYC*, January 1963, pp. 54–57.

[17] Li Ching-fang, *Chou-I Che-hsueh chi ch'i Pien-cheng-fa Yin-su (Elements of the Philosophy of the Book of Changes and Its Dialectics)* (Shantung: Jen-min Ch'u-pan She) (1961), Vol. 1; (1962), Vol. 2.

[18] Wang Ming, *CHYC*, May 1962, pp. 59–68.   [19] *CHYC*, January 1961, pp. 60–68.

[20] See discussions in *Hsueh-shu Yen-chiu*, Canton at this period.

[21] George T. Yü, " The 1962 and 1963 Sessions of the National People's Congress of Communist China," *Asian Survey*, Vol. 4, No. 8, August 1964, pp. 981–990.

[22] Chang Tung-feng, *CHYC*, pp. 61–85.

scrutinises and condemns the preservationists of different hues one by one. He ends declaring that controversy is admissible but, as Mao said, the correct point of view must prevail. The message of Chang's statement was reinforced by articles in other leading journals, among them one by Feng Chih in *Wen-i-pao* [23] and another by Hou Wai-lu in the *Li-shih Yen-chiu*.[24]

V

It was not accidental that in the intermittent battle over the task and scope of intellectual history, the issue of Neo-Confucianism was almost entirely by-passed. To begin with, the body of thought left by the Neo-Confucianists is very extensive and extremely complex. It had resisted systematisation and categorisation under any set of concepts including those proposed by this school itself. Almost all of its thinking and most of its writing is of the aphoristic type and the relationship between its different sections is not necessarily consistent. Also, Neo-Confucianism had already become increasingly unpopular by late imperial times, and due, among other things, to Hu Shih's rejection of it, had fallen out of grace in early republican times to such an extent that the value of including Neo-Confucianism in a university course on the history of Chinese philosophy was questioned.

The recent opponents of Neo-Confucianism attacked not only its intrinsic concepts and values but its use (or abuse) by imperial and post-imperial ideologists. Hou Wai-lu states this problem rather succinctly with reference to Chu Hsi. Chu Hsi's teachings, he says, eventually became the imperially-sanctioned academic philosophy, and thus the Tao Hsueh (traditionalist school) became established. During the last half-millennium, temporal rulers from K'ang-hsi to Tseng Kuo-fan to Chiang Kai-shek used the religious clericalism of Chu Hsi to add bright lacquer to their positions. It must be stressed also, Hou continues, that later conservatives and reactionaries such as Yeh Te-hui, Chang Chün-mai, Feng Yu-lan and Ho Lin all came out of Chu Hsi's school. After the liberation, attempts were even made to mix up Chu Hsi's doctrine with Marxism. And as for Western capitalist sinologues, they have attempted at recent philosophical congresses to construct a modern philosophy composed of Western capitalist philosophy and Chinese feudalist traditionalism.[25] Thus, Hou says, we must not only discuss the

---

[23] Feng Chih, *Wen-i-pao*, April 1964, pp. 14–17. " The foremost duty of the workers in the field of literature is to use historical materialism to explain the phenomena of history and to use the critical spirit of Marxism-Leninism when dealing with Chinese or foreign classical heritage."

[24] Hou Wai-lu, *Li-shih Yen-chiu (Historical Research)*, January 1964, pp. 15–30. " We must firmly grasp the class character of philosophy as the most general principle of Marxism-Leninism."

[25] This, I assume, refers to the East-West philosophy meetings, organised by C. A. Moore.

Chu Hsi of the twelfth century, but we have also to deal with the recent image of Chu Hsi, the Aristotelised Chu Hsi, the Hegalised Chu Hsi and the Chu Hsi adapted to Marxism.[26]

Only two other Neo-Confucianists have been singled out for special treatment and discussion. One is Chang Tsai [27] who, in contradistinction to other Neo-Confucianists, gradually developed into the fair-haired materialist of the school and was almost generally recognised as such. The other is Chou Tun-i, whom Chang Tai-nien also claimed as a materialist misrepresented as an idealist by the Ch'engs and Chu Hsi.[28] In a later report [29] this misrepresentation was said to have been spread further by a conspiracy of capitalist sinologues such as de Harlez, Zenker, Hackmann and Forke.[30] The proposition concerning Chou on the other hand has not found widespread acceptance.

For the rest of the reappraisal of Neo-Confucianism we must take our clues from general surveys and hand-books. Hou Wai-lu's *Chung kuo Ssu-hsiang T'ung-shih* [31] can be taken as representative of the ortho-dox position. Hou almost never strays from the correct point of view and never yields to the lure of tradition. His book is not only the most extensive but presumably also the most authoritative coverage. It super-sedes earlier treatments such as Lü Chen-yü's *Chung-kuo Cheng-chih Ssu-hsiang Shih* [32] (*History of Chinese Political Thought*), and is found simplified and popularised in shorter treatments like Yang Yung-kuo's *Chien-ming Chunk-kuo Ssu-hsiang Shih.*[33] *The Philosophy Reader* com-piled (anonymously) by the Institute of Philosophy of the Academy of

---

[26] Summarised from pp. 596–598 of Vol. 41 of Hou's *Chung-kuo Ssu-hsiang T'ung-shih,* 1962 ed.

[27] For example, Chang Tai-nien, *CHYC,* January 1955, pp. 110–130 and discussion; *ibid.* March 1955, pp. 142–148; April 1956, pp. 136–143. See also *CHYC,* February 1957, pp. 54–69; and *Pei-ching Ta-hsueh Hsueh-pao, Jen-wen K'o-hsueh,* March 1957, pp. 57–68.

[28] *CHYC,* February 1957, pp. 62–63.

[29] See review of V. A. Krivstov's article on the *T'ai-chi-t'u shuo* in *CHYC,* March 1959, p. 41. Chang Tsai and Chou Tun-i are already claimed as materialists in the *History of Philosophy* compiled by the Soviet Academy of Sciences (1957); a report on the treatment of Chinese philosophy in this book asserts that the Soviet scholars followed closely the evaluations of their Chinese colleagues such as Hou Wai-lu, Kuo Mo-jo, Feng Yu-lan, etc. See *CHYC,* April 1957, pp. 110–116.

[30] In another place the conspirators are Legge, Abel Remusat, Forke and Wilhelm.

[31] Hou Wai-lu, *Chung-kuo Ssu-hsiang T'ung-shih. (A General History of Chinese Thought)* (Peking: San-lien, 1962). Neo-Confucianism is treated in two parts of Vol. 4. In the following I assume a rather polemical attitude towards Hou's interpretative methods and results. This, however, should not becloud the fact that Hou's com-pendium is of great value, that the factual evidence presented is rich and on the whole judiciously chosen, and particularly that he does not try, as many others do, to shun issues even if they are inconvenient.

[32] Lü Chen-yü, *Chung-kuo Cheng-chih Ssu-hsiang Shih (A History of Chinese Thought)* (Pekin: Jen-min Ch'u-pan She, 1962). Originally written in 1937, then frequently revised.

[33] Yang Yung-kuo, *Chien-ming Chung-kuo Ssu-hsiang Shih (A Short History of Chinese Thought)* (Peking: Hsin Hua, 1962).

Sciences [84] avoids contradicting Hou's position even in cases where it obviously disagrees.

Boiled down to its essentials, the basic task of the reappraisal of Neo-Confucianism was to show that the social contradictions of the time of its development were reflected in an intellectual struggle. Specifically it had to be shown that the political struggle of Ssu-ma Kuang's old party and Wang An-shih's new party was expressed in and reflected a struggle of materialist and idealist trends. Expressed in class terms, Wang represented the small clans, specifically the oncoming petty capitalists, while the old party represented the great clans (hao-tsu). Wang was of course the foremost representative of materialism. When Wang's political fortunes waned, the social trends which he represented persisted. Later when the Sung was intellectually dominated by Neo-Confucianism, this struggle was expressed not only in the struggle between the old and the new party but also within Neo-Confucianism. Hou takes his clues for an interpretation of the philosophy of the earlier period from the actual or assumed political positions of the philosophers concerned. These clues are at times rather flimsy. The fact that a given philosopher lived for a period of time in Loyang was frequently sufficient to label him since Loyang had been the power centre of the aristocracy since Tang times and the conservatives established something like a government in exile there after their fall from power. Personal associations and exchange of poetry are taken as important clues if no more tangible political involvement can be shown. Differences within the old party, such as those between the Loyang faction, the Shensi faction and Szechuan faction, are judged to be predominantly personal power struggles; the special position of the Shensi school is, however, singled out as also ideologically significant.[35]

Since philosophy is a reflection of politics, the political protagonist Ssu-ma Kuang had to be treated also as the head of the Neo-Confucianist school.[36] This gets Hou into difficulties immediately, for Ssu-ma differs fundamentally from all other Neo-Confucianists in the choice of his hero, Yang Hsiung, and his villain, Meng-tzu, and even Hou acknowledges materialist elements in Yang Hsiung and the idealist nature of Meng-tzu. Hou tries to solve this problem by claiming that Ssu-ma, the clearest case of a reactionary, selected only Yang's idealist and religious elements. And while occasional remarks of Ssu-ma lend themselves to a materialist interpretation, they are deceptive, for his basic

---

[84] Chung-kuo Che-hsueh-shih Tzu-liao Hsuan-chi (Reader in the History of Chinese Philosophy) (Peking: Chung Hua, 1962). Neo-Confucianism is covered in the fourth volume.

[35] Hou, pp. 497–509. The Academy Reader follows this guilt-by-association pattern rather closely.

[36] The absence of Ou-yang Hsiu is puzzling. The Academy Reader does not deal with Ssu-ma Kuang.

attitude is idealistic, particularly his understanding of Heaven, a concept with which he justifies feudal inequities.[37]

Hou's difficulties are clear from the start. A statesman has to be made into a philosopher. An admirer of Yang Hsiung and a doubter of Meng-tzu has to be made into an abysmal idealist. And even then, there remain unresolved dregs which can be explained away only as deceitful devices.

Hou's treatment of Shao Yung is just the reverse. Here we do not have a reactionary politician who has to be shown to be a reactionary philosopher, but a philosopher with a reactionary historical philosophy who has to be shown to be involved in reactionary politics. In the case of Shao this is rather difficult because he never played a major political role, and Hou seems to be rather uneasy in dealing with him. There is so much neatness and logic in Shao's system. He is also the one who, in his poetry, talked the language of the people. All this does not fail to impress Hou, to his own annoyance. First Hou uses the guilt-by-association argument. Then he hits out at Shao as the great deceiver who, with clever devices, manipulates seemingly materialist concepts and accommodates contemporary scientific advances to strengthen his idealist position and thus makes science " the slave of religion." Hou makes a real contribution when he traces Shao's concepts back to the tradition of the apocrypha which was particularly strong in northern Sung times. But Hou is less successful when he tries to show that Shao's li (principle) concept is identical with heavenly fate (t'ien-ming). For Shao the li can be grasped only in things (wu) and not in the self (wo), nor in Heaven. Shao's concept of contemplation of things (kuan-wu) does not mean, as Hou wants it to, an exploration of ordained fate but has rather mystical qualities.[38]

The *Academy Reader* on the whole seems to be much more relaxed in its treatment of Shao. Here, too, Shao is traced back to the *I-Ching* tradition of Han, particularly to Chiao Kan and Ching Fang and then to the *Ts'an-t'ung-ch'i* and Taoist magic. Shao's doctrines of images and numbers, hsiang-shu hsueh (symbolic numerology), is here explained as the method of transforming a subjectively devised logical system into an absolute truth. The *Reader* also points out that Shao calls himself An-lo hsien-sheng (Mr. Optimist), but that his optimism is only superficial, and actually he suffered intensely under the conditions of his time.

Neither of these treatments does justice to some of the special qualities of Shao, such as his intellectual daring which occasionally bordered on the heterodox and his clearly idealist philosophy which

[37] Hou, pp. 511–521.
[38] *Ibid.* pp. 521–535.

makes him to a certain extent a predecessor of Ch'eng Hao and certainly of Lu Hsiang-shan.

The problem of Chou-Tun-i, whom later Neo-Confucianists held in such high esteem, is solved by Hou rather simply by debunking him. Hou claims he was neither an important politician nor a great philosopher. His philosophy is said to be metaphysical and feudalistic, cribbed from the apocrypha, particularly the *I* apocrypha, and influenced by Ch'an Buddhism. Hou has nothing but ridicule for the attempts to make a materialist out of Chou.[39]

The *Academy Reader* gives Chou a little more of his due. More is made of his "strong relations to the old party" and of his position as the originator of the mainstream of Neo-Confucianism. In its interpretation the *Reader* does, however, more or less agree with Hou. Chou is made out to be a strict idealist who was the one to enrich traditional Confucianism with Taoist, particularly magic, ideas. The influence of the *Book of Changes* is considered to be only superficial; the mysticism of the *Tao-te-ching* is seen as a much stronger influence. Also Buddhist influences are pointed out particularly in Chou's concept of desirelessness (wu-yu). His ch'eng (sincerity) concept is made to stand for his acceptance of existing conditions. Thus all his philosophy is devised to serve the authoritarianism of the feudal order of his time.

Except for Chu Hsi himself, Hou devotes his most extensive section to Chang Tsai and the Shensi group.[40] Here he discovers a group of philosophers who did not enjoy the support of the great clans as the Loyang people did. Was not the opposition to Wang An-shih of Chang and his group (except Chang's brother) only weak? Was not Chang the only one who was spared when in Hsi-ning times Wang beat the old party completely off the political stage? Was Chang not living in a border situation where the constant threat of the Hsi-hsia opened his eyes to the political realities of the day? And was not Chang's family much lower in official position than that of the Ch'engs and that of Shao Yung? All this could not fail to set him on the road toward materialism and anti-spiritualism and help him discard the fetters of Chanism and of the two Ch'engs.

Chang thus became the chosen antithesis in the dialectical process in which Neo-Confucianism had to be understood. Chang's concept, on which Hou and others concentrated to sustain this interpretation, is the ch'i concept. Chang does link his ch'i quite closely to material existence (wu); in fact, however, his difference from other Neo-Confucianists is one of degree only and, it appears to me at least, of minor degree. For Chang, ch'i is just as closely linked to the li (principle). He too conceives

---

[39] *Ibid.* pp. 535–544.
[40] *Ibid.* pp. 545–570.

of ch'i in dual state, that of dispersal and that of contraction, the latter leading to the world of existence, the former to the Great Void (t'ai-hsü). Hou has some difficulties explaining away the strongly Buddhist connotations of this term. He does so by declaring that in Chang's understanding it was a general term for the world of time and space.[41] The same is true for Chang's hsiang (image, symbol) concept, which Hou would have Chang understand as something like an attribute of ch'i. With respect to Chang's " two state " concept, which goes back to the *Analects* and to the philosophy of the *Book of Changes*, Hou draws consolation from the fact that the interaction of the two states is spontaneous and not purposive. Thus Hou states that Chang is opposed to idealism and clearly contains a dialectical element.

The application of all these interpretive concepts to Chang's thoughts without doubt seems forced. Now, to be sure, Hou is not the only one to use Western interpretive concepts to explain Chinese philosophy, and it seems unfair to accuse him alone of what appears to me as a methodological fallacy which he shares with so many others, even though Hou and his peers put this Procrustean method to a much more strictly political use. On the other hand, there is very little intellectual attraction in the alternative to beating Hou on his own grounds. It could be pointed out, however, that the cherished materialist Chang, with all his dialectical elements, maintained a political position which Hou, much to his disappointment, cannot possibly claim as progressive. Chang failed, Hou states, in his understanding of the relationship of mind and matter and thus he again fell into the trap of idealism.

The *Academy Reader* makes much more of the point that Chang maintained " the feudal ethics of optimism." Here, too, the by now orthodox doctrine that Chang is a materialist with dialectical elements is accepted, even though there are some minor variations in interpretation. Chang's ch'i concept is monistic, not dualistic, his t'ai-hsü concept is just the sky and not the world of time and space, etc. But of the elements of the contemporary situation which conditioned Chang's thinking, for example, the peasant rebellions, which threatened the dynastic house of northern Sung, are stressed, and thus, the *Reader* states, it is quite reasonable to find that Chang, who proceeds from a defence of the feudal order, would in his writings completely reveal the position of the ruling class.

At the opposite pole from the materialist Chang Tsai, Hou puts the two Ch'eng brothers. Strangely, not too much is made of the differences between the two in their political careers and intellectual attitudes. They are, as a team, the founders and representatives of the idealistic li school

---

[41] Hou takes this to be a restatement of a position taken by Liu Tsung-yuan, a man of whom he makes much as recently as in his 1964 article.

(school of principle) and the heads of the Loyang faction. Hou even opposes the thesis, supported by the *Academy Reader*, that Ch'eng Hao, with the functions he ascribed to the mind (hsin), can be considered a forerunner of the Lu-Wang school. Hou takes pains to show that the li concept of the Ch'engs has nothing to do with the Platonic idea, that it is, on the contrary, derived from the li concept of Hua-yen Buddhism, a derivation which, even if sustained, does not help at all toward an understanding of the li concept of the Ch'engs. He adds that it is spiritual rather than temporal and, of course, richly endowed with feudal connotations. This makes the Ch'engs representatives of religious clericalism (seng-lü chu-i), a term which here, as later on in the discussion of Chu Hsi, assumes great importance.

The *Academy Reader* makes more distinctions in its treatment of the two Ch'engs. There are minor differences in interpretation, even minor dialectical elements discovered here and there. The introspective trend and the inclination toward spiritual exercises as a method of self-cultivation and of transcendental experiences are more convincingly explained. The *Reader* agrees with Hou, not in its labels but in its conclusion.

Hou then proceeds to submit Chu Hsi's speculative (ssu-pien) philosophy to an extensive analysis,[42] characterising his thought as " objective idealism " as against the " subjective idealism " of the Lu-Wang school, a characterisation which has by now found just about universal acceptance. To begin with, Hou links the political fate of Chu and other members of the Tao-hsueh school to the defeatist faction at the courts of the Emperors Kao, Hsiao and Ning. This is not quite accurate, since Chu Hsi was a great admirer of Yüeh Fei. Hou focuses on Chu Hsi's li (principle) concept which, he says, contains the secret of Chu's speculative philosophy. This philosophy posits an absolute and universal principle which at the same time is manifested in every individual object (the famous fan example). Hou claims this is an application of the li-shih (universal-particular or abstract-concrete) formula of the Hua-yen Buddhists and justifies the characterisation of Chu Hsi's philosophy as religious clericalism. Chu represents for Hou the final form of the trend to syncretise the three religions observable since the Six dynasties. Li then is:

(1) Spiritual: in the individual it is identical with human nature, seated in the heart or mind (hsin); in the universe it is identical with endowed fate (t'ien-ming) and it is also identical with the Supreme Ultimate and thereby the origin of all things. Even though the relationship between the subjective mind (hsin) and the objective absolute li is never clarified, it is clearly spiritual in nature.

[42] Hou, pp. 595–647.

(2) Li is the highest abstraction without any concretisation (t'ai-chi and wu-chi).

(3) Li precedes matter and is the mystical origin of matter. The ch'i concept used here is *not* materialistic but something like an operational principle of yin and yang, produced by li. Chu Hsi's system is therefore not dualistic. Li in this sense is something like the logos of the Gnostics.

(4) Li is the supreme force which rules reality " like a man riding a horse." It is limitless in its power, not even limited by its own laws, something akin to the Holy Spirit of the Christians.

Chu Hsi's system is thus pure idealism and not, as had been recently maintained by Feng Yu-lan, an attempt to harmonise idealism and materialism.

Hou next examines Chu's relation to, and grasp of, the natural sciences. Capitalist scholars, Hou says, want to make Chu Hsi the greatest natural scientist and philosopher of nature in medieval China.[43] Also, all those who want to make a materialist out of Chu stress his scientific knowledge. Chu's ko-wu (investigation of things) concept, however, is not scientific in spirit or method, Hou states. Chu was not interested in the exploration of reality and the term " things " (wu) was used by him only as a stepping stone to gradual or sudden enlightenment concerning the highest principle. His speculative discourses pertain very little to things. He did borrow some contemporary data from the natural sciences to adorn his idealistic system. " Things " are an instrument manipulated by Chu not to explore reality but to gain distance from reality. His theories about the origin and the structure of the universe were not progressive in the context of his time, they were a patchwork of current common knowledge to which Chu added a mystical content in order to produce an image of the universe which would fit his religious clericalism.

In the universe thus explained by Chu the divinely established natural law is then linked to the feudalistic class structure and to authoritarian ethics. Hou declares that Chu could not disregard current demands for an equalisation of high and low status and a distribution of wealth, but with a sleight of hand, he postulates harmony as a universal principle for those involved in class struggle. As this principle is eternal, the feudalistic class structure also becomes unalterable. Class differentiation runs like a black thread through all of his doctrines. This is why it was not accidental that future rulers adopted this system.

The *Academy Reader* also calls Chu Hsi an objective idealist and adds that he is also referred to as a dualist. The points taken up by the

[43] This, I presume, refers to Needham.

Reader roughly coincide with those of Hou although they are at times differently argued. On the whole, the *Reader* does not seem to be able to discover anything objective or dualistic in Chu, even though this is not explicitly stated.

In conclusion it might be said that the conceptual and strictly terminological premises on which this reappraisal of Neo-Confucianism was conducted placed pitiable limitations on the debate and frequently diverted the debaters into positions unsupportable by the data of the case. Still, once this terminology is discarded, some of the results appear to be sound. There is no question, for instance, that a sober sociologist would agree that much within the Ch'eng-Chu school can be used to explain and has been used to sustain the structure of imperial China. On the other hand, and this seems to be serious, these premises have pushed the argument into a direction which a historian of philosophy or a sociologist cannot but reject. The artificial widening of the differences between Chang Tsai and the rest of the Ch'eng-Chu school into a dialectical counter-position is a case in point. The beclouding of the differences between the Ch'eng-Chu and Lu-Wang schools is another. These distortions are detrimental even to the Communists' own interests.

This last point might show that the arguments offered in reappraisal of Neo-Confucianism are more than just intellectual exercises undertaken in compliance with the political dictates of the time. It might show that the urge behind these arguments was not just intellectual, nor just political for that matter, but that basic value choices are involved here. A strange, if largely unconscious, fear of archetypal values and an eager, if undiscriminating, hope enticed by utopian values seem to have been the forces directing this choice. Goethe called fear and hope the greatest enemies of mankind.

9

Chinese Communist Attitudes Towards Buddhism in Chinese History

By KENNETH CH'EN

IN the journal *Hsien-tai Fo-hsueh* (*Modern Buddhism*), September 1959, there appeared a long article entitled " Lun Tsung-chiao Hsin-yang Tzu-yu " (" A Discussion Concerning Freedom of Religious Belief "), by Ya Han-chang, which was originally published in the official Communist ideological journal *Hung Ch'i* (*Red Flag*), 1959, No. 14. Appearing as it did in *Red Flag* it is justifiable to conclude that the views expressed in it represented the accepted Communist attitude toward religion. In this article, Ya wrote that the basic policy of the Chinese Communist Party and the People's Republic of China is to " recognise that everyone has the freedom to believe in a religion, and also that everyone has the freedom not to believe in a religion."

Primitive man, according to Ya, was awed and overwhelmed by the forces of nature around him; he felt there must be some supernatural deity behind such forces of nature that must be propitiated by prayers, charms, formulas or sacrifices. Such was the origin of religion and religious practices. Later, society advanced to the stage when opposing classes began to appear, the ruler and the ruled, the oppressor and the oppressed. The oppressed classes, in order to seek relief from such oppressions and sufferings, sought refuge in religion, which promised them the prospects of a better life in a future paradise. The ruling class actively encouraged such a tendency among the oppressed people, for belief in a future paradise would keep the people docile and satisfied with their earthly status. Religion thus became a tool which the oppressors used to maintain their acts of oppression.

With the victory of the proletariat in the Socialist revolution, the masses and the workers would naturally feel that all forms of oppression, even that under the banner of religion, should be abolished. However, even though a Socialist society may be against religion, it cannot control entirely the natural forces in the world that foster belief in a religion. A lengthy period is necessary to educate the masses to the truths discovered by science. Moreover, religion has existed for a long time in the history of man, and it still wields considerable influence over the thoughts and actions of people, even in a Socialist society. Consequently it cannot be wiped out at once. Force should not be applied, for fear that it may dislocate the lives of the people who still believe in religion. With the elevation of the cultural level of the masses, and with the increase in scientific knowledge, belief in religion will naturally decline and will in due time disappear altogether.

It is on these historical and cultural considerations, according to Ya, that the Chinese Communist Party and the People's Republic base their policy of freedom of religious belief. Such a policy, he contends, is entirely compatible with the goals of the Socialist revolution. Ever since the liberation of the entire country, the Government has established offices for the supervision of religions and religious affairs in the central government, in the provinces, and in the cities. All religious institutions, temples, monasteries and historical sites are protected by the government, and all legitimate and correct religious activities are permitted to carry on as usual.[1]

This statement furnishes us with the official attitude on the mainland toward Buddhism as well as the other religions which are permitted to function. It makes it clear that such religions are permitted to carry on only if they confine themselves to their legitimate religious functions under the supervision of the Government. It states that the people have freedom of religious belief, but it also makes clear that the converse is equally important, the freedom not to hold any religious belief. Chinese Communist commentators have interpreted this to include the freedom to engage in anti-religious propaganda.

In view of their critical attitude toward all religions in general, it would be interesting to find out the position taken by the Communist intellectuals on the mainland toward the development of Buddhism in China. Such an inquiry would reveal some good examples of how these writers apply their methods of dialectical materialism to the study of Buddhism. Here I would like to examine the attitudes of these writers under three headings: (1) factors responsible for the development of Buddhism in China during the Northern and Southern Dynasties; (2) the triumph of the Ch'an School during the mid-T'ang period; and (3) the Communist critique of the Vijñānavāda and Hua-yen Schools.

1. *Factors responsible for the development of Buddhism during the Northern and Southern Dynasties.* Non-Communist historians of Buddhism in China in their discussions of this problem are generally agreed that important roles were played by: the breakdown of the centralised Confucian state, thus permitting an alien ideology to enter China and claim the attention and allegiance of the Chinese; the political and social unrest of the period, which drove many people to take refuge in the relative tranquillity and safety of the Buddhist temples, either to find solace in Buddhist philosophy or to escape from heavy military and

---

[1] *Modern Buddhism*, September 1959.

labour burdens; the large numbers of non-Chinese peoples in north China, who were not bound to the indigenous religions and therefore found it easier to embrace a foreign religion, Buddhism, under the active encouragement of the non-Chinese rulers; the religious activities of a few outstanding Buddhist months in China, Kumārajīva, Tao-an, and Hui-yuan, who were able to win converts among the cultured literati; the favourable intellectual climate in China under the Southern Dynasties, which permitted considerable interchange of ideas between Chinese and Buddhist thinkers, as both groups were primarily concerned with similar problems of ontology; and finally, the attraction that Buddhism offered with its promise of universal salvation and the presence of Buddahood in every sentient being.

These factors are not given any prominence by the historians on the mainland now. Practically all of them contend that Buddhism flourished because it was sponsored and encouraged by the ruling class in order to prevent the oppressed classes from thinking too much about their miseries and sufferings. Fan Wen-lan, the veteran Communist historian, gave the following reasons for the acceptance of Buddhism. First, the ruling class, after being driven out of north China by the invading barbarians, migrated to the south. There on the banks of the Yangtze, they looked back longingly to their days of glory and splendour in Lo-yang, and in order to forget their sorrows and disappointments, they sought refuge in Buddhism. Secondly, the bodhisattva ideal in Mahāyāna Buddhism stressed endurance and tolerance to all kinds of sufferings, insults and oppression without any idea of revenge. Such an ideal was favoured by the ruling class, for it was valuable in keeping the oppressed people satisfied with their conditions.[2]

In a long article on Hua-yen thought, published in *Philosophical Studies*, No. 2, 1961, Jen Chi-yü presented his views on the development as follows: " During the period of the Northern and Southern Dynasties, the great and privileged families held powers and enjoyed political, economic and social privileges. To seek pretexts to justify their privileges, to stamp out popular resistance to their role and to propagate slavery and cultivate a docile character, the ruling class had recourse to Buddhism and assisted the religion considerably. At that time, many Buddhist works were translated into Chinese. The common goal of Buddhism was to propagate teachings concerning the blessings of the Buddha land in the future, so that people would not concern themselves too much with the sufferings of the present. People were taught that in the Western Paradise every earnest and pious

[2] Fan Wen-lan, *Chung-kuo T'ung-shih Chien-pien* (*Concise General History of China*), (Peking: 1949) pp. 231–232.

Buddhist was welcome. From this standpoint, we can see that during the Northern and Southern Dynasties, the great and privileged families subjected the people to all kinds of injustice and oppression. Religion was one of their spiritual weapons." [3] A viewpoint similar to that expressed by Fan and Jen is found in Shang Yüeh's *Chung-kuo Li-shih Kang-yao* (*Outlines of Chinese History*), (Peking: 1954), p. 108, where the author wrote that Buddhism held out the reward of a paradise for all the suffering and oppressed people in the world, and hence was encouraged by the ruling class, who wanted the people to forget about their earthly woes.

2. *Triumph of the Ch'an School during the mid-T'ang period.* Students of the Ch'an School in China usually explain the popularity of this aspect of Buddhism as being due to its being in consonance with the practical nature of the Chinese people, and its non-dependence on the accoutrements of Indian Buddhism. The Ch'an masters broke away from such Indian practices as recitation of the scriptures, worship of images and metaphysical speculations; instead they favoured a plain, direct, concrete and practical approach to enlightenment. The Buddha-nature is in all of us, and we need only to look directly into ourselves to find this Buddha-nature. The Ch'an masters also spoke in plain everyday language, easily understood by any common Chinese. Hence the growth and popularity of the Ch'an School. The appeal was predominantly religious.

The Communist writers on the mainland do not accept such an explanation. They explain the popularity entirely on social and economic considerations. According to them, the Ch'an School came into prominence at the end of the seventh and the beginning of the eighth centuries, when Empress Wu Tse-t'ien was usurping power and establishing her new dynasty. In order to build up a new aristocracy which would support and strengthen the new dynasty, Empress Wu began to bestow honours, ranks and titles to newly arisen clans and land-lords, so that they might serve as a counter-balance to the old great families who were supporters of the T'ang Imperial house. Such newly arisen clans and landlords were not connected with the traditional aristocracy but were commoners who had achieved success. This effort to raise one social class at the expense of another was accompanied by considerable struggle in which many of the old-established families were executed.

With the creation of the new aristocracy, a religion beneficial to its

---

[3] Jen Chi-yü, " Hua-yen-tsung Szu-hsiang Lüeh-lun " (" A Preliminary Discussion of Hua-yen Thought "), *Philosophical Studies*, No. 1, 1961. The entire article was translated into English and published in the *Union Research Service*, Vol. 24, Nos. 5 and 6, July 18 and 21, 1961. However, I have made independent translations of the portions I use in this article.

members was necessary. At this juncture, Empress Wu decided that the
Ch'an School was exactly what was needed for the times. Ch'an was
revolutionary in tendency, and this fitted in with the Empress's desire
to create a new society. Ch'an reflected the spirit of the common people.
Hui-neng (638-713) one of the important masters of the period, was a
commoner belonging to the lower ranks of society. The school did not
insist on intellectual efforts and prolonged periods of study of the
scriptures, which only the upper classes could afford; it insisted that the
Buddha-nature was in every one of us, regardless of station, position or
learning. It was, therefore, egalitarian and progressive. Even a
commoner could become a patriarch and preach the law. With Empress
Wu actively supporting the Ch'an School, the aristocracy which she
created followed her example. As the power and prestige of Empress
Wu and the newly created aristocracy increased, so did the power and
prestige of the Ch'an School. In this manner, the dominant position
of the school was assured.[4]

Before the Ch'an School attained prominence, it was progressive and
egalitarian, but as soon as it became the main school of Buddhism, the
Communist writers claim that it changed its nature. It now became
identified with the ruling class, and as supporters of the rulers, it ceased
to be egalitarian but became oppressive. This aspect of Ch'an is clearly
seen in the regulations drawn up by Huai-hai (720–814), which separated
the leaders from the common monks. With this division and separation,
the leaders or abbots were regarded with respect by the ruling class, they
worked hand in hand with the feudal lords to preserve order and keep
the masses suppressed. It was no wonder that the rules of Huai-hai
were compiled again under Imperial orders during the Mongol dynasty
in 1338 after the original list had been lost.[5]

3. *Communist critique of the Vijñānavāda and Hua-yen Schools.*
The Vijñānavāda School in China is based on the translations and
teachings of Paramartha (*c.* 500–570) and Hsüan-tsang (*c.* 600–664).
Its main tenet is that all external phenomena are but creations of the
mind. This idealistic nature of the school drew the fire of the Communist writers. They charge that the school is not only erroneous but
also reactionary. According to them, the Vijñānavāda teaches that all
surroundings and circumstances under which the individual lives are but
manifestations of his consciousness. The miseries that the individual
suffers and the pleasures that he enjoys are created by his consciousness,
and the individual can do nothing about them because they are the
results of his *karma*. If we follow such teachings, then we would have

---

[4] For these views, see Hou Wai-lu and others, *Chung-kuo Szu-hsiang T'ung-shih*
(*General History of Chinese Thought*) (Peking: 1959) IV, pp. 149–155, 262–263.
[5] *Ibid.* 275.

to conclude that the oppression of the peasants by the landlords is not the result of the evils of the feudal system, but only the concrete manifestation of their own inner consciousness. At the same time, one would also say that the persecution and oppression by the landlords are but the external phenomenal conditions created by their inner consciousness. Such a viewpoint is entirely erroneous and unacceptable,[6]

The Communist evaluation of the Hua-yen teachings is found in the article already mentioned, that by Jen Chi-yü in *Philosophical Studies*, No. 1, 1961. This is the most important full length article against Buddhism to appear on the mainland. That the article was published in *Philosophical Studies*, a journal devoted to articles of a scholarly nature, and not in *Modern Buddhism*, the official organ of the Chinese Buddhist Association, where the articles are friendly to Buddhism and are more popular in nature, is of some significance and points to the author's desire to reach the Communist intellectuals with his condemnation of the Hua-yen School. Since the brunt of the attack is directed against Hua-yen idealism, and since practically all the Mahāyāna schools in China are idealistic in their philosophy, one might conclude that the target of the author's criticisms is not just the Hua-yen School but Buddhism as a whole.

The first portion of the article is devoted to a review of the translations of the *sutra* and the writings of the Hua-yen masters in China. Then follows the discussion of Hua-yen tenets. In the last portion we come to the critical remarks of the author.

The main objectives of Hua-yen philosophy, according to Jen, are to attack materialism and to serve the interests of the ruling class. It ignores all the differentiations of the world, it aims to lead men away from earthly struggles, and to persuade men to take no interest in the events of the present but to seek only for spiritual comfort in the future. " The Hua-yen School employs all sorts of devious methods to prove that the present world is not real, that it is unknowable, illusory and relative. Its ultimate aim is to lead people away from the human world to the heavenly world."

" From the viewpoint of Hua-yen, the task of freeing man from the miseries of human life does not require a reformation of the present world; it is only necessary to change our viewpoint concerning the present world. When this is done, the problem is solved completely. . . . The main purpose of the ten profound mysteries is to propound the theory that if one were to adhere to the idealistic world view, and consider all things and events from the religious point of view, then everything would be perfect and everyone would be happy. . . ."

" Such a mass of confused ideas as these mentioned above is but an

6 *Ibid.* 228–229.

array of subjective views piled one above the other, repeatedly stressing that although the world appears to be very complicated, in reality it is very simple, for everything in the world is related to the Buddha-nature and embodies one aspect of the Buddha-nature or Thusness. It holds that all things in the world, good or bad, big or small, are indispensable in making up the world as a whole. In essence, the school is but using detailed verbiage and coarse descriptions to justify the conclusions required by the ruling class, namely, that whatever exists is reasonable. Such a set of theories was designed mainly to provide the theoretical foundations for the corrupt, reactionary, tyrannical, and exploiting system of the T'ang Dynasty. Very naturally the ruling authorities were delighted, and willingly encouraged the development of such a school." [7]

From this attack on Hua-yen idealism, the author proceeds to criticise the Hua-yen principles of interpenetration and mutual identification. " The theory of the four *dharma*-realms is also advanced to meet the demands of the ruling class. . . . The four *dharma*-realms are: (1) the realm of *shih* or things; (2) the realm of *li* or principle; (3) the realm in which principle and things are interfused without obstruction; (4) the realm in which all things are interfused without obstruction. . . ."

" But the Hua-yen denies there is an objective world outside of consciousness. From this fundamental premise, one must conclude that *li* is not the norm of events and things, and *shih* is not objective phenomena. Their so-called *shih* is but a mixed array of individual existences embodying the Buddha-nature or Thusness, and their *li* is but a principle which does not reflect the objective world and which is suspended in the void without foundation. . . ."

" In this theory of the *dharma*-realms, the basic viewpoint is identical with that of their philosophical system, namely, that all things in the world are but reflections or embodiments of the Buddha-nature or Thusness. Regardless of what the embodied individual existences and the general principles may be, they are in harmony, they are not contradictory, and they are mutually complementary to each other. The path leading to emancipation from misery pointed out by the Hua-yen admits and accepts the view that everything in the present is ordained by fate." [8]

On the basis of this analysis of Hua-yen tenets, Jen condemns the school for advocating that we look upon the inequalities and miseries of the world, such as class oppression, tyranny and exploitation, as mere creations of the mind and not connected with the existing social system, and that consequently we need not do anything about them. He also attacks the Hua-yen principles of interpenetration and mutual identification on the ground that they negate the differences between classes and seek to draw people's minds away from inequalities and iniquities. Such a view is contrary to the basic principle of Communist dialectics, the law of contradiction of things, and would permit the ruling class to carry out their tyrannical acts without protest and opposition. The Hua-yen error consists of its concern only with the mutual relations and connections between things, it does not dare concern itself with the contradiction and struggle between opposites. The inevitable consequence of the Hua-yen views is that all things in the world are in perfect harmony, regardless of whether they are right or wrong, good or evil, oppressor or oppressed, landlord or peasant, that all are indispensable links in the network of relations, and that this network is filled with co-operation and equilibrium. Such a world view is thoroughly unacceptable to one who holds to the truths of dialectics and materialism.

In spite of this critical attitude of the Communist intellectuals, some Buddhist activities are being carried on on the mainland in line with the proclaimed policy of freedom of religious belief. The position of the Government is that the followers of Buddhism will be left alone if they obey the official policy of the Government and abide by the pattern of co-existence, by which is meant that the Buddhist monks are not to carry on religious activities outside the Buddhist temples, and the Government is not to interfere with the religious activities within the temples.[9]

For the purpose of bringing together the Buddhist clergy and laymen into an organisation that can be supervised by the Government, the Chinese Buddhist Association was organised in 1953, " to unite all followers of Buddhism under the leadership of the People's Republic in order to demonstrate their love for the Fatherland and to protect world peace." The officers of the association claim that the organisation's chief activities consist of the following:

(1) To serve as a bridge between the followers of Buddhism and the Government;

(2) to train Buddhist personnel;

(3) to promote Buddhist cultural activities;

(4) to encourage Buddhist international co-operation.

Observers outside mainland China have pointed out that while these activities have undoubtedly been performed by the association, they do not constitute the real and essential reason for its existence. Instead, they contend that the fundamental reason for the existence of the

---

[9] In the *People's Daily* for July 21, 1959, appeared the following statement: " In the midst of the democratic revolution, the protection of the freedom of religious belief, the protection of temples and monasteries that abide by the law, and the protection of historical and cultural monuments, must be carried out thoroughly. At the same time, the temples and monasteries should oppose all counter-revolutionary movements, all feudalistic special powers, and all illegal deprivations."

organisation is that it serves as the agent of the Party for the control and supervision of Buddhism and Buddhist activities.

Besides these functions, the association also fulfils another role, this time in the realm of international politics. Since its inception, Communist China has been trying to gain the goodwill of the countries in south-east Asia, Vietnam, Cambodia, Thailand, Burma, Buddhist countries all. If these countries could be made to believe that even in Communist China, Buddhism is not being persecuted, but is permitted to function, they would be more favourably inclined toward the Communist giant to the north. To create this favourable image among the Buddhist countries and peoples of south-east Asia, the People's Republic permits delegations of the Chinese Buddhist Association to visit those countries, and in turn welcomes representatives from those countries. Upon arrival in China, these Buddhist delegations are received by the Chinese Buddhist Association and taken on tours of the Buddhist temples in the metropolitan areas, just to demonstrate that the Chinese Buddhists enjoy freedom of religious belief. To a certain extent, the Chinese Communists have been successful in their attempts to woo the Buddhist countries. For example, a group of Cambodian monks toured China from June 15 to July 26, 1958, to the accompaniment of banquets and speeches in various cities. On the eve of his departure, the leader of the Cambodian delegation told reporters that he sincerely believed the Buddhists in China enjoyed freedom of religious belief, and that what he had seen was entirely different from the rumours he had heard.

Within the limits imposed by the People's Republic, the Chinese Buddhist Association is able to function and to carry on religious activities within the temples which are often subsidised by the Government. Moreover, since Buddhism has had such a long history in China, the Communists could not very well close their eyes to this historical development. Some studies of Buddhism are, therefore, being carried out. This leads us to our consideration of the second problem, what is the Communist attitude concerning the cultural contributions of Chinese Buddhism?

In the search for data bearing on this problem, I have consulted such periodicals as the *Li-shih Yen-chiu (Historical Studies)*, *Che-hsüeh Yen-chiu (Philosophical Studies)*, and the index *Ch'uan-kuo Chu-yao Pao-k'an Tzu-liao So-yin (Index of the Important Newspapers and Journals in the Entire Country)*. I also had a friend in Hong Kong examine the files prepared by the Union Research Institute. With the exception of one article in *Philosophical Studies,* which has already been considered, these efforts did not reveal anything of value. For some reason which is not clear to me, writers on the mainland have not devoted the time and effort to study the history of Buddhism in China that one would expect. For example, no monograph or journal article has appeared discussing that aspect of Buddhism during the T'ang Dynasty which should be of interest to the Communist historians, namely, the economic and commercial activities of the Buddhist monasteries. It would appear that the older scholars of Buddhism on the mainland, such as T'ang Yung-t'ung before he died in 1964, and Chou I-liang, have steered away from Buddhist studies for various reasons, and younger writers are not yet sufficiently advanced in their Buddhist studies to publish. In the end, my main sources of information are first, *Modern Buddhism,* the official organ of the Chinese Buddhist Association, and secondly, the books on Chinese history and thought by Communist writers.

At the outset, it is well to point out that the Communist writers freely admit the extent of the cultural contributions of Chinese Buddhism. One wrote that " if it were not for the large scale introduction of Buddhist *sutras* since the Eastern Han Dynasty, there would not have been the new Chinese culture of the Sui and T'ang Dynasties." [10] Another wrote, " Through the introduction of Buddhism, the fine arts of foreign countries, such as music, lyrics, dances and architecture, were introduced into China. Moreover, through the translations of the Buddhist *sutras,* the study of phonology was promoted in China. Finally, under the influence of Buddhism, the teachings and doctrines of Taoism became systematised." [11] There is also the following summary in a general history of China that is widely read. " With the gradual introduction of Buddhism into China, many new elements were added to Chinese culture. Buddhism itself was, of course, the most important of the innovations. But there were also many other elements whose development in China was either directly or indirectly connected with Buddhism. Such were the new elements in literature, language, thought, architecture, sculpture, painting and so forth." [12]

Turning to specific contributions, the Communist writers have gone to great lengths to point out the influence of Buddhism on Neo-Confucianism. Neo-Confucianism was the intellectual movement which arose in the latter stages of the T'ang Dynasty and reached full bloom during the Sung. It represented the Chinese protest against the Buddhist emphasis on other-worldliness and the illusoriness of all phenomena, and marked a return by Chinese thinkers to their own cultural heritage. The Chinese philosophers of the Sung Dynasty claimed that they could find in the Confucian classics a system of ethics and metaphysics that

[10] Fan Wen-lan, *Concise General History of China,* p. 722.
[11] Chien Po-tsan and others, *Chung-kuo Li-shih Kai-yao (Outlines of Chinese History),* (Peking: 1956), p. 24.
[12] Chou Ku-ch'eng, *Chung-kuo T'ung-shih (General History of China),* (Shanghai: 1959), p. 442.

could take the place of Buddhism. However, while they used terms found in the classics, it is safe to say that they interpreted those terms in the light of their understanding of Buddhism.

The biographies of the Neo-Confucians Chou Tun-i (1017–73), Ch'eng Hao (1032–85), Ch'eng Yi (1033–1107), Chang Tsai (1020–77), Chu Hsi (1130–1200), and Lu Hsiang-shan (1139–93) all indicate that they had contacts with Buddhist monks and were acquainted with Buddhism. Communist writers point out in great detail the influence which the Hua-yen concepts of *li* (ultimate principle or the absolute) and *shih* (phenomena or mundane things) exerted over the thinking of the Neo-Confucians.[13] The Hua-yen School in China was concerned with the fundamental problem of the relationship between the absolute and phenomena. It established two basic principles, that *li* or the absolute and *shih* or phenomena are perfectly interfused with each other, and that all phenomena are mutually related to each other. According to the first, everything in the phenomenal world is a manifestation of the absolute perfectly and completely. Translated into religious terms, it means that the Buddha-nature is in all of us. Since every phenomenon is a manifestation of the absolute, it follows that every phenomenon is related to every other phenomenon. The unity and universality of life are thus affirmed.

Communist writers acknowledge that the Ch'eng-Chu School of Neo-Confucianism was influenced by such Hua-yen ideas. The philosophy of the Ch'eng-Chu School often stressed that substance and function stem from the same source, and that there is no difference between the hidden and manifested. Such a statement means that events and things are but the embodiment of *li* or the totality of the spirit. The Ch'eng-Chu School also holds that all men and things have the Great Ultimate, a view similar to the Hua-yen contention that all is the one, the one is all.[14]

Communist writers point out that the Neo-Confucian School was also influenced by the writings of the Ch'an School. Hou Wai-lu, for

13 Hou Wai-lu and others, *General History of Chinese Thought*, IV, 256 *et seq.*
14 Jen Chi-yü, "A Preliminary Discussion of Hua-yen Thought," *Philosophical Studies*, No. 1, 1961. See also Hou, *Chinese Thought*, IV.259/262, where copious quotations from the Neo-Confucian philosophers are cited. Examples of such quotations are:

(a) "The myriad things are complete in me; not merely is this true of men but also of things." *Erh-ch'eng Yü-lu (Recorded Sayings of the Ch'eng Brothers)* 2.20b, Cheng-i-t'ang edition.
(b) "Things are *shih*. If one can exhaust the *li* that is in *shih*, then there is nothing that is not understood." *Ibid.* 9.1b.
(c) "By observing the *li* that is in *shih*, the *li* of the whole world can be obtained." *Ibid.* 15.9a.
(d) "The myriad things in their entirety is the Great Ultimate, but if we take them separately, then each thing shares in the Great Ultimate." *Chou Lien-hsi Chi*, 1.16a, Cheng-i-t'ang edition.

instance, wrote, " The Neo-Confucians of the Sung Dynasty were really in the same tradition of the Ch'an School of Buddhism. Not only did the Szechuan School of Su Shih and Su Che clearly take its model from Buddhism, but the orthodox wing of the Neo-Confucians, Ch'eng, Chu, Lu and Wang (Yang-ming) also trace their systems of thought to the different schools of Buddhism, especially the Ch'an School. . . . For example, Wang Kuan, who was once a disciple of the Neo-Confucians, but who later switched his allegiance, wrote on the basis of the secrets taught in the inner circles of Neo-Confucianism that the teachings of the Sung Confucians all trace their source to the Ch'an School." [15]

Specifically the system of subjective idealism worked out by Lu Hsian-shan was traced to the Ch'an and Vijñānavāda emphasis on mind or consciousness. The Vijñānavāda School of Mahāyāna Buddhism has as its fundamental tenet that all external phenomena are but representations of the mind. The phrase that Lu Hsiang-shan uses is, " The universe is my mind, my mind is the universe." This is similar to the Ch'an slogan, " Within my nature are the myriad things of the world, the myriad things are embraced in my nature." The conclusion drawn by Hou Wai-lu is that " Lu Hsiang-shan combined the thought of the Ch'an School with subjective idealism of Mencius and Tzu-szu of the Confucian School to form his system of philosophy." [16]

In literature, the contribution of Buddhism to the formation of the literary genre known as *pien-wen* or texts of marvellous events, is emphasised by the Communist writers.[17] The *pien-wen* consists originally of stories told by the Buddhist monks to the crowds who gathered at the temples during festival days. The nucleus of such stories was usually an episode taken from a Buddhist *sutra,* and retold in the vernacular in a greatly expanded and embellished style. In form, the *pien-wen* consisted of prose and poetry in the manner of the Buddhist *sutras.* In the beginning, the *pien-wen* was used for religious propaganda. But it soon became so popular that it was seized upon by non-Buddhist writers, wandering minstrels and ballad singers, who converted the religious themes to those of a popular nature, based on famous historical events or well-known heroes of the past. The *pien-wen* was thus transformed into popular literature, and as such played an important role in the rise of later literary genres such as the drama, novel, stories and prompting manuals used in the theatre.

The contributions to phonology which were discovered by such scholars as Ch'en Yin-ch'üeh and Lo Ch'ang-p'ei in pre-Communist

[15] Hou, *Chinese Thought,* IV.262–263.
[16] *Ibid.* 4.670.
[17] See Ch'iu-lo, " Pien-wen yü Chung-kuo Wen-hsueh," (" Pien-wen and Chinese Literature), *Modern Buddhism,* November 1958; Ch'ang Jen-hsia, *Tung-fang I-shu Ts'ung-t'an (Collected Remarks on Eastern Art),* (Shanghai: 1956), p. 99.

days are accepted by the Communist writers of the present. Professor Ch'en's article, entitled " Szu-sheng San-wen " (" Three Questions Concerning the Four Tones ") was first published in the *Tsing-hua Journal,* September 1934. All the findings in the article are accepted in a short paper published by Chang Chien-mu, entitled, " Fo-chiao Tui-yü Chung-kuo Yin-yün-hsüeh Ti Ying-hsiang " (" Influence of Buddhism on Chinese Phonology "), *Modern Buddhism,* February 1957. It was Professor Ch'en's contention that the three tones in Chinese, *p'ing, shang* and *ch'ü,* were based on the pitch accent used by the Indians in reciting the Vedas, the *udatta, svarita,* and *anudatta.* Likewise, the studies of Lo Ch-ang-p'ei, who pointed out that the thirty *tzu-mu* or phonetic radicals were formulated by the Buddhist monk Shou-wen on the basis of his knowledge of the Sanskrit alphabet, are also accepted by present-day writers in Communist China.[18]

In art, the contributions of Buddhism to architecture, painting, music and sculpture are pointed out, but it is the contribution in sculpture that is most often stressed. This is understandable, for the works carved out of the earth and stone in Yun-kang, Lung-men, Tun-huang and Mai-chi-shan are present for all to see. The cave temples and sculpture in these centres are now considered to be national treasures by the Chinese Communists, and the Government undertakes to preserve and maintain them. In their discussions of such sculptural monuments, the Communist writers emphasise one point above all others, that this type of art was folk art, conceived and executed by the common people and as such must be considered as the glorious contributions of the common people to Chinese culture.[19]

Turning to science, one of the most fertile fields for the study of Buddhist contributions is medicine. Buddhism from its earliest days had stressed the health of the community of monks, and many passages in the scriptures refer to the medicine that the Buddha permitted his followers

[18] Lo Ch'ang-p'ei, " Indian Influence on the Study of Chinese Phonology," *Sino-Indian Studies,* March 1944.117–124.

[19] On the Buddhist contribution to sculpture, see the following articles: (a) Ch'ang Jen-hsia, " Yun-kang Shih-k'e I-shu " (" The Sculptural Art of Yun-kang "), *Modern Buddhism,* February 1958 ; (b) *Ibid.,* " Fo-chiao yü Chung-kuo Hui-hua " (" Buddhism and Chinese Painting "), *Modern Buddhism,* October 1958; (c) *Ibid.,* " Fo-chia yü Chung-kuo Tiao-k'e " (" Buddhism and Chinese Sculpture "), *Modern Buddhism,* December 1958; (d) *Ibid.,* " Mai-chi-shan ti Fo-chiao I-shu " (" Buddhist Art of Mai-chi-shan ") *Modern Buddhism,* February 1957 ; (e) Chin Wei-no, " Sui T'ang Shih-tai ti tiao-su-chia " (" Sculptors of the Sui T'ang Period "), *Modern Buddhism,* January 1963; (f) T'ung-i and Tung Yü-hsiang, " Yun-kang Ti-wu-shih-ch'üeh ti Tsao-hsiang I-shu " (" The Sculptural Art of Cave 50 in Yun-kang "), *Modern Buddhism,* February 1963. As for the stress on folk art, here are some samples. " The special feature about the rock-cut images of Lung-men is that the artists were able to synthesise various forms of traditional art and create a new form of people's art." " The artistic products of the Sui T'ang Dynasties to an even greater extent manifested a superior people's style." *Modern Buddhism,* December 1958.

to use. The master himself called his teachings a therapy to cure the ills of the world, and in the Buddhist pantheon a prominent position is accorded the master of medicine, Bhaishajyaguru. Among the Buddhist monks who went to China, An Shih-kao (second century), Fo-t'u-teng (fourth century) and Buddhayásas (fifth century) were acknowledged masters in the Indian art of healing. Such contributions of the Buddhists in medicine have already been pointed out in the past.[20]

The Indian theory of the four great elements that compose the body, earth, water, fire and wind, and that good health results when these four elements are in proper equilibrium, was adopted by the Chinese. The most prominent of the T'ang physicians, Sun Szu-miao (601?–682), who was nicknamed by his contemporaries the " New Vimalakīrti " because of his interest in medicine, wrote a medical treatise entitled *Ch'ien Chin Yao Fang (Book of Prescriptions Worth a Thousand Gold)*, in which he said that the Chinese should be well-versed in the medical lore of the Buddhists if they wished to understand the virtues of love, compassion and impartiality that a doctor must possess. Moreover, such surgical techniques as laparotomy or removal of the abdominal walls, and trepanation or surgery on the skull, were influenced by Indian methods. It was said of Fo-t'u-teng, for instance, that on certain days he would cut a hole in his abdomen, take out his entrails, wash them, and then put them back.

Further discussion of this contribution in medicine by a writer in Communist China is to be found in an article, " Yin-tu I-hsüeh tui-yü Chung-kuo I-hsüeh ti Ying-hsiang " (" The Influence of Indian Medicine on Chinese Medicine "), *Modern Buddhism*, June 1956, written by Lin Tzu-ch'ing. The writer first points a list of *sutras* dealing with medicine.[21] These are but a few of the translations of medical works which have survived and are preserved in the Chinese Tripitaka. Undoubtedly there must have been many others which have been lost. With so much medical knowledge introduced to the Chinese from India, the influence on Chinese medicine must have been considerable. One of the best indications of this is in the nature of the medical literature which appeared in China. Lin points out that in the bibliographical treatise of the *Sui Shu (History of Sui)* Chap. 13, there are a

---

[20] See the article on " Byo " in *Hōbōgirin*, 3.225–265, especially 257–265; Pierre Huard and Ming Wong, *La Médecine Chinoise au cours des Siècles*, (Paris : 1959), pp. 27–32; Ch'en Yin-ch'üeh, " Hua-t'o Chuan " (" Biography of Hua-t'o "), *Tsinghua Journal* June 1930.

[21] *Taishō*, No. 793, *Fo-i Ching (Sutra on Buddhist Healings)*; *Taishō*, No. 219, *I-yü Ching (Medical Parables)*; *Taishō*, No. 1330, *Lo-fu-nu Shuo Chiu-liao Hsiao-erh Chi-ping Ching (Sutra Spoken by Ravana on Healing Children's Ailments)*; *Taishō*, No. 1325, *Liao-chih Ping Ching (Sutra on Healing Piles)*; *Taishō*, No. 1691, *Chia-yeh Hsien-jen Shuo I-nü-jen Ching (Sutra Spoken by Kāśyapa on Treating Women)*.

number of medical works whose titles reveal some connections with Buddhism.[22]

As for Indian physicians in China, there were two so well-known that they even attended the T'ang emperors. One was Na-lo-erh-p'o-sa, who arrived in 648 and was commissioned by T'ai-tsung to concoct some pills which would bring everlasting life. The other was Lu-chia-i-to, the trusted physician of Kao-tsung, who dispatched him to the four corners of the empire to search for longevity potions.

Indian treatment of eye ailments, such as the removal of cataracts, were followed by the Chinese. During the T'ang, a *Treatise on the Eye*, attributed to the bodhisattva Nāgārjuna, was very popular.[23] In various parts of China, Indian eye specialists were also practising their art of healing. For instance, the famous Buddhist monk Chien-chen was treated for an eye ailment in 748 in Chü-chiang, Kwangtung, by a foreign doctor. The poet Liu Yü-hsi (772–842) also consulted an Indian eye specialist for the removal of cataract, which the doctor performed with a golden comb.[24]

The contributions of Buddhist monks in astronomy and mathematics are mentioned by present-day writers under the Communist régime, but the subject is not given extended treatment.[25] In 1955 a special postal stamp was issued by the People's Republic to commemorate the astronomical and mathematical contributions of the famous monk I-hsing (682–727). This monk charted the stars in the southern skies during an expedition which he led to the southern seas and which went as far as the southern tip of Sumatra. He also determined the latitudes in China by setting up nine stations, the northernmost one in Shansi and the southernmost in Indo-China, and measuring the shadows cast

---

[22] (a) *Lung-shu P'u-sa Yao-fang*, 4 ch. (*Nāgārjuna's Book of Prescriptions*); (b) *Hsi-yü Chu-hsien So-shuo Yao-fang*, 23 ch. (*Prescriptions Prescribed by Various Immortals from the Western Regions*); (c) *Hsi-yü P'o-lo-hsien-jen-fang*, 3 ch. (*Prescriptions of Brahman Immortals from the Western Regions*); (d) *Hsi-yü Ming-i So-chi Yao-fang*, 4 ch. (*Prescriptions Collected by Famous Doctors of the Western Regions*); (e) *P'o-lo-men Chu-hsien Yao-fang*, 20 ch. (*Prescriptions of Brahman Immortals*); (f) *P'o-lo-men Yao-fang*, 5 ch. (*Brahman Prescriptions*).

[23] One line in a poem of Po Chü-i referred to this work. " On the table the pages of *Nāgārjuna's Treatise* is scattered about."

[24] This treatment is mentioned in a poem by Liu presented to the Indian doctor, now found in *Ch'uan T'ang-shih*, ch. 13.

" My two eyes have become blind early,
Although I am middle-aged, I am like an old man.
I look at vermilion and it resembles green.
I am afraid of the sun and cannot stand the wind.
You, my master, know the method of the golden comb.
Can you help me see again? "

The method of using the golden comb for cataracts is described in the *Ta-pan Nieh-p'an Ching*, ch. 8 (*Mahāparinirvānasūtra*), Taishō, 12.411c, 652c; and *Ta-jih Ching Su*, ch. 9 (*Commentary on the Mahāvairocanasūtra*), Taishō, 39.699c. See also *Hōbōgirin* 3.261 for illustrations of the golden comb.

[25] Chao Pu-chu, *Buddhism in China*, (Peking: 1957), p. 30.

by a standard eight-foot gnomon simultaneously during the summer and winter solstice. In the T'ang court there were three clans of Indian calendrical experts, Kāśyapa, Kumāra and Gautama, who helped the Chinese determine the positions of the heavenly bodies and prepare the calendar used by the dynasty.

Finally, the contributions of Buddhism in the practice of magic and on tales of magic are acknowledged and form the subject of an interesting article by Fu T'ien-cheng, " Fo-chiao tui Chung-ko Huan-shu ti Ying-hsiang Ch'u-t'an " (" A Preliminary Investigation of the Buddhist Contribution to Magic in China "), *Modern Buddhism*, May 1961. In this article, the writer points out various feats of Indian magic copied and repeated by the Chinese. Such feats include the following; restoration of a severed tongue, restoration of a piece of cloth cut in twain, spitting fire and burning objects without destroying them. In the biography of Kumārajīva in *Chin Shu* (*History of the Chin Dynasty*), Chap. 95, is a description of the magician swallowing needles. This became a popular feat of magic in China, where some more sophisticated touches were added. For instance, the magician after swallowing the needles would then swallow some thread, and then pull out the thread from his mouth with all the needles strung on it.

As for the tales of magic, one of the best known is the *E-lung Shu-sheng* (*The Goose Cage and the Student*), which Lu Hsün declared was based on a Buddhist source.[26] According to this tale, a certain Hsü Yen was walking along a road carrying a cage with some geese in it when he met a student who complained of sore feet and asked to be carried in the cage. Hsü put him in the cage together with the geese. The student did not shrink nor did the cage expand, but student and geese remained comfortably within the cage. After a while, the student got out of the cage and spit forth from his mouth some wine cups, wine and a feast. He and Hsü enjoyed the feast together. The student then spit out a girl, and the girl in turn spit out a boy. From the boy's mouth came forth another girl. In the end every one returned to the mouth of the spitter, and the utensils also returned to the mouth of the student.[27]

In China such magic acts and tales of magic were usually presented before crowds gathered at the temple fairs. According to Fu, this

---

[26] Lu Hsün, *Chung-kuo Hsiao-shuo Shih-lüeh* (*Short History of Chinese Fiction*) (Hong Kong: 1958), pp. 32–34.

[27] The Buddhist source of this story is the *Chiu-tsa Pi-yü Ching* (*The Old Book of Miscellaneous Parables*), *Taishō*, 4.514a, translated by K'ang Seng-hui in the third century, where we read that a religious student spit out a jar, and in the jar was a girl. While the student went to sleep, the girl then spit out a jar which contained a boy. After sleeping with the youth, the girl then swallowed the jar with the boy. The student then awoke, put the girl back into the jar and swallowed it.

feature endowed the acts and the tales with a collectivist nature and transformed them into sources of entertainment for the masses.[28]

From this review of the Communist attitude towards the cultural contributions of Chinese Buddhism, it is clear that the Communist writers have not differed much from the conclusions arrived at by writers of the pre-Communist era. To a certain extent, this was a disappointment to the author, for he had hoped that they, with their different viewpoints and methodology, would have attacked the problem in their own manner and come forth with some different assessment of such contributions. However, it may be that the position they have taken on such contributions is the only tenable one. The contributions and influence of Buddhism on Chinese culture are historical facts and are imbedded so firmly in the fabric of Chinese life that they are not susceptible of being interpreted differently.

Let us now summarise what we have discussed at some length. The Communists contend that they permit freedom of religious belief in China, and that Buddhism is permitted to function if it stays within the limitations imposed by the state. In their assessment of Buddhist contributions to Chinese culture, the writers under the Communist régime are essentially in agreement with the conclusions of those in the pre-Communist era. It is in their interpretations of the historical development of Buddhism and their evaluation of the Chinese Buddhist schools that we see the Communist historians differing from their non-Communist counterparts. Given the Buddhist insistence on idealism and the harmonious identification of all dualisms, and given the Communist insistence on materialism and on contradictions in society as the supreme law, the strong and caustic attacks against the important Buddhist schools in China should come as no surprise. What is interesting is that the leaders of the Chinese Buddhist Association have apparently chosen to ignore these attacks, for so far no reaction to the critical remarks of Jen Chi-yü has yet to appear in the official organ of the association, *Modern Buddhism*.

[28] *Modern Buddhism*, May 1961. A graphic description of such mass entertainment is given in the *Lo-yang Chia-lan Chi (Description of the Monasteries in Lo-yang)*, ch. 1, *Taishō*, 51.1003b, " Musicians were assembled to demonstrate their art within the temple, while rare birds and strange beasts danced within the courtyard. Acrobatic stunts, deceiving magical acts, and strange skilful feats such as had never been seen previously by people, were assembled and performed before the crowds. Some magicians skinned a donkey in a moment, others dug a well and drew water. Some made dates and melons grow on the spot and became eatable instantly. Such sights were indeed amazing and bewildering to the spectators."

10

Chinese Communist Assessments of a Foreign Conquest Dynasty

By DAVID M. FARQUHAR

CHINESE Communist evaluations of China's foreign conquest dynasties, like those of earlier Chinese historians, have been hostile, at least on the most vulgar level of historical writing.[1] This comes as no surprise, for the conquest dynasties occupied all or part of China by military force and often governed badly. For the Chinese Communist historians these conquerors carry the additional onus of being feudalists, or worse, feudalists who allowed the feudal economy to stagnate. This attitude is particularly marked in the treatment of the more recent foreign dynasties, the Khitan Liao dynasty (916-1124), the Jurchen Chin dynasty (1115-1234), the Tangut Hsi Hsia dynasty (1032-1227), the Manchu Ch'ing dynasty (1644-1911) and the one discussed here, the Mongol Yüan dynasty (1220-1367).

Beyond the business of determining whether particular dynasties are " good things " or " bad things " (i.e. progressive or reactionary), the sophistication of analysis and refinement of discussion by Chinese Communist historians has depended a good deal on the extent and quality of the pre-1949 studies. By all rights, recent Chinese scholarship should be filled with specialists in foreign dynasties, for the last great spurt of traditional Chinese historiography was dominated by men particularly interested in the Mongols and the Manchus. Ch'ien Ta-hsin (1728-1804), Ch'i Yün-shih (1751-1815), Chang Mu (1805-1849), Wei Yüan (1794-1856), Wang Kuo-wei (1877-1927), K'o Shao-min (1850-1933) and T'u Chi (a *chin-shih* of 1892) are not only the most distinguished historians of the Mongols and Manchus, they are also among the chief luminaries of late classical scholarship.

But for some reason—probably 20th century Chinese nationalism— interest in these studies did not extend to the Republican generation of scholars. Only Meng Ssu-ming,[2] Weng Tu-chien, Ch'en Yüan [3]

---

[1] For example Tung Chi-ming, *An Outline History of China* (Peking: Foreign Languages Press, 1959).

[2] Meng, *Yüan-tai she-hui chieh-chi chih-tu* (*Social Classes in China under the Yüan Dynasty*) (Yenching University, 1938), seems to be one of the few full-length modern monographs on Yüan history published in Republican times.

[3] Ch'en wrote the important study *Yüan hsi-yü-jen hua-hua k'ao* (*The Sinicisation of Central Asians during the Yüan*), 8 chüan, (*Li-yün shu-wu ts'ung-k'o pa chung 1-2*, Peiping: 1934) which has recently been translated by L. C. Goodrich as *Western and Central Asians in China under the Mongols* (*Monumenta Serica Monograph* XV, Los Angeles: Monumenta Serica, University of California, 1966).

and a few others [4] devoted themselves seriously to Yüan history. These men are still alive and in China, but to my knowledge none has produced important work since 1949, although Weng seems to be a leader in Mongolian studies (he was the head of the Chinese delegation to the International Congress of Mongolists held in Ulan Bator in 1958).[5] Recognising that their own studies must be based on work done before the Liberation, the communist authorities have reprinted many articles written in the 1920s and 30s on various aspects of Chinese history, but treatments of the Yüan dynasty are not among them.

Today, the most important Chinese Communist work on Yüan history (or more accurately, Mongolian history) is being done by Yü Yüan-an, a Mongol (his Mongolian name is Bayan), and Han Ju-lin, a scholar trained by Paul Pelliot.[6] Both know Mongolian, Russian and other western languages—a fact which alone places them in a new wave of historians in China—and the work of both, at least that part involving new interpretations, has focussed on Chinggis Qan and his epoch. In a sense, then, their concern has been with early Mongolian rather than Chinese history, since Chinggis can be called an emperor of China only by virtue of the courtesy temple name, T'ai-tsu, given him posthumously by his grandson, Qubilai. It is true that Chinggis conquered part of north China, but the states affected—the Hsi Hsia and particularly the Jurchen Chin—are regarded with contempt by these authors, especially Yü Yüan-an, and their defeat is not considered a Chinese tragedy. Chinggis scholars have a peculiar advantage in the fact that the Chinese government has recognised the Mongolian conqueror as an acceptable national symbol for some two million Mongols of the Inner Mongolian Autonomous Region.[7] By contrast, the neighbouring Mongolian People's

---

[4] Feng Ch'eng-chün (now dead), T'ao Hsi-sheng and Yao Ts'ung-wu (both now in Taiwan), Han Ju-lin and Wu Han have all made contributions. Some, like Wu, have subsequently taken up other lines of activity.

[5] Weng is in the Institute ot Nationalities, Chinese Academy of Sciences. The Congress at Ulan Bator was limited to language, literature and folklore studies, and Weng's paper read there contains little of scholarly interest. See " Shih-chi-nien-lai Chung-kuo Meng-ku min-tsu yü-yen wen-hsueh ti fa-chan ho yen-chiu kung-tso ti kai-k'uang " (" A sketch of the development of, and research projects in, the linguistics and literature of the Mongolian nationality in China during the past ten years "), *Studia Mongolica* III, 2.24–30 (Ulan Bator, The First International Congress of Mongolists, 1962), pp. 25-37.

[6] Yü Yüan-an, *Ch'eng-chi-ssu han chuan* (*A Biography of Chinggis Qan*) (Shanghai: People's Publishing House, 1955); Yü Yüan-an, *Nei Meng-ku li-shih kai-yao* (*Outline History of Inner Mongolia*) (Shanghai: People's Publishing House, 1958); Han Ju-lin, " Lun Ch'eng-chi-ssu han " (" On Chinggis Qan "), *Li-shih Yen-chiu* (*Historical Studies*), No. 3, 1962, pp. 1-10.

[7] This is evidenced by the maintenance of the mausoleum (" shrine " would be a better word) of Chinggis Qan at Ejen qoriya in the Ordos region. See, for example,

Republic has never approved Chinggis Qan as an object of patriotism and no book-length biography has ever been published there.[8]

Yü's *Biography of Chinggis Qan,* published in 1955, begins with an outline of social and economic conditions in the middle of the 12th century. This was a period of great change, when the clan system was breaking up and the pattern of nomadism was changing: seasonal migration by family units (*ayil*) was replacing movement by clan units (*küriyen*). But the clan still controlled the nomadic lands and clan institutions like ultimogeniture still prevailed: the Mongolian people were not yet a united " nationality " (*pu-tsu, narodnost'*).[9] The break-up of the clan society projects the Mongols into a slave society in only a very limited way (although elements of patriarchal-slave society are very persistent in the Mongolian as well as all nomadic societies). Though slaves influenced the political and economic sectors for a while, the condition of slavery was not really hereditary; by the second generation they were generally free, whereupon they joined the other free or semi-free commoners (*qarachu*) of the tribe. Slaves (*bogol*) were usually captives taken in battle, but occasionally entire clans or tribes would be defeated, in which case they would become a kind of dependent class within Mongolian society (*unagan-bogol*), rendering tribute and services to the victor tribe while maintaining their separate character.[10]

By the first years of the 13th century the Mongols had entered the early stage of feudalism. A feudal nobility (*noyan*), derived from the rich and powerful *ayil*, already exploited the Mongolian masses with typically feudal forms of exaction, viz. the annual tribute in animals. Feudalism was further developed and clan life further weakened by the appearance of the *nökör* (" companions, comrades "), retainers in the service of the nobility. Outside forces—including contact with more

Rintschen, " Zum Kult Tschinggis-khans bei den Mongolen," *Opuscula Ethnologica Memoriae Ludovici Biró Sacra* (Budapest: Magyar Tudományos Académia, 1959), pp. 9–22.

[8] At least the two chief bibliographies of modern Mongolian books list none: *Mongol ulsad 1913-1944 ond khevlesen Mongol nomyn bürtgel (Bibliography of Mongolian Books Printed in the Years 1913-1944 in Mongolia)* (Ulan Bator: Shinzhlekh Ukhaany Akademiin Khevlel, 1963) and *BNMA uslad 1945-1955 onuudad Mongol khel deer khevlegdesen nomyn tovch bürtgel (A Brief Bibliography of Books Published in the Mongolian Language in the Years 1945-1955 in the MPR)* (Ulan Bator: Ulsyn Khevleliin gazar, 1957). It should be noted, however, that considerable materials about Chinggis have been published in Mongolia, including a modern Mongolian translation of the most important source on him, the *Monggol-un niguca tobchiyan (Yüan-ch'ao pi-shih,* the " Secret History of the Mongols "), by Ts. Damdinsüren: *Mongolyn nuuts tovchoo* (2nd ed., Ulan Bator: Ulsyn Khevleliin gazar, 1957). In 1962 the MPR did deign to celebrate the 800th birthday of Chinggis by issuing a commemorative postage stamp. See *Stanley Gibbons Priced Postage Stamp Catalogue,* Part III (London: Gibbons, 1966), p. 439.

[9] Yü, *Biography of Chinggis Qan,* pp. 3, 6. Ultimogeniture: inheritance by the youngest child.

[10] *Ibid.,* pp. 7–8.

civilised states like the Chin, the Hsi Hsia and the Uighur Turks—and a technological revolution brought on by the newly developed arts of wood- and iron-working, also speeded the evolution of feudal society.[11]

In Yü's analysis of the evolution of Mongolian society up to Chinggis' assumption of power, students of Mongolian history will immediately recognise the overwhelming influence of B. Ia. Vladimirtsov's *Obshchestvennyi stroi mongolov. Mongol'skii kochevoi feodalizm* (*The Social Régime of the Mongols. Mongolian Nomadic Feudalism*).[12] This unfinished, posthumously published book has dominated world scholarship on Mongolian social history, although it has not been accepted uncritically by either Marxist or non-Marxist scholars. But they would probably accept much of the preceding analysis [13]; the important point here is that a contemporary Chinese historian has accepted the theories of a European scholar (a not particularly Marxist one [14]) about a problem in his own national history— surely something of a departure.

In essaying the forces upon which Chinggis Qan fed, Yü notes two as being most important: (1) the Mongol's thirst for peace and unity, brought on by the interminable inter-tribal warfare characteristic of the second half of the 12th century—the worst years for the Mongols; and (2) the need to protect themselves from foreign aggression, in this case the "reactionary and barbaric" *chieh-ting* policy ("diminishing the able-bodied males") of the Chin dynasty, whereby soldiers were sent north every three years to systematically kill Mongols.[15]

Yü reports the famous break between Chinggis and his blood brother Jamuqa without involving himself in the Soviet scholastic dispute over who was the more progressive. According to Yü, Chinggis wanted to win back the peoples who had formerly been part of his father's tribe, some of whom were then subjects of Jamuqa; having accomplished this, he decided to go his own way. There were several reasons why tribal leaders left the older, more noble Jamuqa for his younger brother. Many saw in Chinggis the personification of the "air of a ruler" (*chu-chün p'in-hsing, ti-wang ch'i-hsiang*), able to lead them to victory,

11 *Ibid.*, pp. 6-7, 85.
12 B. Ia. Vladimirtsov, *The Social Regime of the Mongols: Nomadic Feudalism* (Leningrad: Izdatel'stvo Akademii Nauk SSSR, 1934), French translation by Michael Carsow, *Le Régime social des Mongols, Le Féodalisme nomade* (Paris: Adrien-Maisonneuve, 1948). See especially pp. 39-99.
13 See, for example, the most recent assessment of Chinggis, Owen Lattimore, " Chingis Khan and the Mongol Conquests," *Scientific American*, Vol. 209, no. 2 (August, 1963), pp. 55-68. Some points in Vladimirtsov's (and hence Yü's) analysis—the " unagan-bogol " concept, the character of the *noyan* class, etc.—must be rejected or seriously modified.
14 Vladimirtsov developed his concept of Mongolian nomadic feudalism around 1911-1912 after his return from Mongolia, well before any Marxist pressures could be put on him.
15 Yü, *Biography of Chinggis Qan*, pp. 12, 16, 45, 85.

capture rich pastures, livestock, beautiful girls and other booty. Others, like Sacha-beki, representatives of ancient and honourable clans, preferred to put themselves under someone younger and inferior to themselves, whom they hoped to control. Some subordinates of Jamuqa had already made terms with Chinggis before the break occurred.[16] Chinggis found it ultimately very easy to attract the *noyan* of all tribes, because the military and administrative confederation which was the Mongolian state was created by them and their retainers specifically for their own benefit.[17] Many common Mongolian soldiers were eager to support Chinggis, because as subjects of the feudal *noyan* they had to render an annual tribute, supply all their own equipment and rations, and consequently found their sole income the booty distributed to them as a result of war victories. Their mistaken idea that they were fighting for themselves made them heroic in battle. Commoners were further encouraged by opportunities opened to them in Chinggis' new institutions, for example, his elite bodyguard (*kesig*) which admitted sons of both *noyan* and commoner.[18]

To explain the Mongolian conquests Yü Yüan-an claims to draw on F. Engels' *The Origin of the Family, Private Property, and the State*: the early, pre-empire wars against the Merkid and Tatar, for example, were wars of revenge, while the later ones against the Hsi Hsia, Korea, Kwarezm and Chin were for plunder, and thus undertaken to satisfy Chinggis' economic needs.[19] But how had Chinggis Qan managed to conquer these richer, culturally more-advanced states with his inferior numbers and in such a short time? The Qan was a superb military strategist, the Mongolian troops outstanding to be sure, but the real cause lay in the decadence of those various states, whose governments were rotten or seriously divided by internal discord. Some of the feudal lords offered resistance, but they were never able to develop their military capabilities because they oppressed their people, and frightened of the Mongols, caused their subjects to be frightened as well. The states themselves, hostile to each other, could not form a confederation against the Mongols; thus the great expanse of land from Korea to Russia fell.[20]

The real theme of Yü's book is the unification of the Mongolian tribes. This was Chinggis' greatest work, in which he had the support not only of the feudal lords which he represented, but of all the Mongolian people. " Progressive " elements like the Muslim merchants also supported it.[21] Unification ended the tribal wars, consolidated the Mongolian lands, broke the barriers which separated the various

---

[16] *Ibid.*, pp. 19–20.
[18] *Ibid.*, pp. 35, 69.
[20] *Ibid.*, pp. 68–69, 77.

[17] *Ibid.*, pp. 32–33.
[19] *Ibid.*, pp. 44, 68–69.
[21] *Ibid.*, pp. 85–87.

Mongolian peoples; the economic system was strengthened and the herdsman's life became peaceful. The Mongols could protect themselves against foreign oppressors like the Jurchen Chin nobility. The new social conditions created by unification brought increased cultural development—writing, law codes, and new political and administrative institutions, which in their turn helped break down further the old clan relations based on blood.[22]

Chinggis Qan's role in Mongolian history must therefore be considered positive and progressive, Yü maintains. But one must not be "excessive" about his role or attribute merit to him. For one thing, the unification of the Mongols in the 12th and 13th centuries was a historical necessity. An outstanding personality was needed to carry out the task and Chinggis Qan happened to be on the scene; but if he had not been, unification would have been accomplished sooner or later by someone else. Chinggis influenced the speed rather than the character of the process.[23] Moreover, to say that his role in Mongolian history was positive is not to say that it was positive in the history of other peoples: the wars he waged against the non-Mongolian states were clearly wars of aggression. To achieve victory he did not hesitate to slaughter peaceful populations on a grand scale, burn cities and destroy all cultural accomplishments, retarding progress in many of these lands for several centuries, Central Asia in particular. True, some benefits accrued from the cultural and commercial exchange over the Mongolian empire's postal relay system, " but these do not compensate at all for the harm which [Chinggis] brought to the peoples of vast lands, and this is the reason Marxists, when writing world history or the history of various countries, have not given him a positive role." [24]

Having delivered himself of this modestly revisionist analysis, Yü brings us back to Soviet-Marxist historical orthodoxy with a thump in the last pages of the *Biography of Chinggis Qan*. Chinggis after all represented the feudal interests, and any clash between the interests of the people and himself was resolved in his favour. His extended campaigns often brought misfortune to the Mongolian soldiers, who were abandoned in distant places and never able to return home. The countries he conquered were oppressed by his agents, the *darugachi*, who supplied him and his feudal lords with wealth from enslaved peoples.[25] This last unfavourable impression of the Chinggis Qan era is bolstered by quotations from a book of B. D. Grekov and A. Iu.

22 *Ibid.*, p. 68.
23 *Ibid.*, p. 90.
24 *Ibid.*, pp. 89–90.
25 *Ibid.*, pp. 90–95.

Iakubovskii, one of the standard works of Soviet scholarship on the Mongols.[26]

Between Vladimirtsov at the beginning and Grekov-Iakubovskii at the end there is a good deal which is new in Yü's books, most particularly his interpretation of Chinggis' role in Mongolian history as a positive one. His view of Chinggis the man, however, is judicious: he sees neither a great culture hero nor a blood-thirsty monster. New too is much factual information, none of which has been discussed here; the *Biography of Chinggis Qan* is essentially a popular book, but the author has examined many carefully chosen sources not customarily used by Western and Soviet historians. It is, despite its Marxist orientation, one of the few really useful biographies of Chinggis Qan.

In 1958 Yü published his *Outline History of Inner Mongolia*. By that time a new *History of the Mongolian Peoples Republic*, a joint publication of the Soviet Academy of Sciences and the Mongolian Scientific Committee, had been published in Moscow and Ulan Bator.[27] Promoted as the first history of the Mongolian People's Republic written on Marxist-Leninist principles, the latter book has obviously influenced Yü's work, and it is cited numerous times in the *Outline History*. But the two books are quite different in spirit: the work of the academies is self-consciously aware of its official character, evidenced by its dogmatic tone and frequent citations from the works of Marx, Lenin and Stalin. Yü's book largely ignores the Marxist apparatus.[28]

Following the Soviet work, Yü begins the history of Inner Mongolia with the Hsiung-nu of antiquity, after a brief nod to the stone age. He finds them essentially similar to all the other nomadic peoples living in Mongolia down through the Khitan: they were in the primitive or patriarchal-slave stages of social development; they formed tribal confederations, but these had no common territory and were simply devices for mutual aid in time of war. Once these peoples entered Chinese territory and established states they fell under the the influence of Han-Chinese feudal culture and passed directly into

---

[26] B. D. Grekov and A. Iu. Iakubovskii, *Zolotaia orda i ee padenie* (*The Golden Horde and its Downfall*), 2nd ed. (Moscow-Leningrad: Izdatel'stvo Akademii Nauk SSSR, 1950).

[27] Soviet Academy of Sciences, *Istoriia mongol'skoi narodnoi respubliki* (Moscow: Izdatel'stvo Akademii Nauk, SSSR, 1954); Mongolian Scientific Committee, *Bügd nairamdakh mongol ard ulsyn tüükh* (Ulan Bator: Ulsyn Khevleliin gazar, 1955). This book was subsequently translated into Chinese from the Russian edition: *Meng-ku jen-min kung-ho-kuo t'ung-shih* (*History of the Mongolian Peoples Republic*) (Peking: Science Publishing House, 1958). The Chinese translation, which is cited in this paper, is superior to the other versions because the translators have given precise citations for quotations from Chinese books and added other useful material.

[28] A point already noted by Okada Hidehiro in a brief review of the two books: " Shinkan Mongoru-shi nishu " (" Two New Mongolian Histories "), *Shoho* (*Book News*), July, 1958, pp. 13–14.

the feudal stage.[29] Yü notes however, that even peoples like the Khitan who became very sinicised and were virtually converted from a nomadic to a sedentary society, never gave up all of their patriarchal-slave institutions.[30]

The discussion of the age of Chinggis Qan summarises without important change the conclusions reached in the *Biography* and need not be repeated. Yü believes Chinggis's death to be a turning point in Mongolian history: while he was alive his empire kept its integrity; his sons were only high officials who carried out his will in their " fiefs " (*ulus*); but at his death the sons came to regard the territories as their private possessions. By the 1260s the empire was still further divided, for the primitive economic relations (in the form of the caravan trade) were too weak to keep the various *ulus* together; the rulers of these *ulus* came more and more to rely on the local feudal lords and rich merchants, while the emperor, the great *qagan,* was busy with matters in China and the Mongolian homeland.[31] The latter, incident-ally, is now characterised as being in a weakened economic condition because of a loss of population to the wars of conquest. Despite the introduction of agriculture around centres of population like Qara-qorum, this decay continued throughout the Yüan dynasty, as the feudal wars went on and the Mongolian feudal nobility, with their subjects and herds, moved into the Central Plain of North China. Mongolia by the 14th century was deserted, a place where the emperor hunted and spent his summers.[32] Apparently the period of peace and economic growth which Yü attributed to Chinggis' unification in his first book was either extraordinarily brief, or else he has changed his views to conform to the *History of the Mongolian Peoples Republic,* which regards unification—even though it created a Mongolian *narodnost'*—as being essentially destructive to the Mongols' creative powers, chan-nelling their energies into the conquest and enslavement of other peoples, and which denies altogether the existence of a united economic foundation in Chinggis' empire.[33]

Western scholars have always been interested in the reasons for the sudden halt of the Mongolian army's westward advance. The usual explanation has been that the news of the death of the Emperor Ögödei, requiring a diet (*quriltai*) to elect a new emperor, caused the withdrawal of the Mongols from the borders of western Europe. But Yü says that Ögödei's death was merely the occasion, not the cause

[29] Yü, *An Outline History of Inner Mongolia,* pp. 1–14, 16–18. See *History of the Mongolian Peoples Republic, op. cit.,* p. 74.
[30] Yü, *An Outline History of Inner Mongolia,* p. 16.
[31] *Ibid.,* pp. 38, 43.
[32] *Ibid.,* pp. 43–44, 49–50.
[33] *History of the Mongolian People's Republic, op. cit.,* pp. 98, 108.

of the withdrawal; the Mongolian armies had already been so seriously weakened and demoralised by the "heroic struggle" of the Russian people to protect their fatherland, that they had been unable to continue their advance, and the news simply provided the opportunity to withdraw. It was Russia that saved western Europe from the terrors of a Mongolian invasion.[34]

Returning to the Chinese scene, Yü notes the wholesale adoption of Chinese political institutions under Emperor Qubilai, and the conquest of the Southern Sung dynasty, completed in 1279. While mentioning some Sung resistance, he does not describe any of the cruelties of the invasion of South China. Sung was conquered for the same reasons that Chin, Korea and Kwarezm had been conquered before it: the rottenness and inability of the ruling class. Having exploited the people in time of peace, the ruling class was unable to organise them in time of war. Qubilai's conquest was further aided by his reliance on local Chinese feudal lords in the newly-conquered regions.[35]

Yü is very critical of Yüan rule under Qubilai. His foreign wars and the wasteful extravagances of the Mongolian ruling class—elaborate Buddhist ceremonies, the building of Buddhist temples, palaces, and falcon coops—soon emptied the treasury and caused prices to rise. To solve the problem the government began to issue shocking amounts of paper money which soon became worthless and brought great losses to the people.[36] While not denying the inflation of the Yüan currency, Western scholars have tended to emphasise the relative success and stability of the paper issues of Qubilai's times compared to earlier experiments during Sung and Chin times.

Yü notes that Qubilai's successor, Emperor Temür (reign 1295-1307), was an improvement since he stopped the foreign wars and lowered taxes.[37] But the rest of the Yüan rulers and the events of their reigns are hardly mentioned. The Yüan dynasty was destroyed by peasant uprisings and large-scale feudal war among the Mongolian ruling class in the north. Little is known of the latter, and Yü takes few pains to enlighten us. Of the former he notes that there were "several hundred" between 1277 and 1350, always suppressed by a combination of Mongolian army and Chinese landlords. A new wave of rebellions beginning in 1351, however, proved fatal to the dynasty.[38]

In a final section, Yü discusses Mongolian culture in the 12th–14th centuries. His main emphasis is on city- and palace-building, apparently

[34] Yü, *An Outline History of Inner Mongolia*, p. 41.
[35] *Ibid.*, p. 46.
[36] *Ibid.*, p. 48.
[37] *Ibid.*, p. 51.
[38] *Ibid.*, pp. 51–52.

taking up a theme which recently has much interested historians in Outer Mongolia—the development of cities in a nomadic society.[39] He mentions literature briefly (*The Secret History of the Mongols*, the now lost *Altan Debter*, etc.), but gives no mention of early Mongolian translations of and commentaries on Buddhist writings.[40] In all Yü gives 34 pages to Chinggis Qan and the Yüan period; it is not surprising that one finds so little new material in so brief a survey.

Since 1960 the Sino-Soviet dispute has influenced Chinese scholarship on Chinggis Qan and the Yüan dynasty, and that scholarship has itself become an element in the dispute. This can be seen in a recent reassessment of Chinggis by Han Ju-lin.[41] Noting that previous historians have been almost completely negative about Chinggis' role in history, he urges the continued study of this important figure under three rubrics— as a factor in Mongolian history, Chinese history and world history. He begins by documenting, as did Yü, the very unstable conditions in Mongolia in the 12th century which demanded a great pacifier and unifier—a historical responsibility which Chinggis fulfilled completely. Chinggis ultimately conquered all of the other tribes and brought peace to the people; however, his real intention was simply to satisfy his own base desires, and in this he did not differ from other tribal or confederation heads. Why was Chinggis and not some other leader successful? The answer, says Han, must be sought outside of the Mongolian situation, in the Jurchen Chin state to the south. Although the Mongols, particularly the Tatar tribe, were one of the Chin's greatest enemies, the Chin had been able to control them until 1161 with border fortifications inherited from the Liao. After 1161 Chin power declined while the Tatar grew stronger, but they continued expeditions against the Tatar and in 1196 were joined by Chinggis, who was having a blood feud with the Tatar. The Tatar were greatly weakened, and to protect themselves formed an eastern bloc of 11 tribes under Jamuqa. But this confederation lacked cohesion and was unable to stand up to Chinggis with his Chin officialdom and Chin support. With the destruction of the bloc in 1202, rich grazing lands in Külün Buyir fell into Chinggis' hands, greatly increasing his economic power and enabling him to complete the unification of the tribes in the next four years. What had been an aggregation of nearly 100 tribes differing in language, nationality and level of culture became united under a common name. Han will not go so far as to say that there was a Mongolian *narodnost'* only

---

[39] See, for example, the book of L. Dügersüren, *Ulaanbaatar khotyn tüükhees: Niislel khüree* (*On the History of Ulan-Bator: the Capital*) (Ulan-Bator: Ulsyn Khevleliin gazar, 1956).

[40] Yü, *An Outline History of Inner Mongolia*, pp. 52–53.

[41] Han, "On Chinggis Qan," *Historical Studies*, pp. 1–10.

because there was a Chinggis, but he insists that the Qan's contribution to its formation was great. " At least we ought to say that the important role which the great Mongolian nationality played on the stage of world history begins with Chinggis Qan." [42] Unfortunately social benefits which unification brought were nullified by the outlook of Chinggis Qan and the noble class he represented: " Gain through plunder is more glorious than gain through labour." Instead of devoting themselves to animal husbandry they wasted their subjects on foreign wars, while production in the Mongolian homeland declined. [43]

Han also sees many positive features in the Mongolian conquest of China. North China had been badly chopped up into various states which separated not only the various nationalities of China (the Tanggud, Khitan, etc.) but also the Chinese (Han) population which formed the majority of their subjects. Mongolian unification enabled economic development and cultural progress to begin again. [44]

The conquest of North China was a difficult business (what was to Yü Yüan-an quick and easy is long and hard to Han Ju-lin), and Chinggis accomplished it not through any special talents or great military power, but owing to the decay existing in the northern Chinese states. Once Chinggis crossed the Chin borders, for example, unorganised peasant uprisings occurred, and for lack of a respectable central authority, armed landlords began to take over the country. The great horrors of the collapse of Chin Han describes in some detail, but maintains they were only partly of Chinggis' making: the Chin armed landlords and manifold internal contradictions were much more responsible. Moreover, Chinggis soon abandoned his custom of completely slaughtering cities because it proved disadvantageous to everyone. [45]

Han next discusses the advantages accruing to Mongolia from the Chin conquest. The import of numerous Chinese artisans, technicians and farmers greatly increased Mongolian material existence and productive power, but cost the Chinese of the Central Plain great suffering and death. In fact, Han is quite cautious in evaluating Chinggis' role in Chinese history, and says simply that Mongolian rule should not be completely condemned. He finds no social and economic retrogressions in China which are specifically attributable to the fact that Mongolian emperors were on the throne. [46]

Thus far, though one may not agree with everything Han Ju-lin

[42] *Ibid.*, pp. 1–3.
[43] *Ibid.*, p. 3.
[44] *Ibid.*, pp. 3–4.
[45] *Ibid.*, pp. 4–6. On the re-evaluation of the cruelty of the Mongolian conquest of China, see Wang Huai-ling, " Tui ' Chung-kuo li-shih kang-yao ' Yüan-tai pu-fen ti i-chien " (" A critique of the Yüan dynasty section in ' Outline of Chinese History ' by Shang Yüeh "), *Historical Studies*, No. 7, 1958, p. 42 ff.
[46] Han, " On Chinggis Qan," p. 7.

has written, one must agree that it is a sophisticated article, well researched, well argued and balanced, with many original ideas about when and how the Mongolian state first came into existence. His final section on the role of Chinggis in world history, however, is quite otherwise. He begins by relating some of the benefits to the West of the East-West bridge which the Mongolian empire provided, largely in technology (the inventions usually mentioned are the magnetic compass, gunpowder and printing).[47] He then puts aside all caution in a paean of praise for Chinggis Qan, who broke 40 different states out of their isolation and allowed them to become acquainted with a higher culture, Chinese culture.[48]

In both the Yü *Biography* and the Han Ju-lin article, we are clearly confronted by a special phenomenon, the phenomenon of the last few paragraphs. Yü ends his judiciously revisionist book with an unexpected retreat into the orthodoxy of Soviet historical interpretation. Han's equally judicious article (his general interpretation of Chinggis does not differ greatly from Yü's) ends with an equally unexpected flight into extravagance. Yü's retreat is a retreat to safety: in assigning a positive role to Chinggis as a unifier of the Mongolian peoples he has left himself open as a Mongol to a charge of nasty Mongolian nationalism or pan-Mongolianism, a charge against which the last few paragraphs are a protection. Just as surely, Han's last few paragraphs seem deliberately designed to provoke and irritate the Soviets.

The Soviets were indeed irritated. Two of their scholars, R. V. Viatkin and S. L. Tikhvinskii, have responded to Han's article [49] and several other Chinese articles with even more extravagant claims for the benefits of the Mongolian world empire.[50] They are shocked at the sudden change in the evaluation of Chinggis and the Yüan dynasty, the beginnings of which they detect in 1959–62 (they apparently do not know the books of Yü Yüan-an in which several of Han Ju-lin's interpretations are first formulated), and which they characterise as definitely un-Marxian. In this they appear to be correct, at least to the extent that a positive interpretation of Chinggis does not represent Marx's own.[51]

---

[47] See Yü, *Outline History of Inner Mongolia*, p. 39.

[48] Han, " On Chinggis Qan," pp. 9–10.

[49] R. V. Viatkin and S. L. Tikhvinskii, " Some questions of historical science on the Chinese People's Republic," *Voprosy Istorii* (*Historical Questions*), No. 10 (October, 1963), pp. 3–20. Full translation in *Current Digest of the Soviet Press*, XVI, no. 4 (February 19, 1964), pp. 3–10, to which reference is made in this paper.

[50] See, for example, the article by Chou Ku-ch'eng, " On the conditions under which world history developed," *Historical Studies*, No. 2, 1961.

[51] I cannot precisely confirm this. Marx wrote a note on the early Mongols which has been published as " Mongoly v kontse XIV veka " (" The Mongols at the end of the 14th century "), in *Arkhiv K. Marksa i F. Engel'sa*, VI, pp. 169–171. This volume is not available to me and I have been unable to find such a paper in other editions of Marx's works.

While not denying the value of the unification of North China to the Chinese, Viatkin and Tikhvinskii ask: "[to achieve unification] was it necessary to endure the Mongol yoke and for the Chinese people to undergo great suffering? Was the help of Mongol horsemen and slavery necessary to expand 'cultural ties'? What kind of 'high culture' did the Mongols bring to flourishing and highly developed Samarkand? . . . What wide world were the enslaved peoples enabled to see?" [52]

The Viatkin and Tikhvinskii response is to the phenomenon of the last few paragraphs. The quite provocative ideas in the first two-thirds of Han's article do not interest them, nor does the question of Chinggis' varying roles in the histories of different peoples. They ignore his role in the creation of a Mongolian nationality through unification, which Soviet scholarship has heretofore been willing to grant. It is perhaps understandable during the present Sino-Soviet conflict that Chinese talk about the "unification of all the Mongolian peoples" should be unpopular in the Soviet Union, with important Mongolian populations living in three states: the Soviet Union itself, the Mongolian People's Republic (always closely allied with the U.S.S.R.) and China.

Although valuable, none of the books and articles discussed above really deals with the Yüan dynasty, and any Chinese wishing to read about that period of his national history must turn to the brief general histories, or to old-fashioned historical works. Indeed, serious study of the Yüan dynasty, by Chinese and others, can be said to be just beginning. Soviet scholars, for all their certainty that recent Chinese interpretations are incorrect, have contributed even less to the understanding of this period of Chinese history, although their studies on the Mongols themselves have been very important. [53]

Recent Chinese scholarship on the foreign conquest dynasties in general, and the Mongolian-Yüan period in particular, exhibits a number of significant tendencies, including a willingness to learn the languages of those dynasties for which important literary materials survive (Old Turkic, Mongolian and Manchu) [54] and to become familiar at least to some extent with modern European and Japanese scholarship. The influence of Marxist historical categories is obvious, and has sometimes

---

[52] Viatkin and Tikhvinskii, "Some questions of historical science," *op. cit.*, p. 7.

[53] Mongolian studies were created as a discipline in Russia about 140 years ago. But the Chinese language has never been considered a normal part of the Mongolist's curriculum, and this has successfully excluded them from Yüan studies.

[54] Communist Chinese studies on the ancient Turks are of considerable importance. Note for instance, Huang Wen-pi [*T'a-li-mu p'en-ti k'ao-ku-chi (Archaeological Report on the Tarim Basin)* (Peking: Science Publishing House, 1958)]; Ts-en Chung-mien [*T'u-chueh chi-shih (Collected History of the Turks)*, 2 vols. (Peking: Chung-hua shu-chu, 1958)]; Hsiang Ta [*T'ang-tai Ch'ang-an yu hsi-yu wen-ming (Ch'ang-an and the Civilisation of the Western Regions in T'ang Times)* (Peking: San-lien shu-tien, 1957)]; and a number of articles by Feng Chia-sheng—all men of the older generation.

led scholars to formulate new interpretations which do not harmonise with traditional Marxist or Soviet historiography. Significant also is the influence of what one is tempted to call a Kuomintang theory of Chinese history, which in its most extreme form sees the Chinese state as a great multi-national organism. At any given period in imperial history, one or another of these nationalities was dominant—usually the Han, but sometimes the Tibetans, Mongols or Manchus.[55] Thus foreign " barbarian " conquest dynasties were not foreign at all, even in their pre-dynastic phases. Yeh-lü A-pao-chi, Chinggis Qan and Nurhaci are therefore as much figures of Chinese national concern as are Yüeh Fei, Chu Yüan-chang and Li Tzu-ch'eng.

One can find these tendencies in the historical scholarship written before 1949, but not with the present frequency. The new methodologies and interpretations are perhaps less surprising than the persistence of older forms of historical scholarship: the old-fashioned essays written in classical Chinese, the reading and collation notes and the documentary histories.[56] The practitioners of these traditional forms of historiography, mostly older men of great learning, have been subject to frequent criticism in the historical journals by their Marxist colleagues, but at least they have been permitted to publish their work. Whether they will continue to do so under the great proletarian cultural revolution remains in doubt.

[55] Such a view has been expressed by Liu Ta-nien with respect to the Ch'ing dynasty. See Viatkin and Tikhvinski, *op. cit.*, p. 8.
[56] Notable examples are the books of Teng Chih-ch'eng on the Manchus and general history, the books of Feng Chia-sheng and Lo Chi-tsu on the Liao dynastic history, and the book of Ch'en Shu on supplements to the Jurchen Chin history.

11

Chinese Communist Interpretations of the Chinese Peasant Wars

By JAMES P. HARRISON

ONE of the most heated debates in Chinese Communist historiography concerns the evaluation of the peasant movements in Chinese history.[1] As in many other aspects of mainland intellectual life, the issues debated in this question seem artificial. Yet even in terms of the interpretation of Chinese history new problems have been raised, if not solved. More important, in terms of contemporary intellectual history, the discussions of the Chinese peasant wars form an important part of the documentation for the most massive attempt at ideological re-education in human history, the effort to inculcate attitudes of struggle in place of the traditional emphasis on harmony.

Certainly the Chinese place enormous emphasis on the subject:

> The study of these peasant revolts and wars can deeply reveal not only the laws of development of China's feudal society but also the basic Marxist theories of class struggle and feudal society. At the same time the study of the history of peasant wars has very great significance in the elevation of our country's glorious revolutionary tradition and in the education of the people's progressive class struggle.[2]

In short, as a leading historian put it, the " mass nature and revolutionary nature [of the peasant movements] . . . is the historical textbook of the Chinese labouring people." [3]

As Marxists, Chinese Communist historians are committed to the proposition that social history can be understood only as the history of struggles between mutually opposed classes. The radical shift represented by this reversal of the Confucian emphasis on harmonious social relations is, along with the stress on the material basis of history and its progression towards Communism, the most striking of the fundamental departures mainland historians have made from traditional historical

---

[1] Over 400 articles and several books on the subject were published between 1949 and mid-1961, not including a comparable amount of material on the nineteenth-century rebellions. Discussions of the subject have played an especially great role in the revived " hundred flowers " debates since 1958.

[2] Shih Shao-pin, " Discussion of the Peasant Revolutionary Wars in Chinese Feudal Society," in *Chung-kuo Feng-chien She-hui Nung-min Chan-cheng Wen-t'i T'ao-lun Chi (Collected Articles on the Problem of the Peasant Wars in Chinese Feudal Society)*, Shi Shao-pin (ed.) [hereafter *SSP*] (Peking: San-lien Shu-tien, 1962), p. 499.

[3] Hou Wai-lu, " The Development of the Peasant Wars and their Programs and Slogans in Earlier and Later Periods of China's Feudal Society," *SSP*, p. 47.

practices. It is also the most characteristic feature of the specifically Communist revolution in Chinese historiography, since most other basic changes in the interpretation of Chinese history were well under way or complete before 1949 as inevitable products of the modernisation of Chinese thought.[4]

As Chinese, mainland historians naturally look to their own history for the proof of such theories as that of the class struggle. Specifically they look to peasant movements in the history of imperial China as the historical documentation for the enormous task of converting seven hundred million people to an acceptance of the naturalness and efficacy of class struggle. The subject is doubly important to the Chinese theorists because the country lacked a fully developed bourgeois stage and only the peasant wars can demonstrate the place of the class struggle in traditional times. Accordingly, mainland studies of the peasant movements now assume a place of importance comparable to the treatment of the modern bourgeois and labour movements in Soviet historiography as direct forerunners of the revolution.

However, despite the apparent naturalness of exploring the historical roots of Chinese class struggle, concern with the other pillar of Marxist historiography, the necessity to show the economic and social evolution of history and the whole complex debate over the nature of Chinese society, occupied the academic Marxists almost exclusively prior to 1949. Then, as the prospect of a Communist triumph became more likely, the academic Marxists became more concerned with showing revolutionary traditions in Chinese history. At Party direction, increasing attention was devoted to documenting from Chinese history the theory of the class struggle and the inevitable triumph of the masses. As Fan Wen-lan wrote in the preface to one of the many popular tracts on the history of the peasant movements, which began to appear as "liberation" approached:

> For us intellectuals, finding who were the masters of history is of first importance. Because when one discovers the master of history, he also finds the masters of present society. Once we recognise this and always honestly serve [the masses], then and only then can the intellectuals find their bright and happy future.[5]

Some better known historians trained before 1949 have taken an enthusiastic part in recent studies of the history of the peasant wars,[6] but

---

4 Such as the Marxist emphasis on economic considerations in place of Confucian moral determinism and the adoption of a lineal concept of historical development in place of the Confucian theory of cyclical aberrations from a permanent ideal.

5 Fan Wen-lan, Preface to Pai T'ao, *Chung-kuo Nung-min Ch'i-yi te Ku-shih* (*Stories of Chinese Peasant Revolts*) (Harbin: Kuang-hua Shu-tien, 1948).

6 Notably Hou Wai-lu, Pai Shou-yi, Ch'i Hsia and Yang K'uan. However, Fan Wen-lan, Chien Po-tsan and Kuo Mo-jo have all warned against exaggerating the revolutionary nature of the peasant revolts and Wu Han has refused to even speak on the

it is the younger generation, products of the Party line in education, who have contributed the most radical interpretations in the flood of hundreds of articles seeking to prove that "only through struggle is there a way out." [7]

DEFINITIONS

The Chinese Communists sometimes use the term "peasant revolutionary war" (*nung-min ke-ming chan-cheng*) to describe the peasant revolts in Chinese history, but no Communist writer has ever equated these movements with the Communist-led revolutions of the twentieth century. They justify the use of the word "revolution" in terms of the "revolutionary effects" of the peasant revolts in advancing the cause of history, but never maintain that the peasant revolts themselves ushered in a new epoch of history as would be required of a social "revolution." [8]

The usual Communist terms for the peasant movements in Chinese history are "righteous uprisings of the peasantry" (*nung-min ch'i-yi*), which I shall hereafter designate "peasant uprising," and "peasant wars" (*nung-min chan-cheng*). The former are distinguished from the latter primarily in terms of their size. Where peasant revolts were "local peasant riots (*pao-tung*) of relatively small scale, peasant wars were armed struggles of the peasantry against the landlord class on a state-wide scale." [9] Nonetheless, both are "armed struggle" and "the highest form of class struggle."

One student of these "class struggles" distinguishes five types of peasant revolts in Chinese history which may be useful for categorisation: first, the small peasant movement which neither set up any organisation nor promulgated any revolutionary slogans (as exemplified by countless "peasant riots"); second, the large-scale peasant movement which developed an organisation but which was quickly suppressed, such as the movements of Ch'en Sheng (209 B.C.) and Chang Chueh (A.D. 184), or which was transformed into a "feudal war" such as the uprising led by Ko Jung (*c.* A.D. 525); third, the large-scale peasant movement which was infiltrated by members of the governing class and transformed into an instrument of dynastic change, such as the movements opposing Wang Mang, the Sui and the Mongols; fourth, small-scale peasant movements covering several counties (*chou* or *hsien*) but which persisted and

subject. See Wu Han, "More on Meetings of Immortals," *Survey of the China Mainland Press* (*SCMP*) (Hong Kong: U.S. Consulate-General), No. 2477, pp. 5–6, citing *Kuang-ming Jih-pao* (*Kuang-ming Daily*), March 21, 1961.

[7] Su Hsing, "Ch'en Sheng, The First Leader of a Chinese Peasant Revolt," *Chung-kuo Ch'ing-nien* (*Chinese Youth*), No. 72, August 1951, p. 30.

[8] See summary discussion of the "theory of two types of revolution" in Hsueh-shu Tung-t'ai (Academic Situation Column), *Jen-min Jih-pao* (*People's Daily*), March 2, 1965.

[9] Li T'ieh-tso, "The Question of the Special Features of Chinese Peasant Wars," *SSP*, p. 219.

proclaimed a relatively clear ideology, such as the movement in Szechuan in the late second century of our era and the movement of Chung Hsiang and Yang Yao in the second and third decades of the twelfth century; finally, the large-scale peasant movement which struggled in the interests of the peasant class for a relatively long time, such as the movements of the late T'ang and Ming and the T'ai-p'ings.[10]

Similarly, other historians argue that the term " peasant leader " applied only to those who have " merged with the peasant masses " and contributed to their struggle. The term " peasant revolt " or " peasant war " had to be merited and could only be applied to movements whose participants opposed feudal inequities and fought for the good of " the people," [11] according to this view. Therefore, some exceptionally destructive or aimless movements are denied the title " righteous uprisings," [12] particularly if led by ruling class figures, such as An Lu-shan.

In sum, Communist definitions of peasant movements tend to be purposely broad and vague. They use the word " peasant " loosely to include representatives of many different social layers so long as these diverse elements can be shown to have behaved according to the Chinese Communist ideal for the " peasant rebel." [13] Yet, if these definitions are virtually meaningless as historical tools, they do provide a framework for the Communist reconstruction of history.

For a working definition for this paper, which could also serve as a paraphrase of the broader Communist definitions, peasant revolts or wars might be described as

> movements of large groups of rural inhabitants predominantly of lower- and middle-class origin, though possibly with some upper-class leaders, who are mobilised in the belief that they are acting in the interests of the majority of their kind and against the existing government and *status quo*.

According to this type of definition, there were well over a dozen large-scale peasant movements in the two thousand years of imperial

10 Ch'i Li-huang, " The Dual Nature of Peasant Governments in China's Feudal Society . . ," *Li-shih Yen-chiu (Historical Research)*, No. 3, 1962, pp. 134–135.

11 " Anhwei University History Department Holds Discussion of Chinese Peasant War," *Kuang-ming Jih-pao*, April 3, 1961.

12 The revolt of An Lu-shan, A.D. 755, is the most notable exception. According to the Communist historians this is because although An was said to have " used the class struggles of the peasants against feudal exploitation," his movement, " judged by its status, was a civil war, whereas judged by the origin [of its leaders] it was actually a war between different races." See Wang Tan-ling, *Chung-kuo Nung-min Ke-ming Shih Hua (Talks of the History of Chinese Peasant Revolutions)* (Shanghai: Kuo-chi, Wen-hua Fu-wu She, 1953), p. 185, and Feng Chih, " Tu Fu," Chung-kuo Wen-hsueh (*Chinese Literature*), April 1962, p. 31.

13 This is of course analogous to the current inclusion of all who accept " proletarian " leadership and goals in the " party of the proletariat," and to the definition of the " people " as all who accept Party leadership. See Liu Shao-ch'i, *On the Party* (Peking: Foreign Languages Press, 1951), p. 20, and Mao Tse-tung, *On the Correct Handling of Contradictions Among the People* (Peking: Foreign Languages Press, 1960), p. 8.

China, including eight which either overthrew or greatly weakened the ruling dynasty.[14] Smaller peasant revolts were numbered in the hundreds in many dynastic periods.[15]

CURRENT DISCUSSIONS

The first of the problems discussed in the mainland historiography of peasant wars is the causation of the peasant movements. Communist historians considered the exploitation of the peasant class by the landlord class and its political arm, the feudal monarchy, the primary and inevitable cause of the peasant revolts. This theory of causation might be summarised as a Marxist version of the traditional adage " the officials force the people to resist " (*kuan-pi min-fan*). Other economic and natural factors such as land concentration or famine are also mentioned but are considered secondary to, or shaped by, class oppression.

The second topic of discussion concerns the leadership and social composition of the peasant movements. After an early period of insisting that only leaders actually of peasant class origin (*ch'u-shen*) be considered peasant rebels, historians moved to the prevailing view that one could serve the interests of and have the attributes of (*shu-hsing*) the peasant class, regardless of social origin. Thus it could be admitted that " the leaders of the various peasant uprisings and wars were not necessarily all of the peasant class and some were even of classes opposed to the peasantry." [16] Rebel leaders are graded according to the degree to which they advanced the cause of history and served the people.

An Anhwei historian recently suggested five categories of peasant rebels in Chinese history:

> *First*, the isolated hero who never enters into the life of the masses [some would even include the military aristocrat Hsiang Yu in this category of " peasant rebel "]; *second*, the leader of a mass movement who has goals differing from the masses and who gives no help to the peasants [Liu Hsuan and Liu Hsiu of the rebellion against Wang Mang are cited in this category]; *third*, leaders whose goals differ from the goals of the masses but who contribute to the organisation and campaigns of the mass movement [such as Li Mi, *c.* 616, Sun En, *c.* 400, and Sung Chiang, *c.* 1120]; *fourth*, leaders such as those in type three who help the peasants but for their own purposes and who later are completely transformed into representatives of the feudalists such as

---

14 In addition to the well-known revolts against the Ch'in, Wang Mang, the Han, Sui, T'ang, Yuan and Ming and the T'ai-p'ings, there were at least three other major disruptions in each of the periods of the northern and southern dynasties, the northern and southern Sung, the Ming and the Ch'ing.

15 Chien Po-tsan mentions over a thousand peasant revolts in one article: Chien Po-tsan, *Li-shih Wen-t'i Lun-ts'ung* (*Collected Discussions on Historical Problems*) (Peking: Jen-min Ch'u-pan She, 1962), p. 110 *et seq.*

16 Sun Tso-min, *Chung-kuo Nung-min Chan-cheng Wen-t'i T'an-su* (*An Investigation Into Problems of Chinese Peasant Wars*) (Shanghai: Hsin Chih-shih Ch'u-pan She, 1956), p. 89.

Liu Pang and Chu Yuan-chang, and; *fifth*, the dedicated peasant leader who fights consistently for the peasants against the landlords [Huang Ch'ao and Li Tzu-ch'eng are included here, while most would include such T'ai-p'ing leaders as Yang Hsiu-ch'ing and Li Hsiu-ch'eng].[17]

Of course it is evident in this scheme that no rebel could, or did, win the support necessary for the success of a rebellion without "selling out" the anti-feudal goals of the peasant class. Hence according to the logic of the Communist interpretations, the least successful "bandit" would have the best chance of retaining revolutionary purity, and vice versa. This feature of the peasant revolts was well summarised in the traditional saying "he who fails is a bandit; he who succeeds is a king" (*pai-che wei k'ou, ch'eng-che wei wang*). Communist historians seek to cope with this dilemma in their interpretations by citing the inevitable failure of pre-modern workers' movements. They argue that a solution of the contradiction between loyalty to the working class and the achievement of successful revolution became possible only when the working class was itself able to win control of the means of production in the modern socialist revolution.

Analogous to interpretations of the peasant rebels is the evaluation of notable government figures who participated in the suppression of peasant revolts. As a rule, the interpretation of government generals presents no problems since they were "suppressors of the people," but there has been acrimonious debate over the treatment of such leading figures as Ts'ao Ts'ao, Yueh Fei and the great Ch'in, Han and T'ang emperors who seemed to have advanced the cause of history in spite of, or because of, their suppression of revolts. Generally the better known historians such as Kuo Mo-jo have defended the "progressiveness" of such government leaders, but the majority of younger and less well-known writers have sharply criticised any tendency to praise great emperors and generals who, like the above, also oppressed the masses, the "real makers of history."[18] These discussions raise the fundamental problems of the meshing of the Marxist theories of the class struggle with the Marxist theory of historical development.

The manner in which the peasant movements themselves evolved from lower to higher forms of struggle is what the Communists call the "evolution of the peasant wars" (*nung-min chan-cheng te fa-chan*), the third topic of considerable discussion in mainland historiography of the peasant movements. This question is especially difficult in the Marxist consideration of the peasant wars against feudalism, when the feudal

---

[17] "Anhwei University History Department," *op. cit.*

[18] *e.g.*, see Lin Yeh-shu, "On Discussion of the Problem of Evaluation of Ts'ao Ts'ao," *Shih-hsueh Yueh-k'an (History Monthly)*, 1959, p. 9.

system was still performing a progressive historical function as was the case in China from Ch'in through T'ang.[19]

Within the two thousand-year history of "Chinese feudalism" another tendency in the Communist treatment of historical evolution is worth noting, namely, that the Communist historians treat the evolution within each dynastic period in exactly the same way they treat the development of a given mode of production as a whole. Thus, the class struggle eliminates or modifies restrictive productive relations or bad working conditions at the end of each dynasty, permitting the development of productive forces in the next dynasty in the same manner that the social revolution brought on the transition from a given stage of production to another in Western Marxist historiography. Still other problems of evolution concern the changes within each peasant war, particularly after the reigning dynasty had been overthrown, as in the case of the struggles against Wang Mang, the Sui, Yuan and Ming. These peasant wars supposedly evolved from more progressive "anti-feudal wars" to "wars of feudal unification."

Given the stress on historical evolution in Communist historiography, the fourth topic in the mainland treatment of the peasant wars is in many ways the most decisive, the manner in which the peasant wars "formed the real motive force of historical development in China's feudal society." Mainland historians at first interpreted this statement of Mao's in terms of concessions in working conditions wrung from the feudal government, but this interpretation has been criticised as ignoring the deeper currents of history in favour of a "new theory of the dynastic cycle" and as giving too much credit to the ruling class and not enough to the masses. Accordingly, recent interpretations of the "function" (tso-yung) of the peasant wars stress not only the improvement of working conditions, but the peasant's struggle for production and for general influence on the society of the time. There have also been extensive debates on the function of those peasant wars which were followed by chaotic conditions and greater oppression rather than by a new, strong dynasty, such as those of the late Han and T'ang and many smaller revolts.

A final consideration of the function of the peasant wars concerns their relation to racial wars. In Marxist historiography racial antagonisms are interpreted as manifestations of and secondary to class

---

[19] Most historians handle the problem by stating that the peasant wars advanced from early struggles against individual dynasties and feudal lords to struggles against the feudal system as a whole after the middle of the T'ang. Thus, the early peasant wars advanced production by opposition to the *corvée* and excessive ties to the feudal lord, but after feudalism entered its declining stage, peasant movements evolved to oppose such basic features of the system as land-holding and unequal stratification.

contradictions. However, the racial contradictions between the Han and other races of China sometimes play a prominent part in mainland historiography, as in the anti-Mongol and anti-Manchu wars. In both of these cases, the racial contradiction temporarily took precedence over the class contradiction in later stages of the struggles, according to the prevailing view. In short, although racial struggle is not so progressive as class struggle, if it serves Chinese nationalism as in the anti-Mongol and anti-Manchu wars, it is highly praised. In fact these and similar struggles are said to prove that the peasants were "the only true patriots" in Chinese history.[20] They are also said to have laid the basis for the later leading role of the peasantry in the struggles against imperialism.

A fifth topic of discussion concerns the degree of organisation of the peasant movements and the degree to which they could form a peasant government (*nung-min cheng-fu*), representing peasant class interests. In the discussion of this question, as elsewhere in the mainland historiography of the peasant revolts, only an influential minority support the classical Marxist view that in fact the peasants could not represent themselves as a class. This minority maintains that the governments set up by the Chinese peasant rebels were in fact "feudal governments." However, the majority of Chinese historians contend, on the contrary, that many Chinese peasant movements could and did establish an organisation which temporarily represented the peasant class, although all concede that prior to the emergence of the proletariat such "governments" sooner or later became instruments of the ruling class.

Despite the diverse composition of the mass movements in Chinese history, the leading position of the peasant class is affirmed. A recent summary spoke of a "united front of the middle and lower layers of society, led by the peasant class."[21] Others protest that this majority view of the historical role of the Chinese peasants usurps functions reserved for the proletarian class. More accurately, in this prevailing Chinese view, the peasant class is substituted for the bourgeoisie of Western Marxist historiography as the leading class in the struggle against feudalism.

REVOLUTIONARY IDEOLOGY

Discussions of the "revolutionary ideology of the peasant rebels" (*nung-min chan-cheng-chung te ke-ming ssu-hsiang*) are derived from a relatively small number of slogans and statements which Communist

---

[20] *e.g.*, see Fan Wen-lan preface to *Chung-kuo T'ung-shih Chien-pien* (*A General History of China*) (Peking: Jen-min Ch'u-pan She, revised edition 1961), 2 vols., I, p. 66.
[21] Shih Shao-pin, *op. cit.*, *SSP*, p. 503.

historians presume to manifest the wishes of the inarticulate masses throughout the centuries.[22] Implicit in the Communist handling of this problem is the belief that only the working class knows the real wishes of the masses, while traditional and bourgeois historians were either ignorant of these ideals or consciously concealed and distorted them. This type of interpretation also assumes the sincerity of the rebel slogans, although it can be argued that their appeal can be taken to prove popular support for the ideas expressed, regardless of the real aims of the leaders.[23] Another key assumption in the Communist analysis of rebel programmes and ideology is the assertion that the different motivation of the rebels made their proposals different in kind from similar statements and ideas found in classical philosophy and also in the proposals of various "feudal" governments. Therefore, mainland historians argue that where governing class proposals designed to ameliorate glaring inequalities were intended only to preserve political power, similar rebel demands were by contrast used in the struggle against the government to win power for the labouring class, which alone could effect a really new order.

Hou Wai-lu classifies the egalitarian content of these slogans according to whether they implied a better distribution of the property already possessed by the rebels or whether they implied confiscating the surplus property of the rich to relieve the poor.[24] A third category of slogan which is by far the most common simply reflects a negative protest against abuses of the government rather than a positive programme.

In the case of the first great peasant war led by Ch'en Sheng and Wu Kuang, the complaint "are kings, nobles, generals and ministers a race of their own?" (*wang hou chiang hsiang, ch'i yu chung hu?*) is cited to show peasant opposition to hereditary privileges, but is, of course, also well within the Confucian tradition.[25] Rebel slogans decrying the abuse of the Ch'in government are better known. In the case of the Red Eyebrows, their simple legal principle "if a man killed

---

22 Many of these slogans are discussed in Vincent Shih, " Some Chinese Rebel Ideologies," *T'oung Pao*, p. 44, and in Yuji Muramatsu, " Some Themes in Chinese Rebel Ideologies," in *The Confucian Persuasion*, A. F. Wright (ed.) (Palo Alto: Stanford Un., 1960). Norman Cohn's *The Pursuit of the Millennium* (New York: Harper Torchbook, 1961) provides interesting comparative material for medieval Europe.

23 Actually at least one Communist historian has been so bold as to suggest the obvious assumption that rebel leaders used such slogans only for purposes of recruitment and not out of conviction. See Sun Tso-min, " Tentative Discussion of the Nature of Li Tzu-ch'eng's Ta-hsun Government," *Hsin Chien-she* (*New Construction*), No. 3, 1962.

24 Hou Wai-lu, *op. cit.*, SSP, p. 35.

25 This was pointed out in a recent article: Ts'ao Yung-nien, " On the Slogans of Ch'en Sheng and Wu Kuang," *Kuang-ming Jih-pao*, August 14, 1963. See also Vincent Shih, *op. cit.*, p. 154, from whom the translation is taken.

another, he is executed; if he wounds another, he must give compensation " (*sha jen che ssu, shang jen che ch'ang ch'uang*) [26] is similarly cited to show peasant protest against the unequal " feudal laws." It is clearly based on Mohist and legalist principles of equal punishment for all, regardless of social rank.

Communist historians have frequently interpreted the title of the influential text (*T'ai-p'ing Ching*) used by the Yellow Turban rebels as the " Book of Great Equality." Recently, however, many mainland historians as well as most non-Communist historians regard this as a distortion of the original meaning of the term *t'ai-p'ing*.[27] In fact, many now hold that the book was a conservative influence rather than an instigation to revolt.[28] Nevertheless, mainland historians advance evidence of certain welfare measures, if not of egalitarian proposals, as evidence of the continuing peasant struggle for justice in the late Han.

Certain isolated slogans from the period of the Northern and Southern Dynasties and the Sui have also been mentioned.[29] However, because of the dispute over the role of the class struggle in early feudalism and in the absence of many clear-cut slogans for the period, most mainland historians do not stress aspects of positive peasant ideology before the late T'ang. They argue that the peasant movements of the early feudal period were primarily negative protests against specific government and individual abuses, such as the *corvée* and the personal restrictions imposed by the lord on his tenant or serf.

Then after the middle of the T'ang, a " certain degree of conscious opposition to the feudal system " (*fan-tui feng-chien chih-tu te mou-chung ch'eng-tu te chueh-wu hsing*) developed in the peasant movements, according to the prevailing mainland view. The growing class consciousness of the peasants was revealed in the slogans and programmes of rebels of the later peasant uprisings from the late T'ang on. Historians cite the personal seal of Ch'iu Fu (revolted 859), bearing the characters for " equality " (*p'ing-chun*), and the titles taken by Wang Hsien-chih, " heaven appointed equality general " (*t'ien-pu p'ing-chun ta-chiang-chun*), and Huang Ch'ao, " heaven storming, protecting equality general " (*ch'ung-t'ien t'ai-pao chun-p'ing ta-chiang-chun*), as the first

---

26 See Hans Bielenstein, *The Restoration of the Han Dynasty* (Goteborg: Elanders Boktyckeri Aktiebolag, 1953), p. 138.

27 See Vincent Shih, *op. cit.*, pp. 166–167.

28 See " Academic Circles Discuss the T'ai-p'ing Ching . . . ," *People's Daily,* December 15, 1960.

29 *e.g.*, see Chao Li-sheng and Kao Chao-yi, *Chung-kuo Nung-min Chang-cheng Shih Lun-wen Chi* (*Collected Discussions on the History of the Chinese Peasant Wars*) (Shanghai: Hsin Chih-shin Ch'u-pan She, 1955), p. 41, who assert that the fourth-century Szechvan rebel, Li T'e, advocated a policy of " equal opening of land " (*k'en t'ien chun p'ing*) which expressed the idea of " a certain egalitarian . . . Utopian society."

indications of rebel concern with the fundamental issues of social and economic inequality.[30]

Mainland historians cite the rebellion of Huang Chao, along with the revolt of Chang Hsien-chung in the late Ming,[31] as prime examples of the distortion and slander of the peasant revolts in traditional historiography. They charge that the bad reputation of Huang Ch'ao is due to the class bias of the traditional historian since in the words of Sung historians, the late T'ang rebels "hated the officials in particular and killed as many of them as they could," while "the wealthy families were all expelled in a barefoot condition." Yet the same historians, the Communists emphasise, were forced to admit that "when the bandit [Huang Ch'ao] saw impoverished people, he handed out gold and silk to them." [32]

One of the primary sources cited by Communist historians as proof of an alleged peasant concern with the injustices of "feudal China" is the statement of Wang Hsiao-po, who revolted against the Sung in Szechuan in 994. He is reported to have stated: "I hate the inequality between rich and poor. I will level it [the inequality] for you" (wu chi p'in-fu pu-chun, chin wei ju chun-chih). According to the same source, Wang's successor, Li Hsun, sought to carry out this principle by confiscating the surplus property of the rich and distributing it to the poor.[33]

Similar statements describing the activities of Chung Hsiang and Yang Yao in Hunan and Hupei (suppressed 1135), together with the programmes of the late Ming and T'ai-p'ing rebels, form the principal exhibits for proponents of a revolutionary peasant ideology. A contemporary source states that Chung Hsiang told his followers: "The [present] law which distinguishes between noble and commoner, and between rich and poor, is not a good law. If I am able to carry out a law, then noble and commoner, rich and poor, will be made equal" (fa fen kuei-chien p'in-fu, fei shan-fa yeh; wo hsing fa, tang fa teng kuei-chien, chun p'in-fu). Although Chung Hsiang himself was a wealthy landlord, we are told that "small people" (hsiao min) around Tung T'ing

---

[30] e.g., see Hu Ju-lei, "The Historical Function of the Late T'ang Peasant Wars," Li-shih Yen-chiu, No. 1, 1963, p. 117.

[31] e.g., see Sun Tz'u-chou, "An Investigation of Chang Hsien-chung in the Records of Ssu Ch'uan," Li-shih Yen-chiu, No. 1, 1957, and "The Birth of a Graduate Thesis," People's Daily, August 26, 1962. See also James Parsons, "Attitudes Towards the Late Ming Rebellions," Oriens Extremus, No. 2, December 1959.

[32] e.g., see Chou Pao-chu, "Discussion of a Problem in the History of the Late T'ang Peasant War," Shih-hsueh Yueh-k'an, No. 6, 1959. For a Western reference to some of these problems, see Howard S. Levy, Biography of Huang Ch'ao (Berkeley: University of California, 1961), pp. 28, 73–74.

[33] Shen K'uo, Meng Ch'i Pi T'an (Notes taken at Meng Ch'i), Chap. 15. This interpretation is disputed by W. Eichhorn "Zur Vorgeschichte des Aufstandes von Wang Hsiao-po und Li Shun in Szuchuan," Zeitschrift für Deutschen Morgenländischen Gesellschaft (1955), p. 105.

Lake, Hunan, flocked to join him, and they plundered and burned government yamens and killed officials, scholars, monks, sorcerers and medicine men. The shocked recorder of these deeds reported that the rebels excused these actions by "calling bandit soldiers lords, [and by] saying the national law was an iniquitous law, [while] killing men was [a means] of carrying out the [new] law and plunder was [a means of] equalisation" (*wei tsei-ping wei yeh erh, wei kuo-tien wei hsieh-fa, wei sha-jen wei hsing-fa, wei chieh-ts'ai wei chun-p'ing*).[34] According to Communist historians, these statements show the "dreams of peasants for a life of primitive equality and justice and their struggles to liquidate poverty and injustice." [35]

Statements attributed to the essentially religious revolts of Fang La in the Sung and of the White Lotus from the Sung on receive less attention in the documentation of a militant rebel ideology, presumably because there is considerable controversy over their interpretation.[36]

By the late Ming, according to many mainland historians, economic developments were approaching conditions of incipient capitalism. In the Marxist scheme of things such conditions would invariably influence the ideology of the Chinese rebels, but Party theorists no longer allow historians to make too much of the problem of incipient capitalism because of the threat such an interpretation poses to the theory of the imperialist rape of China and to the image of Party uniqueness.

Again, the materials of Chinese history strain at the confines of official dogma. On the one hand, revolts such as those of Yeh Tsung-liu and "the Levelling Prince" (Ch'an P'ing Wang), Teng Mou-ch'i (1442–1450) and of Liu T'ung and Li Yuan (1466–1471) are said to show new economic demands reflecting social and economic developments. The former were among the most important of some seventy-seven so-called "miners' revolts" of the middle Ming and supposedly involved,

---

[34] Hsu Meng-hua, *San Ch'ao Pei-meng Hui-pen* (*Collections on Negotiations with the Northern Dynasties During the Three Reigns*), Chuan 137, pp. 4–5.

[35] G. Ya. Smolin, "Peasant Uprising Under Leadership of Chung Hsiang and Yang Yao," *Problemy Vostokovedeniye* (*Problems of Eastern Knowledge*), No. 1, 1960, p. 60.

[36] For Fang La, see Ch'ien Chun-hua and Ch'i Hsia, "The Uprising of Fang La," in *Chung-kuo Nung-min Ch'i-yi Lun-chi* (*Articles on Chinese Peasant Uprisings*); Li Kuang-pi, *et al.*, eds. (Peking: Sen-lien Shu-tien, 1958) (hereafter Li Kuang-pi, ed.), and Feng Chih, "Did Fang La's Revolt Promulgate Egalitarian Slogans?" *Kuang-ming Jih-pao*, September 29, 1960. See also the recent study of Fang La's revolt by Kao Yu-kung, *Harvard Journal of Asiatic Studies*, No. 24 (1962–63). For a White Lotus song stating: "Only after destroying the unjust will there be great equality [or peace]," see Pei-ching Ta-hsueh Chung-wen Hsi, eds., *Chung-kuo Li-tai Nung-min Wen-t'i Wen-shueh Tzu-liao* (*Literary Materials on the Peasant Question in Chinese History*) (Peking: Chung-hua Shu-chu, 1959), p. 107. For a discussion of the White Lotus ideology in the Ch'ing, see Yang K'uan, "A Tentative Discussion of the Features of the White Lotus," *Kuang-ming Jih-pao*, March 15, 1961, and Shao Shung-cheng, "Secret Societies, Religions and the Peasant Wars," *SSP*, pp. 374–384.

for the first time, large numbers of urban plebeians as well as peasants, while the peasants supposedly made new economic demands in the struggle to open up restricted lands.[37]

On the other hand, orthodox historians criticise efforts to find too great an advance in peasant ideology in the late Ming. Among the recent criticism of the historian Shang Yueh was the charge that he attributed the late Ming egalitarian slogans to the growing influences of incipient capitalism. Rather, orthodox interpreters maintain, these slogans were products of changes within feudalism and not of new forces, of quantitative and not qualitative changes.[38]

In any case, the ideology of the peasant rebels is said to have reached a new stage of development by the late Ming. Some writers state that the egalitarian ideals of the peasants developed from a concern for the equalisation of movable property in the Sung to demands for equal land-holding in the Ming.[39] According to this view, the proposal of Li Tzu-ch'eng and Li Yen for the "equalisation of land and the avoidance of taxes" (chun-t'ien mien-liang) was the first such clear programme advanced by the Chinese rebels. Li Tzu-ch'eng called himself "great general claiming justice for heaven" (fen-t'ien ch'ang-yi ta yuan-shuai).[40] Other late Ming rebel slogans, such as "equal buying and selling" (p'ing-mai p'ing-mai), are also cited as evidence of enlightened rebel policies.

The key issue in the evaluation of the late Ming rebellions, as in the case of the T'ai-p'ings, is of course the degree to which they were carried out and the real intentions of the leaders. In both cases, there are numerous statements attesting to the rebels' destruction of the rich and some attesting to their help of the poor, but as one would expect, there is little, if any, evidence of the systematic execution of an equal land policy. In the case of Li Tzu-ch'eng's revolt, some historians argue that local records recently discovered in Shantung prove rebel distribution of land. However, other historians maintain that the redistribution applied only to movable property, while Li Tzu-ch'eng's programme was mainly directed against burdensome Ming taxes.[41] There is also

---

37 See the articles in Li Kuang-pi, ed., op. cit., and Li Lung-ch'ien, "A Tentative Discussion of Resistance Struggles of the Ming Miner Movements," Shih-hsueh Yueh-k'an, March 1959., p. 34.

38 Liao Ning Ta-hsueh History Department, "Criticise Shang Yueh's Mistaken Views of Rural Class Relations and the Peasant Wars in the Ming and Ch'ing," Kuang-ming Jih-pao, July 21, 1960, and P'an Te-shen, "On the Nature, Features and Function of the Peasant Revolts and War of the Last Stage of Chinese Feudal Society," SSP, p. 194.

39 e.g., Chang Hsing-te, "Features of the Peasant Revolt of Chung Hsiang and Yang Yao," Li-shih Chiao-hsueh Wen-t'i (Problems of History Teaching), No. 3, 1958.

40 See Muramatsu, op. cit., p. 262.

41 Jung Sheng, "A Tentative Discussion of the Special Points in the Peasant Class Struggles of the Ming and Ch'ing," in SSP, pp. 10–12; Hsieh Kuo-chen, "Notes of

discussion of the role of Li Yen, the son of a prominent government official, in devising Li Tzu-ch'eng's programme.

There is no disagreement among Communist historians about the egalitarian nature of various T'ai-p'ing proposals, but there is an enormous difference of opinion as to the degree to which they were carried out, and their " progressiveness " in the light of the conditions of the time, *i.e.*, the extent to which such T'ai-p'ing policies as the land programme were influenced by, and favoured the growth of, capitalism. This characteristic of the T'ai-p'ings is covered by statements to the effect that the T'ai-p'ings were an " old-style [42] peasant movement ' flavoured by ' varying degrees of a bourgeois-democratic revolution." [43]

The problem of the degree of execution of the land programme and other T'ai-p'ing policies is still unresolved but is generally said to depend on the area and the time period involved. Three types of T'ai-p'ing land programme have been defined : first, in a few places the landlord holdings were confiscated and distributed to the poor as well as to T'ai-p'ing officials; secondly, tenants were allowed to take over land deserted by the former owners; thirdly, in most areas, the old systems of landlord-tenant relations were continued as before.[44] Therefore, there was no " fixed land system " in practice, but some revolutionary redistributions were effected when conditions allowed. The prevailing view is that significant parts of the communal treasury system were carried out in the early years of the T'ai-p'ing rebellion, and the land law intended to extend this principle to forms of land-holding. However, since the orders of the T'ai-p'ing leaders were not implemented by local officials, the rebels later compromised with the gentry, who alone were able to administer the newly won territories.[45]

Materials on the Function of the Late Ming and Early Ch'ing Peasant Revolts," *Li-shih Yen-chiu*, No. 3, 1962, p. 145, and Wang Shou-yi, " Doubts About the ' Equal Land ' Slogan of the Late Ming Peasant Army," *Li-shih Yen-chiu*, No. 2, 1962.

42 The term " old-style " (*chiu-shih*) peasant war is used to designate rebellions which conformed to the pattern of " pure peasant revolutions " (*tan-ch'ün nung-min ke-ming*) which erupted throughout the " feudal " period. In other words " old-style peasant revolts " are distinguished from peasant movements of the bourgeois period and especially from Communist-led peasant movements.

43 See articles in *T'ai-p'ing T'ien-kuo Ke-ming Hsing-chih Wen-t'i T'ao-lun Chi* (*Collected Essays on the Nature of the Revolution of the T'ai-p'ing Heavenly Kingdom*), Ching Yen and Lin Yen-shu, eds. (Peking : San-lien Shu-tien, 1961). Seven views on the nature of the T'ai-p'ings presented in this book are summarised by L. P. Delyusin in *Narody Azii i Afriki* (Peoples of Asia and Africa, hereafter *NAA*), No. 5, 1962, pp. 183–186.

44 Ts'ao Kuo-she, " Discussion of the Land and Tax Policy of the T'ai-p'ing Heavenly Kingdom," *Shantung Ta-hsueh Hsueh-pao* (*Journal of Shantung University*), No. 9, 1959.

45 See V. P. Ilyushechkin, " Agrarian Policies of the T'ai-p'ings," *NAA*, No. 4, 1962, and Lung Sheng-Yun, " On the Land Policy of the T'ai-p'ing Heavenly Kingdom," *Li-shih Yen-chiu*, No. 6, 1963, for recent summaries of interpretations of the T'ai-p'ing land programme.

Through the middle of the 1950s, most writers stressed the revolutionary side of the T'ai-p'ing movement, although all acknowledged that no such sweeping revolution could succeed prior to the emergence of the proletariat. The weaknesses of the peasant class and the inevitable failure of the T'ai-p'ings were stressed in important anniversary articles in the *People's Daily* in 1951 and 1956,[46] but it was not until the late 1950s that most writers toned down their praise of the revolutionary qualities of the T'ai-p'ings.[47]

The recent restraint in the evaluation of the revolutionary nature of the T'ai-p'ings contrasts with the opposite tendency in the treatment of earlier peasant revolts and no doubt is explained by the proximity of the T'ai-p'ings to the Communist-led revolution. All Chinese are aware of the significance of the T'ai-p'ing movement and there is no longer the need to dramatise its egalitarian proposals as is the case with the earlier peasant revolts. Rather, the danger is that Party uniqueness may be questioned by too great attention to the revolutionary qualities of the T'ai-p'ings. Therefore, mainland historians are more careful to stress the inevitable failure of the T'ai-p'ings than they are in the case of the earlier peasant movements. These can be praised in order to establish the " glorious revolutionary tradition " of the Chinese people without threatening the monopoly of correct leadership by the Communists.

Most writers insist that while the T'ai-p'ing revolt coincided with and helped to launch a new stage in Chinese history, it nevertheless belonged to the " old-style " peasant wars since the primary contradiction remained that between the landlords and the peasants. This was even more true of the Nien movement (1851–1868), whose real significance according to many historians lay in its extension of the T'ai-p'ing rebellion into north China. In the Boxer revolt, however, for the first time the contradiction between the Chinese people as a whole and the imperialists became dominant. Communist writers still treat the Boxer movement as a peasant war, but one directed against imperialism. Some writers see new ideological content in the peasant movements occurring between the fall of the Manchus in 1911 and 1919. However, the supposed manifestation of this in the slogan " strike the rich to help the poor " (*ta-fu chi-p'in*) occurred also in earlier revolts, including one in South-west China in 1903–1904.[48] Therefore, the May Fourth movement

---

[46] See *People's Daily*, January 11, 1951, and January 11, 1956.

[47] For instance, Lo Erh-kang, in 1957 (according to A. Feuerwerker and S. Cheng, *Chinese Communist Studies of Modern Chinese History* [Cambridge: Harvard Un., 1961], p. 79), declared that earlier versions of his works had exaggerated the " progressiveness " of the T'ai-p'ings. Lo had stated that the T'ai-p'ings had carried out a " kind of field to the tiller policy ": e.g., Lo Erh-kang, *T'ai-p'ing T'ien-kuo Shih Shih K'ao* (*Investigation of Historical Events of the T'ai-p'ing Heavenly Kingdom*) (Peking: San-lien Shv-tien, 1955), p. 205.

[48] See articles of Lai Hsin-hsia in Li Kuang-pi, ed., *op. cit.*, pp. 427, 454, 459.

of 1919 marks the only fundamental division in the Communist historiography of the peasant wars, between the "old-style" and modern Communist-led peasant movements.

There obviously are immense difficulties in evaluating the historical significance of the fragmentary evidences of rebel ideology enumerated above. Yet it does appear that some of these materials will force a greater emphasis on the tradition of protest in Chinese history than has yet been given in non-Communist historiography. Leaving aside the implications for Chinese historiography in general, it is evident that these Chinese Communist views present great problems in the light of Marxist historiography.

The first of these concerns the role of religion in the formation of peasant rebel ideology. Engels and Kautsky did describe mass movements of an analogous nature in medieval Europe, but they attributed the more revolutionary aspects of the rebel ideology to the participation of plebeians, the forerunners of the modern proletariat, and to the role of religious beliefs, "the only language [the people] could then understand." [49] Thus in Western Marxist historiography, heretical religious beliefs played a key role in the ideology of pre-modern mass movements.

The role of religion in the Chinese peasant wars was far less obvious and the degree to which it played a part at all has become another of the key questions argued by mainland historians of the peasant movements. Some writers follow Engels' emphasis and maintain that the role of heretical sects and religions was essential to the organisation of a peasant movement and to the expression of its ideology in pre-modern times.[50] However, since Marx's statement that religion is the opiate of the people is still better known, and because many Chinese peasant movements had no demonstrable connection with religious sects or ideas, many Chinese historians deny any such close connection between religion and class war in Chinese history.[51] A third group, the largest, takes the middle position that the heretical religions were very important in the history of the Chinese peasant movements but were themselves manifestations of class antagonisms.[52] Those who stress the importance of religious ideas in peasant rebel ideology attempt to draw a clear distinction between what is called the religion of the oppressing classes,

[49] F. Engels, *The Peasant War in Germany* (Moscow: Foreign Languages Publishing House, 1956), p. 77; see also K. Kautsky, *Communism in Central Europe in the Time of the Reformation* (New York: Russell and Russell, 1959).

[50] *e.g.*, see Yang K'uan, "On the Function of Revolutionary Thought in the Chinese Peasant Wars and Its Relation with Religion," *SSP*, pp. 321–339, and "More on . . . ," *ibid.* pp. 353–368.

[51] *e.g.*, see Shao Shun-cheng, "Secret Societies, Religion and the Peasant Wars," *SSP*, pp. 369–384.

[52] See Jung Sheng, *et al.*, "Tentative Views on Relation between Peasant Wars and Religion in China," *SCMP*, No. 2370, p. 10, citing the *People's Daily*, October 17, 1960.

which is indeed an opiate used to teach subservience, and the religion of the oppressed, which was frequently used by the masses as a weapon of struggle against the ruling class, as in the revolts of the Yellow Turbans and the T'ai-p'ings. Advocates of the other extreme in this debate deny that any distinction can be drawn between the religion of the upper and lower classes since it was always directed towards the " other world," and that, in any case, religion was either secondary to class factors or missing altogether in the Chinese peasant movements.

PEASANT CLASS CONSCIOUSNESS

A final and crucial consideration in the treatment of the ideology of peasant rebels concerns the degree to which the peasants themselves were conscious of their goals. Mainland historians are most widely split over this issue and their departure from classical Marxism is most evident. The majority of mainland historians manifest what has been criticised as a " fairly universal leftist tendency " in their " irresponsible exaggeration of the revolutionary consciousness " of the Chinese peasant movements.[53] They glorify the ideology of the peasant rebels to an extent which goes well beyond the limits set by most Western Marxist historians, ascribing to them such revolutionary goals as " a fervent wish of thousands of years for a society where there is no exploitation of man by man." [54] Others, closer to the orthodox Marxist insistence on the weaknesses of pre-modern rebel movements, contend that the peasant wars were always " a simple spontaneous struggle against feudal exploitation . . . [and] opposed only the individual landlord, official or . . . emperor . . . and had no way of understanding that their oppression was not simply an individual matter but was [rooted in] the whole feudal economic system." [55]

The debate between exponents of these conflicting views centres around the emphasis on the degree of consciousness (*tzu-chueh*) or spontaneity (*tzu-fa*) manifested in the peasant movements. No Communist historians maintain that the rebels were wholly conscious of revolutionary goals since this could only be true of the modern Communist-led revolution, nor do any say that the Chinese peasantry was entirely unconscious of " feudal " injustices. However, although these arguments concern degrees of emphasis, the various shadings are significant since they determine the final evaluation of the class struggle in pre-modern times. The question was recently summarised:

---

[53] See Sun Tso-min, *Chung-kuo Nung-min Chan-cheng, op. cit.,* p. 2, and Sun Tso-min, " Historicism and Class Stand in the Research on the History of the Chinese Peasant Wars," *People's Daily,* February 27, 1964.
[54] Yang K'uan, *op. cit., SSP,* p. 339.
[55] Ch'i Hsia, " On Several Questions in the Late Sui Peasant Revolts," in Li Kuang-pi, ed., *op. cit.,* p. 110.

How to correctly understand and expound the relationship between spontaneity and consciousness of peasants' wars in such a way that the peasants' revolution is not regarded as a proletarian one, on the one hand, and the revolutionary character of the peasants' wars is not disparaged, and the dividing-line is not blurred between the peasants and landlords on the other, such is a very complicated and difficult question.[56]

In short, Chinese historians wish to stress the revolutionary qualities of the Chinese peasantry, but are constrained by Marxist theory from giving the pre-modern peasantry the characteristics of the modern proletariat.

Certainly the problem of confusing the conservative peasantry with the revolutionary proletariat never arose for Marx and Engels. Regarding the specific question of consciousness of revolutionary tasks, Marx and Engels wrote that this could develop in the last stages of a given mode of production when man became aware of the " one-sidedness " of his working conditions.[57] However, in the case of late feudalism, this awareness would be led by representatives of the bourgeoisie and not by the peasantry. Moreover, the egalitarian slogans advanced during the relatively few [58] medieval peasant revolts were not components of a positive programme but symbols of protest, according to Engels.[59]

In any case, the most important point in the classical Marxist treatment of ideology, in addition to the insistence that ideas derive from economic and social conditions, is the related assumption that ideas be judged according to their appropriateness for a given stage of production. Hence, Marx, Engels, Lenin and Mao have all praised egalitarian ideas in so far as they " express the aspirations " of the peasants, but attacked them in so far as they did not accord with the economic needs of their time.[60] Lenin also denied the ability of the peasantry to be aware of the systematic causes of oppression and hence to oppose the feudal system as such.[61] Even Mao, for all his praise of the " objectively " revolutionary qualities of the peasantry, has condemned the backwardness of peasant ideology in history. He wrote:

The extreme poverty and backwardness of the peasants, resulting from such ruthless exploitation and oppression by the landlord class, is the

56 Ning K'o, " The Question of Spontaneity and Consciousness in the Chinese Peasant Wars," *Extracts from China Mainland Magazine (ECMM)* (Hong Kong: U.S. Consulate-General), No. 311, p. 43, citing *Hung Ch'i (Red Flag)*, No. 7, 1962.

57 K. Marx and F. Engels, *The German Ideology* (New York: New World, 1963), p. 71.

58 See F. Engels, *Peasant War in Germany*, p. 52.

59 F. Engels, *Anti-Duhring* (New York: International, 1939), p. 123.

60 See V. I. Lenin, " The Agrarian Programme of Social Democracy in the First Russian Revolution," 1905–07, *Collected Works* (Moscow: Foreign Languages Publishing House, 1962), XIII, p. 237, and Mao Tse-tung, " Rectification of Incorrect Ideas in the Party," *Selected Works*, I, p. 111.

61 V. I. Lenin, " To the Rural Poor," in *Alliance of the Working Class and the Peasantry* (Moscow: Foreign Languages Publishing House, 1959), p. 32.

basic reason why China's economy and social life has remained stagnant for thousands of years.[62]

However, many of these reservations about the ideology of the peasant class have been brushed aside in recent writings by mainland students on the Chinese peasant wars. Just as Mao developed Lenin's ideas about the role of the peasant in the modern revolution, many apparently younger Chinese historians have applied Mao's enthusiastic appraisal of the revolutionary qualities of the peasantry in the modern Chinese revolution to their studies of the peasant wars in Chinese history. In the last few years, the majority of discussants of the subject have assigned varying degrees of conscious opposition to the feudal system to the peasant rebels in a way which goes far beyond the statements of the classical writers and even of Mao himself.

There have been several approaches to this problem of the revolutionary consciousness of the peasant revolts in recent mainland historiography. Some of the most influential historians, notably Kuo Mo-jo and Hou Wai-lu, have sought to resolve the contradiction between attributing " a certain degree of consciousness " to the rebels and classical Marxist statements by maintaining that this consciousness appeared only in the declining period of feudalism when, according to the Marxian scheme, men might become aware of restrictive working conditions. Hou Wai-lu wrote:

> Following historical development, the peasants' feelings of injustice also developed from lower to higher forms. They [the Chinese peasant rebels] passed from slogans and programmes of religious principle . . . from wild illusions of resistance to poverty and demands for human rights, to opposition to special land rights and to advocating egalitarian ideals, following step by step from the long, exhausting experiences of struggle.[63]

Hence, according to this view, after the middle of the T'ang, peasants moved from hazy conceptions of basic rights and opposition to the *corvée* to demands for equal rights with the feudal governing class, and during the Ming to demands for equal distribution of land. While this interpretation is consistent with the Marxist concept of historical evolution, it poses the peasantry and not the bourgeoisie and plebeians as the leading class in the struggle against feudalism and it describes a revolutionary ideology considerably in advance of comparable developments in Europe.

Other historians deny that the history of the Chinese peasant wars

---

[62] Mao, " The Chinese Revolution and the Chinese Communist Party," *Selected Works*, III, p. 75.
[63] Hou Wai-lu, *op. cit.*, *SSP*, p. 25; see also Hou Wai-lu, " Historical Characteristics of the Peasant Wars of the T'ang and Sung," *Hsin Chien-she*, March 1964.

can be divided into two periods, roughly corresponding to an unconscious earlier stage of opposition to feudal abuses and a post-T'ang stage of a certain degree of conscious opposition to the feudal system. They point out that even in the *Classic of Poetry* (*Shih Ching*), a poem of the early first millennium before Christ questions the justice of nobles obtaining luxuries without work,[64] and that the first peasant rebel leaders questioned the monopoly of important posts and advanced slogans calling for equal laws. Furthermore, the Yellow Turbans raised the land problem and therefore, they argue, Kuo Mo-jo to the contrary, early peasant revolts in China were conscious of more than the mere desire to overthrow a tyrannical landlord or dynasty.[65]

Thus fundamental arguments have arisen over the general evaluation of the degree of consciousness attained by peasant rebels. While all mainland historians obey the Marxist injunction that only the proletarian movement is fully conscious of its revolutionary tasks, while peasant wars were essentially a " kind of spontaneous revolutionary movement " (*i-chung tzu-fa te ke-ming yun-tung*), there are wide variations of opinion as to the amount of peasant class " self-consciousness " permitted within this formula. A representative of the " leftist " interpretation stressing the revolutionary qualities of the peasants defined this peasant consciousness:

> Long confronted with their bitter life and the brutal exploitation and oppression by the landlord class, the peasants would inevitably develop a certain knowledge (although it was obscure, superficial and even distorted knowledge) of their lot and develop their class consciousness. This found expression, on the one hand, in their hatred for the landlord class and the feudal system and, on the other, in their eager longing for liberation and happy life. From this, the peasants developed a strong demand for revolution and, proceeding from their class position and historical position, formed naïve egalitarianism and naïve ideas of equality.[66]

The proponents of a more enthusiastic appraisal of the peasant wars in Chinese history maintain that not only did peasant movements have an objectively revolutionary function, but that " under certain conditions [the peasants] formed a class," [67] and expressed a " certain degree of consciousness." [68] They argue that the peasant rebels did express ideals which surpassed the feudal thought of the time and " gradually acquired a class knowledge of the mutual opposition between rich and poor and

---

[64] *Chung Kuo Li-tai . . . op. cit.*, p. 397.
[65] Liu Chuan, " Tentative Discussion of the Problem of the Goals of the Chinese Peasant Wars," *Kuang-ming Jih-pao*, September 17, 1959. See also *SSP*, p. 127.
[66] Ning K'o *op. cit.*, p. 34.
[67] " Opening of Discussion of Problems of Peasant Wars in Chinese Feudal Society by Historical Circles," *Kuang-ming Jih-pao*, September 20, 1960.
[68] Ning K'o, *op. cit.*, p. 34.

between noble and base." [69] Although the peasants did not have knowledge of the fate of their struggle, they did have a consciousness of their revolt in the sense of having definite goals and plans. Therefore, the peasant movements were not just blind attacks against feudal abuses as stated by some Chinese historians, but were directed against the entire feudal system of exploitation.[70]

Thus, where orthodox Marxist interpretations admitted at most a negative consciousness of opposition by the peasants, the prevailing view in Chinese Communist historiography attributes to the peasants a certain positive revolutionary consciousness. One writer expressed the tension between this interpretation and the classical Marxist view in the following words:

> Of course, in feudal society pure peasant wars were all spontaneous, but following the development of feudalism and the changes in material life, did not the nature of the peasantry change (*nung-min tzu-shen shih-fou yeh tsai pien-hua ne*?), ... was there not a certain consciousness within the spontaneity? [71]

Recent criticisms of exaggerations of the revolutionary quality of the peasant wars by such leading historians as Kuo Mo-jo,[72] Fan Wen-lan [73] and Chien Po-tsan suggest that senior theorists are concerned about the theoretical implications of this type of interpretation. Chien warned that "the peasants opposed feudal oppression and exploitation but did not oppose feudalism as a system." They opposed individual landlords but not the landlord class, the emperor but not the imperial system.[74] Sun Tso-min, the most voluminous writer on the subject of the peasant movements in the mid-1950s, stresses, in a manner consistent with Mao's statements, the "objectively revolutionary" historical function of the peasant revolts, but denies that they had any "subjective revolutionary consciousness." [75] Ch'i Hsia is another prominent historian who often denied to the peasants any significant degree of conscious opposition to the feudal system either in early or later periods.[76]

Finally, in 1961 it seemed as if the Party was finally swinging its weight behind the representatives of views stressing the more backward

---

[69] " Some Problems in the History of the Peasant Wars," *Kuang-ming Jih-pao*, November 7, 1961.

[70] *e.g.*, see Pai Shou-yi, *op. cit.*, *SSP*, p. 185.

[71] Tientsin Teachers' College History Dept., " Regarding a Heated Debate on the Question of the Laws of Development of the Chinese Peasant Wars," *SSP*, p. 464.

[72] Kuo Mo-jo, " On Several Problems of Contemporary Historical Research," *Hsin Chien-she*, No. 4, 1959, and *Kuang-ming Jih-pao*, April 8, 1959.

[73] See " Chinese Historians Meet in Peking . . . ," *SCMP*, No. 2514, pp. 21–22, citing *People's Daily*, May 31, 1961.

[74] Chien Po-tsan, " Some Tentative Ideas Regarding Disposition of Several Historical Problems," *Kuang-ming Jih-pao*, December 22, 1961.

[75] See Sun Tso-min, *Chung-kuo Nung-min, op. cit.*

[76] *e.g.*, Ch'i Hsai, *op. cit.*, in Li Kuang-pi, ed., p. 110.

aspects of the historical peasant movements in a manner similar to its earlier restraining comments on the T'ai-p'ings. This seemed the implication of the most negative appraisal of peasant rebel ideology published up to that time, which to be sure restated Mao's basic position, itself an advance on classical Marxist statements, but which stopped well short of the tide of articles praising the revolutionary consciousness of the peasant movements. The author, Ts'ai Mei-piao, wrote:

> This kind of opposition [movement] propelled history forward and became the true force of historical development, but the peasant rebels did not and could not imagine this. That the peasant revolts struck at the feudal governments of the time and propelled the development of social production was the objective result of the uprisings but was not their preconceived plan. . . . Only with the coming of the proletariat was it possible to know one's class position and self-consciously carry out class struggle.[77]

Despite the relative conformity of this position with orthodox Marxist views of the class struggles of the peasants in history, it soon became clear that in fact the Party was at least temporarily favouring the more enthusiastic appraisals of the historical peasant movements. In the first place, it is evident that the great majority of discussants of these problems continue to oppose the more conservative and orthodox views of the peasant movements. They criticise by name the "second-string" spokesmen of this view, most notably Ts'ai Mei-piao, Sun Tso-min and the earlier Ch'i Hsia, and accuse them of abandoning the "class stand of the workers."[78]

The latter two writers have reflected the pressures of the "leftist" criticism by substantially modifying earlier more negative conclusions. Sun now concedes that at times the peasant rebels did develop a "certain class knowledge" and obtained "glimpses of a new order," although virtually alone among the younger historians he continues to deny that they were conscious of opposing the feudal system as such.[79] Ch'i Hsia recently confessed to having too negative a view of the peasant revolts:

> My mistaken views on this problem were due to superficial methodology but primarily they were due to the fact that [I] had not thoroughly reformed my capitalist class world view and standpoint or purged the

---

[77] Ts'ai Mei-piao, " Discussion of Several Problems in the Debate on the History of the Chinese Peasant Wars," *Li-Shih Yen-chiu*, No. 4, 1961, p. 62.

[78] *e.g.*, see *SSP*, pp. 130–131, 456, 462 *et seq.*; " Tientsin Historians Discuss Some Questions in the History of Chinese Peasant Wars," *ECMM*, No. 308, pp. 33–36, citing *Li-shih Yen-chiu*, No. 1, 1962, and Wu Chuan-ch'i, " We Cannot Say the Peasant Wars are a ' Continuation ' of Feudal Landlord Policies," *Kuang-ming Jih-pao*, April 3, 1964. See also the discussions in *Che-hsueh Yen-chiu* (*Philosophical Research*), No. 3, 1964, pp. 16–34 and pp. 84–85, and in *Che-hsueh Yen-chiu*, No. 5, 1964.

[79] Sun Tso-min, " On the Question of Chinese Peasant Wars Striking the Feudal System," *SSP*, p. 109.

"emperor, general and minister" system of historiography. This made it impossible to investigate creatively the peasant wars with a revolutionary world view and to praise creatively the revolutionary struggles of the peasants.[80]

In addition to the far larger numbers of writers favouring a revolutionary interpretation of the peasant movements, other evidence of Party sanction of this "revisionist" view of history has been the recent publication of statements favouring the revolutionary qualities of the peasant rebels in various Party journals, no doubt partly in answer to Soviet criticisms of the Chinese model of a rural-based revolution.[81]

Hence in recent mainland writings on this subject, the substance of Mao's 1939 evaluation of the revolutionary function of the peasant revolts in Chinese history is in fact compatible only with the most conservative contemporary Chinese position,[82] although it is itself a considerable modification of classical Marxist views. Carrying this evolution of the Marxist view of the historical attributes of the peasantry still further, the vast majority of younger Chinese discussants, instigated by current Chinese policies, try to show the historical roots for a "subjectively" revolutionary peasant ideology as well as for their progressive "objective" role.

The three different interpretations of the degree of consciousness manifested in the Chinese peasant revolts—those denying any conscious opposition to the system as a whole, those arguing that such consciousness did develop but only in the later period of Chinese feudalism, and those who maintain that peasant revolts throughout the history of Chinese feudalism consciously opposed the system to one degree or another—all are mirrored and summarised in the debate generally subsumed under "the problem of the nature (*hsing-chih*) of the Chinese peasant wars."

CAUSES OF FAILURE

Despite the great emphasis on the most radical of these interpretations, it should be noted that all discussants attempt to show the development of the class struggles of the peasants from lower to higher forms of opposition and at the same time to draw a clear distinction between the most advanced peasant wars and the modern proletarian-led revolution. At its crudest level this distinction is made simply by

---

[80] Ch'i Hsia, "On the Question of the Nature of the Chinese Peasant Wars," *SSP*, p. 72. Ch'i has now been accused of going too far to the other extreme and exaggerating the revolutionary consciousness of the Ch'in-Han peasant wars. See Chu Ta-chun, *et al.*, "Criticism of the History of the Ch'in-Han Peasant Wars," *Li-shih Yen-chiu*, No. 4, 1963, pp. 74–75.

[81] *e.g.*, Ning K'o, *op. cit.*, *ECMM*, No. 311.

[82] As expounded by Ts'ai Mei-piao and Sun Tso-min.

repeating Mao's formula that in the absence of an "advanced political party" and such "correct leadership as is given by the proletariat and the Communist Party today, the peasant revolutions invariably failed." [83] There is a certain amount of truth in this, in the sense that in pre-modern times it was difficult at best for the rebel leader to imagine a truly revolutionary programme or, if he did, in the absence of modern communications and propaganda techniques, to win the support necessary for its execution. Yet rather than analyse such aspects, most Communist studies of the peasant movements are content to rest on the classical Marxist statements of the inherent weaknesses of the peasant class. Some of the more sophisticated analyses of the inevitable failures of the peasant movements do explore the reasons for the lack of vision and consciousness of the peasants and their consequent lack of organisation.[84] Others speak of the greater strength of the enemy or of specific military and political mistakes committed by the rebel leaders.

Among the weaknesses of the Chinese peasant rebels, one receives particular attention in mainland historiography. This is what Mao called the "roving insurgent mentality" (liu-k'ou-chu-yi) and is defined as mere wandering with "the view that base areas are neither necessary nor important," and the "wish to go to the big cities and indulge in eating and drinking." [85] This question is clearly related to the key role of the "wandering people" (yu min) in the Chinese peasant movements. Yet, while the Chinese Communists generally praise this Chinese version of the lumpen-proletariat,[86] the "vagabondism" of the roving insurgents has also been called the leading "feature of all Chinese peasant uprisings and the cause of their defeat." [87] On the other hand, Lo Erh-kang praised the mobile tactics of the Nien rebels, while others have attacked the description of rebels such as Huang Ch'ao and Li Tzu-ch'eng as mere "pleasure seekers" as "slanders of the working class." [88] In short, the evaluation of the "roving insurgent mentality" of the peasant rebels varies considerably.

Thus, mainland historians stop short of admitting any really revolutionary accomplishments for the peasant rebels. At most a pre-modern peasant movement might set up a new feudal dynasty by compromising with the ruling class and selling out the alleged aspirations of the

---

83 Mao Tse-tung, "The Chinese Revolution and the Chinese Communist Party," *Selected Works*, III, p. 76.
84 e.g., see Fan Wen-lan's statement that the source of the mistakes of the T'ai-p'ing leaders lay in the tendencies of the peasant class towards cliquism (*tsung p'ai ssu-hsiang*), conservatism and hedonism (*an-lo ssu-hsiang*): *Chung-kuo Chin-tai Shih (Modern Chinese History)* (Peking: Jen-min Ch'u-pan She, 1961), pp. 151–152.
85 Mao, *Selected Works*, I, pp. 114–115, and II, pp. 135–136.
86 Forming, of course, another contrast with traditional Marxist views.
87 Chien Po-tsan, *Li-shih Wen-t'i Lun-ts'ung, op. cit.*, p. 135.
88 e.g., Chang Pao-kuang, "The Problem of Vagabondism in the History of the Chinese Peasant Wars," *SSP*, p. 207.

peasants. Yet the search for the establishment of a continuous tradition of class struggle in China has led Communist historians, in the absence of any significant bourgeois or labour movements, to exalt the historical class struggles of the Chinese peasantry to an extremely high position.

A description of what the Communists term the distinguishing characteristics (*t'e tien*) of the Chinese peasant movements shows the use of certain very un-Chinese Marxist beliefs in the name of Chinese nationalism. Mao wrote in the oft-cited passage from the "Chinese Revolution and the Chinese Communist Party": "The gigantic scale of such peasant uprisings and peasant wars in Chinese history is without parallel in the world." [89] Therefore, the first special feature of the Chinese peasant movements is considered to be their size and frequency. This appears to have some justification. Even if one divides the traditional figures for the size of the peasant armies by ten,[90] one still finds numerous claims of mass movements of 100,000 or more. By contrast the most famous peasant movements of European and Russian history did not exceed one-half that number.[91] Furthermore, the frequency of large-scale rural disturbances in Chinese history seems unparalleled in the rest of the world.

A second group of alleged characteristics of the Chinese peasant movements is considered to be their greater degree of organisation and the broad base of participation in these movements. Both of the above points are explained by arguments approximating those used to show that China was an Oriental society. Some historians point out that all Chinese peasant movements struggled for power against the existing government, unlike the more aimless movements of other countries.

A third set of characteristics of the Chinese peasant movements, according to mainland historians, was the greater militancy of their ideology.[92] This was manifested in the supposedly high degree of class content in their programmes. Furthermore the ideology of peasant rebels in China allegedly often developed without the use of religious disguises or imparted a higher degree of class consciousness to the heretical religions than was the case in other countries. Another aspect of the more militant ideology of the Chinese peasant movements, according to some historians, was their willingness to oppose the existing emperor, unlike Russia and Japan, where the peasants revolted only against the "nobility and individual officials, but never against the

[89] Mao, *Selected Works*, III, p. 76.
[90] A division made by some scholars who have assumed the wish of government commanders to exaggerate the size of the rebels.
[91] Such as the uprisings led by Thomas Muntzer (1525) in Germany and by E. Pugachov in Russia (1773-74). Uprisings of the Muromachi period in Japan and in other areas are perhaps more comparable.
[92] See Pai Shou-yi, "Special Points in the History of the Chinese Peasant Wars," *SSP*, p. 237 *et seq.*

tsar." [93] Finally, the greater class content of the Chinese peasant movements is said to be shown in the clear political slogans and egalitarian proposals outlined above.

Thus the history of the Chinese peasant movements has been analysed according to the theory of the class struggle in the interests of the new ideology. In the light of Marxist historiography, there has been a clear development from right to left in the treatment of the peasant wars in Chinese history. As Mao developed the Leninist theory of the class struggle of the peasants in the modern revolution, the present generation of Chinese Communist historians in turn have applied this theory to Chinese history. The younger generation of historians has developed the teachings of the older generation of academic Marxists in a manner that is at once more Chinese and more radical in its class and revolutionary implications. It is more nationalistic in its stress on the peculiarly revolutionary qualities of the Chinese peasantry, and it is more radical in its unprecedented emphasis on class struggle. It therefore reveals both the chauvinism and Marxist fundamentalism of the Chinese Communists, who believe that their interests are best served by a revolutionary ideology.

Major aspects of mainland historiography revealed in the treatment of the peasant revolts include: the substitution of peasant wars for social revolution as the driving force of historical development; the superseding of traditional Marxist stress on the development of productive economic forces by the Chinese Communist emphasis on productive relations, or the role and welfare of the people [94]; the nature of class struggles and antagonisms in history; the relation of individual leaders to the masses; the evolution of history to the inevitable triumph of Communism; the allegedly "revolutionary character" of the Chinese peasantry, and, above all, the ethic of struggle. Indeed, the greatest significance of the mainland historiography of the peasant revolts, especially in view of the utter contrast between classical Chinese and Communist Chinese interpretations, is the pedagogical attempt to demonstrate the truth that "only through struggle is there a way out."

---

[93] Joseph Stalin, *Complete Works* (Moscow: Foreign Languages Publishing House, 1955), XII, p. 115. However, Engels, in Karl Marx and Frederick Engels, *Selected Works in Two Volumes* (hereafter the *Selected Works*) (Moscow: Foreign Languages Publishing House, 1958), 2, p. 59, noted that the Russian peasants did at times name their own pretender tsar, a fact which corresponds to the Chinese rebels' use of the concept of the mandate of heaven in naming their own candidates for emperor. Accordingly, the question of the existence of "monarchism" (*huang-ch'uan chu-yi*) in the history of the Chinese peasant movements is another problem of considerable controversy in mainland historiography.

[94] This stress on the role of the "people" more than on the evolution of the economy in contemporary Chinese historiography is another side of the "voluntarism" of Chinese Marxism referred to by Maurice Meisner (see "Li Ta-chao and the Chinese Communist Treatment of the Materialistic Conception of History" in this issue).

We may conclude that mainland historiography of the peasant wars has not been an academic success—there have been few studies which have equalled the best pre-liberation efforts in depth and mastery of sources [95]—but that it has been a tremendous popular and educational success, given the goals of the Chinese Communists. Despite the theoretical problems and inconsistencies constantly mentioned above, it is certain that the voluminous writings on the history of the peasant wars have helped inculcate in the average reader a belief in the existence and efficacy of the class struggle. Most of all, Communist ideologists have used the interpretations of the peasant wars to test and train the " world view " of the intellectuals, to induce them to abandon "objectivism " and to embrace the " class stand of the working class."

---

[95] In addition to the many hundreds of articles on the subject there have been four book-length general studies, a few monographs on particular revolts, several collections of source materials and numerous popular pamphlets. There are some good studies (*e.g.*, Mou An-shih, *T'ai-p'ing T'ien-kuo* [Shanghai: Jen-min Chu-pan She, 1959]), but so far the only major contribution of the Communists to the objective study of the peasant revolts has been the collection and editing of relevant documents and in some cases the discovery of new materials (*e.g.*, local records). Perhaps more important to a future understanding of the phenomenon of rural unrest in Chinese history has been the attention given to previously neglected aspects of the revolts.

12

China's Modern Economic History in Communist Chinese Historiography *

By ALBERT FEUERWERKER

IT will be evident to a reader of historical works produced in the People's Republic of China that these writings, in the choice of subject-matter and in its treatment, are decidedly influenced by the current domestic and foreign political "line" of the Communist Party and Government. This is a relative matter, not absolute, but I would suggest that the dominant "class viewpoint" of the first decade of the Peking régime which produced an anonymous history of dynasties without "feudal" emperors or bureaucrats, literature minus the landlord-scholar-official literatus and nameless peasant rebellions as the central matter of China's history, was to a degree correlated with the process of the internal consolidation of power which may more or less be said to have been accomplished with the completion of the collectivisation of agriculture.[1] The more recent "historicist" trend, which while not rejecting entirely its predecessor concentrates on what may be "positively inherited" from the "feudal" past, represents a quickening of Chinese nationalism fanned to a red-hot intensity, one cannot resist the temptation to conjecture, by the increasingly severe quarrel with the Soviet Union. Soviet Russian commentary on recent Chinese historiography, for example, accuses the Chinese of the "introduction of dogmatic, anti-Marxist and openly nationalistic and racist views." The Chinese, for their now relatively favourable view of the thirteenth-century Mongol conquests (which are seen as calamitous by the Russians and other Europeans), for their claim that Chinese "feudalism" is the classical model of this historical phenomenon, and because they exaggerate the role of Confucian ideas and their influence on Western philosophy, are roundly condemned by the Russians for "bourgeois nationalism."[2]

* I gratefully acknowledge the assistance of a Social Science Research Council Auxiliary Research Award in the preparation of this article. An earlier version of this article was presented to a Conference on Chinese Communist Historiography, sponsored by *The China Quarterly*, at Ditchley Park, Oxfordshire, September 6–12, 1964.

1 See Albert Feuerwerker, "China's History in Marxian Dress," *The American Historical Review*, January 1961, pp. 323–353.

2 R. V. Vyatkin and S. L. Tikhvinsky, "Some Questions of Historical Science in the Chinese People's Republic," *Voprosy istorii*, October 1963, pp. 3–20; translated in *The Current Digest of the Soviet Press*, XVI, No. 4, February 19, 1964, pp. 3–10. And for some of the writing which inspired this attack see *Ts'ao Ts'ao Lun-chi* (*Collected Discussions of Ts'ao Ts'ao*) (Peking: San-lien Shu-tien, 1962); Liu Ta-nien,

Movement from "class viewpoint" to "historicism" in Chinese Communist historiography, however, as with the oscillation of a pendulum, brings to bear forces tending to push the historian back to the other extreme of the ideological arc. The momentary pause of the weight of opinion at one extreme of amplitude represents an inherently unstable equilibrium. Too great an emphasis in the historicist phase on what is assertedly Chinese at the expense of what is assuredly Communist carries the danger of abandoning one's forward defences in the great international Marxist-Leninist polemic. Hence the continuing dialogue between the historicist and class viewpoints in recent Chinese Communist historiographical discussions.[3]

The study of modern economic history in China since 1949, like other fields of historical research, has been conducted within the context I have just outlined. By "modern," in what follows, I shall mean the late-Ch'ing and Republican periods, that is the nineteenth and twentieth centuries. If one can suggest that the attitude of the historian may vary between an active pole and a passive one, the treatment of modern economic history in post-1949 China has been singularly passive. Given a context in which the past is to be treated " as we do our food, which should be chewed in the mouth, submitted to the working of the stomach and intestines, mixed with saliva, gastric juice and intestinal secretions, and then separated into essence to be absorbed and waste matter to be discarded," [4] the historian has been occupied in feeding upon a *table d'hôte* menu prepared for him by *le cordon bleu* Mao Tse-tung. Hence the overwhelming passive tone of valuation, appraisement, assessment in recent Chinese economic history. *This* is good—the utopian land system of the Taipings as set forth in the *T'ien Ch'ao T'ien-mu Chih-tu* (*Land System of the Celestial Dynasty*), for example. It was anti-feudal and presaged the Communist society of the future. *That* is somewhat overdone—referring to the assertion that elements of a capitalist economy were already widely present in the late-Ming. So to hold, by exaggerating the degree of China's progress along the trunk road to capitalism, might raise doubts about the historical necessity of a democratic revolution led by the Communist Party.

Absent is an active, concerted, fresh attack on the problems of China's modern economic history which, while not abandoning judgment,

---

"Lun K'ang Hsi" (" On K'ang Hsi,") *Li-shih Yen-chiu* (*Historical Research*), No. 3, 1961, pp. 5–21, where the Manchu emperor is described as " the great feudal ruler who united China and defended her against European penetration "; Han Ju-lin, " Lun Ch'eng-chi-ssu-han " (" On Genghis Khan "), *ibid*. No. 3, 1962, pp. 1–10; Chou Liang-hsiao, " Kuan-yü Ch'eng-chi-ssu-han " (" About Genghis Khan "), *ibid*. No. 4, 1963, pp. 1–7.

3 For brief reviews of these discussions, see *Jen-min Jih-pao* (*People's Daily*), February 25, 1964; *Kuang-ming Jih-pao* (*Kuang-ming Daily*), January 18, 1964.

4 *Selected Works of Mao Tse-tung* (English ed., London: Lawrence & Wishart Ltd., 1954–56), III, p. 154.

is at least in the first instance devoted to analysis and understanding of the economy of a social system whose age and amplitude make it one of the great challenges to modern social science research. To put it another way, much of what bears the label " economic history " would with great difficulty be accepted as that by practitioners outside of China. This is not to say that the history of the economy must be considered in a vacuum, but the characteristic intrusion, even dominance, of political matters before what is specifically economic has been exhaustively comprehended—a paradoxical inversion for the Marxist in any case— robs economic history in China of any independent disciplinary value. The problem, it must be fairly stated, is not merely that Marxism-Maoism is a defective if sometimes useful tool. It is just as much that in this area of learning China remains, as she was before 1949, woefully underdeveloped. The marriage of sophisticated economic theory with sound historical practice, which is a recent union in the West, too, has not yet been consummated in China. The continuities in materials and method from the economic history of the 1920s and 1930s to that of the 1950s and 1960s are too grossly apparent.

II

This is the version of China's modern economic history which is current in the textbooks used in the People's Republic of China. Some of the controversies and unresolved problems which lurk behind this outline will be discussed in Section III.

On the eve of the Opium War, China's feudal society was already beginning to disintegrate. The development of a commodity economy (*shang-p'in ching-chi*) within that feudal society bore within itself elements of capitalism (*tzu-pen-chu-i meng-ya*). After the consolidation of the Ch'ing dynasty, agricultural production gradually recovered from the destruction of the late Ming and early Ch'ing. By the last years of Ch'ien-lung a process of concentration of land ownership was in full swing and many independent farmers lost their land. The life of the tenant farmer was a miserable one, and the " contradictions " between the peasantry and the landlords were sharp; as a consequence many local peasant uprisings occurred. At the same time, " relatively " large handicraft workshops (*kung-ch'ang shou-kung-yeh*) with " relatively " developed division of labour had appeared, and were " relatively " widespread in the large cities. Many of the peasants who had lost their land drifted to the cities where they were transformed into handicraft wage labourers. As a result of the increased circulation of commodities, the integration of the internal economy was well advanced. In these circumstances, even without the influence of foreign capitalism, China could have gradually developed into a capitalist society. But precisely because of the intrusion of the West this was not to happen.

From the sixteenth century, Portugal, Spain, Holland and Britain successively developed trading relations with China. China was passive in this trade, which was carried on largely because of the foreign demand for Chinese commodities. In order to compensate for her unfavourable balance in the China trade, England shamelessly imported opium into China. By the nineteenth century, American trade was second only to England, and the United States, too, brazenly brought opium into China. The large-scale importation of opium seriously harmed the health of the Chinese people, while the outflow of silver to pay for opium severely damaged the Chinese economy. China's prohibition of the opium trade, in the interest of the survival of the Chinese people, was completely justified. England's resort to force in the Opium War, in order by military means to enlarge the scope of her economic incursions, was a completely aggressive act.

The unequal treaties between China and the Powers concluded after the Opium War marked the beginning of China's transformation into a semi-colony. Great changes occurred in the Chinese society and economy from the 1840s. The opium trade grew under special protection, while the health of the Chinese populace was poisoned and the outflow of silver grew to ever larger proportions. Even more important, from the five treaty ports capitalist commodities flowed unceasingly to the interior and dealt a severe blow to China's natural economy. Along with the widening impact of imported foreign commodities, the centre of trade shifted from Canton to Shanghai with resultant major changes in transport and commerce in southern China. Hong Kong, which was ceded to the British, became the principal political, economic and military base for British aggression. In order to pay the Opium War indemnities, the impoverished Ch'ing Government increased the fiscal burden of the populace. The capitulation of the Ch'ing dynasty, which sought only to preserve its rule, to the British was not accepted by the defiant populace. From the Opium War, then, the anti-feudal and anti-foreign aggression struggles of the Chinese people began to coalesce.

The Taiping Rebellion marked the peak of the mid-nineteenth century anti-feudal peasant revolution. It was also characterised by opposition to foreign aggression. The Taiping's *Land System of the Celestial Dynasty* (*T'ien Ch'ao T'ien-mu Chih-tu*) was the most advanced land programme in the entire history of peasant revolution in China until the appearance of the Communist Party, while Hung Jen-kan's *A New Work for Aid in Administration* (*Tze-cheng Hsin-pien*) was the first explicit programme that would have China enter upon the capitalist road. In the Second Opium War, the British and French again forced the Ch'ing Government to capitulate. After that war the foreign aggressors began to concert with Chinese feudal power, and together they suppressed the Taipings. With the destruction of the Taiping Rebellion, the semi-colonial, semi-feudal character of Chinese society was deepened.

Following the Second Opium War, the British invaded south-western China through Burma while French aggression was carried out in Indo-China. Not only were these ancient dependencies removed from Chinese suzerainty and transformed into colonies, but with Burma and Indo-China as bases the British and French invaded the south-western China market. Chunking was made a treaty port after the Chefoo Convention and the influence of the British aggressors spread into the upper Yangtze region. On the one hand, the aggressors penetrated into the Chinese interior in order to enlarge their market. At the same time, in the coastal and riverine treaty ports they began to establish modern industries. At first these were limited to shipyards and the processing of raw materials, but from the 1880s, investment in manufacturing began to appear. While these factories were technically illegal under the treaties, few in number, and often small in size, they gradually eroded the basis of China's self-sufficient economy. Both urban handicraft industry and the peasants' ancillary handicrafts were seriously hurt. These developments, however, also furthered the growth of China's commodity economy, and stimulated both the founding of industrial enterprises by Ch'ing bureaucrats of the "foreign affairs group" (*yang-wu p'ai*) and the establishment of "national capitalist" (*min-tsu tzu-pen*) industry. But the development of the Chinese economy under the growing impact of foreign capitalist aggression was flagrantly uneven.

The arms industry established by the *yang-wu* bureaucrats was assertedly undertaken for two purposes: to resist foreign aggression, and to suppress any uprisings by the Chinese people. In truth, relying upon the support of the foreign aggressors, the *yang-wu* group used the arms industry primarily to stabilise feudal rule. The first purpose, therefore, was merely a cover, while the second was the joint aim of Chinese feudal power and the foreign aggressors. The development of mechanised industry was severely constricted by the feudal system of the Ch'ing dynasty. Moreover, no independent development was possible because for both machinery and technology these enterprises depended upon foreign countries. Such mechanised industry as appeared was the product of Chinese society in the process of being transformed into a semi-colonial, semi-feudal condition, and the semi-colonial, semi-feudal character of this industry was the principal obstacle to its development. The evolution from " official management " (*kuan-pan*) to " official supervision and merchant management " (*kuan-tu shang-pan*) in the organisation of industrial enterprise in the late nineteenth century was principally a change in the method of financing, which sought to put the capitalisation of industry on a business basis and to draw capital from non-government sources. The *yang-wu* bureaucrats, however, continued to dominate modern industry even though management was now increasingly in the hands of "compradore bureaucrats" (*mai-pan kuan-liao*). "Contradictions" arose between the compradore element, which supplied much of the capital and sought to increase its influence accordingly, and the *yang-wu* bureaucrats. The modern transport and communications network which began to be established in this period was also dominated by the *yang-wu* and compradore bureaucrats. *Kuan-pan* and *kuan-tu shang-pan* light industry to some extent stimulated the establishment of private (*min-tsu*) manufacturing enterprises. The workers in the foreign and Chinese factories founded in the last half of the nineteenth century were the first true industrial proletariat in China. At this early point one can already see a sharp differentiation between bureaucratic compradore capitalism, arising out of the *kuan-tu shang-pan* system, and national capitalism whose roots were in the handicraft workshops and in investment by overseas Chinese and small merchants.

China's defeat by Japan in 1894–95 and the resulting Treaty of Shimonoseki opened the way for foreign capitalism, now in its imperialist phase, to step up its political and economic aggression in China. Political spheres of influence were carved out by the powers, and an aggressive export of capital ensued in the form of politically motivated loans, and direct investment in railroads, banking, mining and manufacturing. Between 1895 and 1913 the capitalisation of foreign factories in China (now legal in the treaty ports) increased more than thirteenfold. The shock of the defeat and the failure of the *yang-wu* efforts at self-strengthening led the Ch'ing Government to remove some of the obstacles and restrictions that had hindered non-official undertakings. Both in manufacturing and in mining, national capitalist enterprises experienced unprecedented, but still very limited, growth. The limited effective domestic demand characteristic of any underdeveloped economy was in China curtailed even further by the effects of imperialism on the rural economy and by the competition of foreign-manufactured goods. The shortage of capital remained acute, and the government—which was neither a *bourgeois* state nor an *independent* one—was unable to protect and support nascent Chinese industry.

In the countryside, the semi-feudal, semi-colonial character of the rural economy deepened. The rapid growth of foreign trade after 1895 further undermined peasant ancillary handicraft industry. Chinese agriculture became increasingly commercialised and the peasant dependent upon the international market. Compradore capital, accumulated

221

in commerce or industry, penetrated rural China and in some areas capitalist farming, with hired labour, became important.

The 1898 Reform Movement, the Boxer Uprising, and the 1911 Revolution were the political reflections of deepening economic distress. In 1898 a newly arisen bourgeois class tried and failed to remove the feudal fetters to its further development. The abortive Boxer movement was a great peasant revolution comparable to the Taipings and staunchly anti-imperialist in character as well. Where these two failed, 1911 saw the bourgeoisie (whose origin was the national capitalist enterprises which had developed since 1895) lead the peasantry in a successful effort to overthrow the feudal Ch'ing régime. But if one obstacle to economic development was now removed, the ramparts of foreign imperialism were hardly touched at all by the 1911 Revolution.

From 1915 to the early 1920s, as a result of the outbreak of war in Europe which for the moment reduced foreign pressure on China, Chinese privately-owned consumer goods manufacturing flourished. The expansion of the cotton textile industry and of flour milling was especially notable. Chinese modern banking, too, experienced a considerable growth. This " golden age," however, was only an interlude. Imperialism returned in full force after the war, and even during the war Japanese textile mills and other enterprises expanded rapidly in the treaty ports, like the Chinese taking advantage of the temporary withdrawal of the European nations. Coupled with the resumption of imperialist aggression was the outbreak of endemic civil war, the several contending semi-feudal warlord interests each backed by imperialist powers. Imperialism and semi-feudal reaction, as before, obstructed and suppressed the development of the China economy.

In agriculture, the war and immediate post-war period saw a further growth of commercialisation and some increase in capitalist farming as a consequence of the demand for raw materials by the new industries and in response to changing demands of the international market. The peasantry became increasingly dependent upon a monopsonistic market and were subject, too, to a new spurt of land concentration and increasing rents as the contending warlords grabbed land and heartlessly exploited their tenants. Rural handicraft industry, especially weaving, in some areas (e.g., Kayong in Hopei) came under the control of native commercial capital and in the wartime interlude enjoyed an expansion parallel to that of the treaty port textile mills. But it also was badly hurt by the return of imperialist competition.

In sum, " capitalist relations of production " were strengthened to some extent during 1914–27, but China did not develop into an independent capitalist country. It remained enmeshed in a semi-colonial, semi-feudal nexus which throttled the economy. The workers' and peasants' revolutionary movement under the leadership of the CCP culminating in the "first revolutionary civil war" of 1923–27 marked the beginning of a challenge to this condition of stagnation. Between 1927 and 1937 China's industry and agriculture on the one hand suffered the blows of the world depression and heightened foreign aggression as the imperialist powers sought to move the burden of the world crisis of capitalism onto the semi-colonial countries. On the other hand, the Chiang Kai-shek clique of bureaucratic compradore capitalists under the guise of "economic reconstruction" increased their monopolistic control over commerce, banking and industry, while the semi-feudal landlords with whom they were in league stepped up their exploitation of the peasantry. In the "revolutionary bases" under CCP control, however, "New Democratic" economic forms were being developed which would eventually replace the KMT's semi-colonial, semi-feudal economy. The anti-Japanese war saw the increasing concentration of economic power in the hands of "the four big families," but also an increase in the impoverishment and misery of the peasantry and working class. In the revolutionary civil war of 1945–49 the feudal and bureaucratic capitalist reactionaries and their imperialist supporters, especially the American imperialists, were defeated, and the way opened for China's future rapid economic development. Q.E.D.

III

It is evident from the preceding summary that there are two major preoccupations, themselves related, which permeate the work that has been done since 1949 on China's modern economic history: the transition (or, better, transition *manqué*) from "feudalism" to "capitalism," and the impact of "imperialism" upon China's economy. The historians have been furnished with a characterisation of the nineteenth- and twentieth-century economy as "semi-feudal and semi-colonial," [5] and from this they have derived their specific problems for investigation. One of the leading economic historians has put it this way:

> Comrade Mao Tse-tung's analysis of the conflicts in China's society is our guide in the study of China's modern economic history. His theory that the contradiction between the Chinese nation and imperialism and the contradiction between the broad masses of the people and feudalism were the two principal contradictions, and that the former was the most important, is the guiding principle in our study of modern Chinese economic history. In mastering facts and determining the choice of research themes; we should start from these principles. [6]

5 Like much else in the treatment of China's modern history, the "classical" text for this characterisation is Mao's *The Chinese Revolution and the Chinese Communist Party*. See *Selected Works of Mao Tse-tung*, III, pp. 72–101.
6 Yen Chung-p'ing, "Kuan-yü Hsuan-ts'e Yen-chiu T'i-mu" ("On the Selection of Subjects for Research "), *Hung-ch'i* (*Red Flag*), June 16, 1962; available in English

If China's economy was " feudal " until the nineteenth century, what were the special characteristics of Chinese feudalism? The Chinese Communist historians—and they are, of course, not alone in this difficulty—have had an irksome time with the concept of " feudalism." I need hardly point out that the institutions of medieval Europe and those of Imperial China (which the CCP calls " feudal ") were, in many major aspects, radically different. The Chinese Communists, in adapting the Marxist paradigm of social revolution, have taken feudalism to mean a society based on an agricultural economy and dominated by a land-owning class, and in this protean sense they, of course, find an equivalence among all pre-industrial nations. (Marx, as will be indicated below, in so far as he discussed feudalism, had in mind specifically Western Europe, and his own Teutonist version of the origins of European medieval society.) There still remained, however, the problem of describing the Chinese version of the assertedly universal social stage.

The overwhelming tendencies during the first phase of post-1949 historiography, under the dominance of the " class viewpoint " principle, were either to dismiss the " interlude " from the Ch'in unification (221 B.C.) to the mid-nineteenth century as characterised by " the pro-tracted stagnation of the feudal system which lasted for more than 2,000 years, and during which thought, literature and art could not break free from the patterns and rules set by the various schools of thought, par-ticularly the Confucian school, of the Warring States era," [7] or, alter-natively, to emphasise, following Mao-Tse-tung, the " class struggles of the peasants—the peasant uprisings and peasant wars—[which] alone formed the real motive force of historical development in China's feudal society." [8] In either case there was little analysis of the specifically economic characteristics of Chinese " feudalism."

The Marxist classics have had relatively little to say about the feudal period; their emphasis has been on tracing the origins and development of a capitalism that successfully grew out of medieval society rather than on analysing the antecedent feudal order. Who would not be reluctant to venture forth in uncharted waters? There was, however, in both approaches, an implication that Chinese feudal society was relatively backward, or slower in developing than feudalism in the West. This acknowledgment of relative stagnation was, I believe, in some measure a reflection of the continued influence among Chinese historians of Marx's speculation about an " Asiatic mode of production," even

translation, U.S. Department of Commerce, Office of Technical Services, Joint Publications Research Service, JPRS: 14,595, July 25, 1962, pp. 46–71.

[7] See Kuo Mo-jo, " Kuan-yü Hou-chin Po-ku Wen-t'i " (" On Emphasising the Present and De-emphasising the Past "), Pei-ching Ta-hsueh Pao, Jen-wen K'o-hsueh (Peking University Journal, Humanistic Sciences), No. 3, 1953, pp. 111–114.

[8] Selected Works of Mao Tse-tung, III, p. 76.

though that explanation of China's history had been officially discouraged.[9]

Marx, one recent commentator asserts, clearly believed " that the inner principle of Western historical development has from the start been quite different from that of the East or of Graeco-Roman antiquity." The origin of this distinction was the threefold differentiation of the primitive communal (tribal) organisation of human society into " Oriental, Graeco-Roman and German-medieval forms of private and common ownership." In this trichotomy, Asiatic society—characterised by the absence of private ownership of land and by a centralised despotic state—was historically closest to man's primitive origins. European feudalism developed from the German form of ownership (Marx is naturally a Teutonist on this question) and incorporated an element of personal freedom from barbarian clan society. Because of " its relatively healthy starting-point it embodie[d] new potentialities of growth and human development " and was, therefore, " progressive " as compared with Graeco-Roman and *a fortiori* Asiatic society.[10]

In almost completely disavowing their " feudal past," Chinese Communist historians seem at first to have accepted this inferior status for China. The historian Hou Wai-lu, who is now Deputy Director of the Second Office (Medieval History) of the Institute of Historical Research, in 1954 explicitly argued that the land system in feudal China was one of " landlord ownership by the imperial family " or of " state ownership." [11] While a not inconsiderable amount of empirical work on specific periods or aspects of the feudal land system were published in the intervening years, it appears that a full-scale (there had been scattered articles on 1957 and 1958) theoretical confrontation of the issues raised by Hou's quasi-Asiatic mode of production position began only in 1960. And, not accidentally, these theoretical discussions of the feudal land system coincided with the shift from an emphasis on the " class viewpoint " to " historicism " in Chinese Communist historiography, and with the growing Sino-Soviet rift which fed Chinese nationalistic feelings.

The " Asiatic mode of production " theory *per se* is now explicitly out in China, as it is in the Soviet Union. In the Soviet case, the theory

9 See Karl A. Wittfogel, " The Marxist View of China," *The China Quarterly*, No. 11 (July–September 1962), pp. 1–20, No. 12 (October–December 1962), pp. 154–169; and Feuerwerker, " China's History in Marxian Dress," pp. 339–340.

10 George Lichtheim, " Marx and the ' Asiatic Mode of Production,' " *St. Anthony's Papers, Number 14* (London: Chatto & Windus, 1963), pp. 86–112.

11 Hou Wai-lu, " Chung-kuo Feng-chien She-hui T'u ti So-yu Chih Hsing-shih ti Wen-t'i " (" The Problem of the Form of Land Ownership in Chinese Feudal Society), in *Chung-kuo Feng-chien She-hui T'u ti So-yuh Chih Hsing-shih Wen-t'i T'ao-lun Chi (Collected Papers on the Problem of the Form of Landownership in China's Feudal Society)*, comp. by Department of History, Nankai University (Peking: San-lien Shu-tien, 1962, 2 vols.), Vol. I, pp. 1–20. This symposium reprints 39 papers on this topic and includes a listing of more than 100 others originally published between October 1949 and the end of 1960.

raised uncomfortable questions about the "European" character of Russian society, the post-1917 programmes followed by Lenin, and especially Stalinist policy. For China, however, the issue seems less doctrinal than emotional. On the one hand, the concept of an Asiatic mode of production might be misused, even to the extent of suggesting that China's particular social structure, rather than feudal oppression and imperialist exploitation, was the source of the miseries of the past century. But more important, I believe, is the recognition of the implication of the Asiatic theory that Chinese society, in being different, was also somehow inferior to the mainstream of social development in the West.

While there is still no evident consensus—none has been imposed, and the academic discussions continue—on the question of the socio-economic structure of Chinese medieval society, with respect to the implication of diversity being equivalent to inferiority the whole matter has been turned on its head. It cannot be denied that "feudalism" in China was different from that in the West, but so much the worse for Western feudalism. China's pre-modern society was "feudal," not "Asiatic," even though it was feudalism of a distinctly Chinese type. But it is precisely Chinese feudalism which, because of its temporal priority and its geographic and demographic scale, should be taken as the *locus classicus* of this stage in the development of human society. Such statements as the following by the Hopei historian Wu T'ing-ch'iu have found considerable support:

> China was the first country in the world to enter a feudal society— some 800 or 900 years ahead of the countries of Europe, or 1,000–1,700 years earlier if the Western Chou is regarded as feudal (at that time ancient Greece and Rome had not yet attained a class society). The feudal society in China constitutes an excellent classical model in world history. In establishing a new system of world history, we cannot continue to treat feudal society in Western Europe as the model. Moreover, during the whole period of feudalism, such eastern countries as China, India and Arabia were far ahead of Europe in economy and culture.[12]

Along with this nationalistic assertion of priority and pre-eminence, there has been some attempt to examine the particular dynamics of Chinese feudal society. For there still remained the unwelcome question of why, if Chinese society were superior, it was the West that first made the momentous transition to the "higher" societal form of capitalism. The special features of Chinese feudalism, it is typically argued, which distinguish it from feudalism in the West (and which to the Western observer with the patterns of medieval Europe in mind suggest that pre-modern Chinese society was *not* feudal at all) are these: (1) land in China

---

[12] *Kuang-ming Daily*, April 10, 1961.

could be freely bought and sold throughout the Imperial period; (2) there was no one-to-one correspondence between economic class (*chieh-chi*) and social rank (*teng-chi*); (3) medieval China saw only a very incomplete development of a manorial system.[13]   From these special features, a number of significant consequences follow. Throughout Imperial China independent small peasants, cultivating their own land, continued to exist in large numbers. Even in the allegedly dominant landlord-tenant system, the tenant unlike the European serf was not legally tied to the land and could at least aspire to become a self-cultivating peasant. The facts that the land tax of the independent farmer was generally lower than tenant rents and that rents themselves were principally collected in kind (rather than in labour service as in Europe; and Marx had said that rent in kind was a more advanced form of exploitation than labour rent) are taken to mean that the degree of feudal exploitation in medieval China was less than in medieval Europe. The " surplus " which could in part be retained by the peasant is asserted to have provided the economic basis for the cultural flowering of China from the Han onward, while Europe was still in its " dark ages." Furthermore, because China did not have a developed manorial economy of large, relatively autarchic economic units, from a very early point landlord income was used to purchase commodities (necessities in part, but primarily luxuries) in the towns and cities. A money economy, therefore, allegedly grew up earlier and was more widespread in China than in the West.

If Chinese feudalism was in these respects in advance of Europe, this is not to say that the social system was without its " contradictions," contradictions which strangled it while, from the fifteenth century, Europe marched ahead to capitalism. The Chinese feudal economy, it is asserted, was subject to recurrent crises arising primarily from the ever present *tendency* towards concentration of landholding in the hands of large landlords. This concentration was at the expense of the independent farmers who were the most productive agricultural operators, and at its extreme point land concentration therefore brought on a sharp drop in total agricultural output. Economic crisis typically led to class struggle—peasant uprisings (*nung-min ch'i-i*) which temporarily readjusted the " relations of production " and encouraged the restoration of the " productive forces " which the crisis had undermined. In the

---

[13] See, for example, Hu Ju-lei, " Kuan-yü Chung-kuo Feng-chien She-hui Hsing-t'ai ti I-hsieh T'e Tien " (" The Special Forms of Feudal Society in China "), *Historical Research*, No. 1, 1962, pp. 1–23, which has its own peculiarities but reflects fairly well the general trend of thought on this question at present. The following paragraphs are based largely on Hu's article. There is little indication in recent Chinese publications of any acquaintance with the important work on the medieval Chinese economy of such Japanese scholars as Sudō Yoshiyuki. See, for example, his *Chūgoku Tochiseidoshi Kenkyū* (*A Study of the History of Land Systems in China*) (Tokyo: Tokyo University Press, 1954).

period of " restoration," and that of " development " which followed, the Chinese farmer out-produced his European serf counterpart. This increment in production was the material foundation for China's great cultural achievements. But it was only temporary, for land concentration and the consequent agricultural cycle persistently repeated themselves. Unlike the West, no new development of productive forces such as might lead to a break-up of the cycle occurred.

Paradoxically, this anatomy of Chinese feudalism continues, even the relatively advanced degree of commodity production and money economy in medieval China was tied to the agricultural cycle. The prosperity of handicraft industry and commerce in the cities was directly the result of the urban migration of independent farmers displaced by land concentration who now turned to the crafts and trade in order to support themselves. Industry and commerce flourished precisely in those periods when total agricultural production declined, and the restoration of agriculture after a successful peasant rising generally saw a concomitant decline of the urban economy. In brief, the commodity economy of feudal China was not a product of the growth of society's total production forces, as was the case in Europe, but rather of their suffocation by feudal relations of production.

China had had large urban conglomeration long before the eleventh century when towns began to develop in Europe, but Chinese towns were inextricably a part of the feudal nexus while those of Europe struggled to liberate themselves from the domination of the feudal lords. The inhabitants of Chinese towns were primarily consumers—imperial and local officials, military units and, of course, the landlord-gentry class which expended its land rents on urban-produced commodities. These tended to be luxury goods, often of high quality, but produced in small quantities for the upper classes only. In the West, the new towns were founded on commerce and handicrafts and increasingly sold their commodities to the rural villages. The class struggle in late medieval Europe took the form of a conflict between the urban bourgeoisie whose economic exploitation of the rural areas was on the rise, and the rural feudal lords whose political domination of the towns was being challenged. In China, on the other hand, where the towns were fundamentally administrative, judicial and military centres, and the place of residence of the upper classes in general, the urban centres dominated the bulk of rural China politically and, through the landlord class which resided in them, exploited it economically as well. The class struggle could only take the form of peasant opposition to feudal officials and landlords.

The current Chinese Communist analysis of China's feudal economy summarised in the foregoing paragraphs raises as many questions as it answers, and a detailed critique would take us far afield. For the purpose of this article, I want merely to draw attention to the following three points. First, an attempt is made to explain the basis of China's asserted superiority to Europe in the medieval period without, in any degree, idealising China's feudal society. Secondly, an explanation of the " progressive " role of peasant rebellions is offered. And, thirdly, the whole matter of the development of " capitalist sprouts " (*tzu-pen chu-i meng-ya*) in late-feudal China gets very short shrift indeed.

At an earlier point, say in 1956 and 1957, the assertion that there was a proto-capitalist development in late-Ming and Ch'ing China, the topic to which I now return, would not have been so summarily dismissed. It is of some interest that the controversy about this question was in part a consequence of Mao's re-editing of his writings for the official edition of his *Selected Works* which appeared between 1951 and 1960. In the original (1939) version of *The Chinese Revolution and the Chinese Communist Party*, Mao had emphasised the " stagnation " of Chinese feudal society. In the *Selected Works*, however, he modified this position, and inserted two new sentences which read: " As China's feudal society developed its commodity economy and so carried within itself the embryo of capitalism (*tzu-pen chu-i ti meng-ya*), China would of herself have developed slowly into a capitalist society even if there had been no influence of foreign capitalism. The penetration of foreign capitalism accelerated this development." [14] Exegesis of Mao's new text flowed from many pens, especially from 1954 onward. In that year Professor Shang Yüeh of the Chinese People's University in Peking published a textbook which asserted that incipient capitalist elements were already existent in the Ming.[15] In the next year, 1955, extensive discussion in literary circles of the social background of the novel *Hung-lou Meng* (*Dream of the Red Chamber*) stimulated a spate of articles agreeing that capitalist burgeons were already to be found prior to the Opium War, but differing quite sharply as to the date of their origin and the degree of their development and significance.[16]

For a time, during 1956 and 1957, it appeared that the view represented by the historian Shang Yüeh had won the day.[17] In brief, Shang

14 *Selected Works of Mao Tse-tung*, III, p. 77.
15 Shang Yüeh, ed., *Chung-kuo Li-shih Kang-yao* (*Outline History of China*) (Peking: Jen-min Ch'u-pan-she, 1954).
16 The chief contributions to this discussion are reprinted in *Chung-kuo Tzu-pen Chu-i Meng-ya Wen-t'i T'ao-lun Chi* (*Collected Papers on the Problem of the Incipiency of Capitalism in China*) (Peking: San-lien Shu-tien, 1957, 2 vols.); and *Ming-Ch'ing She-hui Ching-chi Hsing-t'ai ti Yen-chiu* (*Studies in the Society and Economy of the Ming and Ch'ing Periods*) (Shanghai: Jen-min Ch'u-pan-she, 1957). Both collections are edited by the Chinese History Seminar of the Chinese People's University in Peking.
17 See Shang Yüeh, *Chung-kuo Tzu-pen Chu-i Kuan-hsi Fa-sheng Chi Yen-pien ti Ch'u-pu Yen-chiu (Preliminary Studies on the Origin and Development of Capitalist Relations*

and his supporters argued that the late Ming and Ch'ing economy was already proto-capitalist. The central arch of this contention was the assertion of the widespread existence of factory handicrafts (*kung-ch'ang shou-kung-yeh*) which are presumed to have fulfilled the Marxian criteria for capitalist production. Their development, so the schema goes, was preceded by a proliferation of internal and external trade. These market forces acted to bring about an increasing differentiation of handicraft, traditionally a peasant ancillary occupation, from agriculture, as well as an unprecedented concentration of landholding which forced many peasants into newly growing towns where they found employment in factory handicraft. The new " bourgeoisie " of the late Ming (whose ideological leaders, it is explained, were such men as Ku Yen-wu, Huang Tsung-hsi and Wang Fu-chih) would eventually have seized political power in combination with their peasant allies (this is the interpretation given to Li Tzu-ch'eng's rebellion which overthrew the Ming) and then proceeded to prepare the rest of the prerequisites for the development of industrial capitalism, just as their English and French counterparts are alleged to have done. But the Manchu invasion and devastation of the land in the first instance, and the imperialists' aggression and exploitation which followed in the nineteenth century prevented this happy fruition.

Most of the theoretical arguments advanced in the 1950s in support of the position that China's pre-modern economy was in fact evolving in accordance with the Marxist normative stages of societal development had already been tabled in the debates on the nature of Chinese society of the 1920s and 1930s.[18] It may well be that, given the underdeveloped state of the study of Chinese economic history, we have underestimated the degree of commercialisation of the pre-modern Chinese economy. But the step from the posited existence of extensive commerce and advanced forms of organisation in handicraft manufacture to the assertion that the Chinese economy was developing toward an " industrial revolution " is an act of faith rather than a historical-scientific conclusion. Equally significant with the external criticism we might apply is the fact that more recently the weight of authoritative opinion in China has swung away from Shang Yüeh.[19]

in China) (Peking: San-lien Shu-tien, 1956); and his preface to the collection *Ming-Ch'ing She-hui Ching-chi Hsing-t'ai ti Yen-chiu.*

18 See Benjamin I. Schwartz, " A Marxist Controversy on China," *Far Eastern Quarterly*, February 1954, pp. 143–153.

19 See, *e.g.*, Liu Ta-nien (associate editor of *Historical Research*, the leading mainland historical journal), " Kuan-yü Shang Yüeh T'ung-chih wei Ming-Ch'ing She-hui Ching-chi Hsing-t'ai ti Yen-chiu I-shu so Hsieh ti Hsü-yen " (" A Critique of Shang Yüeh's Preface to *Studies in the Society and Economy of the Ming and Ch'ing Periods* ") *Historical Research*, No. 1, 1958, pp. 1–16; a sweeping attack by the modern historians at the People's University in Peking, " P'ing Shang Yüeh T'ung-chih Kuan-yü Ming-Ch'ing She-hui Ching-chi Chieh-kou ti Jo-kan Kuan-tien " (" A Critique of Shang

The remark by Mao just cited, beginning "As China's feudal society developed its commodity economy . . ." follows immediately after a passage that reads, "Chinese feudal society lasted for about 3,000 years. It was not until the middle of the nineteenth century that great internal changes took place in China as a result of the penetration of foreign capitalism." Shang Yüeh's critics explicitly indicted him for contradicting this last passage. Behind their charge was apparently the fear that too great an emphasis upon internal proto-capitalist developments prior to the full impact of Western imperialism in the nineteenth century might divert attention from the villain's role assigned to foreign capitalism in transforming China into a "semi-colonial, semi-feudal" status. This clearly would not fit in with the need, at this stage, of the Chinese revolution, to project a large share of the blame for a century and more of humiliation and weakness onto the "imperialist aggressors." Thus Shang was accused of misinterpreting the nature of the Opium War, of failing to see that it marked the beginning of "the struggle between the Chinese people's anti-imperialist, anti-feudal line which sought to transform China into an independent and prosperous nation, and the imperialist feudal line which sought to transform China into a colony." And this because of his false attribution of a connection between the leadership of the people's struggles in 1839–42 and the "bourgeois urban movement" of the late Ming and early Ch'ing, with the result that "the nature of this Chinese national anti-aggressive struggle is changed into "bourgeois" anti-feudalism.[20] Moreover, playing up the degree of China's economic development along the Marxist normative road to capitalism might raise doubts about the historical necessity of the revolution led by the Communist Party. "If 300 years ago capitalism already held such a secure position," stated the critics of Shang Yüeh, "then the anti-feudal land reform led by the Communist Party could not have occurred. . . . And how could there have been any necessity for the proletariat to seize the leadership of the democratic revolution?"[21]

As the attacks by more orthodox historians increased in severity, Shang Yüeh adopted an ingenious stand. Marx, Engels, Lenin and Mao, when they began to write, he stated, expressed views that clearly were not acceptable to the majority, but these new views were correct ones.

Yüeh's Views concerning the Social and Economic Structure of the Ming and Ch'ing Dynasties "), *ibid.* No. 12, 1958, pp. 21–35; and Li Shu, "Chung-kuo ti Chin-tai Shih yü ho Shih? " (" When was the Beginning of Modern History in China? "), *ibid.* No. 3, 1959, pp. 1–11.

20 Liu Ta-nien, *op cit.*, pp. 11–12.

21 People's University historians, *op. cit.*, pp. 22–23. Shang Yüeh, however, did not give up the fight; see his rebuttal to Li Shu: "Yu-kuan Chung-kuo Tzu-pen Chu-i Meng-ya Wen-t'i Erh-san Shih " (" Some Matters concerning the Question of Incipient Capitalism in China "), *Historical Research*, No. 7, 1959, pp. 25–50.

No layman, of course, has the right to suggest new interpretations in a field where he is not a master, but the specialist in a particular field of knowledge—for example, an historian who has studied carefully a specific historical question—may arrive at knowledge and insights that in the beginning are possessed by him alone. While these views may not be in agreement with the general opinion, the historian who has new ideas about periodisation and the origins of capitalism in China should express them even though they may differ from the " traditional doctrine." [22]

That was it. The assertion that the " traditional doctrine "—the " tradition " that Shang referred to was, as everyone knew, the " thought of Mao Tse-tung "—could be challenged was sufficient to call forth a torrent of political abuse. " In his writings on the Chinese Revolution, comrade Mao Tse-tung has made many penetrating analyses of Chinese history. These analyses are objective truths which have been proved in the practice of the Chinese Revolution. But Shang Yüeh has slandered them and opposed them as merely ' an old and traditional system of historical analysis,' and has set up his own system of private science which is unrelated to the facts and is anti-Marxist. . . . What Shang Yüeh calls his ' new system ' is, however, only the remnants and rotten pieces of the capitalist view of history which he has picked up in a garbage can." [23] In similar tones Shang was attacked as an arch " modern revisionist," who has attempted to revive the capitalist view of history under the cover of " Let the hundred schools of thought contend."

The political implications of the assault on Shang Yüeh are obvious from the label " modern revisionist ": he—like Khrushchev—was guilty of weakening the defences against imperialism by, at least implicitly, denying that " the contradiction between the Chinese nation and imperialism . . . was the most important " contradiction in modern Chinese history. But what of the implications for the academic question of the transition from feudalism to capitalism in China? My impression is that the field has been left in considerable disarray, for the time being at least. While Chinese feudal society cannot any more be described as stagnant, neither it appears is it politically possible to argue consistently that, if left alone, it would have developed naturally to capitalism. One is left only with Mao's brief statement which follows the notorious sentence about the embryo of capitalism in feudal society: " The penetration of foreign capitalism accelerated this

[22] *Wen-hui Pao* (Shanghai), November 1, 1959; summarised in *China News Analysis*, No. 326, June 3, 1960, p. 7.
[23] *People's Daily*, June 13, 1960, p. 7; see also *Historical Research*, No. 4, 1960, pp. 1–22, and No. 5, 1960, pp. 1–48.

development." Here we are introduced to the paradoxical and ambiguous role of " imperialism " in China's modern economic history.

The academic position of Shang Yüeh's opponents is essentially this (although on the specific question of the " primitive accumulation of capital " in China the divergence of opinion is quite broad and discussions continue).[24] In contrast to Shang Yüeh, they hold that origin of the Chinese bourgeoisie and proletariat is to be found not in the seventeenth and eighteenth centuries, but only in the latter half of the nineteenth century. While, to be sure, there were some proto-capitalist forms in the later Ming and early Ch'ing, they were extremely weak. Shang Yüeh's " handicraft workshop," in particular, was the rare exception rather than the rule; such large-scale handicraft production as existed was of the *Verlag* type. It cannot be maintained that there was either a bourgeois or proletarian " class " in the Marxist-Leninist sense in this early period. Indeed, Marx's " really revolutionary way " towards the development of capitalism, in which a section of the craftsmen themselves accumulate capital and become merchants and capitalists, never occurred at all in China. There was no connection, such as Shang Yüeh implies, between the proto-capitalism of the early eighteenth century and China's modern industry. The process of primitive accumulation was fundamentally different in China and the West. Where the antecedents of the European bourgeoisie were handicraftsmen and tradesmen who occupied an antagonistic position towards feudal society, the Chinese bourgeoisie originated initially from the merchants, landowners and bureaucrats who were the controlling strata of feudal society. *Under the stimulus of foreign capitalist penetration of China's economy*, one section of the ruling class began to invest in large-scale industrial production by machinery and was transformed into the upper stratum of a bourgeois class. At a later point, a lower stratum of national capitalists (*min-tsu tzu-pen-chia*), some of whom were not originally part of the ruling class, also appeared. From its very beginnings the Chinese bourgeoisie was characterised by an ambiguous relationship with both the forces of feudalism and imperialism. The proletariat, however, whose growth accompanied not only the slow development of native capitalism but also the earlier and more extensive imperialist investment in Chinese industry, enjoyed a priority in both age and class coherence over the Chinese bourgeoisie.[25]

What the Chinese historians are asserting here is that not only did China become less than independent, a " semi-colony," as a consequence of foreign incursions in the nineteenth century, but also that

---

[24] For summaries of these discussions, see *Ching-chi Yen-chiu* (*Economic Research*), No. 3, 1962, pp. 52–61, and *People's Daily*, August 9, 1962.
[25] *Kuang-ming Daily*, June 23, 1960.

this same foreign impact began the transformation of two millennia of feudalism into something else—" semi-feudalism " embarked on the way to capitalism. To have impaired China's sovereignty was an absolutely evil action; of this there are no doubts. But to have pushed the feudal economy off dead centre, on to the universal path, this is something else again. One can, I think, suggest that the vehemence with which Chinese Communists attack " imperialism " is in direct pro-portion to the positive importance which they themselves give to foreign aggression and exploitation as the moving force in modern Chinese history. In Mao's words, " The history of imperialist aggression upon China, of imperialist opposition to China's independence and to her development of capitalism, constitutes precisely the history of modern China." [26] On the one hand, imperialism is alleged to have stimulated a rupture of the feudal bonds in which the Chinese economy was entrapped; on the other, in league with the feudal forces it deliberately obstructed the full development of the nascent Chinese capitalism which it had fathered. Shang Yüeh unambiguously rejected " the erroneous conclusion that the Chinese bourgeoisie is an outgrowth of foreign capitalist infiltration," [27] but his opponents cannot allow an unsullied pedigree to the capitalist class. They are therefore forced to abandon some part of the autonomy of Chinese history itself. To the abuse which the imperialists will have to bear for real wrongs inflicted, an extra measure of obloquy has to be added for this wound to national pride.

What was the character of the Chinese " capitalism " which appeared in the late nineteenth century as a consequence of imperialist stimulation and which because of imperialist aggression was able to achieve only a partial development? We may approach the discussions on this question by examining one of the rare explicit comparisons of the Chinese experi-ence with that of Japan that the Chinese Communist historians have produced.[28] The problem is to what extent was the " foreign affairs " (yang-wu) movement in China similar to the Meiji Restoration, and the consensus is that the similarities were only superficial. Both " movements " were stimulated by the direct pressure and influence of Western capital, both sought to establish modern factories, mines and

[26] " On New Democracy," *Selected Works of Mao Tse-tung*, IV, p. 123.

[27] Shang Yüeh, *Chung-kuo Tzu-pen-chu-i Kuan-hsi Fa-sheng chi Yen-pien ti Ch'u-pu Yen-chiu* (*Preliminary Investigations of the Origin and Development of Capitalist Relations in China*) (Peking: San-lien Shu-tien, 1956), p. 277.

[28] Huang I-feng and Chiang-To, " Chung-kuo Yang-wu Yün-tung yü Jih-pen Mei-chih Wei-hsin Tsai Ching-chi Fa-chan Shang ti Pi-chiao " (" A Comparison of Economic Development in China's Industrialisation Movement and in the Japanese Meiji Restoration "), *Historical Research*, No. 1, 1963, pp. 27–47; see also *Economic Research*, No. 4, 1963, pp. 62–71, for a report of discussions by the Shanghai Economic Society.

communications, and both drew upon Western technology and technicians. But here the similarities end.

In Japan on the eve of the Meiji Restoration, the Chinese Communist economic historians hold, the development of a commodity economy and handicraft workshops had far surpassed China. And, furthermore, a modern bourgeoisie had already clearly emerged. On this basis, Meiji Japan underwent a fundamental change in its " political superstructure " as part and parcel of the industrialisation effort. The Meiji leaders, in spite of their feudal background, had a clear bourgeois goal, and all of the measures they adopted were designed to promote the rapid development of capitalism. In China, in contrast, the feudal political superstructure remained intact, and the " wealth and power " (*fu-ch'iang*) which the *yang-wu* group sought was explicitly for the purpose of preserving feudal rule. China's early industrialisation was' undertaken by such " feudalists " as Tseng Kuo-fan, Li Hung-chang, Tso Tsung-t'ang and Chang Chih-tung. But this *yang-wu* clique was only a small part, representing local power groups serving their own material and political interests, of the feudal ruling class. As a whole that class opposed even the *yang-wu* movement, and the Ch'ing central government, in contrast to Meiji Japan, not only gave no positive help, but was also a negative factor of considerable weight. The capitalist forces of production introduced by the *yang-wu* clique were throttled by the unchanged feudal relations of production. Where in Japan many former feudal lords were transformed into capitalists as a consequence of the policies of the Meiji government, in China the feudal land economy remained dominant and was much more attractive and safe as an object of investment than was modern industry. In the Chinese enterprises themselves, again in contrast to Japan, feudal management practices were carried over from the official *yamen* and seriously damaged the efficiency of the new industries.

A second area of major divergence between Japan and China in the late nineteenth century, it is also suggested, lay in the contrast between the sense of national unity and purpose, the growing modern nationalism of Japan and the progressive decay of the Ch'ing state. In spite of its anti-foreign slogans, the *yang-wu* clique, like the feudal Ch'ing government as a whole, was dependent upon the imperialists for its very existence. Feudal-cum-imperialist collusion obstructed private capitalist development until the very end of the nineteenth century. Furthermore, the accelerating Chinese-Manchu " national " (*i.e.,* racial) conflict undermined even what little unity the dynasty retained.

Finally, this comparison concludes, while both China and Japan suffered Western capitalist aggression, it was China which was the prime target of the imperialists. Japan, with some of the blow deflected by China, was able to progress within the interstices left by the contradictions among the Western aggressors. The imperialist powers, in fact, deliberately utilised growing Japanese power against both China and Russia, with the consequence for China of a large-scale drain of capital in the form of reparations to Japan.

But the nineteenth-century industrialisation movement cannot be simply dismissed out of hand by the Communist historians. While, as we have seen, the bourgeoisie cannot be allowed a clean pedigree, it (a section of that class, to be exact) nevertheless has a " progressive " role to play in both the " Old Democratic " and to a lesser extent the " New Democratic " revolutions. In some degree a historicist or relativistic approach, rather than one based entirely upon the class viewpoint, is required. The framework for this positive role is erected by modifying somewhat the harshness with which the late-Ch'ing modern industries are treated in the comparison with Meiji industrialisation. Some writers deny that the early *yang-wu* industries can correctly be described as capitalistic—even if they employed wage labour, they did not produce commodities for a market, only military supplies directly for the government.[29] The majority position, however, is that in some measure, because of their techniques of production with modern machinery, utilisation of wage labour and internal management, they were capitalistic albeit it was " official capitalism of the Chinese style." While the motivation and objectives of the promoters were unquestionably reactionary, the techniques they borrowed from the West accelerated the development of modern forms of production in China and laid the technical groundwork for the appearance of privately-owned capitalist industry (*min-tsu tzu-pen chu-i*).[30] Moreover, the *kuan-tu shang-pan* enterprises producing civilian goods for the market which followed the early military industries were increasingly capitalistic in character; this was especially so in the case of light industry such as cotton textiles. Even if the monopolistic *kuan-tu shang-pan* system was subjectively intended to restrain and control private capital, objectively it stimulated complementary enterprises in industry and mining, trained managers, technicians and workers in the techniques of modern production, and to some extent helped overcome society's total opposition to investment in new forms of production. In China's situation in the late Ch'ing, the official and semi-official enterprises were necessary stages

[29] See, for example, Sun Yü-t'ang, comp., *Chung-kuo Chin-tai Kung-yeh Shih Tzu-liao, Ti-i-chi, 1840–1895 nien* (*Source Materials on the History of Modern Industry in China, First Collection, 1840–1895*) (Peking: K'o-hsueh Ch'u-pan-she, 1957), Introduction, *passim*.

[30] See, for example, Mou An-shih, *Yang-wu Yün-tung* (*The " Foreign Affairs " Movement*) (Shanghai: Jen-min Ch'u-pan-she, 1956).

which had to be traversed before private capitalist industry could develop.

The important distinction for the Communist historian is between private capitalist industry and "bureaucratic capitalism." From the bureaucratic capitalism of the late-Ch'ing to that of the 1930s and 1940s there is a profound spiritual, if not material, connection. In both epochs this was the great obstacle to China's economic development, along with its imperialist cohorts, the great enemy of the people. Private capitalism, however, provided the economic basis for the "bourgeois reformers" of 1898, for the "bourgeoisie, petty bourgeoisie and revolutionary democrats headed by Sun Yat-sen," and for those national capitalists who opposed the Kuomintang of Chiang Kai-shek and the "four big families" and made their peace with the "New Democratic" economy of the CCP. They are to be highly, but not uncritically, valued and incorporated into the great historical heritage of the Chinese people.[31] But arising as it does out of the historical situation of nineteenth-century China, even the progressive wing of the Chinese bourgeoisie could not escape a compromising attitude towards the imperialists and the feudal ruling class. Above all, it was under the illusion that aid could be expected from the imperialist powers in the task of establishing a modern and industrialised China. " So long as imperialism exists, the bourgeoisie of any country cannot really lead the people to prosecute a victorious revolution. The proletariat is the only class capable of leading the Chinese people to complete victory in their struggle for liberation." [32]

IV

I have described in several instances, as for example in the quotation which closes the preceding section, the connection that holds between the importunate demands of policy and politics and the study and writing of modern economic history in China today. It may, I believe, also be suggested that in some measure policy has been reciprocally influenced by the ideological positions expressed in current historiography.

In their efforts to " periodise " modern Chinese economic history, the mainland historians, while not in agreement on the sub-stages, unanimously begin by drawing the sharpest possible distinction between semi-colonial, semi-feudal China and New Democratic China on the way to Socialism and eventually Communism.[33] The semi-colonial, semi-

---

[31] On the " critical inheritance " of China's early bourgeois economic thought, see *People's Daily*, May 18, 1962.

[32] *Ibid.*

[33] See Jen I, " Kuan-yü Chung-kuo Chin-tai Ching-chi Shih Fen-ch'i Wen-t'i ti T'ao-lun " " On the Discussions concerning the Periodisation of Modern Chinese Economic History "), *Historical Research*, No. 3, 1961, pp. 122–123.

feudal economy, they state, which was brought crashing to the ground in 1945–49 suffered under the double oppression and exploitation of domestic feudalists and foreign imperialists, who together blocked the development of the Chinese economy. China's stagnation was not the consequence of any significant divergence of her society and economy from the universal evolutionary stages of Marxism. (We have seen that the " Asiatic mode of production " theory is untenable in Communist China today.) All that was required in order to accelerate the " normal " development from feudalism through capitalism to Socialism, etc.— indeed it would be possible even to jump leap-frog over the capitalist stage—was " liberation " from the feudal-imperialist yoke. To put this in another way, what the Chinese economic historians suggest is that the traditional economy had been undermined by foreign incursions, that the semi-modern economic forms which arose as a result of the foreign stimulus did not develop very far, indeed were crushed by the very forces which fathered them. Once the Kuomintang excrescence was removed, the new Peking government faced a *tabula rasa*.

The implications of this overview of China's economic history for policy, especially economic policy, since 1949 have, it seems to me, been profound. It is assumed first that there was nothing inherent in the basic values or structure of the Chinese economy which would prevent rapid economic growth once the onerous fetters on the people's strength were removed. A second assumption followed from the first: the revolutionary civil war of 1945–49 really did remove entirely the obstacles to development. This outlook, I suggest, contributed importantly to the sense of immense optimism and self-confidence with which the Communist government approached its economic tasks after 1949. We may, with hindsight, now see that much of the optimism was misplaced, that revolutionary fervour unaided does not lead inevitably to economic growth. And judging from the aftermath of the " Great Leap," the reorientation of economic policy in what can only be described as a more conservative and cautious direction, the Chinese leadership seems now to have recognised this too. We may wonder what the reciprocal effects, if any, will be on China's modern economic history in Communist China.

Appendix

In connection with the foregoing examination of the Chinese Communist treatment of China's modern economic history, it might be well to describe briefly the range and quality of the publications on this subject that have appeared since 1949.[34] The comments that follow may be

[34] For a more detailed survey see Albert Feuerwerker and S. Cheng, *Chinese Communist Studies of Modern Chinese History* (Cambridge, Mass.: Harvard University Press, 1961), pp. 168–207.

taken as an elaboration of a recent characterisation of modern Chinese economic history offered by Yen Chung-p'ing, Deputy Director of the Institute of Economic Research, Chinese Academy of Sciences:

Since the establishment of the New China, the achievements made in the study of modern economic history have been extremely rich, far surpassing those accumulated in the Old China over many years. However, the development of the various aspects of this work has been very uneven. Briefly, in terms of geographical regions, generally more emphasis has been placed on the several coastal provinces and the few large cities, while the attention given to the interior provinces and their many large villages and densely populated townships has been inadequate. And no attention has been paid to the various national minority areas, the border regions, the Soviet areas and revolutionary bases, Manchuria after 1931, or Japanese-occupied areas after 1937.

With respect to the several sectors of the economy, the emphasis has been on modern industry and commerce, and rather less on agriculture and handicrafts, although the latter accounted for 90 per cent. of the total value of production in the old China. In the matter of relations of production, more attention has been given to the emergence and development of capitalism, and less to feudal land relationships and the development of industrial and commercial trade associations, and almost none has been given to research on the economic history of the national minorities.

As for periodisation, more works have been produced on the Ming and Ch'ing dynasties prior to the Opium War because of the extensive discussions of the birth of capitalism. Inadequate attention has been given to the post-Opium War period. For the century since the Opium War, more research has been done on peasant rebellions and class struggles, but few achievements have been produced in the research into the economic origin and economic role of these uprisings.

If we turn to the forms in which our research has been conducted, we may see that there has been more data collection than production of finished research works. As to the data collected, more consists of extracts from old documents, and less is in the form of completely edited archives. There is a special lack of carefully processed statistical data. Among the written works produced, there are many short articles but few completed books. There are a great number of subjects and a great diversity of levels of synthetic generalisation, but there has been little analytic research within a small scope. The usual problems which have been discussed are all significant, but there are many problems which have yet to be brought up.

In sum, there are too many blanks and too many weak spots. The course of our scientific research has not been smooth, and some projects have not been completed. The foundation of research in our field is relatively flimsy, while the requirements of teaching, scientific research and the ideological front are general and urgent. This is the contradiction with which we are faced at present.[35]

---

[35] Yen Chung-p'ing, " Yuan-yü Hsuan-ts'e Yen-chiu T'i-mu " (" On the Selection of Subjects for Research "). See note 6 above.

Reliable and comprehensive statistical materials for any period of Chinese economic history have been, as is well known, grossly inadequate. The historians of Communist China have not significantly changed this situation. No volume, perhaps, has been more used and cited by economic historians in China than Yen Chung-p'ing's *Chungkuo Chin-tai Ching-chi Shih T'ung-chi Tzu-liao Hsuan-chi* (*Selected Statistical Materials on Modern Chinese Economic History*) (Peking: K'o-hsueh Ch'u pan-she, 1955). This handbook contains 250 statistical tables covering the period 1840–1948 (except for the foreign trade statistics which go back to 1760) and the following topics: Anglo-Chinese trade prior to the Opium War (31 tables), treaty ports and concessions (3 tables), foreign trade (31 tables), industry (47 tables), railroads (30 tables), shipping (23 tables) and agriculture (85 tables). Each section is prefaced with a discussion of the statistics that follow, the substance of which remains refreshingly intelligent (as one might expect from Yen, perhaps the best economic historian in China today) even while it is hopelessly tendentious. Close examination of the tables shows that the statistics are flagrantly selective, that many are trivial in content, that the "index number problem" has not been faced squarely by the compilers, that the data are often too fragmentary to support the sweeping introductory statement about the "semi-feudal, semi-colonial" character of the Chinese economy, and that, in general, statistics about many facets of the Chinese economy prior to 1949 that are both adequate and reliable are still lacking. Statistical data supplementary to Yen's compilation are included in most of the collections of sources to be described presently, and they suffer from similar shortcomings. One gets the impression, however, that a good many unpublished materials from central and local government and private archives are now being processed and, hopefully, may eventually be made available.[36]

Of a somewhat different character than Yen Chung-p'ing's handbook is the reprinting in one volume of the major statistical series for the period 1913–52 compiled by the Nankai Institute of Economics (*1913 nien—1952 Nien Nan-k'ai Chih-shu Tzu-liao Hui-pien* (*Nankai Index Numbers for 1913–1952*) (Peking: T'ung-chi Ch'u-pan-she, 1958)), and the publication from a wide variety of sources of data on Shanghai commodity prices for 1921–57 (*Shang-hai Chieh-fang Ch'ien-hou Wu-chia Tzu-liao Hui-pien, 1921–57* (*Collected Materials on Commodity Prices in Shanghai Before and After Liberation, 1921–57*) (Shanghai: Jen-min Ch'u-pan-she, 1958)). These are relatively comprehensive statistics rather

---

[36] See, for example, the notice in *Economic Research*, May 1958, pp. 89–90, of 39 major projects to collect and compile source materials on the modern economic history of China.

than a tendentious selection, apparently undoctored, and as such should be extremely useful for more refined analysis than the several editors have provided.

The collection and publication of source materials is probably the most valuable service being performed by the mainland economic historians. Certainly, in bulk, this has been their main contribution since 1949. One is tempted to suggest that this emphasis represents a confluence of the "scissors and paste" tradition, a hoary veteran in Chinese historiography, and perhaps the safest way of digesting the past in a society still in full revolutionary transition. In general, although there are exceptions, the amount of explicit commentary accompanying the many new source collections has been minimal. The editors' "argument" is commonly carried only by the selection and arrangement of materials and by outrageously hermeneutic headings and sub-headings. Valuable materials, often not easily obtainable elsewhere, have been reprinted in these volumes, but I have the distinct impression that to date the proportion of newly printed archival materials is rather small—an indication that the Chinese historians have not yet got very far with exploiting the mass of official and private documents that presumably became available after 1949. If the cruder Marxist analysis which accompanies the documents can be disregarded, it may be fairly stated that these source collections lay the foundations for writing the economic history of modern China on a higher level of theoretical sophistication and with a more comprehensive control of the empirical data than was the case in the past.

One very good example of the scissors and paste technique, and of its continuing usefulness, is the compilation by the Department of History at Nankai University of *Ch'ing Shih Lu Ching-chi Tzu-liao Chi-yao* (*A Compendium of Economic Materials in the Veritable Records of the Ch'ing Dynasty*) (Peking: Chung-hua Shu-chü, 1959). From the 1,220 volumes of the *Ch'ing Shih Lu* (covering the period 1583–1911) the editors have extracted and arranged topically and chronologically (with punctuation added and full citations for each item) the passages relating to the Chinese economy. It is usually necessary to refer to the original for the context in which the extracts occur, but what one has in effect is a valuable index to data on the economy in the otherwise nearly uncontrollable bulk of the *Shih Lu*.

Three major collections of source materials on industry in nineteenth- and twentieth-century China have appeared. Sun Yü-t'ang, comp., *Chung-kuo Chin-tai Kung-yeh Shih Tzu-liao, Ti-i Chi, 1840–1895 Nien* (*Source Materials on the History of Modern Industry in China, First Collection, 1840–1895*) (Peking: K'o-hsueh ch'u-pan-she, 1957, 2 vols.) and Wang Ching-yü, comp., *Chung-kuo Chin-tai Kung-yeh Shih Tzu-liao,*

Ti-erh Chi, 1895–1914 (Source Materials on the History of Modern Industry in China, Second Collection, 1895–1914) (Peking: K'o-hsueh Ch'u-pan-she, 1957, 2 vols.) together span the last century of the Manchu dynasty and provide an impressive mass of materials from Chinese (including archives), Japanese and Western sources on foreign and Chinese industrial enterprise in China. Each collection is preceded by a lengthy essay which strings the assembled documents together on a Marxist-Maoist thread and provides a compact industrial history of the period. Of the four parts of Ch'en Chen *et al.,* comps., *Chung-kuo Chin-tai Kung-yeh Shih Tzu-liao (Source Materials on the History of Modern Industry in China),* I have seen only the second: *Ti-kuo-chu-i Tui Chung-kuo Kung-k'uang Shih-yeh ti Ch'in-lueh ho Lung-tuan (Imperialist Aggression Against and Monopolisation of China's Industries and Mines)* (Peking: San-lien Shu-tien, 1958). Part I is reportedly devoted to industries founded by " national capitalists," Part III deals with " bureaucratic capital " from the Ch'ing through the Kuomintang, and Part IV seems to be a general treatment of individual enterprises.[87] In Part II, the data are most extensive for the 1920s and 1930s. The four part collection as a whole then presumably continues rather than merely supplements the Sun Yü-t'ang and Wang Ching-yü volumes.

A source collection similar to the above has been published on handicraft industry: P'eng Tse-i, comp., *Chung-kuo Chin-tai Shou-kung-yeh Shih Tzu-liao, 1840–1949 (Source Materials on the History of Handicraft Industry in Modern China, 1840–1949:)* (Peking: San-lien Shu-tien, 1957, 4 vols.). It unfortunately contains no introductory essay such as is found in the collections on manufacturing in the nineteenth century.

Agricultural history is represented by four large collections of source materials, all of which lack introductory essays and all of which, like the volumes on industry, scrupulously cite sources and include comprehensive bibliographies: Li Wen-chih, comp., *Chung-kuo Chin-tai Nung-yeh Shih Tzu-liao, Ti-i Chi, 1840–1911 (Source Materials on China's Modern Agricultural History, First Collection, 1840–1911)* (Peking: San-lien Shu-tien, 1957); two further collections compiled by Chang Yu-i under the same general title and with the same publisher and date and treating respectively the periods 1912–27 and 1927–37; and Shih Ching-t'ang, comp., *Chung-kuo Nung-yeh Ho-tso-hua Yun-tung Shih-liao (Historical Materials on Agricultural Collectivisation in China)* (Peking: San-lien Shu-tien, 1957, 2 vols.) which begins in the 1920s but concentrates on the post-1937 period and is, of course, limited to materials on Communist-controlled areas. The first part of Volume I of the last item is of particular interest for its data on patterns of mutual aid in rural

87 See *Kuang-ming Daily,* September 12, 1962.

villages upon the foundation of which Communist collectivisation allegedly proceeded.

Among the other collections of newly published source materials, attention should be drawn to the seven volumes that have appeared to date under the general title of *Ti-kuo Chu-i yü Chung-kuo Hai-kuan* (*Imperialism and the Chinese Customs*). Compiled by the research department of the Directorate General of Customs of the Ministry of Foreign Trade and published in Peking by K'o-hsueh Ch'u-pan-she, these volumes consist for the most part of Chinese translations of English-language documents from the otherwise inaccessible archives of the Imperial Maritime Customs during the period of Sir Robert Hart's incumbency as Inspector-General. Intended primarily to demonstrate the " imperialistic " behaviour of Hart and other foreigners employed by the I.M.C., this series is relevant to several significant problems in China's modern economic history, foreign loans to the Manchu government, for example.

Finally, a number of collections of source materials on individual business enterprises have been published, and more are promised. We may stretch this category to include *Shang-hai Ch'ien-chuang Shih-liao* (*Historical Materials on Money Shops in Shanghai*) (Shanghai: Jen-min Ch'u-pan-she, 1960), compiled by the Shanghai branch of the People's Bank of China and covering the period 1840–1952. A large amount of statistical data on such matters as discounts and exchange rates is included, and the volume concludes with quite detailed information on the organisation, assets and liabilities of several individual money shops. Note also, of this same genre, *Nan-yang Hsiung-ti Yen-ts'ao Kung-szu Shih-liao* (*Historical Materials on the Nanyang Brothers Tobacco Co.*) (Shanghai: Jen-min Ch'u-pan-she, 1958), compiled jointly by the Shanghai Economic Research Institute of the Academy of Sciences and the Economic Research Institute of the Shanghai Academy of Social Sciences. The volume draws upon the archives and accounts of the Nanyang Brothers Co., as well as private letters, interviews, memoirs, newspapers and the like, to provide a detailed documentation of the internal history from 1905 to 1957 of the leading Chinese cigarette manufacturer. Data of this kind relating to any Chinese enterprise have hitherto hardly been available. A similar volume of documents on the Chee Hsin Cement Co., likewise a leader in its field, has also been published: *Ch'i-hsin Yang-hui Kung-szu Shih-liao* (*Historical Materials on the Chee Hsin Cement Co.*) (Peking: San-lien Shu-tien, 1963), compiled jointly by the Nankai University Economic Research Institute and the Department of Economics of Nankai University.

Monographic publications (apart from occasional articles in the leading journals, *Li-shih Yen-chiu* (*Historical Research*) and *Ching-chi Yen-*

chiu (*Economic Research*), and the selected volumes mentioned below) have in general not attained the relatively high quality of the source collections I have described. The lack of theoretical sophistication in formulating problems and assembling materials to answer them which characterised pre-1949 Chinese economic historiography has not been overcome by rearranging matters in Marxist categories. Probably the two best works that have appeared—and coming closest to what would be recognised as economic history outside of China—are the revised edition of Yen Chung-p'ing's *Chung-kuo Mien Fang-chih Shih Kao* (*Draft History of Chinese Cotton Spinning and Weaving*) (Peking: K'o-hsueh Ch'u-pan-she, 1955; original edition, Chungking, 1942), and his *Ch'ing-tai Yun-nan T'ung Cheng K'ao* (*A Study of the Yunnan Copper Administration in the Ch'ing Period*) (Peking: Chung-hua Shu-chü, 1957).

A significant part of the monographic work down to the end of 1958 was related to the "capitalist burgeons" controversy discussed above. I shall mention only Shang Yüeh's *Chung-kuo Tzu-pen-chu-i Kuan-hsi Fa-sheng Chi Yen-pien Ti Ch'u-pu Yen-chiu* (*Preliminary Investigations of the Origin and Development of Capitalist Relations in China*) (Peking: San-lien shu-tien, 1956). Other publications on this topic are in general either derivative from his work or in sharp opposition to it.

One has the impression that in their specialised publications the Chinese economic historians often either have not used or have not had access to the voluminous archival materials that surely must have become available to the CCP and Government after 1949. Chang Yü-lan's *Chung-kuo Yin-hang-yeh Fa-chan Shih* (*A History of the Development of Banking in China*) (Shanghai: Jen-min Ch'u-pan-she, 1957), for example, which surveys the period 1896–1937, is based largely on banking periodicals and other published sources and contains little new data. Wu Ch'eng-ming, *Ti-kuo-chu-i tsai Chung-kuo ti T'ou-tzu* (*Imperialist Investment in China*) (Peking: Jen-min Ch'u-pan-she, 1955) is an interesting rearrangement of the known statistics, but the citation of these data is largely rhetorical. It is the accompanying commentary that dominates—the figures can be and are used to show anything or nothing. The same comments apply to Hsien K'o, *Chin Pai Nien Lai Ti-kuo-chu-i tsai Hua Yin-hang Fa-hsing Chih-pi Kai-k'uang* (*A General Account of the Currency Issues of Imperialist Banks in China in the Past 100 Years*) (Shanghai: Jen-min Ch'u-pan-she, 1958). Yang Tuan-liu, *Ch'ing-tai Ho-pi Chin-jung Shih-kao* (*Draft Monetary and Financial History of the Ch'ing Period*) (Peking: San-lien Shu-tien, 1962) is essentially a stringing together of quotations from Ch'ing documentary collections and Chinese and Western secondary sources, in the traditional style, accompanied by a minimum of commentary and without any useful theoretical framework. While the coverage is comprehensive, the treatment of any particular topic is necessarily fragmentary.

As the titles just described will indicate—and there are other volumes and quite a few articles on similar topics—a relatively large amount of attention has been given to the subjects of money and banking, on which Chinese economic historians often concentrated before 1949, and, of course, also to the matter of foreign loans and investments. In addition to the items I have mentioned, there has been some monographic work on nineteenth- and twentieth-century industry, including a number of company histories. On the other hand, much less effort seems to have been devoted to the study of agricultural history, land tenure and land taxation than to the question of incipient capitalism and the beginnings of modern industry. Perhaps because Chinese agriculture was so intimately a part of " feudal " society (which to the mainland historians is coincident with Imperial China), while the Marxist-Maoist classics have had little to say directly about the anatomy of feudalism, it is judged somewhat perilous to venture into an area described only by ambiguous guidelines. In contrast, in order to have a proletariat—and it is an article of faith that a proletariat is *sine qua non* before there can be a Communist Party—there must first be modern capitalist industry. Hence the vigorous search to trace its roots. This, perhaps, accounts for the unbalanced allocation of resources in the current study of modern economic history.

An analogue to the " campaigns " and " movements " which regularly punctuate other areas of life in China is the " academic discussion," that is, certain topics or problems—usually with more or less direct political implications—are periodically set before the scholarly world by its political panjandrums and an invitation issued for wholesale discussion under the still current but much circumscribed slogan of " letting a hundred flowers bloom and a hundred schools of thought contend." The discussions take the form of specially convened national and local conferences and the extensive publication in journals and newspapers of articles and essays on the topic in question. Summary statements, emanating from the cultural offices of the CCP, then appear from time to time in *Hung-ch'i* or *Jen-min Jih-pao* as guidance for the direction which the discussions should take. The debate on the relationship between historicism and the class viewpoint, mentioned at the beginning of this paper, is an example of this kind of academic discussion. Other topics of interest to historians have included " emphasise the present and de-emphasise the past " (*hou-chin po-ku*), the " inheritability and class character of morality," and the " evaluation of historical personages." Of special relevance to modern economic history is the "capitalist burgeons" controversy, thirty-three contributions to Which have been reprinted in a symposium entitled *Chung-kuo Tzu-pen Chui-i Meng-ya Wen-t'i T'ao-lan Chi* (*Collected Papers on the Problem of Incipient Capitalism in China*) (Peking: San-lien shu-tien, 1957, 2 vols.). This kind of collection provides the opportunity to assess the range of academic opinion on a particular topic and, more important, also the level of theoretical competence as many of the contributions are couched in theoretical terms.

I am acquainted only with two post-1949 textbooks on China's modern economic history. Wu Chieh, *Chung-kuo Chin-tai Kuo-min Ching-chi Shih* (*The Modern National Economic History of China*) (Peking: Jen-min Ch'u-pan-she, 1958), treats the nineteenth century only, *Chung-kuo Chin-tai Kuo-min Ching-chi Shih Chiang-i* (*Lectures on the Modern National Economic History of China*) (Peking: Kao-teng Chiao-yü Ch'u-pan-she, 1958), edited by Department of Political Economy, Hupei University, begins with the eve of the Opium War and continues through 1949. These volumes are oriented to such questions as these: What were the stages in the transformation of China from a feudal society into a semi-colonial and semi-feudal society? How was the semi-colonial, semi-feudal nature of the economy intensified and eventually destroyed? What are the characteristics of each of the stages of economic development and change? What of the class struggles that accompanied economic change? They are, however, reasonably well documented, draw to a limited extent on the newly available materials referred to above, and are probably the most detailed consecutive accounts of China's modern economic history now available.

13

The December 9th Movement:
A Case Study in Chinese Communist
Historiography*

By JOHN ISRAEL

COMMUNIST literature on "Contemporary (post-May 4) History" in which China begins a "bourgeois democratic revolution" is more than an ideological exercise; it is autobiographical. The leading character is none other than the Chinese Communist Party (CCP) itself. The emotional involvement of mainland scribes is comparable to that of a public figure writing his biography. Every event from 1919 to the present is regarded in the light of the CCP's role. Communist leadership is even attributed to the May 4 Movement, which antedated the Party's formation by two years.[1] As the editors of the picture history, *The Glorious Tradition of the Chinese Students*, tell their readers:

> The Chinese student movement, which began with the May 4th Movement of 1919, has continually been under the leadership and summons of the Chinese Communist Party and has intimately consolidated itself with the Chinese people's New Democratic Revolutionary Movement against imperialism, feudalism and bureaucratism.[2]

Such assertions should neither be credulously believed nor rejected out of hand, but carefully analysed and evaluated. An understanding of the Party's role is a prerequisite for an analysis of China's recent political history. The historian who examines writings of the self-proclaimed guardians of the world's greatest revolution must come to grips with the problem of the CCP as a causal agent. How important was the Party in determining events? Were Mao Tse-tung and his comrades generating a wave of history, riding the flood, swimming against the current, or drifting with the tide? What has been the Communist Party's relationship to resurgent nationalism that has swept over twentieth-century China?

* The author wishes to express his gratitude to the Joint Committee on Contemporary China of the Social Science Research Council, whose grant made the research for this article possible.

[1] Chow Tse-tung, *The May Fourth Movement: Intellectual Revolution in Modern China* (Cambridge, Mass.: Harvard University Press, 1960), p. 356.

[2] Chung-hua ch'uan-kuo hsueh-sheng lien-ho hui (ed.), *Chung-kuo Hsueh-sheng ti Kuang-jung Ch'üan-t'ung* (Peking, Chung-kuo Ch'ing-nien Ch'u-pan She, 1956, "Editor's Preface").

In studying the United Front period (dating from the CCP's August 1, 1935, declaration calling for unified resistance to Japanese invasion) these problems are seen in their full complexity. The new Comintern policy was designed to gain support of " bourgeois " elements against " fascist imperialism." To form a broad anti-Japanese alliance Chinese Communists eventually interpreted this strategy to include non-Communists from left-wing intellectuals to heretofore despised Chiang Kai-shek. Since the underlying tactic (to identify with and capitalise upon existing nationalism) was highly successful, the historian finds it difficult to evaluate subsequent claims that CCP leadership played a decisive role in the widely supported National Salvation Movement.

The Peiping student demonstration of December 9, 1935, gave its name to youthful patriotic activities that became a vital part of the national salvation drive.[3] Provoked by Japan's attempt to establish an " autonomous " government in Hopei and Chahar provinces, the Peiping outburst soon spread to schools in thirty-two cities throughout China, as well as to countless adult groups. In Shanghai on May 30, 1936, these forces merged in the All-China National Salvation Association.

[3] Peiping was the pre-1949 name for Peking. The following outline is adapted in part from " Chronology " in Nym Wales' [Helen F. Snow] Notes on the Chinese Student Movement 1935–36, mimeo. (Stanford: Hoover Institution on War, Revolution and Peace, 1959), pp. 184–190. For narrative treatment of the subject, see Hubert Freyn, Prelude to War: The Chinese Student Rebellion of 1935–1936 (Shanghai: China Journal Publishing Company, 1939); and Chaps. 4 and 5 of the author's doctoral dissertation, "The Chinese Student Movement, 1927–1937," Harvard, 1963, to be published by Stanford University Press.
November 1, 1935: 11 Peiping schools send manifesto demanding civil liberties to Fifth KMT Central Executive Committee Congress.
November 18, 1935: Peiping Student Union formed.
December 9, 1935: Nearly 2,000 students demonstrate in Peiping to present a six-point petition to Nanking representative, Ho Ying-ch'in.
December 16, 1935: Second demonstration draws approximately 8,000 participants.
January 2–January 21, 1936: Peiping and Tientsin students conduct propaganda tour to rouse Hopei peasants against Japan. From this pilgrimage emerges a hard core of left-wing agitators centred in a Chinese National Liberation Vanguard, a front organisation for the CCP.
January 15, 1936: Conference of educators and students held in Nanking under auspices of Chiang Kai-shek.
February 20, 1936: Government Emergency Law initiates period of severe suppression of left-wing activists.
March 31, 1936: 1,200 youths demonstrate in memorial for Peiping high school pupil Kuo Ch'ing, who died in prison. CCP criticises this display as " left extremism."
April 17, 1936: Peiping Student Union changes its name to Peiping Student National Salvation Union and adopts moderate policies to harmonise with the United Front strategy.
June 13, 1936: Peiping students demonstrate in response to the South-west Rebellion.
December 12, 1936: Leftist-inspired Peiping student demonstration precedes news of Chiang Kai-shek's kidnapping.
May 4, 1937: " Old " (leftist) Peiping Student Union clashes with " new " (rightist) union during an attempted unity meeting.

Writings of national salvation leaders had strong leftist overtones, but so broad was the movement's popular base that, when Chiang Kai-shek was released from his Sian captivity a year later, countrymen who assumed he was prepared to lead them against the foreign foe gave him the most enthusiastic popular reception of his entire career.

NON-COMMUNIST INTERPRETATIONS

From its inception, the December 9 Movement was a subject of lively debate. Japanese officials and newspapers variously blamed the United States Embassy, Chinese faculty graduates of American universities, the Kuomintang and the Communists for incitement to riot.[4] The Nanking Government called the December 9 demonstration by 2,000 students "patriotic" but urged an end to such outbursts after 8,000 joined a protest on December 16.[5] The English-language Press in China generally expressed guarded sympathy, supporting the students' aims though not always their means.

Suspicion of Communist infiltration after the January propaganda crusade by Peiping and Tientsin students to rouse Hopei peasants against Japan dampened the enthusiasm of many hitherto sympathetic observers. On February 20, the Nanking Government promulgated an Emergency Law to Maintain Public Order, followed by an Executive Yüan directive "to prohibit the activities of the Peiping and Tientsin Students' Union on the ground that the union [was] dominated by a few agitators secretly plotting student disturbances."[6]

These charges roused the ire of resident Western liberals who saw in them an attempt to discredit a non-partisan patriotic movement. In a series of articles in the *China Weekly Review*, Mrs. Edgar (Helen F.) Snow (who often wrote under the pseudonym Nym Wales) maintained that "independent student activity" was motivated solely by selfless concern for the nation's welfare.[7] Hubert Freyn supports Mrs. Snow in *Prelude to War* (1939), the only book-length narrative on the December 9 Movement. Freyn, a Columbia-educated Viennese student, accompanied Yenching schoolmates on the propaganda expedition and subsequently wrote:

> the charge of Communism was the convenient bugbear with which to create the impression that the whole student movement was "really" an attempt at staging a red revolution.

[4] See *China Weekly Review* (CWR), Vol. 75, No. 3, December 21, 1935, p. 100; Wales, *Notes*, p. 44; Freyn, *Prelude*, p. 34.

[5] See CWR, Vol. 75, No. 3, December 21, 1935, p. 100; Vol. 75, No. 5, January 4, 1936, p. 163; *North China Star*, December 12, 1935; *North China Herald*, December 25, 1935; *New York Times*, December 10, 11, 17, 1935.

[6] CWR, Vol. 76, No. 1, March 7, 1936, p. 35; quoted in Wales, *Notes*, p. 49.

[7] Wales, *Notes*, p. 49.

The outstanding characteristic of the movement was, however, not any sort of revolutionary aim but the nationwide response of the patriotic appeal pure and simple.[8]

Now, a quarter of a century later, both Snows have reaffirmed their original position. Edgar Snow, in *Journey to the Beginning*, claims that the movement was conceived at Yenching University, inseminated by his wife and himself, not by the CCP.[9] Mrs. Snow goes further, tracing the ideological roots of the youthful revival not to Karl Marx but to Roger Williams. In her *Notes*, she writes:

> Yenching was the *alma mater* of the " new democracy " in China long before Mao Tse-tung thought up this name. . . . Yenching was the flower of American Protestant influence in China under its president, Dr. John Leighton Stuart, and the 1935 student movement was its unique contribution to modern Chinese history, an unconscious *entente* between American influence and Chinese necessities.[10]

The Snows concede that the movement fell into more professional hands during the spring of 1936,[11] but still depict the students as heroes of a patriotic crusade.

THE PARTY LINE: 1935–1949

The first official Communist reaction to December 9 was a proclamation of the Central Executive Committee of the Chinese Communist Youth Corps (CY) in Pao-an.[12] The hiatus of eleven days between the event and the response strongly suggests that Communist leaders were caught off guard. Thus, that the movement was Communist-instigated appears highly unlikely. In any case, since the pronouncement was to be circulated in non-Communist areas, it naturally offered no hint of Party complicity. Rather, it welcomed the student upsurge as a spontaneous display of youthful patriotism, advised the youngsters to unite with workers, peasants and soldiers, and stated that CY was henceforth to be called the " Resist Japan National Salvation Youth Corps," open to all students, Communist and non-Communist.

Hence, the initial CCP reaction, though belated, was one of gratification and surprise. It implied not that Communist leadership already existed but that the Party was ready to assume control. Five years

8 Freyn, *Prelude to War*, p. 21.
9 Edgar Snow, *Journey to the Beginning* (New York: Random House, 1958), pp. 139–143.
10 Wales, *Notes*, p. 2.
11 See Wales, *Notes*, p. 60; author's interview with Edgar Snow, March 22, 1957.
12 " Chung-kuo kung-ch'an chu-i ch'ing-nien t'uan chung-yang wei-yuan-hui wei k'ang-jih chiu-kuo kao ch'uan-kuo ko-hsiao hsueh-sheng ho ko-chieh ch'ing-nien t'ung-pao hsuan-yen " (" Proclamation of the Chinese Communist Youth Corps Central Executive Committee to Students of the Nation's Schools on the Subject of Resisting Japan and Saving the Nation "), *I-erh chiu Yun-tung* (*The December 9th Movement*) (IECYT) (Peking: Jen-min Ch'u-pan She, 1954), pp. 136–139.

later, Mao Tse-tung conceded that the Party had been " in an utterly defenceless position in all the cultural institutions in the Kuomintang-controlled area " before December 9.[13]

Since the early war years, the December 9 Movement has been a source of nearly annual commemorative articles by Chinese Communist writers. These constitute an index, not only to Communist interpretations of the event, but to changes in the Party line, especially with regard to youth. The basic dilemma of the CCP's wartime united front operation was how to maintain independence while co-operating with the Kuomintang. Commemorating the third anniversary of the December 9 Movement, Ch'en Po-ta argued that student sympathy with the Party line had been thoroughly compatible with loyalty to the Central Government:

> These six demands [of the December 9th petition to Ho Ying-ch'in] were completely at one with the spirit of the CCP's August 1st Proclamation. The young students of various places in the entire country manifested enthusiastic sympathy with the proposals of the CCP and the Central Government, and hoped that the two great political parties, the KMT and the CCP, would again join hands in co-operation to save China from extinction.[14]

A year later, when Mao Tse-tung was still trying to maintain the image of unity while hard pressed by the Japanese, a *Tu-shu Yueh-pao* writer stressed the national implications of December 9 [15]:

> Although [it] started as a student movement, because of the functions of young intellectuals in a semi-feudal, semi-colonial Chinese society, the December 9th Movement actually became, in the political life of the nation, a great anti-Japanese movement, anti-appeasement movement, a movement for unity, a movement for democracy, a new culture movement (the New Enlightenment Movement).[15]

Conspicuously absent from this account were the partisan words " Kuomintang " and " Communist." In keeping with the needs of the time, the writer urged wartime youth to eschew the " fierce attitude " of the December 9 period and to " carry out practical work to resist the enemy under the leadership of the Government " rather than to " stupidly succumb to a nostalgia for past battles against broadswords and firehoses." [16]

---

[13] Mao Tse-tung, " On the New Democracy," *Selected Works of Mao Tse-tung*, Vol. 3 (New York: International Publishers, 1955), p. 149.

[14] Ch'en Po-ta, " I-erh chiu yun-tung san chou-nien chi-nien hui " (" Commemorative Meeting for the Third Anniversary of the December 9th Movement "), *Chieh-fang (Liberation)*, No. 58, p. 19, December 12, 1938; reprinted in Mu-tan-kiang shih ch'ing-nien t'uan chou-wei-hui (ed.), *Wei-ta ti I-erh chiu Yun-tung (The Great December 9th Movement)* (WTTIECYT), Mutankiang, 1948, p. 18.

[15] Hsü Li-ch'un, " I-erh chiu yun-tung ti-ssu chou-nien " (" The Fourth Anniversary of the December 9th Movement "), *Tu-shu Yueh-pao*, Vol. 1, No. 10, December 1, 1939, p. 453.   [16] *Ibid.* p. 454.

By December 1944 the situation had changed radically. No longer struggling for survival, Mao Tse-tung now ruled vast areas of China containing more than a hundred million people. Since Pearl Harbour the war had turned against Japan; it would clearly be won in the Pacific, not in China. With four-year-old scars of the KMT massacre of the Communists' New Fourth Army still unhealed, both sides prepared to resume the civil war. Little wonder that a December 9 commemorative article, "Attack and Counterattack," referred not to the war against Japan, but to the contest against the Chungking Government. "The firehoses and broadswords of December 9 whipped up a fierce National Salvation Movement," stated the author. "This was the precious value of the bitter sacrifice that the young students made in the struggle and was the true consequence of the dictators' criminal acts."[17] No longer were students to bury their heads in books or to work "under the leadership of the Government," for:

> A method of solving the problem of a nation's independence and survival must finally be sought in young students' casting aside the books on the table, leaving the tranquil study, and charging forth to battle.[18]

The tenth anniversary of December 9 found China, the victor over Japan, tottering on the brink of civil war. The foremost demand of the Communists at the time was for "democracy," that is, an equal partnership with the KMT in a national coalition government. In this context, a Party publication recalled the heretofore ignored November 1, 1935, student petition for civil liberties; the December 9 movement was now seen as a struggle for democracy:

> Ten years ago, after the telegram from the Student Self-governing Associations of ten Peiping schools demanding that the Fifth Plenary of the Kuomintang terminate its one-party dictatorship and put into practice the Provisional Constitution, the young students of Peiping staged the great December 9th demonstration. The brave youth of Peiping opposed the firehoses, broadswords and leather belts of the Kuomintang authorities and bellowed forth the bitter shouts buried in their hearts for so many years: "Stop the civil war; consolidate against the foreign foe"; "Terminate tutelage; carry out democracy." These were the central slogans of the December 9th Movement at that time.[19]

In conveniently remembering that the November 1 petition had been the curtain-raiser, the writer pointedly overlooked the fact that, by December 9, the orientation of student wrath had turned ninety degrees and was primarily directed against Government foreign policy, Chinese

---

[17] Ch'ung Chi, "Ta-chi yü hui-chi," *Chieh-fang Jih-pao* (*Liberation Daily*) (Yenan), December 9, 1944.

[18] *Ibid.*

[19] Yao I-lin, "Chi-nien i-erh chiu shih chou-nien" ("Commemorating the Tenth Anniversary of December 9"), *Chieh-fang Jih-pao*, December 13, 1945.

puppets and Japanese imperialists. "Terminate tutelage; carry out democracy" had not been among the slogans of the historic demonstration. His account was obviously cut to fit current political exigencies:

> To this day, the slogans of the December 9th period have still not been completely realised. The Japanese bandits, under orders of Kuomintang authorities, still retain their arms; the large army of the Kuomintang reactionary faction still attacks the liberated areas and initiates large-scale civil war . . . we youth of December 9 working in the liberated areas are deeply moved as we hear of the emergence of our fellow-students [in the] anti-civil war movement in the areas controlled by the Kuomintang.[20]

Thus, from 1945 to 1949 Communists solicited support for civil war by evoking memories of a student generation which had agitated for an end to domestic conflict and for unified resistance to a foreign foe.

USES OF THE PAST: 1950–1952

Though Communists no longer found it necessary to recruit youth for civil war after 1949, annual commemorative articles multiplied. Publications such as *China Youth* and the *People's Daily* now interpreted the history of the revolution to a vastly enlarged audience. Titles of *China Youth* editorials—" The December 9th Movement and Solidarity with the Workers and Peasants " (1950); " Lessons that the December 9th Movement Has Given Me in Regard to the Thought Reform Movement " (1951); and " Revolutionary Youth Massively Enlist in Science " (1952)—show that history continued to serve as the handmaid of politics.

However, there were striking differences between pre- and post-1949 histories. Prior to " liberation " an occasional CCP spokesman boasted that the August 1 Proclamation had inspired the movement, and a few even credited cadres with having prepared the groundwork and served as a vanguard. However, the process at work was seen primarily as one of identifying the Party line with the will of the people.[21] As Ch'en Po-ta (subsequently alleged to have been one of the Party's December 9 leaders in Peiping) phrased it, " The students certainly were not, as some have said, blindly ' led by the nose.' " [22]

Once in control of the mainland, the Party no longer found it desirable to cover its footprints in the dust of populism. Instead, it proudly announced that " the organisation and development of the December 9th Movement . . . was the result of the direct leadership of Communists towards the students of Peiping and Tientsin." [23] Analysing

20 *Ibid.*
21 See WTTIECYT, pp. 17–19.
22 *Ibid.* p. 12.
23 Li Hsueh, " I-erh chiu yun-tung yü kung-nung hsiang chieh-ho " (" Consolidation of the December 9th Movement with the Workers and Peasants "), *Chung-kuo Ch'ing-nien (Chinese Youth)* (CKCN), Nos. 53–54, December 9, 1950, p. 22.

the recent revolution, the party of the proletariat now emphasised the importance of class affiliation. No longer were readers of December 9 eulogies permitted to assume that the young vanguards of the petty bourgeoisie had been masters of their own destiny. The triumph of the movement was not theirs, but really " a victory of the correct leadership of the CCP " which had led students down " the road of consolidation [with] the workers and peasants." [24]

However, even after 1949, CCP writers frequently resorted to populistic explanations while reasserting the indispensability of Party leadership. During the early months of the Korean conflict, Peking spokesmen appealed to their citizens on a broad nationalistic platform. Thus, on December 9, 1950, while Chinese " volunteers " battled American forces south of the Yalu, a banner headline in the *People's Daily* exhorted readers to " Expand the Spirit of Patriotism of December 9." The same day, an article in *China Youth* by student movement veteran Yao I-lin [25] tried to reconcile the Party's admittedly tenuous position in Peiping on the eve of December 9 with sweeping CCP claims to hegemony. " Why," he asked, " with such feeble organised power, with such difficult material conditions, were we able to lead this momentous December 9th Movement? " [26] The answer was:

> simply because December 9 represented the demands of the broad masses. . . . In the December 9th Movement, the victor was not the reactionary clique with political power, arms, and all its superior material means and vast organisational strength, but several thousand bare-handed students with the determination to fight a war of resistance.[27]

The application of this lesson to the Korean war was obvious.

A persistent problem of the new régime was its relationship with China's intellectuals. Many had accepted the Party as the only alternative to the KMT, but serious reservations persisted. Some academicians wished to remain aloof from politics and independent of the CCP. These doubts were quite understandable, intimated Liu Chih-lan to *China Youth* readers in her article, " December 9 Taught Me." She had felt the same way when she was a student:

> At that time, of course, I didn't have any particular animus against the Communist Party—the sacrifice in Peking of Li Ta-chao and other revolutionary leaders had made a deep impression on Pekingers—but I felt that the student movement was a patriotic movement and ought to be " pure." If there were Communists in it, I might have nothing to do with it.[28]

[24] *Ibid.*   [25] See note 19, above.
[26] Yao I-lin, " I-erh chiu hui-i " (" Recollections of December 9 "), CKCN, Nos. 53–54, December 9, 1950, p. 21.   [27] *Ibid.*
[28] Liu Chih-lan, " I-erh chiu chiao-yu-le wo " (" December 9 Taught Me "), CKCN, Nos. 53–54, December 9, 1950, p. 26.

Many of Miss Liu's readers had also participated in December 9 and similar activities during the United Front period. No doubt most had believed these to be spontaneous. Now they were to reinterpret their experiences and see themselves not as the creators of history, but as beneficiaries of the magnanimous bounty of the Party. No patriotic experience independent of the CCP was possible.

In 1951, as pressure on China's intellectuals increased, interpretations of the December 9 Movement were geared to the needs of thought reform. The message was: Orthodoxy plus obedience equals success:

> Had it not been for the leadership of the Chinese Communist Party and the thought of Mao Tse-tung, the December 9th Movement might have withered on the vine or might, like several student movements in Chinese history, have flowered without bearing fruit. The leadership of the Chinese Communist Party and the thought of Mao Tse-tung . . . permeated every aspect of the movement. The factual proof of this in the December 9th Movement was that, if at any time or in any aspect it did not correspond to the thought of Mao Tse-tung, the movement of that time or in that aspect would succumb to sluggishness or defeat.[29]

The December 9 period, wrote Party scribes, had been one of intense ideological conflict in which proletarian thinking had overcome petty bourgeois adversaries on the battlefield of China's campuses. Some misguided students had urged a united front based upon the " Kuomintang reactionary Government and bogus KMT student organisations "; others had sought to achieve unity by abolishing revolutionary bodies such as the Peiping Student Union and the Chinese National Liberation Vanguard. Still others had been captivated by petty bourgeois " third road illusions." No less dangerous had been the dogmatic leftists who had isolated themselves by mouthing slogans unacceptable to the broad masses. Only under the omniscient guidance of the Party had the movement steered a correct course between " left adventurism " and " right capitulationism." [30]

A commemorative article of 1952 continued to emphasise ideological orthodoxy with a series of didactic stories about the youth of December 9 by Hsiao Wen-lan, the Party's foremost expert on the movement. The contemporary application of these edifying tales was clear: Party members must ruthlessly criticise and destroy all traces of bourgeois thinking.[31]

---

[29] Hsiao Wen-lan, " Kuan-yü ssu-hsiang kai-tsao i-erh chiu kei wo-men ti chiao-hsün " (" Lessons that December 9 Gives Us Concerning Thought Reform "), CKCN, No. 80, December 8, 1951, p. 1.

[30] *Ibid.* pp. 1–2.

[31] " Tsou-kuo ti tao-lu " (" The Road We Have Travelled "), CKCN, No. 102, December 1, 1952, pp. 3–5.

THE LIMITS OF FLEXIBILITY: 1953–1957

In the same article Hsiao sounded a new note that was to become increasingly resonant in the mid-50s: Intellectuals must participate in "constructive labour" and learn from the workers and peasants. Economically, 1953 through 1957 were the most fruitful years the Peking régime has yet seen. The Korean conflict was terminated, the First Five-Year Plan begun. Agricultural production rose appreciably; socialisation of industry and agriculture was accelerated. This coincided with a period of stabilisation in the academic world which lasted from late 1952 until the summer of 1955, when the anti-Hu Feng Movement and the Movement for the Liquidation of Counter-Revolutionaries once again cast a pall of fear over China's intellectual community. Economic progress and political relaxation reflected and reinforced a mood of self-confidence that overflowed into the disastrous Hundred Flowers Movement, communisation and the Great Leap Forward.

Even in December 1952, a new line, thought reform *cum* economic construction, was evident in an article by former medical student Huang Shu-tse, who had served in the first aid corps on the January crusade and later became a physician in Yenan. Reflected the author:

> Were someone to ask me, "At what time did you become a revolutionary warrior?" I would answer him thus: " . . . not at the time of the December 9th Movement, not when I decided to go to Yenan, and not when I entered Yenan, but after I had received several years of rigorous discipline in Yenan, especially after I had been through the *cheng-feng* movement of 1943." [32]

Huang reiterated the moral of his experience: The man of science must serve the masses and submit himself to ideological remoulding. "Of course," he added, "to this day I must ceaselessly accept revolutionary discipline, ceaselessly remake myself." [33]

The transition to a more constructive line from the militant attitude of the Korean war and the thought reform campaign manifested itself in the terminal paragraph of the December 9 chapter in Wang Nien-k'un's *Talk About the Basic History of the Student Movement*. The 1953 conclusion began, as did the 1951 version, by calling upon students to "promote the spirit of youth of December 9, heroically, selflessly fighting for the survival and independence of the fatherland," but added that students must:

> energetically study scientific knowledge, study culture, study politics. We must combine a heroic, positive political zeal with the study of even

[32] " Wo shih i-erh chiu ch'un-chung tui-wu chung-chien ti i-ko " (" I Was One in the Ranks of the December 9th Masses "), CKCN, No. 102, December 1, 1952, p. 6.
[33] *Ibid.*

more knowledge, so that we may still better serve the constructive enterprise of the fatherland.[34]

By December 1953 the transition was complete. The new mood was
reflected in a two-page *China Youth* essay, the magazine's sole offering
for the eighteenth anniversary of the historic date. (The seventeenth had
been celebrated with five items covering eight pages.) The article was
remarkably free of doctrinal teachings. Not only was no claim made
for CCP leadership, but the very name of the Party was nowhere to
be found in the narrative portion of the text. The author confined himself to a simple account of how Tientsin youth displayed solidarity,
determination and fortitude in carrying on the movement started by their
Peiping comrades-in-arms. A postscript, obviously added by the editor
and totally unrelated to the rest of the article, told China's youth that
they could best " carry on the revolutionary tradition of December 9 "
by " constructing the fatherland " and making " even greater efforts
towards the realisation of Socialism." [35]

The following year, *China Youth* ignored the anniversary of
December 9, so far removed were the economic tasks of the present from
the stirring history of the past.

The period of relative objectivity in commemorative articles during
the mid-50s coincided with a trend towards careful scholarship in the
field of documentary history. Between 1951 and 1956, a series of eight
collections on modern Chinese history were published. Reviewers
noted:

> the selected documents [were] on the whole faithfully and fully
> transcribed, editorial comment [was] minimal, and the traditional
> chronicler's regard for the written record [was] evident in the printing
> of many hitherto unpublished manuscripts.[36]

This statement applies imperfectly to *The December 9th Movement*,
one of six volumes in a contemporary history series published during
the same period.[37] Most if not all the documents in this book had
previously been published, if only in leaflet form. Some were condensed
or abridged for editorial reasons. Though deletions included tirades that
would have sharpened the political impact, editors did not hesitate to
take textual liberties for ideological purposes. One item on the Southern
Propaganda Crusade amalgamated two letters to Tsou T'ao-fen's *Life*

[34] *Hsueh-sheng yun-tung shih-yao chiang-hua* (Hankow: Shang-tsa Ch'u-pan She, October
1951), p. 60; revised edition, May 1953.
[35] Chi Yu, " I-erh chiu ti i-ko tse-mien " (" One Aspect of December 9 "), CKCN,
No. 126, December 1, 1953, pp. 21–22.
[36] John K. Fairbank and Mary Wright, " Documentary Collections on Modern Chinese
History," *Journal of Asian Studies* (JAS), Vol 17, No. 1, November 1957, p. 55.
[37] IECYT, in the series *Chung-kuo Hsien-tai Shih Tzu-liao Tsung-k'an* (*Collection of
Sources on Contemporary Chinese History*) (Peking: Jen-min Ch'u-pan She, 1953–54).

of the Great Masses and made numerous revisions in the interests of orthodoxy.[38] Where the original had castigated the compradore class, the revised version heaped abuse upon landlords as well. Deleted were a reference to a foreign teacher (presumably a missionary), who had sympathised with the young crusaders, and an expression of anti-proletarian romantic heresy that contrasted benighted denizens of the " evil city " to the " sincere and pure " masses of rural China.

Nonetheless, the editor's sins against scholarship were mostly ones of omission. Nothing was added to prove that the CCP had led the movement. Although it was necessary here, as in the modern history collections, to place " China's modern century in a context of Marxism-Leninism " [39] this was achieved by a brief, almost perfunctory, prefatory statement (totally omitted in at least some of the other volumes in the series): " The December 9 Movement was a patriotic movement led by the Chinese Communist Party." Having thus paid his respects to the Party line, the publisher dispassionately explained why the contents of the book failed to substantiate this central thesis:

> The majority of the materials selected for this book were publicly published in Kuomintang-controlled territories. Therefore they were unable to discuss the problem of the Party's leadership.[40]

As a matter of fact, at least three, and probably five, of the selections in this volume were *not* published in KMT areas. One was issued in Pao-an in 1935,[41] another appeared in the Yenan *Liberation Daily* in 1944, a third was taken from a 1953 issue of *China Youth*,[42] and two others, dated November 1948, were probably published in the " liberated areas." The publisher's explanation certainly did not account for the failure of the single post-1949 article selected for inclusion (Chi Yu's " One Aspect of December 9 " [43]) to establish the CCP's claim to leadership. This is especially remarkable since the item dealt with Tientsin, a city where Party notables such as Liu Shao-ch'i and Huang Ching were supposed to have been active at the time.

The actual reason that the contents of Chi Yu's article virtually ignored the question of Party hegemony was not because the article was published in a KMT region, which it emphatically was not, but rather because neither the original writer nor the editors were anxious to establish the point. (The book and the article were published within

---

38 " P'ing-chin hsueh-sheng lien-ho hui k'uo-ta hsuan-ch'uan t'uan hsia-hsiang hsuan-ch'uan " (" The Peiping-Tientsin Student Union Propaganda Corps Goes to the Country to Disseminate Propaganda "), IECYT, pp. 61–69; originally published in *Ta-chung Sheng-huo*, Vol. 1, Nos. 11 and 12, January 25 and February 1, 1936.
39 Fairbank and Wright, " Documentary," p. 55.
40 " Ch'u-pan she kuan-yü pen shu ti shuo-ming," IECYT.
41 IECYT, *op. cit.*, note 12, above.
42 Chi Yu, *op. cit.*, note 35, above.
43 *Ibid.*

three months of each other.) The original article was notably free from forced interpretations and doctrinaire interjections. The strongest propaganda was confined to an introduction and a conclusion, both organically unrelated to the narrative. These sections, including effusive praise for Mao Tse-tung and the New China, did *not* appear in the anthology's reprint. The editors of this volume evidently were stretching objectivity to the limit.

However, Communist scribes had no intention of applying the kind of dispassionate attitude characteristic of their documentary compilations to their commentaries and analyses. In November 1954, eight months after the publication of *The December 9th Movement*, Wang Nien-k'un's *Discussion of the History of Our Country's Student Movement* appeared.[44] Examination of the two works suggests a dual process through which the CCP's ideological aims were served:

1. Documentary collections were confined to items likely to sustain the Party's point of view.

2. These sources were then used in secondary accounts to vindicate foregone conclusions.

This is not to disparage the value of the documentary works, even as employed by Communist historians. A comparison of Wang Nien-k'un's book and an earlier 1951 work on which it was based[45] finds the later volume unquestionably superior thanks to its greater wealth of detail.[46] However, factual elucidation was countered by an expansion of ideologically motivated generalisations. For example, describing the origins of the December 9 Movement, the author amended his previous book with[47]:

> Under the summons of the Party's August 1st Proclamation, under the direct leadership of the Peiping Party organisation, Peiping's students rose to battle.

As noted above, *The December 9th Movement* documents did not provide evidence to support such contentions. Thus, this key thesis of Party historians remained unsubstantiated.

[44] *Wo Kuo Hsueh-sheng Yun-tung Shih-hua* (WKHSYTSH) (Hankow: Hu-pei Jen-min Ch'u-pan She, November 1954).

[45] *Hsueh-sheng, op. cit.*, note 34, above.

[46] Unfortunately, Wang Nien-k'un did not use the documentary collection carefully. Perhaps he was rushing to meet a publication deadline when it appeared. For example, he continued to date the November 1, 1935, Petition as November 5. (See 1953 edition, p. 50; 1954, p. 38.) His numerical calculations (*e.g.*, that there were more than 10,000 students in the December 9 demonstration, of whom one was killed and more than 500 injured, that more than 30,000 students and tens of thousands of townspeople marched on December 16, see 1954 edition, pp. 41–43) are gross exaggerations compared with the non-commital attitude of the earlier editions and the more conservative figures of *The December 9th Movement*. Wang's estimates apparently are based upon WTTIECYT, p. 39, although he has taken the liberty of raising this volume's statistic of 20,000 students on December 16 to 30,000.

[47] WKHSYTSH, p. 41.

Wang Nien-k'un's revised volume was published just as another storm of thought reform was brewing in Peking. A year later, by the time the first edition of Hsiao Wen-lan's anthology, *Commemorating December 9th*,[48] appeared, China's intellectuals had once more reaped the whirlwind. In the summer of 1955, while the collection was being prepared, the new drive for orthodoxy reached a peak with a frenzied attack upon alleged followers of the outcast intellectual, Hu Feng. "Counter-revolutionaries" were marked for "liquidation." The ideological tempest was followed by an economic and social cyclone of rural and urban collectivisation while Hsiao's book was going to press. Moreover, as the socialist revolution accelerated at home, China's prestige among underdeveloped nations was riding high on the tide of the Bandung Conference (April 1955). Thus, Peking was enjoying a period of exuberant confidence when Hsiao's book appeared.

As success bred self-assurance, the régime prepared to adopt a more conciliatory attitude towards intellectuals. The painful re-examination of attitudes *vis-à-vis* this small but vital sector of China's population culminated in Chou En-lai's January 1956 "Report on the Question of Intellectuals," which expressed a willingness to reintegrate this element into the body politic in an active, co-operative capacity. Following relentless self-examination and thought reform, the intellectuals were to join forces with the proletariat in building Socialism. Hsiao's postface applied the lessons of history to the needs of the present:

> At the time of the December 9th Movement, generally speaking, the task at hand was anti-imperialism, anti-feudalism. Then, China was in the period of the democratic revolution. Today, the democratic revolution has already been completed and we have entered the period of the socialist revolution. The central slogan of today is: Everything for Socialism. . . .
> What have these past twenty years to teach the youth of today's new era? The first thing we should mention is the problem of thought reform. Unless one has gone through a violent ideological struggle, unless one has ceaselessly swept away bourgeois and petty bourgeois ideas from the realms of thought, it will be difficult to know oneself and to remould oneself, to know the world and to remould the world. . . .
> One more thing which should especially be mentioned is the problem of deeply penetrating among the working and peasant masses. In the December 9th Movement, the Party told us to consolidate with the broad working and peasant masses. This slogan, in the socialist revolutionary period of today, has not diminished in significance.[49]

Here, then, was a style of Communist history quite different from that of the previous year's documentary, *The December 9th Movement*.

---

[48] Tzu Fang (Hsiao Wen-lan, pseud.), *Chi I-erh chiu* (CIEC) (Peking: Pei-ching Ta-chung Ch'u-pan She 1955).   [49] *Ibid.* pp. 37–38.

In 1955, the primary concern was to instruct, not to transmit. The original, inadequate to the needs of the new era, was revised.

The 1954 collection had reprinted with few changes Hsiao's "Short History," originally published in 1937. In keeping with their concern for textual sanctity, the editors had retained the concluding paragraph of 1937:

> Youth are the sentinels of the nation and the vanguard of the people. At a time when our nation has not yet achieved thorough liberation, at a time when our people have not yet achieved complete democracy, youth must stoutly and bravely carry on this struggle.[50]

The 1955 book reissued the "Short History" but the original last paragraph was replaced with:

> Intellectual youth and young students: the working and peasant masses are the main force; we certainly must consolidate with the main force, become one with them, and form a great army before we are able to destroy Japanese imperialism and change the old China into a new China.[51]

The meaning was thus inverted: Young intellectuals were no longer leaders, but followers, of the "working and peasant masses."

Why was Hsiao willing to make this substantive change in his conclusion but still reluctant to interject concrete evidence of CCP leadership? His reasons are a matter of conjecture, but one may surmise that this expert, with first-hand experience, could not bring himself to believe that the CCP *had* led the December 9 Movement; he refused to go out of his way to prove otherwise.

However, the Party line could not always be slighted. Hence, the title article, "Commemorating December 9," placed new words on the eloquent tongues of the January 1936 propaganda corpsmen. In a 1950 version, Hsiao had stated:

> In the propaganda corps, some revolutionary youth told everybody we must have a people's country; we must have a society of the working people. Only thus would we be able to beat down Japanese imperialism and rescue the country from its dangerous situation.[52]

Four years later, the ideas of the young patriots were so paraphrased as to suggest that they had been unabashed Communist propagandists:

[50] IECYT, p. 29.

[51] CIEC, p. 28.

[52] CKCN, Nos. 53–54, December 9, 1950, p. 24. The same text appeared in the *Jen-min Jih-pao (People's Daily)*, December 9, 1950, and in Hu Hua and others (ed.), *Chung-kuo Hsin Min-chu Shu-i Ko-ming Shih Ts'an-k'ao Tzu-liao (Materials on the History of China's New Democratic Revolution)* (Shanghai: Commercial Press, 1951), pp. 337–346. According to Hsiao, the original was included in *I-erh chiu Man-yü (Chat on December 9)*, 1940.

we must have a people's democratic country. . . . Only by relying upon the People's Army and People's Democratic Régime would we be able to beat down Japanese imperialism.[53]

Most sweeping changes came in an article dating from the early 50s, "Lessons that December 9 Gives Us Concerning Thought Reform."[54] The original text attributed the success of the December 9 Movement to "the leadership of the Chinese Comunist Party and of Mao Tse-tung's thought." The latter was mentioned no fewer than five times in a six-paragraph article. In 1955, the CCP was retracting its earlier claims for the originality of Mao's ideas; in every instance, "the thought of Mao Tse-tung" was changed to "Marxist-Leninist thought."[55]

Ideological motives also prompted other revisions. Attacks on petty bourgeois thought were subdued, heralding the new "soft" policy towards "petty bourgeois" intellectuals. According to the 1951 article, the most important ideological issue in the December 9 period had been the bitter struggle between "proletarian thought" and "petty bourgeois thought." In the revised version, the villain was recast in a more amorphous shape as "non-proletarian thought" or "bourgeois and petty bourgeois thought." Whereas in 1951, non-proletarian and proletarian thought were separated by a great wall called "the demarcation between the enemy and us," in 1955 this phrase was changed to the innocuous "demarcation of thought." If the active co-operation of intellectuals was to be solicited, they could no longer be viewed as intransigent foes.

Further modifications mobilised the article to the needs of the campaign to accelerate Socialism. In 1951, the reader had been told that the December 9 Movement had overcome "left adventurism and right capitulationism." In 1955, the order was reversed, indicating that the primary danger had emanated from the right. In the earlier article, the author pointed to the importance of studying "theory." In 1955, the adjective "revolutionary" told mainland youth precisely what kind of theory would be acceptable.

Hence, the ideological content of the December 9 Movement and the lessons drawn from it were undergoing a metamorphosis late in 1955. Hsiao's commemorative offering in a December 1955 *China Youth* appeared during the transitional period between the renewed anti-rightist drive and Chou En-lai's enunciation of a liberalised policy towards intellectuals. The message was reminiscent of 1952 (thought

---

[53] CIEC, p. 4. [54] CKCN, *op. cit.*, note 29, above.

[55] This article was reprinted with only inconsequential changes in the 1960 and 1961 editions of Hsiao's anthology. Although "the thought of Mao Tse-tung" had once again become respectable, to say the least, and was lauded in a 25th anniversary article in the same collection, this phrase inexplicably remained deleted from the earlier commemorative. This oversight can be attributed to careless editing.

reform *cum* economic reconstruction) but the tone was not as shrill. The ideological dispute was now considered of secondary importance in the December 9 period. Attention was directed to a hitherto neglected educational aspect of the movement; Hsiao told of students establishing night schools for workers and peasants and taking sociological polls.[56] In the same issue, Wei Chün-i eulogised Tsinghua students who, at the time of December 9, had taken upon themselves the education of the proletariat.[57]

By 1956, Party scribes had already reached the outer limits of their flexibility. The moderate tone continued through the Hundred Flowers period. Commemorating the twenty-first anniversary of December 9, the picture history, *The Glorious Tradition of the Chinese Students*,[58] devoted thirty-three of its eighty-four pages to the December 9 period. Here, even the semi-literate reader could not miss the message of the Party implicit in the sequence of photographs. Pictured on page 10 were the Chinese Soviet's April 1932 " Declaration of War against Japan " and the August 1 Proclamation. On the next page were scenes of the Long March. Page 13 began the section on the December 9 Movement. Cause and effect were obvious.

The captions, however, did not make great claims: even a dramatic picture of an orator in the December 16 demonstration was described simply as " Standing on a street-car and speaking to people on the street," without mentioning that the young propagandist depicted was CCP student leader Huang Ching. In keeping with the constructive tone of the First Five-Year Plan, the editor's introduction stated:

> Now students are continuing and developing the glorious revolutionary tradition of the Chinese student movement, studying hard for socialist construction.

During the Hundred Flowers period, no attempt was made to prove that the splendour of the December 9 Movement lay in a " hundred schools contending." In Yang Chi's *Stories of the Chinese Student Movement*, published at the height of the movement, the moral was familiar:

> Revolutionary young intellectuals must consolidate with the broad workers, peasants and soldiers and must be under the leadership of the Communist Party if they are to be able to reach their revolutionary goals.[59]

[56] " Tsou i-erh chiu ti kuang-jung tao-lu " (" Follow the Glorious Path of December 9 "), CKCN, No. 174, December 1, 1955, p. 2.

[57] " Kuan-yü hsueh-sheng ho kung-nung chieh-ho ti wen-t'i " (" Regarding the Problem of Students' Consolidation with the Workers and Peasants "), CKCN, No. 174, December 1, 1955, p. 4.

[58] Chung-hua, *op. cit.*, note 2, above.

[59] *Chung-kuo hsueh-sheng yun-tung ti ku-shih* (CKHSYTTKS) (Nanking: Kiang-su Jen-min Ch'u-pan She, May 1957), p. 23.

That the heady perfume of the hundred flowers failed to permeate the musty pages of December 9 historiography is no surprise. Further liberalisation of Party history would have exceeded the limitations of the Hundred Flowers idea, which was never intended to challenge the Marxist-Leninist *weltanschauung*. History remained a bulwark of this view.

RIGID ORTHODOXY: FROM 1957 TO THE PRESENT

In June 1957, a sudden freeze blighted the hundred flowers; anti-rightists declared open season on rebellious intellectuals. With ideological orthodoxy of paramount concern, history reassumed the tones of the thought reform days of 1951–52 and 1955. An article aptly entitled " Youth Must Resolutely Follow the Communist Party " explained how a small number of students, both inside and outside the Party, had committed rightist errors during the December 9 Movement, and warned contemporary youth against repeating the mistake.[60] *Leftist* errors were not mentioned.

In the excesses of the Hundred Flowers, intellectuals had demonstrated that they were not to be trusted. Party attempts to imbue them with proletarian consciousness had failed. Stern measures were necessary if this was to be corrected. No longer were academicians to be given the preferential treatment promised by Chou En-lai in January 1956. They were now to be mobilised as workers in the hinterland. On December 9, 1957, the *People's Daily* reported that students were celebrating the twenty-second anniversary of the movement by going to the countryside to aid the peasants and by carrying on discussions and symposia with the proletariat. Anniversary articles stressed how youth of 1935–36 had broken down barriers to communication with the countryfolk. One writer pointed out:

> The December 9th Movement points out a truth: only if the intelligentsia resolves to carry out consolidation with the workers and peasants and to carry out duties for the workers and peasants will they be able to become true revolutionaries.[61]

As students by the tens of thousands were sent from classrooms to farmhouses, the experience of their precursors was recalled. According to the Party, there was room for improvement:

> The students of this period had only an elementary understanding: the workers and peasants were stronger than the students; oppression was bad; labour was good. But how labour was good they could not

60 Yang Shu (Hsiao Wen-lan, pseud.), " Ch'ing-nien jen yao chien-chueh ken-cho kung-ch'an-tang tsou," December 9, 1957, CIEC (5th ed.), 1960, pp. 40–42.
61 *People's Daily*, December 9, 1957.

say. They themselves had never taken part in labour; to them, labour was but an abstract concept.[62]

Before 1949, the CCP claimed the December 9 Movement had been largely a spontaneous expression of the *vox populi*. Through the mid-1950s mainland readers were told it had been CCP-led, but even this information generally had either to be induced from the contents or derived from a short preface or postface. For example, in the 1955 edition of Hsiao Wen-lan's article "Commemorating December 9," only a few concluding lines mentioned the alleged impact of the August 1 Proclamation, the United Front, and other aspects of Party leadership.[63]

In the revised 1960 version, references to the CCP's role were woven into the fabric of the text.[64] New phrases were added: "the People's Army and the People's Democratic Régime led by the Communist Party," "the national student movement led by the Chinese Communist Party." The Chinese National Liberation Vanguard was now (accurately) described as "an organisation under the leadership of the Chinese Communist Party." In 1955, youth of December 9 were reported to have "completely accepted" Party policies. Five years later, these same policies were said to have been "both completely accepted and supported."

We have observed that the spirit of the Hundred Flowers did not encompass any relaxation in the assertion of the Party's historic leadership over the revolution. Indeed, a trend towards making increasingly extensive claims began while the exotic blossoms were in full bloom. In Yang Shu's popular history, published in May 1957, the claim was first made that the Peiping Student Union had been a Communist organisation, founded November 18, 1935, "under the leadership of the CCP." Since the body had been responsible for all subsequent student activities, this amounted to a blanket claim of Party hegemony.

On December 9, 1957, readers of the *People's Daily* learned that exactly twenty-two years earlier, "The March of the Volunteers"—later to become Communist China's National Anthem—had been sung in the streets of Peiping.[65] (This flatly contradicted all earlier reports, which stated that the song had first been heard in a Peiping student demonstration on December 12, 1936.)

One year later, a Shanghai *Wen Hui Pao* writer made it known that the historic demonstration had been planned by "comrades of the

---

[62] Yang Shu (Hsiao Wen-lan, pseud.), "Ts'ung chih-shih ch'ing-nien ho kung-nung ch'un-chung chieh-ho t'an-ch'i" ("On the Consolidation of Intellectual Youth with the Working and Peasant Masses"), December 9, 1958, CIEC, 1960, p. 44.

[63] CIEC, 1955, p. 9.

[64] CIEC, 1960, pp. 1–9, *passim.*

[65] *People's Daily*, December 9, 1957.

265

Peiping committee of the CCP working day and night," [66] while an adjoining article declared that the December 16 outbreak and the January crusade had also been Party-organised.[67]

Since 1960, after the failure of the communes and the Great Leap, the one-sided assault on rightism no longer has been appropriate, though more attention still has been given to attacking that excess than to exposing leftist heresies. The most notable characteristic of writings from this period is the dogmatic insistence that students must be orthodox. Without a national goal to replace the great drives and with serious food shortages affecting rural and urban dwellers, orthodoxy and loyalty have become ends in themselves. Mao Tse-tung and Liu Shao-ch'i are quoted at great length to add sanctity to the writing. Footnotes appear in unaccustomed profusion. One article concludes:

> The significant experience of December 9—that we must resolutely advance along the road delineated by the Chinese Communist Party and Chairman Mao, that intellectual youth must consolidate with the broad working and peasant masses and must study the thought of Mao Tse-tung and the policies of the Party—this should still be deeply engraved in the minds of today's youth.[68]

Thus, extravagant claims for the Party's historic role in the student movement—first announced in the era when China was committed to double agricultural output in one year and to surpass England's steel production in fourteen—continue long after the 1958 harvest figures had been officially repudiated and the backyard furnaces dismantled.

The assertion of CCP importance has been a three-stage process: First, to make a general claim; second, to spell out specific details; and third, to support these with personal testimony through the publication of memoirs.

Reminiscences of December 9 (Peking, 1961) contains eleven articles on events and people of the historic movement.[69] Seven have been translated into English in *The Roar of a Nation*, published by Peking's Foreign Languages Press in 1963. Comparing the English with the Chinese, we recall Allen S. Whiting's note of caution concerning "tempting translations . . . offered to foreign scholars." [70] We have

[66] Chang Nan, " I-erh chiu chi Huang Ching t'ung-chih " ("December 9 Memories of Comrade Huang Ching "), *Wen Hui Pao* (Shanghai, December 9, 1958).

[67] " I-erh chiu yun-tung ti ching-kuo " (" The Events of the December 9 Movement "), *ibid.*

[68] Hsiao Te (Hsiao Wen-lan, pseud.), " I-erh chiu yun-tung chien-lun " (A Brief Discussion of the December 9 Movement ", *Kuang-ming Jih-pao*, December 9, 1960, reprinted in CIEC, 6th ed., 1961, p. 54.

[69] Chung-kuo Ch'ing-nien Ch'u-pan She (ed. and pub.), *I-erh chiu hui-i-lu* (IECHIL).

[70] " Rewriting Modern History in Communist China: A Review Article," *Far Eastern Survey*, Vol. 24, No. 2, November 1955, p. 174.

already observed that the English version is shorter by four articles; moreover, some of the translations have been abridged or amended. In principle, this is both natural and justifiable since the foreign reader would likely be bored by some parts of the original material and confused by others. However, a careful perusal of the texts reveals well-calculated ideological reasons for most changes.[71]

The Chinese places greater stress upon CCP leadership. Though the Party's predominant role is made painfully clear in the English, the original labours the point *ad nauseum*. In many instances, the English version has deleted phrases such as " according to the Party's directives . . .," " following the Party's guidance . . .," and " under the Party's strong and correct leadership. . . ." The reader of the English version is less frequently reminded that the student movement was a recruiting ground for the revolution. It is deemed inadvisable to tell him, for example, that " comrades of the underground Party secretly spread booklets on carrying out guerrilla warfare." [72] References to the behind-the-scenes activities of Liu Shao-ch'i are quietly omitted, as is the lead article, Li Ch'ang's " Recollections of the National Salvation Vanguard " (the CCP's foremost North China front organisation).

In both versions, the conclusion of an article on the January 1936 propaganda tour begins:

> In fact the whole area [covered by the agitators] became a guerrilla base in the fight against Japanese aggression.[73]

The Chinese account adds:

> and, under the Party's leadership, the people of the base stoutly carried on a heroic revolutionary struggle.

The English sounds more like the final sentence in the report of a YMCA camper:

> This was indeed an extraordinary month for us young students, who gained such wonderful experience in China's countryside.

The translator has toned down anti-Kuomintang epithets, sometimes deleting adjectives from phrases such as " country-selling Chiang Kai-shek " and " reactionary Peiping authorities." Furthermore, he has taken pains to differentiate between the localistic semi-autonomous troops and police of Sung Che-yüan, whose Twenty-ninth Army was used to quell Peiping demonstrations, and the Central Government forces of Nanking. The Chinese reader is allowed to believe that the

---

[71] Some differences between the two have no apparent political motivation. " Several hundred " and " several thousand " in Chinese are justifiably translated as " many." Less understandably, an article attributed to P'eng Yüan-li in the original is by-lined Shih Li-teh in the English.

[72] IECHIL, p. 146. See *Roar of a Nation* (Peking: Foreign Languages Press, 1963), p. 118.　　　　　　　　　　[73] IECHIL, p. 153; *Roar*, p. 129.

Peiping warlord was nothing more than a lackey of Chiang Kai-shek. The English reader is afforded a more rounded view. Even though the English introduction refers to the " troops, police and secret agents of the reactionary Kuomintang Government " in Peiping,[74] a subsequent footnote says of Sung:

> On the one hand, he represented the reactionary Kuomintang rule in northern China, collaborated with and nestled under the wings of the Japanese aggressors, and took advantage of the contradictions between Chiang Kai-shek and the Japanese invaders to expand his own forces. On the other hand, in face of the demand of the people and his own men for resistance against Japan, he dared not openly surrender to Japan and was even prepared to fight her under certain conditions.[75]

Communist propagandists correctly gauge their audience. They realise that their own people, emotionally anaesthetised by a constant stream of propaganda, will react only to a " hard sell." The foreigner, on the other hand, would likely be revolted by indoctrination of an intensity that seems only natural to the Chinese.

Secondly, though the foreign reader must be told in no uncertain words that the CCP *did* lead the Chinese revolution, he must not regard the process in conspiratorial terms. He must not be allowed to suspect that the Communists are untrustworthy. Thus, references to underground work, secret propaganda and recruitment for the Liberation Army have been minimised. In the English version the Chinese Communists appear more populist than Leninist.

The shrill, doctrinaire tone of *Reminiscences* bespeaks the post-Great Leap desperation just as the more objective *The December 9th Movement* seven years earlier reflected the self-confidence of the First Five-Year Plan. Of course, both operate within the same overall Marxist framework of historiography, share the view that history is a weapon in the class struggle, and insist that the CCP played the hero's role. But the didactic purpose in the earlier volume is served primarily by the choice of articles and a brief statement in the preface, while in the later one, every paragraph is heavily interlarded with propaganda.

The authors of *Reminiscences* have apparently failed to examine the principal documents in *The December 9th Movement*, not to mention unpublished primary sources. Blatant inaccuracies occur in Shih Li-teh's account of the December 16 demonstration,[76] in Li Che-jen's statement that the December 18 Tientsin demonstrators shouted " Investigate the Incident of the Floating Corpses in the Hai-ho " (the bodies were not discovered until April 1936), and in the slipshod use

---

[74] *Roar*, p. iv.   [75] *Ibid.* p. 11.
[76] See Shih Li-teh's account of action at the Hsuan-wu Men in " Chi liu " (" The Rapids "), IECHIL, p. 45; *Roar*, p. 14.

of figures when more nearly precise (though still exaggerated) ones are available in the earlier volume.[77]

One of the least ambiguous acts of historical revision has been to deprecate the role of Yenching University and to focus the spotlight on China College. Yenching and Tsinghua, hotbeds of student ferment, especially in the early days of the movement—Yenching often hosted meetings of the young Peiping Student Union [78]—had historic associations with the United States. Communist authors could scarcely admit that an American missionary college such as Yenching had ignited a patriotic conflagration. China College, on the other hand, with the largest number of Party members (including Ch'en Po-ta) of any Peiping school,[79] was an ideal candidate for the historian's laurels. Though Tsinghua, like Yenching, was tainted with American origins, it had been a Government school and a vortex of contention between radical and pro-KMT forces. Consequently, Tsinghua has been credited, at least, with furnishing dedicated cadres for the Party.[80] On the other hand, the numerous Yenching students who fled to Yenan, served the CCP during the war, and rose to respectable positions in the Peking régime, are generally ignored by Party scribes.

In 1954, editors of *The December 9th Movement* dared to reprint an admission that the movement began at Yenching and Tsinghua because " the political environment at [these] universities in Peiping's western suburbs was a bit better than in the city schools." [81] By 1961, such editorial candour was taboo; it was inadmissible, if not inconceivable, that any good could come from a missionary school. The solution was, at first, to treat the problem summarily, later, to ignore it completely.

An ambiguity in both publications concerns the rural masses' reception of the students. According to one article in *The December 9th Movement*, when students orated on the Japanese threat and the class struggle, " the masses rose up aroused, shouted, leapt, and waved their fists in the air." Anti-Japanese sentiment was at its zenith.[82]

[77] " I-erh chiu tsai T'ien-chin " (" December 9 in Tientsin "), IECHIL, p. 72.
[78] Wang Lin, " Hui-i Huang Ching t'ung-chih " (" In Memory of Comrade Huang Ching "), IECHIL, pp. 167–168; *Roar*, pp. 133–134, mentions the meeting at Yenching on the eve of December 9, but criticises its inadequacies, implying that even if this missionary school was playing an important role in the early stages she was doing it poorly. Wang claims that because of planning mistakes the procession was scattered and the ranks brought together only through the skill of CCP leader Huang Ching.   [79] Shih Li-teh, IECHIL, p. 55; *Roar*, p. 27.
[80] See Chiang Nan-hsiang, " Chi i-erh chiu yun-tung ti chan-shih—Yang Hsueh-ch'eng t'ung-chih " (" In Memory of Comrade Yang Hsueh-ch'eng "), IECHIL, pp. 176–186; *Roar*, pp. 146–159, and P'eng Yuan-li or Shih Li-teh, " Chi Huang Ch'eng " (" A Tribute to Huang Ch'eng "), IECHIL, pp. 187–196; *Roar*, pp. 160–172.
[81] Yang Chün-ch'en, " I-erh chiu yun-tung ti hui-i " (" Recollections of the December 9 Movement "), *Chieh-fang Jih-pao* (Yenan: December 9, 1944); reprinted in IECYT, p. 52.
[82] Chang I-ku, " P'ing-chin hsueh-sheng lien-ho hui k'uo-ta hsuan-ch'uan " (" The

Another account offers a contradictory picture:

> The rural people, at first, did not understand these "foreign students," thinking we had come to evangelise them, because they didn't speak the same language as the common folk. Therefore, those who could speak the local dialect and those with propagandic talents were discovered and everyone studied with them.[83]

Each of these versions is supported and expanded by a later writer in *Reminiscences*. Both, characteristically, use their cases to enunciate political morals. Wang Nien-chi, who agrees that there were problems of communication, finds that more than language was involved:

> The majority of the brigade members, with the exception of some underground Communist Party members *who had a proletarian political consciousness*, were simply acting from patriotic motives, wanted to contribute something useful at this critical period in the country's history, and to preserve individual freedom. These young people still lacked the political consciousness of the need to fight for the complete emancipation of the workers and peasants. As a result, in their contact with the people, they could not share the *class* feelings and talk the common language of the masses.[84]

Wang claims that corrective influence came from "the Party organisation in the brigade." [85] Once in the firm grasp of Party cadres, students visited oppressed families which:

> helped the members to realise that the mobilisation of the masses for resisting Japanese aggression must be integrated with opposition to bureaucratic oppression and ruthless feudal exploitation, and to see that Chiang Kai-shek was the chief representative of the ruling class in China.[86]

In contrast to this story of trial and error followed by redemption through the CCP, an account by Shih Li-teh admits of no difficulties in approaching the peasants. Furthermore, according to Shih:

> On many occasions the peasants became propaganda workers and the students their audience. . . The contacts with the working people broadened their vision and enabled them to realise that, in carrying out

Peiping-Tientsin Student Union Disseminates Propaganda "), *Ta-chung Sheng-huo*, Vol. 1, No. 11, January 25, 1936, p. 273; reprinted in IECYT, p. 63.

[83] Yang Chun-ch'en, IECYT, p. 58.

[84] " Tao nung-ts'un ch'ü " (" Off to the Countryside "), IECHIL, pp. 144–145; *Roar*, p. 115. We touch here upon the problem of wartime peasant motivation, recently the subject of controversy. See Chalmers Johnson, *Peasant Nationalism and Communist Power: The Emergence of Revolutionary China* (Stanford: Stanford University Press, 1962), and Donald G. Gillin, " Peasant Nationalism in the History of Chinese Communism," JAS, Vol. 23, No. 2, February 1964, pp. 269–281. Was there such a thing as " peasant nationalism " or did the rural populace support wartime guerrilla activities as an extension of the class struggle? Available evidence indicates that, *as of January 1936*, students were most successful in reaching the peasants with *economic* issues. Only rural schoolteachers and pupils responded enthusiastically to nationalistic appeals. See Freyn, *Prelude*, pp. 39, 48–49. Areas " softened " by students became important guerrilla areas during the war.

[85] IECHIL, p. 145; *Roar*, p. 115, reads " leaders of the brigade."

[86] IECHIL, p. 146; *Roar*, p. 117.

the revolution, intellectuals can only play the role of an intermediary and that strength is with the people.[87]

Thus, in 1961, confusion as to initial peasant reaction remains.

As of 1961, what impression has the young Chinese reader of his progenitors, the heroes of December 9? If he has read *Reminiscences* and the latest edition of Hsiao Wen-lan's articles, he will probably emerge with the following impression [88]:

In 1935, North China tottered on the brink of doom as the treacherous Kuomintang Government prepared to sell out to the Japanese. As stunned patriotic students waited for the axe to fall, the CCP arrived on the scene.

On August 1, 1935, the Party, which had set out on a correct course under the infallible leadership of Mao Tse-tung after the Tsunyi Conference, called for a united front against Japan. Directed by Liu Shao-ch'i and others in the CCP's North China Bureau, the students of Peiping organised a union and staged demonstrations on December 9 and 16. Following the Party's admonition that the movement could succeed only by going to the workers and peasants, in January 1936 the youngsters formed the Southern Propaganda Brigade and fanned out over the countryside. Initial difficulties arose from inadequate class consciousness as well as linguistic difficulties, but these were corrected by CCP leadership. Students who had undertaken to teach the masses were, instead, taught by the masses. The youngsters' success proved the truth of the axiom later proclaimed by Mao:

> The ultimate line of demarcation between the revolutionary intellectuals on the one hand and non-revolutionary and counter-revolutionary intellectuals on the other lies in whether they are willing to, and actually do, become one with the masses of workers and peasants.[89]

Returning to Peiping, under the leadership of the CCP, brigade members formed the Chinese National Liberation Vanguard, which spearheaded the movement on behalf of the Party. Soon major North China cities had Vanguard chapters and the student tide had flowed over the entire nation. Following the correct United Front line, China's youth steered a straight and narrow course between the Scylla of Right Opportunism and the less lethal but still dangerous Charybdis of Left Adventurism.

These patriotic youth flocked by the thousands to Yenan to submit joyously to severe discipline and thought reform. During the war, under the leadership of the CCP, they made a glorious contribution to the

---

[87] " Chi liu," IECHIL, p. 49; *Roar*, p. 20.

[88] The best-seller and popular movie by authoress Yang Mo, *Ch'ing-ch'un Chih Ko* (Peking: Jen-min Wen-hsueh Ch'u-pan She, 1960), *The Song of Youth* (Peking: Foreign Languages Press, 1964), tells the same story in the form of historical fiction.

[89] *Mao Tse-tung Hsuan-chi (Selected Works of Mao Tse-tung)* Vol. 2 (Peking: Jen-min Ch'u-pan She, 1953), p. 546; quoted in Li Lien-pi, IECHIL, p. 124; *Roar*, p. 108.

struggle against Japan. For their patriotic activities, many were martyred by the reactionary KMT clique; others fell in battle against the Japanese or collapsed on the job from exhaustion. Above all, they surrendered selfish bourgeois individualism and cleaved to the Party.

Go thou and do likewise.

The history of the December 9 Movement naturally enough is written differently on Formosa. The KMT's foremost specialist on the student movement, Pao Tsung-p'eng, argues that student demonstrators were pro-Kuomintang and were opposed to the North China autonomy scheme primarily because it threatened to alienate territory from the Central Government. He states that CCP support was limited to a small group in the Chinese National Liberation Vanguard and goes so far as to assert that the movement gave the younger generation a new realisation of the evils of Communism.[90] In 1962, the founding of a monthly, *Biographical Literature*, provided an outlet for the Kuomintang counterparts of *Reminiscences*. T'ao Hsi-sheng, chief KMT ideologist and former Peita professor, gives the CCP credit for the December 16 demonstration though not for December 9. He believes that Communists staged the parade of December 12, 1936, to coincide with the Sian kidnapping (of which, he assumes, they had foreknowledge) and argues that a lure of free ice skates, not political zeal, attracted mass participation. T'ao takes a cynical view of student motivation; he claims that the CCP could never have formed a popular front in Peiping without " using co-eds as a stimulus and impetus to male students." [91]

On the other hand, the late Ch'in Te-chun (Mayor of Peiping, 1935-37) wrote that " over 90 per cent. of the students were the very purest of patriotic youth." [92] The ex-mayor insisted that he ordered the police to treat demonstrators with utmost courtesy, resorting to fire hoses only to save them from marching into Japanese machine guns.

Such diversity of interpretation is typical. Chiang Kai-shek's opinion that December 9 " was started as a patriotic movement, but . . . came to be utilised by the Communists to advance their neutralist tactics " [93] is challenged by editors at the Ministry of Justice's Bureau of Investigation. These men accept " Red bandit " claims that the movement was a Communist creation. That a leading government research bureau can openly disagree with the President on a question of recent history

---

90 Pao Tsun-p'eng, *Chung-kuo Ch'ing-nien Yun-tung Shih* (*History of the Chinese Youth Movement*) (Taipei: Cheng-chung shu-chü, 1954), pp. 159–167.

91 T'ao Hsi-sheng, " Pei-p'ing erh-san shih " (" Events in Peiping "), part 3, *Chuan-chi Wen-hsueh* (CCWH), Vol. 2, No. 1 (January 1963), p. 8.

92 Ch'in Te-chun, " Chi ch'i-ch'a cheng-wei-hui shih-ch'i ti hui-i " (" Recollections from the Time of the Hopei-Chahar Political Council "), CCWH, Vol. 2, No. 1 (January 1963), p. 21.

93 *Soviet Russia in China* (New York: Farrar, Straus and Cudahy, 1957), p. 67.

indicates, in Formosa's intellectual life, a degree of pluralism inconceivable on the Mainland.

THE PROBLEM OF EVIDENCE

What version of the December 9 story is the most accurate? This question poses a problem of evidence that obfuscates many aspects of the Communist movement, particularly the United Front. During that era, the Party so successfully identified itself with a popular cause that it became difficult to differentiate the two. Now, years later, this same Party claims that it was not merely identified with, but actually led, the crusade.

Where does the evidence lead?

We have demonstrated that the CCP saga of contemporary Chinese history is politically inspired, doctrinaire and biased. This does not necessarily mean that it is incorrect. Indeed, there is much truth in the story. The Party did make an exceedingly good impression on the younger generation of North China. It is safe to conjecture that more students were attracted to Party ranks between December 9, 1935, and the Sian Incident of December 12, 1936, than during any previous year. Educated youngsters were overwhelmingly sympathetic to the Party's demands for national unity and resistance to the invader. To some extent, they shared the assumption that intellectuals, to be effective, must unite with workers and peasants. Communist techniques, including individual and group thought reform, were borrowed.

Communism, however, was not the least common denominator among youth of December 9. Student leaders won mass support by acting as standard-bearers in a nationwide anti-Japanese crusade. When Communist historians focus upon other aspects, they tend to lose sight of the principal component: nationalism.

The most valid criticism of Party history is not that it is false, but that it is oversimplified, teeming not with lies but with half-truths. Let us try to correct some of the more glaring distortions in the CCP version of the December 9 Movement:

1. There is no evidence that the movement was inspired by the August 1 Proclamation. Awareness that this document existed may have been limited to a small coterie of Party members and sympathisers. CCP writers describe its effect upon themselves as electric, as well it may have been. Though handicapped by censorship and police control, they must have made every effort to spread the gospel. But how successful were they? We are told that the proclamation was circulated abroad through the English edition of *IMPRECOR* and in the Paris-

published *National Salvation Times* (*Chiu-kuo Shih-pao*) [94] but we do not know how and to what extent it was circulated in China.

2. As Mao Tse-tung has admitted, the Party organisation in Peiping schools was hopelessly weak when the movement began. It could not and did not play a major role in the initial stage.

A key problem is this activity of the enigmatic Liu Shao-ch'i, allegedly director of the Party's North China Burea and backstage manager of student activities. A secretive man in action, Liu is best known through his writings. Yet his articles, which allegedly guided the student movement during the December 9 period, are difficult to unearth.

Had Liu been active in day-to-day operations, we should expect some reference to his doings, considering the detailed accounts in recent publications of the activities of lesser figures. In view of the wealth of testimony that Liu was in the Peiping-Tientsin area, and the absence of evidence that he was elsewhere, only a cynic would contend that he was not on the scene at all—yet there is no published evidence that he was. From available knowledge of the man, it seems likely that Liu was in Tientsin more often than in Peiping, more concerned with the proletariat of the treaty port than with the petty bourgeois students of the ancient capital.

As for Liu's alleged subordinates (men such as Ch'en Po-ta, Huang Ching, Li Ch'ang and Huang Ch'eng), we have only a few personal recollections and the even more dubious testimony of eulogies and commemorative essays to document their activities. Moreover, even if all the evidence in these sources was valid, it would remain insufficient to support grandiose generalisations about Party control.

3. Yenching and Tsinghua were undeniably foci of the movement in its initial stage. To prove that the CCP initiated the movement, one must demonstrate that student organisations at these universities were Party-controlled. Even Peking's most dedicated ideologists have made no such claims. Rather, they have attempted to prove that China College was the centre of activity. Yet the name of this institution appears neither among the signers of the November 1 Petition nor in the Circular Telegram of December 6,[95] though she was one of the nine founders of the Peiping Student Union.

4. References to "killed and wounded" student demonstrators are grossly misleading.[96] According to eye-witnesses and student union

[94] Wang Lin, IECHIL, p. 167; *Roar*, p. 132.   [95] IECYT, pp. 144, 149.
[96] IECYT, p. 82; WKHSYTSH, p. 41; CKHSYTTKS, p. 19: also see Shih Li-teh. "Chi liu," IECHIL, p. 51; *Roar*, p. 22; "Chiang Kai-shek . . . ordered [his troops] to massacre the patriotic students."
   Reports of fatalities may have originated in leaflets distributed shortly after the December 9 demonstration, quite possibly on December 16. According to one,

reports, there were no fatalities in any demonstration in spite of police brutality. The sole acknowledged martyr, Kuo Ch'ing, died in prison, presumably from mistreatment.

5. The Party boasts that under its direction the December 9 Movement followed the road to consolidation with the rural masses during the January propaganda pilgrimage. Yet the four or five hundred participants in this crusade constituted only slightly more than 5 per cent. of the multitude who had marched two weeks earlier in the December 16 demonstration (for which the CCP also claims credit). Perhaps a like number remained in Peiping to carry out support activities for those in the field. If the Party insists on claiming credit for both the demonstration and the march to the countryside, it must account for the 90 per cent. who abandoned its leadership in the interim.

6. Allegations that "right deviationism" was the principal threat to the Peiping CCP after the Sian Incident are contradicted by contemporary Party and Vanguard documents which indicate that the leadership was much less concerned with "right capitulationists" than with radical elements who endangered the United Front.

7. Communist accounts, in giving the impression that patriotic youth supported the CCP, while only a handful of renegades and reactionaries capitulated to the KMT, fail to explain Chiang Kai-shek's enormous popularity after the Sian Incident. To admit this fact would violate the assumption that the December 9 Movement was "revolutionary," directed against "Japanese imperialism *and the Kuomintang reactionary clique.*" [97] This was not the case (though Ch'en Po-ta exaggerated when he wrote in 1938 that the students' attitude towards the Nanking Government had been one of "cringing supplication").[98] The movement was nationalistic. After shifting to the left it became a minority operation, lacking support of the bulk of Peiping's students. Once Chiang emerged as a leader prepared to resist Japan, the majority eagerly supported him.

Without reducing problems of historical fact to questions of definition, we may clarify matters by asking what is meant by "December 9 Movement." If it is defined in terms of student *political activities* between the November 1 Petition and the Marco Polo Bridge Incident, it was strongly tinged with Communism. However, one must not forget

---

"a hundred or more of us students were killed, wounded and arrested by [police]": "Kao nung-min t'ung-pao" ("To Our Peasant Countrymen"). Another stated: "A co-ed, stabbed in the chest by a policeman's bayonet, later died": "Kao Kung-jen" ("To the Workers"). However, these accounts must be adjudged sceptically since they were neither reaffirmed in subsequent student propaganda nor reported by the sympathetic Press. In contrast, the martyrdom in March 1936 of one youth, Kuo Ch'ing, incited a mock funeral demonstration.

[97] CIEC, 1961, p. 48. Italics added.
[98] WTTIECYT, p. 14.

that within two months after its inception the political activists had dwindled to a minority. Popular participation reached a high-water mark on December 16. Thereafter the numbers diminished. In the nineteen months before the outbreak of war only on two occasions (June 13 and December 12, 1936) did students by the thousands demonstrate on the streets of the old capital.

If " December 9 Movement " refers to the composite of *political and intellectual currents* in the student world during this period, the Communist element shrinks to a fraction, though still a significant one, and nationalism can be seen even more clearly as the unifying factor. In this respect, youth who cheered Chiang's release from Sian and followed the Government to the south-west were as much sons of December 9 as were the dedicated pilgrims who made their way to Yenan.

CONCLUSION: THE DILEMMA FACING MAINLAND HISTORIANS

In 1958, Party spokesman Liu Ta-nien, exhorting mainland historians to " emphasise the study of post-May 4 history," expressed strong dissatisfaction with current Chinese historiography. His words revealed that the bulk of Communist writings on the December 9 Movement did not rank very high in the estimation of Party academicians. Noting the paucity of articles on contemporary history in leading mainland journals, he remarked:

> the majority of those articles are either source materials or commemorative in nature. You could count on the fingers of one hand those men who have really done serious research and reached a definite scientific level.[99]

The output of the seven years since this was written offers little cause for hope. Confronted with innumerable ideological pitfalls, the mainland historian can scarcely be blamed for avoiding attempts at " scientific " history on this subject.

Party scribes will doubtless continue to wield history as a weapon in the political arena by reading into the past an idealised version of the present. Thus, their assumption will remain that students of December 9 must have overcome ideological heresy and political error, united with the workers and peasants, and achieved victory under the Party of the proletariat, for these are the doctrines prescribed for contemporary youth.

Whatever Chinese Communists may write about the student movement, they still have to deal with a gnawing dilemma: how to incorporate a petty bourgeois act into a revolutionary pageant.

[99] Liu Ta-nien, " Hsü-yao cho-chung yen-chiu wu-ssu yun-tung i-hou ti li-shih " (" The Study of Post-May 4 History Must be Emphasised "), *Li-shih Yen-chiu* (*Historical Research*), 1958, No. 5, p. 10.

14

Li Ta-Chao and the Chinese Communist Treatment of the Materialist Conception of History

By MAURICE MEISNER

THE traditional alliance between politics and scholarship that Professor Fitzgerald has referred to as " characteristically Chinese " [1] has become a most explicit alliance in contemporary China. Not only is scholarship to serve immediate political interests, but it must do so within the framework of an all-pervasive ideology. In no field of scholarship is this union more explicit than in the study of history. The application of Marxist-Leninist theory and the " thought of Mao Tse-tung " to the study and understanding of the Chinese past is the appointed task of Chinese Communist historians, and they would no doubt be the first to acknowledge that historiography cannot, and indeed should not, be separated from ideology. The most relevant portion of this body of ideology for historians is, of course, the materialist conception of history. It is from the assumptions of this theory that the Chinese Communist interpretation of history ostensibly begins.

If the Marxist view of history is in fact the prism through which mainland historians look at the Chinese past, then it is quite obvious that, from the outset, they face a most peculiarly difficult problem— quite apart from all the other problems that the application of the materialist conception of history to the study of Chinese historical development may involve. For the major premise of the materialist conception of history—the proposition that " being determines consciousness " [2]—is profoundly inconsistent with the main tendencies of Chinese Communist ideology. In the Maoist world view, the emphasis falls not on the role of objective social forces, but rather on subjective human factors. The ideas and the will of men are more important than the

---

[1] C. P. Fitzgerald, *China: A Short Cultural History* (London: Crescent Press, 1950), p. 389.

[2] " Being " for Marx, of course, is essentially economic being; that is, the stage of the development of the productive forces of society and the manner in which these forces are organised. These productive forces constitute the economic " base " upon which is erected the legal, political and ideological " superstructure." Marx's description of the process of historical change in his " Preface " to *The Critique of Political Economy* is generally regarded as the classic statement of the materialist conception of history.

development of the material forces of production. For Mao Tse-tung and his disciples, "consciousness" determines "being" more than "being determines consciousness."

Yet we are, of course, well aware that the deterministic formulations of the materialist conception are invariably invoked in Chinese Communist historical and ideological writings. Most Chinese Marxist historians have devoted the greater part of their energies in attempting to explain Chinese historical development by reference to the forces of production, and on the basis of objectively-determined social relationships. No less prodigious energies have been devoted to the closely related problem of fitting Chinese history into the Marxist scheme of periodisation. These efforts are perhaps not to be taken lightly, for in the eyes of Maoist ideologists they serve important political and ideological needs. Yet there remains a strikingly ritualistic quality about the way in which the historically deterministic formulas of Marx are employed in Chinese Communist historical writings. Neither the superimposition of a scheme of periodisation derived from Western historical development nor the appeal to the determining, objective forces of history is consistent with, or essential to, the basically nationalistic and voluntaristic content of Maoist ideology. Nor has either of these aspects of Marxian determinism provided answers to what Professor Feuerwerker has called "the problem of meaninglessness" that confronts Chinese Communist historians.[3]

In the pages that follow, I shall be concerned with certain facets of the problem of how Chinese Marxists have attempted to reconcile the historical determinism of Marx with the tenets of their own non-deterministic world view, particularly as this problem is treated in the historical writings of Li Ta-chao in the early years of the reception of Marxist doctrine in China.

Li Ta-chao, it might be noted, was not only China's first Marxist, he was also China's first Marxist historian. In so far as he was not a professional revolutionary, he was a professional historian who taught history at Peking University during most of his Communist career. In so far as his writings were not devoted to immediate political and ideological problems, they were largely devoted to the study of history and historical theory. Chinese nationalism and revolutionary voluntarism were the deepest impulses that governed his interpretation of Marxism (like his disciple Mao Tse-tung), and yet he coupled his nationalistic and voluntaristic predispositions with the determinism and universalism of the materialist conception of history. The manner in which Li Ta-chao treated this theory of history, and the things that he derived from it,

[3] Albert Feuerwerker, "China's History in Marxian Dress," *American Historical Review*, Vol. LXVI, No. 2, January 1961.

clearly foreshadow certain prominent themes and problems in the contemporary Chinese Communist historical world view.

LI TA-CHAO AND THE MATERIALIST CONCEPTION OF HISTORY

" If one wishes to obtain a true view of human life," Li Ta-chao wrote in 1920, " it is first necessary to obtain a true interpretation of history." [4] It is not surprising that Li attached importance to the study of history, for the will to shape history inevitably gives rise to the desire to understand it. Indeed, in the very article in which he first announced his support for the principles of the Bolshevik Revolution in July 1918, Li remarked that " if one can write the history of billions of people, then one can have the authority to move the minds of billions of people." [5] That the study of history was to serve political ends was a conviction that the first Marxist historian of modern China shared with his Confucian predecessors.

Even before his conversion to Marxism, Li's desire to promote action in the present had been accompanied by a need to understand the forces which had moulded the past. In 1915 he had argued against his future Communist colleague, Ch'en Tu-hsiu, that it was necessary for " self-conscious " Chinese intellectuals to participate in politics to achieve their ends. [6] He then turned to the development of a transcendental philosophy which purported to identify the motivating forces of history. The historical world view that emerged from these philosophic speculations was used by Li to support his demand for political participation.

As a Marxist, Li was more committed to an understanding of history than before. Marxism rests on the proposition that an understanding of the general laws of historical development provides the insights into contemporary historical reality which are necessary to guide the activities of men in the present, so to enable them to create the socialist utopia of the future.

Li accepted this commitment with enthusiasm. From 1920 until his death seven years later, his main intellectual interests revolved about the study of historical theory in general and the materialist conception of history in particular. A major portion of his writings during these years were devoted to these subjects, including his only book-length manuscript, *Shih-hsueh Yao-lun* (*The Essentials of Historical Study*),

---

[4] Li Ta-chao, " Shih-kuan " (" Historical Interpretation "), *Li Ta-chao Hsuan-chi* (Peking: Jen-min Ch'u-pan She, 1959), p. 297. (Hereafter cited as *Hsuan-chi*.)

[5] Li Ta-chao, " Fa-O ko-ming chih pi-chiao kuan " (" A Comparison of the French and Russian Revolutions "), *Chung-kuo Chin-tai Ssu-hsiang-shih Tsan-k'ao Tzu-liao Chien-pien* (*Source Materials for the Study of the History of Modern Chinese Thought*) (Peking: San-lien, 1957), p. 1204.

[6] Li Ta-chao, " Yen-shih-hsin yü tzu-chueh-hsin " (" Pessimism and Self-Consciousness "), *Hsuan-chi*, pp. 28–35.

published in 1924.[7] At Peking University he lectured and offered courses on the Marxist interpretation of history and its application to the Chinese past.

Li's special efforts to promote and popularise the materialist conception of history are perhaps surprising in view of his basically voluntaristic and politically activistic predispositions that characterised his pre-Marxian world view. Indeed, it was precisely the determinism of this view of history that Li had quite bluntly criticised in the spring of 1919, in the early stages of his assimilation of Marxist theory.[8] And although his objections to the materialist conception were no longer so explicit in the period after the "May Fourth" incident, when he became more firmly committed to the Communist programme, the fact that he placed an extraordinary emphasis on the factors of consciousness and human activity in his treatment of Marxist theory suggests that his earlier reservations about Marxist determinism were not fully overcome, and that the activist impulses of his pre-Marxian world view remained very much a part of his Marxist mentality.

Yet in his writings on history Li upheld all the deterministic formulas he had implicitly rejected in his reinterpretation of Marxist theory. Time and again, and in a variety of ways, he repeated the view that "changes in the social superstructure completely follow the changes in the economic base, and therefore it is impossible to explain history except from economic relations."[9] Li's purpose in promoting the materialist conception, however, was not to recite these well-known formulas. His aim, rather, was to find support for his own politically activist needs and his voluntaristic interpretation of Marxist theory.

The historical theory of Marx was able, in part, to serve these purposes because it is not only a scheme of periodisation and a collection of "laws" purporting to prove that all of history is determined by the inexorable movement of the forces of production. The materialist conception of history is also a philosophy of history that begins with the assumption that "man makes history" and ends with the vision of a future socialist utopia in which man for the first time fully realises his truly human potentialities. It is a philosophy which views history as the process of man's self-creation in his struggle to master nature, his self-alienation that grew out of this struggle, and finally his attainment of the true self-consciousness that is to make possible the passage of mankind from the "realm of necessity" to the "realm of freedom."

Like Hegel, Marx found an inner logic and an objective meaning in

---

[7] Li Ta-chao, *Shih-hsueh Yao-lun* (*The Essentials of Historical Study*) (Shanghai: Shang-wu Yin-shu-kuan, 1924).
[8] Li Ta-chao, "Wo-ti Mak-k'o-ssu-chu-i kuan" ("My Marxist Views"), *Hsin Ch'ing-nien* (*New Youth*), Vol. 6, No. 5 (May 1919).
[9] *Shih-hsueh Yao-lun op. cit.*, p. 5.

history. History was seen as progress through necessary and ever higher stages of development leading to the inevitable triumph of reason. The content of Marxist historical philosophy is, of course, profoundly different from the Hegelian philosophy of history. While for Hegel the subject of history was the *Weltgeist*, an objective power which moved through the actions of men, for Marx it was men themselves, and the productive forces they had created, which was the true subject of history. But for both Marx and Hegel, history was seen as logically moving toward a final utopian goal, however much they differed on the definition of this goal.

It would be impossible to explain the appeals of the materialist conception of history, or the role that it has played in Chinese Communist ideology, if it is seen as no more than a method to analyse historical reality upon the basis of objective economic criteria and without reference to its utopian goals. For as Croce has pointed out, if historical materialism is deprived of the elements of finality and an inevitable utopia, then it cannot provide support for socialism or any other form of society. It would remain silent, as Robert Michel has written, on " the outcome of the struggle it has traced through history." [10] It is precisely the utopian vision of the future, sanctioned by an analysis of history, that gives the materialist conception its dynamic appeal. It is by this means that the Marxist view of history has served to inspire men to transform the existing historical situation.

The terms " materialism " and " determinism " as applied to the Marxist conception of history are often quite misleading. Marx's " historical materialism " is a unique variety of materialism, for it is based on the premise that all material forces and objects are but the expressions, or materialisations, of human activity. And while Marxism is deterministic in the sense that socialism is seen as historically inevitable, it is a doctrine that demands the participation and activity of men to realise the " inevitable." Marx declared:

> History does nothing, . . . it is not history which uses men as a means of achieving . . . *its* own ends. History is nothing but the activity of men in pursuit of their ends.[11]

The notion that " man makes history " lies at the very core of the Marxist world view.

It should also be pointed out that the Marxist emphasis on change in history (that which is historical in the Marxist sense is defined as that which is constantly changing and in the process of becoming) does not

10 Robert Michel, *First Lectures in Political Sociology* (Minneapolis: University of Minnesota 1949), p. 21.
11 Karl Marx. *Selected Writings in Sociology and Social Philosophy*, edited by T. B. Bottomore and Maximillian Rubel (London: Watts, 1956), p. 63.

refer simply to a variety of evolutionary change. The notion of quantitative to qualitative change, which Marx derived from Hegel, manifested itself in the belief that at certain stages in its development human society undergoes quick and sudden transformations. The Marxist concept of revolution is not simply a matter of the slow maturation of economic and social forces, but it is conceived as a radical break with the past. The socialist revolution is to be a " leap " from man's " pre-history " to his " truly human history."

These were the strains in the materialist conception of history—the belief that man is the producer as much as he is the product of history, the utopian goals towards which the historic process is seen as inevitably moving, and the promise of radical, revolutionary breaks with the past— that Li Ta-chao and his successors could and did draw upon to support their voluntaristic predispositions. In his writings on the Marxist view of history, Li was not concerned—in contrast to later Chinese Communist historians—with the question of historical periodisation, and he was content only to repeat formally the " objective laws " of historical development set down by Marx. But in one essential matter Li clearly foreshadowed the later Chinese Communist treatment of the materialist conception of history; for Li the Marxist view of history was above all a conception which would encourage the activities of men and inspire them to create the future.

This approach to historical theory was already present in Li's first writings on Marxism in early 1919. In the essay " My Marxist Views," Li, while sharply critical of many of the deterministic formulations of the materialist conception of history, nevertheless found that the great contribution of the Marxist view of history was that it recognised that " the realisation of socialism is completely impossible if it is separated from the people themselves." [12] The notion that men make their own history was of the greatest appeal to Li from the very beginning of his Marxist intellectual life.

One of the striking features of Li's historical writings is that he is less concerned with what happened in the past than with the views men hold of the past, and how these views might influence their activities in the present. Thus, in an essay entitled " The Value of the Materialist Conception of History in Modern Historical Study," published in the *Hsin Ch'ing-nien* in December 1920, Li undertook to reconcile Marxian determinism with his faith in the activist role of man in history by emphasising the role of the Marxist view of history as a spur to revolutionary action rather than as a pre-ordained scheme of historical development. He contended that all idealist, pre-Marxist interpretations of

---

[12] " Wo-ti Ma-k'o-ssu-chu-i kuan," *op. cit.*, p. 534.

history are either superficial narrations of historical facts or theological interpretations which paralyse " the moral powers of the individual " by attributing historical events to forces beyond the sphere of human control. All such interpretations of history serve the interests of the ruling classes by teaching the common people that their plight has been predetermined, and by counselling them to bow to established authority.[13]

The materialist conception of history, on the other hand, has a " completely different effect on the human spirit," Li argued, because it searches for the motive forces of history in the actual material life of society; thus it looks to " the nature of the people themselves and certainly not to any outside force." Since the Marxist view of history interprets social change as the result of man's own efforts, it is a conception that gives man " great hope and courage." Man is able to see that

> all progress is able to come only from the unity of progressive people . . . from the self-consciousness of his own power, his own position in society, and from his acquisition of new attitudes.

In all other theories of history man is " only a passive and negative animal," but according to the materialist view of history he becomes " an active and positive element " who recognised his own potentialities and is thus ready to

> put his shoulder to the wheel of life and push directly forward. . . . This concept can make man a person who belongs to himself and a person who can rise up to obtain satisfaction in life and be useful in society.[14]

The appeal of the Marxist notion of man overcoming self-alienation through the achievement of " self-consciousness " is quite evident in this discussion of the influence of Marxist historical theory.

Having interpreted the materialist conception of history to the satisfaction of his own activist needs, Li was not disposed to bother with the troublesome question of the economic preconditions for the exercise of man's self-consciousness. He dismissed in advance any possible criticism of the contradiction between the Marxist axiom that motivating forces in social and intellectual development are basically economic and the emphasis he placed on the independent role of conscious human activity by implying that such objections merely reflect a misunderstanding of Marxism:

> There are some people who misinterpret the materialist view of history by saying that social progress depends only on natural material changes. [They therefore] disregard human activity and sit around to wait for the arrival of the new situation. Moreover, there are other people who are

[13] Li Ta-chao, " Wei-wu shih-kuan tsai hsien-tai shih-hseuh-shang ti chia-chih " (" The Value of the Materialist Conception of History in Contemporary Historical Study "). *Chung-kuo Chin-tai Ssu-hsiang-shih*, pp. 1245–1248.
[14] *Ibid.* pp. 1248–1249.

generally critical of the materialist conception of history who also use this as an excuse to talk [and take no action], and then they say that fatalistic views of human life result from evil influences of the materialist conception of history. This is an especially great error because the influence of the materialist conception of history on human life is precisely the opposite.[15]

In the essay "Shih-kuan" ("The Interpretation of History"), Li develops this theme by emphasising the importance of a "true view" of the past for the life orientation of the individual in the present.

It is not known how the history of humanity began and it is not known when it will end. In this long tide of history [which is] without beginning and without end, there is still myself and my own life. The future and the past are limitless, and thus if I do not clearly examine the nature of history in order to understand its tendencies, then my life would be without a shred of significance. . . . I would be like a solitary boat, being thrown about in a wild and limitless ocean, having lost its way. An interpretation of history, therefore, is really the standard to measure human life.[16]

Li traced the beginnings of "the true interpretation of history" to the European scientific revolution. The ideas of Kepler and Newton, he wrote, gave birth to a new historiography which was developed by Condorcet, Saint Simon and Comte, and which culminated in the materialist conception of Marx.[17] The purpose of the new historiography is "to pluck out from men's minds" the traditional theological interpretations which attribute historical events to forces beyond the sphere of human activity and human control. This is a particularly important task in China, Li argues, because Confucian historiography has instilled in the minds of Chinese a "retrogressive view of history" which looks back to a golden age in antiquity and which emphasises the powers of the gods and the role of great men.[18] These baneful Confucian influences still live in the Chinese present, for Li finds evidence of this traditional "retrogressive view of history" in the thought of such eminent contemporary intellectuals as Liang Ch'i-ch'ao and Chang Shih-chao.[19]

The activist role that Li assigned to historical theory was reflected in the definition of the nature of history that appears at the beginning of Shih-hsueh Yao-lun. History, Li declared,

is the process of human life, the succession of human life, the changes in human life and the evolution of human life. It is a thing of life, activity, progress and development . . . it is not old volumes of books,

15 Ibid. p. 1249.
16 "Shih-kuan," op. cit., p. 287.
17 Ibid. p. 288.
18 Ibid. pp. 290–291.
19 Li Ta-chao, "Shih" ("Time"), Hsuan-chi, pp. 488–489.

old pieces of paper, dead rocks and dried bones. . . . What we study should be living history, not dead history. Living history can only be obtained from human life and cannot be sought in old pieces of paper.[20]

Partly because of this preoccupation with the psychological implications of historical world-views, Li sometimes adopted a highly relativistic position in dealing with the question of what constitutes historical truth. In the same essay in which he claimed that " Marx discovered the true meaning of history," [21] he also wrote:

> In rewriting and revising history do we dare determine what is unchanging truth? History has a life which dead and old records are unable to express . . . [the expression] of this life is completely dependent on the new historical conceptions of later men . . . But although later men arrive at new understandings and make new discoveries, we still cannot know whether that which we now recognise as true will not later be regarded as mistaken. The facts which we recognise as true and our view of truth are certainly not fixed but rather are relative.[22]

Li did not deny that there was an objective historical process beyond man's perception of it, although certain of his statements would seem to almost lend themselves to such an interpretation. In *Shih-hsueh Yao-lun*, for example, he wrote that a historical fact is

> past and cannot be revived. But our understanding of that fact is always in the process of movement and can change at any time. The so-called historical fact is thus the fact that is perceived. Perception is active and has a progressive nature. Even if one had a complete record of the past, it could not be considered historical truth. In order to have historical truth, it is necessary to have complete perception.[23]

Moreover, Li added, " historical truth is only temporary." [24] Further in the same passage Li acknowledged that there is indeed a " real past," but then he went on to argue:

> the real past is dead and gone, the affairs of the past have been made and completed, and the men of the past are dead and can never be revived; a change in these is forever impossible. What can be expanded and broadened is not the past itself but our knowledge of the past.[25]

In an earlier essay Li had put the matter more succinctly: " Facts are dead and unchanging, but explanations are alive and always changing." [26] However, Li was not seriously concerned with the metaphysical problem of whether historical reality exists independently of man's cognition of it. He did, in fact, believe that there was an objective

20 *Shih-hsueh Yao-lun, op. cit.,* pp. 1–2.
21 Li Ta-chao, " Yen-chui li-shih ti jen-wu " (" The Responsibilities of Studying History "), *Hsuan-chi,* p. 480.
22 *Ibid.* p. 483.
23 *Shih-hsueh Yao-lun, op. cit.,* p. 8.
24 *Ibid.*
25 *Ibid.* pp. 8–9.
26 " Shih-kuan," *op. cit.,* p. 287.

historical reality and he also believed, or, as we shall see, at least tried to believe, that there were scientifically discoverable laws according to which the historic process proceeded. But the actual history of the past always remained a matter of far less concern to him than the inter-pretation of the past. In discussing the problems involved in the study of Confucius, for example, his attention was focused not on the life and thought of Confucius but rather on the image of Confucius as this image changed through the centuries.[27] This manner of approach to history reflected Li's preoccupation with the need to create an intellectual and psychological atmosphere that would encourage political activism, a need that his historical writings were intended to serve. It was this preoccupation that lay behind the great appeal of Marx's notion that history is made by men and not determined by " outside forces."

THE PROBLEM OF INEVITABILITY

Both before and after his conversion to Marxism, Li Ta-chao had an unshakable faith in the ability of men to shape historical reality. Yet coupled with this faith (as in contemporary Chinese ideology) was a seemingly contradictory belief in the existence of impersonal and immut-able forces which determine the course of historical development. In his pre-Marxian phase, Li saw the determining principles of history as essentially spiritual forces which moved on cosmic levels and which manifested themselves both in the " egos " of individuals and in a cyclic process of the inevitable rise and decline of nations. Li's belief in a cyclic theory of history had supported his pre-Marxian faith in the inevitability of the rebirth of China and the equally inevitable decline of the materially powerful nations of the West.

With his conversion to Marxism, his idealist assumptions as to the causal factors in history were replaced by materialist assumptions. His earlier view of history as a cyclic process gave way to the view that history moved in a progressive fashion. Correspondingly, his faith in the inevitability of the rebirth of China was replaced by a newly-found faith in the inevitability of world socialism, a process with which Li now identified the rebirth of China.

The influence of Marxism also led Li to proclaim that there were laws of history which could be scientifically determined. He wrote in 1920:

> There is no difference between the study of history and the natural sciences . . . With Marx's materialist conception of history, the study of history has been raised to the same position as that of the natural

---

[27] *Shih-hsueh Yao-lun, op. cit.,* p. 9.

sciences. This accomplishment really opens a new era on the world of historical studies.[28]

In arriving at the conviction that there are scientifically verifiable laws governing objective reality, Li drew not only upon Marx but also upon the whole line of universalistic and optimistic historical thought that began with Turgot and Condorcet and continued with Saint-Simon and Comte. Although Li had read Saint-Simon during the years between 1913 and 1916, when he had studied in Japan, and possibly Condorcet and Comte as well, his interest in Marxist historical theory encouraged him to return to the works of these and other European historical theorists. In 1923 Li published two essays on Condorcet and Saint-Simon, both of whom he regarded as important precursors of the Marxist conception of history. These essays are of interest not only because they set forth Li's views on Condorcet and Saint-Simon, but because they suggest some of the reasons why those of voluntaristic predispositions can also be drawn to the more deterministic elements of Marxist historical theory.

Among the virtues of Condorcet enumerated by Li is " his natural optimism " and his belief that the process of " enlightenment and social progress is unlimited " and that its direction can be predicted.[29] Li observes:

> In Cordorcet's eyes, the study of the history of civilisation has two uses. One is to enable us to construct the factual record of progress, and the other is to enable us to determine its future direction and from this to increase the velocity of progress . . . if the universal laws of social phenomena were known to men, then it would be possible to predict changes. These laws can be sought in the history of the past.[30]

However, Condorcet's search for universal laws of historic development was unsuccessful, not because such laws do not exist, but because his methodology and assumptions were unscientific. He saw social progress as the result of intellectual progress, and thus his efforts to predict the future remained in the realm of philosophic speculations.[31] Instead, Li suggests, it is necessary to look to " the masses of humanity " for the sources of historical progress.

> The human race is wholly dependent upon the result of its own work, which is the accomplishment of the masses of the people. The true subjects of history are these masses.[32]

[28] Li Ta-chao, " Ma-k'o-ssu ti li-shih che-hsueh " (" The Historical Philosophy of Marx "), Hsuan-chi, p. 294.
[29] Li Ta-chao, " K'ung-tao-hsi ti li-shih kuan " (" The Historical View of Condorcet "), She-hui k'o-hsueh chi-k'an (Social Science Quarterly), Vol. II, No. 1 (November 1923), p. 60.
[30] Ibid. p. 62.
[31] Ibid. pp. 61–62.
[32] Li Ta-chao, " Sang-hsi-men ti li-shih kuan " (" The Historical View of Saint-Simon "), Hol, pp. 466–467.

Li finds this Marxist notion in embryo in the writings of Saint-Simon, particularly in Saint-Simon's later historical writings which emphasise economic factors. Saint-Simon, Li declares, "recognised that the productive classes were the basic classes of society and the motivating force of history."[33] Furthermore, Saint-Simon elevated Condorcet's belief in the existence of universal laws of historical development and the inevitability of social progress onto a more scientific basis as he became convinced that,

> the laws of history and the historical process could only be explained by the changes in the organisation of property, and that the society of the future could be foreseen only by (studying) the tendencies in the development of property. . . . Later Marx inherited these clues and built the theory of the materialist conception of history.[34]

Li did not write a separate essay on Comte but he frequently referred to Comte as the successor of Saint-Simon and one of the direct predecessors of Marx. While Li praised Comte's search for "definite laws of history,"[35] he was by no means drawn to the mechanistic materialism of the Positivist outlook, nor does he say anything to suggest that he was aware of the elitist role of the "enlightened educator" that is implicit in the writings of both Saint-Simon and Comte. Like Marx, Li saw history as the product of human activity; unlike Saint-Simon and Comte, he found "the masses" to be "the true subject of history."[36] Taken as a whole, Li's historical writings affirm the view that history is a process of the interaction of man and his material environment, the view that Marx expressed so well in his critique of mechanistic materialism in the "Theses on Feuerbach"[37]:

> The materialist doctrine concerning the change of circumstances and education forgets that circumstances are changed by men and that the educator himself must be educated.

What Li drew from the writings of Condorcet, Saint-Simon and Comte were the beliefs that Marx shared with these historical theorists— the optimistic faith in the intrinsic rationality of man and history, the conviction that historical development is essentially progressive in nature, and the assurance that the triumph of reason, equality and freedom was inevitable.

Above all, Li drew from Condorcet, Saint-Simon and Comte the confidence that the future could be foretold, and this confidence served to reinforce his belief in the inevitability of socialism:

33 *Ibid.* p. 471.
34 *Ibid.* pp. 469–471.
35 See the discussion of Condorcet, Saint-Simon, Comte, and Vico in *Shih-hsueh Yao-lun, op. cit.,* pp. 54–58.
36 "K'ung-tao-hsi ti li-shih kuan," *op. cit.,* p. 63.
37 Karl Marx, "Theses on Feuerbach," in Marx and Engels, *The German Ideology* (New York: International Publishers, 1947,) pp. 197–198.

> Scientific socialism has taken as its basis the materialist conception of history, and by investigating the process of human historical development, it has discovered the necessary laws of history. On the basis of these laws it has advocated the social necessity of socialism. From this it can be said that a socialist society, no matter whether men want it or not . . . is a command of history.[38]

Li's assertion that there are " necessary laws of history " inevitably moving toward the realisation of socialism is not necessarily incompatible with his faith that conscious human action can shape historical reality. The combination of a doctrine of inevitability with an emphasis upon human activity is hardly a unique phenomenon in the history of human thought. The Calvinist doctrine of predestination, for example, taught that salvation was predetermined, that even before the creation of the world God had chosen the elect and condemned the damned. But in Calvinism, as Max Weber has written,

> it is held to be an absolute duty to consider oneself chosen . . . since lack of self-confidence is the result of insufficient faith. . . . The exhortation of the apostle to make fast one's own call is here interpreted as a duty to attain certainty of one's own election and justification in the daily struggle of life. . . . In order to attain that self-confidence, intense worldly activity is recommended as the most suitable means.[39]

Thus while salvation is predetermined, the evidence for salvation is to be sought in activities of men on earth.

This same combination of a doctrine of inevitability with exhortations to activity has also appeared in different forms in many secular philosophies. The Russian " Realists " of the 1860s, for example, men such as Chernyshevskii, Dobrolyubov and Pisarev, firmly believed that society proceeded towards a rational end in accordance with the logical laws and scientific principles of objective reality. Yet this " realistic " faith in objectivity was combined with the demand that a few men of will and perception must transform the world in the image of their consciousness.[40] Marxism itself, as we have noted, is a doctrine that combines a faith in the inevitability of the socialist goal as a result of processes immanent in history with a call to revolutionary action. In Lenin these two elements coexist in exaggerated form. For Lenin's emphasis upon subjective factors—the consciousness and will of the revolutionary intellectual in particular—is coupled not only with the generally deterministic formulations of the materialist conception of history, but also with his own particularly strong need to appeal to a

---

38 " Sang-hsi-men ti li-shih kuan," *op. cit.,* p. 465.
39 Max Weber, *The Protestant Ethic and the Spirit of Capitalism* (New York: Charles Scribner's Sons, 1958), pp. 111–112.
40 For a discussion of the influence of the " Realists " on Lenin, see Leopold Haimson, *The Russian Marxists and the Origins of Bolshevism* (Harvard, 1955), pp. 9–11, 98–100.

" concrete " and " objective " reality and to the ability of men (and particularly himself) to apprehend " absolute truth."

Li was not unaware of the problems posed by the doctrine of the inevitability of socialism. He was even fearful that other men might draw from the materialist conception of history the fatalistic conclusion that the future was assured regardless of their own activities. Thus he was continually preoccupied with the question of the psychological impact of the Marxist view of history. Time and again he felt compelled to repeat that this was a view of history that would encourage " self-consciousness " and human activity and not lead to quietism. As for himself, Li never acknowledged that there existed any contradiction between his belief in the historic inevitability of socialism and his demand for political action. Just as in his pre-Marxian world view, in which his faith in the rebirth of China as the inevitable result of processes immanent in the cosmic forces of the universe was combined with a demand for individual political participation, he now saw no conflict between his belief in the historical necessity of socialism and the necessity of human activity to achieve it. In 1919 he had drawn a parallel between the efforts necessary to achieve socialism and the spread of Christianity. Since the Christian's faith in the coming of the millennium did not hinder his efforts to propagate the gospel, there was no reason why the socialist's belief in the inevitability of socialism should impede his efforts to achieve socialism.[41] Later, in January 1923, Li declared that " the Marxist economic interpretation of history is especially valuable in that it is able to provide people with a belief in the necessity of the realisation of socialism." [42] For Li, as for Marx, Lenin and Mao, the recognition of " necessity " was but the first step in a programme for action.

That a Marxist believes there are determining forces in history that must inevitably produce socialism is of less importance in describing the specific nature of his thought than the manner in which he perceives his determinism. Although Marx no doubt arrived at the desirability of socialism before he proclaimed its inevitability, his economic and historical studies gave him the fullest confidence that socialism would be the necessary result of the contradictions of capitalist society in general, and the arrival of the proletariat upon the historical scene in particular. For Marx, the social and economic structure was an absolute reality which determined the direction of the historical process, a direction that was inexorably moving toward the realisation of socialism.

[41] " Wo-ti Ma-k'o-ssu-chu-i kuan," *op. cit.,* p. 534.
[42] Li Ta-chao, " She-hui-chu-i ti ching-chi tsu-chih " (" The Economic Organisation under Socialism "), *Hsuan-chi,* p. 428.

Li Ta-chao never succeeded in acquiring this Marxist confidence in the determining forces of history. One need not doubt the sincerity of Li's declarations that socialism would be the inevitable result of the laws of history, for he was certain from the beginning that the millennium was approaching. But Li's faith in the forces of history was never firm enough to allow him to test that faith by applying Marxist criteria to a serious examination of Chinese historical realities. His historical studies were always directed to promoting what he regarded to be a true historical world view rather than to the study of concrete historical processes. Moreover, his emphasis on the consciousness and the practical activities of men (and his concomitant de-emphasis on material preconditions) that characterised his interpretation of Marxism, as well as his continued insistence that spiritual reform was no less important than material reform, are additional factors which suggest that his confidence in the workings of the laws of history was something less than absolute. There were laws of history but these laws were not objective forces to which the activities of men had to conform. For Li such laws were but the expressions of conscious human activity and the evidence of their existence were to be sought, in the final analysis, in the consciousness and the practical activities of men.

THE CONCEPT OF TIME

An element of particular significance in Li Ta-chao's historical world view is his concept of time, for it is in this area that he makes a most important departure from the Marxist outlook. In the philosophic system that he had developed prior to his conversion to Marxism, Li had drawn from Emerson the feeling that the present moment is " the most precious thing in the world " and that any given " present " offers unlimited opportunities for human creative activity. The purpose of Li's early philosophic speculations, like his later interpretation of Marxism, was to encourage the activity of men in the here and now, to inspire men to take full advantage of the potentialities existing in the present in order to create the future. Thus he was harshly critical of all mentalities which failed to appreciate the vital forces latent in " now."

Li's concept of time was originally set within the framework of a transcendental philosophy that based itself upon a belief in an unceasing " tide of great reality," a universal spirit of youth that flowed through limitless time and space and through the "egos" of innumerable individuals. This tide moved in a dialectic fashion, manifesting itself in higher and higher levels of " rebirth " which were always expressed in an infinite series of " nows." [43]

---

[43] See Li's essays: " Ch'ing-chun " (" Spring "), *Hsin Ch'ing-nien,* Vol. II, No. 1 (September 1, 1916), and " Chin " (" Now "), *ibid.,* Vol. IV, No. 4 (April 15, 1918).

After his conversion to Marxism, strong echoes of this transcendental philosophy are still to be found in Li's writings. Moreover, his feeling of exaltation for the present moment survived the influence of Marxism virtually intact.

Early in 1923 Li wrote an essay entitled "'Now' and 'Antiquity'" ("'Chin' yü 'ku'") which begins with a restatement of certain of the themes of his pre-Marxism philosophy:

> Both the destiny of the universe and the history of man can be seen as the torrential flow of a great reality [ta shih-tsai] which has no beginning and no end, and which is in continuous motion and circulation. The past is gone and can never return, and the changes of the future will never end. Time has a present and a past, man has a present and a past . . . attitudes toward the present and the past differ, and the debate between the present and the past continues.[44]

It is this "debate between the present and past" with which Li is concerned in this essay. His aim is to combat the influences of what he terms the "recalling the past school" of historiography, and for this purpose he turns to an examination of the writings of a number of seventeenth and eighteenth century European philosophers—such diverse figures as Jean Bodin, Francis Bacon, Descartes and the English theologian George Hakewell—who are lumped together as "the venerating-the-present school." From Bodin Li draws support for his opposition to "the theory of a golden age" existing in the past, and in Bacon he finds confirmation for his view that "the cyclic theory [of history] is the greatest obstacle to the development of knowledge, for it causes men to lose their faith and hope." Descartes is praised for his critical attitude toward the authorities of the past and Hakewell for "recognising that the theory of [historical] regression can numb the vitality of man . . . drown man's hopes and dull his efforts." [45]

The reasons why these and other philosophers of the Enlightenment had "an optimistic and activistic view of history and human life," Li suggests, is that they shared a common conception of time, that is, they "venerated the present." Their views appear to Li to be very much in accord with Emerson's concept of time—a concept that had so greatly influenced Li's pre-Marxian philosophy and which he again quotes in this essay—the idea that "yesterday is beyond recall and tomorrow is uncertain; the sole thing within our grasp is today." This view of time, Li concludes, can serve to stimulate "the efforts of the men of the present to become the vanguard of the future." [46]

In an essay entitled "Time" ("Shih"), written late in 1923, Li attempts to relate more explicitly the manner in which time is perceived

44 Li Ta-chao, "'Chin' yü 'ku'" Hsuan-chi, p. 433.
45 Ibid. pp. 433–444.
46 Ibid. p. 446.

to the way in which history is understood. Here again the reappearance of Li's pre-Marxian world view is quite striking:

> The best part of life is youth and the best part of morning is the dawn . . . heaven and human life everywhere move unceasingly, waxing and waning, in a contradictory and complementary fashion. The dead and the living all enter into the present, the fulfilled and the unfulfilled are just beginning to develop into the future. Time is the vastness of nature without beginning and without end. Time is a boundless great reality. . . . Time is the great creator and also the great destroyer. The stage of history is its creative work-place and the ruins of history are the remnants of its destruction. Life and death, success and failure, and flourishing and decline among men are all but the metamorphosis of time.[47]

The concept of time had an almost mystical significance for Li. Taoist and Western philosophers, psychologists, mathematicians and physicists, have all grappled with the problem of explaining time, but have provided only partial answers. This is because

> the problem of time cannot be studied and, moreover, it is unnecessary to study it. When all is said and done, the problem of time is really beyond conception.[48]

If "time" is so elusive and transitory a phenomenon that it cannot really be apprehended, then one must grasp what he can of it—the present moment. Thus the past and the future, Li writes, exists only in the present. Only the present or "now" ("chin") is "alive."

> Now is powerful, active and creative. If in any given instant there is no activity and no movement, then this instant of the present becomes nothing and the life of this instant is equivalent to death.[49]

This feeling that all moments in time are unique and that each unique moment occurs but once led Li to the view that men are presented with an infinite series of unique opportunities and that in order for such opportunities not to be wasted they must be taken advantage of at the very moments they occur. The ability to appreciate the creative opportunities in the present had very much to do with how history is interpreted, Li believed, for a mistaken view of time inevitably gives rise to a mistaken view of history. The failure to appreciate the present results in a view of history that is

> retrogressive and motionless, (one) which disavows the developing aspects of nature and reality and which looks back to the past and loses the future . . . if you want to know the essence of time, then you must look not to antiquity but rather to the present, and not flee towards the vast and limitless past but rather towards the vast and limitless future. One

[47] " Shih," *op. cit.*, p. 485.
[48] *Ibid.* pp. 485–486.
[49] *Ibid.* p. 486.

who is able to understand the present as the " essence of time " is thereby capable of achieving " an energetic and exciting view of history and an optimistic and striving view of human life." [50]

There is much in Li's concept of time that can be reconciled with the Marxist outlook. The notion that the past lives in the present and that the future is being prepared in the present, as well as the need to look to a utopia located in the future, are elements that are very much in accord with the Marxist world view. But in Marxism, the process leading to the future socialist utopia is disciplined by a relatively strict sense of historical time. The past is highly differentiated in time according to specific and necessary stages of historical development, stages that are the result of the movement of concrete economic and social forces. Not only the past but also the future is differentiated, for the arrival of socialism is placed at a specific point in time—the period of the collapse of the capitalist system.

In Marxism, moreover, the determining objective forces of history apply not only to the past and the future but also to the present. Man makes history, Marx believed, but only under pre-existing conditions :

> men are not free to choose their productive forces—which are the basis of all their history—for every productive force is an acquired force, the product of former activity. The productive forces are therefore the result of practical human energy; but this energy is itself conditioned by the circumstances in which men find themselves, by the productive forces already acquired, by the social form which exists before they do, which they do not create, and which is the product of the preceding generation.[51]

For the Marxist, therefore, not all moments are favourable for revolution; indeed, favourable moments are relatively rare, determined as they are by the movement of the forces of production. It is only at certain crucial times that these forces give rise to the social and political conditions that make revolution possible. Thus in the Marxist world view, as Karl Mannheim has pointed out, time is experienced as " a series of strategic points " [52] and not in the manner that Li Ta-chao experienced it, as a series of equally significant " nows." The activity of the Marxist revolutionary is not to be a matter of impulse but it is to be based upon, and restrained by, the recognition of the determining, objective forces of history, and the concrete analysis of such forces at any given time.

Marxists, of course, have differed profoundly in the prescriptions for political action that presumably have been drawn from their analyses

50 *Ibid.* pp. 487–488.
51 Letter of Karl Marx to P. V. Annekov (December 28, 1946), *Selected Correspondence of Karl Marx and Frederick Engels* (Moscow : Foreign Languages Publishing House, 1953), p. 40.
52 Karl Mannheim, *Ideology and Utopia* (New York : Harcourt, Brace, 1952), p. 219.

of these determining forces of history. But to greater or lesser degrees, the feeling of a need to act in conformity with objective historical forces, and the discipline and restraint that such a feeling imposes upon the revolutionary impulse, has been a characteristic feature of the Marxist mentality.

It is the almost total absence of such a sense of discipline that characterises Li Ta-chao's historical world view. His concept of time largely precluded the differentiation of time on the basis of the development of objective historical forces, because for Li it was the present alone that was vital and creative. In envisioning the process of the realisation of socialism, Li did not look to the objective forces of history but rather to the revolutionary will and consciousness of men. One of the most important elements in acquiring this will and consciousness, he believed, was a proper concept of time, that is, the ability to appreciate the potentialities inherent in the present moment. For Li " now " was pregnant with meaning, and men needed only to grasp that meaning to realise through action the unlimited opportunities latent in " now." Since there is an infinite series of " nows," Li's concept of time was a philosophy of permanent activity.

Li's view of history was no less a philosophy of activity. History was to be studied not primarily to discover the tendencies of objective forces as the basis for political action, but rather to create the proper psychological atmosphere for political action. The role of historical theory was not so much to gain scientific insights into history as it was to provide men with the spiritual energy to create the future. For Li Ta-chao, men, inspired by a " true " historical world view (and a true concept of time) were to shape history; they were not to be bound by history.

CHINESE HISTORY

Although Li Ta-chao often called on historians to study the Chinese past from the point of view of the materialist conception of history, he himself found few opportunities to undertake such efforts. While he lectured on traditional Chinese history at Peking University, where he retained his professorship in the history department until the political repressions of March 1926, the published notes based on these lectures offer little to suggest that specifically Marxist assumptions were fruitfully employed. The major product of his own research on Chinese history—an attempt to analyse very ancient Chinese society on the basis of references in the classics—might just as well have been written without any knowledge of Marxism.[53]

---

[53] Li Ta-chao, " Yuan-jen she-hui yü wen-tzu shu-chi-shang chih wei-wu ti fan-ying " (" The Material Reflection of Primitive Society in Literary Documents "), *Hsuan-chi*, pp. 341–355.

As the leading figure in the Communist Party in North China, the demands placed on Li's time and energies left him with little leisure for serious historical research. And his death in 1927, at the age of 38, cut short whatever opportunities the future might have held to apply his Marxist beliefs to the interpretation of the Chinese past. Yet one suspects that because of his entire preoccupation with the need for a proper historical world view, rather than with any overwhelming concern with the historic process itself, the question of the application of the materialist conception to Chinese history would have, in any case, remained a matter of secondary concern to Li.

If Li lacked the opportunity, and perhaps the inclination, to engage in serious historical research, he was nevertheless not reluctant to express his views on Chinese history in his political writings and in his writings on historical theory. Two themes emerge from these writings which bear upon the questions posed by the Marxist historical outlook, and which are also relevant to the problems encountered by later Chinese Communist historians: first, his rejection of a universalistic pattern of historical development and, secondly, his nationalistic interpretation of modern Chinese history.

The notion that the history of all mankind has proceeded according to the pattern of evolution Marx outlined for Western European history—the scheme of the passage from primitive communism to slavery, feudalism, capitalism and finally socialism, is a dogma to be found neither in the writings of Marx nor Lenin. Marx, of course, quite explicitly denied that his scheme of historical periodisation had universalistic applications. It was, he argued, only an " historical sketch of the genesis of capitalism in Western Europe " and not " an historico-philosophic theory of the *marche generale* imposed by fate upon every people, whatever the historic circumstances in which it finds itself. . . ." [54] And although Lenin had been disposed to magnify the degree of capitalist economic development in Russia, he never argued that Marx's scheme of periodisation was fully applicable to Russian history, much less to the histories of Asian lands. The theory of a unilinear pattern of historical development is, in fact, a distinctive product of Stalinist ideology. By the time the Chinese Marxist Kuo Mo-jo wrote his *Study of Ancient Chinese Society* in 1929,[55] Stalin's control of the international Communist movement had hardened and the

[54] Letter of Karl Marx to the editors of *Otechestvenniye Zapiski* (November 1877), *Selected Correspondence of Marx and Engels, op. cit.*, pp. 354–355.

[55] Kuo Mo-jo, *Chung-kuo Ku-tai She-hui Yen-chiu* (*A Study of Ancient Chinese Society*) (Shanghai: Chung-ya Shu-chü, 1930). Kuo began with the premise that " on the whole, the history of mankind has everywhere been the same. . . ."

unilinear scheme was generally, although still by no means universally, accepted in world Communist circles.[56]

In the early 1920s, however, in its pre-Stalinist phase, " Marxist-Leninist " doctrine did not demand universalistic assumptions, at least as far as the past was concerned, and Li Ta-chao felt no compulsion to make such assumptions. Nowhere do we find Li searching for evidence of a slave society in ancient China; nowhere does he categorise the traditional Chinese socio-economic structure as feudal; nor did he feel the need to look for signs of incipient capitalism in pre-nineteenth-century China. He was content to describe traditional Chinese society only in the most general terms—as an " agrarian economic organisation " that remained " unchanging " for two thousand years.[57] As late as 1926 Li pointed out that private property in land (a form of property relation-ship wholly incompatible with the Marxist definition of feudalism) had been the predominant type of landownership in China since the late Chou era.[58] While Chinese Marxists have since devised various schemes to encompass the traditional Chinese system of private landownership within the scope of "feudalism," Li himself had constructed no such rationalisations.

Far from attempting to fit Chinese history within the Marxist scheme of periodisation, Li stressed the differences in historical develop-ment, and he assumed that Marxist historical theory would be interpreted in a fashion sufficiently broad to take into account the divergent historical patterns of both Eastern and Western civilisations. He called upon historians to construct a new, general " theory of national experience " that would include within its scope all national peculiarities in historic evolution.[59]

Li attributed the differences between the historical patterns of China and the West to essentially geographic factors. He argued that the generally favourable natural environment of China produced a relatively stable and static agrarian system that served as the base for traditional China's distinctive social, political and ideological " superstructure." Conversely, it was " deficiencies in nature " that stimulated commercial and industrial activities in the West.[60]

56 Opposition to the unilinear view was expressed in the Communist debates on the question of the " Asiatic mode of production," which continued into the 1930s. For an account of these debates by a participant, see Karl Wittfogel, *Oriental Despotism* (New Haven: Yale, 1957), pp. 401–412.

57 Li Ta-chao, " Yu ching-chi-shang chieh-shih Chung-kuo chin-tai ssu-hsiang pien-tung ti yuan-yu," (" An economic explanation of the changes in modern Chinese thought "), *Hsin Ch'ing-nien*, Vol. 7, No. 2, pp. 48–49.

58 Li Ta-chao, " T'u-ti yu nung-min " (" Land and the Peasants "), *Hsuan-chi*, p. 523.

59 *Shih-hsueh Yao-lun*, *op. cit.*, pp. 37–39.

60 Li Ta-chao, " Yu ching-chi-shang chieh-shih Chung-kuo chin-tai ssu-hsiang pien-tung ti yuan-yin," *op. cit.*, pp. 47–48.

While Li did not derive these views from Marxism, it might be noted that he could have found considerable support in Marxist historical writings for an emphasis upon geographical and climatic factors in history. Marxists have been quick to deny that geography, which is unchanging, can account for historical change, but the geographical environment is, in fact, the starting point of the Marxist analysis of history. Marx did indeed lay great stress on " the natural conditions in which man finds himself—geological, orohydrographical, climatic and so on." " All historiography," he wrote, " must begin from these natural bases and their modification in the course of history by men's activities." [61] It is well known, moreover, that Marx believed that capitalism could only have developed in the temperate zone.[62]

The importance of geographic factors has been emphasised by many of the successors of Marx. Plekhanov, for example, wrote:

> The peculiarities of the geographical environment determine the evolu-
> tion of the forces of production, and this, in its turn, determines the
> development of economic forces, and therefore the development of all
> the other social relations.[63]

The influence of the geographical environment is, of course, also the basis of Marx's theory of the " Asiatic mode of production," a theory which purports to explain the peculiarities in historical development of at least a part of the non-Western world on the basis of the need for large-scale irrigation works managed by the state.[64] Despite his emphasis on geography as the main factor which determined the differences between East and West, Li Ta-chao did not employ the concept of the " Asiatic mode of production " to explain Chinese history. In his only references to the " Asiatic mode " Li treated it as one stage (the stage preceding slavery) in Marx's general scheme for the periodisation of Western history [65]—the same context in which Marx mentioned the " Asiatic mode " in his well-known " Preface " to The Critique of Political Economy.

Marx's reference to the " Asiatic mode " in the " Preface " is quite misleading, for he clearly thought of " Asiatic society " as more than simply an ancient antecedent of modern Europe. The idea of the " Asiatic mode of production " was a general socio-historical concept (although not a geographical one) that Marx employed to describe traditional Indian and other societies—although he did not, it might be

61 Marx, The German Ideology, op. cit., p. 7.
62 Marx, Capital, Vol. II (Chicago: Kerr, 1912), p. 176.
63 George Plekhanov, Fundamental Problems of Marxism (New York: International
   Publishers, 1930), p. 34.
64 Marx's most complete statement of the theory of the " Asiatic mode of production "
   is in his essay " The British Rule in India," which originally appeared in The
   New York Tribune, June 25, 1853.
65 " Wo ti Ma-k'o-ssu-chu-i kuan," op. cit., p. 532.

noted, apply it to traditional China or Japan for reasons which I have outlined elsewhere.[66] Li-Ta-chao, in any event, was either unaware of this Marxian concept or, as is more likely, chose to ignore it.[67] It did not, in any event, play any part in his view of traditional China.

If Li rejected the notion that mankind had developed in the past according to a single, unilinear scheme, he was nevertheless insistent that the revolutionary future of all mankind would be the same. He had the fullest confidence that the road to socialism would lead to a world unity that would forever destroy all national and racial distinctions that had developed in the course of historic evolution. But if the Chinese past had been different from that of the Western countries and, moreover, if Chinese society had been unchanging for more than two thousand years, what assurance was there that the Chinese future would now converge with the future of Europe and the rest of the world? Li's pre-Marxian belief that future world unity would rest upon the synthesis of Western and Eastern (*i.e.*, Chinese) cultures would clearly no longer do now that he was a Marxist. If China had become part of the mainstream of world history, as he believed, then this had to be explained upon the basis of economic and not cultural factors.

It was here that the agency of foreign imperialism was invoked. It was the pressure of foreign economic power, Li stressed, that transformed China's " unchanging agricultural economic organisation " and the entire social, political and cultural " superstructure " that rested upon it, thereby thrusting China onto the stage of modern world history.[68] More than once he pointed out that it was the forcible entry of Western guns, technology and ideas that awakened China (and all of Asia) from its millennial slumber.[69] The fact that economic changes in China were the result of external rather than internal forces led Li to the conclusion that China was a " proletarian nation " oppressed by international capitalism and for that reason qualified to participate in the world socialist revolution, its still pre-capitalist economic structure notwithstanding.

The admission that foreign imperialism played an objectively " progressive " role in Chinese history is an uncomfortable notion for a Chinese nationalist to hold. This admission, however, did not prevent

---

[66] See Maurice Meisner, " The Despotism of Concepts: Wittfogel and Marx on China," *The China Quarterly*, No. 16 (October-December 1963).

[67] The theory of " Asiatic society " does appear in *Capital* which Li Ta-chao read.

[68] " Yu ching-chi-shang," *op. cit.*, pp. 48–51.

[69] The following statement, for example, appears in a booklet by Li published in January 1923: " Democracy originated in Europe and spread to America, and recently, by means of the power of the machine gun, the steamship, the newspaper, and the telegraph, it has brought a thunderous sound to awaken Asia, which has slumbered deep in despotism for several thousand years." *P'ing-min-chu-i* (*Democracy*), (Shanghai: Shang-wu Yin-shu-kuan, 1923), p. 1.

Li from treating modern Chinese history—as Chinese Communist historians do today—as essentially the history of Chinese national resistance to imperialist aggression. Like his Marxist successors, Li paid particular attention to the T'ai-p'ing Rebellion, which he interpreted not primarily as an anti-Manchu movement, but rather as the opening chapter of the popular struggle against Western imperialism.[70] Virtually every important event in China since the time of the T'ai-p'ings was also viewed by Li through the anti-imperialist prism. Even the more traditionalist movements, such as the activities of the triads and other secret societies in the post-T'ai-p'ing era, as well as the Boxer Rebellion, were seen as part of " the Chinese peoples' national revolutionary history of resistance to imperialism." [71]

The details of Li's interpretation of modern Chinese history need not detain us here, since his views are quite similar to more recent Chinese Communist interpretations. It should be pointed out, however, that Li's purpose was not simply the glorification of Chinese nationalism. He argued:

> From the beginning the Chinese national revolutionary movement was a part of the world revolution. The success of the Chinese revolution will have the greatest influence upon Europe and the whole world.[72]

Li was inclined to place " the beginning " of Chinese participation in the international revolution at a very early period in modern Chinese history. He sought, and claimed to have found, concrete links between certain secret societies connected with the T'ai-p'ings and Marx's First International.[73] Moreover, he drew upon the authority of Marx's own writings on China to support his nationalistic interpretation of the T'ai-p'ing Rebellion.[74] The identification of Chinese nationalism with world socialism was the essential message that Li's comments on modern Chinese history were intended to convey.

CONCLUSION

In interpreting modern Chinese history as essentially the history of Chinese national resistance to foreign imperialism, and at the same time rejecting the notion of a unilinear scheme of historical development, Li

---

[70] See, for example, Li Ta-chao, " Ma-k'o-ssu ti Chung-kuo min-tsu ko-ming kuan " (" Marx's Views on the Chinese National Revolution "), *Hsuan-chi*, p. 545; and " Sun Chung-shan Hsien-sheng tsai Chung-kuo min-tsu ko-ming shih-shang chih wei-chih " (" Mr. Sun Yat-sen's Place in the History of the Chinese National Revolution "), *Hsuan-chi*, pp. 537–544.

[71] " Sun Chung-shan Hsien-sheng," *op. cit.*, p. 537.

[72] Li Ta-chao, " Chung-shan-chu-i ti kuo-min ko-ming yu shih-chieh ko-ming " (" The Sun Yatsenist National Revolution and the World Revolution "), *Hsuan-chi*, p. 562.

[73] *Ibid.* p. 562.

[74] Li Ta-chao, " Ma-k'o-ssu ti Chung-kuo min-tsu ko-ming kuan " (" Marx's Views on the Chinese Nationalist Revolution "), *Hsuan-chi*, pp. 545–555

Ta-chao, if not more enlightening, was at least more consistent than his Chinese Marxist successors. As Professor Feuerwerker has observed, it has become increasingly difficult for Communist historians to maintain the belief that Chinese history proceeded in a pattern parallel to the stages of social evolution that Marx outlined for Western Europe, and, at the same time, describe modern Chinese history as a great drama of anti-imperialist struggle.[75] For if China's historical development paralleled that of the West, how is it possible to explain the fact that China was the victim of Western imperialism without making the undesirable admission that China's backwardness pre-dated the foreign intrusion? It must be further admitted that socio-economic changes in modern China, unlike those in the West, resulted primarily from external rather than internal factors, thus suggesting that China itself was incapable of generating such changes. While no satisfactory solutions to these problems have yet been found, for the nationalist it is more comforting to ignore the problem of periodisation as much as possible and concentrate on the story of the evils of imperialist aggression and the heroics of the Chinese response.

The balance that had been previously maintained in Chinese Communist historiography between these conflicting elements of Marxian universalism and Chinese nationalism has been clearly overthrown in recent years in favour of the nationalist emphasis. In this, historiography has, of course, submitted to immediate political and ideological considerations. If the superimposition of Marx's scheme of periodisation was necessary to prove that socialism was relevant to, and the inevitable outcome of, Chinese historical development during the years when the Chinese Communist Party was still fighting for power, it has obviously become a matter of less concern since 1949. The existence of a presumably socialist régime is in itself sufficient to prove the relevance of socialism. But nationalist and anti-imperialist themes not only fulfil continuing political needs, they also strike responsive chords that are deeply imbedded in Chinese Communist ideology and in the psychology of the Chinese intelligentsia. While the form of the Marxist scheme of periodisation has not been abandoned (partly for the purpose of maintaining some sense of ideological continuity), the content of Chinese history, as it has been presented in recent years, has tended increasingly to diverge from the universalistic pattern. Within the formal structure of the division of Chinese history according to Western-derived stages of development, an increasing number of Chinese socio-economic peculiarities are being found, and the unique riches of traditional Chinese civilisation are being rediscovered. Interpretations which suggest rather

75 Feuerwerker, *op. cit.*

301

fundamental differences from the Western pattern of historical development are now permissible if superiority to the West is somehow implied.

This attempt to recapture the national past has taken many forms. Historians have been called upon, for example, to portray " the bright side " of the traditional ruling classes.[76] An appeal that the anonymous history of the masses be enriched by an emphasis on individual historical figures [77] has more recently come to fruition in the resurrection of the great " feudal " emperors. Indeed, the whole tendency to negate the achievement of the past has ben identified with " the views of the slaves of the compradore-capitalist class," such as Hu Shih and Wu Chih-hui.[78]

The recognition of the role of individual historical figures is, of course, in no way inconsistent with the premises of the materialist conceptions of history.[79] On this point, Chinese Communist historians have recently found no lack of support in the writings of Marx, Engels and Lenin. Nor is there anything in the Marxist view of history that in any way prevents one from appreciating the accomplishments of the past (even though it might be argued that a specifically nationalistic celebration of the past is in conflict with the principles of original Marxism, for Marx viewed nationalism as a manifestation of human self-alienation). Even if Chinese Communist historians were to abandon completely Marx's scheme of periodisation, this would not in itself represent a departure from the premises of the materialist conception of history. For while Marx claimed that his theory of history had universalistic applications as a *method* to analyse historical reality, he specifically denied, as we have seen, that his scheme of periodisation was any more than an attempt to trace the origins of capitalism in Western Europe. The materialist conception of history is in no sense dependent upon the validity of the scheme of periodisation, although the assertion of the inevitability of socialism perhaps is.

The real departures from the premises of the Marxist view of history that have occurred in Chinese Communist historiography are to be found in a quite different area. Although the materialist conception of history is, as most Marxists have traditionally insisted, primarily a method of historical analysis, it is nevertheless a method that begins with a definite set of assumptions. The core of these assumptions consists in the belief that there are, in fact, determining forces of history and objective

---

[76] Chien Po-tsan, " Some Present Problems in the Teaching of History," Joint Publications Research Service (Washington: Department of Commerce), July 29, 1959, pp. 46–48.

[77] *Ibid.* p. 40–41.

[78] Pai Shou-i, " The ' Past ' and the ' Present ' in the Teaching of History," *JPRS*, August 11, 1959.

[79] Plekhanov's celebrated *The Role of the Individual in History* sets forward the generally accepted Marxist view on this subject.

laws of social development to which the activities of men must conform if these activities are to be historically significant; these objective forces and laws, it is further assumed, are to be understood primarily through the analysis of the techniques, the organisation and the social relations of production, and their changes. It is this that constitutes the economic " base " that, in the final analysis, determines the social, political and ideological " superstructure."

However often Chinese Communist historians may invoke the deterministic formulas of Marx, and however ardently they may proclaim the historic inevitability of socialism, the most striking characteristic of the Chinese Communist treatment of the materialist conception of history is that it reflects that same lack of confidence in the determining forces of history that we have observed in examining the historical works of Li Ta-chao. Like him, contemporary Chinese Communist historians are less interested in understanding the past or the present in terms of the objective laws of history than they are in using historiography to promote the proper ideas and the proper actions in the here and now.

This characteristic is quite apparent in the discussions of the slogan " emphasise the present and deemphasise the past," one of the recent guidelines for historiographical work. In part this slogan was intended to encourage historians to devote more attention to contemporary and modern history in their research and teaching. But its primary purpose was not to deemphasise the study of ancient history but rather to " make use of ancient history in contemporary circumstanes." The meaning of this, Chien Po-tsan has informed his fellow historians, is that they are

> to summarise all useful experiences in history according to Marxist-Leninist historical methodology, that is, to summarise such experiences [as are to be found in the history of] productive labour, the class struggle, and the struggle against external aggression in defence of the fatherland in an effort to promote the education of productive labour, the education of the class struggle, and the education of patriotism.[80]

Marxist historical theory is to be applied to the past, in short, not primarily for the purpose of investigating objective historical realities, but rather to present the activities of the men of the past in such a fashion as to stimulate productivity, create the proper political consciousness, and encourage nationalistic sentiments among the men of the present.

That the " past and present " slogan was intended to insure that historiography serves immediate political interests was further made clear by Pai Shou-i:

[80] Chien Po-tsan, p. 40.

The heart of the problem of " past " and " present " is the problem of
how to make use of the " past " at " present." By the " past " . . . is
actually meant one's knowledge of history. Ancient history is " past ";
medieval history is " past "; modern and contemporary history may
likewise be regarded as " past." By the " present " is meant current
politics and contemporary life.[81]

The treatment of the materialist conception of history in Chinese
Communist ideology is in large measure determined by this concern for
the political and ideological needs of the " present," and especially by
those core elements of Maoist ideology which stress the determining role
of the energies, the activities and the ideas of men. Within the framework of these ideological predispositions, Marx's belief that " being
determines consciousness " is turned firmly upon its head, a transformation which requires, in turn, the inversion of all the long-cherished
formulas of historical materialism. The social superstructure thus tends
to be seen as more important than the economic base, political factors
tend to prevail over economic factors, and ideas triumph over material
forces.

This emphasis on political and ideological factors, along with the
purely nationalist themes, constitutes the heart of the Maoist historical
world view and the real content of Chinese Communist historiography,
even though these basic voluntaristic and nationalistic predispositions
are usually coupled with the deterministic formulas of orthodox
historical materialism. Thus while the necessary orthodox rituals are
satisfied by repeating the notion that the " base " determines the " superstructure," ideologists and historians tend increasingly to emphasise that
a decisive role in determining the course of history can be played by
such factors as " subjective dynamism," which is defined as the forces
of the masses mobilised by the party and its ideology.

> Socialist ideology becomes a weapon in mobilising and organising the
> masses and becomes a material force in society . . . it [ideology] becomes
> instrumental in establishing a socialist economic base by acquiring
> political power and by destroying the capitalist economic base with
> that power.[82]

The notion that it is the ideas and energies of men that can determine
the course of history, and not simply the inexorable movement of
economic forces, has been quite clearly communicated to the professional
practitioners of the materialist conception of history. In the December
1958 issue of *Li-shih Yen-chiu*, historians were warned that " it is a
mistake to see only the physical factor and lose sight of the human

[81] Pai Shou-i, p. 29.
[82] Hsu I-jang and Lin Ching-yao, " Subjective Dynamism and the Superstructure Can
under Certain Conditions Produce Decisive Results," *Hsin Chien-she* (*New
Construction*), March, 1959, pp. 44–46.

factor." It was asserted, moreover, that " when theory grasps the masses, it itself becomes a material force." [83]

If the " past " is to serve the " present," then the study of history must serve to reinforce these voluntaristic and nationalistic ideological tendencies. The emphasis on the revolutionary struggles of the Chinese people against feudalism and foreign imperialism which has long characterised Communist historical studies, has suited these needs, for it is an essential part of the lesson that Maoist ideology endeavours to teach. The point of this lesson, of course, is that when the energies of the masses come under the " guidance" of the proper theory and the necessary organisational restraints (namely, the thought and the party of Mao Tse-tung), then these energies and ideas can together create history and overcome all material obstacles. The more recent concern with the role of individual historical figures has the virtue of satisfying nationalist impulses by reclaiming the heroes of the past, and at the same time it facilitates the general shift of emphasis from the realm of the economic " base " to the realm of the political and ideological " superstructure."

What contemporary Chinese Communist historians finally derive from the materialist conception of history are much the same things that Li Ta-Chao derived. First, there are certain strains in Marx's historical writings, such as the belief that " man makes history," that can be drawn upon to support a generally non-deterministic world view. Secondly, there is the continuing need, both psychological and political, to provide some sense of continuity with the Marxist tradition by employing objective historical correlatives for what is basically a subjective system of revolutionary values. Finally, and perhaps most importantly, the materialist conception of history reinforces the belief in the inevitability of world socialism. This belief, however, is more an act of religious faith than it is a belief based upon confidence in the tendencies of objective historical processes and the objective laws of social development. The belief in the historical inevitability of socialism is based primarily upon faith in the energies, the ideas and the will of men. It is the purpose of historical studies and historical theory to encourage these energies and to reinforce this will.

---

[83] Chiang Ch'un-fang, " Ma-k'o-ssu-chu-i tsai Chung-kuo " (" Marxism in China "), *Li-shih Yen-chiu* (*Historical Research*), December, 1958, p. 19.

15

Mao Tse-tung as Historian

By HOWARD L. BOORMAN

> Every society is an arena of social conflicts, and those
> individuals who range themselves against existing authority are
> no less products and reflections of the society than those who
> uphold it.
>
> Edward Hallett Carr, *What Is History?* (1963), p. 65.

THE label " history " is conventionally used with at least two distinct
meanings: history-as-actuality and history-as-record.[1] The events lying
beneath the abstraction termed the social and economic history of the
Roman empire constitute the former; Rostovtzeff's *Social and Economic
History of the Roman Empire* is an example of the latter. Our concern
in this paper is with " history " in still a third sense. When an individual, through either intent or accident, comes to occupy a dominant
position in the history of a people, a country or an institution, his
personal views on history and the historical process assume significance
for the historian. *The Peloponnesian War, Commentaries on the Gallic
Wars, The History of the Russian Revolution,* and *The Second World
War* are important sources not only as records of past events but also
because Thucydides, Julius Caesar, Trotsky and Churchill were themselves involved in the making of history. The recorded views of such
event-making individuals are of intrinsic, albeit uneven, value because
the men had personal knowledge of the events described—because they
were, in short, actors before they were authors.[2]

As background for our inquiry, we pose the topic of the rise to
power of the Communist Party in twentieth-century China as a problem
in multiple causation.[3] One critical element in the pre-1949 competition

[1] See *Theory and Practice in Historical Study: A Report of the Committee on
Historiography,* Social Science Research Council, Bulletin No. 54 (New York: Social
Science Research Council, 1946), p. 133.

[2] On the distinction between the eventful man and the event-making man, see Sidney
Hook, *The Hero in History* (Boston: Beacon Press, 1955), chapter 9, pp. 151-183.

[3] This paper is devoted to discussion of Mao Tse-tung's general view of modern
history, not of Peking's present line on the history of the Chinese Communist
Party. A summation of the present Party line is given in the " Resolution on Some
Questions in the History of Our Party," adopted by the enlarged seventh plenum
of the sixth Central Committee of the Chinese Communist Party on April 20, 1945.
For the Chinese text, see *Mao Tse-tung Hsuan-chi* (Peking: People's Publishing
House, 1953), III, pp. 955-1002; for the English, see *Selected Works of Mao Tse-tung*
(London: Lawrence & Wishart, 1956), IV, pp. 171-218. See also the review article
by Howard L. Boorman, " From Shanghai to Peking: the Politics of a Revolution,"
Journal of Asian Studies, XXIII, No. 1 (November 1963), pp. 113-119.

for national authority in China was the quality of political leadership. One salient element in effective leadership is the ability to relate political and social goals meaningfully to the on-going course of national history. In this key respect, the Communist Party élite around Mao Tse-tung during the 1940s proved more effective than the Kuomintang élite centred on Chiang Kai-shek. It would be naive—though not completely irrelevant—to assert that Mao Tse-tung's party succeeded in gaining the Mandate of Heaven because Mao was a better student of history than was Chiang Kai-shek. But Mao was able to buttress his political case persuasively, in the eyes of significant groups in China, by representing communism as the logical, indeed necessary, consequence of China's historical impasse after the republican coup of 1911–12. Both the course of recent Chinese history and the massive weight which contemporary Chinese historiography accords to the thought of Mao Tse-tung constitute joint warrants for assessment of Mao as student and shaper of history.[4] Of all the individuals, both professional and political, who write on historical subjects in the People's Republic of China, Mao Tse-tung alone may speak with freedom and with unimpeachable authority.

SOURCES OF MAO'S VIEWS ON HISTORY

Before you study history, Mr. E. H. Carr advised in his 1961 lectures at Cambridge, study the historian. And before you study the historian, Mr. Carr added, study his historical and social environment.[5] The historian, whether professional or lay, is himself rooted in a specific milieu, influenced by the specific stimuli of his period, and moved to react to specific problems in history which he deems significant. Milieu, period, and reaction blend, consciously or unconsciously, to shape the historian's outlook. Mao Tse-tung's view of history and historical change is the product of Chinese, not of German or Brazilian, soil. But that view is not simply Chinese: it is the distinctive product of an interlude of massive disorientation in Chinese life marked by the breakdown of Confucian patterns and by the search for new political, intellectual and ethical reintegration.

Mao Tse-tung was born in Hsiang-t'an *hsien* in Hunan province the

---

[4] See, for example, the major speech by Chou Yang, then deputy director of the propaganda department of the Central Committee of the Chinese Communist Party, *The Fighting Task Confronting Workers in Philosophy and the Social Sciences* (Peking: Foreign Languages Press, 1963), especially pages 53–68. Chou's speech was given on October 26, 1963, at the fourth enlarged session of the committee of the department of philosophy and social science of the Chinese Academy of Sciences, the national organisation sponsoring advanced research in the People's Republic of China.

[5] Edward Hallett Carr, *What Is History?* The George Macauley Trevelyan Lectures delivered at the University of Cambridge, January-March 1961 (New York: Knopf, 1963), p. 54.

year before the first Sino-Japanese war of 1894–95 sounded a final, blunt warning to the long-coveted sense of cultural integrity and superiority of the Central Kingdom.[6] A village lad during the abortive 1898 reform effort and the 1900 Boxer uprising, Mao was just short of 18 when the Wuchang revolt of October 1911 toppled the Ch'ing dynasty. As a youthful patriot in Changsha, the provincial capital, he was frustrated both by Hunan's fading strength in China's domestic politics and by China's failing strength in international affairs. With the appearance in 1915 of *Hsin Ch'ing-nien* (*New Youth*), edited by Ch'en Tu-hsiu and others in Peking, Mao rallied at once to its call for national reform and bold action. After his graduation from the First Normal School in Changsha in 1918, Mao, then nearly 25, left for Peking on his first recorded trip outside Hunan. Back in Changsha in the spring of 1919, he was struck with patriotic fallout from the Peking student demonstrations which sparked the May Fourth Movement.[7] The situation in Changsha provided Mao, then only an obscure and impecunious normal school graduate, with new opportunities for action, influence and increased prestige and stamped him as a Chinese of the May Fourth generation, though scarcely a typical representative. It is hardly accidental that, in one of the popular communist versions of Chinese history prepared for Western consumption, he first appears on stage in the summer of 1919 as editor of the *Hsiang Chiang P'ing-lun* (*Hsiang River Review*), the short-lived but well-written journal published by the provincial student organisation in Hunan.[8]

The young Mao's attitude of patriotic protest was well-defined by 1919, two years after the Bolshevik revolution in Russia but still some months before Mao's conversion to Marxism. The formative influences shaping his political attitudes had all been Chinese; indeed, most had been specifically Hunanese.[9] His childhood had been rural, and experience rather than exegesis had taught him that wealth in China was

---

[6] The most recent and informed biography of Mao's political career is Stuart Schram, *Mao Tse-tung* (Harmondsworth, Middlesex, England: Pelican Original, 1966). Other relevant materials include Jerome Ch'en, *Mao and the Chinese Revolution* (London: Oxford Un. Press, 1965); Arthur A. Cohen, *The Communism of Mao Tse-tung* (Chicago: Un. of Chicago Press, 1965); Stuart R. Schram, *The Political Thought of Mao Tse-tung* (New York: Praeger, 1963); Howard L. Boorman, "Mao Tse-tung: The Lacquered Image," *The China Quarterly*, No. 16 (October–December 1963), pp. 1–55; and the symposium "What Is Maoism?" in *Problems of Communism*, XV, No. 5 (September–October 1966), pp. 1–30, which includes papers by Schram and Cohen, commentaries, and concluding remarks.

[7] The definitive discussion of the subject is Chow Tse-tsung, *The May Fourth Movement: Intellectual Revolution in Modern China* (Cambridge: Harvard Un. Press, 1960).

[8] Tung Chi-ming, *An Outline History of China* (Peking: Foreign Languages Press, 1959), p. 316.

[9] For discussion of Mao as a Hunanese, see Howard L. Boorman, "Mao Tse-tung at Seventy: an American Dilemma," *The Virginia Quarterly Review*, XL, No. 2 (Spring 1964), pp. 182–200.

created by manual labour in the fields. No available evidence suggests that Mao's views on history were seriously influenced by his family. The principal early stimuli were rather provided by the traditional Chinese novels. Like countless other school boys in China, Mao devoured the *San-kuo yen-i* (*Romance of the Three Kingdoms*), the *Shui-hu-chuan* (*Water Margin*), and others. Certainly these adventure-laden tales of heroic deeds, clever stratagems, and righteous rebellion against unjust officialdom gripped the young Mao and stretched his imagination.

More systematic appraisal of the patterns and problems of Chinese history came with formal schooling, notably that which Mao received at the First Normal School in Changsha from 1913 to 1918.[10] Too late for solid classical training, yet too early for modern Western-style education, Mao became aware of the Chinese past but was not constricted by it. His chief introduction to traditional Chinese history during his school days at Changsha was doubtless based upon the *Tzu-chih t'ung-chien* (*Comprehensive Mirror for Aid in Government*) of Ssu-ma Kuang (1018–1086) or the abridged and reorganised version of that bulky work prepared in the twelfth century under the direction of Chu Hsi (1130–1200).[11]

Mao was also influenced by free-thinking faculty members at the First Normal School, notably by his ethics teacher, Yang Ch'ang-chi (1870–1920). Yang, whose daughter Yang K'ai-hui was to become Mao's first wife, was a respected local scholar of Changsha who had studied abroad for ten years after the turn of the century in Japan, England, and Germany. While Yang regarded himself as an intellectual rebel in criticising China's indigenous traditions, he nevertheless gave his students solid grounding in Neo-Confucianism as expounded by major Chinese thinkers of the Ming and Ch'ing periods. At the same time, since he styled himself a Neo-Kantian idealist because of his European training, Yang also exposed his students to some Western ethical theory. The Western book which most influenced Mao at this time was a Neo-Kantian work by Friedrich Paulsen entitled *System der Ethik*. A Chinese translation of this work entitled *Lun-li Hsueh Yuan-li* had been prepared by Ts'ai Yuan-p'ei (1867–1940), one of the most prominent intellectuals and educators of the pre-1928 period, and was used by Yang Ch'ang-chi as a textbook. Although the marginal increment of German idealism has perhaps embarrassed latter-day scribes in Peking, the major elements in Mao's formal training were indubitably and overwhelmingly Chinese.

[10] The most useful account of that period is contained in Li Jui, *Mao Tse-tung T'ung-chih te Ch'u-ch'i Ko-ming Huo-tung* (*Comrade Mao Tse-tung's Early Revolutionary Activities*) (Peking: China Youth Publishing House, 1957).

[11] A reprint of the *Tzu-chih t'ung-chien* was published at Peking in 1956 (Ku-chi Ch'u-pan She, 10 volumes).

At the same time, Mao's informal education before 1920 was perhaps as important as that which he received in the classroom. In Changsha, for example, he encountered the ideas of Wang Fu-chih (1619–1692; T. Ch'uan-shan), the famous Hunanese scholar, patriot and materialist philosopher.[12] Wang was renowned for his loyalty to the Ming house and for his refusal to serve the new Manchu rulers when they conquered China in the mid-seventeenth century. Some 200 years later, towards the end of the Ch'ing dynasty, Chinese patriot-reformers drew theoretical support for their modern nationalism from Wang Fu-chih's writings.[13] After the establishment of the republic, Hunanese scholars, including Yang Ch'ang-chi, established a special institute at Changsha, the Wang Fu-chih Study Society (Ch'uan-shan hsueh-she), for the study of his writings. As a student in the city, Mao Tse-tung often attended lectures at the Society, where he imbibed the patriotic fervour and the philosophical and historical iconoclasm of a scholar whose active career had ended in 1650.[14]

Closer in time and temperament to Mao Tse-tung and his contemporaries was the fiery young Hunanese reformer T'an Ssu-t'ung, who had been executed in September 1898 after the collapse of the reform movement of that year.[15] Only 33 at the time of his death, T'an was viewed by the Changsha students as the first Hunanese martyr in modern Chinese history to give his life for the cause of emancipation from the network of traditional obscurantism and official corruption which

---

[12] See the biography of Wang Fu-chih by Ch'i Ssu-ho in Arthur W. Hummel (ed.), Eminent Chinese of the Ch'ing Period, II, pp. 817–819. Brief summaries of Wang's philosophical views are given in Wm. Theodore de Bary et al., Sources of Chinese Tradition (New York: Columbia Un. Press, 1960), pp. 597–606; and Wing-tsit Chan, A Source Book in Chinese Philosophy (Princeton: Princeton Un. Press, 1963), pp. 692–702. J. Gray deals with Wang's historical views in his chapter, " Historical Writing in Twentieth-century China: Notes on its Background and Development," in W. G. Beasley and E. G. Pulleyblank, Historians of China and Japan (London: Oxford Un. Press, 1961), pp. 193–197.

[13] Wang Fu-chih's collected works, the Ch'uan-shan i-shu, were printed at Changsha in 1840–42 and reprinted at Nanking under the auspices of Tseng Kuo-fan, the Hunanese soldier-statesman, in 1864–65.

[14] See Li Jui, note 10 above, pp. 29–30.

[15] See the biography of T'an Ssu-t'ung by Teng Ssu-yü in Arthur W. Hummel (ed.), Eminent Chinese of the Ch'ing Period, II, pp. 702–705. Perhaps the earliest biography of T'an is that by Liang Ch'i-ch'ao, " T'an Ssu-t'ung chuan," still very useful for an account of his participation in the 1898 reform movement in Yin ping shih ho-chi, chuan-chi, I, pp. 106–112. The article by Ts'ai Shang-ssu, " T'an Ssu-t'ung hsueh-shu ssu-hsiang t'i-yao," in Chung-kuo Chien-she (China Reconstructs), IV, No. 2 (May 1947), pp. 49–53, is also useful. Recent materials on T'an published at Peking include Chiang Shang-ssu (ed.), T'an Ssu-t'ung Ch'uan-chi (Complete Works of T'an Ssu-t'ung) (Peking: New China Bookstore, 1954) and a chronological biography by Yang T'ing-fu, T'an Ssu-t'ung Nien-p'u (Peking: People's Publishing House, 1957). Nathan M. Talbott has prepared a doctoral dissertation on the subject at the University of Washington, Intellectual Origins and Aspects of Political Thought in the Jen-hsueh of T'an Ssu-t'ung, Martyr of the 1898 Reform (Ann Arbor, Michigan: University Microfilms, 1956). Takashi Oka has written on " The Philosophy of T'an Ssu-t'ung," Harvard University, East Asian Regional Studies Seminar, Papers on China, IX (August 1955), pp. 1–47.

constituted a natural target for youthful rebellion. Although associated with K'ang Yu-wei during the Hundred Days reform period in 1898, T'an Ssu-t'ung was considerably more drastic than K'ang in his prescriptions for institutional reform and in his emphasis upon revolution against the alien monarchs of the Ch'ing house. His ardent national consciousness and radical denunciation of Confucian orthodoxy made him very popular with the post-1911 student generation in China.

Some of T'an Ssu-t'ung's ideas were embodied in the influential tract entitled *Jen-hsueh* (*On Benevolence*), an ingenious attempt to synthesise Confucian, Buddhist and Christian ideas and to illuminate a new revolutionary ethical code to depose Manchu autocracy, to establish a truly independent China, and to create a social environment in which the Chinese people could give free expression to their creative human capacities.

Mao's evolving and eclectic social thought in the period after the First World War comprised an unusual medley of themes: patriotism, resistance to alien rule, self-discipline, self-realisation, social responsibility, the power of the conscious will to influence events, and others. He came of age politically with the May Fourth Movement of 1919, and the anti-imperialist impulses of that explosion deeply affected his social attitudes. Interestingly, the literary experimentation which accompanied and followed it had less influence on Mao. With really only one major exception, the authors of China's new fiction of the post-1919 vintage years left little mark on Mao's view of literature as a reflector of social change.[16]

That exception was the redoubtable Lu Hsun (1881–1936), the most potent social critic of the period.[17] Himself a rebel torn between his sense of patriotism and his spirit of rebellion against the thou-shalt's and thou-shalt-not's of the Chinese tradition, Mao was dazzled by the satirical short stories and essays which flowed from Lu Hsun's pen. Lu Hsun's first published story, "The Diary of a Madman," which appeared in *New Youth* in 1918, was a stinging indictment of the man-eating nature of traditional Chinese society.[18] Its condemnation of China's great tradition as a self-serving cover for a cannibal feast marked the opening incision in an extended operation through which Lu Hsun exposed and dissected the neurotic psyche of twentieth-century China. Of his later stories, based according to Lu Hsun on "the lives of unfortunate people living in a sick society," *The True Story of Ah Q* (1921)

[16] See Howard L. Boorman, "The Literary World of Mao Tse-tung," *The China Quarterly*, No. 13 (January–March 1963), pp. 15–38.

[17] A bibliography of basic materials in Chinese and Western languages dealing with Lu Hsun is given in C. T. Hsia, *A History of Modern Chinese Fiction, 1917–1957* (New Haven: Yale Un. Press, 1961), pp. 550–552.

[18] *Selected Works of Lu Hsun* (Peking: Foreign Languages Press, 1956), I, pp. 8–21.

emphasised his constant theme: that the Chinese people, to attain maturity, must replace self-delusion and defeatism with self-respect and self-confidence.[19]

Mao Tse-tung shared Lu Hsun's indignation at social injustice and approved of Lu Hsun's impatience with that national evasiveness which did duty for national character in China during the early years of the twentieth century. Yet Mao also saw that his favourite modern author was essentially a social critic, not a social theorist.[20] Mao recognised that Lu Hsun had no cohesive model for a new China, no organisational formulae with which to confront the practical problems of doing something about the pressures which frustrated sensitive Chinese. And Mao turned, therefore, like some other patriotic Chinese of that period, to the alien stream of social thought labelled Marxism-Leninism. Like other key chapters in his biography, the story of Mao Tse-tung's conversion to communism is neither complete nor precise. His initiation into the movement that was to shape his basic estimates of history and historical change was influenced, in part, by personal contacts with two of the pioneer leaders of the Chinese Communist Party and, in part, by actions taken by the new government in Russia after the Bolshevik revolution.

The writings of T'an Ssu-t'ung had influenced Mao's student generation partly because they represented what one of the least tradition-bound minds of the late nineteenth century had been able to evolve as patriotic philosophical synthesis without direct exposure to Western thought. With the May Fourth outbreak, Mao encountered a new generation which marked a sharper break with the traditionalism of Chinese classical learning and a closer movement toward modern nationalism and social radicalism derived from Western models.[21]

At the beginning of 1920, on his second journey from Hunan to north China, Mao came under the direct influence of Li Ta-chao (1889–1927), one of the first Chinese intellectuals to respond to the messianic appeals of the Russian revolution.[22] As Li Ta-chao, then a member of the faculty of National Peking University, quested for intellectual and practical formulae to remedy China's debility, he moved leftward in his political thinking. Mao followed him, reading the *Communist Manifesto* for the first time in Chinese translation and exploring the elementary tenets of dialectical and historical materialism. Having begun the baptismal process under the guidance of Li Ta-chao, Mao

[19] *Ibid.*, pp. 76–135.
[20] See Harriet C. Mills, "Lu Hsun and the Communist Party," *The China Quarterly*, No. 4 (October–December 1960), pp. 17–27.
[21] See the discussion of intellectual generations in twentieth-century China by Benjamin Schwartz, "The Intelligentsia in Communist China: A Tentative Comparison," *Daedalus* (Summer 1960), especially pp. 612–621.
[22] See Maurice Meisner, *Li Ta-chao and the Origins of Chinese Marxism*, scheduled for publication by the Harvard Un. Press.

went to Shanghai, where he had decisive discussions with Ch'en Tu-hsiu (1879–1942), one of the most influential intellectual leaders of the period who was shortly to become the first general secretary of the Chinese Communist Party.

The political attitudes of many young Chinese patriots of the May Fourth period were also strongly affected by the dramatic declaration of Soviet intentions towards China, issued at Moscow in July 1919 and addressed to " the Chinese people and to the governments of China, North and South." [23] In sharp contrast to the pressures exerted on China by the Western powers and manifest in Japan's Twenty-one Demands of 1915, the so-called Karakhan statement proposed the abrogation of all secret agreements and other unequal treaties concluded by the Tsarist government with China and the relinquishment of all its privileges and interests without compensation. When it became known in China several months later, in early 1920, the declaration naturally had a strong appeal for nationalistic young Chinese anxious to free their country of the political, economic and psychological privileges which the major foreign powers then maintained in China. By mid-1920 Mao Tse-tung was convinced of the validity and relevance of Marxism-Leninism and prepared to begin a new career as political evangelist and organiser.

MAO AND MODERN HISTORY

In the summer of 1921 Mao attended the small meeting of intellectual radicals at Shanghai later formally labelled the First National Congress of the Communist Party of China. While Mao had come to his vocation, advancement came slowly, and he was for many years more closely involved with the pressing problems of Communist Party organisation and revolutionary strategy than with historical estimates. During the early 1920s he gained initial experience as communist organiser in his native Hunan; from 1923 until 1927, he was committed to the Comintern-sponsored alliance between the Chinese Communist Party and the Kuomintang, then viewed as the most effective way of carrying through an anti-imperialist nationalist revolution in China. After the debacle of 1927, when the Kuomintang broke the united front with the communists, Mao spent the middle years of his career in the countryside. That was the period that both hardened and humanised the Party structure, brought Mao to its top command, and paved the way for implementation of his revolutionary strategy during the national crisis created by

---

[23] See Allen S. Whiting, *Soviet Policies in China, 1917–1924* (New York: Columbia Un. Press, 1954), chapter 2, pp. 24–41, and Chow Tse-tsung, see note 7, pp. 209–214. The Chinese text of the declaration appeared in *Hsin ch'ing-nien* (*New Youth*), VII, No. 6, May 1, 1920, appendix, pp. 1–3.

the Japanese invasion of China. It was only after the communists established a new territorial base in Shensi province in northwest China following the Long March that Mao turned to definition of the place of the Chinese Communist revolutionary movement within the larger sweep of modern Chinese history. By that time he had begun to assemble his personal brains trust and to delineate the political and military guidelines to national power.[24] The result was a series of pronouncements, articulated during the years between 1937 and 1949, which established the basic framework within which history writing in the People's Republic of China has been confined since mid-century.[25]

[24] Ch'en Po-ta, Chou Yang, and Hu Ch'iao-mu first appeared in Mao's entourage during the early wartime period at Yenan.

[25] The following statements of Mao Tse-tung are useful in studying his views on history:

(1) "The Role of the Chinese Communist Party in the National War," section on "Study." Delivered at the sixth plenum of the sixth Central Committee of the Chinese Communist Party, October 1938.

(2) "The Chinese Revolution and the Chinese Communist Party." December 1939. Mao revised the first section, on Chinese society, in this report, and wrote the second section, on the Chinese revolution.

(3) "On New Democracy." January 1940.

(4) "On Coalition Government." Political report at the Seventh National Congress of the Chinese Communist Party, April 24, 1945.

(5) "How Yu Kung Moved the Mountains." Concluding speech, Seventh National Congress of the Chinese Communist Party, June 11, 1945.

(6) "On the People's Democratic Dictatorship." Essay to commemorate the 28th anniversary of the Chinese Communist Party, June 30, 1949.

(7) Editorials on the United States White Paper, *United States Relations with China*, issued by the Department of State on August 5, 1949. Written by Mao Tse-tung for the Hsinhua News Agency and published at Peking between August 14 and September 16, 1949.

English translations of these documents appear in *The Selected Works of Mao Tse-tung* (hereafter cited as *Selected Works*); the original Chinese texts may be found in *Mao Tse-tung Hsuan-chi* (hereafter cited as *Hsuan-chi*). The editions used are indicated below, with documents numbered as above:

English translations (London: Lawrence & Wishart):

(1) II (1954), pp. 258–261;
(2) III (1954), pp. 72–101;
(3) III, pp. 106–156;
(4) IV (1956), pp. 244–315;
(5) IV, pp. 316–318;
(6) IV (Peking: Foreign Languages Press, 1961), pp. 411–424;
(7) IV (Peking), pp. 425–459.

Chinese originals (Peking: Jen-min Ch'u-pan She):

(1) II (1952), pp. 521–523;
(2) II, pp. 615–650;
(3) II, pp. 655–704;
(4) III (1953), pp. 1029–1100;
(5) III, pp. 1101–1104;
(6) IV (1960), pp. 1473–1486;
(7) IV, pp. 1487–1520.

A useful selection of excerpts from Mao's writings dealing with history was compiled by the Honan branch of the China Historical Society and published in *Shih-hsueh yueh-k'an* (*Shixue Yuekan*). Entitled "Chairman Mao on Historiography," this selection appeared in two consecutive issues of *Shixue Yuekan*, No. 1 (January 1959), pp. 1–36, and No. 2 (February 1959), pp. 1–41. It is divided into five sections: principles of historiography, Chinese society and the Chinese revolution, historical events and historical personalities, war, and cultural problems.

Speaking at an important Communist Party meeting at Yenan, the Chinese Communist wartime capital, in late 1938, Mao set the problem which was to become a recurrent theme in official doctrine in later years.[26]

> Another task in our study is to study our historical legacy and to sum it up critically from the Marxist approach. . . . The China of today has developed from the China in history; as we are believers in the Marxist approach to history, we must not cut off our whole historical past. We must make a summing-up from Confucius down to Sun Yat-sen and inherit this precious legacy. This helps much in directing the great movement of today. Communists are internationalist-Marxists, but Marxism must be integrated with the specific characteristics of our country and given a national form before it can be put into practice. The great strength of Marxism-Leninism lies in its integration with the specific revolutionary practice of different countries. In the case of the Chinese Communist Party, it is a matter of learning to apply the theory of Marxism-Leninism in the specific circumstances of China.[27]

Slightly over a year later, in the winter of 1939–40, Mao elaborated his prescriptions in two significant statements. The first, " written jointly by Comrade Mao Tse-tung and several other comrades," was " The Chinese Revolution and the Chinese Communist Party " (December 1939); the second was Mao's essay " On New Democracy " (January 1940), in which he sketched the anatomy of the system which he projected for China's future.

" The Chinese Revolution and the Chinese Communist Party " opens with rhetoric which might have come from any primary school textbook:

> China is one of the largest countries in the world, with a territory almost as large as the whole of Europe. . . . From very ancient times our forefathers have laboured, lived and multiplied on this immense territory. . . . China is a country with a very large population composed of many nationalities.[28]

China, the gloss continues, is one of the oldest civilised countries, a land known for stamina, industriousness and " freedom-loving people with a rich revolutionary tradition." While Mao recognised the international context of the Chinese Communist movement, he nevertheless developed his thesis within the framework, not of world revolution, but of China's " glorious revolutionary tradition " and " splendid historical heritage."

The periodisation of Chinese history is marked out, with its development corresponding to the orthodox Stalinist pattern and with the stages corresponding to stages in the unfolding of the Chinese revolution. The

[26] The sixth (enlarged) plenum of the sixth Central Committee, late October–early November 1938.

[27] *Selected Works*, II, pp. 259–260.

[28] *Ibid.*, III, pp. 72-73.

historical course of China's development is viewed not only as a series of events, but also, more significantly, as a dialectical process obeying discoverable laws, similar to the laws of geology, in accordance with which a process of change takes place over long periods of time. First is a vague period, lasting some "tens of thousands of years," of primitive communism in prehistoric China. That remote era was devoid of revolutionary upheavals because it was free of classes and of class struggles. After the collapse of the primitive communes came a transition to class society, first to slave society and then to feudalism beginning with the Chou period (conventionally, 1027–256 B.C.).

The great corpus of traditional Chinese history is allotted to the so-called feudal period, defined as beginning with the Chou dynasty and lasting for "about 3,000 years" until the mid-nineteenth century. Despite its extent, diversity and impressive cultural and material achievements, this period is placed by official Maoist analysis in a common mould defined by the economic and social constraints of the feudal system. Under that system, characterised by economic exploitation and political oppression of the mass of the population by the ruling class headed by the emperor and the landlords, the peasants existed virtually as slaves in dire poverty and suffering. For Mao, the recurrent peasant rebellions over the centuries were notable indicators of the sufferings of the mass of the Chinese people in pre-modern times. His 1939 formulation, while certainly controversial, is nevertheless suggestive of a basic theme:

> The gigantic scale of . . . such peasant uprisings and peasant wars in Chinese history is without parallel in the world. These class struggles of the peasants—the peasant uprisings and peasant wars—alone formed the real motive force of historical development in China's feudal society.[29]

While some social progress was registered after each outburst, the nature of the economic and social system in traditional China block reform and prevented progress.[30]

With the impact of the Western powers and Japan beginning in the nineteenth century, Chinese history entered a new phase: that dominated

---

[29] *Ibid.*, III, p. 76.
[30] In the original (1939) text of "The Chinese Revolution and the Chinese Communist Party," Mao laid emphasis on the "stagnation" of Chinese society during the so-called feudal era. The later, bowdlerised version, which is now official, modified that position and inserted new sentences to state that China, as it developed a commodity economy, bore within itself the embryo of capitalism and would have turned into a capitalist society even if there had been no intrusion of outside imperialism. For full discussion of the point, see Albert Feuerwerker, "Chinese Modern Economic History in Communist Chinese Historiography," *The China Quarterly*, No. 22 (April–June 1965), p. 44.

by imperialism.[31] The worldwide expansion of capitalism, which Leninist definition terms imperialism, affected not only the colonial areas like Africa but also " semi-colonial " countries like China. The Leninist analysis, which arrived in the Far East at a formative period in the evolution of modern Chinese nationalism, naturally fell on receptive ears in China. All patriotic Chinese resented the fact that the Central Kingdom, despite its proud heritage, had become a passive target rather than a major actor in international affairs. Thus the official Maoist version of modern history states its case bluntly:

> The history of imperialist aggression upon China, of imperialist opposition to China's independence and to her development of capitalism, constitutes precisely the history of modern China.[32]

That history, in the Chinese Communist formulation, comprises a period of 110 years, beginning with the first Anglo-Chinese (or Opium) war which broke out in 1839, divided by the May Fourth Movement of 1919, and culminating in the establishment of the People's Republic of China in 1949. Viewed in its entirety, this was a period when feudal China, in the Maoist analysis, was reduced to the status of a semi-colonial, semi-feudal country through the military, political, economic and cultural intrusions of the imperialist great powers. Taking advantage of the fact that China was too weak and disorganised to defend its national interests, the foreign powers established a record that was—in Chinese eyes—as consistent as it was humiliating: the Opium war (1839–42), the Anglo-French war on China (1856–60), the Sino-French war (1884–85), the first Sino-Japanese war (1894–95), the invasion of the eight-power allied army of the time of the Boxer uprising (1900), the Russo-Japanese war in Manchuria (1904–05), the Japanese Twenty-one Demands (1915), the Japanese military invasion launched in Manchuria in September 1931 and expanded into general hostilities in July 1937, and the United States intervention on behalf of the Nationalists in the Chinese civil war (1946–49).

As the modern history of China is the record of the transformation of feudal China into a semi-colony through an alliance between external imperialism and domestic feudalism, so the modern Chinese revolution is a reaction to the dilemmas born of that extended crisis. During the period of about 80 years after the Opium war of 1840, the " national revolutionary struggle " of the Chinese people was essentially a political movement aimed at national reform and independence. Its landmarks were the Taiping rebellion (1851–64), the reform movement of 1898, the Boxer uprising of 1900, and the revolution of 1911. The Wuchang

---

[31] An official Chinese Communist summary is given by Hu Sheng, *Imperialism and Chinese Politics* (Peking: Foreign Languages Press, 1955).

[32] *Selected Works*, III, p. 123.

revolt of October 1911 which led to the fall of the imperial dynasty and to the formal establishment of a republican government in China is viewed by Mao as a military coup rather than as a revolution in the Marxist sense. It marked a fuller development of the old-style nationalist revolution but was still essentially bourgeois-democratic, not socialist, in social character.[33]

From the time of China's defeat in the Opium war of 1840 until the early twentieth century, many of China's progressive leaders looked toward the West for the key to national regeneration: Hung Hsiu-ch'uan (1814–64), leader of the Taiping rebellion, which the Chinese Communists label a "peasant revolutionary war"; K'ang Yu-wei (1858–1927), leader of the ill-fated reform movement of 1898 which attempted to bolster the imperial government in the face of growing pressure upon China from the outside world; and Yen Fu (1854–1921), the pioneer Chinese translator who made the first attempt to bring modern European concepts to the attention of the Chinese literati after the turn of the century.[34] Yet, while these and other Chinese of the same period " learned much from the West," they were unable to realise their reform programme because they had no truly effective method for dealing with the Western bourgeois states which were persistently engaged in imperialist aggression against China.[35]

Sun Yat-sen, the symbol if not the father of modern Chinese nationalism, is accorded a place of special honour in Mao Tse-tung's historiography. As a transitional figure, Sun is given high marks for his " clear-cut stand as a Chinese revolutionary democrat " during the period from 1894, when he organised the Hsing-chung-hui and began his anti-Manchu activities, until 1911, when the Ch'ing dynasty was finally overthrown. Sun's long career as a revolutionary leader, the socialist ideas expressed in his later writings, and his policies of alignment with the Soviet Union and the Chinese Communist Party are praised by the Chinese Communist historians. Mao Tse-tung and his associates regard themselves as heirs to the cause of democratic revolution to which Sun was committed.[36]

---

[33] *Ibid.*, III, p. 110.

[34] For a penetrating study of Yen Fu, see Benjamin Schwartz, *In Search of Wealth and Power: Yen Fu and the West* (Cambridge: Harvard Un. Press, 1964). Although it would be deceptive to suggest any causal relationship, it is noteworthy that two qualities which Yen Fu found at the heart of the modern Western ethos—sheer energy, and the public spirit which disciplines energy to socially constructive ends—are now, in a perverse way, the very qualities which some Western observers have found most dramatic in post-1949 China.

[35] *Selected Works*, IV (Peking), pp. 412–413.

[36] See Mao Tse-tung, " In Commemoration of Dr. Sun Yat-sen," *Dr. Sun Yat-sen: Commemorative Articles and Speeches* (Peking: Foreign Languages Press, 1957), p. 10. References to Sun Yat-sen and to his Three People's Principles are scattered throughout Mao's writings.

Yet, while Sun Yat-sen occupied an important place in China's modern century, he was capable of writing only the first chapter in its revolutionary history. Mao's version of that history stipulates, with imprecise dating, that a new phase in the modern Chinese revolution began in the years from about 1917 to 1921. "The salvoes of the October Revolution," Mao stated in 1949 with laudable simplicity but dubious precision, brought Marxism-Leninism to China and marked "a new historical era of the whole world." In China itself, official communist periodisation places the May Fourth Movement of 1919 as the principal line of demarcation running through China's "democratic revolutionary movement," dividing old from new, and preparing the way for fresh developments. The May Fourth Movement set the consciously anti-imperialist mood which became dominant in twentieth-century Chinese nationalism. And, Mao's argument concludes, the establishment of the Chinese Communist Party in 1921 provided an organised political group dedicated to the belief that it was the chosen instrument to lead China forward to a new period in its modern history.

Within the framework of conventional Leninist doctrine, Mao outlined a two-stage revolution, articulated in his statement, *On New Democracy*, in 1940 and reiterated in later wartime speeches and essays. Mao recognised that the pattern of anti-imperialist revolt in a technologically backward country like China made it both possible and desirable for the communists to gain the support of a portion of the bourgeoisie as a pragmatic principle of action. The Maoist strategy of revolution thus called for two stages, an interim period of New Democracy while the Communist Party was contending for national power, to be followed by a socialist-communist period, both under the control and leadership of the Communist Party. In effect, Mao's political strategy during the New Democracy stage prior to 1949 comprised a peasant-based, nationalist-infused, protracted struggle in the countryside, combined with a united front appeal to a broad coalition of urban classes.[37] The New Democracy formula, in short, called for the Communist Party to champion a united front composed of four social classes: peasants, workers, petty bourgeoisie and national bourgeoisie.

That formula governed Chinese Communist policy during the drive toward power in the late 1940s, and its concepts were embodied in the so-called people's democratic dictatorship proclaimed in 1949 when the communists established a new national government at Peking. A central theme in this strategy was that it was based upon the concept that Mao

---

[37] For a detailed analysis, see S. B. Thomas, *The Doctrine and Strategy of the Chinese Communist Party: Domestic Aspects, 1945-1958*, Ph.D. dissertation, Columbia University, 1964, chapters 1-4.

Tse-tung had successfully unified the general theory of Marxism-Leninism with the specific experience of modern Chinese history; that he had, in short, not only carried forward the design of the Russian revolution but also transmuted a set of concepts that were originally and essentially European into a practical framework for political action in Asia.[38]

MAO AND CONTEMPORARY HISTORY

With the completion of the New Democracy stage of the communist-led revolution, modern Chinese history, in Mao's formulation, merged with the history of the People's Republic of China as its leaders embarked upon the task of creating a new social order in China. The objective of the second stage of the revolutionary process was to extirpate all remnants of domestic reaction and to develop China along fully socialist lines. The distinctive pattern of Chinese communism which has emerged since 1949 has been shaped by two elements: first, by China's modern history and by the pre-1949 experiences and bases of power of its communist leaders, and, second, by the conviction that the experiences and aspirations of the communist revolution in China are also relevant to the newly emerging nations of the post-1945 world.

The importance of the non-Western nations in the pattern of contemporary world politics is generally recognised, though the long-range significance of these areas, and the policies to be pursued towards them, are still matters for debate in Western capitals. The role of Mao Tse-tung in contemporary history is based upon the fact that he is not only a successful communist revolutionary but also a major nationalist leader of the non-Western world. The Chinese Communists are well aware of the drastic changes in population distribution and political geography which have flowed from the dislocations of the Second World War, and their political analyses have revealed consistent preoccupation both with these changes and with the relationship of China to them. In 1945, the Chinese Communists portrayed the political concepts of Mao Tse-tung as a major new development of Marxism-Leninism especially pertinent to revolutions in the backward areas. Six years later, in July 1951 on the occasion of the anniversary of its founding, the Chinese Communist Party projected the Chinese revolution as a development of historic significance:

> The classic type of revolution in the imperialist countries is the October Revolution [of Russia]. The classic type of revolution in colonial and semi-colonial countries is the Chinese revolution.[39]

[38] See Donald S. Zagoria, " Some Comparisons between the Russian and Chinese Models," in A. Doak Barnett (ed.), *Communist Strategies in Asia* (New York: Praeger, 1963), pp. 11–33.

[39] See Lu Ting-yi, " The World Significance of the Chinese Revolution," July 1, 1951, reproduced in *Current Background* (Hong Kong: U.S. Consulate-General), No. 89,

Mao Tse-tung's views on contemporary history evade precise definition, since relatively few statements directly attributed to him have appeared since 1949. Because of Mao's unrivalled dominance of the Chinese Communist Party, however, his views are clearly implicit in Peking's major pronouncements of recent years which, though not directly credited to Mao, provide an accurate gauge of the views of the top command of the Chinese Communist Party.[40] As the communism of Mao Tse-tung is a unique phenomenon which may best be appreciated historically in relation to the chaos of China since the First World War, so it must be appraised today in relation to that erosion of Moscow's political and doctrinal authority which has been the most conspicuous feature of the international communist movement since the death of Stalin in 1953. Factors of national interest, ideology, politics and personalities have been intermeshed in the Sino-Soviet polemics which have grown to major proportions during the 1960s.[41] But the major element

July 5, 1951. The same theme is stressed in Ho Kan-chih, *A History of the Modern Chinese Revolution* (Peking: Foreign Languages Press, 1959), pp. 535-536:

> The victory of the Chinese people's revolution and the establishment of the People's Republic of China brought about a radical change in the history of China. It was the greatest event in world history since the October Socialist Revolution of 1917 and the victory of the anti-fascist war in 1945. The victory of the Chinese people's democratic revolution had a great world significance in that it extended and deepened the great influence exercised by the October Revolution upon all mankind.

[40] Peking's pronouncements affecting Western as well as Asian communism began with two major statements in 1956: *On the Historical Experience of the Dictatorship of the Proletariat* (April 5, 1956) and *More on the Historical Experience of the Dictatorship of the Proletariat* (December 29, 1956). Six years later, Peking fired another blast, *The Differences between Comrade Togliatti and Us* (December 31, 1962). Since the end of 1962, Peking's cogently argued summations of the long-range goals of the Chinese Communist leadership under Mao Tse-tung have appeared in a steady stream, highlighted by the massive open letter from the Central Committee of the Chinese Communist Party to the Central Committee of the Communist Party of the Soviet Union (June 14, 1963); the comments in *On Khrushchev's Phoney Communism and Its Historical Lessons for the World* (July 14, 1964); and the definitive projection of Mao Tse-tung's revolutionary strategy on a global basis by Lin Piao (September 3, 1965). Peking's major doctrinal statements of the past decade have usually been credited to the editorial departments of the *People's Daily* (*Jen-min Jih-pao*) and *Red Flag* (*Hung Ch'i*) and have been released simultaneously in Chinese and in English for world distribution.

[41] Western discussion of the Sino-Soviet dispute has grown rapidly in recent years, particularly with the development of the study of international communist affairs as a specialised academic sub-discipline in the United States. A recent summary is given by William E. Griffith, " Sino-Soviet Relations, 1964-1965," *The China Quarterly*, No. 25 (January–March, 1966). The following book-length studies published since 1960 are pertinent, although none has been written from the viewpoint of the Chinese Communist crater looking outwards: Brzezinski, Zbigniew K., *The Soviet Bloc: Unity and Conflict* (New York: Praeger, 2nd ed., 1961); Dallin, Alexander (ed.), *Diversity in International Communism: A Documentary Record, 1961-1963* (New York: Columbia Un. Press, 1963); Floyd, David, *Mao against Khrushchev: A Short History of the Sino-Soviet Conflict* (New York: Praeger, 1963); Griffith, William E., *The Sino-Soviet Rift* (Cambridge, Mass.: M.I.T. Press, 1964); Hudson, G. F., Richard Lowenthal, and Roderick MacFarquhar, *The Sino-Soviet Dispute* (New York: Praeger, 1961); Lacquer, Walter, and Leopold Labedz (eds.), *Polycentrism: the New Factor in International Communism* (New York: Praeger, 1962); London, Kurt (ed.), *Unity and Contradiction: Major Aspects of*

of long-range significance is that the leadership of the Chinese Communist Party, despite China's present relative inferiority in absolute power terms, has created an unprecedented situation in world politics by its defiant decrees proclaiming that Peking is now the most authoritative arbiter of policies and programmes for the international communist movement.[42]

Mao Tse-tung's statements on modern history before 1949 were largely limited to China and were primarily significant for their operational specificity. They involved the effort to show that China had evolved along lines similar to those followed by Western society and is therefore a partner in world civilisation; they were also imbued with a deep sense of the necessity of preserving selected elements in the Chinese cultural tradition to develop and sustain a sound sense of national identity and dignity in the modern period. Peking's pronouncements on contemporary history since 1950 have shown a similar ambivalence between specificity and universality. They have frequently emphasised the necessity for " nationalisation " of general communist theory to further the crusade for psychological emancipation from the West. At the same time they have been generated by a sense of moral fervour about the relevance of the Chinese Communist experience to the quest for modernity in the late-developing countries.

However he may be viewed in the West, Mao Tse-tung, while still alive, has already been hailed by Peking as a truly international figure, a sage ranked in direct line of apostolic succession to the classical theorists of communist-style revolution: Marx, Engels and Lenin. It was indeed significant that it was Mao's favourite military officer who was selected to articulate Peking's major 1965 statement proclaiming Mao Tse-tung to be the undisputed leader of the world revolution. That statement was made by Marshal Lin Piao, Minister of Defence and deputy chairman of the Central Committee of the Chinese Communist Party, on September 3, 1965, the date observed by Peking as the twentieth anniversary of the victory over Japan in the Second World War. Lin stated that Mao's military strategy, which holds that revolutionary bases

Sino-Soviet Relations (New York: Praeger, 1962); Lowenthal, Richard, *World Communism: the Disintegration of A Secular Faith* (London: Oxford Un. Press, 1964); Mehnert, Klaus, *Peking and Moscow* (New York: Putnam's, 1963); Zagoria, Donald S., *The Sino-Soviet Conflict, 1956-1961* (Princeton: Princeton Un. Press, 1962); Zagoria, Donald S. (ed.), " Communist China and the Soviet Bloc," *The Annals* of the American Academy of Political and Social Science, Vol. 349, September 1963.

Although not specifically concerned with the Sino-Soviet conflict, Bernard S. Morris, *International Communism and American Policy* (New York: Atherton Press, 1966), offers a perceptive analysis of the present state of the international communist movement.

[42] See Tsou Tang and Morton H. Halperin, " Mao Tse-tung's Revolutionary Strategy and Peking's International Behavior," *American Political Science Review*, LIX, No. 1 (March 1965), pp. 80–99.

must be established in rural areas so that cities can be encircled from the countryside, is " of outstanding and universal practical importance for present revolutionary struggles." The whole cause of world revolution depends on transferring Mao's strategy to the international arena: with the gradual extension of " revolutionary struggles " on the part of Asian, African and Latin American peoples, the urban areas of Western Europe and North America, despite their superior material and industrial strength, can gradually be encircled and overcome. *Quod erat demonstrandum.*

PARADOX AND PERSPECTIVE

An assessment of Mao Tse-tung's views on modern and contemporary history confronts an initial paradox: that one central element in the materialist conception of history to which Mao has long been wedded— the emphasis on objective social forces as determining elements in history—appears to be profoundly inconsistent with the main tendencies of Chinese Communist ideology as formulated under Mao's leadership. That ideology is powered not only by nationalism and populism but also by a spirit of revolutionary voluntarism, which holds that the ideas and the will of men are, in the end, more important than the development and relationship of the material forces of production. Mao's assumption of the mantle of Marx and Lenin as a prophet of the dialectics of history, like his surge to power in China before 1949, is based as much on will as on material power. These developments stem from the notion that new-born forces, though weak and inferior at the outset, will—given appropriate strategy, stamina, and determination—triumph over decaying forces that are superficially strong and appear to be strategically dominant. Human resolution, in short, can itself become an objective force in history, thereby resolving the apparent contradiction between determinism and voluntarism.

In casting Mao Tse-tung as historian, we do not imply that his views should be assessed by the criteria used in grading professional historians. We do, however, suggest that Mao Tse-tung, like other statesmen of the contemporary world, has a well-developed sense of history, a sense of historical-mindedness, a sense of active involvement with the process of history. Whatever his policies, the statesman must possess an instinct for the grand design, a feeling for the direction in which the world is moving and should be moving. This sense of history may be optimistic or pessimistic, voluntarist or determinist, plausible or absurd—but it must exist. Of the major leaders of the twentieth century, one may instance Lenin, Churchill, Roosevelt, Hitler, Nehru and de Gaulle as men possessed of this historic sense.[43]

[43] See Arthur Schlesinger, Jr., " The Historian and History," *Foreign Affairs*, XLI, No. 3 (April 1963), pp. 491-497.

Like these more familiar figures, Mao Tse-tung has also projected an historical vision, which in turn has reflected his political personality and his political creed. While Mao's analyses of Chinese society and directives for its rejuvenation are couched in the jargon of the class struggle required by communist doctrine, his deepest emotional commitment has always been to China and to its people. From 1919 to 1949, Mao's nationalist impulse was notably consistent. The Chinese people, the argument ran, have long been oppressed. Only armed struggle can end this suffering. Only when communism cleanses China of the nefarious influences of domestic reactionaries and foreign imperialists will China have a revolution worthy of the name. Only with the establishment of a people's government will the men of Han again have the opportunity to release their vigour and versatility.[44] Since 1949 Mao Tse-tung has added a new wing to his structure by representing the leadership of the Chinese Communist Party as the most effective, consistent and responsible spokesman for all deprived peoples of the non-Western world. Only when the militarism and neo-imperialism of the United States are overthrown, the argument runs, will the people of Asia, Africa and Latin America be able to break the deadlock which for centuries has spelled only stagnation, frustration and exploitation for them.

Based as they are on premises which often appear to have little direct relation to historical fact, the views of Mao Tse-tung are not guaranteed to win standing applause from disciples of Liu Chih-chi, Ranke or Nagel.[45] Mao's essentially moral and teleological view of history is nevertheless significant for reasons that are often ignored by conventional Western historians concerned with the critical use of evidence or with the recording of historical data to reconstruct the past *wie es eigentlich gewesen*. Mao Tse-tung's unconventional history is significant, not for historical, but for political and psychological reasons, for what it reveals of the ethos of twentieth-century China and of the animus of a major Asian revolutionary movement spawned by the Russian revolution but radically different from it, fed by the frustrations of semi-colonial status, and nurtured by the Second World War.[46]

Mao Tse-tung's statements on history are clearly not reflections based on professional research. They are political acts through which Mao attempts to shape the present and to provide a blueprint for the future.

[44] See Schram, note 6 above, pp. 103 *et seq.*

[45] Liu Chih-chi (661-721) is the author of the *Shih-t'ung (Generalities on History*, completed in 710), the first formal treatise on historical methodology in China. For Ernest Nagel's views, see his chapter, " Problems in the Logic of Historical Inquiry," *The Structure of Science* (New York : Harcourt, Brace, and World, 1961), pp. 547-606.

[46] See the comments on ideology and history in Communist China by John K. Fairbank, *The United States and China* (Cambridge: Harvard Un. Press, 2nd ed., 1958), pp. 303-306.

The materialist conception of history is above all a dynamic theory which holds that correct understanding of the general laws of historical development is necessary not only to provide insights into present reality but also, and more significantly, to shape the future. Mao's statements on history are designed, in effect, to guide the actions of men and to inspire them to create a fresh future. Both as Chinese and as Chinese Communist, Mao is essentially concerned with history and revolution as process, not as event; his basic concern is with the direction in which China and the world are moving, not with immediate crises or catastrophes.

Like the Chinese Communist Party and the People's Republic of China, Mao Tse-tung is a home-grown product of Chinese soil enriched with some Western vitamins. Since the Boxer catastrophe, the central issue confronting Chinese political and intellectual leaders has been the problem of how best to meet the challenge of the modern world without completely jettisoning the traditional Chinese way of life. Viewed in this context, Chinese communism may legitimately be assessed as a reaction to basic social and economic pressures within China and to major pressures on China from the outside world. At the same time, the nature and direction of this reaction have been shaped by the fact that China's specific dilemmas have been part of the general international process of change conventionally labelled modernisation. Long before Mao Tse-tung arrived at a position where his views on history were relevant on a national basis, the forces of positivism, pragmatism and materialism which have accompanied the spread of modernisation had already struck China.[47] These forces, as well as Li Ta-chao, the Communist Manifesto and the Soviet declaration of 1919, helped to lead Mao to accept Marxism as a valid science of society, Leninism as an effective method for achieving social revolution and dialectical materialism as a modern philosophy of life.

Assessed in the light of Chinese tradition, the discontinuities inherent in Mao Tse-tung's view of history are manifest. Acceptance of the theory of the class struggle as the dynamic factor in human history marked an immense break with conventional Chinese historiography and with traditional Confucian emphasis on social harmony.[48] The messianic

[47] The point is made, for example, in Wm. Theodore de Bary et al., note 12 above, pp. 858-861.

[48] E. G. Pulleyblank has discussed Chinese historical writing in Beasley and Pulleyblank, op. cit. (note 12 above), pp. 1-9, and the historiographical tradition in Raymond Dawson (ed.), The Legacy of China (Oxford: Clarendon Press, 1964), pp. 143-164. Other dimensions of the topic are discussed by Charles S. Gardner in Traditional Chinese Historiography (Cambridge: Harvard Un. Press, 1938; second edition with additions and corrections by L. S. Yang, 1961) and by Arthur F. Wright, "The Study of Chinese Civilization," Journal of the History of Ideas, XXI (1960), pp. 233-255, and "On the Uses of Generalization in the Study of

view of history, which places the ideal society in the future, likewise marked a fundamental change from the cyclical conception and backward-looking focus of traditional Chinese history-writing.

Mao's emphasis on the mobilisation of peasant discontent to spark political change was significantly different from the conceptions held by traditional Chinese historians, and indeed by classical European Marxist theorists. The peasant wars and rebellions of the past may have been the principal motive force of historical development in dynastic China. But since those abortive past revolts showed no way out of China's impasse, they are merely worthy of note in confirming the existence of a revolutionary traditon, not worthy of emulation. Only with decisive political leadership based on the new ideology of Marxism-Leninism and on the new organisation of the Communist Party is it possible to gain victory over the economic and social forces which traditionally held the Chinese peasant in bondage and the Chinese nation in backwardness. In the realm of contemporary history, Mao's projection of China as a model on a world scale, not simply as a major cultural force in East Asia, marks a new and significant dimension in the history both of China and of international communism.

Assessed in the light of Chinese tradition, however, some significant continuities are also apparent in Mao's view of history and in the distinctive pattern of Chinese communism which has evolved since 1949.[49] One conspicuous link with the past is the alliance between history-writing and policy-making, an alliance which has been labelled " characteristically Chinese." In addition to recording data, the historians of traditional China were in effect constructing a body of precedents to guide future generations of bureaucrats in accordance with normative ethical standards. Ultimately, history was regarded, not as a composite portrait of an age, but rather as a mirror of political behaviour.

Mao Tse-tung and his disciples are still devoted to the concept of history as a mirror to guide current policies. In addition to appraising past and present within the framework of what conventional Marxism labels the objective laws of history, the guardians of social morality in

Chinese History," in Louis Gottschalk (ed.), *Generalization in the Writing of History* (Chicago: Un. of Chicago Press, 1963), pp. 36–58. See also John Meskill (ed.), *The Pattern of Chinese History: Cycles, Development, or Stagnation?* (Boston: D. C. Heath, Problems in Asian Civilisation Series, 1965).

49 For general discussion of the problem, see the trilogy by Joseph R. Levenson, *Confucian China and Its Modern Fate*, especially III, *The Problem of Historical Significance* (Berkeley: Un. of California Press, 1965). See also Levenson's review article, " Ideas of China," *The Times Literary Supplement*, July 28, 1966, p. 691. Other views are offered by Frederick W. Mote, " The Communist Chinese Puzzle," *University, A Princeton Magazine*, No. 19 (Winter 1963–64), pp. 14–20; Wolfgang Franke, " The Role of Tradition in Present-Day China," *Modern World*, III, 1963–64, edited by Dr. Walter Hildebrandt, Vlotho/Weser, West Germany, pp. 75–92; and Franklin W. Houn, " The Communist Monolith versus the Chinese Tradition," *Orbis*, VIII, No. 4 (Winter 1965), pp. 894–921.

contemporary China utilise historiography as a tool to promote approved ideas and attitudes, a pattern shown in the political demise in Peking of the prominent historian of the Ming period, Wu Han.

Although the dictates of contemporary orthodoxy in the People's Republic are always strong and frequently overwhelming, elements of the Chinese political tradition have survived in the communist system. Notable among these elements are: the attitude of superiority towards peoples not of Chinese culture, the concept of political unity on a cultural basis, the key role played by military power in the system, the dominant position held by a single leader at the top, and the pattern of bureaucratic autocracy which has persisted for centuries in China. The convulsive developments of 1966 upset many easy assumptions previously held by observers with respect to communist attitudes towards China's classical heritage without, however, providing a clear baseline from which to estimate future trends. In the short run, the officially-sponsored actions of youthful Red Guards throughout China do attack and desecrate the Chinese past, though the primary targets of these actions have been traditional attitudes and apathetic institutions, notably peasant social habits in the countryside and bureaucratic slackness and inefficiency on the part of government, educational and Communist Party officials. In the long run, however, the deep-seated instincts of cultural pride and modern nationalism symbolised by Mao Tse-tung will probably dictate a more pragmatic and selective communist attitude directed to upholding the distinctiveness of the Chinese heritage even within the constraints of the " great socialist cultural revolution." [50]

CONCLUSIONS

As political leader, Mao Tse-tung may in a sense be viewed as a latter-day representative of the self-strengthening movement that began in China after the mid-nineteenth century and gained new form and impetus following China's ignominious defeat in the first Sino-Japanese war of 1894–95.[51] K'ang Yu-wei, Liang Ch'i-ch'ao, Sun Yat-sen and

[50] Variant interpretations of the contemporary Chinese political puzzle are given by A. Doak Barnett, *China After Mao* (Princeton: Princeton Un. Press, 1967); Howard L. Boorman, " Sources of Chinese Communist Conduct," *The Virginia Quarterly Review*, XLII, No. 4 (Autumn 1966), pp. 512–526; Cheng Chu-yuan, " Power Struggle in Red China," *Asian Survey*, VI, No. 9 (September 1966), pp. 469–483; John Wilson Lewis, *Communist China: Crisis and Change* (New York: Foreign Policy Association, Headline Series, No. 179, October 1966); Roderick MacFarquhar, " Mao's Last Revolution," *Foreign Affairs*, XLV, No. 1 (October 1966), pp. 112–124; and Franz Schurmann, " What Is Happening in China?" *The New York Review of Books*, XX (October 1966), pp. 18–25.

[51] This view has been suggested by Jerome Ch'ên, note 6 above, pp. 7–8. See also Benjamin Schwartz, " Modernization and the Maoist Vision: Some Reflections on Chinese Communist Goals," *The China Quarterly*, No. 21 (January–March 1965), pp. 3–19.

Chiang Kai-shek—like Mao himself—have all been preoccupied with the same central theme: modern China's patent lack of " wealth and power." K'ang Yu-wei and Liang Ch'i-ch'ao accorded priority to administrative and educational reform, aiming at the transformation of China's autocracy into a constitutional monarchy. Sun Yat-sen and Chiang Kai-shek sought to harness the power of nationalism and to develop a republican form of government which would at the same time conform to Confucian tradition. Mao Tse-tung has also sought an effective and responsible government, a strong and self-reliant China capable of assuming an international position commensurate with China's heritage and history. Always a Chinese patriot, Mao has worn a different uniform from his predecessors but has been no less committed to the vision of a unified Chinese nation administered for Chinese benefit.

Unlike Stalin, who inherited an operating régime from Lenin, Mao Tse-tung himself was the principal creator of the political-military machine which gained national power in China at mid-century. Like Stalin, he was primarily responsible for the policies which, despite blunders and setbacks, have nevertheless led to substantial expansion of national power in China and to notable growth in China's international prestige and influence.

In carrying out his self-assigned tasks, Mao has relied both on Chinese pragmatism and on communist doctrine, adjusting Marxist-Leninist formulae to a technologically primitive environment in which the overwhelming bulk of the population and the Communist Party is peasant. Mao and the Communist Party which he leads have committed themselves to a herculean effort to wrench Chinese society out of tradition-bound inertia and to thrust it forward into the age of industry and science. The success of that venture is still uncertain; the gap between reality and aspiration is still wide. But Mao's view of history is essentially modern in its estimate that man's social environment can be altered through conscious action; and he has long acted on the assumption that the effectiveness of one's resources should be rated according to their maximum potential for growth, not their current earnings.

A prominent student of modern history and international politics has pointed out that the great revolutions of the modern age, from the French revolution of 1789 to the Chinese upheaval in this century, have been carried forward by men " dismayed, not only at being governed badly, but also and more importantly, at not being governed enough. These revolutions owed their success to the determination and ability of their leaders to seize power, to hold it, and to use it to govern, badly, perhaps, but firmly." [52] The observation is relevant to this inquiry into Mao Tse-tung's views on history and politics. The task of sinicising and implementing Marxism-Leninism in China could only have been directed by a Chinese intellectual of peasant background.[53] That task could only have been led by a man who combined bold historical vision with a grasp of military realities and a sense of the outer limits of political practicality. Mao Tse-tung's legacy derives from the fact that, through decisive political and military leadership, he has transmuted his vision of " history " into a crucial element in contemporary history.

What, then, will the independent Western historian find in the writings of Mao Tse-tung? Clearly, he will discover nothing comparable to Trotsky's classic autobiography or to his *History of the Russian Revolution*.[54] But he will find, notably in Mao's detailed reports and directives of the pre-1949 period, an important record of the moves of an Asian revolutionary party on its way to national power. Better than any outside historian, Mao Tse-tung himself has left an account, unparalleled in Chinese historical literature, of the strategy and tactics of revolution.

---

[52] See Hans J. Morgenthau, *The Purpose of American Politics* (New York: Vintage Books, 1964), pp. 318-319.

[53] See Stuart R. Schram, " Chinese and Leninist Components in the Personality of Mao Tse-tung," *Asian Survey*, III, No. 6 (June 1963), pp. 259-273.

[54] See Bertram D. Wolfe, " Leon Trotsky as Historian," *Slavic Review*, XX, No. 3 (October 1961), pp. 495-502.

16

Some Questions of Historical Science in the Chinese People's Republic *

By R. V. VYATKIN and
S. L. TIKHVINSKY

IN recent years some mistaken tendencies have appeared in the sphere of historical science in the Chinese People's Republic, which are closely connected with the generally incorrect political course of the leadership of the Communist Party of China, a departure from the agreed line of the international Communist movement. In this connection it is necessary to examine critically the state of affairs on the front of historical science in the Chinese People's Republic, to appraise its development objectively and point out the principal erroneous tendencies.

It is clear that all these questions cannot be dealt with fully within the scope of a single article. This is impossible in the first place because historical science is a many-faceted phenomenon, which includes a large number of branches, auxiliary disciplines and extensive problems in the most diverse epochs. Besides, it takes a long time for various concepts to be reflected in major research works or monographs. In this particular case the presence of some new views and tendencies can only be judged by isolated articles and public pronouncements. Finally, the presentation of a sufficiently complete picture of the development of Chinese historiography has of late been interfered with by certain fairly substantial concomitant circumstances that have arisen through the fault of the Chinese side: a sharp reduction in the number of scholarly works of the C.P.R. sent to the Soviet Union, the almost complete cessation in forwarding local publications and learned university notes, and the weakening of scholarly contacts of Chinese historians with Soviet scholars.

Historical science occupies an important position in the general system of the humanities of the Chinese People's Republic. For it, as for other spheres of science, the victory of the Socialist revolution opened wide horizons. During the first decade of the existence of the Chinese People's Republic, historical science undoubtedly made great progress. This was manifested not only in the growth of the number of institutions and

* Translation from the *Current Digest of the Soviet Press*, published weekly at Columbia University by the Joint Committee on Slavic Studies appointed by the American Council of Learned Societies and the Social Science Research Council. Copyright 1964, the Joint Committee on Slavic Studies. Reprinted by permission.

establishments concerned with history and the publication of hundreds of books with the most varied contents, but also in the fact that the majority of Chinese historians accepted the proposition of historical materialism as the basis of their scientific work. This was, therefore, qualitatively a new stage in the development of Chinese historical science, a stage of intensifying and developing Marxist-Leninist historiography, the foundations of which were laid by individual Chinese Marxist historians in the 1920s and 1930s.

The principal trends pursued by Chinese historians in their research since 1949 have been the following: in the sphere of ancient history—the study of the most ancient periods in the history of Chinese civilisation on the basis of new archaeological data, the social-economic and political history of the earliest class-societies (Yin, Chou), the problems of the periodisation of ancient society; in medieval history—the problems of the feudal land tenure, the history of the peasant wars, the history of nationalities; in modern history—the greatest risings of the Chinese People against their oppressors (the Taiping and Boxer movements, the 1911 revolution), the history of imperialist aggression against China; in the sphere of most recent history—the history of the Chinese Communist Party, the history of the wars of national liberation. The permeating theme was the history of the ideas and philosophic thought of China. In many of the areas mentioned important works and research papers which have enriched our knowledge of different periods of Chinese history can be cited. Of all these works the Soviet scholarly world is well informed. Many of them have been translated into Russian or reviewed in Soviet periodicals.

In speaking of the progress of historical science in the Chinese People's Republic, in comparison with the position in the old, semi-colonial Kuomintang China, one should bear in mind the extremely low general level of scientific development from which it had to start and the objective difficulties that stood in its way. Professor Liu Ta-nien, the deputy director of the Institute of Modern History, said in his address at the 1962 conference of Pakistani historians, "Naturally the achievements of historical science in the new China cannot yet satisfy us. Some research work has only begun, or only the foundations have been laid. Research on several important questions still awaits further probing."[1]

At present a considerable proportion of the best qualified Chinese historians are scholars who obtained their training in the old China or in the capitalist countries. It is no accident, therefore, that many of

[1] *Li-shih Yen-chiu (Historical Research)* No. 2, 1962, p. 5.

their works retain influence of the traditions of the old school, with a purely dynastic approach to history and with the emphasis only on the philological analysis of and commentary on ancient texts, or else are marked by another extreme position—excessive sociologising and schematic treatment, without the necessary historical comparisons and conclusions. A number of works show insufficient familiarity on the part of Chinese scholars with the best achievements of world-wide historical science. Young historians who were educated after the victory of the revolution were not always given the necessary guidance and assistance in their research work. All these and other weaknesses and difficulties, however, were overcome gradually in the process of growth of the youthful historical science of the new China. In the period between 1949–1958 the training of historical cadres expanded, collective forms of work were enlarged, the political education of scholarly workers was carried on, numerous works of Soviet scholars and progressive historians of other countries were translated into Chinese, thus exerting a direct influence on the mastering of Marxist-Leninist methodology.

Soviet scholars have always carefully followed the development of progressive historical science in China and welcomed its successes in a fraternal way. After the victory of the people's revolution, Soviet historians and archaeologists who visited the Chinese People's Republic assisted in the establishment of science in the new China. In the USSR a number of important works by Kuo Mo-jo, Fan Wen-lan, Ch'en Po-ta, Hu Sheng, Hua Kang, Shang Yüeh and other historians, as well as collections of documents, bibliographies, were published in Russian translations. The Basic Social Science Library of the USSR Academy of Sciences regularly issues a reference work, *Contemporary Chinese Literature in the Social Sciences*. The journals, *Questions of History, Journal of Ancient History, The Peoples of Asia and Africa*, and other periodicals contain articles on the history of China and reviews of new Chinese publications. The researches of Soviet historians, and above all the works of Sinologists, make wide use of the original works of Chinese scholars and provide historiographic surveys, reflecting the state of studies of one problem or another.

However, facts indicate that the situation that has arisen in the Chinese People's Republic during the past four or five years has retarded the process of growth of historical science in China. It was unavoidable, of course, that a certain part in this respect should have been played by the economic difficulties which demanded great additional effort from the intelligentsia, diverting its powers from scholarly work. But a more serious repercussion on the state of affairs on the historical front in the Chinese People's Republic was exerted by the political atmosphere which pervaded the scientific institutions during these years. Nothing else can explain the substantial decrease in the number of completed research projects, the failure to meet plans for issuing them and other developments in 1959–1962—528 books on history were published in 1959, 260 in 1960, and about 150 in 1962. The publication of many periodicals was suspended, the publication of the collective comprehensive work *A General History of China*, edited by Kuo Mo-jo, which had been planned for the tenth anniversary of the Republic, was not carried out, and so on. The state of historical science, one of the important sectors on the ideological front, has been noticeably affected by the generally erroneous line pursued by the leaders of the Chinese People's Republic in recent years, by the prevailing atmosphere of hostile attacks against the world Communist and workers movement, against the Communist Party of the Soviet Union, and against the Soviet Union itself. These processes are reflected in historical publications either in the form of open attacks on the theses of the Programme of the Communist Party of the Soviet Union, or in the form of individual distortions and misrepresentations with the introduction of dogmatic, anti-Marxist and openly nationalistic and racist views. Even any mention of the achievements of Soviet science is gradually disappearing from the pages of historical journals (for example, this year the news-notes section, which reported major works by foreign, and in particular Soviet, historians, has disappeared from the prominent historical journal *Li-shih Yen-chiu*). What such policy and practice lead to in the concrete sphere of historical studies is best understood by examining how this or that problem is treated by the historians in the Chinese People's Republic. Out of the great sum total of questions, we have selected only the problems of expounding world history in the Chinese People's Republic, the correlation of the general and specific in the historical process; the part played by the Mongolian and Manchurian conquests in the history of China; problems of international relations; questions of the modern history of China and their connection to the national struggle for liberty of the nations of the world.

Acquaintance with world history is a comparatively recent phenomenon for China. The prolonged artificial isolation of the country by its feudal rulers during the later Middle Ages retarded the study of world culture and history. The transformation of China into a semi-colony of the capitalist powers in the 19th and 20th centuries, though it put an end to isolation, led to the penetration of the country by the bourgeois scholarship of the colonial powers, which was carrying out its duty of defending colonialism; the first historiographers of the modern period, K'ang Yu-wei, Liang Ch'i-ch'ao, Yen Fu, and others, followed in its footsteps. With the spread of Marxist-Leninist ideas in China after the Great October Socialist Revolution, the situation began to change slowly, but even the appearance of the first Marxist-Leninist works, mostly in translation, could not significantly alter the general picture.

After 1949 definite work was carried out in this sphere; text-books of world history were produced, books by foreign Marxist historians were translated (in particular 100 books by Soviet historians), the range of research topics in the history of foreign countries was broadened. At the same time it cannot be overlooked that the majority of works by Chinese historians are still, as before, restricted to the history of their own country and to Chinese sources and literature. The appeal of Professor Chien Po-tsan that "One must see both China and the whole world"[2] cannot be regarded as having been answered.

This is confirmed by the contents of the journal *Li-shih Yen-chiu*. During the last four years, out of a large number of scientific articles (about 250) in its issues, hardly more than 10 were devoted to questions of world history (we do not count articles dealing with the history of the relations of foreign countries with China, translated articles or news on foreign science).

But even in such a quantitatively small list of works and pronouncements on problems of world history some Chinese scholars have erroneous theses and views which remain uncriticised and uncondemned.

Let us take, for example, the pronouncements of Professor Chou Ku-ch'eng, of Futan University, the leader of the historians of Shanghai. He is the author of several articles: "Universal History Without the Principle of Universality", "The Conditions in which World History Developed", "Develop the Spirit of Studying Foreign States that was inherent in the Historians of our Country",[3] and others. In these articles the author argues against the Europocentric concepts of bourgeois world history and is in favour of studying the history of all states and peoples, and in this he should be fully supported. However, his assertions that "up to the present all text-books of world history, both progressive and non-progressive, have been Europocentric" and that "the time has come to reject Europocentric world history and to create a new system of world history . . ."[4] sound strange, to say the least, to us Soviet his-

---

2 *Kuang-ming Jih-pao*, December 22, 1961.
3 The articles were published successively in the newspaper *Kuang-ming Jih-pao*, February 7, 1961; in the journals *Li-shih Yen-chiu*, No. 2, 1961, and *Hsin Chien-she (New Construction)*, No. 8, 1962.
4 *Kuang-ming Jih-pao*, February 7, 1961.

torians. For the author, in his struggle against "Europocentrism", nihilistically denies the achievements of Marxist-Leninist historiography, above all the works of Soviet historians, who have done much to unmask the Europocentric dogmas of bourgeois historiography and have produced not a few works that consistently apply the Marxist-Leninist principles to the writing of world history. But Chou Ku-ch'eng pretended that no such works existed in the world. And yet, only little more than a year before, in reviewing the publication of *World History* in the USSR, the newspaper *Jen-min Jih-pao* had written: "The scope of its presentation of world history is exceptionally wide. The history of the countries of Asia, Africa, and the history of the original inhabitants of America and Australia have been restored to their proper place." And emphasised in conclusion: "The successive publication, volume by volume, of the Chinese translation of this *World History* will be an enormous contribution to our study of world history, to the study of Marxist-Leninist theory".[5] It should also be noted how Chou Ku-ch'eng, a specialist in world history, presents the development of the world-historical process. In his scheme attention is focused on cultural influences and interreactions, i.e., aspects that are central to many concepts of the bourgeois historiography, with the difference that Chou Ku-ch'eng emphasises everywhere the special, exceptional role of Eastern culture in the history of mankind. In this sense he is not original, for ever since the time of the rebellion of Meiji, bourgeois Japanese historians have been putting forward theories of "Great East Asia", which were later used by the ideologists of Japanese militarism; we know of theories of "Americano-Europocentrism" proclaimed to the present day by the supporters of the so-called Atlantic community; there are well-known bourgeois theories according to which the Mediterranean zone is the sole centre of world civilisation—"theories" later adopted by Mussolini; and finally, the racist theories of the Fascist Reich also claimed the exceptional role of Germanic tribes in the history of the world. Chou Ku-ch'eng ignores the social-economic factors in the historical process and scorns the universal laws of historical development. Thus the basic principle of the progressive movement of world history as a succession of socio-economic forms is doomed to oblivion.

In referring to the history of the ancient world, the Chinese author persistently underlines the special importance and *Kulturträger* (culture-upholding) character of the wars between the ancient kingdoms. Therefore, in his opinion, the Graeco-Persian wars are significant because they facilitated the spread of Eastern culture to the West, and the campaigns

---

[5] *Jen-min Jih-pao*, November 21, 1959, p. 7.

of Alexander the Great, because they brought Western culture to the East. According to the views of Chou Ku-ch'eng the most important facts in the development of the world in the first fifteen centuries of our era were: the great migrations of peoples that were taking place everywhere; the growing influence of religion among the migrating peoples, and the consolidation of the feudal system as a result of the spread of religion.[6]

In trying to minimise the importance of the contribution of the European peoples to the treasury of world culture of the Middle Ages, Chou Ku-ch'eng compares the flourishing condition of the Arabian Caliphate in the 7th–13th centuries, the culture and sovereignty of the other countries of the East, to the "darkness in Europe". Undoubtedly, the countries of the East made an enormous contribution to the treasury of medieval culture, but why adopt a nihilistic attitude to the history of the already highly enough developed feudal states of Europe (France, England, Germany, Italy, Spain, Kiev Russia, etc.) after the 10th century?

Then the author goes on to explain the reason for the transition of human society to modern times. Here, too, Chou Ku-ch'eng again confines himself to external factors: "Through the Crusaders' campaigns in the East, European traders became aware of the extensive lands and wealth in the East. After this the cutting of communications by land between East and West forced them to go to the East by sea; as a result of the necessity for sailing eastwards many new lands were discovered, which created the initial movement in the transition of world history from the Middle Ages to Modern Times". And again no mention of the rise in European countries of new productive relations, lying at the root of trade and other expansion; a purely idealistic interpretation of the greatest turning-point in the history of mankind.

In a distorted light the author describes the early feudal Mongol Empire, expressing his delight in its military successes. Having recounted the Mongol campaigns in detail and having noted that the Mongols had reached the Mediterranean, he exclaims: "This was a tremendous power, it shook all Europe!" And again the author brings forth the conception of the *Kulturträger* role of campaigns and conquests: "During the flowering of the (Mongol) empire culture developed considerably. . . . Under the rule of the Mongols, scholars from various states to the east and west of the Pamirs had great opportunities of studying Chinese philosophy, literature and art".[7] (Apparently from the ashes of towns

[6] *Li-shih Yen-chiu*, No. 2, 1961, p. 85.
[7] *Ibid.*, p. 88.

and villages destroyed by the Mongols.) Chou Ku-ch'eng uttered not a word of the misery the Mongols' conquests inflicted on the world. And not by accident. For in a subsequent passage the author arrives at still more anti-scientific theses, converting the phenomena of world history and the history of the struggles of states and nations to the plane of purely racial conflict.

In describing the period of the beginning of modern history, Chou Ku-ch'eng declares: "In connection with the successes in the overseas ventures, the European countries assumed the position of leadership previously held by the yellow race of Asia, and since that time an enormous change has occurred in the development of world history." And later: "The leading position of the peoples of the yellow race of Asia was firmly seized by the peoples of the white race from Europe, and therefore the capitalist mode of production developed earlier in Europe than in other parts of the world".[8] This is also mentioned in the author's article in the newspaper, *Kuang-ming Jih-pao*, referred to above.

Thus the Marxist-Leninist principle of historical analysis was replaced by a racial principle. The dethroned "Europocentrism" has been replaced, for the first fifteen centuries at least, by an entirely undisguised "Asiacentrism". It is perplexing that these statements of Chou Ku-ch'eng, published two years ago in the leading historical journal and in the pages of a national newspaper, were not subjected to analysis and criticism by Chinese historians. This can point only to one thing: his ideas receive the obvious sympathy of the editor of the journal and of those who guide its activities.

Closely connected to the foregoing theory of the general course of world history we find the question of China's place in the world-wide historical process, of the correlation between the periodisation of world-historical development and the stages of development of Chinese society, i.e., methodologically the question of the correlation of the general and the particular applied to the history of the Chinese people. These questions were solved long ago by Marxist-Leninist science on both the theoretical and practical planes in connection with treating the history of most of the countries of the world. This is seen clearly enough in the example of the Soviet *World History* which, with enormous and varied material, demonstrated the unity of the world-historical process and pointed out how the general laws of the development of human society operate despite the great variety of their manifestation in specific, individual cases. We used to find a recognition of these truths in Chinese works.

[8] *Ibid.*, pp. 89–90.

However, in speaking of the dialectical unity of the general and the specific, many Chinese authors now incline so much towards the specific that it leads essentially to a slurring over of the general and an argument for the specific. In the opinion of Li Shu, the radical direction of the development of historical science in China "consists of explaining the general laws of development of human society on the basis of the history of China, and in particular the reflection of these laws in the history of China".[9] If all the problems of historical science are to be confined within the scope of the history of China and at the same time a struggle against "Europocentrism" is proclaimed, the whole history of mankind will be concentrated automatically in one corner of Asia and will be separated from the history of other nations, and its processes will seem to be the most important and "classical" ones. We already know examples of this. The Shanghai historian Li Ya-nung wrote: "The slave-owning system of ancient China was vast in scope, far surpassing that of ancient Greece. If the slave-owning order of Greece was classic, then the slave-owning system of China appears all the more 'classic' ".[10] Teng T'o echoes him: "Actually the slave-owning system in China was also classic in a way, classic in a Chinese way. Classicism can find expression in various forms and patterns. It should be said that the slave-owning order of China was even very classic, and it is certainly not possible to consider only the Grecian and Roman slave-owning systems as classic".[11]

In the same way, Chinese feudalism is also declared to be classic. The historian Wu T'ing-ch'iu wrote:

> . . . China was the first state in the world that entered feudal society, having entered it 800–900 years earlier than the European states, or, if West-Chou society is considered feudal, 1600–1700 years earlier (at that time ancient Greece and Rome had not yet entered class society). The feudal society of China constitutes an excellent classical model in world history; in the new system of world history the feudal society of Europe cannot be regarded as the model. At that time, in the feudal era as a whole, the economy and culture of such Eastern countries as China, India, the Arab empire, were far ahead of Europe, and the invasions of the West by the Huns, Turks, Arabs, and Mongols exerted an influence on the whole course of world history . . .[12]

Facts now known to science show that slave-owning relations were not greatly developed in China as a whole, although in the Ch'in and

9 *Jen-min Jih-pao*, July 8, 1961, p. 7.
10 Li Ya-nung, *Western and Eastern Chou* (Shanghai, 1956 [in Chinese]), p. 106.
11 *Li-shih Yen-chiu*, No. 1, 1961, p. 7.
12 *Kuang-ming Jih-pao*, April 10, 1961, p. 2.

Han empires the number of slaves was considerable. It is not a matter of numbers (which Li Ya-nung probably had in mind) that is important when comparing little Greece with big China. It is the essence of the phenomenon that matters, the degree of development of slave-holding relations. And therefore there is reason to call slave-ownership in Greece and Rome classic without downgrading Chinese history and prestige. The numerous articles of Chinese historians on the characteristics of Chinese feudalism speak for themselves in undermining the idea of its classicism. At present, Chinese scholars are carefully summing up all the distinctive aspects, the special features, of the history of China in order to emphasise again and again, not the general, but the particular; it is as though they were striving to secede from, rather than to unite with, the general current of human history. Again, Li Shu sees a difference in the history of China and the history of other, mainly European, countries in that

> China, for instance, did not suffer such a huge disaster as the fall of the Roman empire; in China there was no religious inquisition, therefore, there could be no Renaissance either; literature in Europe has had a real development only in the era of capitalism, whereas literature in China flourished in most periods of feudal society; the peasant wars in Europe erupted primarily in the period of the decay of feudalism and were as a rule notable for their small scale, while the peasant wars in China occurred even at an early stage of feudalism and in such proportions as were unknown to other states; China had Confucius, whose ideas were influential for more than 2,000 years and played a prominent part in the formation of the Chinese national character, whereas in Europe there was no one who could be compared to Confucius.[13]

We have given this lengthy quotation in order to show in what direction the author develops his thought. Here is a blending of concepts and categories from the most diverse systems of ideas: character formation, rebellions, literature, and thinkers—a mixture of debatable and indisputable assertions. No one will deny the distinctive character of many processes in almost every country in the world, including China. But what do individual peculiarities really prove, how do they change the character of Chinese feudalism? In struggling against mechanical imitation and the stereotyped transference of historical concepts from Western countries to China, some Chinese historians exaggerate the originality of separate phenomena without analysing their essence.

But playing at uniqueness does not always lead to a good end. Sometimes it leads to the gravest errors. In characterising the causes of the victory of the Chinese revolution and its peculiarities, Li Shu writes:

> The Chinese nation was able to resist foreign aggression and internal reaction and the Chinese revolution was able to triumph because, *inter alia*, the Chinese nation is among the few foremost nations of the world. When many Western nations, which have become known in modern times as "cultured", were still hunting wild beasts in the forests, our nation had already created a brilliant ancient culture.[14]

Thus we have the idealisation of the Chinese past and a haughty treatment of the history of other nations.

One is struck by a certain duality, the contradiction in opinions of Chinese historians. On the one hand, an effort to emphasise the classical nature of the course of China's development, the typicality of its forms of slave-ownership and feudalism by which the systems of other countries and nations should be judged, especially those which began this course later; and on the other hand an incessant over-emphasising of specific aspects, of those socio-economic forms and ways of historic development that apply only to China. This contradiction can be resolved, in our opinion, only by one thing—a scientifically objective examination of the history of Chinese society within the framework of world history, with regard to the specific features of China's development but on the basis of general laws.

From the emphasis on specific features it is only a step to the exaggeration of China's role and place in history, in the development of world culture. The journal *Li-shih Chiao-hsüeh* (Nos. 8–9, 1961) wrote, meaning China, that "that state should be regarded as the centre of universal history in which the revolutionary struggle possesses the most advanced, the most representative character and which advances in the very front lines of the era and exerts the greatest influence on the progress of world history".

Apparently, it is for this reason that Chinese historians are trying to set up the peculiarities of China as an absolute. Of late, historians of philosophy have begun to devote great attention to these questions. At a meeting of the Philosophical Society in Wuhan a number of speeches were heard on the superiority of certain aspects of Chinese over Western philosophy. It was proposed that all Chinese philosophy of the later Middle Ages should be regarded as a classic example (again classic!) of the development of materialism during the feudal age. The attempt to exaggerate the degree of development of Chinese philosophy

14 *Ibid.*

and culture as a whole, and in particular their influence on the nations of the whole world is also characteristic of the works of Chu Ch'ien-chih, professor of the Faculty of Philosophy at the University of Peking. As early as 1940, in Kuomintang China, he published a monograph on the influence of Chinese culture on Western culture; in 1957 he published a work on the influence of ancient Chinese music on Greek music, and in 1958, a book on the development of Neo-Confucian doctrine in Japan. In an article, "Confucius as Viewed by the Western Philosophers of the 17th–18th Centuries", published in *Jen-min Jih-pao* on March 9, 1962, Chu Ch'ien-chih carefully collects all references by ·the French Encyclopaedists and German philosophers on China and Chinese philosophy, particularly on Confucius, and from these he draws the conclusion that Confucianism has greatly influenced Western philosophy. In Chu Ch'ien-chih's opinion, China was no more and no less than one of the sources of the atheism, materialism, naturalism, and rationalism of the French Encyclopaedists; directly or indirectly the democratic ideas of China became one of the foundations of the philosophy of the great French Revolution; some of Leibnitz's mathematical ideas are connected with the *I Ching (Book of Changes)*, while Kant, Fichte, Hegel, and other German thinkers also felt the indirect influence of Chinese philosophy. The conclusions are very sweeping: influence on nearly everyone—from Descartes to Hegel! The only evidence given for far-reaching assertions consists of a number of statements by European thinkers about Confucius, in which, having only fragmentary information, they often idealised him. But the author of the article does not reveal in what concrete way, in what elements of the philosophical structures of Western philosophers, the influence of China is shown. It is, of course, impossible to agree with these statements of Chu Chi'en-chih. Anyone who is even partially acquainted with the ideas of the French Encyclopaedists, of Leibnitz, Kant, Hegel, and many others, can see the assertion of Chu Chi'en-chih as a perfectly frank exaggeration of the role of Confucian ideas and of their influence on the thinkers of another era—the era of the primary accumulation and development of capitalism in Europe. The substitution for Marxist principles of historical research of the great Han "Sinocentrism" is a blatant concession to bourgeois nationalism, which possessed rooted traditions in the historical science of old China.

It cannot fail to evoke surprise, too, that in the Chinese People's Republic in recent years a thesis has been advanced, unconfirmed by facts, concerning a claim to the discovery of America—a claim originally put forward in 1913 by the Chinese bourgeois nationalistic press.

The Peking newspaper, *Pei-ching Wan-pao*, published in September 1961 a series of sensational articles by Ma Nan-tung in which it was asserted that 1,400 years ago, or about 1,000 years before Columbus, a Chinese Buddhist monk, Hui-sheng, discovered America. The conclusion drawn by the author is typical. He writes:

> Already in the 5th century of our era, the Chinese and Asians established close relations with the nations and countries of America. . . . Thus the friendship between the Chinese and the peoples of different countries of America has been shaped by the deepest traditions. This is a historical fact of colossal importance! Thus it is evident that Columbus was not the first to discover the American continent. However, we must not completely negate the achievements of Columbus. He can be considered the first European to find a new sea route from Europe to America.[15]

As is known, it has been established by historical science in recent years that among the early visitors to the American mainland there were representatives of the peoples of Scandinavia and the West Coast of Africa. Possibly, Hui-sheng was accidentally carried by a storm to the shores of America, but this was of no social significance, and the very mention of his voyage was forgotten for 1,000 years!

The efforts of Chinese scholars to trace the connections between Eastern and Western culture and their mutual influence at various stages of human history, and to show the contribution of the Chinese nation to the civilisation of the world, merit full approval in and of themselves and should be supported by similar researches by scholars of those countries the links with and influences of which are being traced. But in the course of such studies it is necessary to stick to facts and well-founded fully valid evidence. Any subjective exaggeration of the role and influence of the ideas of one country on the history of thought of another country, or even of a whole continent, can do nothing but harm. One must not instil a feeling of patriotism into a nation to the detriment of internationalism. One must not use "historical" precedent of this sort as basis for claim of some ancient "community" of the peoples of Asia,

---

[15] Quoted from a reprint of Ma Nan-tung's articles in the Chinese journal, *Contemporary Buddhism (Hsien-tai Fa-hsüeh)*, No. 4, 1961, p. 46. The basis of these articles, widely reprinted later in the Chinese press, and of similar declarations of several Chinese historians, like Chu Ch'ien-chih already mentioned, who has devoted himself to this sphere since 1935 (see report of Chu Ch'ien-chih's paper read before the University of Peking, in *Jen-min Jih-pao* of June 3, 1962, entitled "Proof of the Original Discovery of America by a Chinese"), is the theory, familiar in the literature of Chinese studies since 1761, but never confirmed, identifying the country of Fusang, which was visited by the Chinese monk Hui-sheng in 499, as Mexico. It is characteristic that in 1913 Chinese bourgeois nationalistic circles raised a noisy discussion of this question in the pages of the Chinese *Geographical Journal (Ti-hsüeh Tsa-chih)*, No. 37, 1913.

Africa, and Latin America or, moreover, as basis for claim that the leaders of the Chinese People's Republic—and they alone—are the champions of the interests of these peoples.

Another question that is worthy of attention is the assessment of the Mongol and Manchu rule over China (the Yüan dynasty 1280–1368 and the Ch'ing dynasty 1644–1912) and the parts played by certain historical figures of these epochs. As is known, in the 13th century the Mongols subjugated China with fire and sword and established the sway of the Yüan dynasty. But the Mongol supremacy in China was short-lived; after only 88 years, as a result of a nation-wide anti-Mongol uprising, the invaders were driven from the country. Less than three centuries later a fresh disaster beset China—the beginning of intrusion by Manchu tribes. Through the treachery of Chinese feudalists, the Manchu succeeded in defeating the Chinese armies and in conquering the whole of China. The Manchu Ch'ing dynasty lasted 268 years and was overthrown in the course of the bourgeois Hsin-hai revolution of 1911–1912. The conquests of the Mongol and Manchu were bloody and cruel invasions by semi-nomadic peoples; they brought incalculable suffering and misfortune to the Chinese population, destroying to an enormous extent the material and spiritual treasures of the people. These facts are well known and have been reflected in the books of Chinese historians. It appears, however, that some time ago the once seemingly unquestionable assessment of these periods began to change. Let us consider the Mongol rule. Formerly, the schoolbooks and histories of China, when telling of the era of the Mongolian yoke, emphasised its bloody, destructive character and the losses inflicted on Chinese society. The rule of the Yüan dynasty was declared to be a period of "stagnation of the feudal economy under the rule of foreign tribesmen"[16] and Chinggis Khan was called an aggressor the like of whom has been seldom known in the history of mankind.[17] This corresponds to Marx's well-known characterisation of the Mongol invasion.

However, in 1960 the period of the Yüan Mongol dynasty was already being called "the period of the great unification of the country". Such an interpretation was reflected, in particular, in the exhibition of the Central Historical Museum in Peking, organised by a group of historians under the guidance of the Chinese Academy of Sciences, and in the course of a discussion of the personality of Chinggis Khan.

---

[16] *A Short General History of China*, under the general editorship of Fan Wen-lan. (Shanghai, 1949 [in Chinese]), p. 453.
[17] *Ibid.*, p. 458.

Formerly, the assessment of Chinggis Khan in Chinese historiography corresponded in the main to his actual role. But in 1959–1962 a sharp turn took place in the direction of the glorification in the Chinese People's Republic of Chinggis Khan and the Yüan dynasty. The very fact of the triumphant celebration of the 800th anniversary of the birth of Chinggis Khan in Inner Mongolia in 1962 and the laying of the foundation stone of his tomb is very significant (by the way, Chinggis Khan's burial place is still unknown and naturally there can be no discussion about Chinggis Khan's remains).

During this period many historians began to deny the negative character of the Yüan dynasty. At a discussion of this question in the Nanking Historical Society, Professor Han Ju-lin formulated the following views:

> The dynasty founded by Chinggis Khan played for the most part a progressive role in Chinese history. At the time of Chinggis Khan's rise, the country was divided between the kingdoms of the Western Hsia, Chin, Western Liao, and Southern Sung. This was a serious obstacle to the development of the social economy of various nationalities and to the advance of culture. Chinggis Khan, having extended his power throughout the central plane, destroyed these kingdoms, which were in a state of decay, broke down the boundaries between nationalities and restored a multi-national state that had not existed since the days of the Han and the T'ang. . . .[18]

The historians who asserted this probably did not stop to think of one simple question: Was it really necessary for the "great unification of the country" for the Chinese people to endure the Mongolian yoke and undergo great suffering. Was the use of Mongolian horsemen necessary, and was slavery necessary to expand "cultural ties"? The logic of the defenders of Chinggis Khan is strange indeed.

The arguments of the champions of Mongolian rule are supplemented by that same Han Ju-lin in an article entitled "About Chinggis Khan". At first, indeed, he does not deny the cruel suffering of the people and the destruction, but then he endeavours in every way to prove the "progressiveness" of the Mongol rule, declaring:

> And so there appeared Chinggis Khan "towering above the world", his chargers broke down the iron walls of forty large and small states, in which the people were confined, and as a result the people beheld a wider world (!) in which to act; they became acquainted with a higher culture from which they could learn. Thus, from the standpoint of the general tendency of historical development, should one deny the role of Chinggis Khan? The abolition of forty states could not, of

[18] *Jen-min Jih-pao*, August 10, 1961.

course, take place without bloodshed and destruction, but are we really to defend the seclusion and isolation of the large and small slave-owners and feudal lords of all these states, or do we approve of the fact that Chinggis Khan destroyed this seclusion and created for the peoples of different nations economic and cultural conditions in which they could associate and learn from one another?. . . .[19]

Again, one may ask the author: What kind of "high culture" did the Mongols bring to flourishing and well-educated Samarkand? How can one speak calmly of the ruin of forty states and indulge at the same time in sophistry, praising the liquidation of isolation and enumerating "achievements" in the dissemination of a few Chinese inventions? What wide world were the enslaved peoples able to see? No, such an appraisal cannot be accepted! The predatory wars of Chinggis Khan and his successors and their bloody rule cannot be justified from the standpoint of historical progress. The Marxist-Leninist appraisal of the activities of Chinggis Khan has already been given in Soviet literature. The academician I. M. Maisky drew fresh attention to this question in his article published in the journal *Questions of History* (1962, No. 5), and there is no need to refer here to these conclusions in detail.

Parallel to this runs the altered appraisal of the Manchu conquest of China, of the whole period of the rule of the Ch'ing dynasty in general, and of the personalities of the early emperors of the Manchu dynasty, K'ang-hsi in particular. Formerly, in monographs and textbooks, the period of the Manchu dominion was called a period of stagnation, isolation, and even "the imprisonment of the people". Fan Wen-lan wrote correctly in the *New History of China*:

> The Manchus who ruled in China were not a numerous people and were economically and culturally backward. In order to exert their dominion over the more advanced Chinese people, the Manchus joined with the small number of leading Chinese feudal lords and with the feudal lords of other nationalities in China. . . . For quite a long period, from the middle of the 17th century, the policy of national repression carried on by the Manchu rulers and the struggles of the people, especially the Chinese people, against this policy were very serious factors in the political life of China.[20]

We find a similar description of Manchu rule in Tung Chi-ming's popular book, *An Outline History of China*, published in Chinese and English in the Chinese People's Republic:

> In political respects, the Manchu government repressed the non-Manchu nationalities of China with exceptional harshness. They were deprived

[19] *Li-shih Yen-chiu*, No. 3, 1962, pp. 9–10.
[20] Fan Wen-lan, *New History of China*, Vol. I, 1840–1901 (Moscow, 1955 [translated from Chinese]), p. 13.

of equal rights. In the regions occupied by the Manchu troops the peasants were driven off their land, and these lands were divided up, some to the aristocracy, some to the troops. The Manchus forced the Hans to cultivate this land and to pay land rent. Under the oppression of the Manchu government and officials the life of the peasants of all nationalities became more and more difficult. . . . All the big posts in the Manchu government were reserved for Manchu aristocrats, Han landowners and Mongol princes, while all real power was in the hands of Manchu aristocrats. Manchu notables occupied all the highest posts in local administration, too, especially the posts of provincial governors. . . . Under the cruel oppression of the Manchu government the peoples of all nationalities found themselves bound to a common fate and took up a common position of struggle against the oppressors.[21]

Many similar evaluations, widely distributed in China until lately, could be quoted. A large number of examples of cruel, inhuman treatment of the Chinese and other peoples of the Ch'ing empire by the Manchu despots can be found in such 17th and 18th century sources as *Ming-chi pei-lüeh, Tung-nan chi-shih, Huang-ch'ao ching-shih wen-pien*, etc.[22] Now, however, diametrically opposed evaluations of the rule of the Manchus are the norm; the Ch'ing period is already being called "the period of development of a single multi-national state", while national contradictions are ignored. Facts concerning the struggle between groups within the landowning class are given pride of place, while the people's anti-Manchu struggle is mentioned only in examining the history of the opening of the Ch'ing period.

Individual historians go even further and suggest that the Manchus should not be regarded as aggressors at all. Thus, in the minutes of meetings of the Committee on the Study of the History of Nationalities, which lasted from April to June 1962, the following opinion of a group of historians who studied the history of national minorities of Liaoning appears:

> Within the large family of our homeland, one should not talk of which nationality were the rulers of the country: this is all a matter between brothers of one big family. The Manchu advance into the districts of the central valley beyond the Great Wall cannot be regarded as "aggression from without", nor must the "Ch'ing army", "the Manchu nation", and China be contraposed.[23]

These historians, therefore, ignore the struggle of Chinese patriots under the K'ang-hsi and Manchu yoke in the 17th century and the never-ending opposition of the Chinese masses to the Manchu Ch'ing rule dur-

21 Tung Chi-ming, *An Outline History of China* (Peking, 1959), pp. 197–199.
22 See *Selection of Authors on New History*, Vol. I, 1610–1815 (Moscow, 1963), pp. 597–657.
23 See the journal *Hsin Chien-she*, No. 7, 1962, p. 68.

ing the next two centuries. Such assertions are nothing but a distortion of history.

Chinese journals contain reports of discussions and individual articles devoted to the Ch'ing dynasty and to the role of the Manchus and their rulers. In this connection Liu Ta-nien's article, "K'ang-hsi",[24] cannot be overlooked. The author credits K'ang-hsi as follows: "During his reign and that of the early Ch'ings in general, the unification of the different nationalities of China under the aegis of the Han nation reached a new stage in its long development." Quite inappropriately he "confirms" this assertion with a quotation from Lenin: "The proletariat cannot support any intensification of nationalism; on the contrary, it supports all that helps to erase national differences, to break down national barriers, all that makes relations between nationalities ever closer, all that leads to the fusion of nations".[25]

V. I. Lenin's article, "Critical Notes on the National Question", from which Liu Ta-nien quoted the above so inappropriately, was written at the end of 1913 in connection with the increase in nationalistic vacillations among Jewish, Ukrainian, and Polish Social-Democrats. It contains sharp criticism of bourgeois nationalism and a clear exposition of the principles of proletarian internationalism. What has this to do with the feudal era, or the reign of K'ang-hsi? Such artificial, dogmatic use of quotations is typical of many historical works of contemporary Chinese historians.

To give K'ang-hsi the credit for organising a joint rebuff of all the nationalities of China to foreign aggression, as Liu Ta-nien does, is to falsify history. What can be meant by foreign aggression against China at the end of the 17th and beginning of the 18th centuries, when the Manchu empire itself was conquering and enslaving other countries and peoples? As for the activities of a few dozen Portuguese, Spanish, and French missionaries, they were invited to China, as is well known, and were well treated by K'ang-hsi himself; they served him loyally and faithfully, helping to produce guns, clocks, maps, required by the Manchus in their campaigns, and also in the conduct of diplomatic negotiations.

Not a single historian prior to Liu Ta-nien ever advanced propositions such as that "with the establishment of the Ch'ing political rule in the whole country, the lack of cohesion between the Manchu nation and the other nationalities of the country and, above all, the lack of cohesion between the Han and Manchu nations tended to disappear, and a process of consolidation took place"; that "this had far-reaching, profound con-

[24] *Li-shih Yen-chiu*, No. 3, 1961.
[25] V. I. Lenin, *Essays*, Vol. XX, p. 19.

sequences for the development of Chinese history"; that "all this is the most important achievement of the governments of K'ang-hsi and the early Ch'ing".[26]

In trying to construct a "theoretical" basis for the over-estimation of the history of the Ch'ing dynasty, that same Fan Wen-lan, whose correct thoughts we referred to above, now made the following statement during the discussion of the relations between nationalities in the history of China:

> Expansion of territory must not be considered aggression, and weak and perishing nationalities must not be declared the objects of aggression or be sympathised with. The actions of a strong nation or state directed at expanding its territory correspond to the laws of social development of its time . . . all that is rotten does not deserve sympathy; all that corresponds to the laws of social development is worthy of respect. . . .[27]

By such assertions, generally speaking, any aggression can be justified.

Many historians of the Chinese People's Republic expressed their disagreement with Liu Ta-nien's appraisals of K'ang-hsi and with his other views referring to Mongol and Manchu rule, but the mere fact of the appearance of such articles and addresses, constituting a revision of the role of the Mongol and Manchu conquests and of the historical personalities who symbolized the cruel oppression of the Chinese people by conquerors, is evidence of the development of dangerous erroneous tendencies in Chinese historiography.

Pretensions and erroneous tendencies can also be clearly discerned in articles dealing with the history of China in modern times. Let us take as an example the long leading article, "Various Problems of the Modern History of China", by one of the leaders of historical science in the Chinese People's Republic, Professor Liu Ta-nien, published in the journal *Li-shih Yen-chiu* (No. 3, 1963), in which the stages of the national struggle of the Chinese people for liberty, from 1840 to 1919, are examined in detail. It is characteristic of the author's way of thinking that in the first place he completely ignores the international significance of the revolution of 1905–1907 in Russia, which, in the words of Lenin, inaugurated an epoch of the "awakening of Asia"; and the struggle of the Chinese people during that period is depicted as entirely free from

---

26 It is well-known that in American and English bourgeois literature on China, the idealising of the Government of K'ang-hsi is widespread. Both Samuel Couling in *The Encyclopedia Sinica* and Fang Chao-ying in *Eminent Chinese of the Ch'ing Period* spare no colours in painting the image of such an "enlightened ruler". Samuel Couling, *The Encyclopedia Sinica* (Shanghai, 1917), pp. 266–268; Arthur W. Hummel, ed., *Eminent Chinese of the Ch'ing Period, 1644–1912* (Washington, D.C., 1943), pp. 327–331.

27 *Hsin Chien-she*, No. 1, 1962, p. 52.

any external ideological influences. At the same time this struggle is depicted by Liu Ta-nien as some kind of "classical model", which the peoples of Asia, Africa, and Latin America should copy today. The general conclusion of Liu Ta-nien's article is as follows:

> The societies of the major countries of the world that are in transition from feudalism to capitalism have two courses before them. The first is an independent course of development. The second is the rise of capitalism after the conversion of the country into a colony and semi-colony. Consequently, there are also two types of bourgeois-democratic revolutions. The first is a type of revolution directed only against the feudal forces in that country. The second is that in which, besides the anti-feudal, a serious anti-imperialist direction is also visible. The democratic revolution in China belongs to this second type and is a clearly expressed classic example of it. . . . The democratic revolutions on the English and French patterns are already museum pieces, but at present the democratic revolution on the Chinese pattern, like a prairie fire, threatens imperialist dominion in the countries of Asia, Africa and Latin America. They are at present at the stage at which China stood at the time of the Hsin-hai revolution, and some of them are still at the stage of the Boxer movement.[28]

We will not delay here to discuss the anti-historical parallels which Liu Ta-nien draws in his article. It should be obvious to everyone that it is illegitimate to equate the present stage of the national liberation struggle of the peoples of Asia, Africa, and Latin America with the period of the bourgeois revolution of 1911 in China or the Boxer movement of 1900, which started before the epoch of the "awakening of Asia".

Leaving out of account Lenin's appraisal of the bourgeois-democratic revolutions and their peculiarities, Liu Ta-nien tries to impose on his readers his own "conception". In this connection it is appropriate to recall that V. I. Lenin, in his article "On the Right of Nations to Self-determination", distinguished two epochs in the development of the bourgeois-democratic revolutions. For Western Europe this was the period of 1789–1871, which was "an epoch of national movements and of the establishment of national states".[29] The epoch of bourgeois-democratic revolutions began for the countries of Eastern Europe and Asia in 1905 in connection with the first Russian revolution. "In Eastern Europe and in Asia", Lenin wrote, "the epoch of bourgeois-democratic revolutions only began in 1905. The revolutions in Russia, Persia, Turkey, China, the Balkan wars—this was a chain of world events only a blind man can fail to see as the awakening of a *whole series* of bourgeois-democratic national movements: efforts towards creating nationally independent and nationally unique states".[30] Thus V. I. Lenin specially

28 *Li-shih Yen-chiu*, No. 3, 1963, p. 7.
29 V. I. Lenin, *Essays*, Vol. XX, p. 377.
30 *Ibid.*, p. 378.

underlines a *whole series* of bourgeois-democratic national movements, including in this series the revolution in Russia, in Persia, in Turkey, and in China. Like the blind man, Liu Ta-nien prefers to see no other revolutions but the Chinese one, rather than to see a whole series of bourgeois-democratic national movements. He asserts that

> the experience of the Chinese revolution during these eighty years [The reference is to the period from 1840 to 1919—Authors], especially the experience of the anti-imperialist struggle, no matter whether negative or positive, is indispensable to the revolutionary countries of these regions [Asia, Africa, and Latin America—Authors]. In studying the modern history of China, one's whole attention must be devoted to the satisfaction of these requirements.

Here Liu Ta-nien is clearly calling upon the Chinese historians specialising in the modern history of China to extract from the various events in the history of China from 1840 to 1919 recipes suitable for immediate application in the revolutionary practice of the peoples of other countries in our day.

The foisting of a purely "Chinese way" of development upon the peoples of Asia, Africa, and Latin America, irrespective of the level of their economic development, their historical traditions, the existence of their own Communist parties, etc. (which is characteristic of the views of the leaders of the Communist Party of China), is taking place simultaneously with the defamation in every possible way of all that is "European". While urging everyone to undeviating observance of Marxist-Leninist propositions in historical science, Liu Ta-nien at the same time allows himself great methodological and terminological liberties in the article just mentioned. He asserts, for instance, that after "the May Fourth movement" of 1919, "China was converted from a feudal society into a society of the people's revolutionary movement, led by the working class", and introduces the idea of a "purely peasant war", etc.

Both in Liu Ta-nien's article and in other works of Chinese historians on China's past, artificial efforts are made to modernise some phenomena of the past, to transfer categories of other eras arbitrarily into the present day, and to apply mechanically the experience of the class struggle of the 19th century to contemporary conditions and aims of class struggle.

The incorrect tendencies in historical science in the Chinese People's Republic, some of which have been noted above, weaken the united front of the struggle against bourgeois ideology and impede the fulfilment of one of the most important tasks of Marxist historians—the struggle against reactionary historiography and against the ideology of anti-Communism. In recent years some negative phenomena on the front of Chinese historical science have been actively used by reactionary bourgeois historiographers, particularly the American, for criticism of Marxist-Leninist historical science as a whole and for anti-Communist propaganda.

It is known, with what joy at one time the bourgeois opponents of Marxism-Leninism received some erroneous phenomena in Soviet historical science, connected with the personality cult of Stalin, particularly the idealising in historical literature of individual personalities, and the incorrect appraisal of the role of Ivan the Terrible and of some other historical figures. After the 20th Party Congress, Soviet historians removed these accretions and showed that these phenomena had nothing in common with Marxist-Leninist historical science or with the genuinely scientific method of studying historical reality. Now the bourgeois falsifiers seize upon "evidence" presented to them, voluntarily or involuntarily by Chinese historians. Making use of matter in Chinese newspapers and journals in which attempts are made to re-examine tendentiously some active figures of the past, such as Ts'ao Ts'ao and Chinggis Khan, American historians (such as, for instance, A. Feuerwerker, well-known for his open hostility to Communism, who has in the last few years written on the subject of contemporary Chinese historiography) endeavour on the basis of "new materials" to accuse Marxist-Leninist historiography of political pragmatism.

The enemies of Marxism and the opponents of the Socialist camp report the bourgeois-nationalistic tendencies in Chinese historical science with particular glee. Thus Feuerwerker, mentioned above, gloats in his article, "China's History in Marxian Dress",[31] that during the discussion that has arisen among Chinese historians on Fan Wen-lan's article on the forming of the Chinese nation, every author spoke against the propositions of Marxism-Leninism. Feuerwerker remarks that the assertion by Chinese historians that the Chinese nation was formed in some kind of special way coincides with the concept current among bourgeois historians of the radical difference between West and East.[32] Bourgeois historians also follow with close attention the mistaken conceptions of some Chinese historians regarding the nationality question in China, the treatment of certain questions in a spirit of Great Han chauvinism, the efforts to "link the non-Chinese nationalities to the Hans". Feuerwerker points out that Chinese historians make no distinction between the era of pre-monopoly capitalism and the epoch of imperialism; he writes in this connection: "The contrast between Lenin's account of the distinctive traits" of imperialism and "the vagueness of Chinese Com-

---

[31] Albert Feuerwerker, "China's History in Marxian Dress", *American Historical Review*, 1961, No. 2, pp. 323–353 [Chapter 2 of this volume].
[32] *Ibid.*, p. 332.

munist historians is so obvious that we can scarcely believe that the Chinese do not realise this".[33] The Chinese historians' deviation from the Leninist definition of imperialism is so much to Feuerwerker's liking that he even expresses the hope that it may be possible for bourgeois historians to "come to terms" with Chinese historians and to find a common language on the basis of their mutual rejection of Lenin's theory of imperialism.[34]

In conclusion, some questions of practical work must be referred to. The leaders of historical science in the Chinese People's Republic pursue a policy of isolating Chinese historians by all possible means from scholars of the Socialist countries, from the historical science of the Soviet Union, from the progressive science of the world.

Chinese scholars have refused to send their delegations to a number of international scientific congresses (e.g., the 11th International Congress of Historical Sciences in Stockholm in 1960, the 25th Congress of Historians of the East in Moscow in 1960) in which historians of the Soviet Union and other Socialist countries and many foreign Marxist scholars took part. The bilateral contacts with historians of the Soviet Union and other Socialist countries are being disrupted. Thus during the negotiations on plans for scholarly collaboration in 1961 between the Academies of Sciences of the Chinese People's Republic and the USSR, the Chinese declined the Soviet offers of collaboration in carrying out joint studies on the subjects, "The History of the International Workers' Movement", "Outlines of the New History of China", "The History of Philosophy"; in 1962 they refused to discuss a proposal for co-ordinating research on the subject, "The History of Socialistic Development in the People's Democracies", and later, even refused to discuss plans for joint research in 1963. As a result, since 1960 not a single Soviet historian has been able to undertake an official scientific journey to the Chinese People's Republic in accordance with the plan of collaboration between the Academies of Science of the USSR and of the Chinese People's Republic. It is significant, too, that the Chinese did not offer to send any Chinese historian to the Soviet Union.

Through the fault of the Chinese the exchange of books between the libraries of the Chinese People's Republic and the Soviet libraries has been severely and unilaterally reduced. Up to and including 1959 the literature received from the Chinese People's Republic by the libraries belonging to the system of the Academy of Sciences of the USSR averaged 53–54 per cent of the Soviet scientific literature that was despatched to the Chinese People's Republic. But in 1960–1963 the litera-

---

[33] *Ibid.*, p. 334.
[34] *Ibid.*, pp. 352–353.

ture received from the Chinese People's Republic was cut by half and at present represents no more than 25–26 per cent of the quantity of books forwarded to the Chinese People's Republic.

If we turn to the history of the exchange of books with the scientific organisations of the Chinese People's Republic, it should be noted that during the 1950s the academic libraries of the USSR carried out much work in supplementing the supplies of the Chinese scientific libraries. In 1955 alone the library of the Academy of Sciences in Leningrad despatched 67,000 volumes and a large number of microfilms of the publications of the USSR Academy of Sciences to the academic libraries of the Chinese People's Republic. Similar work was performed by the Basic Social Sciences Library of the USSR Academy of Sciences for the academic and university libraries of China. However, while up to 1959 the Chinese also endeavoured to supplement the supplies of Soviet libraries with Chinese literature and sent valuable old editions and many periodicals in addition to current literature, in 1960, 1961, and the first half of 1962, the arrival of literature dropped sharply (to 10 per cent of that of 1959), while the despatch of Soviet books to the Chinese People's Republic remained at about the former level. In 1960 the Library of the USSR Academy of Sciences received out of 129 journals only 15 full sets; 54 were not received at all, and the rest arrived with many issues missing. In 1961 not a single monograph was sent from China to the Library of the USSR Academy of Sciences in Leningrad, and of 88 Chinese journals promised only 12 were received. In addition, delivery of the basic scientific reviews ceased.

The delivery to the Soviet Union of such periodicals as *Chin-tai shih tzu-liao, Li-shih Chiao-hsüeh, Wen Shih Che, Shih-hsüeh, Yüeh-k'an, Chiao-hsüeh yü Yen-chiu*, and others came to an end, as did the delivery of all provincial and university publications.[35]

The fact that the journal *Li-shih Yen-chiu*, beginning with No. 1 in 1963, ceased to publish an index of its articles in Russian and English, should also be regarded in the light of the policy of erecting a "Chinese Wall" round historical science in the Chinese People's Republic.

Need it be said that such practice on the part of the Chinese scientific institutions leads to the gradual isolation of the historians of the Chinese

---

[35] At present the Libraries of the USSR Academy of Sciences despatch to the Chinese People's Republic 23 sets each of academic serial editions, 16 copies of all monographs of academic publications, and a large number of academic reviews. For instance, the Basic Social Sciences Library sends China 215 titles, or 815 complete sets of journals, but receives 43 titles, or 214 complete sets. The Leningrad Library of the USSR Academy of Sciences sends several copies of all academic reviews. Almost all scholarly literature published in the USSR, including provincial and university publications, is supplied to the libraries of the Chinese People's Republic.

People's Republic from the scholars of the USSR and can only do harm to the development of historical science in China.

The Soviet people entertain deep fraternal feelings for their friend and neighbour, the Chinese people. Our party and government, expressing the will of the entire Soviet people, spare no pains in strengthening fraternal friendship with the peoples of all Socialist countries. We are united by the struggle for the triumph of Communism; we have a single goal, the same hopes and aspirations. This is why the disruptive actions of the Chinese leaders undermine the traditional friendship of our peoples and evoke feelings of legitimate indignation in all Soviet citizens. The situation on the front of historical science in the Chinese People's Republic also causes us increasing concern of late. The aim of the authors of this article is to draw the attention of the Soviet scientific world to some harmful and mistaken tendencies of a bourgeois nationalistic nature which have appeared in recent years in the historical science of the Chinese People's Republic. At the same time they do not wish to belittle the importance of the work that has been and is being performed in present circumstances by Chinese Marxist scholars, in studying various periods of their native history. Soviet historians, with all the Soviet people, unanimously support the Lenin policy of the peaceful coexistence of states with a different social order, a policy that guarantees the victory of the great cause of Socialism and peace, and heartily approves the treaty signed in Moscow on the 5th August, 1963 for banning nuclear tests in the air, in space, and under water. The declaration of the Soviet Government, published on the 4th August, 1963, says:

> No contrivances or onslaught can alter the course of the foreign policy of the Soviet Union outlined by the great Lenin, and further developed by the decisions of the 20th and 22nd Congresses of our Party, in the programme of the Communist Party of the Soviet Union, and unanimously approved by the whole Soviet nation, by the international Communist movement. Guided by this course, the Soviet Union will continue unswervingly to pursue the policy of peace and friendship between peoples; it will strive for general and complete disarmament, for the peaceful solution of international problems, including those concerning the security of Europe, for the triumph of the Lenin principles of peaceful coexistence.[36]

Soviet historians, as well as the entire Soviet people, are firmly determined to strengthen and deepen fraternal friendship with the peoples of Socialist countries, with the great Chinese people.

[36] *Pravda*, August 4, 1963.

17

How to Appraise the History of Asia?

By LIU TA-NIEN

By LIU TA-NIEN

REACTIONARY BOURGEOIS SCHOLARS OF THE WEST DISTORT THE HISTORY OF ASIA

Asia is one of the cradles of the world's oldest civilizations. The Asian people have their honoured place among the people of the world. They have made outstanding contributions to the world's advanced cultures, both in ancient and modern times. Many of the winds of change in the modern world have swept out of Asia. Rich historical records and material remains furnish eloquent proof of the fact that Asian history has its brilliant and important place in the history of world civilization.

But, it must be said that for quite a long time the history of Asia has not, in general, been appraised objectively. Reactionary bourgeois scholars of the West and their followers have in many ways wilfully distorted Asian history and minimized its importance. Up to the present time, one cannot discern any decisive change in this regard.

Unscientific Attitude

The majority of Western historians still have an entirely unscientific attitude towards the history of Asia. They have no real interest at all in a true scientific appraisal of that history. From their writings, one finds it hard to get a real picture of many important Asian events, even harder to understand how history really develops.

Histories of Asia, of the East, and of the various Asian countries written by such Western bourgeois scholars usually propagandize two concepts. Firstly, that Asia has been "barbarous," "backward," "immoral" and "uncivilized" in all its ages. Secondly, that the progress and civilization of Asia in modern times have been favours generously bestowed on her by the West. Deliberately distorting Chinese history in the U.S. White Paper of 1949, Dean Acheson, the former U.S. Secretary of State, wrote: "Then in the middle of the 19th century the heretofore impervious wall of Chinese isolation was breached by the West. These outsiders brought with them aggressiveness, the unparalleled development of Western technology, and a high order of culture which had not accompanied previous foreign incursions into China."[1]

That is how the Western bourgeois scholars generally approached Chinese history as well as the history of Asia. Did the West brutally invade Asia? This is not apparently what happened; the West "brought . . . a high order of culture" with it to bestow on Asia. The second concept is stressed in dealing with the modern history of Asia while the first concept is stressed in regard to both ancient and modern times. It would be unfair to say that such historical writings on Asia by venal bourgeois scholars of the West possess no striking features. These works invariably fling mud at the peoples of Asia and their culture, while doing their best to ignore or whitewash the innumerable crimes committed by imperialism in Asia. This is their most striking feature.

In the present paper, I propose to confine myself to modern Asian history. How shall we appraise it? We must analyse all problems in this field in accordance with the standpoint of historical materialism.

Two Aspects of Asia's Modern History

The modern history of Asia (18th century to the present time) records many events and struggles. But the main current of that history can be summed up in one sentence: This was a period of criminal activities by colonialist marauders and imperialists, invading Asia and turning it into a colony or semi-colony, and of struggles waged by the Asian people to oppose and expel these invaders and their lackeys. This is the central theme of the modern history of Asia. All other struggles are inevitably subordinate to the struggle between these two opposites, and their course of advance inevitably hinges on circumstances in that developing struggle.

Invaded and dominated by Western colonialism, Asia lived through a dark period of history. This lasted for more than a century.

Colonialism and imperialism changed the colours of the maps of vast areas of Asia. From westernmost Persia and Turkey, through Afghanistan, Pakistan, and India to Burma, Indonesia, and the Philippines in Southeast Asia and the countries of Indo-China, to China and Korea in the East—with the exception of Japan in the extreme East—these countries and nations with ancient cultures were successively turned into colonies or semi-colonies of Portugal, Spain, Holland, Britain, France, Russia, Germany, and of the arrogant, present-day imperialism of the U.S.A. They were dismembered, their territories were cut away or an-

[1] U.S. Department of State, *United States Relations With China*, 1949, p. v.

nexed, and their sovereign rights were seized by foreign hands. The final concentrated expression of the seizure of a nation's sovereignty by the imperialists is seen in the ruthless plundering of its material wealth.

Colonialist penetration and conquest in Asia, and the reducing of Asian countries to colonies and semi-colonies was accompanied by crimes and tyranny unprecedented in history. The rule of the colonialists and their lackeys is more ruthless and terroristic than that of ancient Rome. More than 100 million Asians were killed. Whole populations were wiped out. Magnificent palaces, temples and other structures, some of the finest in the world, were destroyed or reduced to ruins. Historical records and valuable works of art were put to the flames. Production stagnated or declined, industry and agriculture remained backward, and social development was retarded.

In his 1834 report describing how the British machine-building industry had disrupted Indian social life, Lord Bentinck, the then British Governor-General of India, said that "the misery hardly finds a parallel in the history of commerce. The bones of the cotton-weavers are bleaching the plains of India." And this admitted crime was only one of those, uncountable as the sands in the Ganges River, committed by the colonialists. What part of the vast lands of Asia is not littered with the bones of Asian people murdered in modern times by the colonialists?

This phase of the history of Asia stands out glaringly. It is wrong not to give an adequate exposure of it or to relate its true facts. It is impermissible to conceal or gloss it over.

Record of Anti-Colonialist Struggles

However, this picture of darkness and decline is only part of the reality of modern and contemporary Asia. The whole picture of these times in Asia contains a record of magnificent and militant struggles of the oppressed. The Asian peoples are by no means standing on the flanks of the historical stage as unimportant actors; they are at the forefront or take the centre of the stage, playing one of the leading roles in the drama of history. It is wrong to belittle this aspect of Asian history; it is all the more wrong to deny this aspect of Asian history.

Modern Asia is, first of all, the most extensive battlefield in the anti-colonialist struggle being waged by the people of the world.

The Asian people began their struggle against colonialism when Portugal, Spain, and Holland first invaded Asia. The more ferocious became the subsequent attacks by the colonialists, the fiercer the people's resistance grew. The modern history of the various Asian countries is a lengthy chronicle of the people's struggles against colonialism. The insurrections of the people against foreign aggression and oppression and against feudal rule in their own countries have been almost continuous in the past centuries.

The struggles of the Asian peoples were formerly waged independently, but in the 19th century they began to be interlinked and one upsurge of the national-liberation struggle after another has followed. The first upsurge was in the middle of the 19th century. Among the large-scale struggles of that time were the Babist Revolt (1844–52) in Persia, the Taiping Revolution (1851–64) in China, and the revolutionary uprising of the Indian people (1857–59). There was a succession of resistance movements in other parts of Asia. Marx at that time pointed out: "The revolt in the Anglo-Indian army has coincided with a general disaffection exhibited against English supremacy on the part of great Asiatic nations, the revolt of the Bengal army being, beyond doubt, intimately connected with the Persian and Chinese wars."[2]

At the end of the 19th century, a second upsurge of national-liberation struggles took place in Asia. The nationalist movement led by Malkom Khan (1890–91) in Persia, the revolt against the tobacco monopoly by the Persian people (1891), the people's uprisings in Assam and Manipur (1891) and the nationalist movement led by B. G. Tilak (1895–97) in India, the anti-French uprising led by Hoang Hoa Tham of Viet Nam (1891–98), the Dong Hak Party Uprising of Korea (1893–95), the resistance struggle of the people of the Ottoman Empire, the early Young Turkey Movement (after 1894), the Philippine revolution to overthrow Spanish rule (1896–98), the Chinese revolutionary movement led by Dr. Sun Yat-sen (after 1895), and the Yi Ho T'uan Movement (known as the "Boxers" in the West [1899–1901])—all these are major manifestations of this upsurge. The broad masses of the labouring people and the political forces of the bourgeoisie took part in these struggles. Their common characteristic was that their spearhead of struggle was directed against imperialism.

The year 1905 was followed by the third upsurge of the national-liberation struggle. The Persian revolution (1905–11), the anti-British struggle by the radical wing of the All-India National Congress (1905–08), the Turkish revolution (1908–09), and the Chinese 1911 revolution to overthrow the Ch'ing Dynasty (1911–12)—all belong to this time. In commenting on the significance of this upsurge, Lenin said: "Hundreds of millions of the downtrodden and benighted have awakened from medieval stagnation to a new life and are rising to fight for ele-

2 "The Revolt in the Indian Army," *The First Indian War and Independence 1857–59*, Eng. ed., Foreign Languages Publishing House, Moscow, p. 40.

mentary human rights and democracy."[3] This was described by him as "the awakening of Asia."

The anti-colonialist struggle of the Asian people at that time not only encompassed vast areas but drew unprecedented numbers of people into the battle. The struggle was extremely fierce, with one upsurge following another. That is why we say that modern Asia became the most extensive battlefield of the anti-imperialist struggle of the people of the world. Africa and Latin America were also important battlefields of the world anti-imperialist struggle. The people's struggles in Egypt and the Sudan alarmed the imperialist world and voiced support for each other and were linked with the people's struggles in Asia because they all had a common aim.

Of course, many of those revolts, uprisings and revolutions were quickly crushed. But this does not in the least diminish their significance. The frantic attacks launched against them by the colonialists and imperialists faced the Asian people with a question: whether or not to dare to fight and deal with and defeat the aggressors. The answer of the Asian people is: dare to fight and dare to make revolution; believe in the justice of your cause and be assured that your strength and wisdom will prevail over the aggressors. The "authority" of the colonialists has been held in contempt, and the spirit of revolution has developed. Each struggle waged by the peoples has paved the way for their next struggle. The colonialists and imperialists turned Asia into a bastion of the colonial system, and each struggle waged by the peoples has made another breach in the walls of that bastion, presaging its final and complete collapse. In their steadfast struggle, the masses of the people have become more awakened and grown stronger, while one by one the reactionary rulers are being driven off the stage of history. Thus, even if the people's struggles failed, the people have won in the final count. This is why these uprisings and revolutions have left their indelible mark on history.

Two Main Currents in Modern Asia

Two major historical currents of the world meet together in modern Asia.

Since World War II, there have been great developments in the history of the people's revolutionary struggles in Asia, Africa, and Latin America. These areas have become the focus of various types of contradictions in the world. Imperialist rule in these areas has steadily

[3] Lenin, "The Awakening of Asia," *Collected Works*, Eng. ed., Foreign Languages Publishing House, Moscow, 1963, Vol. 19, p. 86.

weakened, and one after another great movements of the people's revolutionary struggles have emerged and developed vigorously. The national democratic revolutionary movement in Asia, Africa, and Latin America and the international socialist revolutionary movement form the two major historical currents of the present-day world.

With the coming together of these two massive forces of world history in Asia, no force on earth can now prevent Asia from advancing with giant strides. Since World War II, more than 50 countries in Asia and Africa have declared their independence. In Asia, independence was declared by some ten countries, including Indonesia, India, and Pakistan —countries with large territories and populations, which were subject to colonial rule for several centuries. Since World War II, the People's Republic of China, the Democratic Republic of Viet Nam, and the Democratic People's Republic of Korea have embarked on the road of socialism. These are changes of epoch-making significance in the history of Asia as well as in the history of the world.

Significance of the Chinese Revolution

Among the changes which have taken place in Asia since World War II, the victory of the Chinese people in their democratic revolution and the start of the socialist era in Chinese history are historical events of the first magnitude. They have not only influenced Asia but have deeply influenced the whole world. The Chinese revolution has, in the first place, fundamentally changed the world's balance of forces between revolution and counter-revolution, between the socialist camp and the imperialist camp. The victory of the Chinese revolution delivered a crushing blow to imperialist domination. Yesterday's great rear of imperialism has been turned into a base area, into a forefront of the anti-imperialist struggle. Everything is turning into its opposite. China's area is approximately the same as that of Europe. China's population is larger than that of Europe. The forces of the world's revolutionary camp obviously exceed those of the world's counter-revolutionary camp.

In the second place, the victory of the Chinese democratic revolution and the advent of socialism in Chinese history have set a brilliant example for the colonial and semi-colonial countries of the world. The victory of the Chinese people over imperialism and its lackeys and the founding of the People's Republic of China have greatly inspired the people of many colonial and semi-colonial countries in their struggle for national independence and the complete victory of their people's democratic revolution. The Russian October Socialist Revolution served as an example for revolution in the oppressor nations, that is, for revolution in the imperialist countries; while the Chinese revolution set an example for revolution in the oppressed nations, that is, the colonial or semi-colonial countries. In studying the changes in Asian history since World War II, we need to make an adequate appraisal of the path as well as the influence of the Chinese revolution. For it is of significance for the whole world, far beyond the East or Asia.

While the Asian people are attacking the imperialists and carrying history forward, the imperialists and reactionaries are not sitting back with folded arms. Since World War II, far from abandoning colonialism in Asia, Africa, and Latin America, the imperialists are hanging on wherever they can. In this regard, U.S. imperialism is the most cunning and desperate. In face of the powerful struggles of the people of the world, the U.S. and other imperialists and colonialists have been compelled to change some of the old methods of direct colonial rule and introduce the "new" methods of neo-colonialism. They foster puppet regimes and practise various subtler methods of colonial control; organize military blocs and build up military bases, and plunder the wealth of countries by means of economic "aid" and various other forms of economic "exploitation." They engage in "spiritual" infiltration and cultural aggression; organize subversion and engineer military coups d'etat; they engage in direct armed intervention and launch large-scale armed aggression. U.S. armed aggression against Korea and the current U.S. armed aggression against Viet Nam and Laos are only two of these examples.

In brief, imperialism has not perished; the anti-imperialist struggle of the Asian people is not over. Asia has been and still is a stormy battle-front of the anti-imperialist struggle.

The modern history of Asia today appears at once more complicated and simpler than ever before. On the one hand, it has witnessed the impact of the two great historical currents of the national democratic revolutionary movement and the international socialist revolutionary movement; on the other, it is seeing the death-bed struggles and desperate attacks put up by U.S. imperialism and all the old and new colonialists.

Focal Point of Struggle

Asia has become a focal point of struggle in the present-day world. The struggle between the two opposed forces mentioned above, its development and outcome, has a bearing not only on the destiny of the Asian peoples but on the destiny of the peoples of the whole world. The modern history of Asia is by no means a local question but a question that concerns the immediate course of world history. In commenting on modern world history it is impossible to get to the heart of things if one avoids mention of the two above-mentioned historical currents. Similarly, in commenting on the modern history of Asia, if one avoids touching on the operation of the two big currents of history in this area, on the relentless struggle between revolution and counter-revolution, which affects the whole picture of world history, one will not be able to give an insight into the truth of things.

What conclusion is to be drawn from the above analysis? It is that since the invasion by Western colonialism, there actually exist two Asias: one is a dark and backward Asia under colonialist and imperialist rule, and the other is a great and militant Asia, making brilliant advances. They exist side by side, but stand sharply opposed to each other. There is little truth about this in the works of those reactionary Western bourgeois scholars. By exaggerating Asia's backwardness, they try to cover up and whitewash the unprecedented crimes and obscurantism of the rule of the colonialists and their lackeys in Asia; using the same methods, they have also tried to obliterate knowledge of the struggle of the Asian masses and to denigrate the people's role in carrying forward mankind's history. The dark things in the history of Asia have been masked and falsified by them; the bright things have been obscured by them.

Now, with the fabrications and distortions exposed, the history of Asia presented to us is one which encompasses not only enslavement, darkness, and humiliation on the one hand, but struggle, and great and brilliant advances on the other. The veil has been torn off and the true features of history are being revealed. As time goes on the opposing forces and the trends of development of the two Asias will be revealed more clearly.

In this short review I cannot deal with the outstanding contributions made by the Asian people in the cultural and spiritual fields, or with the fact that the feudal society of the Asian states was itself pregnant with the embryo of capitalism and that, even without invasion by Western capitalism, they would have gradually developed into capitalist societies.

COLONIALISM'S WESTERN-CENTRED HISTORY

Reactionary Western bourgeois scholars invariably refuse to admit that history other than that of Europe—to which North America is now added—has much importance in the history of world civilization. The golden rule followed by such Western bourgeois historical science is that history must be centred on Europe or West Europe. This "theory" is rotten to the core, but it is still being spread and still enjoys a certain audience.

Take the following lines from *Modern History* by two American authors for example:

> From the time of the ancient Greeks and Romans down to the present day, the leading roles in the drama of human history have been taken by the white men of Europe. It was in Europe, the smallest of all the five continents, that what we call modern civilization arose; that the common people first dared wrest the sceptre of government from diademed autocrats; that nations learnt patriotism; that inventors harnessed nature's forces to drive machines of iron and steel or to move man's ships and cars; that bullets and explosives were first made deadly weapons of warfare; that scientists explored the heavens with their telescopes or learnt the secrets of chemistry, physics, biology, and medicine; that public schools and automatic printing presses opened to all the kingdom of knowledge.[4]

It uses insulting labels for Asian and African peoples, speaking about the "retrogressive yellow race in the Far East" or the "illiterate African Negroes." This pernicious propaganda is widely spread in cheap editions.

The absurdity of this theory held by many Western historians manifests itself in teaching practice, which simply excludes Asia from world history. Chester Bowles states in his *Ambassador's Report* that lectures given at American schools on so-called "world history" start from Egypt and Mesopotamia, go on to Greece via the Island of Crete and then through Rome, to end in France and Britain. Students are asked to memorize one hundred of the most important dates in "world history." Only one of them concerns Asia—1857, when Commodore Perry, an American naval officer, "opened up" Japan.

The way the Western bourgeoisie looks at world history is just the way the ant, described in the fable, looks at the world. The ant thinks itself ruler and sole master of the world. In its eyes everyone else is insignificant. The historical idealists have surpassed all records in this respect.

For quite a long time, such historians have described Europe or West Europe as occupying the centre of world history. This is simply a product of the views of the egocentric, out-and-out aggressive forces of Western capitalism. It strikingly reflects the view of Western colonialism, which constantly commits aggression against the Eastern countries and seeks to enslave the peoples of Asia, Africa, and Latin America. In

[4] Carlton J. H. Hayes and Parker Thomas Moon, *Modern History* (New York: Macmillan, 1928), p. 651.

ancient times, imperial Rome looked on the Germans and Gauls (French) as "inferior races" and "barbarians" and concluded that these peoples should for ever submit to the rule of the "superior race," namely, the rule of the Roman Empire.

Bourgeois Historians Serve Their Class

This is exactly how the Western colonialists regard the peoples of Asia, Africa, and Latin America. They look on Asia as a place without any "genuine civilization" or history, as a place to dump their goods, plunder raw materials, and exploit cheap labour. The European-centred approach to history is a blatant reflection of such a colonialist view. According to this view, the Western colonialists' domination of Asia and all other "backward" regions is perfectly reasonable. This is how bourgeois historians serve their own class. This is exactly how matters stand, whether or not those historians are aware of it.

Social consciousness is determined by social being. Decadent conceptions will all finally and inevitably be shattered by convincing facts. This outcome is only a matter of time. The struggle being waged by the peoples of Asia, Africa, and Latin America to transform the world is shaking the earth. No matter how he may try to seal himself off from the outside world, no one can escape this cataclysm. Confronted with this fact, these Western bourgeois ideas of a world centred on Europe or West Europe will come to a quick end.

When we say we must oppose such ideas of a European-centred world, we naturally do not mean that the history of Europe should be treated with indifference—not in the least. To do so would cause people to swing from one anti-scientific extreme to another.

The history of Europe enjoys a fixed position. The bourgeois revolution in the Netherlands in the 16th century, the British bourgeois revolution in the 17th century, and especially the French bourgeois revolution at the end of the 18th century added lustre to the history of Europe. The French bourgeois revolution particularly did a great service to the bourgeoisie. It can be said that the 19th century as a whole passed under the sign of the French revolution. The era of ascending capitalism and bourgeois revolution in Europe witnessed a rapid advance in world history. There is not a shadow of doubt about this. However, no sooner did it gain power, than the European bourgeoisie began to change quickly into a conservative and reactionary class. With the advance of the proletarian revolutionary movement in Europe and the development of the national democratic revolutionary movement in the East, the European bourgeoisie has become more and more reactionary, clinging desperately to the world order, which is based on backwardness, barbarous cruelty, privilege, and the exploitation of man by man.

It is because the advanced European proletariat entered the historical arena that the history of Europe has continued to advance. Holding high the banner of socialist revolution in utter opposition to the desires of the bourgeoisie, they continue to carry the history of mankind forward. The proletariat of Asia will always be grateful to the advanced proletariat of Europe.

The proponents of a European-centred world have been energetically publicizing the leading role of Europe, but judging from so-called Christian civilization, and the like, which many people talk so glibly about, they do not, in fact, really know where the progressive nature of Europe lies. This is why the bourgeois remains a bourgeois.

Our Tasks as Historians

As the subject of scientific research, history has its objective course as well as its objective laws of development. Events do not change according to the likes and dislikes of historians. It is unthinkable that any serious historian should "transform" history in accordance with his subjective ideas. In appraising Asian history objectively, the aim is to restore its original features, which have been besmirched and distorted, not to prettify or whitewash them. In studying the history of a region or an age, we must adhere to historical materialism and oppose historical idealism. The same holds good for the appraisal of Asian history. It is futile either to embellish or to blacken history; this would be an anti-scientific approach.

History is all-inclusive. The development of the social productive forces and class struggle, oppression by the rulers and resistance by the masses of the people, the dark and backward things left over from the past, the bright and forward-looking things representing the advancing line of history—all these are closely interwoven, sometimes sharply distinct and sometimes obscured in a maze of confusion. The historians' weighty duty is to give an accurate judgment on these questions, putting things in their right place and correctly expounding their mutual relations.

To present the history of Asia in the light of this requirement, we hold that the following essentials must be fulfilled:

First, we must elucidate the world significance of the long and bitter class contradictions and class struggle in this region;

Second, we must give the masses of the people their rightful place in history;

Third, we must affirm all the bright and new-born things which represent the line of the advance of history;

Fourth, we must unremittingly repudiate and expunge all distortions and fabrications of Asian history by the Western colonialists and their followers.

The history of Asia has long been described as dark and circumscribed. But, in fact, those who break out from the blind alley of bourgeois idealism and lift their heads see a magnificent sight, and vast new vistas unfold before them.

The history of Asia forms an integral part of world history. A scientific appraisal of Asian history will help the people of the world to a correct understanding of world history and of the present situation. In spite of all difficulties, the oppressed people throughout the world are waging a struggle to transform the present situation and the world. It is imperative that they understand the present situation in the struggle of the people throughout the world and have a scientific approach to world history. The rewriting of the history of Asia to elucidate its true features will help people to free themselves from mental enslavement by imperialism and fully emancipate their minds. Therefore, it may be put this way: the way one looks on the modern histories of Asia and of Africa and Latin America is not only a question of one's approach to history, it is also a question of one's approach to the present struggle.

Index